Light &
Liberty

Light & Liberty

A HISTORY OF THE EETPU

John Lloyd

Weidenfeld and Nicolson
LONDON

Printed in Great Britain by
Butler & Tanner Ltd, Frome and London

Contents

Illustrations

Buxted Park, 1987.
General Secretary Eric Hammond, 1987.
Women on strike for union recognition, 1955.
Contracting strikes, 1954.
Overhead linesmen in the Hurricane, 1987.
Electronics technician Wendy Packer, 1988.
The Executive Council in Centenary Year, 1989–90.

I am indebted to the following for permission to use their photographs: The jacket cover (Carlos Vaz), C. H. Stavenhagen (Patrick Stavenhagen), Walter Citrine (S&G Press Agency), Walter Lewis (W. E. Hainge), Harry Turner (Ray Critchley), Ballot in Bristol (Les Etherington), 1965 TUC Delegation (Paul Bevis), Eric Hammond (Denzil McNeelance), Overhead linesman (David Bennett).

All the other photographs are from the union's own resources; however, I am particularly indebted to Derek Davis for the photographs of the union's properties, the centenary executive council and the restoration of some of the older photographs in preparation for the printer.

Abbreviations

ACAS	Advisory, Conciliation and Arbitration Service
ACT	Association of Cine Technicians
AEU	Amalgamated Engineering Union
AFL	American Federation of Labor
AMEE	Association of Managerial, Electrical Executives
ASE	Amalgamated Society of Engineers
ASLEF	Associated Society of Locomotive Engineers and Firemen
ASSET	Association of Supervisory Staffs, Executives and Technicians
ASTMS	Association of Scientific, Technical and Managerial Staffs
ASW	Amalgamated Society of Woodworkers
AUEW	Amalgamated Union of Engineering Workers
BEA	British Electricity Authority
BIF	Building Industries Federation
CEA	Cinema Exhibitors Association
CIO	Congress of Industrial Organisations
COHSE	Confederation of Health Service Employees
CSEU	Confederation of Shipbuilding and Engineering Unions
DJIC	District Joint Industrial Council
ECA	Electrical Contractors Association
EEF	Engineering Employers Federation
EESA	Electrical and Engineering Staff Association
EETPU	Electrical, Electronic, Telecommunication and Plumbing Union
EETU–PTU	Electrical, Electronic and Telecommunication Union – Plumbing Trades Union
ELECTRA	Electrical, Electronic and Communications Association
EPEA	Electrical Power Engineers Association

ESU	Electricity Supply Union
ETU	Electrical Trades Union
EWA	Electric Wiremen's Association
FEST	Federation of Engineering and Shipbuilding Trades
GFTU	General Federation of Trade Unions
GMWU	General and Municipal Workers Union
ICFTU	International Confederation of Free Trade Unions
IPCS	Institute of Professional Civil Servants
ISTC	Iron and Steel Trades Confederation
JIB	Joint Industry Board
JIC	Joint Industrial Council
LEMA	London Electrical Masters Association
LMBA	London Master Builders Association
MFGB	Miners Federation of Great Britain
MSF	Manufacturing, Science, Finance Union
NALGO	National and Local Government Officers Association
NATE	National Association of Theatrical Employees
NATKE	National Union of Theatrical and Kine Employees
NFEA	National Federated Electrical Association
NGA	National Graphical Association
NJIC	National Joint Industrial Council
NSFU	National Sailors and Firemen's Union
NUGMW	National Union of General and Municipal Workers
NUJ	National Union of Journalists
NUM	National Union of Mineworkers
NUPE	National Union of Public Employees
NUR	National Union of Railwaymen
PTU	Plumbing Trades Union
RETRA	Radio, Electrical and Television Retailers Association
SDF	Social Democratic Federation
SOGAT	Society of Graphical and Allied Trades
TASS	Technical and Supervisory Section (of AUEW)
TGWU	Transport and General Workers Union
TUC	Trades Union Congress
UCATT	Union of Construction, Allied Trades and Technicians
WFTU	World Federation of Trade Unions

Acknowledgements

This book is a history of the Electrical, Electronic, Telecommunication and Plumbing Union (EETPU). Its main focus is the history of the electrical section of the union, which was known up until 1968 as the Electrical Trades Union (ETU). The Plumbing Trades Union amalgamated with the ETU in 1968, and their honourable past has been dealt with by John French in his book *Plumbers in Unity*.

I have numerous debts of gratitude in the writing of this book. First and foremost, I must thank the EETPU executive council for encouraging me to write it in the first place. Second, I must thank all my colleagues in the EETPU, too numerous to mention by name, who have set me on the road to whatever understanding of the union this book reveals. They have talked to me at length about their past, sometimes aware that I would bring it into the story, sometimes not!

I need to thank John Brewster and Laurel Francis for making sure that important books and documents came my way. I am particularly thankful for John French's efforts in sorting the Trial papers into some sort of order. Howard Sallis was generous in giving me key statistics on Electricity Supply issues, and the staffs at Colindale Newspaper Library and the London School of Economics were ever helpful. I am indebted to Roy Moore at Ruskin College for his interest, and to Patrick Stavenhagen for marvellous stories about his father, backed up with priceless pamphlets and an original copy of Walter Crane's 'Cartoons for the Cause'. It is also important to stress that nothing would have appeared without the patience, encouragement and professional skill displayed by David Roberts, Martin Corteel and Hilary Laurie at my publishers, Weidenfeld and Nicolson.

One technical matter. I have tried to avoid imposing footnotes on the reader. Nothing is more likely to destroy the concentration than being required to rummage in the back of the book for the source of quotations and ideas. I hope that the occasional academic reader will overlook my turning down this opportunity to demonstrate the fabulous width of my reading! I have appended a short 'Note on Sources' which lists the general books I have leaned on heavily for background and the provision of the framework within which the union's history unfolds. Nevertheless, it would be churlish not to mention Joe Wild's *Souvenir* of the first fifty years of the union's history and *Light and Liberty* by Gordon Schaefer. I am particularly indebted to John Vickers' 1952 book *The Story of the ETU*. I have also benefited from reading Roger Rosewell's unpublished account of the union's history.

This book is the history of the union as an institution. Obviously, there has not been time to narrate the parallel stories of the development of electricity and electronics in industry; neither has it been possible to describe at every turn what was happening in other unions and other parts of the Labour movement, even when such comparisons would have thrown some light on the affairs of the ETU. There simply has not been space.

Several people do deserve my thanks by name. Dave Rogers is the EETPU's national officer for technical matters and productivity services. To him I am deeply indebted for his constant patience with my technical ignorance. His tolerant and amused explanations of just what electrical and electronic workers are up to has deepened my regard for the central role such people play in all our lives. Terry McCarthy has kept me alive to the fact that this is a story that needs telling, and that the EETPU's struggle against all comers is a genuine triumph for working-class democracy. Yvonne Forsyth has typed the many versions of the book: she has done it with great professionalism and her interested comments have sustained my own concentration in getting it done at all. Lynn Williams has made sure that during the months when I have been away for much of the time, obsessed with the contents of this book, the EETPU's industrial relations training courses have kept going regardless. He has borne the doubling of his workload with a dedicated cheerfulness that will make him a delight to work with once more on a daily basis.

Finally, the largest debt is owed to my family. My daughters Katherine and Jenny have helped by constantly reminding me that family life is the only thing more important than writing this book – although I forgot that from time to time. My wife Susan has supported me in the dark moments when I thought I would never finish. She also provided me with a willing audience as exciting historical discoveries – at least exciting for me – revealed themselves.

The mistakes and misinterpretations have all been made accidentally; they nevertheless remain all my fault.

For Susan,
Katherine and
Jenny

BIRTH OF THE ELECTRICAL TRADES UNION

THE ELECTRICAL TRADES UNION (ETU) was founded at the Crown Hotel, Blackfriars Street, Salford, just across the River Irwell from Manchester, on 30 November 1889. This delegate conference of electrical workers was the first broadly national convention, with delegates present from Birmingham, Blackburn, Sheffield, Leeds, Stockport, Guide Bridge (on the outskirts of Manchester), Warrington, Cork, London and Manchester itself. They met in profoundly ironic circumstances. Parts of Manchester and Salford were plunged into darkness that weekend by a gasworkers strike which immobilized the gas street lights. The gasworkers strike committee was operating from the same hotel. Upstairs, the ETU was taking the first steps towards organizing the workers in the new technology.

The conference could not have been of one mind, however. The only decisions of substance taken were to adopt the name 'Electrical Trades Union' and to agree a set of rules based directly on the premier craft union of the time, the Amalgamated Society of Engineers (ASE). No decision was reached on the location of a general office, the nature of an executive council, or the personalities of the union's officers. This was to be postponed for a year, until the union's constituent parts could agree on an integrated constitution at a conference to be held in Liverpool in December 1890.

Nevertheless, the decisive first step was taken. The union was to become a national society, replacing the two tiny but distinct unions which had emerged during the 1880s in London and Manchester. Electrical trade unionism emerged distinctively in parallel with the developments of the electrical industries in late Victorian Britain. This is not the place to trace the history of the use of electricity in industry: it has been done elsewhere. However, it is important to understand that the electrical industries developed from the outset along divergent paths. The early history of the union reflects those separate industrial developments. The Manchester Society was initially based on the emerging telephone and telegraph industries and was called the 'Amalgamated Union of Telegraph and Telephone Construction Men'. Within five years, it found its best recruits in the electrical engineering companies like Mather & Platt's, who installed and commissioned the same dynamos and electric motors which they manufactured.

The London union, called by 1889 the 'Union of Electrical Operatives', was also closely concerned with the use of electricity in the infant telephone industry. Most of the government departments and large city institutions were starting to use telephones in an appreciable way, and this produced a new industry with a new workforce. Here, too, the original telephone industry base of the union was to change rapidly. The construction and engineering industries of London were to produce the majority of recruits for the union within five years of its founding.

Sidney and Beatrice Webb wrote the first edition of *The History of Trade Unionism* in 1894. It was their proud boast that Sidney Webb had interviewed every important trade society in existence at that time. His original notes survive in the archives of the London School of Economics. The picture they reveal of the early electricians – particularly in London – is revealing. Webb noted that before 1880, the whole of the electrical trades in London were in the hands of three large, first-rate firms of proper electrical engineers, whose workmen enjoyed excellent conditions and good wages. Conditions changed in the early 1880s for the entrepreneurs who were attempting to mix scientific adventure with commercial acumen. Webb notes the gradual arrival in the electrical industries of 'every little ironmonger, jobbery gasfitter or builder who began to call themselves an electrician and do the work. Consequently, competition became very keen.'

The new companies, frequently dominated by the traditional building skills of carpentry and plumbing, began to organize the work with an electrically-skilled supervisor directing the work of labourers. This replaced the amicable relationships in the first electrical companies based on respect for the first practical use of electrical knowledge. The new companies drove down the price of the early electrical contracts so that the traditional companies felt obliged to impose wage cuts in the winter of 1883–4. Webb reveals that the workers affected used to meet in the Paul's Head Tavern in Finsbury in London. They did not set up any formal organization at this stage and paid no subscription to any society. Yet they did apparently insist that they would not work for less than 8d per hour. Neither Webb's notes, nor the sketchy early records of the union, reveal any hint of the success or otherwise of this informal pressure group.

1889: New Electrical Unions in London and Manchester

Webb immediately jumps in his handwritten notes from the problems of the mid-1880s to 1889, where his account can be augmented by the earliest union records. Webb insists that the London workers set up a body called the 'London Society of Electrical Workers' while, quite separately, a similar organization emerged in Manchester called the 'Amalgamated Union of Telegraph and Telephone Construction Men'. On the evening of 5 October 1889, twenty-two telephone and telegraph workers met at the Crown Hotel to review the possibilities.

The London Society remained local to London; the Manchester union quickly spread to those towns who attended the first delegate conference. An account does survive of the first formal meeting of the union in Manchester on 2 November 1889. The minutes of this meeting refer back to the secretary, Phil Carroll's, visit to Liverpool on 30 October and the first rule-book has on its frontispiece the words 'established October 1889'.

At its first meeting at the Crown Hotel on 2 November, the main business was to be the organizing of the delegate conference that took place on the thirtieth, suggesting a new title for the Union – the Electrical Trades Union – on the recommendation of Phil Carroll. However, the men who attended on 2 November clearly had other priorities as well. Twenty-two-year-old Tom Brennan was elected drinks steward. Only he was allowed to fetch and carry the members' refreshments in and out of the meeting. The branch meeting also revealed a great seriousness in the rules they adopted to contain boisterous behaviour. The union was not going to be simply a drinks club.

'No drinks were to be paid for out of union funds' and 'there were to be no 3d whips', both common practices in Victorian trade societies. In concentrating on the forthcoming conference, the meeting authorized the printing of 150 copies of the Manchester rules, along with fifty explanatory leaflets to accompany the mailing of the rule-books. Their optimism was further underlined by the ordering of 1,000 membership cards.

The London union traces its foundation meeting to October 1889 as well, although it is impossible to say whether it was a matter of days before or after the Manchester meetings. *The Electrician* for 11 October 1889 reported the following meeting.

A meeting of electrical engineers and linesmen of whom it is estimated there are about 3,000 in London was held last Saturday at the Paul's Head, Paul's Street, Finsbury to discuss a proposal as to the means for the formation of a society in London on the trade union principle. The workman who was elected to the chair wished his name, as did also the speaker whom he followed, to be suppressed in view of future reprisals from the firm of which they were employed. In opening the proceedings the chairman said he was very much surprised that such a union as was then under discussion, had not been formed before.

As a matter of fact their leaders had been responsible for the delay, but now that they had commenced in earnest they could see plenty of useful work before them.

Throughout the trade wages were far too small, considering the danger they had to incur when they started out in the morning. There was not one of them who could say with any certainty whether he would be alive in the evening. He did not believe in strikes, but he did believe that when their union was duly established, it would do the valuable work in the way of calling an independent arbitrator in the event of a trades dispute ultimately taking place ... A letter was read from the Manchester union, urging the London men to amalgamate, and it was decided the union should be formed.

The Electrician editorial drew the following conclusions from these events.

One effect of the recent great strike has been to give a new impulse to the formation of trade unions and considering the dimensions which the electrical industry has now obtained, it does not surprise us that the artisans employed in it are following the fashion. The reasons assigned are not as intelligible or as manly as we could have wished, one of them being that the electrical workman never knows if he will come home alive – an uncertainty which most of us endure with perfect resignation.

A good deal of the pernicious nonsense now being prevalent amongst workmen about offering a united front to the money bags of the capitalists was reported at the Paul Street meeting. Nonsense which, if the men are as we should expect electrical workmen to be, they ought to forswear as soon as possible. The gist of the matter probably is, however, that electrical trades are in that prosperous condition which is generally the signal for a rise in wages. Perhaps, on the whole, this is not a matter to alarm us greatly.

It is probable that the great dock strike was indeed the stimulus for electrical trade unionism, as one of the trades present at the great strike meetings, who were caught up with the dockers' struggle, were the telegraph construction labourers employed round the London docks. They were demanding 4s a day for working from 6 a.m. to 5 p.m! These extracts give some useful information; not least the fact that Manchester men knew of this inaugural meeting in London at the same location that Webb shows had long been a haunt of electrical men. Reading this in future years, many employers would probably consider *The Electrician*'s disdainful dismissal of the whole initiative as hopelessly complacent.

The First Conference – The Divisive Issues

The Manchester rules that were submitted to the first recognizable conference on 30 November 1889 had two contentious areas that prevented their wholesale adoption by the conference. Firstly, there was no clear definition of the objects of the union or which groups of workers the union was trying to attract. By looking at the contributions to debates within the union of the early 1890s, it is clear there were arguments between the Manchester and London unions on the very nature of the new union. The Manchester men preferred to create an electrical version of the ASE. They wanted an exclusive craft society, based on apprentice-trained skilled craftsmen who could collectively resist encroachment on their work. The London men clearly had a very different vision. They wanted to organize the electrical industries, not simply the electricians. They feared the role of labourers and other partly-skilled workers in taking away the 'bread and butter' parts of the craftsmen's jobs. In their view, the craftsman was best protected by organizing the less skilled grades around him.

These fundamental attitudes on the part of both early societies was to re-emerge in different forms throughout the union's history. In 1889, it also took a second controversial turn that nearly led to the failure of the union as a national society in its earliest stages. The 1889 Manchester rules made provision for various 'friendly society' type benefits. Many early trade unionists thought that the only way to attract and retain members was to advance them a range of financial benefits. The Manchester rules offered unemployment pay of 10s per week for six weeks and 5s per week for a further four weeks. They also offered accident benefit of 7s per week for six weeks and 4s for a further six weeks. Funeral benefit was crucial for all trade unionists, who lived in fear of the disgrace of a pauper's burial: £5 would be paid to the member's next of kin and £3 paid to the member if his wife died.

Most controversial of all, as far as the London men were concerned, was the Manchester insistence on providing sickness benefit of 7s for six weeks and 4s for a further six weeks. Accounts of the London union's meeting at the Paul's Head Tavern on 19 February 1890 hark back to the controversy this proposal must have caused at the inaugural conference when they instructed their secretary to 'write to the Manchester union to the effect unless they do away with the sick benefits, they cannot see their way clear to amalgamation.'

Objections to sickness benefit were two-fold. Firstly, it was notoriously difficult to control expenditure on it: and its very existence therefore required a craft-society level of contributions. Secondly, this level of contribution – 6d per week, when wages for the 'skilled' men rarely reached 6d an hour – was expensive. This was particularly irritating to the London membership whose ambition to recruit all grades in the electrical industries was absolute. They had launched their union amidst the tumult associated with the birth of the dockers', gasworkers' and other 'general' unions for all grades of workers: the dockers' contributions were 4d per week by 1890, out of which they financed strike benefit and funeral benefits. It is fair to speculate that the prevailing view of the union in London in early 1890 would have sympathized with gasworkers' leader Will Thorne's views. He wrote in 1890 that he did 'not believe in having sick-pay, out-of-work pay and a number of other pays. We desire to prevent so much sickness and men being out of work. The way to accomplish this, is firstly to organize, then reduce your hours of labour and work. That will prevent illness and members being out of employment.' In order to organize the whole industry, the London union (by now called the 'Union of Electrical Operatives') wanted to soft-pedal craft exclusivity, recruit as widely as possible and confront the employers in a militant, 'class conscious' way. The London union's sense of its own righteousness could not have been deterred by its visit to the headquarters of the ASE in January 1890. The ASE executive considered the application of the electricians to be allowed to join them. They loftily wrote back that unfortunately 'electrical workers have not the necessary qualifications demanded of new entrants' to the ASE. They were advised to form a union of their own, and the engineers (68,000 strong, and by far the biggest union in the country by 1890) were kind enough to donate one of their own minute books to help the electricians on their way.

It is not unreasonable to conclude from this that the London and Manchester societies therefore had little alternative but to activate the principal decision taken at the Crown Hotel in Manchester on 30 November 1889. By August 1890, a set of rules was registered with the Registrar of trade unions and friendly societies. These rules, printed first in 1891, set out a broad base of electrical trades to recruit amongst, along with dropping the sickness benefits, thus satisfying the Londoners. At the same time, the rules introduced a set of objects for the union that clearly gave great weight to the status of the trade and little recognition of the revolutionary potential embraced by the 'new unions', thus satisfying the Mancunians. The ETU was in business.

2

THE FIRST RULE-BOOK: SETTING THE PATTERN

THE NEW RULE-BOOK that the union endorsed at Liverpool in December 1890 was a sophisticated rule-book designed for the mature organization of the ASE with its complex regulation of the branch-district-national relationships topped off with perfectly serious rules for the administration of branches in Canada, South Africa and Australia.

All of this was for the distant future as far as the electricians were concerned. On 1 January 1891, the union had seven branches (London, Manchester, Liverpool, Leeds, Dewsbury, Hanley and Sheffield). The Manchester section of the union brought six of the branches into the ETU, with London providing the other. Between the six northern branches, there were 400 members and the London branch contributed 170 members. Manchester had a cash balance of £222, while London contributed a further £75. The union therefore had an initial membership of 570 with total funds of £297.

Objects of the Union, 1890

These first members set out a comprehensive set of objects at the front of the rules. The union had been 'instituted' for the purpose of 'resisting any attempt to curtail or take away any of these privileges which are, or may become, the custom of the trade.' This comprehensive defence of past and future exclusivity was then joined by the ambition to 'assist our members in recovering wages in dispute and obtaining justice against any unfairness practised towards them in connection with their employment.' It is hard to imagine today that simple refusal to pay a man's wages, particularly after he had been dismissed, was a regular feature of some employers' industrial relations in 1890. The third objective in the first rule-book was to assist members to gain employment. The fourth objective was to provide unemployment, 'distress', accident and funeral benefits, but no sick benefit.

The statement of the purposes of the union was followed by detailed attempts to define which grades of workers could join the union and the exact procedure for their admission. There were comprehensive regulations for the opening of branches and the precise duties of branch officials – particularly with regard to the handling of money in the branch. Attempts were made to define the relationship between the branch, district committees, the executive council and the delegate conference. Good behaviour at meetings was to be guaranteed by an extensive list of non-acceptable activities that attracted suitable fines and other penalties. Profound opposition to piece-work was formally included in the rule-book. Contribution levels were set and the list of the benefits of the union laid out.

A clearer understanding of the effectiveness of this constitution can be gained by setting out some of the detail of the 1890 rule-book alongside the results of debates at the 1891 and 1893 rules revision conferences. These early conference records are fragmentary, but they do serve by implication to highlight the areas of constitutional debate in the early years of the union.

Developing the Rules – 1891 and 1893 Rules Revision Decisions

The purposes of the union were laid out in some detail – certainly much expanded on the original Manchester union's 1889 rules. In the 1890 rules, the union firstly set itself the task 'of resisting any attempt to curtail or take away any of those privileges which are or may become the custom of the trade'. This determination to stake out their own ground in a new, dynamic industry is quite breathtaking. With £297 behind them, organizing only a tiny percentage of the workers involved in an emerging, entrepreneurial, indistinct and experimental industry, the modern trade unionist can only marvel at the sheer cheek of the pioneers of the ETU. The purposes of the union were laid out to include recovering wages due to members through the legal process; to help members gain employment; to provide unemployment, accident, funeral and distress benefits (but not sickness benefit); and for 'regulating the relationship between workmen and employers'.

The desire to dedicate itself to collective bargaining was not present in the 1889 rules from Manchester and marks the determination of the union to rise above the status of a friendly society. Within these 'purposes' of the union lie the compromises of earlier arguments. The Londoners would not allow the funds to be dissipated by paying out sickness benefit. The Mancunians were anxious to emphasize the 'trade' nature of the union rather than an industrial type of organization. At the 1891 and 1893 conferences, the purposes of the union remained intact in their original form. However, the question of sickness benefit would not go away. N-E Coast district secretary Arthur Senior was the delegate representing (and voting for!) all three North-Eastern branches of Middlesbrough, Sunderland and Newcastle. He was supported by Blackburn's delegate, T. Malaney, when they demanded the inclusion of sickness benefit as a 'purpose' of the union. The conference rejected this 21–4.

This initial argument, about what the union was for, found reflections throughout the rule-book of 1890 and all the rule-books to follow. There has always been a debate in the union – sometimes intensely fought – over just who was good enough to be an ETU member. For some, membership of the union was always a privilege that marked the electrical worker off from the rest of industrial society; for others, membership of a wider union reflected their desire for electrical workers to protect themselves by throwing in their lot with all other workers within the same industry.

The 1890 rule-book was again a compromise: first, qualification for membership was that a man should be 'a competent workman' who was a dynamo winder, erector or tender; an outdoor or indoor installation linesman and wireman; an accumulator and battery maker; an instrument maker; fitter and inspector; or a telegraph and telephone wireman or linesman. Crudely put, these would be the appropriate 'skilled' grades in their 1890 equivalent. It is highly significant that there is no attempt here to define 'competent' in the rules, least of all by the formal provision of proof of apprentice training. Secondly, the rule for membership qualification in 1890 then defined a further acceptable grade of worker – 'labourers who have worked for over six months in telegraph, telephone, electric light construction and maintenance.'

This two-tier basis of the union's membership between 'craftsmen' and 'labourers' has long produced a fine tension in the union between those who believe strength is based on exclusivity and those who think that important elements of a craftsman's job could be 'picked up' by 'labourers'. These people could then undermine the potential strength of the craftsmen in disputes and hold down the wages of qualified skilled people. The early ETU members recognized that this posed a danger to their determination to stake out craft boundaries for electricians. It must have been a painful paradox for the proud and frustrated Victorian electrician. He wanted the world to recognize the growing skills on which the new world order was to be based. The only way he could gain status through decent pay, conditions and standing in industry was to extract such things from employers. His union alone recognized the exclusive nature of his skills. However, he could often understand that his union's effectiveness could be outflanked by underpaid, semi-skilled people doing bits and pieces of his job. Therefore, his union's only option was to recruit those very grades of labour that apparently gave the lie to the craft exclusivity the electrician sought.

The 1893 conference debated the boundaries of the union's membership in some detail. Despite some opposition from London branches, the union included 'electric appliance makers' after instrument workers in the 'skilled' grades list. They then turned their attention to the question of labourers in the union. Branches from the North-East Coast, Cardiff and founder-branches, Salford and Bolton, moved that no labourers be allowed in the union at all. That was rejected by the conference, 20–6.

One lone voice, Blackburn's delegate, T. Malaney, wanted to let labourers into the union immediately, without a six months qualifying period. He was beaten 21–1 – presumably his own vote!

The real crux of the debate came, though, when the Salford branch proposed a new clause that would have attempted to impose a definition of competence via the introduction of apprenticeships.

The proposition was that 'no member shall be considered a competent workman until he has served a term to the trade as follows: if at the time of commencing work he is over seventeen and under twenty years, he shall serve four years; if over twenty years, three years.' This was lost 16–10. The episodic and anecdotal 1893 conference report does not give any details of the debate. Indeed, it does not even tell us who Salford's delegate was. Members elected to conferences sometimes chose not to have their names revealed in the conference minutes for fear of employers identifying them as union activists and persecuting them for it.

Joining the Union

Joining the union was a complicated procedure that reflected the essential craft bias in the union, whatever arrangements were made for labourers. A prospective member would have to be nominated by two fellow electricians who had been members of the union for twelve months. After 'tidying up' changes in 1891/3, the new member had to be proposed at a regular meeting night two weeks before his admission meeting. However, the rules also allowed people to be recruited at open meetings of non-union men. In the normal way, men from the same department in a company or municipal authority would propose and second the new member, and pay in on the new member's behalf 1s at the nomination meeting. Two weeks later, the new member would have to pay a further 1s 6d. With hourly rates between 5d–8d, 2s 6d was a fairly stiff entrance fee. His proposers would have provided the branch with written details of the new member's age, address and length of service in the trade. The proposer and seconder could be fined for knowingly nominating someone who was useless in the trade and the new member could be required by the branch to produce 'a certificate of competence' from his employer or colleagues at work. The early branches were also insistent that only members under the age of forty-five could be 'free' members – entitled to benefit – as they did not want to have to pay out unnecessary benefits to older men! He had to be there the night he was proposed and the night he was admitted. The branch could demand a certificate of good health from the new member – again to avoid excessive demands on the benefits of the union. He must then sign the 'form of proposition' to be followed on admission by signing the proposition book. (Membership forms are still colloquially called 'prop-forms' by the union's activists.) Members seeking readmission had to go through an investigation of the original causes of their leaving the union, and all cases had to be referred to the executive council. Each new member would then receive an entrance card and a subscription card to keep the record of his payment. All new members' proposition forms had to be sent to head office where they were laboriously recorded in massive membership roll-books, which still survive.

Constitutional Powers of Branches, District Committees and the Executive Council

Modern trade unionists would find it difficult to recognize the constitutional relationship existing in 1890 between branches, regional committees and the national executive of the union. There was no money to fund full-time officers throughout the country. There was no research, technical, educational or clerical support in existence. There was little concept of a national power being deployed in support of local trade union activity. It is easy to forget that the union did not have a single local office, a single paid official, a single telephone. Travel was difficult and expensive, communication almost exclusively by post.

It is inevitable, therefore, that the first rules of the union had to allow for virtual autonomy on the part of local branches in matters of recruitment, finance, and negotiation with employers. However, the union learnt the lessons of the 1830s and 1840s when unrestrained local trade union activity had bankrupted national trade union organizations. By adopting a version of the ASE's rules, they attempted a balance of obligation between local branches, district committees and the executive council. This balance was forever under pressure from branches who wanted more control over their own affairs and those branches and individuals in the union who saw that a truly powerful union would only result by organizing a national power, equipped to support all the members in a wide variety of emergencies.

The 1890 rules tried to get the balance right by stating the general principle first. Branches 'shall be subject, in accordance with the rules, to the control and direction of the general governing bodies of the union and their officers; every branch, however, shall appoint its own officers and conduct its own business in the manner set forth in the following rules ...'. Even so, this general principle was challenged at the 1893 conference and its removal was only defeated by the relatively narrow margin of 16–10.

Ordinary branch meetings were required to start at 8 p.m. on a fortnightly basis. Special meetings were to be held on a quarterly basis – still known as quarter nights – in January, April, July and October each year. The branch would be presided over by a president and each branch would also have the following office-holders – a secretary, a treasurer, a doorkeeper, auditors, check-book keeper, and money steward. Together, they would form the branch committee which would meet between and before the fortnightly meetings. The main business of the branch was to collect contributions and pay out benefits. It also acted as a clearing-house for information on employment prospects and local dealings with employers providing, of course, that such employers would allow the branch officials to 'wait on them' with a view towards negotiating wages and agreeing to the local working rules cards drawn up in the branch.

Branches used to frequently meet in public houses. A study could be made of the relationship between drink and the British trade union movement in general!

At the end of 1891, eighteen of the union's branches met in pubs. The London branch and the union's registered office was at the Clarence Hotel in Aldersgate. Manchester met at the Star Hotel in Great Ancoats whilst Salford continued to meet at the Royal Commercial Hotel in Chapel Street. The East Greenwich branch in South East London met at the Old Friends in Woolwich Road. This pub still has on its walls a photograph of the handcart delivery men's union's contemporary banner depicting on the banner itself the fact that the branch met at the pub! The Hull branch met at the Dog and Duck Inn in the High Street. It is clear, though, that a strong temperance influence was at work in the rest of the union's Yorkshire areas. The Sheffield, Bradford and Halifax branches met in coffee rooms.

Glasgow met in Nelson's Temperance Hotel in Ingram Street. Sunderland favoured a coffee house, but the other great early centres of Liverpool (the Old Double Doors) and Newcastle (the Black Boy Inn) favoured a more lively type of refreshment.

However, the early union's law-makers were aware that drink could be a factor in disrupting branch meetings. At the 1893 conference, the Newcastle and Sunderland branches proposed that 'the doorkeeper shall not admit any member who is under the influence of drink'. This produced a tied vote, 13–13, and president Edwin Johnson voted against the proposition, so it fell. It was probably felt the rules were sufficient to handle unruly members. For instance, conduct of a 'very aggravated nature' would attract on the spot fines of up to 20s at the branch meeting. The alternative interpretation, that the president and half the delegates at the 1893 conference wanted to encourage drunks to attend branch meetings, is surely ridiculous. Fourteen of the branches met on Saturday nights – reflecting the need to maintain fragile confidentiality. It also reflects the fact that the working day was originally so long, that it was often unrealistic to expect members to attend on a workday evening. Also, the social side of the branch's life was important to the early membership and Saturday was the only free evening, presumably allowing members to combine union business and a social evening on the same night.

Years later, in 1905, when the union first published a magazine called the *Eltradion* (a bizarre title, assembled out of the words ELectrical TRADe unION) it led to a discussion about the use of pubs as meeting places – possibly an idealized version of events.

Our own society strictly enforces an unwritten law upon all its branches whose meetings must take place on licensed premises to the effect that the landlord of the house is to be paid an agreed rental for the use of the room, and with that duly paid, all obligation on the part of the members, save keeping decent order, ceases. No servant of the landlord is permitted to enter the meeting. No drink is allowed to be called in; the meeting is strictly a temperance meeting. When it is over, members are free to do as they please outside the meeting room, and generally they make for home, knowing they are under no obligation to contribute to 'the good of the house'.

Apart from worrying about members drinking away any benefits they got at the branch, the *Eltradion* went on: 'Without holding extreme views on the temperance question, we look upon the growing tendency in that direction as a good omen ... for nothing but good can accrue from an absolute divorce between liquor and labour.' Clearly, that 'tendency' did not make much further progress.

The Role of Branch Officials and the Union's Committees

The rule-book of 1890 and the slight changes produced at the 1891 and 1893 conferences imposed very specific responsibilities on the branch officials. Most were elected twice a year on appropriate quarter nights, although the branch secretary was elected annually now at the December quarter night.

No officer could hold office if he owed the union over 5s or if he had not been in the union a full year. All members were required by rule to accept nomination to office or be fined 6d unless they were over forty-five or lived more than three miles from the 'club room'. If elected, and they refused to serve, they were fined 1s. These fines would not be applied if the member had held some sort of branch office in the previous year. This rotation of office as a feature of democratic trade union government emphasized each member's responsibility to take part in the union's affairs. The president was required to sign the minutes, keep order and impose the fines! Important as this job clearly was, branch life has tended to revolve round the branch secretary from the union's earliest days.

The branch secretary was required to enter all contributions into the branch ledger and onto the members' subscription cards. (The treasurer, the check-book keeper, the money steward and the branch auditors all had financial responsibilities too. The need for constant vigilance to prevent mistakes and corruption is all too obvious in the union's early financial history.) The secretary had to keep all the union's books and documents, enter into cor-respondence, and read the branch copies of his replies to queries. He was required to send out notices reminding members they were over 5s in arrears and he had to post copies of these notices in the 'club room'. He had to produce agendas for the branch committee and full branch meetings, pay out all the cheques for branch officers' payments and all the union's benefits to members. He was responsible for issuing membership cards and had to keep a record of all the travelling members who had set off from his branch and keep records of hospitality and support offered to those who called at his branch. He was responsible for accrediting branch members as delegates to everything from executive council to special delegate meetings; he was also responsible for paying their expenses.

His duties did not end there. Not later than the second of every month, he had to send in details of jobs available locally, listed in his 'vacant book', to the union's general secretary at the registered office. Included in his report on the vacant book, he had to provide a review of job prospects and the general state of trade.

Each quarter, he had to prepare for the quarter night meeting a com-prehensive set of accounts including income/expenditure, arrears, exclusions and admissions, benefits claimed and by whom etc., and send it to the registered office. Furthermore, the annual report had to be sent in after the December quarter night. The requirement to have such annual reports ready within eighteen days of the quarter night was to be more honoured in the breach than the observance.

For his troubles, the branch secretary was to be fined 5s for any inadequacy under the rules. His reward was to be paid 3d per member per quarter.

There were complicated checks and balances built into the rules in order to effectively supervise the activities of the secretary. Each branch elected annually in December a branch referee. If any member was dissatisfied with the secretary's or any other branch officer's behaviour, he could appeal to the referee who had direct access to the executive council and general secretary.

The clearest indication of the seriousness with which the branch had to check and cross-check the handling of contributions can best be seen in the procedure for paying money into the branch. In larger branches – with over seventy members – a money steward would collect money from the members and bring it to the branch where the check-book keeper would check the members' cards and enter details of payments into the branch check-book.

Once the treasurer was satisfied that the detailed notes in the check-book added up to the total cash to be banked, the treasurer would make out a paying-in slip to be paid into the bank, signed by him and crossed in the presence of the check-book keeper (who in small branches of under seventy did the money steward's job as well). Only then could the secretary write up in the branch ledger which contributions had been paid and sign the members' cards.

Further control was supposed to be assured by the election of branch auditors. Written into the rule directly was the stern admonishment to branches – 'The branches must be most particular in their selection of auditors, as, if need be, they can arrest all confusion and mistakes in the books and prevent any fraud being practised on the union.' The president was required to read this rule to each half-yearly meeting at which the auditors were elected. In summary, they had to double-check all the financial transactions done by the secretary, treasurer and check-book man, and report to the branch quarterly and yearly. They would be paid 1s per audit for up to 100 members, with a further 6d per extra fifty members per audit.

The branch treasurer was also closely involved in this circular game of check and counter-check of each other's activities. He was also elected annually in December and paid 2s 6d per quarter for fifty members in the branch and a further 6d for every extra fifty members. He had to advance £20 guarantee before being allowed to take up his duties. He was specifically instructed in the rules only to pay cheques produced by the branch secretary with the branch stamp on them. He could not advance cash to the secretary on any cheques unless signed by the auditors and counter-signed by the branch president. No travelling benefits could be paid without the member having a travel card. He had to keep records of all benefits paid. Finally, the branch books could be inspected 'at all reasonable times by any member or person having an interest in the funds of the union'. As we shall see, all of this did not prevent grave financial scandals from periodically rocking the union. Nevertheless, the actual constitution required great effort as well as great integrity from its branch officials. The first annual report in 1891 probably evaluated the work of the first generation of branch officers fairly when it said:

> We have had the usual amount of hard administrative work that is naturally expected in the management of a new union, especially with a body of men that have never before been organized, amateurs at the work, in managing and organizing a new body of workers. We (the executive) found it very uphill work ... but this difficulty has now almost disappeared, thanks to the help of several of our London and provincial branch officials.

The branches were to be grouped together to form district committees for the purpose of co-ordinating and regulating the collective bargaining functions of the union. District committees would be formed of between seven and eleven branches with equal representation from each branch, if possible. The executive council was to decide the areas for each district committee to cover. No district committee delegate could work under the rates he was party to setting for the rest of his colleagues, and he had to report to his branch concerning district committee decisions or be fined 1s each time he didn't! The district committee was to be run by a district secretary, elected by the members in their branches, who had to make quarterly reports to the branches and inform branches of all their decisions on wage rates, 'working rules' etc. Each district committee had a 'referee' member in the same way as branches did to keep an eye on the secretary, who was paid 1s 6d per meeting if he had under six branches. If his district had six to twelve branches, it attracted a payment of 2s per meeting.

The main function of the district committee was to set up sub-committees and appoint delegates to deal with employers on questions 'likely to cause dispute in order to reach amicable settlements'. However, the early union recognized that some branches were too far apart to be grouped together. Therefore, the function of organizing such negotiations as took place was performed by the individual branch committees. By 1892, there were only four district committees operating – London, Yorkshire, Lancashire and the North-East Coast. Most of the branches had to operate on their own. Despite the slow growth of the district committee system, it was clear that, for most members, the branch and district committee were the vital institutions in the attempt to govern their relationships with each other and with the employers. The executive council and general secretary's role were very different from any modern equivalent. The ETU executive council from 1890–1907 was elected from among its London membership only, although the elections were held in all the branches. This was done for reasons of economy – the infant union could not begin to pay for the travelling expenses involved in a national executive meeting in London or anywhere else.

In this respect, the ETU local executive council paralleled contemporary craft unions. In 1890, the ASE had a London executive; the Typographical Association had a Manchester executive and the boilermakers' executive was elected from amongst that union's Tyneside membership.

The executive council was composed of nine members who had to live within ten miles of Charing Cross. (The London district committee wanted this restriction tightened at the 1893 conference to insist that executive council men lived within ten miles of Charing Cross at the time of their nomination, rather than move to London in the event of their election. This was defeated, 17–4, on the instigation of the Manchester branch. This attitude of Manchester's is interesting to compare with their attitude to the geographic qualifications involved in running for president of the union some years later in

1916.) Indeed, the 1893 conference insisted that if provincial members were elected to the executive council, the members of the whole union had to be levied to defray the expenses of the executive council men until they had been found a suitable job in the London area. It is difficult to judge from the fragments of early records how many of the first executive elected under the 1890 rules were Londoners. Certainly, the first general secretary, Dick Steadman, was a 32-year-old Londoner, who went on to become the branch secretary of the important London City branch.

Thomas Cannon, the first chairman of the executive, worked for the National Telephone Company in London, as did three other members of the first executive. It is impossible to say where the remainder came from; however, there is no record of levy income to pay for provincial men to come to London, so we may assume an exclusively London basis of the first executive council.

It is important to emphasize that the union's first executive council had nothing like the status and position within the union enjoyed by its successors. It was local to London and had restricted powers of its own. It was responsible for printing and publishing stationery, taking occasional legal action to recover wages held by employers, keeping a list of members, interpreting the rules when they were silent and, most significantly, it had powers over finance. Even on this issue, the rules carefully circumscribed its responsibilities. The executive council could raise money by levy from the members to fund strikes or to make other donations, once the members had been balloted. It could also suspend branches for financial irregularity; it could send in to errant branches 'special auditors' to examine the branch books and take whatever action was necessary, including legal action, to get matters straightened out. The executive also handled arguments between members and employers, if required, and used its influence in writing in support of members applying for higher wages. In practice, this must have clashed with the more direct role of district committees.

Members who felt that the branch had not been sympathetic to them could appeal to the executive council, whose decision could be challenged and overruled only by the delegate meeting. However, as this was only to be called following a ballot vote of members, very few, if any, individual appeals ever reached the delegate meetings. The executive could also grant special 'benevolent' grants to individual members in distress.

The executive councillors were paid 1s 6d per evening meeting and 2s 6d for an all-day meeting, plus fares. Their secretary, the general secretary, was originally a lay member (Dick Steadman). He had to attend to the correspondence of the branches, issue monthly reports to the executive council, district committees and the branches. He was responsible for counting ballots, distributing membership cards, keeping the list of members; he would deal with the legal aspects of the union's status as a registered union and direct unemployed members towards parts of the country where work was available. He was also responsible for issuing the quarterly and annual reports of the union.

Arthur Walker was originally elected as the union's first full-time official at the union's delegate conference in Blackfriars Road on 21 November 1891. Future general secretaries were to be elected by ballot vote in the branches, but there was no fixed term of office. Walker was expecting to stay in office for life: these hopes were to prove over-optimistic, as was his pledge to the conference, reported in the *Workman's Times*. He 'trusted that they would never have cause to regret the confidence they had reposed in him; but, on the contrary, they could have the best expectations of his services amply justified.'

Delegate Meetings

The last part of the constitutional jigsaw was to be provided by the delegate meeting. Every June, each branch had to decide whether to have a delegate conference of the union the following Whitsun weekend. Each branch and district committee could submit propositions to the delegate conference: each branch sent one delegate; those with more than 100 members could send two delegates. No delegate meeting could 'abrogate the principles of the union' which were defined as retaining donation, accident and funeral benefit (unless agreed by seventy-five per cent of the members in a ballot). However, the delegate meeting could overrule the executive council so that 'whatever is agreed at the delegate meeting shall be binding on all the members'.

Benefits of the Union

The benefits of the union were actually described in the rules as part of the 'principles' of the union. The contributions were 6d per week. (The 1893 conference voted 14–13 to stop them rising to 7d.) This was nowhere near the premier craft union, the ASE, whose contributions at this time were 1s per week. However, they exceeded the 2d or 3d of the newly-formed general unions by a clear margin. The ETU could therefore fund a modest level of benefits. The pre-eminent benefit was to be unemployment benefit – or 'donation' benefit, as it was called. If a member became unemployed, he had to sign the vacant book at the union's branch rooms every day, unless he lived over ten miles away when he had to provide a certificate of unemployment signed by two other members or 'respectable householders'. If he refused a job, notified to him by the branch, his entitlement was withdrawn. If he failed to sign the vacant book, he lost a day's benefit for each failure to do so. The donation benefit was 2s per day (12s per week) for twelve weeks. The member had to explain to the branch the circumstances of his unemployment, and if it was due to 'neglect of work, drunkenness or disorderly conduct', he would be refused benefit. If he lost his job because he was a union representative, he would be paid his wages until he found another job for a maximum of a year.

Strike benefit was paid at whatever rates the executive deemed appropriate. The executive council had to decide on this within eight weeks of the strike and could extend the benefit to a year. The first recruitment leaflet said they would have 'special rates of pay for special cases'. They listed nine types of strikes that would be supported, including strikes against piece-work, wage reductions, 'unjust or tyrannical rules of labour' and 'the introduction of labourers to do the work of mechanics'.

Accident benefit was paid at the rate of 10s per week for fourteen weeks and 7s for another fourteen weeks. Funeral benefit was £10 for the member and £5 in the event of his spouse's death. Even here, the London region's uneasiness with the provision of benefits out of funds was emphasized by their 1893 conference proposition that funeral benefit should be funded separately by branch levies on a branch-by-branch basis. This was defeated, 15–11, largely as a result of Manchester's insistence. This benefit, of course, is still funded to this day from the union's central funds. Leaving aside the question of the union's first strike, the 1891 annual report shows the following benefits paid out. £47 18s 1d was authorized in the branches for unemployment benefit. However, on examination, the individual branch returns for 1891 only itemize £23 0s 1d from three branches as unemployment benefit. Only seventeen out of twenty-five branches were included in the 1891 report – an early example of the besetting sin of ETU branch bureaucratic slovenliness. Similarly with accident benefit. Walker's 1891 annual report says £30 9s 2d was spent on accident benefit. Only two individual branches itemized accident benefit to a total of £9 0s 8d. Presumably the rest was spent by branches whose returns were late. The branch returns do not detail Walker's report that one £5 grant was paid out as funeral benefit to a member's wife. The union paid out only 9s to assist men in travelling in search of work. £34 10 0d was paid in benevolent grants for members in 'distress', presumably by executive decision, as again there are no details in the branch accounts of the types of 'distress' that benevolent grants were paid for.

The Importance of Provident Benefits

Whatever difficulties are caused for the modern reader in inching his way through their actuarial confusion, the pioneers of the union were quite certain of the great value of these 'provident' benefits. This was the era before the Welfare State was even dreamed of: pauperization, starvation and the workhouse were all real alternatives for Victorian workers – even relatively skilled ones. 1891 was a year of general economic prosperity in Victorian Britain; this prosperity was not to last, but the benefits provided by the union to its members clearly gave the pioneer leadership cause for some pride. Arthur Walker wrote in the first annual report: 'We were told by many that a union was not required. We ask – has not the first year's work of the union justified us in forming a society for electrical workers?' He then significantly goes on to discuss the benefits paid as the foremost justification of the union's first year in existence.

Look at the benefits paid out; notably that of unemployment benefit. There is something much more important than the amount paid. It is the fact that this benefit creates an independence amongst men; it prevents men through unfortunate circumstances from selling his labour below its value to unscrupulous employers, who are ever willing to take advantage of a depressed market ... Again accident benefits – just think what has been done; we have prevented men and their families becoming pauperized by appealing to their parish authorities, also by avoiding the necessity of getting rid of household effects to raise the wherewithal to support body and soul. Also it tends to stop the system we wish to see ended; that is, the passing around of a contribution sheet or public house benefit cards.

This was clear justification for such benefits and it was to remain a dominant philosophy in the union until the Second World War transformed the position of the union's benefits with the advent of the Welfare State.

By the end of 1891, the union was ready to face the world. It had 1,123 members in twenty-five branches – an increase of 553 over the year. The accounts for the seventeen branches (934 members) whose returns were included in the first report's analysis showed an income of £1,015 14s 1½d and a balance of £422 2s 4½d of income over expenditure.

They were keeping expenditure to a minimum. £118 6s 3d went on provident benefits. They appointed a full-time general secretary at £2 os od per week only in November 1891. A conference had been held at Blackfriars Street to tidy up the rules and to appoint the full-time general secretary. A system of government was agreed, and a rough compromise arrived at, in favour of craft-type trade unionism.

They even fought and lost their strike.

The Brighton Strike, October 1891

The union's early membership was heavily dependent on the telephone industry. Many of the members worked for the different regional bases of the National Telephone Company. Several members of the London executive worked for the company in London, including R. J. Steadman, the City branch secretary, who was also the first part-time general secretary of the union. The Brighton district of the company had long been notorious for its poor pay, long hours and arbitrary working conditions. One of their employees, Alfred Ewer, wrote to R. J. Steadman in April 1891 about the company and asked for the union's help. Steadman persuaded Ewer to join the union and to set about organizing a branch of the union in the town. Early in May, Steadman travelled to Brighton to open the branch. Nineteen of the twenty-one employees of the National Telephone Company joined the union, and with Steadman's help, they set about drawing up a more 'realistic' schedule of wages, hours and conditions for submission to the district manager. The members met with the company on several occasions throughout the summer.

In early September, the district manager offered the workers a reduction of one hour from their working week and promised to consider their other claims on wages etc. early in 1892. The general secretary, Steadman, took a delegation from Brighton to see the National Telephone Company's senior management in London. The national management supported their local management. Consequently, the union's executive council instructed the members to hand in notice of strike action on 9 October 1891, to be made effective on 15 October if there was no response from the company. There was no response, and the strike commenced, with every union member coming out on the fifteenth. The first ETU pickets took up position during hurricane-like weather that smashed along the south coast all that week. R. J. Steadman was sent to Brighton to conduct the dispute. During the first three weeks of the strike, a further four employees of the company joined the strike, including the factory boy. In the first week, there were fifteen members on strike. At its height in the third week, there were twenty on strike, receiving 12s a week strike pay, plus 3s a week picket duty money. At this stage all seemed to be going well. Unemployed men and army reservists were drafted in by the company, only to be paid by the union not to break the strike. £9 18s 5½d was spent on feeding, accommodating and sending home such blacklegs, to great effect. During the second week of the strike, the union got word that the company was assembling a special gang of experienced telephone men drawn from various towns on the Kent coast.

These men were met by the pickets, led by Alfred Ewer, thirty miles from Brighton, and persuaded not to destroy the strike. The men entered Brighton where they were treated to a great feast by the delighted strikers and sent home the next day 'amidst the cheers and hearty wishes of a number of strikers and their friends'. The official report of the strike thought at that stage the union was winning the strike. The company could not get skilled labour. More important, the strike was not bankrupting the infant union at all. Seventeen branches produced special levies of £114 18s 9d. Manchester sent £20 4s 6d.

Even more encouraging than the formal branch levies were the expressions of voluntary financial support from within and without the union. City branch had a whip-round of £10. The Eastern, Western, City of London and Dewsbury districts of the National Telephone Company contributed.

Other ETU workforces also contributed to the strike fund. The Newcastle upon Tyne Electricity Supply Company, Edison Swan Appliance workers at Ponders End in London, Messrs Immish, Messrs Gooldens, Messrs Holmes & Son on Tyneside, and Barnes & Morris in Bath, all organized collections among ETU members. In Brighton itself, there was an encouraging response. The ETU members at the Brighton and Hove Electric Light Company contributed 4s 9d. The Brighton branch of the ASE, the house painters and decorators and the Amalgamated Society of Railway Servants all contributed to the strike fund. Even R. J. Steadman contributed 2s 6d himself and executive councillor W. T. Tebb raised 16s 9d among his friends in London.

The total income to support the strike in the autumn of 1891 was, therefore, £139 17s 0d. This was an enormous sum – given that the total income paid into all branches in the whole of 1891 was approximately £1,015.

However, despite the financial support, the support of other unions and the effective picketing in the first three weeks, by the end of the fifth week only six remained on strike. The report of the dispute submitted to the members was clearly devastated by this collapse of a promising situation.

We were gradually but surely defeating the district authorities, when one or two of our own members began to waver – although assured of the permanent support of the union if defeated. But like a great many men who have never travelled any distance, they would sooner lick their chains at home, rather than become free men away.

By this time, the returning strikers taught unskilled blacklegs the rudiments of the job and the strike was practically over. The union continued to pay strike and benevolent grants to the loyal members until they found jobs outside of Brighton at much better wages than they could get in Brighton. Six men stuck it out to the end: Edward Bennett, Thomas Gifford, Walter Hall, William Knight and Ernest Milam, whose brother George went back to work. The final name was Alfred Ewer who organized the branch and the strike, and was to contribute again to the union's life. The last striker drew his final benefit on 19 February 1892 before being placed in a new job by the union.

The total cost of strike pay, benevolent grants and the travelling expenses incurred in sending the beaten loyalists off to other jobs came to £104 9s 0d.

There were other organizational tasks during the strike that cost a further £50 1s 4½d. The part-time general secretary had his wages paid while organizing the strike and also accommodation and travel expenses. There were rooms to rent, telegrams to send, delegations to send to London. It may well be that the experience of the strike finally convinced the union of the need for a full-time general secretary and in November 1891 A. J. Walker was elected. We do not know if Steadman stood down because he did not want the job, or whether he was stood down because the union's delegates at the 1891 conference blamed him for the failure of the Brighton strike. It is more likely that the former was the case as Steadman was to reappear as general secretary in the dark days for the union of 1895.

The strike cost the union only £14 13s 4½d over and above the money raised specially to pay for it. Although the dispute was lost, the union was able to sustain and organize a lengthy strike without destroying itself in the process. They must have taken great heart from this first strike. However, they were going to need their new found self-confidence as catastrophe loomed in the following years.

3

ON THE EDGE OF DESTRUCTION,
1892–5

THE NEXT TWO YEARS were to see this promising start gradually degenerate into a crisis that very nearly proved terminal. Although 1892 was a year of extraordinary depression throughout manufacturing industry, the union's membership rose marginally to 1,183 and its income rose by half to £1,571. However, the impact of depression, carrying on into 1893, produced a huge increase in arrears of contributions amounting to £255, a four-fold increase in unemployment benefit to £167, an increase in other benefits from £5 9s 0d to £66 17s 6d. The union was worth, per head, 7s 10d compared to 10s 0d at the end of the previous year.

In the light of recriminations against the executive in London throughout 1893–4 it is clear from the 1892 report that the general secretary, Arthur Walker, anticipated the impending financial crisis at the end of 1892. He wrote in the annual report:

> The society cannot be expected to pay out the whole of the benefits, as set forth in the rules, unless members pay £1 6s 0d per year at least, instead of an average of £1 1s 1d, as a present ... We also appeal to the members to do their duty, to keep paid up as closely as possible; otherwise there will be no other way out of the difficulty than ... increasing the contribution ... It is absolutely necessary that we should act prudently, and not be led by impulsive action. We must look to our members to help us in this, which will enable us to build up a good fund, so that we may be better prepared to take action should circumstances require. If we adhere to this policy, we shall be able to accept the prosperity which will accrue without excitement – and the difficulty without fear.

The events of 1893–4 show that few people paid any attention to Walker's warnings. So deep was the crisis that no report for 1893 was issued: the next annual report, for 1894, was not issued until March 1895. The evidence for what happened to the union in those years is fragmentary. We have to depend on the 1894 report for a summary of the accumulating problems of 1893–4: there is a brief report of the May 1893 delegate conference at Newcastle, before the crisis broke. Joe Wild's fiftieth anniversary booklet, published in 1939, consulted Manchester branch and district committee minutes which are now, tragically, lost.

These three sources tell a story of financial diaster and accumulating regional rivalries between London and its executive council on the one hand, and the Lancashire-based branches on the other.

The union virtually disappeared in 1893–4. The trade depression that started in 1892 produced demands on the union's funds for unemployment pay (donation benefit) that the union simply could not sustain. Neither could it resist employers or persuade employers to improve conditions on a widespread basis: for many potential members there was no point in joining an obscure, insolvent and irrelevant organization.

The complete lack of faith in the union's leadership was largely centred on the northern branches. The London-based executive council was criticized for incompetence throughout the 1893 conference. The Manchester branches proved to be their main tormentors, with Tommy Brennan their most vocal critic.

It is clear that Manchester's criticisms revolved around money matters. At the conference in Newcastle in May 1893, the executive council were represented by William Gooday. He moved that the Manchester delegates should not be allowed to participate in the conference as they had not remitted all their funds to London over and above 2s 6d per member in their branches. This was a rule requirement required by the 1892 conference held in Leeds. Clearly, Manchester flatly refused to throw good money after bad. The conference voted, 12–1, against Gooday's proposition. As there were twenty-seven delegates in attendance, it is possible to assume from the high number of abstentions that many delegates knew Manchester to be technically in breach of rule, but probably justified in their refusal to hand money over to the executive council.

Manchester and Salford joined forces to call for the 1892 report to be rejected on the basis of financial irregularities. The conference minutes are cryptic to the point of suggesting conspiracy and fraud.

Manchester delegates asked for explanation regarding the amounts forwarded to the general office and the amounts credited in annual report. Explanation could not be readily given.

Tommy Brennan then persuaded the conference that the report must be amended and only then distributed to the members with a proper explanation for all the errors that were in it.

Manchester knew that it had remitted £46 1s 4d to the head office in 1892.

It could only have imagined the worst when it saw in the annual report that they were only credited with having sent £32 18s 0d. It was not until the 1894 report was issued that an explanation for this single issue – and other items affecting half-a-dozen other branches and funds – was forthcoming. Apparently, some of Manchester's money had been recorded under a different heading of 'income for management grants in the second half of the year' and the rest was mistakenly omitted from the Belfast strike fund which Manchester contributed to. According to the executive, then, the money had not disappeared. However, even if the Manchester membership were persuaded that no conspiracy existed – and we have no way of knowing if they were so reassured – they must have been concerned at this evidence of sloppy book keeping.

The 1893 Conference at Newcastle: The North/South Divide

The conference supported Arthur Senior's insistence on reaffirming the union's rule that the general secretary must keep a list of the members and make the books available to all with a legitimate interest in them. It is clear that the tide of anger was running hard against the executive and, increasingly, with the general secretary. The executive, represented at the conference only in the form of the hapless Gooday, suggested that branch working expenses should be funded out of an additional levy on each branch's members to form a branch management fund. This was thrown out, 23–4, with only Gooday's own branch at Greenwich and the three other London branches voting in favour. The rest of the delegates lined up behind a motion that 'drew the attention of the executive' to the fact that the weekly contribution of 6d was meant to pay for everything – benefits, expenses, branch administration etc.

Manchester was not ignorant of the financial difficulties the union was in, and put forward its own suggestions that contributions should rise to 7d per week. As so often happens in trade union government, there must have been a peculiar alliance of opponents to this scheme. Londoners voted against, disappointed at not getting their branch management funds. They also probably thought 6d was too much, let alone 7d, reflecting the original craft–class war union debate at the union's birth. Again Manchester did not propose to use the extra income to pay extra benefits. In any case, the proposal was lost, 14–13.

Manchester sponsored a whole range of other suggestions that directly implied criticism of Walker and his friends on the executive in London. When his reappointment was 'carried' by the conference, Brennan moved a reduction, of 5s a week from his £2 salary. This aggressive suggestion was too much for the conference. The opposite proposition, supported by London branches, to raise his wages by 5s was defeated. So was Brennan's proposed reduction, and the conference voted, 22–5, to keep his wages the same as they were.

The Manchester branches eventually withdrew a motion calling on the head office to be moved to Manchester from London; they successfully denounced the executive for its handling of the Newcastle strike the previous year when a handful of ETU members had supported an ASE dispute at the Elswick works of Sir William Armstrong. They raised the shambles of the executive's failure to answer correspondence – particularly in the way they delayed their approval for the Lancashire district rates set by the Lancashire district committee. They could not have been too pleased by the conference's narrow rejection of the suggested Salford rule change to institute an apprenticeship basis for membership. There was further suspicion of the London leadership when they successfully carried a suggestion that the conference should elect a 'select committee for the purpose of the supervision of the minutes, after the same have been compiled by the general secretary'. It is no more than idle speculation; but Bill Gooday and Arthur Walker must have been relieved to return to London on 20 May 1893 after a conference like that.

Joe Wild's fiftieth anniversary 'souvenir' of the ETU's history is our only remaining source of other information about the union's dark age. There are no executive council minutes available; there are no London branch minutes available; there was no journal in existence. All we have is Joe Wild's half-page account based on his consultation of the Manchester branch and the Lancashire district committee minutes.

Manchester branch tried to nominate 26-year-old Tommy Brennan for general secretary: but even they could not have anticipated the devastating effect of the London-based executive's next important decision in September 1893. The financial crisis forced the executive to use its powers under the rules to institute a levy of the members. They insisted that each member should be levied 3d per week, to commence in January and finishing in March 1894. The Manchester branch condemned this decision. It proved a disaster. Rather than produce sufficient funds to cover the union's debts, it accelerated the headlong rush of members straight out of the union. So great was the chaos that no report for 1893 could be compiled. Manchester itself appealed for funds from the executive to keep going. During the last few weeks of 1893, the union lost 266 of its thousand or so members. Richard Steadman summarized this depressing turn of events. 'Our members ... preferred running out of our union ... leaving their comrades to pay the debts they had helped to contract.'

The Lancashire district committee initiated other responses to the looming crisis in London. On 4 November the district secretary, Tommy Brennan, wrote to the executive claiming that their correspondence was not answered and the local branch remittances were not being acknowledged. On 18

November, the district committee delegated the Salford branch secretary, T. Jackson, to inspect the books in London. His report to the committee in December was 'received with reserve'. The district wanted the right to appoint a provincial auditor of the executive's accounts and demanded that the union should even go as far as opening up an office in Manchester.

1894 saw the union's fortunes further deteriorate. The 'bottom line' for the union by December 1894 was horrific. The membership fell to 402. The income fell to £773. The union's liabilities were £91 in excess of their assets.

Manchester continued to discuss the possibility of moving the head office from London to Manchester; it remains a mystery why they did not break up the national union at its most vulnerable moment. Perhaps they were impressed with the London executive's response to the crisis throughout 1894. By 23 July, the union had already paid out over £200 in unemployment ('donation') benefit. The executive balloted the members to suspend this benefit for a full year. The members agreed, 118–108. There was much greater enthusiasm for making Arthur Walker's job as general secretary part-time by 153–33. On 15 March the executive amalgamated the City, Lambeth, Paddington, King's Cross and Kensington branches into one, London Central, thus saving considerable money in branch expenses. All of this was in response to the plummeting membership after the impact of the third levy in the spring months of 1894. One further source of reassurance was the executive's appointment of a general treasurer, as the rules allowed, from outside their own London-based number. Arthur Senior was appointed; he was the North-East Coast district secretary and prominent at the 1893 conference. It will be remembered he moved the resolution implicitly condemning the way the books were kept. His influence, and the executive's new-found determination to save the union, lead to further cost cutting. Only London Central, Greenwich and Ponders End branches remained in the capital. The only provincial branches kept open were Bolton, Loughborough, Salford and Wolverhampton. All the others which had even survived 1893 were closed for 'not complying with their orders and to general neglect of branch officials in carrying out their duties'. Preston, Glasgow, Newcastle, Nottingham, Manchester, Birmingham and Dewsbury all shut in early 1894. Tommy Brennan's name had disappeared from the union's records in December 1893, when he was expelled for arrears. Edwin Johnson, who had chaired the 1893 delegate conference and became a full-time organizer for one week, was dispensed with in 1894.

Arthur Walker's Disgrace

It would appear that Walker's shortcomings were not restricted to inefficiency in correspondence and accounting methodology. He was also corrupt. Arthur Senior discovered in November 1894 that the Wolverhampton branch had given Walker £2, Bolton had sent in £2, and the balance of funds from the closing Newcastle branch of 6s 4d had also been sent to Walker. None of these payments appeared in the books. Senior was sent to Birmingham a week later to investigate the collapse of that branch: when closing down the branch, Walker had appropriated their closing balance. The auditors expressed the view that Walker had stolen £21 9s 3d in 1894 alone. Perhaps the instincts of the Manchester membership had been correct in 1893. Walker was dismissed and Richard Steadman reappointed general secretary in his place.

It is sad that the fragmentary early records of the union only produced real data concerning Arthur Walker at the moment of his last disgrace. He was central to the foundation of the union. He was elected president of the first executive council at the conference that made the union a national institution in December 1890 in Liverpool. He was the first full-time general secretary elected in November 1891. He must have been one of the first advocates of the exclusive, proper and distinct skill of electricians. The union's first slogan was – 'Every Electrician in his own Union'. Walker worked hard to launch a union that would give that slogan some substance. His abrupt disappearance from the union's life was tragic for Walker and devastating for the members' failing confidence in the union as a national organization.

4

BACK FROM THE BRINK, 1895–9

THROUGHOUT 1895, THE UNION crept ever closer to complete extinction. By the end of the year, membership had fallen to 236. The union had virtually disappeared in the North of England. Bolton had thirteen members, Salford twenty-eight. Otherwise, the only non-London branches were Wolverhampton (sixteen) Loughborough (thirty-seven) and Dublin (whose initial eighty-three members fell to twelve by the end of the year). In London, the Central branch had halved in strength to 101, Greenwich had twenty-nine members and Ponder's End (in North London) shut completely.

The financial position was desperate. The union was still paying off debts to their printers, auditors and solicitors covering 1893–5. At the end of 1895, the executive council/head office funds showed liabilities of £31 15s 6d to set against a cash balance in hand of £1 8s 11d. The balance of aggregate branch funds had risen slightly to £187 16s 2½d. The union had fewer members and less money than at its founding conference in Manchester in 1889.

The executive council's response to this crisis was reckless, startling and, eventually, wholly successful. They decided to ballot the members on the advisability of having a full-time official once again whose main task would be organizing and recruitment. The members voted in the autumn of 1895, 106–7 to upgrade the job to full-time, and the executive appointed Francis Ernest Sims to take up the post from 1 March 1896, replacing the part-time, stop-gap, general organizing secretary, R. J. Steadman.

Francis Sims was the first electric light wireman to become general secretary of the union: Walker and Steadman had been telegraph/telephone wiremen. A Londoner, Sims was thirty years old when he moved into the one-room office at the union on 2 March 1896 in Club Union Buildings in Clerkenwell Road in London. The union's ambition to succeed in the impossible task of establishing a new union was re-launched.

Changing the Rules: Saving the Finances

First and foremost, control over the union's expenditure was ensured. The union's executive reregistered their rules on 21 November 1895, to come into force on 1 January 1896. The executive could not afford to call a rules revision conference: in any case, there were only six branches in operation. The new rules made key changes with financial implications. First, the executive emphasized its own powers to levy every member if the funds of the union were below £1 10s 0d per member, to a maximum of 2s per head. Secondly, they insisted on each branch sending to the head office any surplus branch funds every quarter. Third, they integrated the 1893–4 3d levy (that nearly destroyed the union) into a new contribution of 9d per week for full benefit members (those from twenty to forty-five who were entitled to all the union's provident benefits). The new rules introduced a lower contribution for members who joined the trade section of the union (assistants, and older skilled men up to fifty-five) and the over-age section of men over fifty-five. The trade section members paid 4d per week for legal aid, strike/lock-out benefit and a reduced funeral benefit of £5. The over-age members got legal aid and strike/lock-out benefit only, but paid only 3d per week.

The new rules were to be introduced when the union had only 236 members. Presumably, there were few members left who did not understand the financial crisis and therefore did not complain at the wholesale reduction in benefits brought in under the new rules. Funeral benefit came down from £10 to £7 for full benefit members who joined after 1 January 1896, and the entitlement to funeral benefit for members' wives was abolished. Accident benefit came down steeply. Twelve shillings per week for fourteen weeks, followed by 7s per week for another fourteen weeks was reduced to one payment of 10s per week for fourteen weeks. After that, the executive council could donate at their discretion a one-off payment. Donation benefit (unemployment) was similarly reduced to 10s per week for a maximum of twelve weeks. Branch finances were to be better supervised by executive council-appointed auditors, rather than continue the practice of branch members auditing their own branches' accounts.

Strike Rules and the Ponders End Fiasco

Most significant of all, the new rules curtailed the circumstances in which local strike actions would have to be paid for through national funds. This new rule was probably in reaction to the disastrous strike in the late summer of 1895 at Messrs Edison & Swan at Ponders End in north London.

The annual report for 1895 clearly implies the executive's resentment at the conduct of that dispute: 'In the matter of the Ponders End dispute, it may well be hoped that the ingratitude shown by those chiefly concerned will not be copied.' At this place, the fifty or so members at Edison & Swan, manufacturing lamps and lamp exhausters, came out on strike for higher wages. A settlement was reached, and the union spent just short of £118 on strike pay and the expenses involved in the strike. This sum was roughly equivalent to sixty members' contributions for a whole year.

No sooner was the dispute settled than, according to the annual report again, 'the members of the local branch forgot the services rendered them,' and the branch was closed before Christmas 1895. Branch secretary Robert Parrott wrote to explain to the executive council that the branch had ceased to function because all the members 'were too busy working overtime to attend to branch affairs'. Richard Steadman's report commented that 'it would be a sheer waste of time and space to comment on such members or on such an explanation'.

The new rules were clearly aimed to give the executive control over strikes and the payments that had been made on the say-so of district committees and branches. The new rules allowed all 'defensive' strikes, where employers attacked the union, to remain 'official' by definition. Any strike to prevent a move to lower wages or lengthen hours of work would be supported by the executive. However, where members felt inclined to join a 'movement' for better conditions, they had to follow a new procedure.

District committees – or branches where district committees were not functioning – had to summon members to a meeting on a district or branch basis. Each member present was given two slips of paper with 'yes' or 'no' written on it. After lengthy discussion, all the members would vote, and the strike would only be legitimated if three-quarters of the members at such a meeting voted 'yes'. Even then, that decision had to be sent to the general secretary to put before the executive in London. If they approved, then all the branches had to take a ballot vote of the members to authorize the planned strike action. Even if that hurdle was climbed, the new rules allowed the executive to decide that 'the time, the state of trade or other circumstances are unfavourable for such a strike and the executive may refuse to authorize it.'

These new rules steadily, if unspectacularly, rebuilt the union's finances in the last years of the century.

Table 1 shows that the drastic action in 1895–6 stopped the financial collapse of the union, and carefully rebuilt the union's finances as the membership slowly recovered.

Table 1

Type of Benefit	1894	1895	1896	1897	1898	1899
Benevolent	4 19 6	16 10 0	4 0 0			
Funeral	5 0 0	15 0 0			34 0 0	53 0 0
Travel	9 10 7		2 15 6	2 4 6	9 2	4 19 3
Accident	17 15 0	10 12 4	3 14 8	4 10 0	1 15 0	3 8 4
Donation[1]	200 18 11	12 8 0	53 0 0	45 16 8	61 8 4	129 7 0
Contingent[2]	1 0 0	12 0 0		9 12 9		11 6 0
Strike[3]		18 8 0		16 15 0	2 10 0	10 19 0
TOTALS	£239 4 0	£84 18 4	£63 10 2	£78 18 11	£100 2 6	£212 19 7
Membership at year's end	402	236	392	635	702	952

[1] 'Donation' benefit is unemployment benefit (in 1894, it was suspended in July, and not reintroduced for 12 months).

[2] 'Contingent' benefit was 'victimization' benefit.

[3] 'Strike' benefit does not include the amounts raised by special levies to sustain long strikes involving considerable numbers of members.

Sims Tours the Country 1896–7

The executive council and the new general secretary were determined to re-establish the union in 1896–7. It will be recalled that the only branches in existence at the end of 1895 outside the London area were at Bolton and Salford, Dublin, Wolverhampton and Loughborough.

Francis Sims set out from London for a sixty-day tour, trying everywhere he went to set up branches and establish the union once again. He held three meetings in Nottingham, but no one joined. He was similarly unsuccessful in Loughborough and Leicester. However, he spent nine days in Wolverhampton in June and after leafleting factories and advertising in local papers, a meeting was held at the Duke of York in Wolverhampton for all and any electrical workers. The Wolverhampton branch was suitably stimulated and by the end of the year its membership had risen from eighteen to fifty-nine.

Sims then went on to Salford. This must have been a crucial visit. The north-western base of the union in Salford and nearby Bolton had only forty-one members between them at the start of 1896. And yet among the survivors were the intensely anti-London critics of 1893–4. Arthur Senior was now secretary at Bolton. Ex-district secretary Jackson was president of Bolton. Alf Rogers was president of Salford.

The 1895 annual report, published in the spring of 1896, announced Frank

Sims's intention of touring the country on a grand organizing mission. It appealed for the 'cordial assistance of officers in branches and members alike'.

Clearly, Sims was well received. He was given a vote of confidence at the Bolton branch on 6 July.

On Friday 10 July, the Salford branch organized a 'well-attended' meeting for electrical workers at the Royal Commercial Hotel in Chapel Street, Salford. Sims was asked to speak and was supported by speakers from Manchester Trades Council. On Saturday 11 July, the two branches combined in a 4,000 strong funeral procession for the Operative Spinners' general secretary, John Fielding, at Bolton. They marched behind a cart full of new electrical appliances, and the union clearly took pride in having its place on a big march among forty other trade unions.

Whatever encouragement he received in the North-West was tempered by another disaster, this time in Sheffield. Sims organized two meetings in mid-July, mainly aimed at the local authority undertaking of the Sheffield Electric Light and Power Company. The company reacted by insisting on overtime to scupper the Wednesday evening meeting. The meeting was rearranged for Saturday. This time the company directly threatened the workers concerned with dismissal if they joined the ETU. Only six turned up and Sims left Sheffield a frustrated man.

This 'some you win – some you lose' experience continued throughout the year. London Central was successful in recruiting during the autumn, and new branches were established in Norwich and Bradford. All the founding documents from Norwich survive, and form the oldest set of individual branch records. However, the electrical workers of Leeds remained indifferent. Sims did not even bother to call a meeting, having been given no encouragement at the factories he visited. Chelmsford was the same in early 1897. However, large meetings in Liverpool and Birmingham produced viable new branches in late February and early March 1897.

The First Signed Agreement, Wolverhampton 1896–7

It is clear that the executive council and Francis Sims both viewed his first task as recruitment. His original title was general organizing secretary. However, he was also expected to negotiate with employers, and his first success was in Wolverhampton in November 1896, building, no doubt, on the successful recruiting he did in the town in June that year.

It is important to remember that the early ETU had virtually no formal, organized collective bargaining strength. It had no members, no money, and no negotiating expertise amongst its leadership. Its early successes are all the more remarkable for that.

The union's strength in Wolverhampton lay in its membership at Thomas

Parker's; the majority of members were armature or 'all round' winders at this important electrical engineering works. The members at Parker's asked for the services of Francis Sims to help them negotiate a minimum wage of 26s for all men over twenty years of age who had been at work for a year.

The standard working week in engineering in 1896–7 was fifty-four hours, and so the demand was for a minimum wage of round about 6d an hour. The 1896 annual report, written by Sims himself, reveals so clearly the atmosphere of those early 'negotiations'. It is worth quoting in full.

The members at Wolverhampton, being anxious to better their condition in the firm of Messrs Thomas Parker, asked and obtained permission of your council to allow your organizing secretary to attend their meeting on Saturday 28 November, in order to advise them as to what steps were best to be taken in order to approach the firm in question with a view to obtaining a minimum wage of 26s for all men over twenty, and who had been twelve months or more in the trade. The members having volunteered to levy themselves in order to pay your organizer's expenses and not come on the funds of the union, the executive council readily gave their permission. The secretary visited Wolverhampton from 27 November to 1 December. A most enthusiastic meeting was held at the branch house on Saturday, 28 November. A committee meeting was held on Sunday evening, 29 November, which was attended by Brothers W. Emery, A. B. Blocksedge, Jones, J. Lynch, J. Boucher and Fletcher. The organizing secretary was further instructed as to rates of wages and conditions of work at Messrs Parker's and was requested to wait upon this firm at 10 a.m. on 30 November, with a view of laying the request of the members before them for a minimum wage of 26s and discussing other complaints. Brothers J. Lynch and J. Boucher volunteered to attend at the works on the morning in question in order to back up the statements made by the secretary if required. The secretary duly attended at the time appointed and, after sending in his card and waiting some time, was allowed to see Mr Parker. After stating his business, that gentleman at first refused to discuss the matter with your secretary on the ground that he did not believe he was representing the men's opinions correctly. Finally he consented to discuss the alleged grievances providing your secretary could get six of his men to attend as a deputation at half-past one o'clock. Unless that number could be obtained, he would not be prepared to meet the secretary. This proposition was accepted by your secretary, and we are pleased to state that we were able to get seven members working in the shop to attend at the time agreed upon. The interview duly took place and lasted over one-and-a-half hours. Mr Parker at first refused to allow your secretary to speak on the main question and tried to intimidate the deputation, but finding that they were not frightened and stuck to their demands, he allowed your secretary to state the case on behalf of the union, and contented himself with a sharp cross-examination of the members of the deputation. Finally, he decided to give his answer to our requests at the end of the week, but emphatically refused to communicate his reply to your secretary, who has much pleasure in testifying to the splendid spirit shown by the members of the deputation in refusing to allow Mr Parker to bully or brow-beat them.

Later in the report Sims reveals that he had to return to Wolverhampton in March 1897 to finalize the issue.

On Monday 8 March, the secretary saw Mr Parker, of Thos. Parker Limited, at the request of the firm, in order to come to some definite understanding with regard to our demands on behalf of Wolverhampton members. The interview lasted one-and-three-quarter hours, and we have much pleasure in announcing that, as a result, an agreement was signed between the general secretary and Mr Parker, in which the firm conceded unconditionally the demand for a minimum wage, and, in addition, agreed to other concessions of an important nature, which has considerably improved the conditions of sixty-three members in that firm. This would not have been possible had not the officers and members of the branch worked hard to back up the position taken by your secretary in his conduct of the negotiations between this office and Messrs Parker.

Sims and the executive were clearly impressed with the Parker's membership levying themselves to pay for Sims's visit, illustrating the depth of the financial crisis in the union. It is also clear that a strong degree of courage was needed by the local men who volunteered to accompany Frank Sims in his interview with Mr Parker. Most interesting of all is Mr Parker's reaction. He saw Sims after keeping him waiting, but refused effectively to deal with him until his own workers would stick up for their case – which they did. It is also significant that it was not until March the next year, nearly four months after the first approach, that a settlement was reached, and the first agreement signed between an ETU official and an employer.

Early Political Moves

Sims could also see that the increasing use of electricity in municipal electricity supply undertakings could provide a useful source of recruitment. Curiously, the same paragraph appears word-for-word in both the 1895 and 1896 reports.

It may here be pointed out that members in the provinces have at their command an effective means for promoting the general interest, *viz.*, by insisting through the various trades councils and similar bodies that in all municipal electric supply undertakings the union rate shall be paid to the whole of the workers employed. We have noted with regret the indifference shown to electrical workers by various municipal authorities throughout the country, our rules and conditions being, in many instances, utterly ignored, although other trades have their union rates and conditions fully observed. We look to the members themselves for an alteration of this state of things, and urge branches to persist in demanding from the local authorities full recognition of the union conditions and rates of pay. If this policy were adopted by those within our ranks, the moral would not be lost on those outside, and we might reasonably hope to see our ranks swelled and our usefulness increased in proportion.

This passage shows two main themes. First, the normal way of 'negotiating' was to send to the employers the union's 'working rules' for the town. Each craft or group of workers would set down on a card what they believed to be fair conditions for the town. Each member of the union was expected to work only for the conditions and wages printed on his card. Each branch secretary kept stocks of other towns' 'working rules', so that if members obtained employment far from home, they would not undermine the local trade union standards that were in force in the new town to which the worker travelled. Nevertheless, few employers went out of their way to accept the card.

Sims's complete failure in Sheffield has already been noted. He was clearly anxious that this new source of employment should be fertile recruiting ground for a union that was finding it difficult to establish itself in already entrenched industries.

Second, it is interesting to note the birth of political action within the union. Sims wanted the union's branches to affiliate to local trades councils with a view to pressurizing local authorities into recognizing the working rules for electricity supply workers. It must have been particularly galling that the ETU was completely ignored, while others were properly recognized. Clearly, the general secretary attached great importance in his organizing work to the power of example. He needed success as a boost to further recruitment. Hence the lengthy description of success at Thomas Parker's; hence the importance attached to local political pressure on local authorities.

5

A FUTURE THAT WOULD NOT COME

IT HAD BEEN SIX years since the union had held a conference and the 1895 rules had been drawn up for the members by the executive in the aftermath of the union's near-extinction in 1894. A rules revision conference was called for the 1899 Easter weekend at the Royal Commercial Hotel in Salford.

The conference was chaired by Alex Calipé, who had been on the executive since 1894, and was general treasurer throughout the period. He was frequently branch secretary of London Central, the largest branch in the union, and also conference delegate for his branch. The executive was represented by Joe Pearce, the president, and Sims, the general secretary. Bill Gooday, a founder member of the union in 1889, represented his branch, Greenwich. He had been a delegate to every conference, a branch secretary and on the executive council since 1891.

Many others who had made substantial contributions to the early days of the union were delegates at this conference. Arthur Senior from Bolton and Alf Rogers from Salford were there: so was Bill Jackson, a Salford delegate and the Lancashire district secretary. Alf Ewer was there from London Central. The conference looked at details of benefits and contributions. Funeral benefit went back up to £10 for both full benefit and trade section members, and the £5 benefit for a wife's funeral was reintroduced. Strike pay was set at 2s 6d a day. Donation benefit (unemployment pay) was fixed at 12s a week for twelve weeks. London Central were opposed by every other branch when they suggested that all money over 2s 6d per member should be sent to head office. The branches allowed the executive council to levy the branches for national running costs, and they were adamant that the executive council should not have more financial power over the branches. If the new benefits cost too much in the future, the executive council were authorized to raise contributions to 10d for full benefit and 5d for trade section members.

Much more fundamental was the debate on the objects of the union which was clearly tied up with the central debate later on the apprenticeship question. We have already seen how the union was confused in its collective mind as to the nature of the union. Was it an industrial union, organizing all grades in the electrical industries, or was it an emerging craft union to parallel the large, experienced and socially powerful unions like the engineers, plumbers or carpenters? Or was it a hybrid of the two?

The new rule-book's 'objects' of the union came down heavily in favour of adopting the culture and outlook of the classic craft union. This 1899 conference was not to know that the battle to define the union's status was far from over; indeed, it had hardly begun. 'The objects of the ETU are by mutual effort to place ourselves on a foundation sufficiently strong to prevent further encroachments on our trade rights and privileges.' It was highly significant that they decided to delete the phrase 'to rescue our trade from the low level to which it has fallen'.

The new rule went on 'we propose to establish an apprentice system'. This proposition was carried without opposition, on the suggestion of the North-West delegates Senior and Rogers – whose branches had been pressing an apprenticeship-based union since the 1893 conference. It was left to the executive to design a precise system.

The new rule continued, 'to maintain a higher standard of skill'. The union was anxious to raise the status of the electrician and the industry he worked in. The low wages of an electrician, compared to, say, a carpenter, was the most obvious reflection of this lack of status. Unionized electricians were pleased to get $8\frac{1}{2}$d or 9d an hour compared to the commonplace 10d of joiners and carpenters. Non-unionized electrical workers in the Midlands were earning hourly wages as low as 5d per hour. However, the union was keen to justify much higher wages by lining the union up with other attempts to raise the status of the craft. This concern even went as far as upbraiding the membership about time-keeping. It was imperative to keep the ideas of competent workmen and union workmen in the forefront of the employer's mind. The 1900 annual report was to say in this context: 'We hope, for the union's sake, that members will improve (their time-keeping) and also, when at work, that they will take more interest in what they have to do and prove to the employers that it is to their advantage to employ union men.'

The objects of the union then went on in the same vein to include the aim of 'encouraging the formation of schools of instruction in various branches for teaching the practical application of electricity and for trade education'. Again, various union reports just after the conference mention the need to attend public classes in order to keep abreast of technical change. The union even accepted the offer of Mr Mitchell, the Southern district manager of the National Wiring Company who would lecture ETU men on house wiring methods 'in order to stamp out bad work'. It was to be eighty years later that the logical climax to the pioneers' dream of a union technical 'school of instruction' would be brought to fruition at Cudham Hall.

The union's slogan on their attractive letterheads, designed by Alex Calipé, the general treasurer, was 'Defence, not Defiance' (interestingly enough, the same slogan was widely used by the contemporary plumbers union). The rest of the union's objects in Rule 1, Clause 2, echoed this craft-union ideology. The union was to 'generally cultivate feelings of friendship among men of our craft, to settle all disputes between employers and employees by arbitration (where possible) and to assist each other in sickness and distress, to secure employment, to reduce the hours of daily labour, to secure adequate pay for our work, and by legal and proper means to elevate the moral, intellectual and social condition of all our members.'

However, an alternative set of 'objects' for the union to pursue was submitted, which had been originally moved by executive councillor Pegg at the London Central branch. It reflected the confident Marxist inspiration of the Social Democratic Federation (SDF) when it said: 'The objects for which this union is established are the socialization of the means of production and exchange, to be controlled by a democratic state in the interests of the entire community, and the complete emancipation of labour from the domination of capitalism and landlordism.'

The conference was unanimous in its reaction to this; it rejected it.

Two other main decisions of the 1899 conference were to haunt the union for the next twenty years and be instrumental in preventing its growth in that period.

Firstly, Bradford branch were only articulating continuing disappointment and suspicion of the London executive when they suggested a national executive. Each branch, they suggested, would have an executive councillor. The executive would meet quarterly, three times a year in London and then rotate once a year to large provincial towns. The branch said in its motion: 'We consider some plan of this kind should be adopted, to do away with the farce of voting for the executive council when we know nothing.' The conference rejected this unanimously as being 'impracticable' but they did accept the point of substance when the executive council members were each allocated a region of the country with whom they were expected to keep in touch as their representative. This never really got off the ground, and certainly did not lead to growing provincial confidence in the London-based executive council.

Secondly, Battersea branch attempted to get the conference to see that the rule about admitting members 'under the rate' was a guarantee of minimal growth for the union. Battersea wanted the union to let men go into unorganized works and work below the working card rate in order to recruit into the union dissatisfied potential members. The rest of the conference thought that this policy would inevitably lead to a lowering of wages for current members of the union, and threw Battersea's suggestion out. The union was going to find it difficult to recruit men who were earning below the rate because they were below the rate! If they did not join, organize and perhaps defy the employer, then, how were they ever going to achieve the working card rate and how was the union going to recruit them?

6

TWO STEPS FORWARD, ONE STEP BACK

Bolton and Sheffield 1899–1900

THE FIRST SUCCESSFUL STRIKE in the union's history was pursued with Bolton Corporation's electric lighting department in August 1899.

The strike's genesis was straightforward. Mr R. Baker, the Corporation's electric fittings superintendent, ordered two ETU members, J. Wilcox and R. Isherwood, to work overtime on 3 August at ordinary time rates. When they refused to do so, they were sacked, and the other ten ETU members came out on strike the following day.

The annual report for 1899 and Joe Wild's *Fifty Years of the Electrical Trade Union* concentrate on the eventual successful outcome. On Friday 11 August, the Corporation signed a written agreement with the union that covered the overtime rates and also introduced an agreed, comprehensive working rules agreement. The men returned to work on 14 August.

However, F. E. Sims produced for the monthly report to members for August 1899 a 3,000-word report on the strike. The details contained in this report reveal a great deal about the union's style and limitations at the turn of the century. It also reveals a story of internal bickering, local pride and skilful manoeuvring.

As far as Sims was concerned, the first he knew of trouble in Bolton came through the post on 3 August. The branch secretary, Arthur Senior (who was also Lancashire district secretary and a prominent member of another small union, the Scientific Instrument Makers Society), wrote to Sims in London. He pointed out that the Bolton branch had drawn up proposed working rules for Bolton Corporation where twelve of the branch's thirty-four members worked in the electric fittings department.

Their proposals had been rejected twice in the summer of 1899 by the electricity committee of the Corporation. They would not pay enhanced rates for overtime. They would not increase working-out expenses, even though the ETU members were increasingly being asked to work beyond Bolton's boundaries. The members had been advised by the branch secretary not to work overtime and to await further instructions from the executive council.

Sims thought that this was news to him, and he put the correspondence down on the agenda for the executive council meeting scheduled for 9 August.

On the morning of 4 August, Sims received a telegram from Senior which announced the dismissal of Wilcock and Isherwood and the instant strike response of the other men. Sims consulted with Alex Calipé, the branch secretary of London Central, and the union's treasurer, before catching the overnight train to Bolton. He arrived there at 10 a.m. on Saturday 5 August and proceeded to the club house (the Queen's Hotel, Bradshawgate).

It is easy to imagine the atmosphere at the meeting from Sims's account. He wrote that the members on strike were 'in a state of great excitement'. Like generations of officials to follow him, however, Sims had to draw everyone's attention to the fact that they had gone about everything in the wrong way. 'I told the members that I thought they had been very unwise in coming out the way they had done, without giving due notice (to the employer), especially as no intimation had been given to the executive committee of there being any dissatisfaction among the members employed at Bolton Corporation.'

The whole issue then began to turn on branch secretary Arthur Senior's conduct of the whole affair. Senior's view was that the executive had sanctioned the Lancashire district committee's 'electric light wireman's card' and so were inevitably bound to support any action to support its imposition. Clearly, Senior's inability to warn the members that the executive did not know of their problems was going to prove troublesome. Sims went on: 'The members all stated that they thought the executive were fully aware of the trouble they had been having with the Corporation, and were greatly surprised when I told them we were ignorant of any grievance.'

Francis Sims had arrived in Bolton, had an argument with the strikers, and no doubt made it quite clear to Senior just what he thought. The members' case was weakened by the impetuous nature of the dispute and the lack of notice given of strike action. Equally, it did not pay any attention to the rules of the union. Either the members should not have worked to such 'under the rate' conditions and wages in the first place or, having done so, should not have gone on strike without going through the complex 1895 strike authorization rules discussed in the previous chapter. It was clearly clever use of words, nothing more, for Senior to argue that as the executive council had agreed the district card, any strike in defence of its conditions was automatically 'official'.

Notwithstanding these intitial problems, Sims then set about dealing with the dispute itself.

Sims and two experienced strikers, Messrs Stringer and Woodcock, left the Queen's Hotel and went straight round to interview Dr Panton, the chairman of the electric lighting committee of the Corporation. Dr Panton and some of the strikers were convinced all along that Senior had never managed to get round to sending him the full story of their complaints. However, Dr Panton refused to discuss the matter with the delegation and told them to go and see Mr Baker, the superintendent.

The two members with Sims thought this was a bad idea: Sims insisted and went to Baker's house where his wife told him he was away, but fixed up for Sims to see him at noon on Sunday 6 August. Sims reported: 'I had a long and angry discussion with Mr Baker. I told Mr Baker we were sorry for the hasty action the men had taken and that, in order to come to a settlement, we were willing that the men should return to work unconditionally, pending a settlement ... but he flatly refused ... and said that not one of the men who had come out should ever put his foot in the shop again; that he was sick and tired of the union. He could get on with the sixty-six gasmen, but not with our men.' He had made arrangements to recruit new workers in Manchester and Liverpool and did not care what the dispute cost, he would not have the men back. Sims talked for about an hour with Mr Baker and then left him, pledging that despite the union's preference for a negotiated settlement Mr Baker left him with no option but to 'fight to the bitter end'.

Sims then spent the Sunday, Monday and Tuesday calling on all the great and good in Bolton who might help effect a settlement, always in the company of one or two of the strikers. He went to see Mr Champneys, the secretary of the Bolton Building Trades Federation, who agreed to arrange meetings with the Corporation. Councillor Toothill, secretary of the Bolton Trades Council was on holiday, but his wife pointed Sims towards the deputy chairman of the electric light committee, councillor J. Berry JP, who was also a member of the premier craft union in the town, the ASE. Councillor Berry lectured Sims and the delegation on the mistaken way the members had come out without notice. He also threw in for good measure his personal disgust at the ETU also withdrawing the apprentices – 'a thing which was unknown in the Lancashire district.' However, he would 'see what he could do'.

Sims also had to keep the strike going and minimize the problems likely to arise from Mr Baker's threats to replace the strikers. Five hundred posters were put up all over Bolton telling men to keep away from the strike-hit Corporation department. Two hundred and fifty similar posters were distributed in Manchester and Liverpool. All twelve strikers were detailed as pickets – six to watch the two railway stations for likely blacklegs, and six to visit the thirteen jobs the Corporation were doing. Two men arrived from Liverpool, but after Sims paid a flying visit to Liverpool to persuade Liverpool Corporation (the employer concerned), they were withdrawn. In the *Man-*

chester Evening News on 7 August 1899 there appeared the following suspect advertisement.

Electro Wiremen Wanted (non-society) for client nine miles out. Apply to offices of Maves, Farrell & Co, of 26 Victoria Street, Manchester.

Sims immediately sent another member, R. Makin, who was not on strike, but on holiday from another Bolton firm, to apply for the job at the Manchester address. It was indeed an old friend of Baker's, attempting to supply labour which he now said he would stop doing. Sims then went on to 'leave a note with the landlord' at the club room asking for Manchester and Salford to come to Bolton for help. For some reason this request was ignored, as was the telegram Sims sent the following day.

Sims must have been pleased with his success in turning back the replacement labour: he must have been less pleased with Arthur Senior. Senior had missed Monday's meetings and the strike meeting that night because he had to go into Manchester to his other union's meeting of the Scientific Instrument Makers Society. When Senior eventually surfaced on Tuesday evening, it was only to admit to Sims that he had had no correspondence between himself and the Corporation over the previous twelve months – but that all the work had been done, if only by 'personal interviews'.

Sims's scurrying round now paid off. The Building Trades Federation met in the Oddfellows Hall at 8 p.m. that Tuesday night. Sims, Senior and two strikers, Treacher and Stringer, attended for the ETU and the other unions represented were the House and Ship Painters, Operative Plasterers, Wood Sawyers and Machinists, the Carpenters and Joiners – along with the president of Bolton Trades Council.

Sims must have cringed. 'Our action in the causes that led up to the dispute and the stupid way in which the local secretary (Senior) had conducted the negotiations was freely commented on.' Nevertheless, the Federation agreed to write to Baker to set up a meeting between the Building Trades Federation and the Corporation which was arranged for Friday 11 August. This took place with only Sims present for the ETU, alongside the other unions' representatives. Mr Baker conceded the issues involved in a two-and-a-half hour meeting and the men were due to start back on 14 August.

The agreement, signed for the union on Tuesday 15 August, is worth reproducing in full because it illustrates perfectly the late Victorian style and content of industrial relations.

BOLTON CORPORATION ELECTRICITY FITTINGS DEPARTMENT
RULES FOR WIREMEN

Rule 1. That 50 hours constitute a week's work made up as follows, *viz*: Commencing 7.30 a.m. until 5.30 p.m., and on Saturdays 7.30 a.m. until 12.30 p.m. Meal hours, 12 to 1 o'clock. The starting place each morning to be from the gas offices, or otherwise, at the discretion of the superintendent. Overtime to be paid as follows, *viz*: Time-and-a-quarter for the first two hours, time-and-a-half afterwards until 7.30 a.m. on the following morning; except in the case of Saturday, when time made after 12 o'clock midnight shall be paid for as double time until 12 o'clock midnight on Sunday. New Year's Day, if working, to be paid at the same rate as Sunday. Double time to be paid for working on Good Friday and Christmas Day. Single time if not working on those days. Christmas Day to be paid a day of 9 hours, irrespective of what day this may come on.

Rule 2. The standard rate of wages to be 9d per hour, with a minimum of 8d per hour.

Rule 3. The time sheet, stating the number of hours made, must be signed by the party on whose account the work is done, or by the person in charge. All fittings and other materials to be booked before leaving the stores, and returned materials to be given in to the storekeeper, and not left about the premises, the time occupied in booking being allowed to the fitter.

Rule 4. Fitters to be allowed travelling time every morning until the work is finished. Fitters to continue working until 5.30 p.m. Tram, train, or bus fares being allowed wherever practical. In all cases of fitters finishing their work, or having cause to take their tools to the shop, to be allowed travelling time.

Rule 5. Each fitter to be provided by the department with a bass of tools, together with a price list of the same; and shall receive a lent tools ticket with any extra tools supplied to him, and shall be responsible for all such tools or their value. In case of the superintendent sending for any tools, he shall send a note for same.

Rule 6. All fitters to give in their numbers before 7.40 a.m. each morning at the offices.

Rule 7. The department shall not employ more than one assistant for each man, and no assistant to be taken on after attaining fifteen years of age.

Rule 8. Any fitter breaking materials which in the opinion of the superintendent is carelessness will be charged for.

Rule 9. Assistants under twenty-one years of age are not to be interfered with in the event of any trade dispute.

Alteration of Rules. No alteration to be made in these rules by either party without giving three calendar months' notice.

Signed on behalf of the Electricity Committee, Bolton Corporation, August 15th 1899.
J. E. Panton, Chairman
John Berry, Vice-Chairman

Signed on behalf of the Electrical Trades Union.
James Treacher, President
James Stott, Secretary

Witness on behalf of the United Building Trades Federation.
Mark Kemsley

Arthur Senior's Embarrassment

The dispute was a great success for everyone except Arthur Senior. He was replaced as branch secretary after the embarrassing meeting with the Building Trades Federation and the revelation that he could not produce any correspondence on this issue, despite the argument having dragged on for nearly a year. At the executive council meeting on 23 August, after Sims's report had been discussed, the chairman of the executive, Joe Pearce, moved a vote of censure on Senior which was carried unanimously by the executive. The resolution noted that after considering how Senior 'had conducted the business with the Corporation representatives, we consider his conduct deserving of severe censure and record our disapproval of his action and general negligence.'

Senior fell into arrears and was excluded from the union at the end of 1899. Yet he was one of the pioneers of the union, whose eventual disgrace cannot totally obscure his important commitment to the union in its earliest days.

He joined the Newcastle branch on 28 September 1891 when he was twenty-nine. He moved around in the next eight years to Kings Cross, Ponders End and Bolton branches. He was the North-East Coast district secretary and later the Lancashire district secretary. He was a voluble and constructive conference delegate in 1893 and 1899. The executive sent him to several branches in 1895, 1897 and 1898 to sort out financial malpractice. He was warmly regarded by Sims on his grand tour in 1896 as he set about rebuilding the union after its near extinction. Perhaps Arthur Senior's failure to operate effectively during the Bolton strike was due to his dual membership with the Scientific Instrument Makers Society. In any event, members of that union overwhelmingly refused to amalgamate with the ETU in the autumn of 1899. It might just be that Arthur Senior's revenge could be seen in that ballot vote.

Sheffield, March 1900

The Bolton Agreement became the model for other local authority electrical undertakings. Sheffield was to be the next town where Sims could chalk up a significant success. He held a meeting at the Yorkshire Stingo on 24 October 1899. The usual formula applied. Present were about thirty local electrical workers and members of the union from Salford, Middlesbrough and Bradford. The meeting was then addressed by Sims himself. However, this time he must have been boosted by Mr Northern from the office staff of the National Telephone Company – an erstwhile opponent of the union at its birth – who chaired the meeting. And in stark contrast to his first visit to Sheffield in 1896 this time Sims had no less a figure than Councillor Richardson, the Sheffield

City auditor, to talk to the meeting. Councillor Richardson, according to the executive council minutes of 1 November, 'made a stirring speech in our support, and assured the men that he and the other members of the Corporation would do their level best in the way of supporting improvements in the conditions, work and wages, provided that the Corporation received the support of the E T U.'

With support like this, it is hardly surprising that a branch of the union quickly got off the ground in Sheffield.

Throughout the autumn of 1899, the local branch and the union's executive pressed the city authorities to make a reality of councillor Richardson's commitment at the founding meeting. Pressure was certainly required. The Corporation reduced the working week from fifty-six to fifty hours, without the consent of the men and also refused to pay any overtime rates, just as Bolton had done. In early December, Mr W. Johnson, the manager and engineer of Sheffield Corporation electric supply department, wrote to the union suggesting the adoption of a fifty-three hour week and time-and-a-quarter for just the first two hours. The Sheffield branch then drew up a comprehensive set of working rules, which were eventually the basis of the agreement signed in Sheffield on 12 March 1900, 'with the result that practically the whole of our demands on behalf of our members were conceded.'

It is interesting to compare the Sheffield agreement with the Bolton settlement wrung from Mr Baker. The wages at Sheffield were to be a minimum of $8\frac{1}{2}$d per hour, compared to Bolton's 'minimum 8d, maximum 9d' per hour.

Bolton men had to put themselves out a little less than their Yorkshire colleagues. They worked from 7.30 a.m. to 5.30 p.m. from Monday to Friday in Bolton, but 7.30 a.m. to 6.00 p.m. in Sheffield. The dinner hour, unpaid, in both towns was from 12 p.m. to 1 p.m. On Saturdays, the Sheffield men had to work right through to 1 p.m.: in Bolton, they finished at 12.30 p.m.

Both sets of workers would be paid to travel to and from a job, and in Sheffield, if the job was one-and-a-half miles away from the headquarters of the electric light department, they would be allowed time off work to ensure they were inside the one-and-a-half mile radius at the normal stopping time.

Sheffield's overtime rates were slightly more generous than Bolton's. Bolton paid time-and-a-quarter for the first two hours, and time-and-a-half for all hours worked then until 7.30 a.m. the following morning. Sheffield, on the other hand, paid time-and-a-quarter for the first two hours, time-and-a-half for the next two hours and double-time through to the next day. Both towns paid double time on Sunday and bank holidays (although these were apparently restricted to Easter and Christmas Day in Bolton).

The union had success in stipulating that there should not be any 'assistants' under the age of fifteen in Sheffield, where, if they were still employed after five years, they would be 'entitled' to the wages of a fitter. In Bolton, however, although agreeing along with Sheffield to only one 'assistant' per fitter, they insisted that no 'assistant' would be started after he attained his fifteenth birthday: this implies quite young boys working as electrical assistants in Bolton. Bolton went further than Sheffield in providing a wide range of tools – although Sheffield actually agreed their fitters could 'sharpen tools which have been in use on any work in connection with the department in works time.'

These two agreements were both printed in the 1899 annual report as examples to the rest of the union. Their details vary slightly, but they reveal a pattern of concerns that must have been universal for the early membership of the union. The union sought to establish its district rates, overtime entitlements, hours of work, ratios of apprentices (or assistants) to qualified members, travelling payments and tool allowances. These first two formal agreements must have been a great fillip to the new union.

However, the agreement in Bolton did not guarantee the supportive mutual respect from the employers that their very signing seemed first to imply. Mr Baker was clearly not impressed with the August deal he had put his name to. He sacked one of the men, the shop-steward Albert Woodcock, for complaining about Mr Baker's friends, the gas fitters. Woodcock objected to gas fitters fixing electroliers and doing wiremen's work on Corporation jobs. Baker had apparently then sent out large numbers of boys without fitters, sometimes having boys supervising boys right outside the agreement. He also employed twelve non-unionists and then actively urged them not to join the ETU.

Sims had to return to Bolton at the end of October 1899 and get a meeting with the full Trades Council, the Building Trades Federation and the electric light committee of the council to get the Bolton agreement back on the tracks. This was successful – so much so that Joe Wild could write forty years later of Mr Baker and the Bolton relationship:

It is pleasing to add that our subsequent relations with Mr Baker, until the time of his death at an advanced age, were of a most cordial nature. Since the signing of the agreement, negotiations with the Bolton Corporation have always been marked by goodwill on both sides, and remain so up to the present (1939).

One Step Back – Edinburgh 1900

The Bolton and Sheffield settlements gave the union great heart; they were widely reported to the membership to show just what the union could do. By the end of 1899, the union had opened twenty-five branches throughout the country. New branches had been opened after Sims's organizing work in Dublin, Huddersfield, Nottingham, Middlesbrough, Sheffield, Fulham and Stratford in east London. Indeed, organizing was becoming such a time-consuming, but rewarding, part of the union's work, that the members voted in November 1899 to elect a second full-time official, called the organizer. He was to be paid the same as the general secretary (£2 10s 0d a week) with 5s daily expenses. He was to work the hours according to whichever district's working rules card he was covered by. He had to be elected every three years and submit a fortnightly report to the executive. Three members were nominated by the branches. Joe Pearce, the president of the union's executive, was nominated by nine branches, an armature winder from Bradford called Morgan was nominated by Greenwich branch only (who got into the spirit of things by nominating all three candidates). The third nominee was Alfred Ewer, an electric light wireman who was the leader of the Brighton strike in 1891 and the 1899 conference delegate from London Central branch. Both Pearce and Morgan refused nomination, so Alf Ewer became the union's first organizer at the executive council meeting on 20 December 1899. Pearce resigned from the executive at its next meeting to take up a job in Northwich, Cheshire, and so one of the union's earliest pioneers drifted temporarily out of activity.

Ewer meanwhile was pitchforked into the next significant dispute for the union: after Bolton and Sheffield, the union's active members may have become over-confident.

This time, the union was seeking to establish itself effectively on the east coast of Scotland, based in Edinburgh.

In July 1899, G. Bailes, who was an armature winder at D. Bruce Peebles Tay Works at Bonnington in Edinburgh, was sacked for alleged incompetence and Robson, a fitter, was sacked by the same company for refusing to put a piece of wood in the key-way of a 250-unit armature. The union took up both cases and, in the enthusiasm generated, formed a branch in Edinburgh on 14 July; and on 15 July, Sims helped the armature winders at Peebles to draw up a proposed set of working rules for submission to the company.

By the end of the year, the branch had over fifty members and Sims congratulated the 'energetic' secretary, J. E. Cuthbertson, who organized a splendid smoking concert for the branch members in November that year.

However, despite successful recruitment and social events, D. Bruce Peebles was not interested in recognizing the union. Eventually, Sims was implored to travel to Edinburgh in March 1900 to try to get the company to accept the terms of the working card drawn up the previous July. It was important for Sims and the union to do well at Peebles. Firstly, success would mean an important breakthrough in eastern Scotland. Secondly, Sims was keen to show that armature winders and other electrical engineering grades were as important to the union as the numerically dominant electric light wiremen (contracting electricians).

Sims met the manager of the winding department, Mr Pickstone, on Saturday morning, 3 March. Mr Pickstone did not object at all to the terms of the working card 'but he would not sign or bind himself to anything as it was against the traditions of the firm to enter into any agreements either with masters or men.'

Sims met the members on the Monday and they decided that if the company did not concede the issue by 13 March the union would withdraw its members. On the morning of 13 March, six members were summarily dismissed for agitating for a strike. They were marched straight out of the works where they found ten policemen who, in Sims's words 'were watching the premises for fear they would fall down'. The rest of the members came out in support, and the dispute started.

However, it was never quite solid. By April there were twenty men on strike. Four members went back to join two who never went on strike in the first place. Curiously, the foreman and deputy foreman were Brothers A. and J. Hart who were ex-members of the union at its Greenwich branch – and J. Hart had even been on the executive in the mid-1890s.

Blacklegs were imported into the firm, including a man called Ridgway who was an acrobat and conjurer by profession! The dispute was lost, despite its being sustained formally for months – but it remains interesting for several reasons. It was Ewer's first test as an organizer and he seemed personally to come out of the dispute quite well. He was sent to Edinburgh the moment Sims returned at the outbreak of the strike in mid-March 1900, and was there until the executive effectively conceded defeat by withdrawing Ewer at the end of May.

He was indefatigable in organizing meetings in support of the strikers throughout Edinburgh. He was made responsible for organizing the levy-based support for the strikers. He kept up a spirited correspondence in local newspapers in defence of armature winders, who were attacked by an anonymous company spokesman as springing 'from that section of the great unwashed which comprises "sticket" joiners, plumbers, telephone labourers and hare-brained wiremen – all of whom having failed in their own particular branches drifted to armature winding.' Although the company formally denied they thought this of their men, it was left to Ewer to defend the strikers' qualifications and apprentice training.

The strike was punctuated by one serious and one frankly bizarre court case. In April, the union won the back wages of the six strikers summarily dismissed on 13 March, despite the ASE district secretary, J. Sliman, giving evidence for the company! The dispute degenerated into farce, however, when the blackleg acrobat and conjurer, Ridgway, issued a summons against F. J. Cottrell, a striker originally from Greenwich, for using obscene and indecent language against him as he went into work through the police cordon and picket line.

Ridgway said that Cottrell and his friends swore at him in the presence of his son, who supported Ridgway's story. However, Cottrell and all his friends insisted that they were talking about the fall of Pretoria, in the Boer War, which had been in the news that day. Furthermore, they were fed up with Ridgway rattling the coins in his pocket as he passed the pickets each pay day whilst at the same time putting his fingers to his nose! Cottrell and friends also said they could produce witnesses to Ridgway's oft-stated claim that he would pay £50 to get the pickets locked up: and the final straw for Cottrell must have been Ridgway's frequent habit of calling across to Cottrell and his friends that they were 'a lot of daft cockneys'.

Confronted with this evidence, the judicial Baillie Baxter, who tried the case, found it 'not proven'. By 27 June the twenty remaining strikers had been found other jobs, all over England in some cases, and the levy was ended as was the voluntary hardship fund. However, the funds were not subscribed to with the usual enthusiasm, and the company had successfully repudiated union recognition.

The steady, if unspectacular, progress of the last years of the nineteenth century was interrupted by yet another scandal involving the incompetence and dishonesty of the general secretary.

Alf Rogers, the Salford branch secretary, attended executive meetings in London during both October and November 1900. He complained bitterly to the executive that Sims had failed to handle a dispute with Mather & Platt's in Manchester, who were apparently trying to reduce outworking allowances. Rogers had first raised this subject in April, and in August Sims and he had met the company to present the full working card. Sims had promised Mather & Platt's that he would prove that other firms were already paying the working card rate of 38s for fifty-three hours for winders and 37s 6d for wiremen.

Nothing had been done, and the executive unanimously resolved 'that this council deplore the negligence of the general secretary in reference to the Manchester correspondence, and request that he take steps to prevent anything of a like nature occurring again.'

Within two months, the executive had received similar complaints from Greenwich and Liverpool branches. The watchers were gathering around Sims. In December executive councillor and auditor Brixey from the Battersea branch was reporting that Sims's accounts and the general office books did not add up. Sims failed to convene the pre-Christmas executive altogether. At the first executive in January 1901, the proceedings opened with a bang. Alf Ewer, the organizer, resigned, saying he could no longer tolerate the 'maladministration' of Sims. Bill Gooday, now the chairman of the executive, and therefore president, asked Sims direct if he had settled the Mather & Platt's business with the Salford branch. Sims replied that he had not. Gooday asked why the executive had not been convened. Sims replied by giving two months' notice of his resignation. Ewer consequently withdrew his, accepted the job of general secretary, pending a new election, and it was decided to hold a ballot of the members to decide whether the union should sustain two officials or revert to one.

Incompetence was not Sims's only crime. By February 1901, under great pressure and accusations from Salford of executive responsibility for Sims's thieving, the executive council decided to prosecute Sims. Ewer and Calipé spent nearly 300 hours between them clearing up the books that Sims had left at Club Union Buildings. The executive council paid each of them £3 for this extra evening work that produced the evidence to convict Sims on 12 March 1901.

Sims was sent to prison for six months. At his trial he revealed that he had stolen over £100. His excuse was that it was difficult to live on his low wages of £2 a week (actually he was paid £2 10s 0d) and the absence of sufficient expenses to cover his travelling, organizing and hospitality expenditure.

The judgment on Sims has to be ambivalent. He stole a comparatively huge sum of money – the best part of a year's salary. As we shall see, his subsequent attempt in the autumn of 1901 to set up a breakaway union did not endear him to his erstwhile colleagues.

However, when he took over in 1896 the union had under 300 members, six branches and no money. At the time of his arrest, the union had 950 members and £1,000 in the bank. Joe Wild, presumably after consulting Jimmy Rowan, the general secretary from 1907 to 40, had this to say of Sims: he was 'a man who did not shirk the hard work and rough routine which his duties involved ... a capable general secretary and a splendid organizer ... though lacking 'in some of those moral qualities without which no amount of hard work can be an adequate substitute.'

Sims wrote to Ewer in 1903 for a reference as a trade unionist as he planned to emigrate to America to join his brother. Ewer's reply does not survive. The only other time Sims re-enters the union's life is for a brief period when he was readmitted to the union in 1913 as an ordinary member.

7

SLOW GROWTH AND SPLITS: EMERGING FROM THE SHADOWS

THE ELECTION FOR A new general secretary in April 1901, was clearly a Manchester–London conflict. Alf Rogers, the Salford branch secretary and then Lancashire district committee secretary, got 122 votes. Alf Ewer, however, won decisively with 244 votes. Salford kept up the pressure on the executive, and must have been annoyed to have their request for a conference in 1902 turned down. However, the members decided to retain the second job of organizer. The executive decided to start the new organizer in Manchester. Alf Rogers won the election against a relative unknown, S. Fairfax, 352–21, in June 1901.

Alf Ewer ought to have known that he was not taking the union over in auspicious circumstances. The union had few members and was unlikely to recruit many more. He himself showed his awareness of the problem in his first quarterly report to the members in June 1901. First, he denounced the apathy of the members. Evidence for this was widespread. The membership had fallen slightly to below 900. Turn-out in the general secretary and national organizer elections was approximately forty per cent. The London district secretary had reported to Ewer 'the London members do not take enough interest in the work of the district committee. The delegates from some branches are more often absent than present. Some branches change their delegate too often, thereby retarding the work of the committee.' This apathy was compounded by the twin evils of parochialism and lack of responsibility. The members 'must put aside the selfish ideas of only helping the members in their branch ... funds must be cheerfully supplied to the executive council' for the purpose of distribution to poorer branches and individuals.

Older members would not take up branch office and then wrote Ewer furious letters about inexperienced people holding office! Fundamental problems pressed in upon the union. Ewer wrote: 'There is no doubt that before us lies a very critical period, and we shall need to stand shoulder to shoulder and fight as other trades have fought. We have not only gigantic trusts being formed in all directions, but we have associations of smaller employers being formed, whose sole object is to defeat the aims and intentions of trade unions.' If the members worked together 'we shall soon become a powerful organization and be enabled to deal with not only the unemployment question, but also prevent the encroachment of other trades and the victimizing of our members by unscrupulous employers.'

Much of the apathy was due to the complete inability of the union to decisively influence negotiations in the members' favour. No one should be surprised at this. The union had no members. Bill Gooday wrote in the summer of 1903 that the union did not have five per cent of the eligible workers in London. He had held six organizing meetings in six weeks that summer; attendances were awful, and the current membership didn't turn up either. He put this disastrous failure to recruit down to the 1899 rule that only people receiving the rate of $9\frac{1}{2}$d in London would be admitted. Gooday reckoned eighty per cent of London electrical workers were working for $8\frac{1}{2}$–9d an hour, so the union could not recruit them even if they did turn up to his meetings!

What I consider the only possible way to organize the electrical trade in London is to admit all and sundry, no matter what rate they are at present receiving, provided they are competent workmen. Let them still remain in shops where they are at present employed until we see an opening elsewhere and then draw them from the job.

Early in the century, the union was also confronted, as all unions were, by the malevolent influence of low economic activity and unemployment, the paralysis of the strike option following the Taff Vale Judgment in 1901, which threatened any union organizing a strike with bankruptcy, and the continuing example of the crushing of the ASE in the great lock-out of 1898. It was a vicious circle. The union had no members because it had a non-existent national reputation: with such a low profile, who would want to join it?

In January 1900, the union circulated fifty letters to the electrical firms in Manchester, with details of both their winders' district card and the wiremen's equivalent. Only one company wrote back and accepted it. P. R. Jackson & Co and Messrs Royce referred it to the local Engineering Employers Federation (EEF). Two companies provided the cruellest cut of all. Geo Hill & Co and Messr O'Brien & Co replied by saying they were not prepared to recognize the cards – not least because they 'were unaware of the existence of the ETU'.

By 1904, the general secretary was still obliged to urge caution on the members in even admitting to their membership of the ETU. He wrote:

In order to assist the members generally in finding employment, they are requested not to look for work in large parties, nor to wear the union's badge when applying for work; and to aid them in keeping employment, when found, they are directed to use the information that they are members of the society with the greatest discretion.

Jimmy Rowan, on his election to the post of national organizer in September 1904, was to bemoan the difficulty in enforcing the district rates that were printed in everyone's local working card:

This difficulty is due, not so much to the falling off of trade, as to the increasing practice of employing unskilled and cheap labour to do the work that should be done by wiremen and it is absolutely necessary, if wiremen are to maintain their position and rates of wages, that we must have better organization in order to cope with the endeavours of employers to reduce the standard of work and wages. There is no doubt that the class of work which is being done in some districts is a disgrace, both to the employers and the men they employ. It is our duty as trade unionists to do all we can to alter this state of affairs.

This was a further pressure on the union – the low quality of work due to the unqualified nature of the new workforce. The union was anxious to establish in the employer's mind a strong connection between high quality work and union rates of pay. Only this combination would improve the status of electricity in its competition with gas for street and house lighting. Only this combination would give the union some control over entry to the trade and the terms and conditions of work within the new industry.

Technical education held the key. Alf Ewer urged the membership in June 1905 to go to evening classes – before anyone else did! 'There is not the slightest doubt but that the present overcrowding of the trade, and consequently, the cutting down of the price of labour has been largely brought about by the technical classes which have been open to every Tom, Dick and Harry that have presented themselves.' Rowan would speak of the widespread failure to confront the problem of the 'flood of apprentices and handymen who are being rushed into the electrical trade.' His organizing reports were a catalogue of disappointment. Stafford was useless due to the 'selfish individualism of the men'. In Rugby, the British Thomson-Houston Co would only pay the hourly rate if the men worked piece-work to achieve it! Loughborough's armature winders were passive and Birmingham was the worst.

Conditions I found very bad – the wiremen totally disorganized and the district rate ignored by the employers who are paying anything from 5d per hour. I attempted to bring the men together, but they appear to be apathetic. In fact, they have got so low that they are afraid of trying to rise. The armature winders, on the other hand, are well organized and the wages earned will compare favourably with any in Great Britain – an object lesson in itself.

And this was also true. Throughout Britain, small pockets of organization existed where straightforward relationships with employers produced agreed rates of pay and acceptance of the union's working rules. These established standards in the locality served employers well by preventing other contractors from undercutting contract prices because of cheap wages. Nottingham was such a town. Leicester was another (with the notorious exception of Gent's, who were excluded from tendering for the telephone exchange contract in 1905 after ETU pressure on the local council).

In Manchester, Bolton, parts of east London, Glasgow, Liverpool and Newcastle, the union had *de facto* recognition of its card in scattered local authorities, winding shops in engineering, some shipyards and government construction contracts.

Throughout the period the union kept the local authority and government area under strict review. They frequently complained to the Admiralty about cheap electrical work in the dockyards, and attempted to establish their working rules as the district rate for the purposes of 'fair wages' comparisons that were legally obliged to be paid on government work. This vigilance was the real basis of the union's entry into the political world. The union was almost universally represented by its branches on local trades councils and building workers federations. In London, they sent delegates to the National Association for the Extension of Workman's Trains, the Workman's Housing Council, the London Labour Conciliation and Arbitration Board and the General Federation of Trades Unions (GFTU). This body was not a trade union centre in the modern sense of attempting to co-ordinate trade union policy for the whole movement. The ETU looked upon it as an insurance society above all: they paid in at the rate of 3d per member per quarter and received a strike pay supplement of 2s 6d a week on top of the union's own benefit of 15s. The Trades Union Congress (TUC) in those days was not the body it is today. The ETU sometimes sent a delegate, and sometimes did not, depending entirely on the state of the funds. All of these bodies provided in their separate ways two main types of assistance to the struggling union. They gave the ETU a reputation of being the electrical union in an area of industry where many wanted to claim the work as an extension of their more traditional callings. Secondly, they gave the early ETU representatives the industrial and political contacts and experience that alerted them to advantages and openings for the union.

Most significant of all, the union had decided to send Sims to the founding conference of the Labour Party (Labour Representation Committee (LRC) as it was then known, in February 1900). After the original conference the executive council circulated LRC pamphlets throughout the year and took every opportunity to support the new party. However, in 1901 and 1902 they did not affiliate to the party or send a delegate to the conference on the grounds of expense. In 1903, they balloted the union to affiliate formally. The union voted, 255–66, to pay 1d per month levy to the LRC.

Sims and other members of the executive were clearly convinced socialists – notably Bill Gooday who was the first ETU speaker at a Labour Party conference when he spoke at the 1903 LRC conference of the need for 'class-war'. However, the leadership's personal support for iconoclastic Marxism was restrained. The defeat of the SDF resolution at the 1899 conference shows the union to have been sensitive to the need not to over-politicize its industrial message.

They were convinced of the need for independent political representation. The 1900 annual report made this very clear.

We appeal to the members, one and all, to take more interest in local matters, such as the works of trades councils and the elections of guardians, school boards, district and borough councils and also the imperial parliament; and wherever possible to help return members of their own class to represent them, as by so doing, they will be represented by men who will know their wants and desires.

However, it is highly significant that the same paragraph goes on to say that such elected men would be the type:

who will see that the trade union clause is inserted in all contracts and conformed to by the contractors ... we must insist on all municipal and government work being done under trade union conditions, and the only way to accomplish this is to return men of our class to sit upon those bodies, and advocate, wherever possible, that the work shall be done direct and without the aid of a contractor.

By 1903, the leadership were bringing wider political messages to the members' attention. Ewer wrote in the quarterly report to members in March 1903:

In times past we have been able to effect improvements by the means of strikes, but owing to the actions of the Law Lords in recent cases, this valuable weapon has been rendered impotent. But the workers themselves are to blame for this, simply because they forget themselves, their wives, and their families, and on every opportunity, go to the ballot box and vote for the employing class to make the laws to govern them.

The union's sense of national identity was also boosted in 1902–3 by the purchase of its banner and the introduction of the union's distinctive lapel badge. The banner was demanded at the 1899 conference: it was to take two national levies of the members to raise the necessary funds for its purchase; no sooner had the money been originally raised then it was spent on the 1900 Edinburgh strike relief. In the event, this was probably sensible, as the banner took over three years to come to fruition. Alex Calipé suggested that Walter Crane be approached to design the banner at an executive council meeting in

November 1899. His design was submitted in April 1900 and the executive indulged themselves with some 'minor alterations' to the design and then accepted it. A regular, one-sided correspondence was then struck up with the great man – who at last replied in September 1901, apologizing for the delay and asking for further advice and time. The union replied by asking him to guarantee the banner would have all the fittings and asked for a price. At the mention of money, Crane replied within a week or so, and said that he would paint the banner on both sides on silk and supply it complete with all the fittings for £100. The executive were appalled and wrote back, asking 'if he could do it for less, as we are only a small society'.

The negotiations became lively. Within a fortnight Crane wrote to ask how much they had got. The executive replied £75. However, they had to ballot the members for a second levy to raise the money once more. In October the members voted, 403–91, to impose a 1s per member levy – at a time when the hourly rate of pay was rarely 9d and usually around 6–8d. Walter Crane now knew he would be paid and promised to keep his price to £75 'if possible'. The banner arrived by May day 1902 and Crane was paid £80 for his services. It was formally unfurled at a Bohemian concert in Finsbury Town Hall on 14 June 1902 in the presence of the mayor of Poplar and Will Crooks MP, an early LRC member whose election campaign that year in Deptford was funded in part with £4 of the ETU's money.

The banner has survived; however, it is probable that it is a copy of the original, produced in 1906 or 1910 when the union ordered copies to be painted. The original can still be seen in the union's emblem – or certificate of entry to the union – which was based on a photograph of the original banner taken in 1902, and adapted as a membership certificate. Walter Crane produced his most enduring symbol at the centre of the banner's design, the angel of liberty; it was a symbol that was adopted on many other banners throughout the golden age of trade union banner-making before the First World War.

It is hard to underestimate the banner's symbolic importance to the union. There was no television, and no media barrage to be utilized in advertisement of the union's very existence. The banner was the only public expression of the union's sense of its own status – and as such, a Walter Crane banner of such distinction was an important investment of the union's money. The angel of liberty was then adopted in the form of lapel badges and watch-chain pendants at 1s each in 1903. A union journal was issued – the *Eltradion* – in April 1905 to give a further boost to the union's national impact, and the angel of liberty featured on the cover. In time, 'Light and Liberty', the slogan on the banner, was to replace 'Defence not Defiance' as the union's rallying cry and the union's journal sold photos of the original Walter Crane banner at 1s each for a 6″ × 4″ print.

The union was therefore able to gain a degree of credibility through its activities on the broader stage of the LRC, trades councils, the Building Trades Federation and other bodies. However, its growth was decisively held back by other trades and their unions looking upon the emerging electrical industries as a useful source of extra work and membership for them.

Much of the 'bread and butter' part of an early wireman's work was to fix the narrow gauge pipework before running wires through the casing or barrelling between the source of the electricity at the one end and the appliance, meter, lighting, bells, etc. at the other. Originally, the bare wires were cased in wood. Later, the enclosed wires were run through metal pipework, sometimes called 'barrelling', 'pipework' and, later, 'conduit'. Throughout this period, in ship-building, on building sites and in engineering works – let alone the emerging electricity power generation and distribution business – it was the erection of the casing or barrelling that interested engineering fitters, plumbers, pipefitters and carpenters. The 1901 annual report spelt this problem out as far as the joiners were concerned. Alf Ewer was frustrated that in the first twenty years of the industry, when wiremen fixed their own wood casing,

the Carpenters Society never wanted the work, even when offered it ... the skilled joiner looked on it with contempt. But now, the electrical industry having grown into a great business, they are, whenever possible, pushing the wireman to one side and not only fixing the casing, but running the wire and fixing the fittings ... we shall have to fight and fight hard to maintain our trade rights and privileges.

The union's records are full of this type of thing; rivalries were persistent in the early 1900s in Birmingham as gas fittings were replaced with electrical fittings. In the shipyards, other trades constantly tried to take the barrelling work from the wiremen. In 1901, the General Smiths, Fitters, Bell Hangers and Whitesmiths Society attempted to fit the entrance bells and calling bells at Battersea Baths. Bolton branch in 1901 were furious that plumbers did electrical work. Swansea felt the same in 1904. There was an aggregate meeting of members on 29 July 1901 from all over London to discuss the problem of taking work from the carpenters by force. These rivalries between skilled workers were compounded by accusations of labourers doing skilled work and foremen working overtime on the tools. These questions sometimes called for desperate remedies. In September 1901, a contracting company called Salman & Gluckstein wrote to the union's executive and asked what the ETU's response would be if the smiths, fitters and bell hangers went on strike in order to regain the barrel-work that Mr Ewer had been kind enough to identify on the site as specially constructed for electrical work? More important, what should he, the engineer of the firm, do? The executive council minute endorsed Ewer's reply: 'The secretary told him to ask the Fitters' Society to send him more men and if they refused, the manager would be justified in taking on non-union men, providing the trade union price was paid.' The members were instructed to accept this: 'it was agreed that we claim the fixing of all barrel, to be used for electrical purposes and that the members on the job be informed of this as well as the engineer.'

Relations with the ASE remained fairly cool, although in Birmingham throughout this period there is little evidence of the friction that occurred elsewhere and occurred in Birmingham with other unions.

In Belfast in 1905 Jimmy Rowan was to denounce the ASE, 'owing to them trying to poach our members. They are using a new name for wiremen, *viz.*, electrical fitters; but it is only a thinly veiled excuse to get mechanical fitters on electrical work in the shipyards.' The ASE set up electrical branches in the Belfast area, and this sort of behaviour must have conditioned the executive's response to the ASE's offer of absorbing the ETU into their enormous union in the same year. Fred Donaghue moved, and the executive council unanimously passed:

Further, that when we can see any necessity for, or benefit to be derived from, joining their Association, we shall not be slow in taking advantage of their offer; also, that while believing that the greater the unity, the better for the workers, we are of the opinion that we are quite capable of catering for the needs of electrical workers.

This picture of sporadic local influence and self-conscious attempts to cut an increasing national figure was altered for the better in 1906. In that year, the union joined the Federation of Engineering and Shipbuilding Trades (FEST) which was the forerunner of the Confederation of Shipbuilding and Engineering Unions (CSEU). The union paid £10 to affiliate nationally, and the general secretary, Ewer, was automatically invited on to the executive council. They then needed to obtain recognition from the EEF, which they secured in August 1906. This decision came as the logical conclusion to the union's members starting to work a new payment system in engineering and shipbuilding called the premium system of payment.

The union had always been ferocious in its apparent opposition to piece-work schemes: but in many parts of the heavy engineering industry, in towns like Barrow and Manchester, over fifty per cent of ETU members were working some variation of piece-work or bonus payment. The organizer, Jimmy Rowan, was convinced that on this issue, if it co-operated with the new scheme, the union could recognize the reality of its members' lives, and use that co-operation to achieve national recognition from the EEF. The executive put the 1905 Carlisle agreement between the ASE and the EEF to its own members.

The conditions attached to the premium bonus system were: that the time rate should always be paid, that overtime and nightshifts should be paid on the same basis as for time work, that a time limit for jobs could only be re-negotiated when methods of manufacture were changed and that the system should be a permanent one. Only if these conditions were met could bonuses be paid for higher output. These propositions were already on the table from the Manchester EEF to the members, and in November 1905, the union voted, 150–120, to adopt such a scheme. Having accepted this method of payment, having joined FEST, when Rowan met Mr T. Biggart, secretary of the EEF, the union was admitted to the recognition procedure agreement offered by the Federation – without the obnoxious anti-union clauses that had years before caused the great lock-out of 1898.

It is undeniable that slow progress was being made. By March 1907 membership had risen to 1,363. National and local negotiations produced elements of credibility for the union. However, throughout this period the union was dominated by an atmosphere of the most unpleasant personal bickering, criticizing and lack of trust in each other that must have deflected the union's active members from the real trade union purpose of representing their members.

Much of this was due to the continuing lack of confidence in the London executive and their occasional cross responses to Manchester's concerns within the union.

In March 1902 Alf Ewer replaced the disgraced F.E. Sims as general secretary and Alf Rogers – the Salford branch secretary who had done most to expose Sims – was elected organizer, by 352–21, over an unknown member called Fairfax. The executive then decided to have Rogers based in Manchester, 'for the time being', and not to change his base without three months' notice. Tragically, by June 1901 Rogers was dead. A further election, which went to two ballots, was held. In the second ballot, Londoner Bill Gooday beat Salford's new champion, Bill Harrison, 241–106. Gooday promptly announced that he would not be moving to Manchester as his family in London 'were better among friends than strangers'. The executive gave three months' notice that the organizer's base was to return to London.

The executive tried to explain this decision on the basis that the organizer was needed in weaker areas of the country, not Manchester, which was 'already a fairly strong branch, indeed, the strongest in the union'. Relations degenerated for the next two years. In March 1902 when the executive accused the Salford branch of shielding their now dead branch secretary Rogers from accusations of stealing £5 15s 2½d, Salford wrote back, 'we would be prepared to make good the deficit in the branch funds, provided the executive council would make good the deficit caused by the late general secretary!' The pressure on Gooday eventually told. He wrote in his final quarterly report of lack of assistance as he travelled out of town. He was sick of small meetings – 'talking to tables and chairs is not very encouraging; you cannot make much impression on wood.' On 13 April 1904 Bill Gooday resigned. He immediately pinpointed the 'bickering' as the reason. 'One thing is certain. I have left no stone unturned and have always done my best. Angels can do no more.' He was returning to the National Telephone Company at a salary below that he gave up to take the job in 1901. 'I have sacrificed a great deal more than a large number are aware of. When one knows within his own mind that he has done justice to the union and finds that in the provinces certain members are ever ready to pick holes when one is not present, it is more than one can stand.'

Manchester's agitation continued on a range of issues. The president of the union, Jack Pearce, now became the focus of Mancunian anger. First, he was the chairman of an electrical contracting co-operative, called London Electrical Engineers, which had commenced trading in 1902. Criticism was immediately forthcoming. Pearce, elected to the executive, was accused of being an 'employer' and therefore ineligible for the executive. A ballot vote narrowly rejected this view, 219–216. Pearce was allowed to appeal for funds and investment from the members. He then got the union to ballot the members about direct investment in the co-op in September 1903. The members rejected this, 166–153. Pearce's co-op collapsed.

Fragments of letters dated 1904–5 from Pearce to Ewer survive. He writes to borrow money – £1 here, £1 10s 0d there, constantly giving the impression that his ship was coming in. It is probable that these loans were part of Ewer's casual attitude to the union's funds that was to cause so much trouble in 1907. Manchester's fury with Pearce and the executive was further fuelled by increases in expenses awarded to Gooday as organizer, and paid to Pearce who visited British Thomson-Houston's works in Rugby on behalf of the union. In 1902, the Manchester branches appealed against the executive's raising expenses. The members carried the appeal – but also voted to increase the expenses!

In 1904, the Manchester members forced a ballot on the location of the head office, which Pearce, now chairman of the executive, and as such, president of the union, skilfully opposed. The members voted for London in October 1904, 241–154.

Again in 1902, this unpleasantness spread to the executive itself when that year's president, Fred Donaghue, left the presidental chair to urge his fellow executive members 'to strive to bring about a better trade union feeling'. He did this at the October executive meeting in the wake of a frankly bizarre episode. Fred Trevis from Lambeth branch had been elected treasurer at a barely quorate executive meeting by 3–2 in April 1902 in place of veteran Alex Calipé. However, the general secretary, Alf Ewer, would not give Trevis a key to the office, as Calipé had had for years. Lambeth branch protested to the executive, which elicited this explanation from Ewer as to his reasons for withholding the key: Ewer said he could not be held responsible for the union's property if Trevis had a key 'especially as Brother Trevis had been twice refused access to the building when intoxicated and under those circumstances, did not approve of Brother Trevis having a key.' Trevis resigned and Calipé resumed the treasurer's position.

Trevis then led a frivolous campaign of harassing the two officials with specious financial inquiries and demands by a procession of members to see the books.

Around the turn of the century, there were three small attempts to set up alternative electrical unions. The small Scottish ETU, whose leading light was Bob Prain, eventually to hold high office in the ETU itself, brought the breakaway union back to the Glasgow branch in 1900, after four years' separation.

More serious were the antics of F. E. Sims after he had served his prison sentence at the end of 1901. He set up the Electric Wireman's Association (EWA) in London. Their manifesto, handwritten in Sims's writing, claimed that they would admit only competent wiremen, and would not tolerate drinks or dishonesty! 'There would be no out of work pay, no inner circles and cliques and the rules would not be elastic.' These were direct criticisms of the ETU, where suspicious examination of allegedly 'excessive' claims, for unemployment benefit, were a regular feature of branch and executive correspondence. The cliques and arguments between members were well-documented and the organizer location controversy was just the most spectacular example of 'elastic' rules. An account has survived of one of the EWA's recruitment meetings at the Alma in Parsons Green in West London on Sunday 1 December 1901. There were twenty-five wiremen present, twelve of whom were ETU members. Sims was there, and it was addressed by a Mr Bishop. The meeting was clearly dominated by Donaghue's insistence that if more joined the ETU its apparent failings would soon be a thing of the past.

All the following speakers were active ETU men, speaking strongly against dividing electrical opinion in London. Brixey, his son, and Frank Whitehead (who was to serve on the executive in later years) urged unity on the meeting which ended in farce and confusion for the EWA.

Mr S. Higgins, one of the supporters of the new union, objected to the clause in Mr Bishop's address, where drunkenness at work was to be selected for special punishment, as he felt it personally! After several other irrelevant remarks, the chairman asked him to resume his seat.

With extraordinary recruitment meetings like these, it is no surprise that the EWA only achieved membership levels of twenty-four in 1901 and fifty-four in 1902 and disappeared in 1903 when Sims left for America.

Potentially more serious was the development of the Electrical Winders Society. This arose out of the Greenwich branch allying itself with the Mancunian critics of the executive over the question of paying Gooday higher expenses. Behind it was the feeling that the London ETU hierarchy was not interested in the problems of Siemens armature winders in Charlton, who formed the basis of the Greenwich branch. The branch's champion was Owen Choppin who served on the executive in 1902 until he was expelled, along with fellow councillor Charlie Bowles, for refusing to give up branch books to the executive. They then set up the Electrical Winders Society which often talked to the ETU about a merger and that was eventually achieved in 1917. (The Electrical Winders Society never had more than 140 members.)

These rival organizations came to nothing: and the chief threat to the union's stability remained its own remarkable capacity to create internal antagonism between groups of its own members.

In April 1905, the whole executive resigned in response to an appeal to the members by Manchester against the delegation fees paid to Pearce in going to Rugby for the union. The executive was re-elected in June, with virtually the same personnel. A gesture was made in electing Morris, originally a Manchester man, as president. But if that was meant to mollify the northern membership, the executive's support for a full-time officer for London undid all the good work. An original ballot in April 1905 to fund a London organizer out of the general funds was carried, 194–178. But so furious were the Mancunians that appeal followed appeal to withdraw this support, despite George Dibdin, from Battersea, having won an election in October 1905, 90–30, over Fred Donaghue to become the first local official elected in the union's history. The executive council further inflamed opinion by suggesting that as the organizer, Jimmy Rowan, now operated largely out of his home town in Salford, what was so wrong about London having its own official? In July 1906, the members voted to withdraw central support for Dibdin's salary by 244–135 votes. The executive gave in immediately to their friends in the London branch (now one large branch and not five small ones), and accepted their opinion that the turn-out had been so low in the first ballot that a second one was called for! In October, the final ballot resulted in seven branches being in favour of a London full-time official grant, 11 against, and eight branches didn't vote. The anti-London bias was revealed in the final vote of 260–203. Dibdin's salary had to be sustained by levy until he became simply a London branch official once more in 1907.

The Emergence of Jimmy Rowan

The story of the ETU had by now become inseparable from the character and actions of its organizer, Jimmy Rowan.

Jimmy Rowan was born of Scottish descent in November 1871. He went to work at the age of ten, but his first 'proper job' was as an armature winder at Mather & Platt's in Manchester at the age of sixteen. He worked there for four years before setting off round Britain, following his trade for the five years of 1892–7. He returned to Salford and Mather & Platt's and joined the union on 28 August 1897. By late 1898 he was Salford's branch secretary, and he first appears in the union's records urging the executive to do something about the plumbers in Manchester doing electrical work; he was also irritated on behalf of the branch at the executive delay in signing the local working rules. By January 1903, he was well known enough to be sent to the ailing Blackburn branch to check their accounts on behalf of the executive. By 1904, he had a solid record of achievement in this most solid of the union's regions. He was president of the Salford/Manchester branch, the delegate to the Manchester Trades Council since 1900, the secretary of the Fair Contracts Committee of the Trades Council and a member of the emergency sub-committee of the Engineering Trades Committee in Manchester. He was a member of the Building Trades Federation of the city and was always proud to be a founder member of the Manchester Labour Party, being elected to its executive in 1903.

It is impossible to know how far he was involved in the persistent criticism of the London executive council. It is obvious, though, that he must have been aware of the criticism as he presided over the meetings of the branch that originated so many of the attacks on the executive. In April 1904 Bill Gooday was hounded out of his organizer's job by 'provincial' opinion. The election to succeed him was held in August, and it featured the first published election addresses in the union. The other candidates were all wiremen from London – Harold Oakleigh from Battersea, John Pratt from east London and the errant, 'intoxicated' ex-treasurer Fred Trevis, who had been on the executive in London since 1900.

There is a curiosity about the ballot paper. Jimmy Rowan, the armature winder from Manchester, was credited with nine years' membership of the union, which meant he was supposed to have joined in 1895. The union's register shows his date of entry as 28 August 1897. Rowan's election address was dour and to the point. It listed the committees he had served on, and little else. Trevis, on the other hand, wrote flamboyantly about the union being 'foremost' in the world and his great concern about the trade being 'overrun by incompetent workmen'. Much good it did him. Pratt got seven votes, Oakleigh thirty-seven, Fred Trevis seventy-eight and Jimmy Rowan beat them out of sight with 291 votes.

Jimmy Rowan was a slightly shorter than average stocky man with fair thinning hair and a taste, certainly in later life, for the accomplishments of the committee-room and a keen awareness of political survival skills. In the first three years of his career as the union's second full-time official, there is no obvious ground on which the London executive could chase after him: he was not implicated in the 1904 debate about moving the head office of the union – indeed the only office – to Manchester. There was no scandal attached to his expenses. Only once in his period did the executive inquire as to his reasons for visiting Salford when he should have been recruiting in Newcastle.

In his early days as organizer, the membership rose from approximately 1,000 to nearly 1,500 in three years. He was the first to know this was not good enough. His organizing reports upbraided his fellow workers for being feeble in defence of their own rights. He was also responsible in 1905–7 for the growing impact of the union in the northern heartlands of engineering and shipbuilding and was an acknowledged expert in the deepening sophistication of bonus payment systems. He was occasionally capable of a droll remark. For Rowan, 'trade unionism in Dublin is like the sea – a lot of ebb and flow about it'. Above all, he had that fierce awareness of the special skill of the electrician and the world's unreasonable refusal to acknowledge that skill. He was keen to permanently replace the phrase 'wireman' with 'electrician' or 'electrical fitter'. However, in 1907, Jimmy Rowan wrote that 'the term electrical fitter is a good one – far too good for the class of men who are mainly using it at the moment'. He was referring to mechanical fitters who erected the occasional dynamo or did mechanical work with firms of electrical engineers. Rowan ridiculed

the absurdity of these pretensions when compared with the demands of an electrician's calling – 'connecting and erecting dynamos and motors, installing telephones, fire alarms etc., fixing and connecting accessories such as switches and motor starters, general wiring for the above, knowledge of all lighting, including arc lamp construction.'

Also, the electrician must

go anywhere where electrical apparatus of any description is installed, and locate and repair faults to the same, which necessitates a general knowledge of the various uses and part each item plays in the whole. It will be seen that a 'wireman' has a part to play that is closely allied to a Jack-of-all-trades – with this one exception: he must be master of all.

However much the union's prospects were to be improved by the election of a competent and persuasive official like Rowan, the tension between Manchester and the London executive was intensifying in the spring of 1907.

Manchester branch sent a letter by express post to the March executive. It made several pointed demands of the general secretary, Alf Ewer. They challenged his expenses claims. They demanded to know why he was paid £1 an issue for being the 'editor' of the union's magazine *Eltradion*. They demanded proof of the spiteful executive allegation that Manchester members were coming to London and deliberately working under the rate. They wanted to know how much money was being kept to one side in a 'dispute fund'.

They demanded an end to the 'mutilation' of their resolutions in the executive council minutes. They were furious that Ewer would not distribute their case to support yet another ballot on the question of moving the head office to Manchester.

By April they were triumphant. The members voted in a fifty per cent poll to go to Manchester, 452–242.

On 9 April, Alf Ewer wrote to the branches to explain the pressure he was under.

> The great quantity of type-written matter which has to be sent out after an executive council meeting prevents me sending out in time for Monday meetings of branches, the number of pages being sent out today being nearly 600, without letters to branch secretaries and other societies. If each branch secretary will realize that there are twenty-six other secretaries beside himself, an idea may be obtained of the amount of work to be carried out by myself and a lad in the general office.

The executive were clearly riled by the pressure too; they rounded on Rowan – wanting to know why he was trying to get circulars out to Manchester employers typed at general office: the executive would sanction that only if the Manchester district committee asked for it – not Rowan! They hinted at his excessive train fares, for which he got a half-hearted apology in the minutes, and refused, until Rowan complained at the executive, to pay him for work done on Sundays.

The whole crisis was resolved in dramatic circumstances. Without telling his wife or his oldest friend, Alex Calipé, Alf Ewer disappeared on the night of 1 May 1907 and boarded ship for Australia.

The president of the union, George Dibdin, first London full-time official, whose salary had been paid by levy in 1905–7 and who was now a Labour councillor in Battersea, took over the reins and a flurry of executive meetings set out to deal with the situation. Rowan was summoned to London to take charge and the executive set up – with a rare display of sensitivity – a three-man investigation team with senior provincial figures in a majority. Fred Trevis, from London, was joined by Robert Ferguson, the Glasgow branch secretary, and Jack Ball, the secretary of the Manchester branch, representing the Lancashire and Yorkshire district committee. The inquiry team reported to the executive on 21 May 1907. Between May 1906 and 27 April 1907 Alf Ewer had stolen £144 1s 2d. He had requested money from the treasurer for office supplies and other requirements, and then not spent all the money, but kept part of it. Just over half of the money came from uncrossed cheques from branch secretaries that Ewer put in his own pocket. There was no accusation of corruption (indeed, when he retired in 1913, Calipé was to be praised for his integrity), but the treasurer was censured for making out cheques to Ewer and not to the recipients of the union's bills. No one had properly checked Ewer's personal expenses and fares claims. The committee's report was accepted and sweeping administrative changes made to prevent such things happening again.

Alf Ewer, like Sims, had done great service to the union in its darkest years – dating all the way back to the first strike in Brighton in 1891. There is, though, no forgiveness for officials who steal union money.

In the next few weeks, Rowan had to launch the process of the general secretary election. Calipé was to say years later, 'I don't want to eulogize Rowan, but it was owing to my persuasive tongue that he accepted [the nomination for] the office, which in those days meant making a sacrifice.' The arrangements had to be made for the first conference to be held since 1899 at Sheffield in August and Ewer had left behind complete chaos in the magazine's finances. On 11 July 1907, Jimmy Rowan was elected general secretary of the ETU with 446 votes. George Dibdin managed eighty, Alan Garner, a socialist from Merseyside who was to serve on the executive council for a decade, got forty-nine.

8

'A POWER IN THE LAND', 1907–14

1907 HAD SEEN THE election of Jimmy Rowan as general secretary and the general office of the union move to Manchester. The first conference to be held in eight years met at the Caxton Rooms in Trippett Lane, Sheffield on Sunday and Monday, 4 and 5 August 1907. The process of irreversible and improving change was to continue.

The conference voted to end the one-town executive council, and create at last a truly national leadership. This was the brainchild of Robert Ferguson (newly elected national organizer in a contest with the hapless George Dibdin). He had laid the groundwork in a vitriolic correspondence in the *Eltradion* with George Butler, a London executive councillor, whom Ferguson called 'a red-hot socialist and an irresponsible extremist'. Ferguson suggested, on behalf of the Glasgow branch that the executive council should be elected by the whole union, but each of the six geographic divisions alone should nominate the candidates. The general president should be elected by the whole union as should the general treasurer. These two 'general' officials, along with the general secretary, should form an emergency committee to process the daily work of the union between quarterly executive meetings. The total cost would be £6 2s 6d in fares etc. per quarter.

Interestingly enough, given every early leader of the union's memories of the 1907 conference being the wonderful, decisive turning-point in the union's history, the actual decision was a damn close-run thing. Great fear was expressed that the three general officials would dominate the union; or that in a strike situation, over-frequent executive meetings would bankrupt the union in travel expenses alone! Jack Ball, Manchester's branch secretary, was fulsome in his praise for 1907 in his 1914 presidential address to the union's conference when he said: 'Those of you who were present at the Sheffield conference in 1907 will remember how the debacle was prevented by the awakening of the democracy of the union for the first time.'

However, Jack Ball had led the cautionary element in 1907.

He was in favour of the principles laid down but considered the scheme was premature and should be deferred until such a time as we were able to have a truly representative executive council. On economic grounds, the experiment was unwise at present and should be left over for more details to be furnished.

Equally, the suggestion of full-time general president and treasurer was defeated in favour of allowing the executive to choose its own chairman, and the union's president, from outside their own number. However, the real disaster was prevented when the conference refused to cede executive powers to district committees. The concept of national government of a national institution survived the conference and in September Ferguson's scheme as amended was carried in a membership ballot by a large majority. When Jimmy Rowan left Club Union Buildings on 29 December, Dibdin came to say farewell and noted the forlorn offices, devoid of everything save the electric light fittings and the 'rather woe-begone telephone'. Many of the original pioneer leaders of the union would not be going to 26 Cannon Street, Manchester, to meet the new executive council which first met in January 1908. Alex Calipé, executive councillor and treasurer since 1893, was the most prominent of the ex-leadership: however, he gave his blessing to the new arrangements in a valedictory letter to the membership in December 1907. He said he was dropping back into the rank and file:

... among the fault-finders ... the ETU has too many critics and too few workers ... you are not the officials, and the executive ... having been elected by the whole of the membership, have a right to exercise their decisions ... I sometimes think that members of the ETU don't know the meaning of the word 'executive' ... that the whole of the members were called together in different parts of the country for the purpose of refusing to obey the executive's findings ... I think the salvation of the ETU is a real governing body and would advise greater powers being given to the executive council, not, as in the past, curtailing them.

Jack Ball, the first president of the new executive, said of Calipé: 'He is earnest and enthusiastic with a manly and consistent purpose. The grand moral of Brother Calipé's thirteen years of service is to show the possibilities of incorruptible integrity – an example that is open to other men.' Alex Calipé remained an active member of the union in London, and concentrated, after 1908, on a political career as a Labour councillor in Southwark. He would occasionally lecture in branches all over London, but only on local government topics, not on union controversies. He died in January 1929, having been in the union for thirty-five years. He had one curious qualification. Because the trade developed so much in his lifetime, he took the City and Guilds exams twice!

The period from 1907–14 saw the union at last emerge as 'A Power in the Land' – a phrase first used in February 1913 by James Buchan, the president of the Fulham branch. The membership growth from 1907–10 was unremarkable; it rose from 1,539 to 1,871. These three years were times of great hardship for all workers – and in 1909 over ten per cent of the union's membership was unemployed. But in the years 1911–14 the position radically changed.

The general improvement in the economy, the startling awakening of the Labour movement in its widest sense and the accelerating use of electricity in every possible guise produced a much easier background for the union to operate against. By 1914, the union's membership had risen to 8,195 in 106 branches.

The union changed in this period out of all recognition from the petty, squabbling irrelevant organization of the early days of the century. Its economic impact was at last meaningful; its new leadership was of real stature, and even its differences began to reflect questions of some consequence.

Several themes continued to divide the membership. Paramount among these issues remained the inconclusive question of who was a typical ETU member and whom the union should admit to its ranks. Deep in this debate lay the seeds of all the other sources of tension within the union; lay the seeds of its relationship with other unions; lay the explanation for the different tactics used in relationships with employers; lay the seeds of the conflicting political attitudes that emerged before the First World War; lay the 'problem' of London that haunted the union until the 1970s. Deep in this debate lay the origins of faction fighting, political war and organizational restlessness that would dominate the union's life into the future.

Skilled and Semi-Skilled Men: Who Should Be in the Union?

Skill is very subjective. Jimmy Rowan was certain that substantial numbers of his men had it. He and president Jack Ball were articulate representatives within the union of the view that union members must become qualified workers in order to become well-paid men. The employers, above all, must respect the union's integrity and genuine concern that higher pay for skill was the union's just reward for its defence of a high standard of skilled work.

Rowan wrote in early 1909 that the extension of skill owed much to the new work involved in maintaining and servicing the installations other electrical workers had manufactured.

It was the rule not very long ago that after the installation of electricity, either for traction or power, no skilled labour was necessary for maintenance – anybody could run it. But the bottom has been knocked out of this contention and the management of those concerns are finding that skilled labour pays and is cheaper in the end ... It is probable that the number of men employed on maintenance, taking into account central and sub-stations, electric traction and power plants, exceeds the number of men employed on new work – wiremen and winders combined.

He also saw quite clearly this link between the expansion of the industry, skill, high wages and quality of work. He wrote in June 1907:

> Electricity has come to stay and is displacing many of the older trades ... the terms and conditions made during the great extension of the trade will have the greatest bearing on its future prosperity or otherwise ... In order to make the best article, we must have the best men; in order to have the best men, we must thoroughly train them; to have thoroughly trained men, we must crush out the trend towards the handymen, and have a thorough apprenticeship system.

Of course, employers prefer cheap to better labour, but in unionized works

> he looks for the best workers he can get for the money he has to pay. This means that ability is the first thing looked for in a workman, and with so-called cheapness forced out of sight, the result is the workman himelf (whether he likes it or not) is forced up to a certain standard of ability, or to go to the wall.

Throughout this period, the union supported the City and Guilds (of London) Institute's first set of examinations in wiremen's work as a marvellous way of guaranteeing standards in an industry anxious to do away with handymen and replace them with qualified people. In most big cities outside London, the union initially supported the local Electrical Contractors' Association (ECA) initiative in the registration of firms and operatives, in an attempt to overturn the falling safety reputation of electricity due to 'cowboy' installations discrediting the trade. Both the union and employers thought that registration would prove, to municipal authorities in particular, that the industry was concerned about competence. Registration was a disaster the moment the employers in Birmingham, Newcastle and Manchester started to register operatives on the basis of their suspected trade union membership and insisted on knowing where people had worked before and why they had left. There was only one result if a member had left because he would not work under the rate or had been withdrawn on strike by the union.

For many activists in the union, this attitude to joint responsibility for the improvement of the industry's standards was genuine. It was best expressed by Tom Milburn, the president of the Manchester branch, when he wrote to the union's magazine in September 1908. This letter is all the more remarkable for the way it could have been written sixty years later at the dawn of the Joint Industry Board for Electrical Contracting. Tom Milburn wrote that the ECA must recognize the ETU and:

... not a mere formal recognition, but one under which the sections of the industry would get to work in harmony with each other and seek to abolish some of the evils which at present exist, creating efficient machinery to watch over the industry ... and if successful, the time will arrive when the national bodies on either side will join hands together ... They will be prepared, whilst recognizing each other's claims and individuality, to work together for the welfare of the industry. That we work to this end and show the industrial world that we have a sincere regard for the well-being of the industry, and are prepared to work for the same, is the hope of, Yours fraternally, Tommy Milburn.

Much of the union's rhetoric urged 'unity', 'federation', or 'joint action'. However, there was an increasing awareness of how skill separated people at work. Rowan wrote in February 1908 that 'the social grading of labour which has grown up through ages of time, coupled with their various interests embodied in customs and conventions, have not yet been overcome'. Branches complained throughout the period that their skills were undervalued. Typically, East Ham complained in 1913: 'The majority of trades get 1s an hour; the painters, even, get 10½d but we get 9½d.' It was this emerging sense of their own value in the years leading up to the First World War that fuelled the deepest-set dispute within the union.

For years, the union had argued about taking in lesser-skilled electrical workers. In 1907, the craft tendency in the union had triumphed. 'Assistants' were debarred from the union. Only 'competent' workmen who had been three years in the trade, as well as bona fide apprentices, would be eligible for membership. Throughout the period from 1908–14, the union debated reversing this élitist trend. The two sets of arguments were straightforward.

Everyone understood the point made by Charles Macaskie, a Plymouth dockyard electrician, when he wrote to the journal in June 1914.

Our branch of industry differs peculiarly from the other trades, and it is necessary that this difference should be recognized and allowed for by our union – that whereas the only entry to such crafts as joiners, fitters, masons, smiths etc. is via apprenticeship, electrical workers always have been – and are today – recruited from a vast medley of occupations. Bona fide ex-apprentices are, perhaps, the exception rather than the rule.

Macaskie drew certain conclusions from his perceptive grasp of the bewildering variety of origins displayed by electricians. He was opposed to letting them in the union unless they were real craftsmen. The admission of 'auxiliaries' into an auxiliary section could lead to such people overwhelming the skilled men in the workforce and 'installing' themselves as the ruling power of the union. Such people would dilute the power of the union in wage bargaining. If the union wanted to set skilled rates at 10d, what was the point in admitting men earning 7d an hour who would be happy to pinch skilled work off craftsmen at 8d an hour. Macaskie's view was that this process would keep down skilled men's wages. This itself would lower the status of the union as a skilled union, and the ETU would quickly become known as a labourer's union.

Alan Bond, the Sunderland branch secretary, had made the same point, with some passion, in December 1911. 'Just fancy,' he wrote to the *Electrical Trades Journal*:

... bringing labourers into the ETU and placing them on the same footing as ourselves. The idea of it is ridiculous ... A man who has been working as a craneman or as a jointer's mate thinks he knows sufficient about electricity to tackle a job himself, so he applies for a job, and incidentally mentions he is in the ETU. If he gets the job and turns out a rotter, the employer straight away judges all union men by the one he has had, and is in future prejudiced against us. Besides, are these men not catered for in the various labourers' unions? I think they are, though apparently others do not. Then again, we are all, I think, doing our utmost to organize the electrical tradesmen and to make the ETU a power to be reckoned with; but I would like to know how many electricians are going to join the ETU and be on the same footing as the labourers working with them? Perhaps one of these labourers would get into office and become, perhaps, the president of the branch and get bragging about it among his workmates. It would immediately lower the electricians to the level of labourers ... The union, by admitting these men, would immediately lose prestige and become nothing more than a labourers' union.

He went on to say that apprentice-trained electricians were none too happy about the union admitting men who had simply been three years at the trade and could claim some sort of 'competence'. The auxiliary section would add insult to injury and Bond finished this classic piece of fierce craft pride and prejudice by urging the union to 'return this new section back where it came from and read a burial service over it once and for all'.

That is exactly what the union did. In 1911, the conference urged the members to accept the principle of the auxiliary section (with great reservation expressed from Manchester and Glasgow). But the members refused to endorse the executive's rule change to bring it about and, on a second ballot, rejected the whole principle, 858–578, in the summer of 1912.

The problem would not go away: it had powerful friends. From 1908 until the First World War and beyond the fastest growing centre of ETU activity was in London. With the general office moved to Manchester, London decentralized its branch structure. (This decision forced George Dibdin to resign his district responsibilities in favour of the new branches running their own affairs.) By March 1908, London had London Central, East, South-East, briefly, South-West and pre-eminently, West, which opened on 21 January 1908.

Socialism, Revolution and the Emergence of Political Faction

London West branch was to provide the focus for uncompromising and energetic syndicalist ideas and revolutionary rhetoric throughout the union. Particularly from 1910–14, as the branch grew in size, it split and split again, setting up branches full of ex-London West activists in Brentford, Fulham, London South-West and London North-West. These branches were dominated by Bill Webb, the branch secretary, whose forceful personality and revolutionary fervour were to become influential in the union as he became London district secretary, executive councillor and elected full-time official.

The emergence of revolutionary political ideas from the London West branch meeting room at the Bush Hotel in Shepherd's Bush marked out a new dimension to the arguments over the auxiliary section. London had always suffered more than any provincial town from the 'rag-tag and bobtail' element calling themselves 'electricians'. There was no apprenticeship scheme anywhere in London for the trade. Perhaps only ten per cent of the appropriate workers were in the union. The London West branch zealots were not dismayed. They were convinced that the French political philosopher, Sorel, and the American unions associated with the Industrial Workers of the World had the answers to London's problem in the electrical industries. The union must recruit everyone into the union and use strikes and other forms of action to 'expropriate the expropriators'. This meant that they rejected the craft élitism and the industrial co-operation outlined by Tommy Milburn in his 1908 letter, quoted on page 74. Bill Webb's view – oft-expressed – was strongly in favour of the proposed new section for these fundamental political reasons.

Are we never to realize that we have to organize our class and not our craft only? We want to uplift the bottom dog, and by so doing, uplift ourselves ... You are not going to deny to these poorer brethren in our industry the benefit of our organization. They are part and parcel of us, of our class, of our trade, and that trade will be the main factor in the industrial history of the twentieth century. Brothers all – help us make the ETU the controller!

The emerging class-conscious London electrical workers were to provide the union with huge problems in their incompatibility with their provincial comrades for decades to come. But on the question of the need to organize auxiliary electrical workers into the union, they were at one with the leadership of the union. Jack Ball expressed the whole argument in favour of the auxiliary section in his devastating presidential address to the 1914 rules revision conference in Manchester on the day that the First World War broke out.

Before we can stop the influx of unskilled labour into the trade, we shall have to control unskilled labour, and the only way to do that is to open the gates for them to enter and organize them after our own ideas, or they will organize themselves without our control, or be picked up as they are now being by other societies ... We shall [thus] protect the interests of our apprentice members in this way much better than by observing a sort of masterly inaction ... We embrace the ship, engineering, building, tramways, mines and maintenance work. Let us go forward for absolute control of the whole of the electrical industry and every man engaged in it, so that no worker can be exploited to the detriment of another, skilled or unskilled.

The argument about the auxiliary section was also involved with the gathering confidence of the union's organizing work in the electricity supply industry in the same period. By March 1912, Webb had started to recruit anyone he could get his hands on in the growing supply industry: his political debt to the syndicalist ideas, expressed as industrial unionism in Britain, was apparent in his insistence in 1912 that 'the present coal strike would be a mere flea-bite compared with a general strike at all the generating stations in London alone.'

The rule-book frustrated Webb enormously: one particular occasion stands out. In July 1913, the union organized the Colchester Corporation electricity supply concern. They recruited stokers, labourers and switchboard attendants. Very few were skilled and eligible for full benefit status in the union. National organizer Jack Kinniburg was eventually forced to exclude the labourers and stokers from the union because they were not skilled enough. The skilled men promptly left in sympathy, and Webb's attempts to gain control of the supply industry were frustrated.

The 1914 conference set up the auxiliary section and this time did not ballot the members: the conference itself set out rules for the section that came into force on 1 January 1915 along with the other rule changes. The new rules were respectful towards craft suspicion: the new auxiliary worker had to have been in his job for two years and be a temporary lightman, arc lamp trimmer, electric crane-driver, electric winch driver, accumulator erector, jointer's mate, dynamo attendant, telephone linesman or other electrical worker. Still Manchester and parts of Glasgow objected; still London was unanimously in favour, and the auxiliary section was carried into the rules at the conference 56–11. The contribution was to be 6d per week; for this, the auxiliary member got an extra 5s a week unemployment pay to top up his state benefit to 12s, strike pay of 10s per week, legal aid, victimization pay and funeral benefits of £5. The central fear of the craft élite was somewhat assuaged by the decision to exclude auxiliary members from elections for full-time office or the important branch functions of secretary, president, treasurer or district committee delegate. They could only hold the less vital jobs like doorkeeper, branch auditor, vice-president and no more than two seats on the branch committee. They added to this rather forbidding attitude by then intensifying the 1911 definition of a skilled craftsman, requiring five, not three years' 'competence' at the trade itself. The next great row on membership was to be the issue of transfer from auxiliary to craftsman. Craft élitism was merely shifting its ground and not conceding the issue that the revolutionary egalitarians required of it.

Collective Bargaining, Strikes and Arbitrations

The period 1910–14 transformed the ETU from an obscure and irrelevant sect to a recognizable part of the emerging collective bargaining system in Britain. All the union's publications reveal this growing sense of confidence – particularly after the economy turned the corner in 1910 and opportunities for the electrical industries grew. Tom Stewart, elected as a second national organizer in 1913, wrote in early 1914: 'Our standing in the trade union movement compares favourably with any other trade, as is proven by the fact we have no difficulty in getting interviews and conferences with any employers on questions that affect our members.'

The union had survived 1908–10 with little fundamental dislocation at a time when wage reductions produced strikes and lock-outs in other industries. The union did not lose money or have to impose levies; they were therefore ready to enjoy the negotiating success that was achieved before the First World War. 1911 for Jimmy Rowan was 'the best year in the history of the ETU'. 1912 'will be long remembered as the first year in which we forced ourselves upon the employers in many districts. We demanded and obtained, not only recognition, but more concrete monetary advantages.'

This increased economic effectiveness of the union was due to the interaction of various influences. In its negotiations, the union's leadership was anxious to establish the full-time officials as the legitimate leaders of wage 'movements'. Spontaneous outbursts of industrial action were frowned upon. The union still required the members directly concerned to meet, be two-thirds in favour of a dispute, have the support of the executive council and a positive ballot of all the members before they would sanction strike benefits.

Typically, unofficial strikes on Merseyside and Glasgow in 1912 were refused support by the executive until the members returned to work – when the officials then took up the wage demands involved and secured an advance. Equally, the union used its membership of the FEST to join in with joint craft union negotiations throughout the two industries: however, they were cautious concerning their independence. They refused to join the Building Industries Federation (BIF) nationally by 613–367 in 1913, on the grounds that it would devalue the non-contracting sections of the membership and give the impression that the union was merely another building union, or, worse still, part of an industrial union. They would not vote – despite Rowan's support for it – to join the National Shipyards Agreement by 902–235 votes, on the grounds that the ETU would become just another shipyard union. However, negotiations in the contracting industry became the beacon by which all other deals and rates were to be judged. There was an enormous breakthrough in Manchester in November 1908. That year, the working rules card was not dreamed up by the union and then circulated in the usual, vaguely hopeful way to the employers in the district. In 1908, it was negotiated by the union with the ECA in order to cover *all* the leading contractors in the whole district. This agreement arranged pay rates, hours of work, overtime, travelling allowances, the apprentice/craftsmen ratio and dirty money payments. Jack Ball, Manchester branch secretary and president of the union, summed up the significance of this district agreement when he wrote:

It may be taken for granted that we all realize, more or less vaguely, that the value of collective bargaining is in the stability it ensures to both parties. It is coming to be recognized as good policy to deal with the same form of organization and more and more to make that organization responsible, so far as may be, for meeting the obligations that are assured by it for the workers it represents. Success or failure depends upon the loyalty with which the two parties adhere to the terms agreed upon. By the agreement, we have erected a base on which to build, and to admit the introduction of improvements. These will give us, not, indeed, 'the millennium' but the advantage of knowing where to start and who to start with, when considering the advisability of making application for better conditions. It is the means to an end, and possibly it may lead to a national trade agreement.

That 1908 prophecy of Jack Ball's was to be some years in coming. However, the capacity to negotiate district rates with the ECA spread from Manchester with alacrity. By 1914, contracting conditions were becoming a useful standard of comparison. On the Tyne and in Glasgow, the engineering and shipbuilding rates were the same as contracting. In 1914, the contracting rates were accepted by the London EEF as the appropriate engineering rate. The great delight for the union in this comparison becoming the norm was that it quickly reduced the capacity of the other unions to set the rates for electricians; if they could not set the rates, it took some of the pressure off from other unions claiming to represent electricians. It is little wonder that Ball and Rowan were to be tenacious in their defence of the contracting rates in future years.

In the shipyards, local organization was already developing out of the branch room and directly into the electricial shops. The executive approved the Clyde district committee definition of the duties of 'Shipyard delegates' in September 1913 – although point-blank refused to pay shop-stewards for doing them!

Shipyard Delegates Duties

1 To see that every man starting in the shipyard is a trade unionist.
2 To have a show of members' cards at intervals of about a fortnight or so, and if any member is in arrears, to persuade them to pay up.
3 To represent the men in any grievance that may arise from time to time.

In February 1913, the Birkenhead branch reporter to the journal, Alan Duncan, explained how shop-stewards were first elected at Cammell Lairds.

The men from Messrs Cammell Lairds held a meeting in order to elect an official shop delegate, and a number of assistants from among themselves. The honour fell to Brother Forester, a late member of Liverpool branch, to act as official delegate. We wish him every success and may he prove to be a very capable diplomat. The position of shop delegate in a large works is a very responsible and far-reaching one, as many misunderstandings can be nipped in the bud by a tactful delegate.

Clearly the system worked. The new district committee chairman, Walter Citrine, was to write that month: 'The ETU is becoming an institution in the Mersey district. The non-unionist is regarded as a phenomenon.'

Standards were also advanced through the union's traditional support for local council electrical projects – particularly in the building of electrical supply plant. The union would frequently expose the ECA as a cartel which attempted to prevent municipalities directly developing their own electrical installations.

However, their support for public ownership was tempered with cruel experience of it in practice – particularly in a series of disputes and arguments led by Tom Philpott, London district secretary, whose experience of dealing with the London County Council (LCC) Tramways left him a jaundiced man. The language is offensive to a modern audience – but this report of Philpott's from August 1911 is instructive.

The complaints that reach the London South-East branch about nigger-driving, the task work, the tyrannical conduct of the foremen and the general discontent ... on the LCC Tramways ... makes one think whether, after all, this idea of municipal employment of the workers is so grand after all. Compare the apparent conditions in general between the municipal employers and private employers in London. It looks odds on the private employer. To my sorrow, I have had a fair amount of dealings with both, and experience has shown that when you lay a case before the private employer, he will, or his manager, fix it up for or against you in five minutes. I take it that his time and money is his own and he will not waste it squabbling with you. On the other hand, when you lay a case before a municipal body, you are not quite sure whether you will get through with it before you draw your old-age pension. There is this official and that official to be consulted, this committee and that committee to consider it, pages of letters to write, and above all, you must have more patience than Job. I will say that we have always received the utmost courtesy from the chiefs and I think it is rare that they cause friction. Most of the trouble is caused by that genius – the understrapper ... With the private employer one good foreman to a group of men is all that he will afford. With the other it is difficult to know which there is most of – officials or workmen ... there is waste with the municipal employers not generally found to exist with the private employers. An enormous amount of time and materials is wasted by the lack of proper method and administration by these understrappers. We have known them to waste half a day and much material and then chase the men for the other half of the day to try and get out of the muddle!

I was led to believe that if we got municipalization, we got away from the profitmonger with all the attendant evils. I am not out to discuss what might be, or deal with ideals. Looking at the facts, and taking into consideration that the municipal councils press the private contractor to pay trade union rates of wages to his workmen when executing any work for them; at the same time, they are often the biggest offenders themselves, in this respect where their own workmen are concerned! When it comes to 'sweating' the workers, the councils can all do their share, the LCC in particular. Under the present conditions, and as things are today, give me the private contractor before the municipal employer.

Notwithstanding this growing struggle with the bureaucracy of the LCC, the union was usually anxious to organize the local council employees and use their position to influence other employers in the town or district. Jimmy Rowan was a clear supporter, too, of arbitration as a better means to settle disputed wage applications than strikes. He was particularly anxious to advance this idea in the rising tide of militant action between 1911 and 1914. Throughout this hectic period, Britain was arguably closer to an open workers' revolt than at any other time in its history before or afterwards. There were furious, violent and memorable strikes on the docks, in the mines, on the railways, throughout the shipyards and in the engineering and construction industries. The ETU were involved peripherally in most of the well-known disputes in the mines, the transport strikes and the shipping disputes. They were centrally involved in the construction strikes of 1914.

It is clear that Jimmy Rowan and Jack Kinniburgh saw this great question of industrial struggle in different ways. Kinniburgh emerged in this period as the most dynamic, persuasive and forceful leader the ETU produced. He was an assistant wireman – or mate – when he joined the union in Glasgow in 1900 at the age of twenty-three. He worked in the shipyards and became ETU delegate to Glasgow Trades Council. Having achieved skilled status, he was the first Scottish representative on the national executive council elected to serve in 1908.

Robert Ferguson, the national organizer since 1907, was suddenly forced to resign on health grounds in February 1910. He had served as a national figure for only two-and-a-half years – but he had been the architect of the national executive scheme and the organizer of the Clydeside shipyards – making the Glasgow branch briefly the largest in the union in the period just after his death. Jack Kinniburgh replaced him in August 1910. He was a huge man, over six feet tall, with dark eyes and a long drooping moustache. He towers over conference photographs and dominated the branch life of the union. He presided over the explosive growth of the union in the period up to 1914, and was responsible for much of it. He was revered as a negotiator and applauded as chairman of hundreds of branch 'smoking concerts'. These were the main social events organized by branches – sometimes for a good cause and some-times as a recruitment event. Members would gather to entertain each other with 'turns' performed by members of the branch, their relatives or their friends. Jack Kinniburgh would usually recite the narrative poem 'The Uncle' at such 'smokers' and finish the meeting by giving an uplifting address on the need for trade unions, socialism and the emancipation of the working class. On some issues, he did not agree with his colleagues in the leadership. He opposed Jack Ball, the president, who thought that high provident benefits including a pension, would keep members in the union.

Jack Kinniburgh stood for a 'fighting union'. He thought the state should provide provident benefits and the union existed, therefore, to prosecute the conflict with the employer. He came very close to embracing the syndicalist ideas that were the staple diet of London West branch. Sympathetic to spokesmen of the SDF, he was a member of the Independent Labour Party from being a teenager. He often revealed a critical attitude to the parliamentary Labour Party's 'inactivity', accusing in public the party's leaders of failing the workers. During the First World War, he was to gradually distance himself from his more iconoclastic friends in London – but in the pre-war period he was on fire. In the April 1912 issue of the *Electrical Trades Journal*, he wrote glowingly of the new position provided by the ferment associated with the 1912 miners' strikes, particularly in South Wales. 'The Government is apparently alarmed at the increasing solidarity displayed by the workers and are losing their heads over the matter. While the worker was content to let the strike weapon be at rest, and only go in for political activity as represented by the Labour Party, everyone was happy! But once the workers realized their industrial power, all the forces of the Crown are out to beat their men.' He bemoaned the arrest of 'syndicalist' newspaper sympathizers. His own execu-tive colleagues were more hard-headed. They refused to give anything to the financial appeal of syndicalist hero Tom Mann, when he was arrested for allegedly speading sedition among the troops!

Jimmy Rowan fired a shot across Kinniburgh's bows when he wrote in the same edition of the journal in clear response to Kinniburgh's flirtation with industrial action for political purposes.

As a result of the coal strike, we have been treated by the press to a vast amount of piffle on 'syndicalism' and other 'isms', and they are trying to convince the public that the strike is the result of some new force, under varying disguises, that is at work in the country. The fact is that the only difference between this and previous strikes is that the miners are well organized, the question is a national one, and all the men are stopped.

As for showing the power of organized labour to stop the industry of the country, the strike has been a success; but whether the results justify the large amount of suffering involved is a debatable question. It certainly does not tend to encourage the views of those who advocate a national stoppage of work as the means of curing all evils. The fact cannot be ignored that the worker fights on his stomach and the employer on his bank book ... the only addition to the power to strike that appears at all practical is political action ... and it does seem feasible that a combination of the two would achieve better results.

By 1914, the union was producing a national leadership team of real substance. Jack Kinniburgh occasionally topped the poll above Jimmy Rowan in TUC or Labour Party delegate elections. He was re-elected unopposed in 1913. In 1914, Rowan crushed Eddie Fisher, 1,366–267, with Tommy Parr from Plymouth getting 138 votes.

The third national figure to dominate the union as it emerged from the shadows was Jack Ball. He spent his early working life in America and Canada as an electrician, and on his return to England, he was recruited into the union on 8 October 1898 at the age of twenty-eight by Jimmy Rowan. He was foreman electrician for Whipps & Co on the Eccles Town Hall wiring contract at the time, and worked as a foreman or charge-hand on many contracts, including the Crossley Sanatorium and the Stuart Street Generating Station in Manchester. Early in 1901, while working for Lightfoot Bros on the Manchester Skin Hospital contract, he signed on full-time for the hospital and became its first X-ray operator. Throughout his life, Jack Ball was to be a distinguished lecturer and demonstrator of the use of X-rays. His devotion to his work would eventually lose him his fingers and kill him with the cancers suffered from exposure to radiation. He was the Manchester branch secretary and president in the early 1900s. When the office moved to Manchester in 1907, he was also elected president by the rest of the executive council. From 1912, he was elected annually by the whole membership and chaired the union's conferences from 1911 onwards. He was more like Rowan than Kinniburgh in his general political attitudes, and his battles with the London-based left were to be a feature of the union's political evolution throughout the 1920s and 30s. His great strength was the dignity and gravitas he brought to the union, which was partly due to his status as a pioneer radiographer, but also due to his firm grip of chairmanship that he exercised to the full. The happy coincidence of Ball and Rowan in the two senior union offices for twenty-three years was one key feature in the union's growth towards maturity and influence.

During this period, political divisions emerged in the union that were to dominate its counsels for decades to come. In the London branches, particularly in those branches close to London West and its leadership, the dominant trade union philosophy was one of industrial unionism, closely allied to syndicalism. Men like Bill Webb were admirers of Tom Mann, knowledgeable of the personalities and struggles of the American Industrial Workers of the World; they were energetic organizers, intense propagandists, genuine revolutionaries. Webb was often in company with men like Fred Billett and Fred Alford, active on the London district committee, officials in the branches that grew out of London West in the years before 1914, and failed candidates for national office. They clearly co-ordinated resolutions, packed meetings, sent delegations to Manchester and wrote to the *Electrical Trades Journal* as an organized group. Bill Webb himself was admired by everyone who came across him; Jack Kinniburgh deferred to his recruitment activity when he wrote in 1911: 'I fancy that if there were many Brother Webbs about, the organizers would have to form a protective union or else lose their trade.' Fred Alford said, as an ordinary member of London West that 'some men are victims of circumstance, but Webb seems to be master of them'. Jimmy Rowan approved of Joe Wild's assessment that he was a 'very live wire' and 'a great force' in the union. More unusually, Sir George Askwith, who was a leading civil servant in the First World War associated with the arbitration process of the Committee on Production, wrote this of Webb in 1922: 'I have heard uncomplimentary remarks about Mr Webb, who sometimes may be brusque, but he acts with decision.'

Pre-eminent among these men from the Western branch was C. H. Stavenhagen. He was born in Twickenham in 1887, the son of a German father and Irish mother who had married in South Africa and were enthusiastic Victorian imperialists. Stavenhagen was the second of six boys, all of whom were named after Disraeli's cabinet ministers or other Victorian great men. C. H. Stavenhagen was named Cecil Herbert, after Rhodes, but never used the names. He was known to all, including his wife, as 'Stave'. Stavenhagen was introduced by his father to a family friend who got him an apprenticeship at the Office of Works. However, it was not a formal, indentured apprenticeship. He joined as a boy and picked up the skill as he went along. However, by going to night school, he became a qualified electrical engineer. He first joined the London West branch on 14 April 1908, aged twenty-one, as a 'machinery designer'. By May that year, he had sent in to the union's magazine the first of many articles on political philosophy that attempted to get to the heart of the evils of capitalist society. He and his wife were committed members of the SDF, the only party he ever joined. He was articulate, persuasive, even inspirational to his political supporters. He was grossly rhetorical to his political enemies, and he had plenty of those in the union. He left the union in the summer of 1909 and went to Australia to visit one of his brothers. However, unemployment was as difficult there as it was in Britain, and he returned home. He rejoined the union on 27 June 1911, as a 'machine constructor and installer'. He was clearly not a conventional electrical craftsman; Jack Kinniburgh was delighted he rejoined. He wrote in the journal in July 1911, 'I am glad to record the fact that we have got Brother Stavenhagen (who, it will be remembered, used to write some splendid articles to our journal), to rejoin again ... I must congratulate the Western branch on having three members of ability in the persons of Brothers Webb, Alford and Stavenhagen.' In working for the Office of Works with men like Jock Muir, Stavenhagen could at least see a more amusing side to the idea of revolution.

During 1913, St James's Palace in Whitehall was rewired throughout. At lunch time, the electricians would eat their sandwiches gathered round the Throne of England. Jock Muir and Stavenhagen would then briefly mount the Throne to provide their fellow sparks with uplifting socialist lectures from an unrivalled source of authority!

Stavenhagen was by now a committed syndicalist, but also took a passionate interest in Irish affairs – he was known to the police who sent him straight back to England when he tried to visit Ireland in 1916. The titles of his articles from 1911–14 give some idea of his political stance: clearly, Jimmy Rowan, as editor of the journal, would not print them after March 1914. Stavenhagen wrote on 'Strikes and Evolution', 'The Necessity of Hate', 'Life', 'Solidarity or Craft', 'The Class War' and 'Class War, a Rejoinder'.

He wrote powerfully – perhaps too powerfully for modern taste, but his views were to earn him high elected office in the union during the First World War and afterwards.

In 'The Necessity of Hate' in 1912 he wrote:

Let us preach the doctrine of hate, and let us define the principle of its philosophy ... the hatred of all that is ugly ... We are fighting with an ever-rejuvenated, ever-increasing hatred of this vulturous system of masters and slaves, kings and vassals, place-men and place-hunters ... The curse of the ugly is upon us; the path of its sluttish movements is seared and rendered foul; its ghoulish, spectral features create in us a terrible despair. All that is left to us is this hate, hate, hate!

In the essay 'Solidarity or Craft' he only wanted members who were 'born fighters, clear thinkers and bitter and unrelenting antagonists of that degenerate system of society which breeds and thrives on the sweating and rapine of the working-class'.

His remedy was simple, powerful, demanding. In 'The Class War' he urged the membership:

Be bitter: be relentless: forgive nothing. Look round with eyes bloodshot with suffering, with implacable hostility, with callous horny hands and Strike! Strike like a hell of demons for the freedom of humanity! Strike with a steam-hammer punch for the greater unionism, international solidarity and world comradeship!

One final example of the fury with the economic and social system that drove these men on was provided by London district committe chairman John Buchan, in his Fulham branch notes of July 1913. He was describing two meetings; the first was a Caxton Hall rally of London electricians. The second, a reception at the India Office where Buchan worked for the Office of Works.

On the 2nd of June a mass meeting of the electrical workers of London was held at Caxton Hall. It was a good gathering of earnest men, not all, by any means, trade unionists, but all seemed to know that things were not right with the world, that they ought not to labour hard, and in return get a mere pittance in the shape of wages. Then again when there is no labour they are free, ah! free to starve. Speeches, gay and grave, a wonderful effort by Ben Tillett, all struck the right note and were listened to with the utmost interest, and the points made were thoroughly appreciated. Great good for our union ought to result from the meeting, and it should be followed up. Another, say, early in September, when things are getting busy, and perhaps by that time some definite statement will be made as to the time and method of getting that increase of wages that is so long overdue. Twenty-four hours later the writer was at a gathering of an altogether different character. In a working capacity I watched the guests arrive at the India Office for the Prime Minister's reception. In that great marble courtyard the 'Fat Ones' of the world assembled. 'Winnie' was there, with his pretty wife, doing perhaps one of the hardest day's work of her life, shaking hands with 'fat'. There, again, was John Burns, with his gold epaulettes and medal. God knows what for! Admiral's cap under his arm, one hand in his pocket, doubtless jingling the 'thirty pieces of silver'. Haldane was there, 'Marconi' George was there, but why go on, they were all there. Women with jewels worth a king's ransom; men, many of them that a self-respecting docker would refuse to shake hands with. The scene made me feel sick, and my mind went back to that gathering of the night before. There we had a great body of men met together to try and get better conditions – a living wage. Here was an inane, senseless exhibition. Hundreds of men and women, crowding in, shaking hands with some big wig or another, then off to swig champagne, claret cup, and other little drinks that the workers indulged in. How I should have liked every wage-slave in these isles to have seen these things with my eyes. I wanted to call out, so that all could hear – 'Creatures, your sisters in the brickfields of Staffordshire are carrying burdens of over two hundredweight all day long for wages. Good heaven! Wages of a shilling a day. Your brothers in the Black Country have got tired of trying to live on

18s a week, and are striking for a wage of 23s a week. And you, cast in the same mould, calling the same maker God. What are you doing? Instead of being here in your fine feathers, you ought to be moving heaven and earth to prevent such things being. You 'Things', that you are, have you not read history? Have you forgotten the lessons of the French Revolution, and such-like happenings? Do you think the people will always be able to stand it? But there, enough, these things sicken one.

This hatred of capitalism found expression within the union through energetic recruitment and organization – particularly in London. This in turn produced strong support for the auxiliary section and determination to confront the employers, culminating in the great contracting strikes of 1914 in London and Liverpool. The prosecution of all those strikes from 1911–14 brought mixed benefits to the union. Its capacity to fight undoubtedly attracted recruits and a degree of respect from the employers. It also created another flashpoint between the union's cautious, northern leadership and particularly the London militants. Their political inspiration and determination to press on with disputes which were outwith the rules or simply failures produced a recurring sense of crisis within the union.

This is not to say the union was unwilling to dispute issues with employers. There were perfectly normal attempts to secure advances in wages or to defend the right to organize. In 1912, the year, it will be remembered, that the union first 'forced ourselves upon the employers', there were many advances of wages up and down the country. In Glasgow, $\frac{1}{2}$d an hour increase was achieved, along with the linking of the contracting rate to the shipyards and engineering shops. Belfast forced two rises of 1s per week. Manchester, the Tyne, Nottingham, Birmingham and Southampton all enjoyed rises on the hourly rates. Most significant of all was the dispute in Leicester in the summer of 1912. The union's application to the ECA for an increase in wages of $\frac{1}{2}$d an hour for ECA firms was referred to a Board of Trade Arbitration for the first time. The arbitrator, Mr Clement Bailhache, refused the claim on 14 June, on the grounds that the Leciester contractors would be at an unfair disadvantage if they had to pay more than the Derby and Nottingham contractors. Rowan refused to be disappointed by this setback, and was clearly impressed with the arbitration process, not least when it secured $\frac{1}{2}$d an hour rise in Leeds. Efforts were redoubled to organize Nottingham, and by early 1913, wages were raised in both Leicester and Nottingham by negotiation, strikes and eventually a second, successful arbitration at Leicester. Strikes failed in Bradford – where F. E. Sims reappeared on his return from America. He was readmitted to the union and became the Bradford strike chairman. The London East workers in the docks failed to gain anything from a solidarity strike with port workers in London. At Earl's Court in April, twenty-seven members refused to work overtime at single time and were sacked, while twenty-five others came out on strike in sympathy. Kinniburgh had a difficult time with the executive who were concerned that there had been no ballot. However, as it was in defence of established conditions on the working card, the strike was official. London West were impressed with Kinniburgh, who, they felt, 'is to be congratulated on the really splendid manner in which he handled the strike. He acted like lightning, travelling this vast city like a native, knew where to get reinforcements, got them, and won a great fight, leaving his able lieutenants, Webb and Buchan, in full possession.'

In Manchester, militance triumphed again. Jack Ball had negotiated a $\frac{1}{2}$d rise with the ECA in early 1912, only for the individual companies to refuse to pay it. The resulting strike was won – but Ball was furious with the employers. 'We had to fight treachery of the grossest description ... from the conference room, we turned with a flag of truce honourable to both sides only to receive a stab in the back ... Gentlemen of the ECA! Next time we shall keep our face to the fore!'

These disputes brought to the union's negotiators an experience and expertise in negotiating and presenting an arbitration case whose successes they could place in contradiction of the Stavenhagen-inspired revolutionary rhetoric. Jack Ball best summed this up when he wrote:

The demagogue bellowing like a bull, red in tooth and claw, relishing the sordid facts of life, leaves us in the grip of a merciless and hopeless materialism. It brings a dreary emptiness to the mind ... [revolutionary] nostrums and platitudes are as old as the hills, but always new to the ignorant, the emotional and the sloppy sensationalist. Let us act as well as hate. 'Light and Liberty' can only be won by the steady application of the mind to various details and difficulties. It is hard work – minus the limelight and the glory ... It may do on a wagon in Hyde Park or Tower Hill – but it will not win a wages dispute.

By the end of 1913, wages throughout the country were settling down at around $8\frac{1}{2}$d an hour for fifty-three hours in average towns like Leicester, Leeds and Glasgow. In Liverpool and Manchester, rates were slightly higher at 9d–$9\frac{1}{2}$d and hours shorter at fifty to fifty-three. They had all recently enjoyed small increases in pay. London was the exception. It was paid $9\frac{1}{2}$d an hour for fifty-three hours, and as the year ended, it was ready for a fight. Jack Kinniburgh was permanently stationed in London from 1 February 1913, following the decision to have a second national organizer – not a London organizer, much to the fury of the London branches whose membership had risen from 212 in 1910 to 1,537 in 1913. The second national organizer, elected with 904 votes in January 1913 at a second ballot, was Tom Stewart. He, too, was a Scotsman and a shipyard man, who had served for two years as the Scottish executive councillor. He beat the colourful, argumentative, George Olley who was at this time back in east London after working and organizing on Merseyside and in Newcastle. He got 704 votes. Tom Stewart kept to the North and his native Scotland, leaving Jack Kinniburgh to concentrate on London.

The members were acutely aware of two things. First, the rate of 9½d an hour had remained unchanged for fourteen years. This, they calculated in the Fulham branch, meant a decline in real standards of 8s per week. However, they were also well aware of their comparative lack of organization which allowed bricklayers to be paid 11d an hour, carpenters 11½d, and plasterers a full shilling per hour.

Frank Wood, the London North branch secretary, told Kinniburgh the size of the problem when he wrote in February 1913:

Every other town, almost, in Great Britain, is asking, or going to ask, or has got, an increase in wages, but London. London, the hub of the universe. London where there are 10,000 electrical workers of whom just over 1,000 only are members of the ETU – and of these 1,000 only about 100 are live members and take an active part in the work of trades unionism.

Throughout 1913, preparations were made to launch a wages movement at the end of the year. In February, an aggregate meeting at the Chandos Hall demanded a full-time London organizer to lead the coming fight. District secretary Jack Potter had lost his electrician's job through having too much time off to do his union work. In April, Kinniburgh had preliminary meetings with Mr Tate of the London ECA. During the summer the electricians helped the plasterers in the strikes called to refuse working with non-unionists. Kinniburgh made it clear to them that the ETU would require their solidarity when the time came.

Alongside these preparations, great meetings were held all over London to recruit and organize for the coming struggle. On 2 June the Caxton Hall was filled. The meeting was chaired by George Dew, the secretary of the London Building Industries Federation, and had star speakers of the day – Ben Tillett, James McDonald of the London Trades Council, Fred Knee, the secretary of the London Trades Council, Hugo Beazley of the plasterers, Henry Adams of the bricklayers, and Jack Kinniburgh. Jack Potter had stirred the meeting with rumours of the electrical contractors' threatening to reduce the paltry 9½d to 9d! The meeting was highly successful and Jack Kinniburgh's 'fine, fighting speech' was helpful in raising the temperature before the fight. Throughout August, Kinniburgh held open-air meetings with help from the London Trades Council. In September, 950 packed into Fulham Town Hall to hear Kinniburgh again. On Tuesday 28 October, 700 attended a meeting addressed by Jack Potter at the Club Union Hall.

Throughout the period, the union organized itself through the enforcement of trade union membership by strikes. This tactic was usually favoured by 'moderate' opinion as well as by London syndicalists. Manchester district committee kept up pressure on the executive throughout 1913 to reverse its 1912 decision not to automatically make official any closed shop strike. The executive stood firm on this general principle; however, they were quick to recognize, retrospectively, closed shop strikes. They said frequently that this was only in circumstances where 'our membership of federations like the BIF, or FEST obliged us to support others and temporarily ignore ETU rules'. This was a distinction that was lost on workers on strike and their leaders, whose enthusiasm to build organization was not to be denied. They argued that the union had ordered men off jobs in support of the plasterers' refusal to work with non-unionists in 1913. They had withdrawn men at Earl's Court, Ewart & Sons and in the great transport workers' strike in the London docks in 1912. Avon docks had struck against non-unionists, as had Merseyside shipbuilders. It was the only way to render impotent the growing employers' demands for union members to work with whoever the employer chose.

All these influences came to bear on a dispute which erupted in early September 1913. Eighty ETU members working for the Office of Works in London went on strike without consulting the district committee, much less the executive council. Jock Muir and John Buchan, part of the West London branches' syndicalist leadership, were involved. They claimed official support on the grounds they went on strike to force the removal of 'blackleg' painters – just as they had previously successfully removed a blackleg plasterer. This dispute deepened into a running battle with the executive, just like the disputes about the auxiliary section, the meaning of industrial unionism and the rights of the executive to control the behaviour of members, branches and district committees. Clearly, the political leadership of the strike enjoyed the position, and bombarded the executive with correspondence and deputations on the issue.

The executive refused to authorize strike pay. Fulham branch claimed the strike was about 'the most vital principle of trade unionism'. London Central denounced the executive's 'dilatory attitude'. Months later, on 15 June 1914, at the height of the London building industry strike, the executive received a forlorn letter from A. F. Reddall – the secretary of the dispute committee itself. He told a very different story. The men had been told that the London Building Industries Federation and the ASE were withdrawing all their men, so the electricians had better come out too. With the men out, they then discovered no such call had been made. When they protested to the ETU London district committee, they were then told that the dispute was now about the general question of blackleg joinery being introduced on to Office of Works jobs. By this time, other trade unionists were left alone in work, leaving some 'ticket men' at work and some outside, making it impossible when the strike was over to clear out all blacklegs. The letter finally complained of endless and futile deputations to see the ETU district committee, and demanded that the executive allow them to go back to work.

The executive told Kinniburgh and the district committee to end the strike.

Throughout the strike, the London district committee and the branches kept up a storm of abuse; the opposition only fizzled out after January 1914 when Fulham, London South-East, London West and Brentford were told that no money would be available to pay other benefits if the strike pay paid out was not repaid to the union. And still Fulham tried it on. In May 1914, they were caught paying Office of Works strikers benefits under the guise of London building industry strike benefit. They grudgingly had branch collections to repay the funds, but the whole episode was symptomatic of the deepening sense of anarchic and unconstitutional behaviour by the London branches and district committee.

The Great Strikes of 1914: London and Liverpool

The claim of the London contracting membership for an hourly rate of 11d was lodged with the ECA in London in November 1913. The claim was official and some sort of trouble expected. The union's leadership were keen to proceed cautiously and took the precaution of sending the claim to each of the 500 electrical contracting companies in London. Other events, however, interfered with the carefully prepared wages movement that Kinniburgh had designed. Just before Christmas 1913, the members working on the Pearl Insurance Building in Holborn, along with other unions, came out on strike against the employment of non-unionists. Jack Kinniburgh was the chairman of the London Building Industries Federation in 1914, and took a key part in the struggle that now ensued. The London Master Builders Association (LMBA) resorted to the imposition of the 'Document' on London building workers of every trade. This was a letter that workers signed, and gave to their employers, where they promised to work with people whether they were members of a union or not.

When thousands would not sign, the employers locked them out. This great dispute in the London building industry formed the background to the electricians' more direct struggle with the electrical contractors.

On 9 January, the newly-organized London Electrical Masters Association (LEMA) wrote to the London district committee, formally breaking off negotiations on the wage claim submitted. LEMA was a new body of contractors formed specifically to deal with negotiations with electrical workers. LMBA willingly ceded to LEMA the responsibility for dealing with the electricians' pay and conditions by March 27. They hoped thereby to split the building workers by encouraging the separation of negotiations. From the ETU's point of view, it gave them much more direct responsibility for shaping their own destiny. LEMA tried to push the union to the sidelines with a childish and provocative 'stunt'. They wrote to every employer in London, enclosing an official announcement which was posted on all sites.

NOTICE

The London Electrical Masters Association, being desirous of improving the status of all electrical workers (whether connected with any organization or not), and the general terms of employment and wages, desire you to send a delegate or delegates to meet them, each delegate to represent about twenty men. At a meeting which will be held on Tuesday 27 January, 8 p.m. at Caxton Hall, all matters with reference to employment will be openly discussed, when it is hoped that a committee of the men and LEMA will be formed to draw up a code of working rules, fix a scale of minimum wages and settle other terms of employment.

The London district committee reacted fast. They issued 3,000 copies of the union's claim in the form of a revised working rules card, and booked the Farringdon Hall for 26 January 1914 to discuss tactics at an aggregate meeting.

The Farringdon Hall meeting was a sensation. Nearly 1,500 electrical workers attended: over 100 were recruited into the union. Jack Stokes, chairman of the London Trades Council spoke, as did Messrs Kinniburgh, Potter, Webb and Harry Rolf from London East. Curiously, although not originally invited by the London district committee, Charlie Bowerman MP, the secretary of the TUC parliamentary committee, spoke too. John Buchan, president of the London district committee, was in the chair, and the meeting agreed to oppose the employers' tactic of removing the union from the negotiations the following evening.

The Caxton Hall meeting was a sensation in its own way: the Office of Works activists had obtained tickets by a roundabout route. The government department had not been sent an invitation by LEMA. Jock Muir and his friends persuaded Simpsons, the financial services company that was lending money to the Government for the job that Muir & Co were working on, to apply for direct representation at the meeting. On the same day as the meeting, 27 January, LEMA gave Simpsons seven tickets for the meeting. When the meeting started, the men from Simpsons were challenged – on the grounds that none of the employers could recall hearing of such a significant electrical contractor called Simpsons employed 150 people. Lionel Tate, the secretary of LEMA, eventually agreed to accept their credentials. The employers' chairman and secretary then made speeches about the desirability of working without the union and formally moved their proposition that a committee of men and masters should be elected by the meeting to deal with wages and conditions in London. The men from Simpsons took over the meeting; they moved an amendment 'that any negotiations must necessarily take place through the unions representing the electrical industry'. This was moved by Jock Muir and seconded by Ebber of the obscure Association of Electrical Station Engineers (a forerunner of the Electrical Power Engineers Association (EPEA)). The amendment was carried to wild applause. After the meeting, Mr Tate passed Jock Muir in the street, and stopped and asked the identity of the Simpsons company. When Muir explained that in reality they indirectly employed the Office of Works militants, 'Mr Tate's face was a picture', according to John Buchan's account of the meeting.

This triumph for the union was not greeted by everyone within the union with unanimous applause. Frank Wood, the London North branch secretary, wrote:

I attended both the meeting at the Memorial Hall and also that of the masters at Caxton Hall. The men's meeting was by far the most orderly I have attended so far, and reflected great credit on all concerned. I cannot say the same remark applies to the other meeting at Caxton Hall. There were several unseemly interruptions of speakers and not the courtesy shown to the chairman as was his due, as, I must say, he was strictly impartial. I regret the line of argument that the non-unionists in the hall were a lot of numskulls or that they could roundly abuse the masters to their faces. . . .

Throughout February and March the employers took up a determined stand, clearly aimed at breaking the union. The national leadership moved heaven and earth to keep the negotiations alive, while the London district committee and its branches were insistent on early industrial warfare.

On 3 February, Kinniburgh withdrew all ETU men from sites where the master-builders 'document' was being imposed. LEMA responded by refusing to negotiate further. Jimmy Rowan travelled to London on 13 February to brief the parliamentary committe of the TUC and to meet the London district commitee, who agreed to accept Rowan's instructions on the Office of Works strike pay issue. He expressed himself pleased with 'a much better understanding' between executive and district committee. On 4 March, Jack Potter wrote to Rowan saying it was 'irksome' that action was still delayed, and that the executive should threaten Tate and LEMA with strike action. LEMA virtually guaranteed it when they published their unilateral working rules on 6 March. There was no problem in raising wages to $10\frac{1}{2}$d an hour by July; however, they now insisted on their own version of the 'document'. 'No exception shall be taken to the employment or non-employment of any workman in the electrical trade on the ground that he is, or is not, a member of a trade society. Neither shall any exception be taken to the employment of a workman in any other trade on the ground that he is, or is not, a member of a trade society.' The crisis deepened when the BIF withdrew all of its workers from all LMBA firms, whether they were imposing the obnoxious 'document' or not.

LEMA were busy stoking the fires. They also introduced two new semi-skilled grades – 'pipefitters' to do the conduit erection, and 'improvers' to act as mates. These people were to be paid at 9d and 7d per hour and represented a clear attempt to cut down on the numbers of skilled electricians required. Three aggregate meetings were held at Caxton Hall in March. Jimmy Rowan and Jack Ball attended; the executive met in London. The third meeting, on 27 March, voted 583–59 to reject the employers' terms and demanded a strike to start on 1 April.

On 30 March, the sub-executive council were still trying to get a settlement. 'Providing the employers are willing to concede the advance as offered,' Rowan wrote to Potter in London, 'and are agreeable to not *enforcing* the rules we object to, we are not prepared to sanction a stoppage of work at the present time, as, due to the dispute between LMBA and the other building trades, we are in a specially unfavourable position and our claims cannot have fair consideration until such a dispute is settled.'

Later that day, Jimmy Rowan, Jack Kinniburgh and Jack Potter met Mr Cash, the vice-chairman of LEMA. After ninety minutes, the employers refused to move: Jimmy Rowan attended the London district committee that night and the strike began on 1 April 1914.

On 7 April 1914, the first claims for strike pay were received at head office. Just about 500 members were on strike. One hundred and sixteen were in London West branch alone; eighty-five at Fulham, eighty-five at London Central. Fifty-four members were out from London North, sixty-four from South West, forty-five from North West, and handfuls in the East, South-East Croydon, Woolwich, East Ham and Brentford branches. The first week's strike pay amounted to over £580.

The executive attempted to meet Tate, or to get him to deal with Potter. LEMA refused to negotiate with anyone who did not have authority to concede the principle of the 'document' as a pre-condition. The London branches were suspicious of Rowan's attempts to negotiate; they seemed oblivious to the rising cost of the strike. From 22 June, the whole membership agreed in a ballot, 1708–487, to levy themselves 6d per week until the strike ended. By mid-June, the strike had cost £4,506, and the union postponed claims in engineering and on the tramways because of the impossibility of supporting any action in those industries. On Merseyside such considerations meant nothing. The electrical contractors replied to the union's claim for 1d an hour with the ultimatum that, unless members worked to the wages and conditions currently being paid, the employers would *reduce* wages by ½d an hour from 20 June. Liverpool electricians, led by Citrine, went on strike with enthusiasm. By mid-July the strike in London was costing around £330 per week, and Liverpool £230 in strike benefits.

In London other employers rapidly paid up 10½d. There was great help from other unions that impressed Kinniburgh, with builders' labourers refusing to work with non-union electricians and attempting to survive on 4s a week strike pay from their union. The Majestic Cinema in Clapham finished the electrical installation over the Easter weekend with non-union labour. The other building trades refused to work on the Tuesday after Easter until Kinniburgh persuaded the management to rip the whole electrical work out and start again with union labour – which they did! The branches did their best to place strikers with non-LEMA firms, local councils and those large, erstwhile anti-union firms like Higgins & Griffiths in the City that quickly paid the rates. The strike in Liverpool was solid and well organized. Nevertheless, men get overexcited in the middle of a dispute and can get things out of proportion. The Mersey district committee asked the executive council to take legal action against a local contractor, Mr Pulford, for slandering the chairman of the district committee, Walter Citrine, 'by informing numerous parties that he is only a labourer!' The executive council wisely decided to take no action.

The financial strain was now enormous. The strike pay had fallen to a weekly total of £213 in London and £100 in Liverpool by the last week in July, but hundreds of members were claiming unemployment pay, victimization pay and lock-out benefit as the building workers strike dragged on. The crisis deepened. The longer the 6d levy went on, the less it brought in. The members rejected the proposition to raise it to 1s 6d per week, 1,712–904.

On 28 July, the employers from LEMA offered to pay 10½d, withdraw the 'document' and have an eight-man joint ETU-LEMA committe look at other grievances for a six month trial period. The district committee unanimously recommended this and the members accepted it, 464–320. In Liverpool, the victory came on 29 August with the employers conceding a ½d an hour rise without any other pre-conditions. The strikes were costly to the memberships in the two towns. One hundred and forty-nine members drew unemployment benefit on Merseyside: in London, no less than 510 members were paid unemployment benefit. In the capital, the strike involved the personal lives of many of its leadership – past, present and future. Old stagers like Calipé, Brixey senior and Brixey junior, G.H. Butler, Brebner and White from Battersea were all involved. Philpott, Bill Day and a future president of the union, Hugh Bolton, were out of work for weeks. John Buchan, Jock Muir, Bill Webb, Fred Alford and future assistant general secretary, Matt Greenwell, were all on strike and then unemployed during 1914. Jack Kinniburgh's new brother-in-law Billy Bucke was out, too. Altogether, London branches paid out £6,844 in dispute benefit in 1914 and £1,735 in unemployment benefit.

The final judgments on these strikes in 1914 complete the picture of a union that was ready for the modern industrial world. Rowan wrote that the seven months of strikes and lock-outs in London cost the union £7,000. 'Although the effect of the dispute was to set up a joint committee ... it is very doubtful whether the results achieved were equivalent to the self-sacrifice of the members, many of whom were brought practically to the verge of starvation.' The Liverpool strike presented Rowan with a much more cheerful aspect. 'It cost us just over £1,000, but there was no doubt in this case of the money being wisely and well expended. There was also a thoroughness shown in the management of this dispute that has never been previously equalled and which had its effect on the favourable settlement attained.'

Jack Ball said to the conference on 3 August 1914: 'We have spent a lot of money: it has been costly, but we have gained what money cannot always buy – influence, prestige and respect.' The lights were going out all over Europe that same day.

9

THE UNION AT WAR, 1914–18

THE FIRST WORLD WAR produced a four-fold growth in membership. It also produced a deepening gap between the London district committee and the national leadership in Manchester and issues associated with the war produced political schism in the union that was to be reinforced, widened and made permanent by the fall-out from the Russian Revolution.

The 1914 conference in Manchester met the week war broke out. It unanimously denounced the war before turning its attentions to revising the rule-book. The most significant changes reflected attempts to accommodate the dramatic growth in membership in 1914 to 8,145. Contributions rose to 1s for full benefit and 6d for the new auxiliary section that was finally instituted at this conference. The extra income would be necessary for the funding of further full-time officials.

Tom Stewart was the second organizer, elected in 1913. At the end of the same year, the union decided to have an assistant general secretary to take on the growing burden of administrative work at 137 Gt Clowes St. Bob Prain won the election on the *third* ballot from Horace Coulthard, 818–783. This election was exceptionally close all round. Coulthard had been general treasurer of the union, re-elected annually since the head office moved to Manchester in 1908. He must have been part of the sub-executive council 'Manchester oligarchy', as Stavenhagen referred to them. He had led on the first ballot by 374 votes to Glaswegian Bob Prain's 264, to Fred Alford's 231 votes. In the second ballot, Coulthard led again, by 507–466 for syndicalist Londoner Fred Alford. Prain got 406. However, Alford withdrew from the final ballot 'with the deepest regret and after considerable temperamental punishment. My aged mother has not taken kindly to the prospect of my going to Manchester, at this, the autumn of her life. I therefore choose duty in preference to place'.

This decision of Alford's prevented a declared industrial unionist from securing a good chance of election to high office in the union. Bob Prain consequently made it to the final ballot and won by forty-four votes. Coulthard took this badly. He wrote that he was upset to lose by 'a majority of forty-four, and only by a particularly heavy vote of Scottish branches, who polled 350 votes out of my opponent's total of 834'. Coulthard denounced the third ballot rule and deplored the absence of a 'conscious electorate' with under thirty per cent of the membership voting. Coulthard fell into obscurity. He stood for the Manchester executive seat in 1917 and came bottom of the poll with thirteen votes.

He did a little better in 1918 when he challenged his successor as treasurer, Peter Irvine, the Trafford Park branch secretary. However, the result was the same. Irvine got 3,279 votes to Coulthard's 543.

Bob Prain, on the other hand, was to be periodically re-elected assistant general secretary every time until 1942. He was a dour, methodical man, largely interested in administrative matters, and in particular the Approved Society. Following Lloyd George's 1911 legislation on the early social security benefits of unemployment pay, maternity benefit and sickness benefit, the trade unions were 'approved' societies for distributing the benefits to members. Seventy-five per cent of the members chose the union to be their approved society in 1912 – but the percentage was never to be so high again. However, the extra work for Jimmy Rowan produced, as far as he was concerned, 'a most trying and weary time for all concerned'. This alone justified Bob Prain's election to help out at the beleaguered head office. Bob Prain's honesty was legendary. His own personal expenses claims were models of their kind. As late as 1939, he would attach every single bus ticket to the expenses form to prove his claims.

The 1914 conference extended the growth of the officials corps significantly. Any district with over 800 members could levy the members in the district for a full-time officer's fund. The general funds of the union would contribute £1 a week, the levy the rest, up to the salary level of £2 2s od. He would be elected every three years. The districts could vary this wage if they preferred, but the rule was not widely used. The first district official elected in the union under the new rules was Walter McLennan Citrine. He was elected in October 1914, and was arguably the most illustrious son of the ETU. Brought up on Merseyside, Citrine joined the Liverpool branch of the ETU on 9 October 1911. He was to go on and become an assistant general secretary of the union in 1920 before taking up the same job for the TUC on 1924. It belittles his career to say simply that he was general secretary of the TUC from 1926 until after World War Two when he became a member of the newly nationalized Coal Board. In 1947, he became chairman of the British Electricity Authority, until 1957. Throughout his life, he was a prolific writer on trade union and political affairs. His most famous book, the definitive *ABC of Chairmanship*, published in 1939, was based on a short pamphlet on the subject he first produced for the Merseyside branches in 1913 that was incorporated in its essentials into the union's 1914 rule-book.

Citrine was the first district official. By the end of 1915, Jack Potter in London and George Olley on Tyneside had joined him. The fourth district official, elected on Clydeside in July 1915, was Archie Stewart, who beat J. J. Melville in an unpleasant, personal campaign, by just one vote! It was clearly desirable that the union should have district officers who could give the membership the benefit of professional negotiating skills. However, the *district* elections, producing another set of lively and legitimate local leaders, were not wholly to the union's advantage as they weakened the sense of national discipline and unity of purpose that Ball and Rowan were seeking. Jack Ball was to deplore, in 1916, the effects of the introduction of district full-time officers on the members. 'Witness the spectacle in many centres where an all-time district secretary has been appointed. If there has not been any trouble before, there will be now. Conspiracy is soon afoot to oust and get his job. No matter how ably he fills the position, the job is the thing.'

The early officials had it hard; endless hours for pay and expenses that roughly equalled the basic pay of the contracting electrician, whose access to wartime overtime was enormous. Citrine had a one-room office in Don Chambers in Paradise Street in Liverpool. When Bill Webb replaced Jack Potter in 1917, he operated from 76 Gray's Inn Road. Citrine bought a second-hand typewriter, and not all districts could even afford a full-time officer. Manchester could probably use the head office officials – but there were active district committees in Belfast, Birmingham, Edinburgh and Sheffield who had to do without full-time help through the early years of the war.

The union's experience of the war can best be understood by examining several themes throughout the war years. First, there was the question of the membership's and leadership's general attitude to the war and the extent of pacifist opinion in the union. There were three main issues throughout the war – dilution of skilled labour at work, the problem of the army's voracious hunger for men for the front and conscription, and the conflicting experiences of arbitration and the emergence of the Whitley system of Joint Industrial Councils (JICs). Overlaying all of this was the growing sense of permanent opposition emerging in parts of London. It seemed that all of these issues produced a 'leadership' and provincial response, and a considered, politicized and always stridently opposite view in the capital.

No one expected the war to last beyond Christmas 1914. It was not until early 1915 that it became apparent that the end of the war was a long time off; and it was then that opposition started to express itself. The union had denounced the war in that 1914 conference resolution; however, like the majority of workers throughout the land, the electricians' patriotism was placed firmly in the service of the State. Galsworthy and Chesterton provided fiery articles for the journal to plead the case for 'poor little Belgium'. The Labour Party joined the Government in July 1915 to everyone's approval (except Jack Kinniburgh, who thought the coalition compromised Labour's political independence).

By June 1915, over 1,000 ETU members had volunteered for the colours, and the journal was regularly used to publish letters from well-known union figures like the ex-secretary of Newcastle Central, Sergeant W. T. C. Charlton, Norwich branch secretary Bert Cannell, who wrote from the Gallipoli beaches, and John Philpott – the brother of ex-London district secretary Tom Philpott. His letter, published in August 1915, summed up the patriotic content of all such letters when he finished by writing 'you do your bit in the munition questions; I will do my bit by making use of them to effect'. There is little evidence of out-and-out jingoism in the union's records (although Salford and Trafford Park branches demanded in late 1917 that the union should refuse to work with Germans, Turks and Austrians for at least seven years after the war). Throughout, there was a steady determination not to let down the boys at the Front. Jimmy Rowan was not an emotional man; but he was clearly moved by a visit to Ypres in October 1915 as part of a delegation of Manchester munitions workers' representatives. He reported:

> Every ruin of once beautiful Ypres seems to cry aloud for vengeance. No one can go through its ruined streets without coming away with his heart hardened against the country responsible for this destruction.... We came away with the unanimously avowed intention of advocating that everything humanly possible should be done to increase to the fullest extent the production of guns and shells, realizing that the defeat of militarization in Europe is more dependent on this factor than all the others put together.

This was to remain Rowan's attitude throughout the war; but the executive were not insensitive to the handfuls of members whose German names got them interned for the duration. They were transferred to the honorary section of the union, where they could retain membership until the war was over, when they would take up paying membership and its rights again. Their families were supported by small benevolent grants. The members voted, 1,020–672, to levy themselves 6d per quarter, in order to pay the reduced contributions of members on active service to keep their cards clear. Throughout the war, even when the leadership was critical of Government policy on dilution, conscription and the possibility of a negotiated peace towards the end, the executive would not support strikes that would confront the Government or interrupt the munitions flow. Even in the dark days of war-weariness in 1917, branch resolutions in favour of 'helping our Tommies by running this war to a successful conclusion' (Loughborough) were the prevalent feelings. In December 1917, Glasgow West branch urged 'the executive council to ask the

Government to put down peace meetings with a strong hand'. They wouldn't go that far, but the executive refused to join any campaign to obtain the release of conscientious objector Fred Scrace. This generally pro-war attitude was most severely tested in June 1917. During this year, anti-war sentiment grew to such an extent as to allow a Labour conference to send peace delegates to a conference in Stockholm. Members of the National Sailors and Firemen's Union (NSFU) in Aberdeen refused to carry the delegates to the conference, to universal disapproval in most other unions. Although deploring the Government's refusal to give the delegates travel documents to Stockholm, the ETU executive only voted 4–3 to denounce the NSFU anti-pacifist stand.

On the other side of the argument, the union's Parkhead branch in Glasgow – at the centre of the Clydeside shop-steward movement of that year – sent a resolution to the executive to adopt:

That the members of the ETU declare against a further prosecution of the war, recognizing that nothing can compensate for the wholesale slaughter of the young manhood of the civilized world. Realizing that a continuance of the reigning militarization means only a further enslavement of the workers, they repudiate all schemes for the partial exemption of the favoured classes of industry and, in the interests of the workers of the world, demand peace.

At the July executive, twenty-five branches had sent in resolutions that rejected the Parkhead motion; but eighteen branches had supported. A ballot vote of the members, however, was to be more conclusive, but not overwhelming. One thousand and forty-two voted for the 'immediate cessation of the war'. Two thousand two hundred and eighty-one voted for 'the successful prosecution of the war' in September 1917. This support for the war was all the more surprising, given the Government's changes to the conscription regulations in late April 1917. These made certain that a much higher percentage of ETU men would be taken into the army. Indeed, Parkhead branch were relying on just this to get their anti-war resolution through. They wrote to the journal in May 1917: 'This is where we get the true vote on conscription. The man over military age may desire a continuance of the horrible carnage, but what a large number of our members will change their opinions ... now the new order is in force.'

Throughout the war, visits to the Front in workers' deputations made as deep an impression on other ETU representatives as the first had done on Rowan. Frank Morrison of Edinburgh went, as did Rowland Penrose, the Leeds branch secretary and first full-time official for the West Riding of Yorkshire in 1918. In January of that year, the general president, Jack Ball, Peter Irvine, the treasurer, and organizer Tom Stewart were nominated by the executive to visit the Front, despite Stavenhagen's view that 'this terrible international tragedy does not warrant its being debased into a pantomime entertainment for sightseers'. Further nominations were collected from every executive division to visit the Front, except from the South, West and Central London division of Stavenhagen, who told Rowan they would not participate in the election of 'war tourists'. Nevertheless, the members did not support conscription in a ballot, and the executive voted to demand the unconditional release of committed Marxist campaigner John McClean in 1918.

Throughout the war, the members' views of the conflict were coloured by the rising likelihood of their having to go and fight in it. At the outbreak of war, virtually all outstanding disputes (including the ETU contracting strike in Liverpool) were quickly settled, and the union joined in the general declarations of industrial peace. Despite early industrial dislocation leading to a surge of unemployment, this proved so short-lived that by mid-1915 there was not a single member of the union unemployed. The problems of labour shortage in the priority munitions industries now became the greatest challenge for unions everywhere. Prices rose, wages became devalued and thousands of Clydeside workers came out on unofficial strike in February 1915. By March 1915, the Government moved in hard with legislation that became law in July – the Munitions of War Act. The Act's provisions were complemented by the Committee on Production, set up in March 1915 to reorganize the munitions industries. They arbitrated on labour disputes, organized labour shortage problems and dealt with employers' demands to make the best of productive capacity by getting trade unions to drop their protective customs and accept the 'dilution' of the trade through the use of semi-skilled labour.

Jimmy Rowan attended the treasury conferences under Lloyd George in March. He was a member of the National Trade Union Advisory Committee that was set up afterwards. There was agreement that dilution and compulsory arbitration in disputes would be accepted by the unions. In return, it was promised that pre-war practices would be restored at the end of the war. This understanding, added to taxes on excessive profits in munitions, was made legally enforceable in the Munitions of War Act in July, with Lloyd George moved to the new Ministry of Munitions.

Changes in Trade Union Practice – the Wartime Contribution

Throughout the war, the union was to argue its case at the Committee on Production, to take part in negotiations in Whitehall on ways to help the war effort or advance the members' interests in these vital industries. This contact with Government officials, civil servants and leaders of opinion must have been wholly new for the union's officials. They seized the opportunity of improving the union's reputation and standing through being able to demonstrate its influence. Jimmy Rowan wrote of this effect, and other key implications of war for the union, at the height of the war in March 1916.

The needs of the war have brought a revolution and mark a new era for the trade unions. Before the war, we had reached the point of being recognized by the law as a necessary evil. Years of hard work, hard fighting, and the expenditure of millions of money had won certain rights for combinations of workers. Since the war started, a complete change has taken place. The trade unions have been taken into consultation by the Government, not necessarily for the good of the unions, but because the Government found they could not successfully carry on without the active support of organized labour.

Due to national needs, organized labour has agreed to suspend many of the most important safeguards they have built up. In doing so, they have the pledged word of the governing authorities that their temporary sacrifices will be restored, by law if necessary. The recommendation of the Treasury conference in March 1915 have been embodied in the Munitions of War Act. Regulations having the force of law, in the forms of circulars L2, L3, and L6 have been put into operation, ADMITTING THE RIGHT OF CRAFTSMEN TO CRAFT WORK, an innovation which may have far-reaching effects in the future. The Munitions of War Act, on the other hand, has taken away, for the time being, most of the liberty of the individual. It is at present illegal to strike on war service work. It is illegal for an employer to offer a man on such work another job, making it impossible for a man to improve his position by the means usually at his disposal – by selling his labour to the highest bidder ... there is a limit on employers' profits ... these changes must all have a far-reaching effect, not only on the relation of employer to employee, but on the part of the State to both. Many of the measures taken are putting into partial operation ideas of collective ownership that have been advocated for years by the best reformers, but which required national need to bring into operation. The State has controlled the railways; it has controlled the engineering and shipbuilding establishments. It has built huge national factories. It has taken over part of the ships. What can be shown to be necessary for wartime in this respect can equally be shown necessary for peace times. All wars are not necessarily between nation and nation.

The Munitions of War Act produced considerable concern arising out of the illegality of industrial action and the immobility of labour within munitions factories. However, it also offered opportunities. Jimmy Rowan welcomed compulsory arbitration before the Committee on Production. The introduction of compulsory arbitration 'does not mean that trade union activity has come to an end, but rather, that trade unionists will require to be more active. The advocates of compulsory arbitration assert it means the substitution of scientific trade unionism for brute force as indicated by the lock-out in the hands of the employer and the strike in the hands of the men.' He was also anxious that skilled men should volunteer for war service work in the munitions factories –

and in this way keep out dilutees if there were serious shortages of skilled men. He was bitterly angry with some employers who abused the regulations that made it difficult for members to leave a 'controlled' munitions establishment. No employer could engage a man who had worked within the previous six months at a munitions factory and left that work without that employer's permission. Some employers were suspending men and not giving them clearance certificates for up to six weeks. In this way, they could not get another job and also lost wages while suspended. Equally, a union member could be sacked, but there was no comeback on the employer, which the Clyde district committee thought particularly one-sided.

There was to be even more opposition to the introduction of conscription when the Military Service Bill was introduced into parliament in January 1916. To start with, the army took only young, single men. As the appetite of the trenches grew, however, the age limit was raised, married men were taken and various exemptions for skilled classes of workers were limited. This whole process further intensified the pressures at work to introduce more and more dilution of skilled work, the introduction of women in previously unheard of occupations and the introduction of disabled soldiers returning to work. This gave the opposition forces within the union two intertwined issues – dilution and conscription – on which to build a growing campaign against the executive council and leadership of the union.

Class War on the Executive Council 1915–16

It was a campaign that reached new heights in the autumn and winter of 1915–16. It was a campaign led once more by the industrial unionists in West London. It was C. H. Stavenhagen's greatest success; but the executive council eventually emerged as a stronger force than the London district committee.

During 1915, the executive council were joined by two Londoners who were usually found to be in opposition to the rest of the council. The intensity of the opposition was largely due to the changes in electing the executive introduced after the 1914 conference. When the 1908 executive was first elected on a national basis, there were six divisions in which the candidates were *nominated* by local branches, but *elected* by ballots in all branches for all districts. In the London context, this effectively meant that the strident industrial Marxists/syndicalists had little chance of being elected. Tom Philpott, the London district secretary, was elected from 1910–14 with comfortable majorities over challengers like Bill Webb or Fred Alford. But the growth in membership led to the executive being expanded to nine seats, with each division voting just within its own divisional election. There were now two seats for London and the South of England. Frank Whitehead, an electrician with Battersea Borough Council, won the seat that covered South East and

South West London along with all of Southern England when he beat Tom Parr, the Plymouth branch secretary, 83–29. The other seat covered Central, Eastern and West London. H. E. Oakleigh who had sat on the first national executive from 1908–10, got eighty-four votes. Bill Webb, with 135, was just beaten by Stavenhagen with 139. There was no doubt what this meant in political terms. 'I have told London members this, not once, but some scores of times, and I told them that when they sent me to the executive council, they sent me on a class-war basis, and that if this was not the case, I was not the man to vote for.'

Stavenhagen dominated the deliberations of the union in 1915. His fierce opposition to the war, his wild opposition to the Munitions of War Act, his deep fear of conscription and his intense hatred for the president, Jack Ball, and the rest of the executive, produce some of the most vivid, even vitriolic, documents in the whole history of the union.

The Government were desperate to get electrical fitters into the Devonport dockyard, and in the autumn of 1914 were prepared to pay the conventional 38s for forty-eight hours, along with the £1 a week subsistence allowance that they were paying at the Sheerness dockyard. By June 1915, the Government were refusing to pay the extra £1 in the dockyards, and the union's executive did not call for strikes as twenty-eight men working at the Portsmouth dockyard replaced those who left in disgust at not being paid the allowance. The law was clearly against the executive, but Stavenhagen and the London district committee used this case to embarrass Rowan and the executive mightily. 'What right,' thundered Stavenhagen, 'have these men, to one of whom we willingly pay 70s per week with 35s country allowance, to take any action whatever to help the damned government of bosses to reduce the already restricted living wage of our members?'

His reaction on the executive to the passing of the Munitions of War Act was to denounce Rowan and Ball for attending the treasury conference with Lloyd George. He then organized aggregate meetings in London to call for the resignations of Ball and Rowan for agreeing to the legislation, despite a 6–1 executive endorsement of their actions. In July 1915, Stavenhagen tried to persuade the executive that the TUC should 'approach the central trade union organizations throughout the world to have an international congress in a neutral country to consider immediate measures, such as an international strike, to bring about the cessation of hostilities'.

Ball said that this was 'a disgraceful exhibition of cowardice'. Ball made it clear he would support conscription as the lesser evil to German victory in the war and pointed out that 'German socialists are just as much inclined to be cruel and double-faced as are the German militarists'. For Ball, 'the only way to cure a mad bull is by superior force and skill'. All of this was on top of endless rows about unauthorized circulation of criticism of the executive by the London district committee, and evidence of Stavenhagen's revealing the executive's business at district committee and aggregate meetings. He also kept on about the 1914 sell-out, and the alleged betrayal of the Dublin striker in 1915 who was fined £5 for leaving a 'controlled' establishment, with the executive refusing to pay his fine or his fares home.

Archie Stewart was elected by one vote from J. J. Melville in July 1915 as Clyde district secretary. The rules required him to resign as Scottish executive councillor, but the executive asked him to stay on until he took up his district secretary job later in the year. This infuriated Stavenhagen, but he allowed himself to second a resolution at the May executive that disciplinary action should be taken against members who illegally circularized the union without executive permission. On 27 October, an aggregate meeting at Chandos Hall formed a committee to circularize the union with a pamphlet that denounced the general secretary, general president and executive members who voted not to ballot the members on their acceptance of the Munitions of War Act, their let-down of London in 1914 and their sell-out on the dockyards subsistence issue, and asked the help of other districts to ensure their dismissals. The resolution that put this policy to the Chandos Hall meeting was moved by Jock Muir and C. H. Stavenhagen! Further, the London district committee had got the long-suffering Jack Potter to write to Lloyd George telling him to ignore the executive council delegation on the working of the Act, as they did not represent the London area since they did not have a London district committee delegate on the deputation.

The executive council that met on 15 November 1915 had had enough. They suspended the London district committee forthwith, although they exonerated district secretary Jack Potter. They expelled from the union the leading members of the committee – Messrs Condon, Rogers, Weston, Jock Muir, Matt Greenwell, John Wyatt, John Buchan, Hugh Bolton and, inevitably, C. H. Stavenhagen. This was carried 8–0, with even Whitehead voting for and Stavenhagen abstaining in his own execution.

Alan Garner and Archie Stewart moved, for the benefit of the members outside, no doubt: 'That in the opinion of this executive council, there is a section of the London members who are attempting to break up the ETU. Certain members have plainly stated so.' This was a clear reference to Stavenhagen's reply that 'it suited his purposes to be expelled'. The resolution went on:

The whole of the actions of the executive council and officials in respect of the matters mentioned in the resolution passed at the London aggregate meeting have been faithfully reported in minutes and circulars issued to the branches – that a campaign of slander and abuse is being engineered against the ruling authority of the union (which is a democratically elected body). The sole purpose of this can only be the disintegration of the union as a national body, and the attrition of provincial branches, and those London members who are not in favour of such a campaign, is hereby drawn to the only possible result that can accrue from such a process.

If all that excitement was not enough for one meeting, the next item on the agenda, taken in Stavenhagen's absence, was even more explosive.

The post of general president was elected by the whole membership every December for the following year, but the rule governing the election procedure produced the next great crisis. Clause 92 read: 'The president and treasurer shall be nominated for the ensuing year by any of the branches, and be elected by a vote of the whole union, concurrently with the election of [executive] councillors. The president and treasurer shall reside within a radius of twelve miles from the general office. . . .' Jack Ball was to write later that what this meant was that the executive had decided that the residential qualification applied at the time of the *nomination*, not just after a president was *elected*. This had been in the rule-book for seven years, and had not been challenged at either the 1911 or 1914 rules revision conferences. Indeed, J. J. Melville asked at the conference in August 1914 for a ruling as the stark words of the rule were relatively ambiguous. He was told it meant 'nomination'. Indeed, the whole union was then to know, as the October 1914 executive ruled A. Simmonds' nomination for president – sent in by none other than London West branch – as out of order on precisely these grounds. The president had to live already in the town where the head office was located, and Simmonds lived in London. The reasoning behind the rule was that the union did not want to incur travelling or removal fees for an incoming president, and, as the president was a working member, it did not think it reasonable to guarantee him a job in the town.

Whatever people thought about the rule, or the justifications for it, it was not going to stop Stavenhagen using it as a devastating *cause célèbre*. At the 15 November executive meeting, the executive council confirmed the sub-executive's decision to refuse the nomination of J. J. Melville, of Glasgow South branch, for president, on 27 October. On 31 October, Stavenhagen wrote to nineteen branches, and fifteen of them sent protests to the executive. Woolwich and London North-West sent copies of the letter to the executive. The letter said:

To my fellow-members,
I hope the active member of your branch will strongly attack the sub-executive for rejecting the nomination of J. J. Melville of Glasgow South branch, for general president. This member, who has exhibited great activity of the progressive order, and who supports the policy and interests of the vast majority of members, has been wrongly rejected. Clause 92 in our rules does not only stipulate that a *candidate* shall reside within twelve miles of Manchester. It only states that the elected *president* must

do so. Melville has signified his willingness to sacrifice personal considerations, and move to Manchester if elected. I urge your branch, in the interests of fair play, to send a resolution to the next full executive council meeting ... demanding that his nomination be accepted as it is in perfect order. Ball, the existing president, is up for re-election, and was, if you please, party to the trickery involved in Melville's rejection. Members, please note!

Yours fraternally
C. H. Stavenhagen

The executive voted 8–o to reassert the 1914 decisions about the rules and deprecate Stavenhagen's accusations of 'trickery' against Ball. Jack Ball was furious. He called this letter 'a dishonourable and subtle attempt to undermine the integrity of the sub-executive and the general president.'

The situation became more heated: London West pointed out that the executive were in breach of natural justice in expelling the London district committee without any sort of hearing. The executive was hastily re-convened on the twenty-eighth, and it was pointed out that the circulars complained of were issued by the committee elected at the Chandos Hall, as individuals, not as official district committee business. The members were ordered to withdraw from this committee and the executive decided, therefore, to cancel the expulsions, but impose a twelve-month ban on being on the district committee, and included district chairman Joe Vaughan, who had chaired the aggregate meeting on 27 October. As far as Stavenhagen was concerned, they laid new charges against him for circulating the members without executive council permission and libelling Ball with the accusation of 'trickery' over J. J. Melville's nomination. He was expelled. The voting was unanimous. He remains the only member of the union to be expelled twice in a fortnight.

However, on 22 January 1916, the executive had to accept branch appeals from London West, Glasgow South and Fulham that a ballot vote be taken on three issues: that the London district committee men who were suspended should be allowed to hold office again; that C. H. Stavenhagen should be readmitted to the union; and that the executive council's interpretation of the presidential residential qualification, Clause 92 of the 1915 rules, be rejected.

There was a huge campaign throughout the union on these issues. Stavenhagen issued a 6,500 word pamphlet entitled 'Executive Council – Boss-Props!' This is full of spectacular abuse in vintage Stavenhagen style, as is the accompanying letter that went out with the pamphlet. A flavour of it is sufficient. Stavenhagen appealed for his reinstatement by saying 'I ask you to give me the common justice denied to me by the human cattle and traitorous charlatans of the executive council by reading my attack on these creatures. ... With these few words, I leave you to judge the carefully considered statements and documentary evidence adduced against the boss-props.'

On 11 March 1916, the results of the ballots were given to the executive. The members voted, 1,325–647, to reject the executive's interpretation of the twelve-mile radius at the time of *nomination*, in favour of a twelve-mile residential requirement after *election*. They also voted, 1,008–960, to lift the suspension on the prominent London district committee members. And most sensational of all, despite the abuse, the faction-organizing, the pro-industrial unionism, the pacifist propaganda, they voted to reinstate C. H. Stavenhagen, by 1,012–964.

Curiously, the union did not then disintegrate. Stavenhagen was reinstated for the rest of 1916 as an executive councillor with Bill Webb making way for his political friend. Indeed, so as not to run against Webb, Stavenhagen transferred to London South West to run against Walter Day in Division No. 1, later that year. He lost. He only got forty-eight votes to Day's eighty-one and his old running partner Whitehead's seventy-one. This in itself turned into another major row. London Central and Woolwich's ballot returns were late and disallowed. Fulham forced another ballot on the whole membership who voted, 1,587–1,262, to allow the votes to be counted. This resulted in Day being turned out by Stavenhagen as he now had eighty-six votes to Day's eighty-one. C. H. Stavenhagen returned, yet again, to the executive in May 1917, where he served until his resignation in April 1919. A ballot vote of the members in May 1916 voted, 1,616–490, not to transfer the head office to Glasgow. This clear vote of confidence in the leadership was reinforced when Rowan beat Webb in the June general secretary election, 1,829–694. Prain was re-elected against John Wyatt, another London district committee stalwart suspended over the Melville/Chandos Hall events, by 1,811–353. J. J. Melville's career in the union ended in the late summer of 1916 in disgrace and death. Tom Stewart and the newly-appointed professional auditors, Wade & Co (who charged all of £30 to do the 1915 accounts in total for a year), discovered 'systematic fraud' in Melville's branch, Glasgow South. He had falsified the books, kept uncrossed money orders, pocketed cash collected in the absence of the treasurer to the tune of £347 1s 10d. Here again a reputation for effort, organizing and determined pride in the skill and value of electricians was set at nought through routine thieving. Melville had been within one vote of being the Clyde's first district secretary. He had been within three votes of the executive council seat at the end of 1915. He was lay district secretary and branch secretary in two Glasgow branches since joining the union in 1903. His disgrace was compounded by tragedy. He went into hospital for an exploratory operation and died on the operating table, aged forty-four.

The response of the members to the three ballots shows just how polarized the union had become. Oldham branch secretary Peter Skipworth wrote: 'The result of the three recent appeals is an absolute disgrace to the union – not twenty per cent of the members voted – and on such important matters, too.

You are allowing the trade unionist to be ousted by the socialist. You are endangering the craft union which has placed you, as an electrical worker, on such a sound basis.'

E. R. Lee, the Small Heath secretary, Birmingham district president and soon to be executive councillor, was even more specific, accusing Stavenhagen and his supporters as 'the clique who are trying to run the great smash'. He also highlighted a worrying feature of the union's balloting procedures. His branch only sent in fourteen ballots for the appeals. Branches were not allowed to send ballots out to the members at home any more. Only people who could prove they were out of town at the time of the ballot were excused having to attend the branch in person. Only these members got a postal vote. Archie Stewart found it all too much in Scotland, and resigned as full-time official and went back on the tools in a huge armaments works near Carlisle at Gretna Green, where he set up the new branch in the town and became its secretary.

There is no doubt that some were very pleased with the turn of events. Parkhead branch wrote in their notes to the journal in April 1916. 'General pleasure is expressed locally at the reinstatement of Brother Stavenhagen. Members who attended a public meeting he addressed in Glasgow some weeks ago found some difficulty in deciding whether to address him as "Brother", "ex-Brother" or "Mister". The members will, I am sure, be greatly relieved.' Not surprisingly, London West took the same attitude. 'What a welcome Brother Stavenhagen had on his return to the branch, and more than one brother said thank goodness – he is not a traitor to his fellows, as some tried to make us think and believe.'

Conscription, Dilution and Wage Strikes 1916–18

The capacity of the union's members to divide with some passion was next exercised over the conscription issue, which came to a head in the early summer of 1916, just as Stavenhagen had been reinstated and the next great campaign started over the general secretary election between Rowan and Webb.

Most people were opposed to the extension of conscription because it made them more likely to be called up for the war. The London district committee had a good scheme in response to the advent of conscription. Men like Fred Alford had been called up under the Military Service Bill and had gone into a line regiment. The London district committee attempted to negotiate directly with the Government to get such men transferred to technical corps where they would see comparatively less of the action. The executive's view was that they didn't wish to pursue this line at all; they wanted their members to stay in civilian employment, not least to prevent the steady growth of dilutee labour. When the executive had debated the issue at the end of 1915, in the midst of the expulsions furore, Stavenhagen and Whitehead had moved a complete rejection of conscription. Then an amendment was moved to this, demanding a ballot vote of the members on the issue. The amendment was lost 4–1, and so was the motion, 4–2! This left the leadership technically without a policy – a position they no doubt preferred to what happened next. The delegation to the Labour Party conference voted against conscription, but then voted to refuse an endorsement for strikes on the issues! The grounds for this, Jimmy Rowan argued, were that they had no mandate from the members.

By May 1916, the executive had had letters from Walter Day, from Fulham, London West, Glasgow West, Greenock, Wallsend and Woolwich branches demanding a conference on the desirability of rejecting conscription. The executive decided to ballot the members on the basic question – 'Do you approve of the Military Service Bill?' The members were also asked, via their branches, if they were against the bill, what could the union do about it. The members voted 1,356–748, against conscription (at the same quarter night, they were busy re-electing Rowan). The suggestion of the usual branches for a 'down-tools' policy in support of anyone taken for the army was defeated, 5–4, on the executive after Rowan produced the necessary legal advice. The executive also refused to vote for affiliation to the 'no conscription' council. Bill Webb was determined to see the good side of his election defeat in terms of this 'success' for the anti-conscription movement in the union. He wrote to the membership through the journal.

Whether you voted rightly or wrongly is your concern – you voted, that's the main thing. There were 700 of you for industrial unionism, 700 of you for the class-war, 700 of you for the right of the ETU to control the electrical industry.

In three years' time, what today is a large and uninfluential minority will have become an overwhelming majority. Let us hope that ere long, Brother Rowan will be on our side.

You were grand on the military question. You will have *no* military compulsion, *no* industrial conscription. You justified everything that Brother Stavenhagen and myself said about you on the executive council and have proved that your executive council had not their hand upon your pulse, or if they did, their reckoning of the beats was not good enough.

Your vote on *that* question was a greater issue than voting for Jimmy Rowan or Bill Webb. You will not be slaves, neither you nor your children, and for that, I also thank you.

Jimmy Rowan must have smiled at this. Anyone would have thought Webb had won. Walter Citrine was to write that such ringing declarations must have meant little to Rowan. In *Men and Work*, Citrine wrote: 'Jimmy Rowan took things philosophically. He could have papered the walls with the letters of censure he received. [He was] . . . pretty hard-boiled.'

Rowan preferred to deal with the very real issue of fear of conscription in a different way. On 28 September 1916, along with other skilled unions, he secured an excellent agreement direct with Lloyd George that would excuse members from direct fighting service.

All member of the union who were skilled before 15 August 1915 would be enrolled as war munition volunteers. These men would be issued with a trade exemption card that excused them military service at the front. No man could be rounded up for service, as often happened at the time, if he possessed this card. The Ministry of Munitions would then decide, in consultation with the union, whether they were suitable for civilian work or technical corps work in the army. They also took on board the old London district committee proposal to get named men transferred from line regiments to technical corps.

The issuing of trade exemption cards in the last months of 1916 was a powerful recruiting agent for the union, which was constantly beset with fears of dilution. The ECA on Merseyside horrified Citrine with the suggestion that they ought to be able to take girls to technical schools and train them from scratch in three months. They could then work and earn 15s (compared to the skilled rate of 40s). Perhaps then they could study for City and Guilds exams and on completion of that qualification get the skilled rate. They were to promise not to marry for two years and give up their jobs instantly to any returning invalid craftsman. The employers backed off at an 'enormous' meeting which decided by an overwhelming majority to give no further consideration to the scheme, much to Walter Citrine's pleasure. It was a good night for him. He was overwhelmingly re-elected district official the same evening.

The trade exemption card proved irritating to the army hierarchy and the whole arrangement was suspended in the early summer of 1917. The executive narrowly refused to sanction strikes in support of the reinstatement of trade exemption cards, by 5–4. The members had voted, 1,461–903, to oppose all further dilution in non-military establishments, but once again the executive could not support strikes against the schemes and also rejected London-based calls to refuse to sit on the committees that would organize the employment of disabled ex-servicemen in the cinema and electricity supply industries.

In the spring of 1917, union members throughout the country were increasingly irritated by rising prices and the uneven supply of food (as the submarine war intensified in the North Atlantic). The operation of leaving certificates and the announcement of the introduction of dilution into civilian work further infuriated ETU members and other skilled workers. The ending of trade exemption cards – a breach of a direct Government promise – further guaranteed a record number of wartime strikes up to 1917.

During the first four months of the year, there were strikes on Tyneside, the Mersey and Barrow, particularly when the Schedule of Protected Occupations was published in April. This list was much more restrictive, although allowing appeals to country-wide Labour Enlistment Complaints Committees, which included trade union officials. When the Dilution on Private Work Bill was published on 27 April, uproar ensued. By 6 May, 60,000 were on strike in Lancashire. By 16 May, thousands more joined them in Sheffield, Rotherham, Derby, Coventry, Crayford, Erith, Woolwich Arsenal and throughout London. Over 5,000 ETU members were among them.

The unions sought to have the bill withdrawn; the Minister of Munitions, Dr Addison, would only offer to consider union amendments and to 'consult' the union on its own particular problems. The minister saw a large delegation on 23 May from the ETU, with the full executive and representatives of the local strikes represented. The same day, however, the crisis was eased by the Government releasing local strike leaders from prison, and setting up a Commission of Inquiry. Even before that date, men were drifting back to work, partly frightened of legal sanctions against the strike under the Defence of the Realm Act.

The ETU's executive had voted, 8–1, to condemn the withdrawal of trade exemption cards and the introduction of dilution on private work. However, they voted, 5–4, against calling strikes to enforce the policy. Two of the majority – Alan Garner and Ted Lyson – were actually on strike themselves, but along with their colleagues were fearful of Government action against the union's funds if they voted for official strike action. Both Scottish executive members – Waterson and Smith – and both London representatives – Webb and Day – were not concerned with the legal position outlined by Rowan. Webb emphasized the atmosphere of crisis when he wrote in July 1917: 'Rows and rumours of rows are rife, and one never knows what is likely to happen. The sooner this Government realizes the members of the ETU are not to be played with, the better it will be.'

Nevertheless, the second half of 1917 was to see the decisive turning point of another kind in the union's wartime experience. In the summer Churchill became Minister of Munitions, and dropped the dilution of private work. Leaving certificates had already been abolished, and by the autumn, the Government was anxious to do something about the wages problems of munitions workers. By 1917, wage rates were running only fifteen per cent behind the rise in the cost of living. But wage rates are never the same thing as earnings. During the war, some groups of workers had much higher earnings than in peacetime, for a variety of reasons. There was less 'broken' or 'waiting' time on war work. There was more access to premium shift work or night work. Fewer employers were worried that higher production might mean over-production and therefore employers were less inclined to reduce piece-work prices. The rapid mechanisation (and electrification) of production processes led to higher output, but also helped earnings by reducing the amount of time wasted in setting up the process and by often increasing the production runs away from small batch production. In many industrial households there were two or more wages coming in as women worked more frequently than ever before.

One group of workers felt left out of these developments. Skilled time-workers often earned less than payment by results (PBR) piece-workers in semi-skilled production areas. Some unions, including the ETU, had clauses in their rule-books against piece-working on principle (although it was often ignored – as was the union's formal opposition to huge amounts of overtime). Some industries had only a patchy introduction of PBR and the Government wanted industry to encourage more of it. However, they were conscious that such developments would make the skilled timeworkers' position worse.

On 14 October 1917, key grades of engineering and foundry timeworkers were awarded a twelve-and-a-half per cent bonus to compensate them for falling behind both the cost of living and comparable grades working piece-work.

Rowan was to explain as early as October 1917 just what problems this gave the ETU.

Much misapprehension has been caused by the very vague terms of the Minister of Munitions respecting the advance of twelve-and-a-half per cent to fully skilled timeworkers engaged on munition work or work in connection therewith. In the first place, it might be pointed out in advance that this advance is not a general one, and has nothing to do with the application for general advances on the ground of the increase in the cost of living.

It is as the result of an anomaly created by dilution, through which workers brought in to tend machines were receiving higher wages than those who taught them to do the work and those that kept the machines in working order for them. Such a position of affairs naturally caused grave irritation, and in the Munitions of War (Amendment) Act, power was given to the Minister to increase the rate of such skilled timeworkers.

It is in the application of the Order that trouble has been caused; first, by omitting certain trades, such as electrical fitting and armature winding, and second, by making it a condition that only those, no matter what their trade, who are receiving the rate of a turner or fitter shall be entitled to the twelve-and-a-half per cent.

Within weeks, Rowan had got electrical fitters and armature winders included on the list, but problems still existed for those working in and around munitions establishments for contracting companies; Walter Citrine reported from Liverpool on the 'utmost confusion' amongst shipbuilding employers who would ask ETU members if they classed themselves as 'electrical fitters'. If they did, they got the bonus. The Mersey Ship Repairers Federation defined their electricians differently. As far as they were concerned, they were 'wiremen', not 'fitters', and so were not entitled to the bonus. For Citrine, it proved the importance of 'what's in a name?' 'It goes to prove we must concentrate on getting the term "electrician" recognized by the Government in place of the words "electrical fitter" as the meaning given to it by the governmental authorities is of such a limited nature that it embraces only a minute portion of our members.' On the Clyde, the employers were quick to concede the union's claims for electricians on war work.

The last two months of the year were bedlam. From the ETU's point of view, the twelve-and-a-half per cent led to wage movements way beyond the munitions industries (interestingly enough, deepening the electrician's sense of himself as an electrician first rather than a steelworker, public utility worker or engineering worker). By January 1918, the union had got the award throughout most grades in engineering, shipbuilding, contracting and electricity supply. Sir George Askwith's verdict on the ETU's campaigns at the end of 1917 is instructive. As chief commissioner of the Committee on Production, he saw plenty of the claims arrive on his desk. Writing of this period in 1920, he said: 'The principal union (the ETU) had its headquarters in Manchester, whence no control was exercised over London and other big cities ...' Because some of the electrical employers (great power companies, municipal authorities, private manufacturers, electrical contractors) were within the coverage of the Ministry of Munitions and some were not, chaos reigned. There was extensive prevarication between the Ministry and employers as to how to deal with the union's claims. Sir George Askwith wrote: 'The delays had driven nearly all the men into the principal union and that union, under energetic leaders – particularly in London – was proceeding to use methods of pressure to bring in all non-unionists and adherents of members of rival unions.'

Throughout London, at the turn of the year, strikes broke out to enforce the twelve-and-a-half per cent. On 5 January there were power stations, newspapers and the great arsenals at Woolwich, Enfield and Waltham Abbey out on strike, along with numerous building sites and the Office of Works. On Monday 7 January, an aggregate meeting of the members met at Holborn Hall, to hear the results of the crisis meeting that day with Sir George Askwith. That meeting had lasted nine hours, with Stavenhagen, Rowan, Kinniburgh and Muir rushing to Holborn Hall to let 2,200 members know the results, leaving Bill Webb and Sir George Askwith to jointly draft the award.

Stavenhagen announced the union's success in getting the twelve-and-a-half per cent extended to electricity supply and contracting and quickly asked the searchlight maintenance crews to return to their anti-zeppelin work. Just after 9 p.m. Bill Webb arrived.

He had ... the decision in writing of Sir George Askwith in reference to the twelve-and-a-half per cent and he gave a detailed report of the proceedings from the time a previous aggregate meeting put it in his hands the previous Thursday. He said that the ETU had that day won a victory bigger than ever it had won before . . . and it had turned out the right way as far as the result was concerned. He suggested that the meeting accept the award of Sir George Askwith and return to work the following day. The meeting unanimously adopted the secretary's report and it was agreed, with four exceptions, to return to work the next morning.

It was moved, seconded and carried unanimously that the twelve-and-a-half per cent bonus be paid to the London district secretary (Bill Webb).

The meeting closed at 10.30 p.m., and this was the end of 'a perfect day'.

National Negotiations, New Styles of Collective Bargaining, National Joint Councils

The May strikes in engineering in the spring of 1917 involved over 5,000 ETU members. The twelve-and-a-half per cent strikes in the winter of 1917–18 probably involved considerably more in the contracting and newly-emerging electricity supply memberships. These exciting events, however, overlay the emergence of recognizable forms of collective bargaining in the union's major areas of interest. The real significance of the last full year of the First World War lay in the establishment of national negotiating arenas in which the union would negotiate rather than fight its way to economic emancipation.

It will be remembered that the union's way of proceeding before the war was to present a group of employers with the union's 'trade card', on a district basis. The 'trade card' would contain the wage levels and basic terms and conditions of employment. The employers would either accept the card, or alter it or, more likely, completely ignore it. In these circumstances, if the union felt strong enough, a strike would commence to enforce the 'trade card'. They were not negotiated annually, or re-presented at any fixed time – only when the union was strong enough to impose its will on the employer. This also explains the early ferocity of closed-shop strikes. Action against the employer only stood any chance of success if there was no replacement labour available to him. The early union activists were therefore determined not to be undermined by foremen, charge-hands or 'boy' labour (apprentices or simply young dogsbodies). They just *had* to join the union.

The real significance of 1917–18, then, lay in the emergence of negotiating as the union's first line of approach – a point well understood by Citrine when he wrote in August 1917 of the need for the union to be 'as efficient in the field of collective bargaining as electricity has been in the productive world.'

Towards the end of the war, Government and civil service were thinking of what a 'reconstructed' Britain was going to look like. There was even a ministry planning the return to civilian life. Part of this planning involved the organization of industrial relations. It is widely recognized in the modern world that trade union membership grows when the government of the day encourages collective bargaining. The Government of Britain in the First World War encouraged collective bargaining to replace the 'stand-offish' trade card system. It was building on the normal evolution of relationships that were strained by the pressures of war. It was inefficient to have constant argument in engineering, shipbuilding and the munitions industries, about wage rises justified by fast-rising prices. Most problems arose on a district basis, thus throwing up more and more applications to correct anomalies which quoted other district variations. From early 1917, it was agreed to examine the wages and prices spirals on a quarterly basis at national level, before deciding on national wage advances. In the autumn of 1917, the ETU came to a similar arrangement with the National Federated Electrical Association (NFEA) for the electrical contracting industry. At a stroke, the union had national negotiations replacing regional applications in its central, important industry. Before the war, it will be remembered, the EEF in London had agreed to pay contracting rates to electricians installing or overhauling equipment in their works. This meant that only the ETU governed this crucial wages yardstick that had significance far beyond the building sites of England.

The union was therefore part of every significant negotiating body in the war manufacturing industries and master in its own contracting house. Government smiled benignly on these developments, and then accelerated the process in a more formal way of their own. During the summer of 1917, J. H. Whitley, the speaker of the House of Commons, started to produce different reports that would make 'suggestions for securing a permanent improvement in the relations between employers and workmen'.

The Whitley reports recommended permanent National Joint Industrial Councils (NJICs), composed of employer and trade union representatives. The national body would preside over the work of regional or District Joint Industrial Councils (DJICs), who would be similarly based on joint representation from employers or their associates and the trade unions concerned. They also urged similar joint arrangements in works committees at establishment level. There would be a permanent industrial court for arbitrating in trades differences (replacing the Committee on Production which peace would render irrelevant). These committees and councils were warmly received by most union leaderships.

Rowan took decisive action throughout the last months of the war to involve the union in this new style of collective bargaining. He had a good war, personally. He had joined the early Treasury conference in March 1915. Rowan may well have been in Lloyd George's mind when he wrote that Prime Minister Balfour 'was surprised to find the workmen's representatives talked so well ... he saw these stalwart artisans leaning against and sitting on the steps of the throne of the dead queen, and, on equal terms, negotiating with the government of the day ... [Balfour] was bewildered by this sudden revelation of a *new* power.' Rowan had led countless appeals to the Committee of Production. He had led FEST delegations to Ministry of Munitions negotiations. Throughout the war, the ASE could usually be depended on to distance itself from the other unions; this led to a leadership vacuum for the smaller unions when dealing with government agencies. Rowan is often found to be moving resolutions, proposing delegations, urging action on the Federation in their dealings with Sir Allan Smith at the EEF and the Shipbuilders and Ship Repairers Associations.

In late 1917, the EEF recognized the rights of shop-stewards to represent members in federated shops. These shop stewards became a new workplace focus of the union's activity, and during 1918, the union's head office started to co-ordinate directly their approaches to the Committee on Production.

The movement for setting up JICs throughout industry involved the ETU's heartland industry of electrical contracting in the summer of 1918. The executive voted, 8–2, in June to put the constitution to the members in a ballot. Here, Rowan was clever. He persuaded the executive council to make the ballot one of general principle, and the members voted 3,779 to 2,088, to accept the general principle of JICs. This enabled the leadership of the union to join in any or all JICs that emerged in late 1918 and early 1919.

Using this mandate, the first meeting of the NJIC for the electrical contracting industry was held at the Hotel Metropole in Leeds on 22 and 23 January 1919. A junior minister from the Ministry of Labour, C. J. Wardle, wished them well, and the meeting started.

Bearing in mind the ferocity of contracting strikes in London and Liverpool before the war, the arrangements for the whole industry made that day were amazing. The NJIC agreed not to allow the Association of Supervisory Electricians to join the council, thus guaranteeing exclusive recognition to the ETU. They reduced the working week to forty-seven hours from fifty-three, without loss of pay. Rates were set at the pre-war hourly rate times fifty-three, plus the war bonuses, divided by forty-seven to arrive at a new hourly rate. On top of that, the men kept the twelve-and-a-half per cent bonus. They were entitled to one forty-five minute break a day, the NJIC agreed to review wages in the light of the cost of living three times a year and the 'document' had gone for ever. The NJIC issued a declaration on union membership that said the industry's 'ultimate object is to eliminate both the unorganized employers and employees'.

There was opposition to the NJIC from London. The delegation to the first meeting was a powerful one. Jimmy Rowan was to be joint secretary and Jack Ball vice-chairman of the NJIC. Jack Kinniburgh went, and the executive council were represented by Archie Stewart, and C. H. Stavenhagen. The union's full-time officials were also invited – Alf Beardmore from Birmingham,

John Milan from Belfast, George Olley from Tyneside, Walter Citrine from the Mersey, Peter Irvine from Manchester, Bob Reid from Glasgow, and Bill Webb from London. Imagine the leadership's embarrassment when Webb refused to turn up at all, on London district committee instructions; an embarrassment that only intensified when Stavenhagen made a scene after the opening pleasantries, denounced NJICs as a sell-out of workers' interests, and stormed out of the meeting.

In the first year, the council spent a good deal of time arranging powers and duties and settling the relationships between DJICs and the NJIC. However, Rowan's first year internal report was pleased with the progress made at the NJIC's six meetings.

The reduction in the working week to forty-seven from forty-eight or fifty-three hours (depending on region), meant everyone got a wage rise plus a reduction in hours. The absorption of apprentices returning from the war was achieved and a joint advisory committee appointed to advise the City and Guilds (of London) Institute on its syllabus and examinations for electricians. Joe Collins was the union's representative on this first, national, technical committee to which the ETU would make distinguished contributions over future decades. The 'document' supporting non-unionism was gone, and a new system of wages emerged. The union wanted to have a national flat rate. Regional variation in wages was enormous – hourly rates ranged from 1s 2d to 1s 9d. It was impossible to have a national rate, but they set up a 4-grade zoning of the country. London still stood aloof, blaming the executive council for holding back their wages while refusing to sit on the NJIC in direct contravention to the national ballot vote. Fulham and Fleet Street branches vocally complained about the district committee attitude. Midlands executive councillor Joe Collins and Scotland's Archie Stewart issued a pamphlet throughout London after their committee of inquiry found that the district committee action had 'segregated London from the rest of the country – a condition of things to be deplored in any democratic organization'. London would not take up its place until late 1920 when the negotiations returned for a while to the direct talks between the NFEA and the ETU, with the forum of the NJIC being only infrequently used.

Nevertheless, despite this wholly characteristic obstructionism from the London district committee, Rowan's report on the first year's work of the NJIC was happy with the new rates. Mersey district rate on Grade 'A' was 2s 0d an hour: Manchester and South Wales were in Grade 'B' and got 1s 11d. Grade 'C' paid 1s 10d for ETU men in Belfast, Birmingham, Leicester, the North-East Coast, Yorkshire, Derby, Blackpool, the Eastern Counties, Bristol and Bournemouth. The rest of England and Wales, in Grade 'D', got 1s 9d. (Scotland did not join this system as it retained its comparative links with engineering.) For many electricians in the less organized parts of the country, these rates were huge increases on their previous standards. Initially, employers would only pay 3d an hour increase at most, paying the rest in early 1920. Rowan was delighted. 'In these particular cases, it was the biggest general advance ever come to, and in districts where our chances of the success of direct action were very remote' – however much London felt it was held back by such attitudes of class collaboration.

During the last months of 1918, progress was also being made in the electricity supply industry.

The Power Workers' Charter 1918

During the First World War, demand for electricity probably doubled. Contemporary estimates of national consumption reveal an increase in growth from 2,100 Gigawatt-hours (GWh) to 4,000 GWh. However, the growth figures varied: in the munitions areas, where ninety-five per cent of power supply was electrical by the end of the war, it was a spectacular increase. Rotherham's output went up thirteen times. Coventry trebled its generation and Sheffield's output rose from 26.5 GWh in 1914 to 177.5 GWh in 1918. London, however, only generated fourteen per cent more by the end of the war. However, national load factors rose noticeably as existing plant was properly exploited. They went up from twenty-four per cent in 1914 to thirty per cent by 1918, with Birmingham doing as well as thirty-nine per cent by 1917. The industry still suffered from competing ownership between private and municipal undertakings, although some councils were co-operating in taking supply from a single efficient station and sharing load by linking up the different stations (Lancashire and Cheshire were especially progressive in this regard). The Government's desire to concentrate manufacturing industry's mind on munitions led to companies being required to take public supply rather than build their own power houses, and the Cabinet's Electricity Services Sub-Committee had further powers to insist on alternating current being the norm, and to examine all potential building plans in the industry worth over £500.

This emphasis on getting full value out of over 600 independent generating stations, with sixty-six in London, produced great strains on the workforce in the industry. Numbers employed had risen from 20,000 in 1907 to approximately 34,000 in 1918, operating in units of between 100 and 1,000 people. The unions had made almost no impact on the industry before the war. Less than five per cent of the workers were organized. There were dozens of different wage rates and Citrine explained many years later that even basic information was hard to come by when he wrote:

... collective agreements between electricity supply undertakings as a whole and individual trade unions or groups of unions, were unknown.... Conditions in the industry were so varied and so little known that we had to first ascertain the facts. ... I remember the confusion that arose when we tried to find out how much a plumber jointer got. There were about a dozen rates of pay – even in London – and throughout the country there were all sorts of arrangements.

Throughout 1915 and 1916, it became obvious that the power industry ought to be a fruitful recruiting ground for the union. Jack Kinniburgh, 'that big piece of humanity wearing a wide brim Trilby hat,' according to Eric Hainge, branch secretary of Aston branch, opened the first station engineers branch at The Swan with Two Necks in Withy Grove, Manchester in early July 1916. On 15 November 1916, London station engineers (LSE) opened with fifty members, forty-eight of whom were auxiliary section members. LSE issued their own nine-point manifesto as a recruitment weapon. They wanted a twenty per cent pay rise, because there had been no rise in pay rates for switchboard attendants in either power stations or sub-stations since 1903! They demanded upgrading of switchboard staff, a forty-eight hour week instead of fifty-six, access to the LCC superannuation scheme, the payment of the higher grade rates to someone who worked on higher rated jobs than his normal duty, the unconditional reinstatement of returning war volunteers, the restoration of skilled men over dilutees after the war and the payment of maximum rates of pay to all employees in a particular grade, rather than have several rates for the same grade.

They wanted to present the supply authorities, and not just the LCC tramways operation, with a complete trade card. By February 1917, members were joining the union under the impetus of further dilution from returning invalid ex-servicemen. By March 1917, over fifteen per cent of London supply workers had been diluted. Harold Morton, the first secretary of LSE No. 1, based on the South Bank of the Thames, had chapter and verse of this problem. He wrote in an internal report in January 1919 of these early problems:

A sub-station whose normal personnel was three charge-hands and three assistants was being run by two wounded soldiers doing continuous twelve-hour shifts, seven days a week for a third of the normal staff's wages. On their complaining they were informed 'You of course receive a pension' and were refused permission to leave under twelve months' service. Thus the patriots who exploited them were posing as their heaven-sent guardians, and incidentally pocketing two-thirds of the normal running costs.

By the end of March 1917 a committee representing thirty-five grades of power workers had drawn up a station engineers' card, basing the wage claim on engineering rates plus that industry's war advances based on piece-work earnings which were denied supply timeworkers. The supply authorities were indifferent to the claim. Railway power worker Jim Memberry wrote later 'these applications were absolutely ignored' and the whole thing was referred to the Committee on Production on 5 September 1917. The Association of Municipal Electrical Authorities, representing thirty out of the seventy-six undertakings and the ETU were represented, but Sir George Askwith recommended involving a wider selection of the employers and unions alike. The trade card talks were suspended while elsewhere the unions were pursuing the twelve-and-a-half per cent awards throughout the autumn of 1917, and the supply workers self-confidence was boosted by the winning of the twelve-and-a-half per cent in January 1918.

The employers spent a considerable time meeting in the winter to draw up schedules of rates throughout London, and in January the unions did the same, eventually submitting their suggested schedule to the employers on 5 March 1918. On 17 June, the employers offered seventy-five per cent of the union's schedule across the board – so long as the payments could be postponed until the war ended! Sir George Askwith was prevailed upon to tell them that this was certainly not a reasonable condition to apply to any offer. The employers replied by saying that if they were going to have to pay up in the near future, their offer now was reduced to only sixty-six per cent of the union's schedule. Jimmy Rowan did not mince his words at the next round of talks on 27 June when this further offer was made. 'The rates you offered on 17 June were refused. The revised rates are a *ten per cent reduction* on the 17 June offer. Therefore, they are hopeless and no further negotiations will proceed from the union on the offer.' Nine months of negotiations had led nowhere. The employers' clear disdain for the unions was astonishing. However, two aggregate meetings threatening strikes produced a further, formal reference to the Committee on Production which was held on 19 August at the Central Hall, Westminster. There were over 200 employers and union representatives at the hearing, with Sir George Gibb in the chair. The employers wriggled to the end. They claimed that the Committee on Production was a war committee responsible for war payments; it had no right to pontificate on general wages and conditions problems as represented by the power workers' claim. Sir George Gibb would have none of that, but before the case got underway, there was uproar.

Jimmy Rowan had formally moved the claim for war advances of 3s 6d per week, including for the technical grades like station superintendent, resident engineer and the shift or charge engineers. Harold Morton was there, and he reported:

At this point, the union's attention was called to representatives of the Electrical Power Engineers Association (EPEA) who were present, sitting on the employers side. Brother Rowan at once protested that they were not named in the list of employers' representatives present. Mr Beaumont (representative of the municipal undertakings) stated: 'They are here to give evidence against the claimants, i.e. the unions.' Sir George Gibb asked who they were, what they represented and what they wanted. They replied: 'We came here on the invitation of certain representatives of the employers side, to contest the claim of the ETU to represent the staff engineers.' ... So startling was the announcement that the unions decided on an immediate adjournment to reconsider the whole position.

The four unions' fourteen delegates had a furious exchange; they voted, 8–6, to continue the hearing, but minuted their own anger – that the long-drawn-out negotiations had only been used by the employers to produce a bosses' union in the EPEA who were giving evidence against the bona fide unions on the one hand and claiming representation rights for the higher technical grades on the other.

It took all of Sir George Gibb's persuasive effort to set up further negotiations between the unions and the employers at a very high level. There were sixteen union representatives on this new industry-wide London negotiation team – seven from the ETU (Rowan, Webb and station engineers, Harold Morton, Vic Needham, Jim Memberry, Bill Westfallen and a member called Plowman whose activity in the industry stops after this conference). The employers' team was high-powered; their chairman was the appropriately named Mr C. Sparks and included power station representatives from municipal and private companies, along with leading managers Fell and Rivière from the LCC tramways and Roger Smith from the electric railways.

At last, negotiations became purposeful. There were twenty-seven meetings between 20 August and 18 September. They reviewed seventy-eight grades of workers, and failed to agree a rate and a grading for only seven. They agreed the payment of the highest rates for people who did work out of their own grade. The final review of the outstanding problems took place at the Committee of Production on 22 October 1918, now chaired by Sir William McKenzie.

This meeting, too, nearly ended in uproar with the appearance of the National Union of Railwaymen (NUR), claiming to be heard for power station workers and linesmen on the electric railways and underground in London. Their own constitution with the railway companies was read out to them, where they specifically were excluded from representing such people. They rather sheepishly withdrew.

On 8 November 1918, the committee issued their famous Award No. 2772, which settled the wages, backdated to 19 August 1918, at 10½d as basic rates for an electrician. It dealt for the first time with the problem of standardizing rates and grades all over London, applying to generating, transmitting, distributing and maintaining power supply. Wages rose – in some cases from 5d an hour to 10d per hour. Suburban undertakings had to pay what everyone else paid. The award standardized training periods and instituted proper apprenticeships. The union did not get everything. The forty-eight hour week was denied and technical grades were given to the EPEA to represent in the future, which infuriated Rowan. However, the EPEA did claim to represent 174 out of 196 charge engineers in London compared to the ETU's 42. The railway power men were covered by a further award, No. 2773, which was published on 5 December 1918 and was similar to No. 2772 except wage rates were slightly lower to take into account concessionary fares on the railways.

These negotiations, led by Rowan, supported with Webb's statistical analysis, resulted in the award No. 2772 becoming known as 'the supply workers' charter'. It became the basis of all the future negotiations on supply wages, not only in London, but throughout Britain. Its publication coincided with the formation of the NJIC for electricity supply, which was the thirty-third NJIC/DJIC structure to emerge from the Whitley system. It first met on 1 May 1919 and published by 1920 rates of pay and conditions throughout its twelve districts that owed everything to award No. 2772.

The union's membership during the war rose from 8,195 in 1914 to 31,345 by 1918, producing by then an annual income of over £55,000 per year with £66,000 in the reserves. Recruitment in electricity supply produced some of that new membership growth.

At the end of 1916, the two station engineer branches had 126 members between them. On the day Award No. 2772 was published, this figure had risen to 2,079 in two years. There were ten station engineer branches in London for over 1,600 members, and the other 400 were in station engineer branches in Birmingham, Glasgow, Liverpool, Manchester and Sheffield.

The union was reaping the benefits of its reputation. With prices rising, there was an urgency about wage claims that did not exist pre-war. As the union fought and achieved wage rises, its reputation was enhanced and more people joined. Collective bargaining and the emergence of national negotiations and NJICs further enhanced national trade union officials at the expense of local leaderships in the branches or district committees. Unemployment was virtually non-existent and fear of the employer was at a lower level. Dismissal for trade union membership became less likely. Throughout the country, trade union membership grew apace. The ASE grew by ninety per cent from 1913 to 18. The ETU grew by over four times, faster even than the general workers' unions recruiting in new areas of membership.

Rowan turned his face to the post-war world when he wrote in the 1918 annual report:

The past year has, on the whole, been a good one for the ETU, not only for the numerical and financial progress, which has been considerable, but for the general advancement and recognition of the union as a whole. We are inter-mixed with every industry in the country and have to preserve the identity, conditions, and rights of the electrical section in all. In doing so, we have to face a certain opposition, much of it due to a misguided conception of industrial unionism. This lays it down that an electrician employed in a steel works shall have his wages controlled by the steel smelter, an electrician in or about a coal mine by the miner, an electrician in a theatre or cinema by the doorkeeper or pianist, and so on. ... The training and skill of an electrician is made subservient to the producers in the industry. The wages of the electricians, they being in a small minority, have been, when left to the tender mercies of the majority, fixed on an unfairly low basis.

During the past few years, we have made considerable headway in rectifying this by organizing the electrician, wherever he may be employed and demanding the proper rate for him. Having done so, we can calmly wait time's verdict on our actions.

10

THE AFTERMATH OF WAR 1919–21

Amalgamation with the Amalgamated Engineering Union

THROUGHOUT THE MOVEMENT GREAT things were expected of the process of amalgamation immediately after the war. Stronger, financially prosperous, united unions would now 'win the peace'. Jimmy Rowan and Peter Irvine had met with the ASE as early as August 1918. The ASE sponsored talks throughout 1919–20 in a series of attempts to encourage the amalgamation of the large number of small skilled engineering unions. Jimmy Rowan attended the steering committee meetings; the full executive council and both national organizers attended the amalgamation conference on 29 May 1919 at York.

The great war-horse of syndicalist labour in Britain, Tom Mann, had recently won election as the general secretary of the ASE at the end of his career. He was appalled at the 1917 decision of his union to retreat into craft exclusivity and exclude from membership the ASE's equivalents of the ETU's auxiliary section. He admired the 'open' constitution of the ETU, and courted the ETU particularly hard. Joint mass meetings were held in Manchester, London and Birmingham at which Tom Mann and Jimmy Rowan shared the pro-amalgamation platform.

However, the actual instrument of amalgamation was widely reported to be a craft document that would destroy the growing auxiliary section. The London district committee passed a resolution on 4 September 1919 which was convinced that the amalgamation was 'detrimental' to ETU members because '(i) it perpetrates the craft system of organization (ii) that ... no men will be eligible for membership who are employed in the boiler house of a power station, none of our auxiliary members employed in cable factories, post office etc.; therefore, it is going to split the industrial organization of the ETU.'

The station engineers rarely made common cause with the district committee against the executive. But on this occasion Harold Morton could see all his hard work in achieving the organization of the power industry into the ETU go up in smoke.

Of course, it was precisely this pro-craft tradition in the organization that was so attractive to craftsmen. After the war years' experience of diluted labour and the growing aggression of the new general unions, many electrical craftsmen were attracted by the possibilities of a newly-constituted Amalgamated Engineering Union (AEU). A third group simply saw the need to increase the unity of workers in defence of wartime gains in status and influence. Jack Kinniburgh was foremost in holding this view when he wrote in the summer of 1919: 'The question of amalgamation is the most important one before us at present ... as upon it depends greatly our economic advancement ... it behoves our members, who constitute the average youngest membership of any union, to be in the van of progress.' Kinniburgh's fellow national organizer, Tom Stewart, was of the same mind. 'There is no reason for separate unions catering for the same industry, and the quicker the workers realize this the better for themselves. Amalgamation is one remedy to cure the existing evils of too many unions.'

Rowan toured the union, particularly trying to reassure his members that the auxiliary members would be saved by the provision of 'section 3' of the new union's structure. This was specifically intended 'to cater for men, who, owing to age, trade or disability, are not eligible to enter the higher [skilled] sections.'

The law affecting trade union amalgamations in 1919 was very strict, despite the wartime Government's relaxation of the rules in 1917. For an amalgamation to be successful, the union had to produce a majority in favour of twenty per cent of the votes cast. Furthermore, there had to be at least fifty per cent of the members voting.

On 30 October 1919, the returns were scrutinized by Manchester district committee officials Stopford and Irwin. 40,581 ballot papers had been sent out to the union's 292 branches. Seventy branches did not send in returns of any sort. This was a clever way to undermine the ballot by deliberately depressing the turn-out. In London, the heartland of opposition to the craft basis of the union, London West and London North West, did not send out ballots. Four station engineer branches (but not Morton or Bussey's) did not vote. Left-controlled branches like East Ham, Joe Vaughan's Hackney and Walthamstow also didn't vote. Throughout the country, other branches with their own reasons for opposing the amalgamation, based on craft rivalry, did not return voting figures. They included significant towns like Southampton, Cardiff, Edinburgh West, Salford, Rotherham, Nottingham and Aston in Birmingham.

Despite seventy out of 292 branches not taking part, there was a turn-out of 19,246 votes. This was an agonizing 1,044 votes short of the fifty per cent figure (20,290) required.

Those that did vote were decisive in their choice. They voted, 13,029–6,147, to go into the AEU. The executive council examined the scrutineers' report on 9 November 1919. It was clear that the wishes of the members had been frustrated by the deliberate non-participation of the seventy branches concerned. The pro-amalgamationists on the executive urged that the deadline for accepting returns from the seventy branches should be extended and the branches *told* to hold the ballot. This was supported by four executive council men – Jack Collins from Ireland, Joe Collins from Birmingham, James Bellamy from Sheffield and Manchester's Bill McKay. It was opposed by five – the London syndicalists Bolton and Muir, with Liverpool's Illingworth, and the two Scottish executive councillors, Archie Stewart and J. Dennison. But the story did not end there. Tom Mann visited the next executive on Sunday 7 December. He appealed to the ETU to ballot again, not least to help the emerging AEU broaden its class appeal beyond 'craftism'. The executive eventually agreed to do this, confident that the new union *would* accept auxiliary members, but reassured that such members would not dominate the new union. This set of contradictions was reflected in the second ballot which was declared on 25 July 1920.

Rowan was clearly determined not to be outflanked by deliberate abstention this time. The head office instructed branch secretaries to post a ballot to every member with a stamped addressed envelope, to be returned to the branch secretary. The executive council also insisted that these instructions overruled any branch or district committee decision not to participate in the second ballot. The circular went on: 'It is the inalienable right of each member to vote for or against, or remain neutral, as he individually desires, but each and every member must be given the opportunity of deciding for himself.'

Steps were taken to publicize these postal ballot arrangements in the *Daily Herald*, and fierce discipline threatened against branch secretaries who urged non-participation. The ballot was to be taken at specially summoned meetings in early June 1920. By mid-May, the London district committee was circulating other district committees with unofficial anti-amalgamation circulars. Forty-seven branches (twenty-two in London) had still not issued the ballot papers. The executive issued notices of suspension against the branches concerned.

Twenty-five branches did not send in any returns at all. Some sent in childish, obstructionist returns. London South West (whose branch secretary was Stavenhagen's friend, F. H. Whitehead), LSE No. 8, LSE No. 4 and Chatham all sent in returns indicating that no ballot papers had been issued and none received!

Scrutineers Butler and Irwin were appalled. In their report to the executive they wrote:

The scrutineers are of the opinion that this ballot has not been conducted in the true spirit of trade unionism and would point out to the executive council that at least one of the London branches circularized its members not to have anything to do with the amalgamations ballot. Further, we would point out the foolishness of quite a number of members sending empty envelopes in to the scrutineers. (We take it that this was not an oversight.)

We are also of the opinion that it is quite time that some members of the ETU were taught how to play the straight game of cricket.

To be legal, the ballot needed a fifty per cent turn-out. This would have needed 23,077 votes. 18,983 were returned, 4,094 short of the legal requirement. What was even more galling was the fact that the margin of those voting in favour had grown. 13,307 voted for amalgamation, 5,636 against. Strangely enough, the executive agreed without a vote to accept the returns. Opinion in the country was harder to placate. Albert Oates, later to be a distinguished district secretary and councillor in Sheffield, wrote to the magazine, furious with the cynical manipulation of these crucial ballots.

I beg to say much indignation was rife amongst our members over the result of the ... amalgamation ballot, which was a direct insult on behalf of a section, who, imbued by a spirit of dominance, brought dishonour to the cause. ... Permit me to point out that the difficulties that a powerful section of our union, both by influence and action, brought to bear against ... the executive council does deliberately deny the rights of the majority.

Gorton's branch secretary, Dennis, felt the same when he wrote 'those trade unionists who talk about democracy should allow every member of the trade union to vote'.

Amalgamation proposals with the AEU run through the union's hundred years' history like a silver thread. It is ironic that the effective alliance between the legal requirements laid down by misanthropic government and the cynical use of this law by left-wing extremist elements in the union in 1919–20, prevented the will of the membership being translated into action. Amalgamation in 1920 between the AEU and the ETU would surely have altered the course of both Labour and the British historical experience in the twentieth century.

Opportunities for expansion

Even without the amalgamation, the aftermath of the First World War seemed to offer the union great opportunities to expand. Despite the often brutal opposition of the MFGB through closed shop strikes, the union opened branches throughout the coalfields. Scotland – despite the Lanarkshire coal-owners admitting recognition was not on due to the opposition of the Scottish

miners – and South Wales proved particularly promising; the colliery electricians were still treated lamentably, with the miners taking the view that
craftsmen's wages could not exceed underground miners' pay. This left colliery
electricians far behind their contemporaries in the trade.

Jack Kinniburgh was tireless, too, in organizing the electrical workers in
the steel industry; again, South Wales was a particularly strong area of
recruitment with the Llanelly branch persuading ASE electricians at the
Bynea steelworks to join the ETU. Here, the steel workers' new union, the
Iron and Steel Trades Confederation (ISTC), was hostile to the ETU, but
less effective than the miners in preventing recognition of the union and its
capacity to negotiate for electricians independently. By October 1920, the
ISTC recognized the ETU's rights nationally to the electricians, armature
winders and electrical fitters in the industry, while still trying to recruit the
mates and boiler-house men themselves.

Most promising of all, the union recruited widely in the growing enter-
tainments industry – particularly in the cinemas, where every community had
at least one small movie theatre. The staff would consist of a musician to
accompany the silent films along with a projectionist who often doubled as
the administrator and maintenance man. Dublin, Manchester, Hull and
Glasgow were joined by London during 1919 in setting up branches for the
cinema operators. Their conditions were often awful. Bob Prain wrote in
February 1921: 'One of our London operators protests he has too much work
to do. He works twelve hours a day, and from 8.0–10.0 p.m. on Sundays.
Between times, he sweeps the hall, looks after the boiler for the hot water
apparatus, repairs seats, sticks up bills, serves in the bar and then spends the
rest of his time contemplating how fortunate he is in getting £3 10s od in
wages per week.' For junior operators in larger cinemas rates could be as low
as £1 10s od.

It was the projectionists who were usually electricians or, at least, required
to pick up electrical skills to use alongside various other duties. Here, too,
their progress was restricted by constant warfare for members with the National
Association of Theatrical Employees (NATE).

Immediately after the war, attempts were made to reopen the union's
organization among post office telephone engineers. They had been the original
base of the union's membership in 1889–91, and, by 1919, their wages were
£1 a week behind the electricians, who were often brought in on parts of the
post office work on contract. Branches were opened throughout London just
after the war, and hundreds of members enrolled, particularly in London.
However, the Government was very conscious of the revolutionary reputation
of the ETU, and successfully urged the post office authorities to refuse
recognition to the ETU. Rowan and Kinniburgh took the argument as far as
the Prime Minister's office. Lloyd George refused to 'interfere' and the

membership steadily eroded, particularly with the onset of mass unemployment in 1921.

Progress was also made on the railways – particularly in the supply and distribution of electricity to the London underground and suburban lines. Equally, the union stood firm against the NUR who sought to exclude them from the railway workshops, and negotiations throughout this period hinged on organizing rights in the workshops for craft unions in the face of NUR insistence on one union for the whole industry. This was to bring the union close to the engine drivers' union, the Associated Society of Locomotive Engineers and Firemen (ASLEF), who looked upon themselves as a craft union surrounded by malevolent unskilled NUR grades. The first formal inter-union agreement that the ETU signed was with ASLEF, promising mutual help if either's negotiating rights were attacked by the employers. Although the agreement was apparently aimed at the employers, it was clearly pointed, too, at the NUR, showing them that pressure on the employers would be met on two fronts. The agreement was never activated, but proved useful to the ETU as it expanded its craft tradition into the stronghold of industrial unionism.

The executive council, too, stood firm when the London district committee attempted to co-operate closely with the NUR in the capital. The London district committee may well have approved of the *industrial* nature of the NUR; they clearly did not approve of the NUR's moderate leadership under Jimmy Thomas. It was therefore easy to appeal to railway workers on the craft basis put forward by the national leadership.

The growth in membership was still astonishing. By the end of 1920, the membership had risen to 57,000. Nearly 20,000 were in London alone. 14,400 were auxiliary workers; in London, there were over 7,000 auxiliaries, which amounted to nearly the same number as the 8,000 skilled full benefit members in London.

Throughout 1920, great strides were made in improving the conditions of the membership. In some industries, like contracting, the union adopted NJIC or Whitley approaches, accommodated the political opposition of the London district committee, and had a hybrid decision-making process that recognized national negotiations with the employers as a way of persuading London to add its weight to the idea of *national* negotiations as opposed to local deals. Electricity supply was always much happier with the philosophy of NJICs. This was due to the spirited defence of the JICs methods by the station engineer leaders in London. Harold Morton wrote several articles in the *Electrical Trades Journal* denouncing a single piece by the anonymous 'BB' who was clearly opposed to the negotiated, painstaking approach favoured by LSE's secretary Morton. BB thought JICs were 'retrograde', reeked of 'compromise', did not help workers improve their living standards and prevented the realization that 'the first thing to be done is to smash the capitalist system'. In response, Morton made a firm defence of compromise. He deployed the classic condemnation of revolution when he wrote in August 1920:

BB states the fundamental relationship between capital and labour will never be changed while the present capitalistic system prevails, as each interest is dramatically opposed – quite so. It only reiterates a truism, but BB must remember that life is only a compromise with death, and the only alternative is international upheaval. With all actions there is a reaction, and the reaction may be even worse than the wildest or sanest prophets might dream. ... No; catchwords, phrases and paragraphs will not alter the woes of the worker, but a steady and sane educational propaganda will ... the whole issue must be approached from a real appreciation of the everyday difficulties.

From the union's leadership's point of view, one of the most pressing of 'everyday difficulties' was the high turnover of membership. The union was rightly enjoying this period of rocketing membership. However, although the ETU recruited 19,851 new members in 1920, it also had to exclude 11,343 for arrears. Negotiating through JICs helped enormously in preserving the union's rights and influence for a workforce that turned over frequently.

Nevertheless, despite the union's successful adoption of the new era's negotiating machinery through JICs, militance and class-war as a basis for industrial decision-making were not wholly out of fashion. From the end of the war to the middle of 1921, the union was involved in some spectacular disputes. It learnt much from them; not least, the limitations involved in opposing employers and government alike with strikes they could not be allowed to win.

The Albert Hall Dispute, November 1918

In late November 1918, the *Daily Herald* booked the Albert Hall to hold a post-war rally led by *Herald* editor, and later Labour leader, George Lansbury. There was a contract to hire the hall and the money had been paid when the authorities governing the hall cancelled the booking. They objected to two recent Labour movement bookings (by the NUR and the Labour Party) being unacceptable due to 'demonstrations of a revolutionary character' taking place. Home Secretary Brace and Prime Minister Lloyd George ignored Lansbury's impassioned pleas that they should intervene to defend the right to free speech.

The London district committee stalwart, Jock Muir, had rung the *Herald* for fifty tickets for the rally, only to be told of its cancellation. On the morning of Saturday, 23 November 1918, Bill Webb and a group of members removed the fuses from the Albert Hall, and told the management of the Kensington area's power company that in the event of anyone replacing them, the whole of that area of West London would be blacked out.

The Albert Hall authorities immediately conceded the issue, and let Lansbury have his rally which filled the hall with thousands locked outside. Every speaker congratulated the ETU who had effectively used industrial power for political ends. Bill Webb and Jock Muir both addressed the meeting. Jock Muir enjoyed the opportunity to explain the union's radical credentials, enormously boosted by the whole episode. He told the ecstatic rally: 'Electricians believe life is not a vote – it is an action, or series of actions ... we require power – power to live, power to expand, power to grow.'

The Government were now very conscious of the ETU's political power: with an atmosphere approaching hysteria at the Home Office, considerable police time was employed watching the key London militants throughout the 1920s. The Albert Hall strike was essentially a gesture. However, there were other issues that the Government were taking more seriously. Stavenhagen went to Ireland during the 1916 troubles. The Albert Hall issue involved Muir and Webb, who were also watched. Cabinet minutes and Home Office papers reveal that other leading London militants like Ben Bolton and Joe Vaughan were also frequently followed.

On 11 January 1919, the whole executive council was summoned to the Ministry of Labour. Sir David Shackleton had at one time himself been the Weavers' Union general secretary. He was blunt and to the point with the executive. He said that the ETU were involved in, or were threatening, industrial action on issues that were not trade disputes. This was an important legal distinction. If action was taken that was a 'trade dispute', under the 1906 Act, the union could not be sued for any damages it caused any company, authority or individual. However, if the Government either prosecuted the union for actions which were not trade disputes, or brought in legislation that specifically banned 'political' strikes, the union would be liable for massive fines and perhaps even imprisonment for the militants concerned. Sir David Shackleton said that he had in mind the union's performance at the Albert Hall a month before, strikes at the Woolwich Arsenal, and letters from Bill Webb threatening strikes if Fred Scrace, the Fulham conscientious objector, was not released from prison. Lastly, the Government would not tolerate general disruption planned again at Woolwich Arsenal on the evidence of Brother Arnell, Woolwich branch secretary, demanding the release of all 'political prisoners', the immediate demobilization of ETU members and the release of all conscientious objectors. Sir David Shackleton told the executive that, at the moment, the Ministry of Labour was handling this problem. However, other departments (i.e. the Home Office and the police) would be involved if the union did not impose some discipline on local activists going beyond the bounds of *industrial* disputes in favour of political strikes.

This set of clear instructions to mend their ways from the Government did not prevent further action being taken over the question of the forty-hour week. The executive had supported moves throughout engineering, contracting and supply to negotiate the forty-seven hour week. Militants in the union in Belfast, the Clyde, Edinburgh and London were adamant that the executive should demand action to impose forty hours, or forty-four hours as far as Belfast was concerned. Strikes broke out.

Strikes for Shorter Hours and the Defeat of Syndicalism

On 1 February 1919, the executive met to consider these strikes in Glasgow, Edinburgh and Belfast, in pursuit of shorter hours, and a strike in the Port of London where 450 ETU men were out for higher pay. None of these strikes had troubled with a ballot. All of them were still technically out-with the union's rules. Jimmy Rowan left his sick bed to bring the executive the formal advice that he had minuted, that the executive council's 5–4 approval for the strikes was outside the rules. The executive re-convened on 9 February to consider the deepening crisis. An aggregate meeting in London on 3 February had denounced Kinniburgh's opposition to the strikes and demanded a total stoppage of London members if the Government did not immediately legislate for the reduction in hours to forty. The Government instantly issued an order in council, No. 43c, to prevent strikes in supply. Harold Morton was not having any of it; especially considering how the district committee went about attempting to manoeuvre the station men into a strike. The district committee called the 3 February aggregate meeting for 7.30 p.m. Morton was only told at 5.30 p.m. that day to notify 284 station men in his branch. Morton later wrote to the executive that 'the whole business was done behind our backs ... the decision to strike for forty hours was taken before the ink was dry on the forty-seven hours agreement for station men.' The newspapers were full of threats to plunge London into darkness – but the power station men knew nothing about it. Jim Memberry wrote that his 'members had been misled many times by the district committee, who had brought men out without notice of any kind and had caused our union to be known as a Bolshevik organization.'

A campaign was raised against the executive for sanctioning the strikes without having a ballot – as Morton put it at a special hearing in front of the executive on 23 March, 'the only authority we could appeal to had themselves supported unconstitutional action and we could not expect proper treatment from them'. Letters of complaint came from LSE branches, Manchester Station Engineers, Willesden, Aston and Hayes branches. Birmingham district committee, Manchester Central and a dozen other branches all complained of the executive flouting the rules. Newcastle Central, though, made a crisis out of the issue by insisting that the union be balloted for or against the executive's decision. In May the result was announced. 4,021 votes condemned the executive, 3,425 supported them.

All strike pay was stopped, and all fines and expulsions for members who worked were rescinded. The executive councillors who had voted for the strikes, Bolton, Illingworth, Dennison, Bellamy and Stavenhagen, all resigned. The first four were persuaded overnight to withdraw their resignations. Stavenhagen stood by his principles. He had campaigned on the issue as one of confidence. He told the executive council his reasons for joining the others in resigning – and he was the only one to carry it through. 'As in such a critical position as arose at Belfast, the Clyde, London, Edinburgh and elsewhere, on the question of the forty and forty-four hour week, it is absolutely impossible to adhere absolutely to rules, if to do so is to seriously injure class unity. As the carrying of the Newcastle appeal virtually imposes such a traitorous position upon us, we are . . . resigning forthwith.'

He left the executive on 12 May 1919, never to return. He continued to be elected to the London district committee, where his colourful resolutions dominated the agenda. He continued to urge the cause of industrial unionism, and even designed a scheme for London which would produce six sub-committees of the district committee, one for each significant industry, serviced by a full-time official. In outline, this is precisely the modern organization of the Electrical, Electronic, Telecommunication and Plumbing Union (EETPU) in London. He took part in the campaigns against the executive council, threatening to resign if the 'malicious and reptilian efforts of the sub-executive council to spread the rumour that the district committee accounts were not in order' was allowed to continue. On 13 January 1921, he got 1,646 votes to top the poll for the London district committee. One week later, the district committee minutes reveal, he resigned. On 20 January 1921, he told the district committee: 'Circumstances have arisen which make it impossible for him to satisfactorily carry out the duties of a district committee delegate until July next, and, in consequence, he regretted to have to tender his resignation.' He never returned. He disappeared from the union's life completely. He bought a small electrical wholesalers in West London. However, he kept in touch with Muir and other London left-wingers for decades after, when he entertained them and their families at his home in Fulham for Sunday lunch. That, along with his two goldfish, Lenin and Trotsky, were the only political gestures he made after his resignation.

Why he went so suddenly and why he stayed away has never been properly explained. He was without question the most iconoclastic revolutionary the union ever produced. He was admired by Citrine, who successfully campaigned for him to write technical articles for the journal long after his flamboyant politics had exasperated the 'Manchester oligarchy' as he called Ball and Rowan. He remains an enigma. He had close links with Irish nationalists and socialists. He was falsely accused of accepting £500 from Trotsky himself. He was a conscientious objector. He was a great inspiration in the union's early organizing days, but nothing was so extraordinary about him as the way he left the union at the height of his powers. His family provide the most obvious and truthful reason for his sudden retirement from trade union life. He was blacklisted all over London from the end of the First World War and did not work at all from 1919–21. Consequently, he set up a small electrical fittings shop in Kensington Church Street (where a regular traveller in Osram lamps was the young Jules Thorn, one of Stavenhagen's old work-mates at GEC's building in Kingsway, where Stavenhagen shared a work bench before the war with Belling, Thorn, Mullard, Ellis and Lee!).

He became a moderately successful electrical contractor, installing appliances and doing the necessary wiring work that often went with early consumer electrical goods. His company, Climax Radio Electrical Co, collapsed in 1927 when bankrupted by a main contractor's own financial collapse. Between then and the Second World War he was a manager of the electrical contracting side of a reasonable-sized construction company in Fulham. During the war, he ran a boarding house for workers transferred to the Vickers aircraft works at Weybridge. He retired in 1948 and lived in Surbiton and near Southampton where he died aged ninety-two in 1980.

Throughout 1919, the union's exuberant growth and activity knew few bounds, whether deployed through strikes, or the more sophisticated developments in collective bargaining; by 1920, however, the willingness of members to fight in the period was to meet its first implacable opponent at Penistone in South Yorkshire.

The Taste of Defeat: Penistone, 1920

Cammel Laird's had an engineering works at Penistone, and the union's membership in June 1920 of around 400 were in a position to demand a closed shop from the company. Organizing meetings had been held and virtually 100 per cent membership assured. Then it was discovered that a foreman called Nicholson, who had been in and out of the union twice before, refused to join. On Friday 4 July, Sheffield district committee secretary Mathews was on an organizing trip to Scarborough. On the Sunday, the district committee met hurriedly in Sheffield and confirmed the result of the mass meeting of the men concerned that decided to go on strike until Nicholson joined the union or left the job. On 17 July, Mathews tried to extend the dispute by asking first the Yorkshire Power Company and then members in local power stations to cut supply to the factory at Penistone. Neither would help. Equally, the EPEA showed their unwillingness to help when they too refused to take action in the dispute and sent Mathews a stern little homily into the bargain. Local EPEA secretary H. Price, wrote: 'The onus of keeping men on the streets rests with the men themselves in their acting in such a rash and unconstitutional manner.'

The EEF took an extremely dim view of this essentially trivial and local dispute. The EEF, under its charismatic if dictatorial leader, Sir Allan Smith, had been concerned throughout the latter years of the war and its aftermath at the loss of managerial control in the engineering industry. Here at Penistone was a good issue to regain the managerial prerogative the previous years of consensus had taken away from them. The ETU was claiming to dictate who the employers could or could not have as a foreman, depending on the union's acceptance or non-acceptance of their trade union status.

Jimmy Rowan and Jack Kinniburgh met Sir Allan Smith and others at the EEF on 29 July. The employers bluntly put forward a two-sentence basis for settlement. 'The ETU do not claim that foremen shall be members of a trade union. The ETU agree to recommend that the men on strike at Penistone return to work so that the cause of the stoppage may be investigated in accordance with the provisions for the avoidance of disputes.'

Rowan tried to get a compromise – he accepted that the union did not claim all foremen everywhere should be union members. He also agreed to a conference on the subject to sort out the general principle involved. However, he suggested that the EEF should support the suspension of Nicholson to allow the men to return to work while the general issues at stake were discussed. The employers point-blank threw this out. Sir Allan Smith then announced that they would lock out every ETU member in every federated establishment. The Federation obtained a 9–1 majority of its affiliated companies and the lock-out was enforced on 19 August.

At the TUC in Portsmouth in early September, the ETU delegation was a permanent national strike committee. Occasionally the other unions in engineering attempted to mediate at national level while picking off ETU members locally – a point made amidst uproar by Jock Muir in his specific attack on the Workers Union.

During the last weekend in August, the union had taken the dispute to the Government. Jimmy Rowan told Congress:

We have done everything on our side *not* to continue the dispute. Last Saturday and Sunday we sat with Dr MacNamara and Sir David Shackleton (from the Ministry of Labour), with Sir Allan Smith for the employers, to arrive at a settlement of this dispute. Dr MacNamara spent one hour of the whole two days with us. The whole of his time was spent with Sir Allan Smith and his colleague in framing different sorts of wording to get an agreement with them. They definitely refused.

Indeed, when the Government offered to set up an inquiry under the industrial courts procedure, the EEF flatly refused to attend. Jack Kinniburgh made a characteristically thundering speech, calling Sir Allan Smith 'the embodiment of capitalism in this country. He is cool, calm and calculating. He puts a proposition to you, and you can take it or leave it.'

Tom Mann supported the ETU on the principle involved, and also instructed all his local ASE branches not to recruit dissident ETU members who were locked out. He, too, thundered from the rostrum.

It all hangs upon the one point, that the employers insist upon forcing down the throats of the members of the ETU their determination that from now the ETU shall accept the foremen they appoint without any voice at all in the matter. In my judgment, I say to Labour that this is a vital matter of principle.

The resolution to support the ETU was passed unanimously 'by acclamation'. Not for the first or last time, conference hall rhetoric was not too helpful in the painfully real world outside. The courts ruled that none of the union's members was entitled to unemployment relief, although no one apart from the Penistone membership was directly involved. It looked obvious that the other men had to be entitled to relief, having been locked out. The courts ruled, however, that they *were* involved, through their membership of the union. Lack of funds for the locked-out men weakened resolve. Members in Sheffield itself, Rugby, Chelmsford, Lincoln and Leamington were reported to be leaving the union, returning to work, or demanding explanations from the executive as to why they were in dispute. Electricity supply shop-stewards in London were threatening sympathetic strike action in support of their engineering colleagues. Will Thorne, veteran leader of the National Union of General Workers (forerunner of today's General Municipal and Boilermakers Union), publicly laid some very careful thoughts before the ETU, at the same congress. He said that a strike of London supply workers would not be totally effective, as his union's members saw no reason to get involved. The loss of power to the railways in London would involve railwaymen who had no quarrel either. It is difficult to see how Sir Allan Smith would be deflected by strikes in power stations, and, finally, 'neither this Government nor any other government will allow London to go into darkness.' Given Rowan's understanding of the latter point, based on the Government's 1919 concern of the misuse of industrial power in the power stations, Thorne's analysis was a powerful, practical corrective to disaster. On 16 September, the Penistone members went back to work on precisely the employers' terms that were tabled on 29 July, leaving Rowan to take some comfort from the fact that it left the union free to 'concentrate on the real issue in engineering, the shortfall on wages'.

In the October 1920 issue of the *Electrical Trades Journal*, shorn of his conference-induced passion, Jack Kinniburgh reflected soberly on the end of the lock-out. 'I was very satisfied when we arrived at a settlement, as the issue being fought, i.e. non-union foremen, was not a very popular one with our members, which no doubt, was partly the reason Sir Allan Smith and his colleagues snapped it up and made an attempt to segregate us from the rest of our fellows in the engineering industry.' Kinniburgh (and Tom Mann) thought that the *real* lesson of Penistone was that had the union's members not been cheated out of amalgamating with the engineers' union, a joint fight, even on that issue, might have been successful.

Nothing could hide the fact that Penistone was a complete defeat. What they did not know was that more of the same was on its way.

There was one last piece of excitement in 1920. In August, the union's active members joined 'councils of action' to insist on no war with Russia – particularly in London: but the possibilities for confident class aggression were about to come to an end. It had been a heady period. From 1918 to the end of 1920, trade union membership had risen in Britain from 6.46 million to 8.25 million. The density of union membership had risen from sixteen per cent in 1910 to forty-eight per cent of the workforce in 1920. Big general unions, like the Workers Union and the General Workers, dominated the movement. The coal and cotton unions had shrunk from forty per cent of the total in 1910 to twenty per cent of this much larger total in 1920. The triple alliance between the miners, railwaymen and transport workers seemed to offer a practical way to organize devastating industrial power in support of each of the three groups of workers involved.

Depression and Disaster, 1920–21

By the end of 1920, the first signs of depression were becoming apparent. By mid-1921, industrial production had fallen by twenty per cent from its mid-1920 level. Unemployment among the insured population rose in the same year from 2.7 per cent to 17.9 per cent. Wholesale prices fell by thirty-three per cent and were still falling. From November 1920 to November 1921, the retail price index fell by twenty-four per cent. It was an economic collapse without precedent since the Industrial Revolution.

It nearly overwhelmed the ETU. The first five months of 1921 virtually bankrupted the union. The first employers to confront the union were the Scottish ECA. They notified the union that they were withdrawing from the NJIC and reducing wages. Walter Finlay, secretary of the Scottish ECA, wrote to Rowan on 19 February that 'a reduction of 3d per hour is essential and that this reduction should be given effect to for the first full week in March. ... You may therefore take it that you have our final position in the matter.' On 24 February, Rowan presented a claim for an increase of 3d an hour to the NFEA. Mr Cash, for the NFEA, replied with a demand for a twenty per cent cut in hourly rates! After a long debate, the employers agreed to postpone imposing the cut until further talks were held before the start of

May. The situation in Scotland was more pressing and the executive had to decide what to do. They were well aware that this first attempt to reduce wages was being watched by others. They balloted the whole union, who decided, 6,066–4,525, to levy the whole membership 1s a week (6d for auxiliary members), in order to boost strike pay by £1 a week above its normal 15s. The strike started on 5 March throughout Scotland. What a dreadful week for Rowan. Having finally broken down with the Scottish ECA on 3 March, he then had to attend meetings at the EEF on the ninth and the Shipbuilding Employers Association on the tenth to listen to more massive reductions for all workers in these industries. Sir Allan Smith for the engineering employers proposed cuts that abolished the wartime bonuses of twelve-and-a-half per cent for timeworkers and the seven-and-a-half per cent for piece-workers, and, in addition, took back the 1920 increases of 6s for timeworkers and fifteen per cent for piece-workers at the end of June 1921. Sir Alexander Kennedy, for the shipbuilders, proposed to reduce wages by 6s per week and fifteen per cent off piece-work prices at the end of April.

Disaster built upon disaster. A conference of Scottish delegates in Perth on 8 April were insistent that though the strike was solid – particularly in Glasgow, where thirty per cent of the contracting companies did not reduce wages, and Edinburgh – if the executive did not improve strike pay by a further £1 a week, negotiations should be immediately opened up with employers. Walter Citrine was despatched to hold meetings in the weaker areas of Dundee and Aberdeen; the Clyde members at work were levied further and a central committee representing the four main areas in Scotland set up (although picketing fees and payments to the strike committee were seriously restricted).

On Sunday 10 April, the executive reviewed the crisis in the mining industry; the miners were faced with wage cuts and were expecting to strike themselves, along with their partners in the triple alliance, the railwaymen and the transport workers, on 16 April. The executive issued instructions that no member should do anything 'detrimental to the miners, transport workers, railwaymen or any other body of workers while on strike.' On Friday 15 April, the heavyweights in the triple alliance demanded the miners keep negotiating, and when they refused, withdrew their promise of sympathetic action, leaving the miners to fight alone. The executive also tried to tie their support for the miners to the recognition of the union in the collieries where the ETU was ignored, and issued instructions to withdraw the electricians from the pits. The London district committee wanted a general strike and all branches to have a strike committee. When the sympathetic action failed to materialize on 15 April, 'Black Friday', only the London district committee wanted to join in. Matt Greenwell went down to the LCC power station at Greenwich which generated for the trams and underground, and got the forty-one ETU members out on strike, to be followed by hundreds of members of other unions, on the grounds that touching the coal in the station was 'detrimental' to the miners' interests.

Morton and Bussey had little difficulty in preventing the strike spreading to other power stations, despite Bill Westfallen in his new unofficial magazine, *Electron*, attacking Morton and Bussey, accusing them of wanting to be full-time officers for the station engineers only. Bussey, of LSE No. 10, had had enough. He said on 16 May: 'The station engineer members were described as the storm troops of the movement; but they are now realizing that the storm troops got devastated in the struggle. Consequently, they were thinking of going in the reserves.' Rowan met Mr Rivière, the LCC chief engineer, who had moved 150 blacklegs promptly into Greenwich power station. He said that he would take the strikers back, in the fullness of time, although he was going to stand by the men he had and the ETU men might have to wait! An aggregate meeting of station engineers completely refused to strike in support of their brethren at Greenwich.

Three months later, in July 1921, of the forty-one ETU men, only three had been re-engaged. Less than £100 was raised all over London in that time, to Webb's complete embarrassment. Rowan and Webb tried to interest the TUC and the London Labour Party in helping the Greenwich strikers. They were politely ignored. Perhaps the most direct humiliation was Mr Rivière's eventual offer to reinstate a further eight electrical workers as tram-conductors for the LCC. The Greenwich dispute was another total defeat for the union. It split the union in London, where the station engineers increasingly resented the cavalier attitude of the London district committee. It is clear that there was no meeting of minds between the active and ambitious trade unionists like Morton and Bussey and the determined political revolutionaries represented increasingly by Bill Westfallen, a station engineer himself from the railways. He wrote in the August issue of *Electron* that the failure of Black Friday and the events surrounding it were due to:

... two main causes. One of which is the lack of a class-conscious outlook in the average member, and the other is the reformist policy adopted by our so-called leaders. The latter is, to some extent, responsible for the former ... and until we are prepared to subordinate all other interests to our class interests, we shall never be able to compel those whom we elect to speak for us to do likewise.

On 20 April the union's executive joined the full-time officials in York to meet the NFEA to see if they still wanted to pursue contracting wage cuts in England, Wales and Ireland. They did. They proposed two cuts of five per cent, one on 9 May and one on 9 July.

The union's delegation was nineteen strong – with ten full-time officials, Rowan, Stewart and Kinniburgh, plus six members of the executive (Bellamy, Bolton, Finn, Foster-Curtis, Illingworth and Morrison). They argued all day.

They voted, 8–6, with five abstentions to recommend the cuts to the members in a ballot. However, when the executive council met alone, later, to formally sanction this they voted, by five (Bolton, Muir, Morrison, Illingworth and Bellamy) to three (Finn, Foster-Curtis and Bellamy), to refuse to put it to a ballot at all. Instead, members were to vote at special meetings by a show of hands and if the reductions were imposed while the meetings were being arranged, then strike they must. With the first five per cent cut due on 9 May, this did not leave much time. They then decided that the same method should be used in the shipyards to decide the nature of the resistance, if any, to the shipbuilding reductions of 6s or fifteen per cent due in two instalments on 7 May and 4 June.

Chaos ensued. When the union's rules revision conference opened at Blackpool on 16 May, the whole week was dominated by the comings and goings associated with the strikes and threats of strikes in contracting, shipbuilding, the engineering industry (due to reduce wages on 16 June) and the lesser industries of cablemaking, steelworking, and the Greenwich dispute.

Jack Ball's presidential address noted how the union conferences so often coincided with a great crisis in the union's affairs – particularly comparing 1921 with 1907, the conference that made the union a national body. The conference set out to review the whole position, and Jimmy Rowan laid out the details of all the disputes currently in force and those looming on the horizon in engineering and electricity supply.

Regional reports only confirmed the gloomy picture. In Wales, steelworkers' wages had been reduced by 19s 1d a week, although their £5 a week compared well with the NFEA rate of £4 15s 3s and the shipbuilders £4 2s 9d, after their reductions. Jack Kinniburgh said that the other unions' compliance in cablemaking wage cuts made resistance impossible. District secretary on the Clyde, J. D. Higgins, was even more pessimistic. The men had been on strike in contracting for over ten weeks. The augmented strike pay had had to be stopped for financial reasons and ordinary benefits were exhausted. Nine hundred men were still on strike and he just did not know how many more would be out that week to resist the shipbuilders' cuts. He was particularly fearful that the unemployed would be taken on in the strikers' place. Bill Webb reported over 1,500 out in London's contracting industry and the shipbuilding section had answered the call with the exception of just four. In Belfast, though, the shipbuilders had voted to accept the reduction and the contractors were still working. Only two thirds of the men affected in Manchester were out, and many of them were wavering. Particularly acid was Bill Noble from the Tyne. He reported that high unemployment in the area meant a degree of disappointment in the contracting section at the change in policy from the York meeting on 20 April, which accepted the NFEA cuts, and the executive council meeting in Manchester on the twenty-fourth which effectively decided to oppose them. If that was not hard enough to swallow, Tyneside shipyards had just taken men on again after five months' lay-offs, and now they were being urged out on strike. Noble said that the executive policy was 'not popular in the Tyne area.' In Southampton, the shipyard men were not happy and recommended bringing the power workers out in their aid. In Sussex, 132 men were on strike, but were very 'windy', and likely to give in soon. In Liverpool, all 450 men involved, along with the apprentices, were solid. Throughout the country, non-federated companies in contracting were still working; but a clear picture emerged of disenchantment with the effects of the executive's turn-around between the York and Manchester meetings in April.

The executive then put to the conference that *they*, the delegates, should decide what to do next. This infuriated H. McFall, the Liverpool man who had done so much in organizing the full-time electricians at sea; he thought it was 'cowardly' of the executive to put it to the conference. Harold Morton was of the view that the executive should resign. All the Scottish speakers in the debate said that all the strikes in Scotland would collapse very quickly without financial aid. Bussey and Morton both said they were fed up with station engineers being used to win others' disputes for them – and particularly objected to the mounting evidence of district committee idiocy at Greenwich. Telegrams were read during the debate that men were going back to work in droves on the Clyde, in Birmingham and Belfast (including seven members of the district committee and the district president). The debate degenerated into farce. There were four motions, including one, which was carried 33–6, condemning the executive. After a full day amending and withdrawing amendments and motions, the result was that all members on strike should return to work on Monday 23 May 1921, and accept the reductions demanded in all cases.

This collapse intensified by the end of the month with the acceptance of the draconian reductions in engineering, along with all the other unions involved.

These dreadful events for the union were dominated by the two related issues of unemployment and the union's financial position, which effectively settled the issue for everybody. Unemployment was accelerating out of control. The demand for unemployment benefit – and then strike benefit – reduced the union to its knees. At the end of 1920, the union had a cash balance of £52,122. By the end of March 1921, it had fallen to £38,789. From 31 March to 14 May, the balance had nose-dived to just £10,595. To balance this expenditure of over £28,000 in six weeks, the union's income was just £2,690 (although a further £10,000 was due for administering benefits for the state benefit schemes). The Co-operative Bank would lend the union £1,000 for six months to pay one more week's benefits, and that was it. There was just one road to defeat without financial resources. Jack Ball as usual told the truth, painful as it was. 'The essential basis of war is money. Carried to its logical conclusion, with money we win, without money we lose.'

11

CONFRONTING FINANCIAL DISASTER, WAGE REDUCTIONS AND INTERNAL SCHISM, 1921–6

JIMMY ROWAN'S ANNUAL REPORTS had difficulty finding new words to describe the disastrous years of 1921–3. Nineteen twenty-one was 'a black year'. Nineteen twenty-two was 'no less black than its predecessor'. 'The only solace we have is that things were so bad in 1921 and 1922 that they could not possibly have been worse in 1923.'

Financial Collapse and Recovery, 1921–3

The chief cause for all this gloom was the level of unemployment, which gave the employers the essential background against which they could insist upon wage reductions from severely weakened trade unions. In shipbuilding, forty-four per cent of the workforce was unemployed. In construction, the figure was twelve per cent. Engineering, which now collected separate figures for electrical engineering and the infant motor industry, had unemployment rates of between seven and ten per cent. The electricity supply industry was seven per cent down (although that was more due to the development of technical sophistication than lack of activity). All these influences affected the union's membership. By the end of 1923, it had fallen to 26,165, forty-six per cent of its 1920 record level of 57,292. All unions had declined over the same period – the miners were seventy-seven per cent of their 1920 total, the steelworkers sixty-four per cent. The most spectacular collapse occurred amongst the general unions, where the Workers Union had fallen to twenty-eight per cent of its 1920 level in three years. The decline in membership in the ETU was less severe in its skilled section (full benefit and over-age members). This was fifty-four per cent of its 1920 level, almost exactly equal to the AEU's fifty-five per cent.

The economic effects of unemployment on the union itself were entirely predictable. It devastated the finances. We have seen how ill-judged, chaotic resistance to the 1921 pay cuts melted the £77,000 reserves in a few short weeks. £75,444 was paid out in 1921 on unemployment benefit alone; £26,407 was spent on strike pay. In 1922, benefits were halved, and then abandoned altogether from March to August. Even so, £23,000 was spent on half-benefits for unemployed people. These half-benefits had a clever twist about them. The union paid half the 15s a week – but paid them for twice as long as the usual fifteen weeks. Only £710 went on strikes. Expenditure exceeded income in 1922, and the general funds were reduced to £6,360 by the end of the year. Nineteen twenty-three was little better, adding just £337 to the balance, having paid out £15,391 in unemployment pay and £243 in strike pay.

The union would probably have collapsed completely had they not taken aggressive steps to rectify the casual and wilful ways in which money was spent throughout the union. For this, the union was to be eternally grateful to Walter Citrine. Citrine was elected as a second assistant general secretary in July 1920. On the first ballot Archie Stewart got 1,253 votes, and two Londoners, Fred Alford and George Humphreys, got just over 1,000 each. There were ten other candidates and so, although Citrine got 4,865 votes, a second ballot was needed against Archie Stewart as Citrine's vote was not fifty per cent of the votes cast. In the second ballot he got 6,239 to Archie Stewart's 3,282. In some respects, Lord Citrine's later reputation as the man who took British trade unions out of Trafalgar Square and into government belies his early reputation inside the ETU. He was no stranger to industrial action on Merseyside, defending the May strikers in 1917, and battling against the pretensions of the EPEA. When he left Liverpool to go to head office in early 1921, he was given a tremendous send-off at the Gainsboro' cafe, where he received a leather-bound set of Dickens's novels and a cheque for £41. He recommended Stavenhagen as the technical editor of the journal. He was an early enthusiast for the Russian Revolution. He wrote years later: 'I had been enthused by Lenin's picture of an electric republic. . . . I accepted . . . almost at its face value, without critical reservations, practically everything which emanated from Russian official sources. . . . I was convinced that our news-papers simply couldn't tell the truth about events in the Soviet Union.' He became disillusioned later when the Russian authorities called the TUC leaders 'lick-spittles' etc., but that was not until 1926. However, he always said he believed in the class struggle, if not the class-war, and on election to his new national job his work brought him into conflict with the union's real class-warriors in London.

He was expected to reform the administration of the union, and reform it he did. He told the story to Les Cannon, the union's president, in 1967, of the first day he arrived at the union's offices in Manchester. He spent a lot of time talking to Rowan and Bob Prain, and when it was time for the office to close Citrine said that he would stay behind and familiarize himself with the union's filing system. He asked Rowan where it was. Rowan replied, 'The filing system is just putting her hat and coat on, and leaving the offices,' as the general secretary's clerical help, who was the only one who knew where anything was kept, left the office! Citrine wrote long articles in the early 1921 issues of the journal concerning the incoherence of much branch–head office correspondence. He showed the union that just to read each day's incoming mail took the three head office officials one-and-a-half hours every day to plough through over 100 letters. The clerical pressures on the union were immense, with over 50,000 pieces of correspondence needing to be filed per annum. They also had to despatch circulars, acknowledgements, receipts, minutes; write up reports, executive council minutes; write the journal and deal with its printers, and then go to committees, conferences and negotiations. To make a system of all this, Citrine introduced the methodology of the business world into the union's administration. He got branches to write on one subject per letter and to properly quote references to any previous correspondence. He instituted new systems of ordering stationery, introduced cheaper ways of sending telegrams, indenting for funds and dealing with applications for benevolent grants. His shorthand note-taking skill was much in demand at union conferences.

These general skills and sharpened efficiency at head office was the first line of defence as the unemployment and strikes of 1921 savaged union funds. However, inspired by Citrine, the union's leadership responded to the financial crisis in a variety of ways. Firstly, the executive appointed Archie Stewart as a special auditor on 9 January 1921. He did the job until 23 February 1923, and saved the equivalent of his national organizer's salary several times over. The union lost thousands of pounds over this period from straightforward stealing by branch officers and, less frequently, other officials. Stewart was empowered to visit any branch or district committee to audit and investigate their accounts. He turned up some casual, some criminal, attitudes to money – particularly where the officers of the London district committee were concerned. In April 1921, Stewart looked at the Ponders End strike at the Enfield Cable Company. R. L. McLaughlin was one of four 'organizers' elected in London. A deputation had visited him on 25 March from the factory, saying they were ninety-nine per cent organized, and so he and the district committee sanctioned a strike to start on 5 April in common with other unions. When McLaughlin got to Enfield, he discovered seventy per cent of the 'members' were not in the union as they had no cards. In complete contravention of the rules, he then issued cards to people 'who could not sign their own name'. He borrowed £260 from the district committee's account to pay the first week's strike pay, blaming head office for withholding the necessary cash. He paid the striking apprentices 8s per week (not 6s, as was the rule) because the Workers Union were paying 8s! In total, he paid out £589 16s 0d and couldn't account for it. Archie Stewart then talked to the treasurer of the local Ponders End branch, Ryder, who put a different gloss on things. McLaughlin did not attend the branch to pay out the strike benefit – he went to a pub instead. The head office *had* sent the required money, but, of course, sent it to the branch for the accredited 102 members the union had – not the 540 'members' McLaughlin paid out in the pub. He then promised the strikers that the district committee's private 'contingent fund' would pay up any further sums, despite, by rule, no one being allowed benefit who had only just joined the union. The strikers promised to return any benefits 'later' if they were not entitled to them and McLaughlin accepted this. He was later surprised to learn that all the strikers later joined the Workers Union after the strike and forgot to pay the ETU back.

McLaughlin was undaunted. Stewart's report to the executive quoted his response. McLaughlin 'did not look upon the trades union movement from the point of view of a business organization, but looked upon it as a phase of the class struggle.'

Earlier that year, Stewart went to London with Citrine to get to grips with the London district committee finances in the round, and were met with obstruction and abuse. They were not allowed to use the London office and they had to get a court order to force the officials to let them look at the books. These were finally made available on 8 March.

The two men examined the books for 1920 and the March quarter of 1921. Their conclusions, presented to the executive in July 1921, were damning. First and foremost, they found over £1,300 had been paid out in delegation and committee fees. Jack Potter, who had been district secretary before Webb's election in 1915, pointed out in February 1921 what was going wrong.

There is an enormous number of often unnecessary and frequently inflated deputations, especially of district committees.... I am credibly informed that it is not unusual for ten to eighteen delegates to be appointed to meet two or three employers. Another remarkable fact is that no sooner is a local full-time official appointed, than delegation expenses rise by leaps and bounds. These men are appointed to run a district; committee-men go with them, either to state the case, or act as warders to see their charge errs not from the path of rectitude. And in *their* wake follow the inarticulates to learn elocution and the business. On top of these come a multiplicity of committees, sub-committees, councils and what-not. We could teach the Soviet Republic something.

All these delegations were quite lucrative and disgracefully accounted for in London. Each delegate would write his claim for fees and expenses on a scrap of paper and sign for the gross sum received. The scraps were then thrown away and no details then survived in the receipt book. Seven members, including Ben Bolton, Bill Westfallen and Harold Morton, received over £100 a year each. On top of this, they then got delegation fees from their branches. Westfallen received £3 2s 0d a week from the union in this way – and Harold Morton got £2 13 0d for his work in the power stations.

The Londoners concerned were then paid out of district committee funds – not out of the full-time official fund which was levied and accounted for separately. By paying them from district committee funds that are sent from head office, 'the London district committee has a retinue of part-time officials ... paid from the general funds of the union ... the members throughout the country are paying heavily for the services of these part-time officials.' Their printing and postage costs were extortionate, sending their minutes and memos to all and sundry, often way outside London. The executive decided in future to vet all claims, to order head office to control stationary costs and to stop the district committee meeting all day in the week and to revert to evening meetings which cost less.

Archie Stewart found endless small defalcations and handled the various prosecutions or internal audits involved. McLaughlin had to answer to losing over £87 at a dispute in 1920 at Pirelli's in Southampton, where he had first made class-conscious payments in pubs without any record of where they had gone. In November 1921, the London district committee was briefly suspended – mainly for calling strikes and paying benefits without ballots or consulting the executive council.

However, in late 1922, Citrine and Stewart were back in London to investigate the dubious finances of the London district committee's radical magazine *Electron*. This magazine is of interest for several reasons. It was published monthly from August 1920 to June 1922. Its first editor was Stavenhagen and then, in 1921, Bill Westfallen, under the 'guidance' of the London district committee. The photograph of Walter Crane's original banner from 1902 was featured on the cover. It was uncompromisingly revolutionary in tone. Westfallen wrote in the January 1921 issue: 'Capitalism stands at the moment like a pyramid on its apex: one big push would bring the whole fabric crashing to the ground. We believe the ETU, by virtue of the youth, vigour and high idealism of its members – its ramifications and its unmistakable industrial power – is destined to become one of the most powerful factors in that push.' It included articles from most of the London organizers which give vivid accounts of recruitment battles and strikes. It printed gently sarcastic letters from Harold Morton, laughing at Westfallen's vision of Morton as 'a hopeless incompetent, out selling the members and hobnobbing with the bosses' and demanding the editor to stop throwing 'mud' at the station engineers. It was keen to emphasize the value of the Red International of Trade Unions and filled its pages with a mixture of plain news on local negotiations and systematic abuse of the national officers in Manchester. Jack Ball was *the* target for what he later described as 'blatant, vulgar and bitter criticism of the executive council and its general officials which seems to have always characterized the leaders of the ETU in London.'

However, it was written with some intelligence. It published technical articles and in one such article on the generation of electricity, it wrote this in August 1921:

> What with the motive power won from rivers and from tides, from wind and from sun, the statisticians who, ten or twenty years ago, foresaw the exhaustion of the coal supply within a few centuries, are likely to have to revise their estimates on a basis of the restricted use of coal for the chemical industries only; for as a source of power, its days are undoubtedly numbered.

It clearly evoked some loyalty amongst its readers. Perhaps it is not simply coincidence that when the communist leadership of the union in 1950 renamed the *Electrical Trades Journal*, they called it the *Electron*.

However, the distinctly non-communist Walter Citrine was more interested in where they got the money from to print it. First, it became quickly apparent that the London district committee contingent fund (from which they incidentally paid strike benefits that the rules would not allow conventionally) was short by £191 12s 5d. John Wyatt, the assistant district secretary, who had come out of London West with Bill Webb back in 1908 and founded, and was the first secretary of, Woolwich branch, had simply stolen some of it and paid the rest out to fund the *Electron*. He was sacked by the executive and eventually prosecuted. Rowan was furious a month later when Wyatt admitted in court forgery with intent to defraud, but pleaded that it was an accident as he was not well at the time. The jury acquitted him. Within a week, Wyatt admitted to a further deficiency of £20, and the executive expelled him from the union. He went quietly. This still left the *Electron* owing, at the end of 1922 when the union's funds were just over £6,000 in total, £1,079 in its own right. It had 'borrowed' £573 from the district committee and full-time official funds, along with £505 owed to the printers. Westfallen, Webb, Wyatt and Bolton had signed the printers' agreement, and the union formally repudiated *its* involvement in that debt. The whole of the district committee was held responsible for repaying the union funds, and Webb was blamed for that – although not too much. 'Webb was technically responsible for the lax financial administration, but is in no way connected with the contingent fund deficiency.'

Throughout the period, Stewart in particular had to pursue branches who were simply late with their returns. In 1921, over 121 branch returns were over six months late, spread across sixty-four branches and district committees. The annual reports were not published until July the following year – and by 1925, the Registrar of Trade Union and Friendly Societies was so fed up with this slovenliness that he threatened to take the union to court.

One way of raising money was to levy the membership. However, Rowan knew how the 1893 levy nearly destroyed the union at birth; he had direct experience of failing to raise the levy during the 1914 strikes. In February 1921, the executive tried to finance the enhanced strike pay for the Scottish contracting strike that was to come by a 2s levy, to be paid at March quarter nights, and then levied members a further 1s a week in March – but this collapsed in May, during the strikes. By 1922, the position had become impossible. Rowan wrote 'no general levy was imposed [in 1922] on account of the fact that there was such a large proportion of the membership unable to pay even their ordinary contributions, and the remainder do not seem to have any enthusiasm for paying anything beyond the bare contribution.'

Other financial measures were taken. The salaries of the branch and full-time officials were cut throughout 1921 and 1922, so that by the end of 1923, the wages of the district secretaries varied from £218 per annum in Sheffield to £319 in London, with Birmingham paying £256, Manchester £275 and the Clyde £286. Grade 'B' contracting electricians' wages had fallen to 1s 6¼d an hour – which gave them an annual basic wage of around £185. London electricians were paid 1s 8½d which gave a basic annual wage of around £200. Average earnings for all manual workers in 1923 were around £150 per annum. Most officials, though, did what Bill Webb did. His wages were reduced from £7 a week to £6 3s 0d in 1922, but he could boost his earnings by around 15s a week with expenses and delegation fees when he left the office. This range of salaries from £218 –£319 was due to the strength or otherwise of local levies for the full-time official funds. ETU salaries were not over-generous when compared with the Workers Union district officers who were paid just over £278 per annum and the Municipal Workers who paid their officials between £234 and £312.

Other economies were taken. The journal was suspended for several months in the winter of 1921–2. Delegations to the TUC and the Labour Party were cut to one delegate appointed by the executive to save on balloting costs. We have already noted the suspension and then half-payment of benefits. The union quietly ended its affiliation to the GFTU. Curiously, the most obvious and tangible austerity measure was the decision in November 1921 to issue in future an annual, instead of quarterly, membership card from 1922. The card was light blue for the skilled sections and pink for the auxiliary.

All of this paled into insignificance compared to Walter Citrine's finest achievement. On 1 January 1923, the union introduced the final part of his scheme to centralize the finances of the union. The scheme had been approved in a ballot in the summer of 1922, by just 2,867 votes to 2,517. Many branches and districts feared, rightly, that the centralized finance scheme meant exacly what its title implied. East Ham and London East even went to court to hold onto the rights to spend their money how they pleased. The scheme was in four main parts. All income into the branch had to be sent to head office (via the Co-op Bank from September 1922). All expenditure by the branch had to then be indented for from head office, who would authorize (or not) the appropriate payments. Further discipline was assured by only paying branch officers' salaries (e.g. 5d per member per quarter to the secretary and 2½d per member per quarter for the treasurer) from head office, *only* on receipt of their quarterly returns. No one ever got rich by being a branch secretary. Harold Morton, branch secretary of LSE No. 1 branch, was paid £3 16s od for the last quarter of 1923. Jim Kearns, branch secretary of Salford, got £15 14s od from his 275 members. Arthur Chowns, branch secretary of Burton-on-Trent, saw his branch nearly, but not quite, expire in 1923. His sixteen members gave him a quarterly pay out of 6s 8d.

Jack Ball was always of the view that centralized finance saved the union. Certainly, Citrine's administrative and financial reforms, and the executive's strictness with benefit payments, did the trick. In 1921, the union spent £180,727 (with £75,444 on unemployment benefit and £26,407 on strike pay). By the end of 1923, expenditure had fallen to £47,611, with £15,391 going on unemployment benefit and £243 spent on strikes. Walter Citrine left the union on 7 January 1924, to take up an appointment as assistant general secretary at the TUC. Suitable tributes were registered to the man who was unchallenged in the members' esteem. He was re-elected unopposed in 1923, and his sheer talent certainly demanded a broader stage. A legend is still handed down inside the union that Rowan was more than happy to see the young Citrine take off to the TUC. No one likes having someone quite so clever as one's 'assistant'! Citrine retained his membership of the union always, and he was awarded the ETU's gold badge in 1947 and the EETPU's gold badge amidst emotional scenes at the biennial delegate conference of the EETPU in 1975 when he was aged eighty-seven.

The union's reaction to mass unemployment in the 1920s took several forms. John Wyatt led marches of unemployed ex-servicemen from Woolwich to the Western Electricity Co in North Woolwich and to Siemens in Greenwich. The men were organized by their ex-NCOs and marched through the streets in military formation. Wyatt would then attempt to shame employers into taking men on, and at least at Siemens, persuaded himself that this demonstration was responsible for putting on an extra shift at the works. The district office ran a priority register for placing members as work became available. Webb was placing thirteen people a week by the end of 1923, but the cost of administering the scheme made it difficult to sustain. The unemployed members were organized into self-consciously political cadres, and were allowed to use the union's London offices: whether it helped them get work is hard to judge. The national officials and the London officials had co-operated in an imaginative way in the autumn of 1921. They complained endlessly to the chief electrical inspector that many government and public buildings were dangerous due to the state of the wiring. They involved the NFEA and NJICS to approach government and civic authorities direct. Rowan was invited on to a joint committee on the encouragement of the use of electricity which had on it representatives from the NJIC's for supply and contracting, the British Electrical Manufacturers Association, the Cablemakers and the Electrical Development Association. Even the London district committee did not mind tapping into Rowan's private network of contacts when Wyatt got the general secretary to ring the army generals concerned with Woolwich Arsenal to introduce new labour rather than continue with endless overtime. Jimmy Rowan was now truly a man of standing, having been made a Justice of the Peace at the end of 1920.

By the end of 1923, the worst was over and the union had survived as an institution. Membership rose by 3,000 in the following three years, and the Citrine-centralized finance reforms were finally taking effect. In 1925, a small balance of £25,349 had been built up, largely by restricting expenditure. Half-benefits continued to be paid, and branch secretaries' salaries were now fully paid on the basis only of the remittances they sent in. This had a side-effect of improving the veracity of the union's stated membership figures, as Jimmy Rowan dryly pointed out in his annual review for 1925. During the year 'quite a number of dead members were buried; it can be said that at the end of 1925, the shown membership was nearer the actual than for many years.'

However, if the union as an institution had survived, the road back for the members' standard of living from 1921 to 1926 was a long one.

Collective Bargaining in Retreat 1921–6

Reductions went on apace in 1922 outside the union's main industries as well. McLaughlin signed a sixteen per cent reduction with the Port of London Authority, and there was a small reduction signed with the Newspaper Proprietors Association (NPA). Comparatively, wages remained reasonable in Fleet Street. Electricians and AEU fitters were paid £5 10s 0d for a forty-four hour week on days and £7 0s 0d a week for a thirty-eight-and-a half-hour permanent night shift. Rotating shifts produced £6 15s 0d for a forty-two hour week. Bill Webb managed to talk the NPA out of increasing the hours of work and even persuaded them to concede an extra day's holiday.

Brother Farr of the Press branch stated that not only members of his branch, but of the AEU particularly wished him to express their very great appreciation of the work Brother Webb had put in on behalf of the Press men. He stated that the AEU men especially realize that they have to thank almost wholly the ETU delegates and officials for the rates and conditions that they are at present enjoying in the Press houses.

Bill Webb's popularity was also unassailable amongst his own members. In early 1923, he won the district secretaryship again by 1,323 votes to S. Edgell's 400 and Fred Alford's 189. Throughout this period, Webb took on the reputation of an informed, analytical negotiator – to add to his fearsome reputation in police circles as a dangerous revolutionary. He was untouched by the endless feuds over district committee finance and the scandal attached to the *Electron*. He made a formidable team with Rowan when negotiating on No. 10 DJIC for London supply workers.

However, the national picture showed little improvement for electricians in the main industries organized by the union. Cuts and more cuts were the order of the day in engineering and shipbuilding. By 1923, wages fell in shipbuilding to eighty per cent of their 1920 value in real terms. In engineering and construction as a whole, it was ninety-four per cent, but in electricity supply they were 107 per cent of their real value. Electrical contracting and electricity supply were both protected to a degree by sliding scale arrangements arrived at in the autumn of 1921. The English contracting members were protected, after the early cuts, by the formula that moved wages one per cent for every three points that the Board of Trade Cost of Living Index moved.

This produced rates for English contracting of 2s 3d for Grade 'A' in London, down to 1s 8¾d for Grade 'D's small towns and rural rate. At its lowest, in late 1923, the rates fell to 1s 8½d for Grade 'A' down to 1s 3¾d per hour for Grade 'D'. In February 1924, the road back started with the restitution of the two five-per-cent cuts made in 1921. Wages rose to 1s 10d for Grade 'A' and 1s 4¾d for Grade 'D'.

Things were much worse in Scotland. The Scottish ECA had withdrawn from the NJIC set-up. They imposed cuts with a cheerful ferocity, fully capitalizing on their smashing victory in the spring of 1921. They came back for a further 2d an hour off in August 1921 and refused a sliding scale arrangement, meetings or arbitration. They came back yet again to drive the rate down a further 2½d by February 1922 to 1s 7½d. There was nothing the union could do; Bob Prain reported to the executive that he 'pointed out to the employers, that without a doubt, they were using the present trade depression to impose upon our members reductions in wages which could not possibly be imposed in normal times; and the frequency with which these reductions were being made was also bitterly complained of.' Such truths did not alter the Scottish ECA's determination to press on. By May 1923, the rate was down to 1s 5d an hour. In September, they asked for it to go down to 1s 3d. Again, all the beaten union could do was complain piteously. 'The representatives of the union informed the employers that they could not recommend the proposals, but would submit them to the members concerned. They were further informed that their action in respect to wages had always been of a brutal character, and no doubt their attitude on this occasion would again embitter the men employed in the industry.' The union was paralysed in Scotland. Shipbuilding on the Clyde was devastated. The arrogant excesses of the Scottish ECA were taking cruel advantage of the collapse of the union's membership, throughout the country. A breakaway union, the Scottish Electrical Workers, recruited dissident contracting and shipyard men on the Clyde. By 1925, the union had organized a strike at Greenock to clear them out; the second part of the strategy was achieved only with difficulty as ex-members of the Scottish Electrical Workers made their reapplications to join the ETU. Many branches objected to the returnees. Tom Stewart was at the centre of fighting off what he described as the 'bogey' Scottish Electrical Workers. He must have been aware that the problem was merely a symbol of the ineffectiveness of the ETU in Scotland, where despite the strength of the electricity supply section of the union, the same could not be said of contracting, 'where the non-unionist question was acute'. By the end of 1925, Scottish membership had fallen to 2,150, compared to 5,926 at the end of 1920. Whole towns were not represented at all – Falkirk, Kirkcaldy, Cowdenbeath, Rosyth, Dunfermline – and the historic Glasgow branch at Parkhead was closed. If the union's fortunes in Scotland had taken a serious knock, in Ireland they were completely overwhelmed.

The background of the troubles associated with the Black-and-Tans and the birth of the Irish Free State rebounded on the union. Jack Ball showed his disgust in the union's journal at the tyranny visited by the British army on the people of Ireland. Twice, the union's Dublin branch meetings were invaded by soldiers, looking for Fenians. In July 1920, the union's membership was balloted nationwide on its support for a general strike to force the evacuation of the British army from Ireland. The members were not interested, by 5,640 votes to 1,408. Organization in Ireland disintegrated. The executive councillor, Jack Collins, resigned in August, saying he 'had no other course left owing to the action of the members on the question of withdrawal of the army of occupation and other matters.' The union's full-time official in Dublin, O'Duffy, was proved to be quietly transferring Dublin branch members into the Irish Engineering and Shipbuilding Union, but his salary was not stopped until just after Christmas 1920. The smaller branches of the union in Ireland – Dundalk and Cork – along with the cinema operators in Dublin moved over wholesale to other Irish unions. In October 1920, Jack Kinniburgh established that there were 220 members and fifty-four apprentices left in the whole of Dublin's three branches, with everyone refusing to pay levies and running up huge arrears of contributions. The leadership of the Irish Engineering and Shipbuilding Union were all, according to Kinniburgh, prominent ex-members of the ETU. No delegates were sent to the Irish TUC due to the 'unsettled' conditions. The inevitable happened in September 1921. The union closed down completely in Dublin, never to return effectively until the union's amalgamation with the plumbers in 1968 reintroduced the EETPU to Southern Ireland as the amalgamated union's Area No. 3.

Electricity supply, too, was protected to an extent by a sliding scale arrangement on basic rates. Here, $\frac{1}{2}$d an hour was taken off for every six point fall in the Board of Trade Cost of Living Index, revised every three months. By 1924, circumstances in the industry were moving the union's way. Technical improvements in power stations and sub-stations alike were halving the costs of each unit of electricity supplied, especially as '30–40,000 horse-power super-stations', as Rowan called them, became more common. He frankly recognized that it could lead to less men employed per location, but that it greatly strengthened the security of employment and the entitlement to higher wages for those who remained. It took months to progress a claim throughout the procedure. On 14 March 1924, the union applied for a 10s increase to every grade in the industry. This was refused, but referred to each DJIC. The claim was re-presented nationally and eventually, with conflicting strike mandates, six DJIC workers' sides voted for strikes and six voted against. It was therefore decided in December 1924 to accept certain concessions by the employers – particularly the suspension of the sliding scale agreement. In certain regions, the 10s advance was granted, in others nothing at all (but that was usually in those regions which had no cuts at all in 1923; the North-East Coast DJIC, in contrast, had lost twelve-and-a-half per cent off the rate in 1923). The whole negotiations took the best part of the year and were inconclusive if not detrimental to the members concerned.

A flavour of mid-1920s negotiations, though, is provided by Rowan's report to the executive of the special court he attended within the NJIC set-up to discuss the 10s application.

The court was public, and I can at once say I am of the opinion that from the point of view of getting increases in wages, these public exhibitions are useless. From a point of advertising they are good. On behalf of our side, I put up the application, which was fairly well received. Before the court started, I received through Brother W. Webb, London district secretary, a detailed copy of advances and reductions sharing the percentages between the fluctuations of wages and the cost of living in the London area. Before I received this, the five representatives of the workmen's side had come to the unanimous opinion that it would be unwise to call evidence, but in view of the expression of opinion of Brother Webb and Brother Morton, who had prepared this table, we agreed Brother Morton should be placed in the witness chair. He was the only witness called by our side.

The other side were represented by Alderman Walker, their chairman, followed by witnesses for their side. It can be said at once that the witnesses put up to oppose the claim nationally were of more service to us than they were to their own side. In fact, it reached such a pitch that Alderman Walker got up and complained to the court that we were building up *our* case on his witnesses. This was true, because they had access to figures that we could not possibly obtain.

Rowan was proud of one fact. Wages in supply were virtually the same as the contracting rates. These industries were dominated by the ETU – contracting exclusively so. Conditions were far worse in engineering and shipbuilding, where the nature of the EEF presented the forty-one unions in the industry with a formidable foe.

Rowan and Kinniburgh never forgot the humiliation of Penistone, which returned to haunt the union in the great dispute in engineering in the spring of 1922.

The AEU was interpreting the new overtime and nightshift agreement in a way that infuriated the EEF. The union told district committees that the clause that expressed the view that overtime should not be worked systematically and that no craftsman should work more than thirty hours a week, gave the union rights to say how much overtime should be worked in an attempt to absorb unemployed members. A handful of other manning disputes, and the AEU's insistence on stopping apprentices working at payment-by-results schemes, provoked the EEF into insisting that the management should impose whatever changes they liked, and the union should complain or negotiate the issues afterwards. In a ballot the AEU members rejected this. The EEF then promptly locked out the AEU nationwide on 11 March and rounded on everyone else, locking out the other unions on the same issue on 2 May. Rowan was furious. The issue had been provoked unilaterally by the AEU, and the other unions had to take or leave whatever arrangement Sir Allan Smith came to with the AEU. After the strikers returned in June, largely on the employers' terms, Rowan said 'it was a storm in a teacup between a single trade union and the EEF that should have been calmly settled months before the lock-out took place.' He thought it highly significant that in the next year after the dispute, there was not a single complaint raised by the EEF with the ETU on the rights of management to make decisions.

However, the effect of the dispute was to raise yet again a war between the executive and London. McLaughlin from the London district committee attended the FEST conference called to consider the lock-out in mid-May and urged the calling out of electricity supply, sewage and water workers in support of the locked-out engineers. He made blood curdling claims that the spread of 'epidemic disease' would bring the employers to heel. These remarks embarrassed Rowan, who missed this part of the meeting, and hastened the resolve of the FEST unions to vote, 30–19, not to extend the dispute and led to the General Workers deciding to accept the employers' memorandum!

It also finally put an end to the lingering hopes of a third ballot on amalgamation with the AEU, whom the executive blamed for the dispute and the huge financial crisis it plunged the union into for the second year running, leading directly to the suspension of all benefits in the summer of 1922. Jack Kinniburgh was also very disillusioned by the dispute.

A lot of exclusions from our ranks took place through the management functions dispute, and although we were informed by resolutions from some quarters that our engineering sections was boiling over with a desire to fight – and they were only kept back by the laxity of the officials – those of us who travelled the country had other opinions!

It coloured their assessment of the EEF. Jimmy Rowan wrote that the EEF:

... have probably the keenest and most intelligent men in the business world in Europe. In addition to this, they are certainly the meanest. In all their dealings, no sentiment is allowed to interfere with business, and the great aggregations of capital, such as Metropolitan Vickers, Armstrong-Whitworth and other groups, can only see justice through the coloured glasses of their capital issues.

Problems arose, then, in attempting to advance 'reasoned argument with this soulless body'. Negotiations were pointless. Although they were, in Rowan's view, 'conspicuously unsuccessful' in 1924–5, the union was pleased that no further decision on working hours, let alone wages, was allowed to take place. There was a further dimension to the frustration in engineering and shipbuilding, and that was the complete lack of mutual organization on the trade union side. The union's members voted, 2,012–1,629, to leave FEST in February 1923. The AEU insisted on working alone, and the enfeebled Federation, dominated by stricken general unions, no longer inspired the craft-based ETU. Rowan had no regrets. 'It has been made patent to the employers that there is no solidarity on the workers' side of these sections [of the union movement]. As a matter of fact, there is open hostility that has been advertised to the employers themselves.'

Amalgamation with the Enginemen, Firemen and Electrical Workers, 1923–4

In early 1924, the union balloted on yet another attempt at amalgamation. This time, they were trying to absorb the smaller but significant 22,000 strong Enginemen and Firemen's Society. After months of discussion on a suitable formula that paid sufficient attention to this union's largely semi-skilled membership, the ballot was held. The attraction for the ETU was that this union had a small number of craftsmen but a large proportion of semi-skilled power station workers in membership. Although there was no systematic branch abstention, like there had been with the AEU, once again the fifty per cent turn-out figures were not achieved. The enginemen and firemen voted, 6,033–3,081, for the amalgamation (forty-two per cent turn out) and the ETU membership voted positively in a low turn-out, 7,088–1,437 (twenty-nine per cent turn out). This was all the more galling when the enginemen and firemen linked with the Transport and General Workers' Union (TGWU) in 1925. The TGWU were to provide stiff rivalry in power industry recruitment battles for years to come. One last impact of the failure to amalgamate with the enginemen and firemen came at that year's 1924 rules revision conference when the union's contributions were actually reduced to 1s for skilled full benefit members and 6d for auxiliary members. High auxiliary contributions included unemployment benefit, which many thought a contradiction in terms. Low-paid workers like ETU auxiliaries and enginemen and firemen wanted a 'fighting union', so the argument ran, with low contributions and no benefits except strike pay.

Amalgamation with the Transport and General Workers Union 1925–6

This move in the mid-20s to abandon amalgamation with the craft-based AEU and turn to the enginemen and firemen, albeit with little success, reached its logical conclusion in extensive talks with Ernie Bevin's new giant TGWU. Jimmy Rowan had got to know Bevin personally when Rowan joined the general council of the TUC in 1924, elected at last, no doubt with TGWU support. Throughout 1925, the TGWU cropped up in the deliberations of the ETU. First, Rowan was with the general council of the TUC on 'Red Friday' – 30 July 1925 when the Government gave in to concerted threats of supporting action from other trade unions to support the miners if their subsidy was withdrawn by Baldwin's Government. Received wisdom is that the unions were ready to fight. Rowan privately wrote very differently about 'Red Friday'. His view of the Central Hall meeting concerned was that 'it was quite evident from the commencement of the proceedings that no demands for direct action would be received with favour, and the representatives of the general council who took part in the debate confined themselves to making a strong appeal for financial assistance ... to provide the sinews of war.' The ETU was ready to support the miners – despite the miners' extremely belligerent attitude in preventing the ETU organizing colliery electricians. The executive ordered members that night not to move or unload coal stocks in power stations and that all colliery electricians should place themselves under the instructions of the MFGB as to whether they continued to provide safety and maintenance services during any strike that materialized. With Baldwin's extension of the coal subsidy while the Samuel Commission looked at the demands for miners' pay reductions, that solidarity was not required. Yet.

Earlier that month, the ETU had been keen to join the new 'industrial alliance', dominated by the TGWU, which was going to provide real help to the unions concerned in the event of an attack by employers on any of them. The miners, railwaymen, transport workers, AEU, boilermakers and FEST were involved. Rowan attended the drafting committee for the constitution of the alliance; Bevin was the secretary. The lessons of Black Friday in 1921 had been learnt. There would be graduated industrial action in sympathy strikes for one of the signatory unions 'notwithstanding anything in [the unions'] agreements and constitutions to the contrary, and to act as directed by the general conference.' Jimmy Rowan reported to the membership in support of this new body: 'The suggested constitution was formed on very powerful lines, and, in the opinion of those intimately connected with the movement, should prove a tower of strength to the organized workers of the country.' The executive approved of the alliance; so did the members in a ballot declared on 23 August, 3,021–204.

In May 1925, the union's membership had decided to send the head office back to London by 3,507–2,354 votes. London was clearly where the leadership spent most of their time anyway, but for six years the union was to delay the move on the grounds of expense. In 1925, they could not afford suitable large houses in Hampstead in Maresfield Gardens or Wedderburn Road – £4,500 was too much for them. The City and the West End were right out. Their new friends in the TGWU offered the executive a suite of offices at their new headquarters in Smith Square, Transport House, at £650 per year. This was too expensive for the electricians. In April 1925, the TGWU had written to the ETU offering formal amalgamation talks, based on plans drawn up by TGWU Financial Secretary S. Hirst. These were discussed in the autumn of 1925 and made good progress – progress that was not halted when Ben Bolton discovered that Transport House was being wired up by non-union electrical contractors. This was put right by Ernie Bevin himself. By Christmas 1925, only two issues were left outstanding between the two unions. The ETU wanted to sustain unemployment benefit for its skilled members and wanted to continue to excuse unemployed members from paying contributions. Notwithstanding these 'minor' issues, the ETU negotiating team reported to the executive 'the approval of our side of the sub-committee at the exceedingly fair manner in which the TGWU had met our side.'

On 18 March 1926, the executive accepted the final amalgamation proposals, and a ballot was due in June with an executive recommendation to accept. The TGWU were offering the union a degree of autonomy as the Electrical Trades Group of the TGWU. The ETU had to pay T&G contributions, but to receive T&G Scale 'A' benefits, the ETU had to pay a lump sum to the T&G equivalent to thirty-nine weeks' contributions for the whole membership, approximately £32,200 on 1925 figures. (Given that the balance in the general fund at the end of 1925 was only £16,188, 'buying into' the TGWU was always going to be problematical.) The ETU group would then have to create a separate fund to provide unemployment, accident and funeral benefits. The political fund was to go straight into the TGWU fund, but the ETU affiliations would be honoured.

The officials of the ETU would do well out of it. They would all be guaranteed jobs by the TGWU at their current salaries until December 1927, when they would be reviewed. Even more attractive, the officials would benefit from the T&G pension scheme for full-time officials, a benefit that no ETU official then had. The union would continue separate affiliation to the TUC. Its influence, though, within the TGWU would be minimal. The Electrical Trades Group would have just one seat by guarantee on the TGWU general executive council. This body only met quarterly, with no guarantee of access to the much smaller Finance and General Purposes Committee which met more frequently. They had, though, access to the powerful general officials of the union like Ernie Bevin, the general secretary.

If the failure of the amalgamation of the ETU with the AEU in the early 1920s was one of the great 'ifs' of British Labour history, so was the failure of the ETU's proposed amalgamation with the TGWU. As we shall see, the General Strike in May 1926 ruined the finances of the TGWU, but devastated the already flimsy financial resources of the ETU. The two unions met in June 1926, when both realized that 'the financial arrangements suggested in the original document were now out of the question.' In both October and December 1926, the question was further deferred on financial grounds.

The ETU and the Labour Party

Towards the end of 1925, it is possible to discern an emerging pattern of political life within the union. We have already noted that F. E. Sims was present at the founding conference of the Labour Party, and that delegates were sent to the early conferences, finance permitting! Before 1914, the union tended to side with the radical 'new-unionists' within the conference in preference to the older skilled craft organizations. In 1903, Bill Gooday had seconded the defeated motion in favour of class-war as a basis for the Labour Party's activity. Jack Kinniburgh was frequently complaining about the lack of genuine political commitment by the parliamentary party. However, during the First World War, Rowan and Kinniburgh had used Labour's participation in the coalition government to exercise union influence. Political activity locally was equated with raising living standards in municipal employment. Direct works for local authorities were proof that the workers could do better than capitalists. Direct labour on Camberwell Library in June 1921 cost £510 compared to the cheapest private tender of £524. It also provided ninety-three electric points compared to eighty-five for that money, along with twice the number of switches at eighty-five, automatic power plugs and a heating radiator. This triumph was hailed by Charles Treanish, when he wrote in *Electron*: 'Direct labour will not in itself achieve the millennium, but will, in a small measure assist in undermining the structure of capitalism, whose collapse, to judge by the economic situation of today, is already overdue.'

The union had narrowly voted to endorse the political fund rules laid down by the registrar in 1913, when it became a legal requirement to separate out the political fund and allow members to opt out of paying if they wanted to. In December 1917, they voted in a twenty-one per cent poll, by 875 (fifty-seven per cent) to 653 (forty-three per cent) to spend the fund on supporting candidates for Parliament in what was clearly understood to be a referendum on the Labour Party performance in the House of Commons. The union's turn-out was low, and London West incurred the wrath of the executive for circulating the union against the use of the political fund for the Labour Party. Other skilled unions had fairly small turn-outs – the engineers had twenty-one per cent, with a sixty-two per cent to thirty-eight per cent majority; the carpenters had a thirty-six per cent turn-out, but voted less enthusiastically for the Labour Party by fifty-three per cent to forty-seven per cent. The miners had the largest turn-out at sixty-five per cent, but voted by precisely the same margin as the ETU (fifty-seven per cent to forty-three per cent) in favour of Labour. The gasworkers and the railwaymen were more emphatic (eighty-seven per cent to thirteen per cent and seventy-five per cent to twenty-five per cent respectively). The ETU's commitment, then, to Labour, was directly in the mainstream of trade union opinion, despite its own internal radical opposition. In 1918, Walter Citrine ran, unsuccessfully, as Labour candidate for Wallasey in the General Election. Joe Vaughan and Bill Webb both won LCC seats in London in 1922, for Bethnal Green and Rotherhithe respectively.

By 1925, one can see the results of this commitment. Two hundred and seventy-six branches were active in that year. Only eighteen failed to collect the 1s a year political contribution (equal to one week's contributions at that time – a level of contribution still the rule in 1989). A crude idea of the level of membership paying the political levy can be gained by looking at the 1925 political fund contributions which were marked separately on members' cards and collected in cash at the branches: £927 was collected, which equates to 18,540s. Given that Jimmy Rowan thought the 1925 membership figures of 29,241 were the most reliable in the union's recent history, it would seem that, making allowances for slovenly collection methods in the branches, something over sixty-five per cent of the membership were contributing to the political fund. However, if the overwhelming majority of branches were collecting money, only 150 branches out of 276 spent any money on politics at all. Each branch could spend political money on approved political causes – such as affiliation to the Local Party and supporting its candidates and campaigns – particularly for local government office. Fulham branch spent £21 18s 11d that year, and were the highest spending branch. Manchester Central spent £20 18s 7d. All the branches in Birmingham, Newcastle, Liverpool, Manchester and London spent money on political activity. There were some significant towns and cities that did not. Derby and Nottingham, the Lancashire branches in Burnley and Bolton, the Yorkshire branches in Huddersfield, Dewsbury, Doncaster and Leeds South all spent nothing.

The ETU and the Communist Party – a New Basis for Opposition

The real political change within the union in the years between the First World War and the General Strike was the emergence of political opposition to the leadership of the union centred on the British Communist Party and its associated organizations. The Communist Party was founded on 1 August 1920, dedicated to producing a revolution in Britain on the Russian model. As far as trade unions were concerned, the Communist Party had a clear view of what had to be done. Lenin had told them, in a letter to Sylvia Pankhurst in 1920:

It is essential for a Communist Party that it should be intimately and continuously associated with the mass of the workers, to take part in every strike, to answer all the questions which agitate the minds of the masses. This is above all necessary in a country like England, where so far ... the socialist movement and the labour movement in general have been exclusively guided by cliques drawn from the aristocracy of labour, persons most of whom are utterly and hopelessly corrupted by reformism, whose minds are enslaved by imperialistic and bourgeois prejudices. Without an uncompromising struggle against these elements, without the total destruction of their authority, without convincing the masses that these leaders are absolutely rotten with bourgeois ideas, there can be no question of a serious Communist Workers' Movement.

Under Lenin's instructions, the Communist Party was to attempt to affiliate to the Labour Party in order to ginger up its commitment to socialism, and work within the trade unions to do the same.

Some early British communists had favoured a separate principled distancing from 'reformist' trade unions, the Labour Party and Parliament. They were defeated by this early decision to enter the established unions from without in order to turn them towards revolution.

Three main bodies were set up by the Communist Party to advance their cause within the unions. First, during that dreadful depression of 1921–3, the National Unemployed Workers Committee was set up to propagandize on behalf of the unemployed. This body was given facilities by the union's London district office. More generally, communists organized separately in each individual union a campaign to get British unions affiliated to the Moscow-financed Red International of Trade Unions. The defence of the first workers' revolution in Russia, and the dissemination of world revolution after the Russian example, were key aims of the early communists. This 'international' was in contrast to the Social-Democratic 'reformist' International based at Amsterdam.

On 24 February 1921, the London district committee voted unanimously to affiliate to the Red International, with Bill Westfallen and Joe Vaughan moving and seconding the resolution. In March, they sent the London bureau of the Red International £5. On 28 April, Harry Pollitt, the boilermaker who became secretary of the Communist Party, addressed the London district committee, and the first signs of opposition appeared. Harold Morton 'protested against hearing Brother Pollitt, as he considered that the business on the agenda was of more importance to the members than an explanation as to the aims and objectives of the Red International.' Morton then walked out! The district committee could not have cared less, and invited Pollitt to speak to a conference of ETU branch delegates in London on 5 May. Already, eighteen branches were affiliated to the Red International in London. Predictably, the list included London South West, North West, Tottenham, Hackney and Brixton.

At its April meeting, the executive council moved quickly, acting on a complaint from Ernest Bussey's LSE No. 10 branch that the district committee had affiliated without balloting the members. The sub-executive had asked the branches nationally for 'an expression of opinion' and affiliation was opposed to eighty-nine branches and supported by fifty-three. The whole issue was referred to the 1921 rules revision conference in May, which was held in the midst of financial catastrophe and widespread industrial disputes involving thousands of the union's members. The conference voted 33–11 to hear a delegate from the 'Third International', despite protests from both Bussey and Morton. On the Thursday evening of the conference, the redoubtable general secretary of the ASE, Tom Mann, turned up to urge, not the cause of amalgamation with the ASE, but affiliation to the Red International.

Walter Citrine took the speech down in shorthand. Mann was quite clear what the Red International was for. 'Now that the Russians were taking the lines they were doing, we should all be willing and anxious to be identified with that great work.' A 360 delegate conference had met in London on 7 May, with local ETU men there. Mann thought that as the crisis in the engineering industry was international in context, the workers must organize similarly, and he was, 'personally of the opinion that this Russian revolution has come to stay, and it is just as true that it will extend right down therefrom until the whole of civilization is covered by it.' Several questions were asked – would sending a delegate to the Third International imply approval of the Russian Government? What was the attitude of the British Communist Party to the issue? Would sending a delegate imply opposition to parliamentary democracy? Mann replied in classic terms. He 'could not give the official attitude of the Communist Party' but 'it was true that the Communist Party was the only party taking an active part [in the coal strike] at the present time' and that affiliation 'would not mean that the ETU would be implicated as an anti-parliamentary body, but it would show that they were no longer relying on parliament as the agency whereby changes could be brought about.' Finally, Mann was of the view that 'the Communist Party did not attempt to dominate the industrial side, and there should be general harmony between the two. The object was to create revolution as speedily as possible, peaceably if possible, violently if necessary.'

On this menacing note, the special evening session of the conference finished with Rowan fulfilling the standards of the time by moving a vote of thanks to Tom Mann. The following morning, Bussey and Morton moved that the union did not affiliate to the Red International. Jock Muir, George Humphreys and the same G. H. Butler from Battersea, (whom national organizer Bob Ferguson had called an 'irresponsible extremist' back in 1908) all spoke in favour. Conference voted, 31–15, not to affiliate.

Even so, the London district committee took the union's banner to a Red International demonstration in Trafalgar Square on 3 July and by August 1921, forty-nine branches in London (out of a total of 101) were affiliated.

In early 1922, the executive banned the use of political funds for affiliation to the Red International, but still the London district committee took 'voluntary collections' in branches to send delegates (Westfallen, McLaughlin and Haskell) to the 14 January conference of the Red International. By 1924, activity on behalf of this body cropped up again when the executive slapped down the Plumstead branch for giving money to the Red International and again took the opinion of branches. Only thirty-eight bothered to reply, and the executive confirmed the branches 25–11 decision, with two indifferent, not to affiliate. Ben Bolton voted against this, showing that communist influence in London predominated, and it was not long before the London district committee voted to affiliate, in February 1925, to the recently founded Minority Movement. This was a more serious and direct domestic attempt to bend trade unions to the political cause of the Communist Party.

Seaman George Hardy was the acting secretary of the Minority Movement when he told the communist international body for organizing foreign trade union activity, the Comintern, in Moscow in March 1926, just what the current role of communists was within British trade unions. This speech provides the key to understanding the different, specialized and wholly determined attitude of communists within the trade unions. He was realistic enough to deal with unions as they were – small, weak, led with a lack of authority by the TUC, squabbling for members. 'It is only by our comrades and parties recognizing and carrying out the tasks in the trade union movement that we are able to gain influence amongst the masses. It is only by preparing our comrades to accept the smallest trade union position that we can ever expect to achieve anything.' The Minority Movement, in each union, was based on three types of organization. First, they recruited individual members. Second, they would persuade these members to get their trade union branches to affiliate and third, 'our Minority groups, organized round the communist nuclei in the factories, bringing in ever wider groups of workers, in order to strengthen ourselves at the very base of industry by building workshop Minority groups.' In the attempt to involve as many as possible, the Minority Movement steered clear of overt communist theorizing about the dictatorship of the proletariat in an attempt to bring the 'workers to us and consolidate them into a fighting organization'. All strikes, particularly unofficial ones were a good opportunity to harass the official trade unions from within. 'In the unofficial strikes that have happened, there is no question as to where the communists will be. They will be with the workers in their fight, official or unofficial, but the blame must be where it belongs, on the shoulders of the reactionaries, to strengthen our influence and weaken the bureaucracy of the trade union movement.' Care had to be taken not to weaken Minority Movement prestige through backing foolish unofficial strikes – but 'our problem is to gain influence in the trade union movement against the reactionary right-wing officials, to force them into official strike action wherever and whenever it is possible.' Organized electoral faction-fighting emerged in the ETU in just this way when Tottenham's Lyons openly organized branch nominations for Matt Greenwell and Joe Vaughan to run against Tom Stewart and Jack Kinniburgh in March 1922. In the search for good recruits, Hardy particularly singled out working with 'syndicalists', because, 'after all, the revolutionary industrial workers are far preferable material to work with to these apathetic workers who are vacillating on the outside of any movement ... with the revolutionary industrials we have much in common; yet all the time, we must point out the absolute necessity for a Communist Party.' They were conscious above all for the need to work within the existing movement and not isolate themselves outside. 'We are very careful in our agitation not to lead the working-class to believe that we are in favour of creating a separate organization.' Indeed, they were constantly supporting moves to give the TUC general council real authority in the movement. Starting with 'fraction' work in the branches, building factory groups, working in multi-union committees 'will help us break down the barriers of craft unionism which is so prevalent in the British trade union movement. This will lead to industrial organization becoming a fact.' By operating in this way, the Minority Movement sought to take political power for the Communist Party by mobilizing the industrial powers of individual unions, co-ordinated by a powerful TUC.

George Hardy's speech, widely distributed in 1926 by the old 'reactionary' seamen's leader Havelock Wilson, is interesting for several reasons. It shows clearly just how the Communist Party set out to achieve its aims through work in the trade unions. In 1924, the Labour Party refused the Communist Party's application for affiliation and tried to prevent communists from standing as Labour candidates. The ETU executive voted against banning trade union delegates who were communists from being delegates at Labour Party conferences and also voted to allow Fleet Street branch to send Joe Vaughan £5 for his Bethnal Green council election because, although he was a communist, he was also in the Labour Party. Bill Minor, the Welsh and Midlands executive councillor, voted against both propositions, along with Tom Corbett, the Barrow-based Liverpool and Lancashire executive man.

The branch secretary at Fulham, C. J. Stark, resigned in April 1925 due to pressure on him from branch members to pay money to the Minority Movement, and after considering this and other examples of branch financial support, the executive voted, 5–3, in December to ban branch affiliation to the Minority Movement. Scotsman Morrison and Londoners Westfallen and Humphreys were the Minority Movement supporters.

Throughout the union, the Labour Party was supported in the first Labour Government of 1924, when it took office without power in a minority government. When the Government fell in the autumn of 1924, the left-led London district committee was true to its pro-Labour lights, even if it was more inspired by Harry Pollitt's desire for Communist Party affiliation than Ramsay MacDonald's social democracy. A circular issued to all branches on 23 October 1924 read:

The attention of members is drawn to the importance of the General Election and every member who has the right to vote should exercise that right and in their own interests should vote straight for the Labour Party. The actions of the Labour Party whilst in office may not have been altogether what we have desired, but they certainly have attempted to do something in the interests of the working-class movement.

Political battle lines were drawn within the union by the end of 1925. A conventional, if radical support for the Labour Party tradition was to be confronted by the largely London-led communist conspiracy. Activist loyalties became obvious, and policy choices predictable, depending on their position in the political faction fight. Decades were to pass before this political inspiration was to be relegated to tolerable levels of influence within the counsels of the union.

The financial uproar constantly attached to the London district committee was less a matter of personal corruption – although the casual approach to expenses and borrowing from one fund to support another sometimes suggests something pretty close to corruption: it was essentially a question of political attitude. Swashbuckling struggle with every last penny deployed behind a fighting working-class would be contrasted with the bureaucratic rule-making of the executive. It was no better when each branch sent a delegate to the district committee: they remained political rallies of up to sixty-five delegates. In such gatherings, faction politics emerged between the leading station engineer branches (who resented their power being used at the drop of a hat in every sympathetic action dreamed up by the communist supporters on the district committee) and the majority group dominated by active and committed men of the Red International. Every contemporary issue was forced into this political strait-jacket, bearing in mind the left's ceaseless concern to expose the national leadership as craven and defensive. NJICSs would have been rendered useless without Harold Morton's stirring defence of them against the revolutionaries who could not bear the idea of small success in the here and now disrupting their helter-skelter progress to the final revolutionary moment. The whole idea of craft, skill and excellence in the work itself was alien to the London leadership whose priorities in everything were highly political. Not everyone enjoyed this. Throughout the period, anything up to thirty-three per cent of London branches would not contribute to the full-time official funds that produced such wholly fanatical men as Wyatt and McLaughlin, along with more balanced but ferocious political men like Bill Webb and Matt Greenwell. The hatred could reach farcical depths. In May 1921, after the district committee had been accused of over-spending on stationery, they were instructed to obtain their cheaper duplicating paper from head office. When it was used by the particular duplicator in the London office, the printed results were a mauve smudge. Walter Citrine, arguably the greatest mind produced in British unions this century, wrote back to the London district committee when he saw these minutes, to accuse the London officials of deliberately smudging the paperwork in order to make an issue of it in London and thereby discredit the executive council! Much more serious, but still indicative of the profound political distance between the executive and London was the setting up in February 1922 of a separate station engineers' sub-committee of the London district committee. The full committee fought it, but the executive imposed it eventually, to the delight of the majority of non-revolutionary power workers. The district committee had 'authority' over the station engineers' sub-committee, subject to executive council approval. Further requirements were demanded of them. 'It must be understood that the London district committee have no power to call strikes or instruct members to cease work without first carrying out the rules, *viz. ...*' a shop question to be balloted by members in the shop – but a general question must be balloted across the whole district. Local or sectional disputes had to be put before the station engineers sub-committee before it went to the full district committee. If the sub-committee and the full committee disagreed, the executive council would adjudicate. Only the station engineer branches would elect the seven-man station sub-committee. This agreement helped modify the worse excesses of the use of station engineers after the disastrous 1921 Greenwich strike.

ETU Elections in the 1920s – First Signs of Concern

Throughout this whole period a growing concern for the executive was the state of the union's democratic processes. As the membership grew larger, it had become much less involved in the union. There never was a golden age when all the members went to every branch meeting and participated in every ballot. However, with determined and deliberate revolutionaries in power in London, the executive council issued in April 1922 a discussion document on the union's own democracy which shows quite clearly the leadership's concern that low participation led to the hi-jacking of the union by political factions.

They looked at balloting systems. The union could send ballot papers direct to members by post. They could then vote at the branch. Or perhaps, if the union also enclosed a stamped addressed envelope, the member could send his ballot back direct. (This was actually done in Southampton in January 1921. Two branch secretaries were candidates for the district full-time officer, and in order to avoid natural suspicion if the two candidates were distributing the ballots, the district committee organized a ballot and for a stamped addressed envelope to be sent to each member and returned to the district committee. They were told this was too expensive and out-with the rules and that they were not to do it again.) The 1922 executive discussion paper suggested it might be possible to get shop-stewards to distribute ballots at work or simply to collect them from members. Or they could just issue ballots to those who attended specially-summoned meetings.

Their main criteria were valid. 'It should be remembered that the object of the ballot is to allow members to register their votes secretly, and to obtain an accurate record of the views of the members.' Even though all other unions just let people vote only at meetings, [that method] 'had the difficulty that it disenfranchises those members who cannot attend such meetings.' However, all the other methods were open to corruption, or, if they involved individual postal ballots, would be too expensive for a union on the verge of bankruptcy. This debate was held in the columns of the anti-executive London-based

Electron. LSE No. 6 branch wrote into the magazine, echoing the executive's concern: 'Many members think that the postal ballot is the most democratic manner in which to ascertain the verdict of the members, especially as a large number of members are prevented by work from attending the branch.' Average turn-outs in London elections rarely exceeded twenty-five per cent of the membership, but 'others argue this method places a veto in the hands of the "deadheads".' The branch correspondent 'L M' knew what the priority ought to be. 'The confidence of the rank and file will only be retained by giving to each the knowledge that he will receive the same power of registering his opinions as another.'

After receiving a derisory number of replies on the subject in the following month, the union confirmed its 1914 election system of special meetings with an allowance for shift workers and travelling men. They had to apply to the branch secretary for a ballot to send back to him by post. He in his turn was obliged to provide the branch scrutineers with his membership figures, the numbers of those voting at the meeting and the numbers and names of postal votes distributed and received. This honest but inconclusive attempt to improve the union's democracy was clearly taken in response to the crude wrecking of the AEU amalgamation ballots and the abuse of strikes without ballots. There was a political need to balance the left control of London with high participation in other regions to maximize the provincial and largely non-revolutionary vote in the union. In the executive council elections at the end of 1923, 110 out of the union's 280 branches did not take part in the election at all. It was going to be decades until postal balloting would take a firm hold of the union's election tradition. In the meantime, the flawed process of election and ballot malpractice would corrupt the union.

The Death of Jack Kinniburgh, 1925

There was in 1925 a human tragedy that the union could do nothing about. On Sunday, 19 April 1925, Jack Kinniburgh died, aged forty-eight. At the executive on 2 May, Jack Ball read a prepared speech on this dreadful event, which was minuted in its entirety. Clearly moved, Ball told the executive council:

Brother Kinniburgh is dead ... whose fierce, free spirit and thunderous voice from many a platform stirred the sluggard blood to life and action, now lies cold and calm in an untimely grave. . . . Beneath his somewhat rugged exterior, he carried the warmest of hearts ... his Bohemian temperament never learnt to store up treasures on earth. . . . The members will miss him as no man has ever been missed before. Farewell, brave Brother Jack Kinniburgh. May the blessing of whatever God there be, rest upon thy soul.

Ninety branches, six district committees and dozens of other unions, employers and NJICs sent in their condolences. The executive granted his widow one full year of Jack Kinniburgh's salary, which was entirely unprecedented from a union that did not even give its officials a pension.

Eight branches complained about this, largely left-wing branches from London. Among them was Brixton branch, whose secretary, Condon, moved the London district committee's apparent condolences when first they heard the news. These people were ignored. The judgment on Kinniburgh by his contemporaries can only be supported. He organized and recruited more towns and more industries than any other single member of the union, before or since. He was an inspirational speaker and hugely popular as a man to be with when the smokers were on and the picnics needed a guest of honour. There remains some difficulty about his politics. Jimmy Rowan's note of appreciation said he had been a member of the SDF since he was fifteen. Jack Kinniburgh himself wrote in June 1909, explaining his frustration with the Labour Party in Parliament that: 'In conclusion, allow me to say that I hope no member of the Independent Labour Party will want my life for the great offence of criticizing the Labour Party, because I would remind them that I was a member at the beginning.' A member of what? Certainly, he was ever-critical of Labour's cautious performance in Parliament. However, Kinniburgh moved away from his pre-First World War syndicalist stance; it is probable that his personal experience of the spitefulness of the London district committee and his own success in getting things done through NJICs mellowed his views somewhat. He remains one of the giants of the ETU.

12

THE GENERAL STRIKE, 1926

On 'Red Friday', 30 July 1925 the Government had prevented a miners' strike by subsidizing miners' wages with £23 million, pending an inquiry chaired by Sir Herbert Samuel into the coal industry's problems. The Samuel Commission reported on 10 March 1926 that 'we came reluctantly, but unhesitatingly, to the conclusion that the costs of production, with the present hours and wages, are greater than the industry can bear.' With seventy-three per cent of coal produced at a loss, 'the way to prosperity for the mining industry lies along three chief lines of advance: through greater application of science to the mining and using of coal; through larger units of production and distribution; through fuller partnership between employers and employed.' Samuel said that the employers were justified in their demand that the national minimum wage must fall – 'not a permanent lowering of wage standards, but a temporary sacrifice by the men in the industry, other than the worst paid, in order to avoid the possible unemployment of hundreds of thousands of them.' The miners had been promised support in the summer of 1925 by the emerging industrial alliance, of which the ETU was an enthusiastic part. It now demanded support of the General Council of the TUC, whose role as the 'general staff' of the trade union movement now led everyone to expect it to lead significant disputes of this nature. The miners were determined not to allow any wage cuts or any increase in hours worked. The subsidy was due to run out on 30 April 1926.

A special conference of trade union executives was called for Thursday 29 April at the Farringdon Hall in London. The sub-executive council attended for the ETU. Jimmy Rowan was on the general council of the TUC, so the delegation was composed of Jack Ball, Ernie Irwin, Bob Prain and Matt Greenwell. Arthur Pugh, the president of the TUC, described the problems arising out of the Samuel report. Although the Commission had said that wage cuts and extensions of working hours were necessary, they should not be imposed before the industry had reorganized itself into more productive and efficient units, as outlined in the bulk of the report. The General Council – or its Industrial Committee (of senior TUC men) – intended to negotiate further in an attempt to persuade the coal-owners and the Government behind them not to reduce wages instantly and thereby precipitate disaster.

On Friday, 30 April, the conference re-convened at 11 a.m. The day dragged on as negotiations continued. The delegates waited. Bob Prain wrote that weekend: 'The delegates stuck to their places with a grim determination to see the matter through and to show the other side that they were prepared to stay on all night if required to do so. The time was passed with song and story, the delegates providing some really fine turns.'

All this was forgotten when the Industrial Committee returned just after midnight. Jimmy Thomas of the railwaymen said that the Government's refusal to do anything, and their insistence that the miners took a reduction before any other reforms were considered, was a declaration of war. Ernie Bevin, the TGWU general secretary, then presented the delegates with the General Council's recommendations for co-ordinated action. He asked the executives to consider them carefully; as the time was 1.30 a.m., it was decided to re-convene the conference the following day, Saturday 1 May, at noon. The sub-executive of the ETU then met the following morning before the re-convened conference and endorsed the TUC proposals. These required various industries to stop work 'as and when required by the General Council'. The tactic was not to all come out at once, but to steadily draw more and more industries out so that the Government could gauge the depth of purpose in the movement, its solidarity, its determination. Transport, the press, iron and steel, metal and heavy chemicals and all building workers (except housing and hospital work) would be in the first 'wave'. There should be no interference with sanitary or health services, but 'the General Council recommend that the trades unions connected with the supply of electricity and gas shall co-operate with the object of ceasing to supply power. The Council requests that the executives of the unions concerned shall meet at once with a view to formulating common policy.' The whole thing was to be co-ordinated under TUC control, with all the unions, including the miners, placing their powers in the hands of the General Council and pledging to follow TUC instructions. The sub-executive went into the re-convened conference at just after noon, and a dramatic roll-call took place of unions pledging their powers to the General Council in acceptance of the paper put before them the previous night.

A note of nervous humour was raised when the first union to so pledge itself was the National Union of Asylum Workers. The ETU voted with the enormous majority to back the miners.

The full executive council met at the Shaftesbury Hotel at 10 a.m. on Sunday 2 May. 'It was generally recognized that never before in the history of the trades union movement had the country been faced with such a decision as that reached at the conference and the ultimate consequences could not be foreseen by any man.' They elected three representatives to be the ETU men on the TUC sub-committee for the gas and electricity industries. Joining representatives of the plumbers, the engineers, the general and municipal workers, the enginemen and firemen's section of the TGWU and the Workers Union were Jimmy Rowan, Bill Westfallen (fresh from his enormous victory in an election as the latest London district official) and Harold Morton. Morton alone voted against giving the General Council powers of control. He was to say in July 1926, in a letter to Rowan, that the TUC's leadership of the strike 'shows that any future possibility of united action is doomed before it starts'. Throughout that day, the executive were in session until 7.30 a.m., waiting for Rowan to pop backwards and forwards from TUC headquarters in Eccleston Square. They eventually dispersed to their divisions and sent the general officials back to the Manchester head office to co-ordinate matters, leaving Rowan and the two London executive councillors, Westfallen and Morton, to deal with the TUC electricity and gas sub-committee.

Bob Prain sent out 286 telegrams at 11.45 a.m. on Monday 3 May, attaching copies of the General Council document, with the clear intention of telling all members to wait for TUC instructions.

The committee representing the power workers in London covered by the DJIC No. 10, over Jim Memberry's signature, issued the following, also on 3 May:

> The General Council of the TUC have instructed all electric power house employees to remain at work until further instructions from the TUC. If electricity is used for power purposes, it must be reported to the committee sitting at the Workers Union offices at 12a Anchor Street, Piccadilly. The only power men to cease work are: Lots Road, Neasden, Greenwich, Dumsford Road and Stonebridge Park [the tram and railway generating stations].

The London district committee was not going to be held back by any concept of staged pressure building on the Government. This was the moment. They were going to make the best of it. Bill Webb, on behalf of the district committee, wrote to every branch secretary and shop-steward in London. This letter was endorsed by the Committee the following day. It read:

> On the instructions of the General Council of the TUC and YOUR EXECUTIVE COUNCIL, every member of the ETU must cease work at 12 midnight, tonight, Monday May 3 1926. . . . No member of the ETU must remain at work unless he has the written consent of the London district committee to do so. The London district committee rely upon the loyalty of its members upon this momentous occasion. EVERYONE *MUST* CEASE WORK.

No mention here of waiting for TUC instructions concerning the generality of power stations – 'everyone must cease work'! By the morning of 4 May, the London district committee was issuing and denying work permits. Bermondsey Borough Council were allowed to feed their hospital from an auxiliary set on the agreement of the borough engineer to let a jointer take out the link to the remainder of the local supply. Liberty and Company, and the Associated Press and the PLA sub-station in the Albert Docks were refused cover for their pumps. Throughout the country, the strike was enthusiastically supported. In Birmingham, a poor place for organizing, Walter Lewis, the district secretary, was surprised at the response by members and non-members alike. The tramways came out instantly. Cadbury, Dunlop, BSA, GEC and the Railway Carriage Works were among the big manufacturing concerns that went on strike, although smaller shops, already on short-time, were not so keen. The Wolverhampton and Coventry power stations came out, although the Birmingham men were not withdrawn until two days before the strike ended. There was extra excitement in Birmingham when the police raided the union's offices in Corporation Street and arrested the ten-man emergency committee, including Walter Lewis, and all were fined £10 by local magistrates for public order offences. Lewis must have looked back on this episode with amusement in later years when he was Mayor of Birmingham and a senior manager in the newly-nationalized electricity supply industry.

On the Clyde, there was great unity in the engineering and shipbuilding centres, but twenty-eight out of thirty-six wiremen and winders employed at the Coplawhill Car Works for Glasgow Corporation Tramways went back to work four days before the strike ended.

Nevertheless, the trackway linesmen and the subway electricians stood firm. The position was 'absolutely solid' in Edinburgh, where executive councillor Morrison led 'nine wonderful days of amazing solidarity, splendid comradeship, and what enthusiasm!' according to the local branch reporter to the union's journal. Manchester was 'blackleg free', although brother V. Leigh of Manchester Central lost £2 10s 0d when his insurance company refused to compensate him fully for damage to his motor-cycle while riding as a courier for the local strike committee. The executive told him to get the money from the Manchester district committee.

New district secretary on the Mersey, George Chadwick, was delighted.

The response from all sections on the Mersey was extraordinary, despite all the difficulties presented by the absence of transport and press and communication. In many instances, our members who may have been in doubt as to whether they were actually affected, ceased work in order to be sure; one could not have wished for a greater exhibition of loyalty than that which was displayed.

Throughout Wales, the striking electricians were particularly solid especially in the area round Swansea. However, the colliery electricians striking alongside the miners were denied access to the relief funds collected in some parts of South Wales. In Glynneath, the local miners only allowed the electricians one meal per day. Frank Johns, district secretary, put this right and later uncovered a contracting employer putting about rumours that he, Frank Johns, was offering to supply strike breakers – but no one took it seriously. Further curious behaviour by employers was revealed by the Manchester Electricity Committee. J. T. R. Eadington, the secretary of Manchester Station Engineers and a founding member of the local Minority Movement, was astonished when his members received congratulations from the Electricity Committee for not going on strike. They were simply not called out: the strike was so comprehensive in the city that it was not necessary to strike the power stations as well. Yorkshire district secretary Penrose had a lively time being transported everywhere on the back of Leeds Central member J. Mason's motor-bike. The whole West Riding was solid, as was Sheffield, once they got started. They held a mass meeting on Saturday 8 May, at the Trades Hall in Charles Street to elect a twenty-four member strike committee. The delay was due to the impossibility of members travelling from outlying districts, so the early action was taken on the instructions of district secretary Albert Oates. The iron and steel industries were effectively stopped and, as elsewhere, strict picketing shifts instituted.

There was one major source of concern throughout the strike – electricity supply, particularly in London. The General Council policy was to allow the supply of electricity for public and private lighting, sanitary, health and food services. Jimmy Rowan told the sub-executive in his first post-strike private assessment of the strike on 23 May that this provided the main difficulty.

The dispute had been in operation for fully a week before the fact could be impressed upon the people concerned that it was an utter impossibility to separate the supply of power from lighting. The matter was further complicated by the fact that due to blackleg labour being introduced on trams, many men employed in electricity supply in the provincial towns resumed work in the generating and sub-stations.

Bob Prain had tried to get some guidance on the point about separating light and power from Citrine at the TUC – who after all ought to have understood the problem if anyone did! Citrine admits in his memoirs that this distinction was causing problems amongst people who might be on strike themselves and thinking power workers supplying light had it easy.

The enthusiasm for the strike in the London ETU produced many problems. On 5 May, Bill Webb had presented local municipal and private company stations in London with the news that all power stations would stop at 3 p.m. that day, if they did not agree to isolate the public lighting and prevent the supply of power to industry and commerce. A handful of Labour authorities said yes. West Ham, Battersea, Poplar, St Pancras, Bermondsey, Woolwich and Walthamstow all agreed to supply only to 'essential services'. In Stepney, Clement Attlee, MP, was chairman of the Borough Electricity Committee, and he handed over to the workers at the generating station the responsibility for making sure no unauthorized electricity was used outside the lighting and hospital service. (Spiteful court action was taken by a local company against Attlee for this, and he was fined £300 – an imposition only removed on appeal in 1928.)

On 7 May, all other stations in London were told to stop work, in line with Webb's instructions two days before. Bob Prain's assessment on 9 May of the result of this was brutally frank. 'Immediately this was done, naval ratings were brought into the stations, and these ratings, along with the EPEA, have managed to carry on as if nothing had happened.' Exactly the same thing happened in Newcastle. Paul McArdle, the district secretary, reported that 'the company manned the stations with staff from their offices, including members of the EPEA, with the result that they ran the service as usual ... again, there were many cases where men had come out on strike, joined up with the special constables, and in some instances were sent back to their own job to work!'

Halfway through the strike, London and the executive found new grounds for their customary disagreements. The sub-executive was anxious because the London district committee had not followed the General Council's cautious approach over strikes in power stations. The sub-executive wrote to the London district committee on 9 May, requesting London to 'loyally carry out the decisions arrived at and the instructions issued by the TUC General Council'. Rowan had been personally embarrassed. He said on the ninth to the sub-executive council: 'There was a very fine spirit throughout the whole of the trades unions employed in electricity and gas ... [but] a good deal of resentment had been shown at the actions taken by the ETU, in many cases without consultation with the General Council and in some cases actually against their instructions.'

Bill Webb was not having any of that. He wrote back on 11 May:

I have been instructed by the committee to draw the attention of the sub-executive council to the fact that Brother Rowan himself was present at a meeting of the London district committee on Tuesday evening last (4 May) when the whole circumstances of the committee had the full support of Brother Rowan. In addition, Brothers Webb and Westfallen were associated with Brother Rowan during the whole of last week and he knows how thoroughly the London district committee disagreed with the weak and vacillating attitude taken up by both the advisory committee [of which Rowan was the chairman] and the General Council. The London district committee sent a deputation to the central strike committee and told them how they disagreed with their policy. In conclusion, I have been instructed to draw your attention to the instructions issued by the General Council calling A GENERAL STRIKE for 12 o'clock midnight on Monday 3 May 1926.

Yours fraternally

W. J. Webb

The problem of the EPEA was now extremely serious. Rowan loathed the EPEA – and had done so ever since they were put up by the employers at the committee on production in 1917–18 to prevent the ETU extending its influence into the technical grades in power supply. Throughout the 1920s he would draw attention to their apparent preference for status and hierarchy over decent wages and their willingness to support the employers in supply against the bona fide trade unions in the industry. Rowan wrote of them at the end of May:

... this association has shown itself at last in its true character – namely, a blackleg agency. In the recent 'general' strike, they issued a detailed series of resolutions which could leave no doubt in the minds of anyone as to their intention. For instance 'the essential public services in connection with the supply of electrical energy should be maintained'. Again, 'the Association deprecates the introduction of volunteer workers into the electricity supply industry, but in the present emergency, this executive committee agrees that to maintain the essential public services it hereby instructs its members to co-operate in the government scheme for the maintenance of such services.'

Rowan urged everyone concerned 'to treat them for just what they are – employers' satellites'.

There were many other casualties during the general strike. The Sheffield annual district dinner had to be cancelled, and much trouble was caused by trying to trace just who had bought tickets in order to refund them their money. Strikes by electricians at the power station near the *Daily Herald* offices, where the TUC's official paper, the *British Worker*, was published, meant that the TUC's own strike bulletin had to be produced with 'black' electricity supplied by naval ratings and volunteers! The *British Worker* cast something of a spell over the ETU. The electricians who worked on it were supposed to pay their wages into a strike fund. Not one of them did, and in July the five who still hadn't paid up were fined £2 each by the branch.

On Wednesday evening, 12 May, the sub-executive met to consider the implications of the telegram from the TUC instructing affiliates to return to work. The General Strike was over. Members were told to return as soon as possible on 13 May. The disappointment was intense throughout the union, and not just amongst those who hoped that the General Strike would lead to the overthrow of Baldwin, the Tories and the whole capitalist system. Jimmy

Rowan gave sanguine leadership in the weeks after the strike. As a General Council member and long-time colleague of Citrine's, he knew what had happened on all sides. On 23 May, he told the executive that:

... it was quite evident that very strong efforts were being made by certain members of the General Council to reach a solution of the difficulty at any cost and reports were continually being received by the General Council of large numbers of men who were returning to work, particularly on railways. On the Tuesday before the strike was terminated (11 May) information was received that over 80,000 workers who were in dispute had resumed work in London alone.

He was genuinely sympathetic to the view that when Herbert Samuel came back from holiday and suggested a formula for ending the lock-out and continuing the Government subsidy, the TUC were entitled to believe he was acting with a nudge and a wink from Baldwin.

The General Council were definitely assured by the negotiating committee that the letters to and from Sir Herbert Samuel and the memorandum of the terms of settlement, which were submitted to the General Council, would be accepted by the Government, and that providing the General Strike would be declared off, the lock-out notices would be withdrawn. Had this been done, then the object for which the strike was called would have been achieved, because the strike was called on account of the owners posting notices to lock out men unless they accepted longer hours and reduced wages.

Certainly Ernie Bevin thought this to be true. Rowan quoted his letter to the miners, 'the terms of the memorandum were put forward to the General Council and finally accepted by the Government as a basis for negotiations'. Either the negotiating committee wilfully misled the General Council or the Government and Baldwin confused the issue sufficiently for misunderstanding to creep in. Or Baldwin simply ratted on a deal.

Jimmy Rowan had one last aspect of the strike to dwell on, when he wrote in January 1927:

Nearly everyone has been more or less obsessed with the inquest into the reasons for the General Strike, and also the reasons for the calling off of the General Strike. There have, however, been so many reports, including even two in this number, [of the journal] that not much further need be said except as to the future. In the past the miner, or to be more accurate, the coal-getter, has been a very selfish person. Originally, his work was of the most arduous character. Inventions and science came to his aid, not because the coal-owner worried about the coal-getter, but because he found out that invention would increase his profits, and from time to time machinery was introduced until today the coal can be said to be mined, raised, and distributed by machinery. During the whole of this evolution the miner did not move forward, but always kept to the slogan that there was only so much money to be got out of a ton of coal, and if any of the interlopers, such as mechanics, electricians, etc., got any more money, it must be at the expense of the miner. Thirty years ago a ton of coal sold for 10s; it now sells for 50s, but the miner got no more out of a ton of coal despite his slogan. A most absurd one, and probably one of the principal reasons why the miner has been through so many tribulations. The ETU have been especially hard hit on account of the fact that electricity has been one of the principal aids toward labour saving in the mines. The remarkable thing is that during this evolution the miners insisted (very often by brute force) in preventing any real efforts being made towards improving the condition of the electricians employed in and about mines; in fact, in some areas they placed electricians on the labourers' scale of pay, and when the electricians organized, to obtain a wage commensurate with their skill, they were met with concerted opposition from the MFGB. One of the results of the late dispute has been to bring publicity upon this sort of thing, and it is now definitely certain that the varying sections employed in the mining of coal will require to be treated better in the future than they have been in the past, and towards this end the Miners' Federation will have to alter its prehistoric methods or expect further opposition, not only from employers, but from their fellow-workers.

The aftermath of the strike hit the union hard. The union entered the strike with around £25,000 in assets and cash. They had nearly 15,000 members on strike at some stage over the nine days. Between 10 May and 1 June, the union paid out £18,222 in strike pay alone. They paid every member who was on strike for at least six days one week's strike pay of 12s. This resulted in lost membership in the railway workshops where the NUR paid strike pay of 24s per week. Many men were victimized – over 500 were not taken back by the end of the month. The union paid victimization benefit initially to them all. However, their average wages of £3 6s 0d each were hard to sustain, particularly as the TUC voluntary fund was not going to contribute. The union's own voluntary levy raised a pathetic £732 7s 5½d nationwide.

The London district committee were playing fast and loose with the money once again. Each member of the district committee was entitled by rule to strike pay (12s a week) and 1s a day picket/committee fees. The London district committee paid themselves nine days' 'strike committee fees' of 1s per day. They added to that nine days' 'food allowances' at £2 5s 0d a day, plus three committee attendance fees at 5s each and three food allowances at the committee at 5s each, making a total pay out for nine days of £4 4s 0d each!

The problem of victimization was acute and serious. To start with, the 1924 conference had reduced auxiliary contributions to 6d and consequently abandoned unemployment benefit for them. Motherwell branch were plagued with men who were victimized or made unemployed by the strike, who were denied state benefit because they had been involved in the General Strike. The branch secretary wrote that his branch 'were of the opinion that some of the sympathy which has been extended to the miners should be extended to these particular auxiliary section members'. London station engineers were appalled by the particular ferocity of municipal supply companies. They took men back, but ignored their previous service which entitled them to higher pay. Brother J. Cousins, with twenty-eight years' service, saw his wages fall from £5 1s 6d a week to £4 3s 9d. The job of the full-time officials was unenviable in the months after the strike: begging for men's jobs back, being unable to prevent petty vindictiveness, watching loyal members penalized.

Typical of dozens of contemporary reports is this one of Tom Stewart, national organizer, working in Aberdeen at the end of June 1926.

As you are aware, there are eighteen of our members who have not yet been started since the General Strike. These men were employed in the generating station, and have several years' service to their credit, but Mr Bell, the city engineer, has selected the men who had to get their jobs back. Aberdeen made a good show during the strike, every man came out, and it had been arranged that every man would go back as they came out, otherwise there would be no resumption of work. However, Mr Bell had to be taken into consideration and the game he played by sending letters to individuals broke down the resolution the men arrived at, hence the rotten position today. I have had the greatest difficulty I have ever experienced in getting an interview with Mr Bell, and he only saw me out of courtesy knowing that I came from Manchester. My interview was of short duration – only lasting a few minutes. He told me very plainly that he would not discuss anything with me, and as I represented the men in question, I could go and find them work. There is no use in going into details of what I said to him, but he will have a rough passage on Monday at the council meeting. I have interviewed all the Labour members and put our case before them, and one of them who is on the electricity committee had a kick up with Bell on Friday afternoon, because he would not discuss the matter with an accredited trade union official. I have done all that is possible, and the men are quite satisfied that I can do no more, unless those who are started are prepared to strike again. I am of the opinion that the matter has been too long in being dealt with to be able to influence the men in that direction. The members don't blame the union in any way; they are quite satisfied with our efforts on their behalf and are now awaiting the action of the Labour group on Monday.

Rowan's final judgment on the General Strike was published in June 1927, in the executive's annual report to the members. He thought that the mistake was calling a 'partial' strike, not an all-out strike from the start; that the miners should have accepted the discipline of following the General Council, as everyone else had to. For the union in the future, it showed that neither negotiations alone or sheer power alone was enough. The one must be supported by the other. The General Strike cost the union £22,956 in strike and victimization pay and £13,365 in unemployment pay, despite having to suspend benefits yet again. It left the union with the paltry sum of £4,089 as a balance, which covered up a deficit position in which the branch and head office benevolent funds were owed £5,600 and the TUC were owed £2,000. Still the abiding memory was of solidarity, the commitment, the comradeship. 'It is to our credit that we entered whole-heartedly into the struggle and got out of it so well.... Incomplete as the strike, it was the most complete exhibition of solidarity ever put up by the working-class in any country at any time.'

13

COMING OF AGE, 1927–39

THE FIRST PROBLEM THE unions had to face after the strike was a legal assault on their capacity to act effectively.

The 1927 Trades Disputes Act was unanimously resented by the trade unions as a clear example of Government vindictiveness, imposed on the defeated trade unions out of spite. The Act banned civil servants from being in trade unions affiliated to the TUC. This had some effect on the ETU, particularly in the royal dockyards. In 1926, the Chatham branch had fifty-six members, almost exclusively in the dockyard. By 1929, it had fallen to twenty-two. Portsmouth was even more affected. Portsmouth No. 2 branch was the dockyard branch, and had 254 members in December 1925. It had 250 in December 1926. By 1927, this had slumped to twenty-five. Portsmouth No. 1, the general town branch, amalgamated with No. 2 branch to produce a total membership in the town of ninety-nine, compared to 344 at the end of 1925. In Plymouth, one of the union's earliest sources of membership before the First World War, the ban on dockyard membership produced an interesting effect. In the months after the General Strike, Ben Bolton did two organizing 'missions' to the West Country where he recruited widely in Plymouth among the power workers and contracting membership, holding up his success throughout the region as an example. Consequently, the Plymouth branch membership actually grew in this period from 250 in December 1927 to 389 by December 1929. Less pleasing, though, the Act probably finally killed off the union in the post office. Telephone and telegraph workers had founded the union; rejoined it periodically after the war. Now they were banned from joining it.

The Act also banned unions from penalizing members who did not strike from expulsions and fines. The union never admitted as much, but throughout the late 1920s, the executive were frequently recommending that branches took members back into the union or readmitted lapsed members despite their apparent misdoings, often in the General Strike itself.

The Act banned sympathetic strikes and outlawed general strikes. Here, the absence of evidence is evidence itself. After the General Strike, the persistent attempts of the London district committee to use the power stations on behalf of every group of workers 'in struggle' petered out. Overtly sympathetic action that characterized the early twenties was probably not going to happen because of the increasing caution displayed by the station membership itself. However, the legal situation was no doubt brought to their attention by the employers, who insisted as a condition of restarting the NJIC/DJIC machinery, particularly in London, on a formal agreement that the supply industry would not be involved in other people's disputes.

Closed shops were banned in local government. In June 1932, the members at Poplar Borough Council were trying to organize a strike to force a plumber-jointer called Fowler into the union, and the executive disowned the letter district secretary George Humphreys sent to the council supporting the strike threat, on the legal issues involved. The most enduring irritation in the legislation was the change in the political fund rules, from 1 January 1928, where the Government insisted that trade-union members contracted *into* the union's political fund, rather than contracted *out* personally and individually.

This had the effect of seriously depressing the political fund of the union. By 1931, when the union had 31,322 members, 5,610 more than in 1927, the annual income for the political fund had fallen from £818 to £650 in the same four years. Given that the branches retained two-thirds of the 1s levy, the union's head office could never do more politically throughout the 1930s than pay the union's affiliation fees. They simply could not afford to run sponsored candidates for Parliament at the same time, despite widespread branch requests to do so.

Jimmy Rowan's judgment of the Act was conventional, if strongly felt.

It at one fell swoop cut off all civil service workers from their fellow-workers and prevented any attempt at collective action on their part. Admiralty, War Office, post office and other employees, by this pernicious Act, were told they could either sacrifice their jobs or their freedom. Because they were not able to accept the sacrifice that would necessarily be entailed in fighting the Government, they have for the time being to forgo their freedom.

Industrial Developments and Union Growth in the 1930s

The 1927 Trades Dispute Act set the legal background against which the unions tried to re-establish themselves after the General Strike. However, the enduring image of the period between the General Strike and the outbreak of war in 1939 is one of idle decline and mass unemployment. This image is largely drawn from the long-term collapse of the old staple industries in Britain, coal, cotton and shipbuilding. In coal, the productivity of British mines rose eleven per cent between 1927 and 1939. In Silesia and the Ruhr, the comparative figures lie between seventy-three and eighty-seven per cent. Three coalfields, South Wales, Scotland and Durham, largely relied on an export trade that was now dominated world-wide by Polish, German and American coal. The profits available to small, inefficient, unco-ordinated British coal-owners did not allow the high rate of mechanization that was necessary to make British export coal competitive. The result was further twists in the cycle of deprivation that devastated whole communities in the coalfields. The same effect was observed in shipbuilding for periods of the 1930s when Jarrow – 'the town that was murdered' – entered our language as a byword for economic collapse.

No picture of 1927–39 is complete without giving due emphasis to this enduring reality of depression: however, it is not the whole story. From the point of view of the ETU it was not the whole story at all.

In 1925, a small Government committee headed by Lord Weir examined the shortcomings in the national interest of the electricity supply industry. The final report, and the bill introduced by the Government to remedy the faults identified, were both published in March 1926, and the Electricity Supply Act 1926 received the Royal Assent on 15 December that year.

The nation needed electricity produced at a constant voltage that would allow interconnection of districts and – one day – transmission up and down the entire land. It needed higher fuel efficiency and it needed cheaper, more plentiful electricity to stimulate the economy. The Weir report, quoted in Leslie Hannah's definitive study of the industry, *Electricity Before Nationalization*, said: 'Of the 438 generating stations owned by authorized undertakings, not more than about fifty can be regarded as being of really suitable size and efficiency ... the percentage of stand-by plant is unduly high and the load factor is unreasonably low. Interconnection is not carried out as a definite policy ... and the resultant loss to the country has become heavy, and becomes daily heavier.' The Act set up the Central Electricity Board (CEB) with powers to direct the generating of electricity, to buy it and to sell it back at cost price plus the costs of setting up a national 'gridiron' to interconnect localities at the new, standard, modern voltage of 132 kV. Although this public duty done, without too much direct interference with private ownership, it did not please Tory MPs, led by George Balfour, who resented this sophisticated, arms-length public control of the industry. But Clement Attlee, MP, was impressed. He was Labour's spokesman at the committee stage of the bill and his praise for the bill was generous to his political opponents. 'We are not considering this merely as a means of getting richer or merely enriching a certain industry or even merely as increasing the economic welfare of this country. We regard it as a vital service that is to be used for the social development of this country.' In this spirit, Attlee joined with Government supporters against Balfour's die-hards, and was not too appalled that full-scale nationalization was not achievable.

By 1929, work on the grid was underway, and the electricity pylons began their long march across the British landscape. Most aesthetes decried them, although most communities were grateful for the power they brought, with its promise of domestic comfort and industrial regeneration; 150,000 tons of steel and 12,000 tons of aluminium were used, all of it made in Britain with work-starved Scottish shipyards building pylons. Perhaps 120,000 jobs were created before the last pylon was erected in the New Forest on 5 September 1933. Power stations were built to have the increased capacity suitable for a new relationship with the national grid. These new stations like Ironbridge, Liverpool's Clarence Dock and Battersea raised the level of thermal efficiency in the stations to unheard-of levels – in Battersea's case, to 29.1 per cent. By 1935, 148 stations were operating under CEB control, if not ownership. The increasing efficiency per ton of coal burnt (from 443 kWh in 1914 to 566 kWh in 1939) and the capacity to interconnect, freed the locations of new industry in the 1930s from the necessity to get cheap power by placing factories exactly on the coalfields.

Contemporary poets were aware of the change that electricity brought, a change that probably implied social development alongside the physical impact the industry made on the countryside. Stephen Spender wrote *Pylons* in 1933.

> The secret of these hills was stone, and cottages
> Of that stone made,
> And crumbling roads
> That turned on sudden, hidden villages
>
> Now over these small hills they have built the concrete
> That trails black wire:
> Pylons, those pillars
> Bare like nude, giant girls that have no secret
>
> The valley with its gilt and evening look
> And the green chestnut
> Of customary root
> Are mocked dry like the parched bed of a brook
>
> But far above and far as sight endures
> Like whips of anger
> With lightning's danger
> There runs the quick perspective of the future

This dwarfs our emerald country by its trek
So tall with prophecy
Dreaming of cities
Where often clouds shall lean their swan-white neck.

With the grid completed by 1934, the use of electricity dramatically increased. Every process and activity was affected. Public supply sales of railway electricity rose, with railways no longer building their own facilities, and the electric mileage outstripped the steam on the Southern railway as the towns of Brighton, Portsmouth, Sevenoaks and Eastbourne steadily connected with London by electricity throughout the 1930s.

Street traction sales rose sixty-three per cent between 1921–39. Tram mileage fell a third between 1929–33, but 2,500 trolley-buses helped consumption to keep rising. Public supply sales of electricity from 1921–39 to industry rose from 2,081 GWh to 11,672 GWh, indicating industry's preference now to rely on public supply. In the same period, commercial use rose from 403 to 3,117 GWh. Domestic use exploded from around 300 to well over 5,000 GWh, while the domestic price fell from 5.75d per kWh in 1920 to 1.6d in 1938.

Wiring costs per house fell from between £11–20 in 1919 to £5–6 in 1936. After the mid-20s, electric wiring, at least for light, was installed as a matter of course. By 1936, eighty-four per cent of supply undertakings were advancing credit terms for new building and rebuilding work, both on estate schemes and for individuals. Between the wars, private houses with electricity rose from around half-a-million homes of the very rich to eight million or more by 1938, with an average annual rate of increase of 600,000 houses throughout the 1930s. Not all had more than a simple lights circuit. But the provision of domestic appliances, spawning the new manufacturing industries of consumer electricals, rose appreciably for those whose supply included electric sockets. Seventy-seven per cent of homes had electric irons. Forty per cent had vacuum cleaners, twenty-seven per cent had electric fires, sixteen per cent had kettles, fourteen per cent washing machines. Nine million radio sets were in use. The success of the grid cannot be over-emphasized in Britain's economic history, and from 1920–38, the industry was responsible for seven per cent of the total capital formulation in Britain over that period, the sum of £597 million.

In broad outline, the implications for the ETU between the wars hardly need emphasizing. The spread of supply had huge effects in doubling the electricity supply workforce to around 90,000. The contracting industry gained enormous stimulus from the electrical side of the housing boom. The tremendous increase in the manufacture and installation of turbines and industrial motors, and other heavy engineering products, along with the new impact of the motor industry produced huge electrical opportunity. The manufacture, installation and servicing of domestic appliances was to provide a whole new set of industries for the union to recruit in.

New industry sprang up throughout the period, encouraged and supported by cheap, accessible electrical energy. Nearly three million new houses were built in the 1930s, and the people who lived in them bought electrical goods, motor cars and furniture supplies. Much of this expansion was based in the South-East, and in particular, the London suburbs. Industrial expansion in the North-West and west of London was particularly striking, with industrial estates at Park Royal and Wembley (on the site of the old exhibition area, near the stadium) typifying the expansion of industry along the arterial roads out of London. When the Great West Road was opened by King George V, it attracted new industries like Smith's Crisps, Maclean's Toothpaste, Trico-Folbert windscreen wiper manufacturers, Firestone Tyres, Curry's cycles and radios and the Gillette razor company. All of these industries needed electrical installation and supply by contractors; all needed maintenance of electrical machinery and office equipment. The electrical age was finally born.

The most powerful image of the 1930s, though, remains the utter misery of the old industries, devastated by unemployment. In 1937, unemployment in Wales was still over twenty-two per cent with only six-and-a-half per cent in London and the South-East. Compared to the 1921 crisis, more people were unemployed in the 1930s. As the figure rose from 1.2 million in 1929 to over 2.7 million in 1932; it did not fall much below 1.5 million until rearmament and war put the people back to work in 1940. However, the number actually *in* employment fell only by 300,000 from 1929–33, compared to a fall of 2.5 million in employment in the 1920–2 period. The edge of the depression was not so sharp, either. Industrial production declined by only ten per cent between 1929–33, compared to the twenty per cent fall in 1921 alone. Wholesale prices fell by around a quarter compared to a half from 1920–2, and retail prices fell fifteen per cent compared to around thirty per cent in the earlier 1920–2 depression. The electrical industries, particularly the building of the grid, provided something of an effective if unintentional counter-cyclical economic stimulus. All of these influences – falling prices, change in the industrial base, a depression counterbalanced with expansion – produced steady gains for the ETU throughout the period 1927–39.

Membership and Finance, 1927–39

The statistical tables of the union's membership and finances for this period show the slowly evolving maturity of the union. In 1927, in the wake of the General Strike where timidity and victimization, the collapse of the union in Scotland, and the failure to recruit in new industry produced a 3,300 fall in membership (eleven-and-a-half per cent), the union's membership stood at 25,712. By the end of 1939, it had risen to 70,065. There was a slight dip in 1931 and 1932 when progress was arrested. The union's membership fell by just 1,400 in these two desperate years to a plateau of 30,021. However, this four-and-a-half per cent fall over the two years compared to an eight per cent fall in the membership figures for the movement as a whole as unemployment climbed to its 1932 pinnacle of 22.1 per cent. From 1933 to the outbreak of war, the union more than doubled in size from 30,100 to 70,065. Unemployment was falling, although 'full employment' was only achieved well into the war, yet the rate of growth per year for the ETU each year was between twice and three times greater than the growth rates for the movement as a whole. This increased membership found a solid reflection in the financial management of the union. Jimmy Rowan's annual accounts are full of the most precise details of the union's finances. By 1939, the union's balance of funds was £203,062, compared to the balance carried forward in 1927 of £7,208. Yet Rowan's long stewardship of the funds since 1907 gave him a real determination to control small expenditures with the methodical approach that he shared with Citrine when centralized finance first made the union viable in the mid-1920s. The union's finances were at last secure enough to pay for the reorganization scheme that started in 1935, providing office and representation facilities from officials all over the country. They were strong enough to sustain the cinema strike expenditure in 1938 of around £15,000. They could pay out throughout the 1930s unemployment benefit – £22,836 in 1931, £15,836 in 1933, £15,863 in 1939. One very real frustration for the officials was the members' regular refusal in ballots to pay for a superannuation scheme for officials: McLaughlin retired in May 1930 from the London office, and got one month's wages as a retirement present. London North West objected to even that! The executive also had to make ex gratia grants to the families of officials who died, and that caused much embarrassment. During the 1930s many of the union's original pioneers died. Alex Calipé had died in 1929, but Fred Trevis and Bill McKay, Joe Collins and Bill Gooday were all remembered in official obituaries during the 1930s. Tom Stewart, national organizer since his election in December 1912, died on 20 May 1936 at the age of sixty-five from throat cancer.

Tom Stewart was a workhorse. There was no organizing job he could not or would not do. He rarely got involved with the political madhouse in London, as Kinniburgh or Bolton had to do; Tom Stewart was a Scot, and did most of his organizing in the North of England and Scotland. His less spectacular contribution to the union ought not to be underestimated. He organized dozens of new locations for the union, and performed the ordinary negotiations for thousands of members, particularly those members who were rarely reached by head office officials and before the spread of national negotiations. His record lives on in the records of the union, but he also left a physical reminder of his career that is still in use by the executive council of the union today. When the union moved back to London in 1930, Tom Stewart presented the president of the union with a large brass bell for bringing the executive and the union's conferences to order. It is engraved with the words, 'A gift from a Scot', and has had plenty of use during some of the warmer discussions within the executive council's boardroom!

Tom Stewart's wife, in the absence of a superannuation scheme, was given six months' salary. So was Bill Westfallen's wife when he died in January 1938. Westfallen had been ill for months, tired out and exhausted. His contribution to the union in London was warmly spoken of by his political opponent Bussey, from the president's chair, at the 1938 conference in Torquay. Westfallen was undoubtedly a member of the Minority Movement, and a regular delegate to the London Red International of Trade Unions – possibly a full member of the Communist Party as well. He edited the ill-fated left-wing journal in London, the *Electron*, and greeted the General Strike as the opportunity for the destruction of capitalism. However, on his election as a junior official in London (when he beat Harold Morton in April 1926 by 2,024 votes to 736) he became a literate and powerful official, particularly for the station engineers, and especially for the supply workers in the railway companies in London. His stature rose in the union following the appalling scandal that surrounded the discovery in July 1929 that Webb had stolen over £600 from the union. This was a particular shock to Westfallen, who had been a political and personal friend of Bill Webb's since the First World War. After this scandal Westfallen's work in the London office was never characterized by the confrontations between the executive (on which he sat from 1925–6) and the London district committee that disfigured the early 1920s (and for which Westfallen was partly to blame!) and the late 1930s which nearly led to a breakaway union emerging in London. If his health had survived, it is arguable that the electoral changes that befell the union following the Earl's Court dispute might not have happened.

Two further changes occurred to the union's leadership regionally, brought about by tragedy. Albert Oates, Sheffield district secretary and local councillor, died in September 1938. He was a strong advocate of the moderate skilled man from the North. He was frequently complaining about the disruption that seemed to be evident in London, and supported Rowan manfully on occasion by writing to the union's magazine and supporting Bussey and Lewis's reorganization scheme at the conferences of the union. George Chadwick, the Mersey district secretary, after well over a decade in the post, beat Frank Foulkes for the job in January 1936, 659–253. By 13 July, he was dead, leaving a wife and nine children. His family received the six months' salary, and Frank Foulkes won the resultant election over the local executive councillor, McKernan, in August 1936, 645–415, and the communists now had a second power base outside London. The changing structure of the union's membership is well demonstrated by looking at the arrival on the scene of branches of the union in 1939 that did not exist in 1927. Barnet, Bexleyheath, Dagenham, Elstree, Hounslow, London Studio No. 1, Oxford and Reading show the south-eastern basis of growth. Add to that huge increases at Hendon – up from thirty to 370 members of the period – with Luton going from thirteen to 327 and Coventry Central from thirty-five to 334, and the fact emerges of growth for the ETU where new industry was growing. But that would leave an incomplete picture. Traditional industrial branches grew fast too. Bolton's membership rose from 175 to 316, Dundee's from 132 to 261, LSE No. 1 from 388 to 579, Manchester Central from 196 to 501, Sheffield Central from 240 to 617 and Wigan from 60 to 219. Everywhere it was the same story – the growing use of electricity and the growing power of the ETU.

Independence and Reorganization: the Structural Changes 1929–35

It was this rapid growth that convinced most ETU activists that there was no need to amalgamate the union with any other. Jimmy Rowan confronted the 1936 policy conference at Scarborough with the issue, saying that he freely 'confessed that he had been an amalgamationist for forty years and was still of the opinion that there were far too many trade unions and not enough trade unionists.' Half the union's time was spent fighting other unions – it competed with the enginemen and firemen in supply and with the MFGB in collieries, with the AEU everywhere, with the NATE in film studios, and with the General and Municipal Workers Union (GMWU) in the semi-skilled supply grades. Bussey explained that exploratory talks were being held with the TGWU again – some twelve years after the deal was all but signed and sealed in 1926 – and that ought to help the union's crusade in the collieries and cinemas.

Only two of the forty-two delegates were convinced. The others voted resoundingly against amalgamating with anyone. The ETU was off on its own.

It had become obvious during the early 1930s that the union had to change its internal organization if it was to properly take advantage of the opportunities presented by industrial expansion.

The 1929 conference at Blackpool did try to get to grips with the real problem: the union was organizing nationally and yet only had effective administration in those districts where they levied themselves to provide full-time officers to co-ordinate the union's work. At the conference, the suggestion to extend the districts to areas covering the whole country to have access to full-time officers was defeated 19–15. There was a coalition of interests against the idea. The Minority Movement delegates feared an increase of full-time official influence in the union, and the London supply delegates were adamant that higher contributions to finance the scheme would destroy the union's membership in supply. They had real fears here for the position in the power stations where the Workers Union amalgamation with the TGWU had revived fears of inter-union competition for semi-skilled membership in the industry.

The whole situation would have been lost, had not Ernie Bussey, seconded by Birmingham full-time official, Walter Lewis, not urged an emergency motion to set up a reorganization committee to examine and recommend to the membership a new system of area organization. The committee, elected by the conference, was very experienced. The chairman and one of the executive's representatives was the excitable Jack Lyons from London. However, it also included Walter Lewis and Ernie Bussey, Albert Oates from Sheffield, the Welsh district secretary from Swansea, Frank Johns, and George Humphreys from London. The other executive councillors added to the committee were Turnbull, Illingworth and Rowan.

The implementation of the reorganization scheme was delayed for several years. It took nearly six years from Bussey's proposal to set up the reorganization special committee, which he made at the May 1929 conference in Blackpool, to its implementation on 1 January 1935. Firstly, the issue was delayed by the immense upheaval in moving the union's head office – four years after the ballot vote instructed it should be done. The union bought offices at 11 Macaulay Road, Clapham, for £2,450 at the turn of the year in 1929–30. This large house in a leafy suburban road had plumbing and central heating installed by Fretwell Heating Co on the recommendation of the general secretary of the Plumbing Trades Union. The first meeting of the executive council was held there on 26 July 1930. Jack Ball's opening remarks urged upon the executive the hope that 'the close attention to the business of the union which had been displayed amidst the noise, dirt and grime of Withy Grove, would be extended amidst the more congenial circumstances of Macaulay Road.' The president, indeed, was the prime casualty of the move to London. Jack Ball had always prided himself on the fact that he was a working member of the union (although not many electricians obtained the Certificate and Diploma of the Society of Radiographers). He reluctantly chose to remain at his job in Manchester and gave up the presidency of the union at the end of 1930.

However, the 1930 conference unanimously elected Jack Ball life vice president, on the suggestion of Rowan, who had originally recruited him in 1898. Ball attended the executive regularly until he died in April 1943, and the union used him as a delegate to the City and Guilds advisory committee for the training of electricians and he went to Russia in 1937, where he was boyish in his enthusiasm for the apparent triumphs of the Soviet five-year plans. He gave lectures to the branches on radiography (which led to occasional disputes about who should pay his train fares between branches like Blackpool and Bury and the head office). The period of his presidency was exactly the same period as the city of Manchester played host to the general office of the union – 1908–30. During those twenty-two years, the union had become a significant and distinct part of the British Labour Movement. Jack Ball was part of the leadership team that did that. His special passion was reserved for protecting and enhancing the power of the executive council over the district committees. In 1921, he said in Blackpool:

The opening of our ranks to embrace all and sundry has caused a complication of interests which can only be served, and turned to account, by an absolute system of national government in all things and everything, industrially and financially. Past conferences have had the tendency to transfer power and authority from the executive council to the branches and district committees. Well, I seriously warn you this is leading us astray. ... You must adopt the principle of central control. ... All administration of branch and district or divisional areas must come under the supervision of the executive council.

At the 1924 conference, he emphasized the point again.

If you want confidence and security, efficiency and reliability, then our experience teaches us we must centralize, not only the financial system, but the authority – the power and control of the whole administration of the union ... This agenda ... is full of the demoralizing influence of the disrupter ... if we cannot get away from our localities, we shall remain mediocrities.

There was nothing mediocre about Jack Ball.

The reorganization committee reported to the executive on 12 May 1930. The executive, instead of putting the report to a ballot, recalled the 1929 conference to Brighton, to go through the report at the Royal Pavilion from 18–20 August 1930. Jack Ball presided over his last conference, as Bussey and Oates moved the proposals of the committee.

Firstly, the conference agreed with little trouble to empower the executive to shut small branches which were unviable in size, and allow assistant secretaries in branches of over 100 members. The first major row – which nearly devastated the scheme – was the conference's refusal to reduce the percentage of the members' contributions that would be paid out as salaries to the branch officers. Secretaries would get six per cent of contributions, not seven-and-a-half per cent, treasurers would be paid two-and-a-half per cent, not three-and-three-quarter per cent, assistant secretaries two per cent, not two-and-a-half per cent. The committee were proposing an all-in contribution for everyone – no levies for benevolent grants or full-time official funds etc. This would ease the workload on branch officers, and along with centralized finance, justified the reduction in the payments to branch officers! This new contribution would be 1s 2d – an increase of 2d for full benefit members, while the auxiliary section would rise from 7d to 8d. Harold Morton described these reductions in the branch officers' payments as 'an insult to the finest body of men in the union' and the proposed reductions in branch 'costs' (as Bussey saw it) was beaten, 18–15. However, they did pass the contribution rises, and incorporated the separate 'sea-going' section into the full-benefit section. In a fit of guilt, the conference did not put up the delegation fees, in order to improve the actuarial balance of the committee's proposals. The conference quietly allowed auxiliary members to hold any office in the branch while still restricting their election as officials. District committees were to have one delegate per branch, while in London there would be four district committees for the different quadrants of the city with a small central committee to co-ordinate policy with a district president elected by the whole membership. This proposal was meant to alleviate the pressure on full-time officials in London, who had to look after the full district committee, its sub-committee, the station engineers, and other industrial sub-district committees and sub-committees. On top of that, they had to provide the secretarial facilities for the two supply DJICs, Nos. 9 and 10, operating in the district, the trade and disputes committees in contracting, the railway committees and so on. Administrative delay was appalling and the district committees in London were expected to relieve this. Elsewhere, there would be thirty-two, not eighteen district committees, with ten new areas covering the whole country. In each of the areas would be the full-time officer, elected in the area but paid by the head office's central funds from everyone's 'all-in' contributions and answerable under rule to the executive council. The three Minority Movement delegates objected to this removal of control of the official from the district to the executive. Everyone else voted for it. The officials' salary level was set at £300 a year (with £338 for London organizers and £364 for the London district secretary). It was agreed to call a conference every two years to discuss 'policy' issues and to revise the union's rules every six years, not three, as in the past. The election period for the new area officials was to be five years and not three years: Bussey tentatively talked about the GMWU example of executive appointment of officers. This suggestion was not formally put to the conference; neither was it recommended to make the president's job full-time.

The 1930 re-called conference set the modern structure of the union: it finally wrenched the political control of the officials from the districts to the executive of the union. It separated policy from rule revision at the conferences and fixed the timing of conferences and periods of election. It provided the funds to make available full-time officials throughout the country and not just in those districts which could afford local levies. Not for the first time, a conference of branch secretaries was conscious of the contribution made to the union by, of course, other branch secretaries, and retained their higher payments.

However, the report was rousingly criticized on one important ground. Morton led the charge. He insisted the report dealt 'wholly with the administration of the *present* membership of the ETU'. The committee's report was a 'full-time officer's charter', to receive a decent salary (at the proposed expense of the branch secretary!) and then have all his work done by the branches and district committees. No attention had been paid to getting officials out on the road organizing, and leaving just two national organizers doing that was wholly inadequate. No attention had been paid to improving the union's publicity and propaganda machine and no attention had been paid to introducing an 'industrial section of the union' that would have a very low contribution to allow the union to organize the less-skilled workers and women workers.

Bussey was undeterred by the opposition of his old friend in London.

The proposals before you are an attempt to knit the fibres of our organization closer together under the control of the executive council so that the greatest service can be rendered by the full-time official to the membership. At the same time [we shall be] extending the democratic control of the branches, through their district committees and our biennial conferences so that at all times the voice of the membership shall be expressed.

Rowan thought the whole thing was 'the most revolutionary report that had ever been dealt with by a delegate conference'.

Morton's disapproval was not expressed in voting down the whole package; firstly, he won his main point over the branch secretaries' salaries. Second, he persuaded the conference to allow the members to vote on the report at the right time, before it was introduced.

By July 1931, a special committee of the executive had reviewed how best to implement the reorganization scheme following its approval in a ballot vote, 4,414–3,625. A delegate conference was held at the Lecture Hall in Queen Street, Blackpool, to discuss the special committee's report in September 1932. Ernie Bussey was now in the chair as the union's new president, and explained that the only remaining problem was to introduce the scheme at a moment when it did the least damage to the union financially. After all, the union was proud of its capacity to pay full unemployment benefit throughout the depression (rising from nearly £8,000 in 1929 to over £23,000 in 1931), and nothing must interfere with this. The conference made one or two small changes to the scheme: the London Central committee would have two delegates from each quadrant district committee, making a total of eight with a London-wide elected president. All full-time officials period of office would now be five years, not three, starting from the time the scheme came into force when their current periods of office ran out. Because the financial situation needed careful monitoring, conference left the date of implementation of the scheme to the executive council.

In early 1934, the executive finally decided that the union's growing financial strength looked relatively well founded, and the May 1934 conference at Blackpool endorsed the recommendation to institute the scheme on 1 January 1935. Incidentally, the conference also agreed to expand the executive from nine to eleven seats; the two extra seats were established by increasing London and the Home Counties to three from two, and by establishing Wales and South-West England and the West/East Midlands as two separate seats.

After one year's operation, the situation was reviewed and presented to the August 1936 conference in the form of a special report accepted by the executive council. The total cost of thirty-two district committees and ten area offices with thirteen full-time area officials was £10,603 for 1935. This compared to £9,002 spent on sixteen district committees and thirteen full-time officers in 1933. This increase, though, was more than covered by the rise in membership over the same period from 31,100 to 40,271. There were some pointed references to the excessive number of delegation fees being paid in Birmingham, West Wales and, inevitably, in London. The suggestion was that area officials should do more of the negotiating and reporting to members – not district committee officials.

Jock Muir, president of London Central committee, had had 127 days' expenses at 3s 6d a day, ninety-nine full days' and twenty-seven half days' loss of time allowances, making a total, with fares, of £121 2s 7d. The committee and conference were, however, greatly pleased that the administration costs per member had fallen and that most members and branches were now getting used to asking for the area official rather than simply feel that all their problems would be answered by participation in district committees.

The analysis of the union's membership figures in this report is revealing (see table 2): it can also be confusing, as the ten area borders were not the same as the thirty-two district committee borders and they in turn were not the same as the groupings of branches that formed the eleven executive council electoral divisions!

London's rapid growth produced sheer organizational problems that were not completely assuaged by the provision of four district committees, the central committee to 'co-ordinate' all this and three full-time officials. Partly to help the situation in London, the conference agreed to set up an eleventh area, based on Southampton, which covered the South Coast towns from Falmouth to Brighton. C. J. Osborne was the first elected official there in 1937 under the new scheme. By the outbreak of war, further reforms had been instituted to ensure the provision of greater full-time officer cover to a wider catchment area. In 1938, Harry Madden was elected to a new office at Middlesbrough, J. J. Hall set up in Preston, and J. Sim opened up an office

Table 2

Area No.	Region	Area Office	Area Official on 1.1.1935	No. of Members on		Increase	% Increase
				1.1.1935	1.1.1936		
1	N Ireland	Belfast	S. T. Ellis	954	1,143	189	19.8
2	Scotland	Glasgow	W. M. Bissell	2,450	2,824	374	15.3
3	North East	Newcastle	P. McArdle	2,402	2,595	193	8.0
4	W & N Yorks	Leeds	R. Penrose	1,222	1,430	208	17.0
5	S Yorks	Sheffield	A. Oates	1,715	2,026	311	18.1
6	Merseyside	Liverpool	G. Chadwick	1,740	2.042	302	17.4
7	Manchester	Manchester	J. Kearns: J. J. Hall	4,024	4,589	565	14.0
8	W & E Midlands	Birmingham	W. Lewis	1,682	2,148	466	27.7
9	South Wales	Cardiff	W. Minor	2,478	2,783	305	12.3
10	London & SE	London	A. Coster W. Westfallen G. Humphreys	15,339	18,250	3,121	20.1
TOTALS				34,221	40,271	6,050	17.7

in Edinburgh. S. C. Richardson improved coverage of the Midlands by opening an office in Leicester and by the end of 1939, a fourth official, Bill Benson, joined Humphreys and Coster in the London office, along with Walter Stevens, who had been elected at the end of 1937 for the first time. For a while, from 1934 to 1939, they were joined by the general secretary of the Lift and Crane Workers Union, Bert Bromilow. His union amalgamated with the ETU in January 1934, bringing 400 members (of whom 200 were unemployed).

Growth in membership produced a suitable organizational response. Ernie Irwin and Bill Turnbull were always adamant it could have been introduced before January 1935. The rest of the executive were more cautious: they wanted to make sure the growing stability of the union was going to last. Far too many of them remembered the near collapse of the union in 1921 and the traumas associated with the General Strike. There can be little doubt that the provision of the first team of full-time officials produced real benefits in terms of recruitment, local prestige and organizational coherence. Their status was enormous. Rowland Penrose in Leeds was a legend for his smart dress sense, bowler hat and habit of marching round building sites shouting 'All in? All in?', waving his umbrella in encouragement. Full-time area officials carried more prestige locally than did lay executive councillors. These were the men to give leadership as the union's negotiating role grew in the thirties and into the war years.

The Road Back: Collective Bargaining, 1927–39

From the General Strike to the outbreak of war, the collective bargaining fortunes of the union varied from sector to sector of industry, and from region to region of the country. One general conclusion does emerge quite clearly: where the union was in charge of its own destiny – in contracting, and to a great extent in electricity supply – workers' conditions were not as bad as in those industries like shipbuilding where economic depression and the weakness of the other unions prevented militant progress. The engineering employers in 1931 launched a savage attack on workers' standards that took years to recover from. Piece-work earnings rates fell from thirty-three-and-a-third per cent to twenty-five per cent. Double time would only be paid on Sundays. The first two hours of overtime would only be paid at time-and-a-quarter, not time-and-a-half. Nightshift premiums were reduced from time-and-a-third to time-and-a-sixth. Overtime rates on nightshift were to be time-and-a-quarter for the first two hours and only time-and-a-half thereafter.

By 1934, the application for 2d an hour by the unions resulted in the acceptance of a miserable ½d in two instalments! Rowan correctly identified the problem as the negotiations being dominated by the weakest trade union and the most miserly employer in the industry. 'Before the war,' he wrote in 1935:

... the system of getting advances in wages was to negotiate locally and only in the event of a failure to agree, to reach the Employers' National Federation. During the war, and mainly owing to abnormal conditions, principally the rapid advance in the cost of living, applications were made of a national character. The employers continued this procedure in respect to the many reductions which have taken place. The result is that in the present application, the least progressive and even retrograde firms are set off against those sections of the engineering industry which are prosperous and making very substantial profits – particularly the electrical engineering and motor car industries.

In 1936, six months of negotiations produced a marginally better rate of night shift premiums (time-and-a-fifth, not time-and-a-sixth) and 3s per week on the war bonus. It was rearmament in 1937 that produced the first significant gains as the industry got back to work generally, and not just in the 'new' industries. A further 3s on the bonus was granted and day rates for shift workers rose from time-and-a-quarter to time-and-a-third. Holidays with pay were introduced. In 1938, Rowan was pleased that 'demand was never higher for electricians' and in 1939, a further 2s was awarded on the bonus. A cry of frustration to leave the national agreement was not supported at the 1936 conference, simply because the union had no power to impose its will on the industry; instead great things were hoped for from the newly-established Confederation of Shipbuilding and Engineering Unions (CSEU).

This picture of steady decline in wages with a recovery from 1936 to the outbreak of war is repeated in the shipbuilding industry, where unemployment hit the hardest throughout the period and lasted the longest. Once again, the union was convinced that if it had had the power to act alone, it could have been more successful in the shipyards, however depressed they were. The union did make sure that they were assured of the maintenance and installation work associated with the introduction of electrical welding processes into the industry in 1935. Wages were kept low in the industry because the majority unions in the shipyards had nowhere else in industry for their members to go; it was low wages or the dole for shipwrights and most boiler makers. Electricians, however, did often have the option of working in the local power supply undertaking or on building sites, if available. Nevertheless, small improvements tended to parallel the same improvements in engineering. On 1 April 1936 (what Rowan called 'a very appropriate date') 2s was put on the war bonus and four per cent on the piece rates. Holidays with pay and small increases on bonus and piece rates followed in 1937 and 1938. Huge amounts of overtime in the rearmament industries led to increased earnings. This completely deflated the official campaigns for the forty-hour week, an agitation that occupied trade union officials throughout the decade to precious little effect.

The picture was somewhat brighter in the industries where the union had greater influence, although the employers in electricity supply provided equally stern and opinionated opponents. The industry expanded enormously in this period; and wages (at seventeen to eighteen per cent) were a tiny fraction of the successful industry's costs. Power station productivity, in particular, rocketed. In 1922–3, 0.28 GWh was generated per employee: in 1937–8, the figure had risen to 1.25 GWh.

As distribution of electricity reached out into every part of the country, the numbers employed rose, and there was always a rush to get into this 'sheltered' employment. This in itself led to the employers resolutely refusing to pay their workers what they could afford; they paid instead what other employers were paying. However, the union had serious problems in its attempts to oppose this attitude. First, it is probable that between only a quarter and a third of the industry's workforce were unionized before the war – and even if the NJIC manual grades are examined, it is probable that just over fifty per cent were in trade unions. The ETU was the largest union, but the lower grades and some skilled men remained with the enginemen and firemen section of the TGWU. The poisoned relationship with the EPEA hung in the air. The Birmingham district committee was so frustrated with not getting high wages out of prosperous local undertakings that it asked the executive to abandon its membership of the NJICs and DJICs. Rowan's reply, on 23 March 1930, based on his lack of respect for the other unions, is interesting.

The plain reply to the Birmingham district committee is that it would be to our disadvantage to leave the council on account of the fact that it would be possible (as has happened before) for a treacherous move to be made on the part of one or two of the unions to endeavour to come to an understanding with the EPEA which would leave them to give away the operative staff (mainly controlled by the ETU) to the EPEA for consideration of the other grades which the EPEA do not want.

It was only in the late 1930s that engineering earnings started to outstrip electricity supply, due to rearmament. Up until then, supply rates remained fairly static. With a falling cost of living index, living standards were improved over the whole period. In 1928, there was a $\frac{1}{2}$d rise and the sliding scale was suspended, which kept wages at a higher value as the cost of living index fell. In 1929, the employers agreed rises for distinct grades of workers in larger power stations, establishing national conditions and the important principle of higher pay for higher technology, but in 1930–31, national bargaining nearly broke down altogether. The employers attempted to impose wage cuts in line with outside industry, irrespective of their own profitability. In 1930, wages fell by $\frac{1}{2}$d an hour (which was much better than if the sliding scale had *not* been suspended in 1928 – a further 1d an hour would have gone in 1930 if it was still operating). Wages were then left alone until June 1931. In March that year, the unions wanted not the suspension, but the abolition of the sliding scale. The employers would only agree to this if the unions added the extra 1d reduction so that they were 'square'. The compromise demand of $\frac{1}{2}$d reduction was rejected by the unions. The employers posted notices to enforce reduction nationwide of 1d. The Ministry of Labour stopped that by recommending that the industrial court should examine the issue if local DJIC negotiations failed, and the notices were withdrawn. For twelve months, there were no reductions as the local bargaining and industrial court hearings took place. Six localities agreed no change at all. One took a reduction of $\frac{1}{2}$d and the industrial court imposed a $\frac{1}{2}$d reduction in six others.

The union was furious that the industrial court supported the idea that it was wholly legitimate for the employers to prefer outside comparisons rather than their own profitability as the standard to judge the industry by.

In May 1934, most of these cuts were restored and the 'A' grades got $\frac{3}{4}$d an hour extra in 1938. Throughout the period, conditions of employment were demonstrably good. This is what made the industry attractive in an era of high unemployment, and militated against industrial action in pursuit of higher wage rates. Access to overtime and the absence of short-time working were great bonuses in the 1930s. The industry led the country in the provision of holidays with pay (partly to compensate for seven-day working). Some companies provided pensions for workers, sick clubs and sports facilities. Despite this frustration at not being able to extract the wage levels from the NJIC that they thought they were entitled to, the union was not going to hand to the employers a justification for ignoring the union completely by leaving the NJIC. They had a vested interest in supporting a body that was considered too generous by significant local authority employers like Glasgow and private companies like the London Power Co, both of whom did not take part in the NJIC in the thirties.

At the bottom line, the stability of the industry was to the workers' advantage and the union knew it.

Developments in the contracting industry were more impressive, even though the problems facing the industry made life difficult for the union. First and foremost, the housing boom in the 1930s produced a new generation of 'cowboy' contractors who would take on an enormous number of young men to be supervised in gangs by a skilled man. Sometimes these lads would be called 'apprentices', but they would be given no training and discharged at the end of contracts.

However, the union's negotiating success tripped itself up here. 'Our past practice,' Rowan wrote in 1936, 'of endeavouring to force as high a rate as possible for youths coming into the trade is being modified, on account of the knowledge gained that a high wage for youths simply attracts a greater number to this work, thus accentuating the problem; it may be found in the end that a reasonable wage governed by a limitation of numbers will be the eventual solution to the difficulty.' Organization was difficult, due to the temporary nature of work-sites. Equally, the employers' organization, the NFEA, did not have each and every electrical contractor in their association. This produced genuine problems for both employer and union. There was no chance of establishing holidays with pay if the non-federated companies did not have to bear the cost. The same thinking applied to the need to provide proper apprenticeships and not simply exploit boy labour. The union tried hard to use its influence to make sure that municipal contracts went to the better-paying NFEA companies. Hugh Bolton (curiously called Ben Bolton by his friends) would make this vigilance part of his duties. He stopped Belfast City Council in 1927 giving over £5,000 worth of work to non-federated companies, and his report of policing an 'assisted wiring scheme' in Newport, in South Wales, is typical of the period.

This work, at the inception of the scheme, was carried out by the Corporation themselves with directly employed labour, but due to the efforts of the people opposed to this principle, political pressure was applied which resulted later on in the work being given out to private enterprise.

The work consists of five-point installation, and the contractors are allowed the sum of £2 5s 11½d prime cost of material per house, plus 1s 9⅝d per hour for labour. The contractor is allowed sixteen hours for each house, which works out at £1 8s 10d for labour. This brings the prime cost to £3 14s 9½d to which has to be added the allowance of twenty-two-and-a-half per cent for profit. This makes the amounts paid to the contractor, £4 11s 7½d. It will be obvious that if the contractor can force the men to do these houses in less than sixteen hours, then this means much additional profit to him ... it is unfortunate that trade union officials have to devote a great deal of time to seeing that these contracts are carried out to specification when it is the duty of Corporation officials to do this work.

Throughout the period, the comparative position of the contracting electrician was improved. In 1929, the employers paid 1d an hour to London electricians only, in the face of considerable unrest and outbursts of unofficial action. London electricians had a justifiable feeling that their better organization would enable them to exceed the rates laid down for them in the national agreement. The executive was keen to sustain the national agreement in everyone's interest: and in 1930, they got the forty-seven hour week reduced to forty-four and a new sliding scale agreement was agreed that replaced the four-monthly review of the cost of living with an annual review of movements in prices over the past three years. This had the effect of sustaining wages at the height of the depression based on 1928–9 figures. Prices were tumbling and ¾d was added in 1930 to all four rates.

However, just as the industry came out of the depression in 1933, the previous three years' cost of living figures dragged earnings down by 1½d per hour by April 1933. This intensified the feeling in London and Liverpool that they could do better locally. The executive put to the members the reassuring argument that the 1933 London rate of 1s 7¾d (plus the five per cent) *was* ¾d an hour less than the 1923 rates. Nevertheless, prices had fallen by a *half* in the same ten years. Further negotiations in 1934 and 1935 provided small increases for everyone, and satisfied Liverpool to an extent by putting 1d an hour on their Grade 'B' in lieu of 'travelling allowances'. The 1934 negotiations can be taken at random for providing, in the heart of the negotiations, an impassioned plea by Ernest Bussey for the new status and the new recognition due to the modern electrician. On 16 August 1934, Bussey told the NFEA:

... it is useless going back to pre-war days. Whatever rates of pay were paid at that time, we can never return to them. The desires and aspirations of our people are not those of pre-war days. They claim, and rightfully so, a larger measure of attributes of life than our predecessors had or desired. Education, improved environment, has had its beneficial effect on the life of the people, and with it the demand for a higher and freer economic life. Our people desire to have something more than a bread and butter existence. ... All that could be expressed by me in respect to the training and sacrifice of our members to fit them for their part in the industry. ... I ally myself with [our general secretary and assistant general secretaries] in respect to this aspect of the problem.

In 1935, mates became a part of the London agreement in an attempt to stem the tide of boys entering the industry. Steadily, negotiations were becoming more sophisticated. Attempts were made to produce national working rules from 1935 onwards, with only scant success however. Again, in 1935, the union took a bold step in an attempt to make its rates of pay, agreed with the NFEA, impregnable. It applied to the Government to have the national rates imposed by legislation, so that the non-unionist and non-federated contractor could not stand outside the negotiations and undermine the standards set. (In the end, the Government would not do this, even though it had done something similar for the cotton industry.)

1935 was something of a decisive year: the union was convinced of the basic prosperity of the industry. The employers said that the expansion was due to local authority and grid-led expansion where the extra electricity generated led only to growth in the use of electric cookers and water heaters, most of which were installed by municipalities. The union explained that pressure was mounting in London and Liverpool for district negotiations. It is quite clear from the verbatim negotiations that neither side wanted the break-up of the national agreement, and the employers eventually came up with a compromise. They would set a new basis for the sliding scale, and the cost of living would be reviewed annually in order to adjust the rates. In return, wages would rise. This arrangement was accepted on a ballot vote, and small increases were assured in 1936, 1937 and 1938. The increase due in March 1938 was actually paid six months earlier. By 1939, the electrical contracting craftsman was being paid 1s 10½d in London (Grade A), 1s 8½d in Liverpool (Grade B), and 1s 7d in Grade B2 and 1s 6¼d in Grade C. He enjoyed a new 'zoning' agreement which abolished Grade D and transferred wholesale groups of members in smaller towns into the new Grade C, with all Grade 'C' workers going up into 'B2'. The rates at September 1939 were set as the new base for the cost of living formula adopted – 5d a week increase for every point rise in the cost of living index.

In 1937, Rowan was confident that in contracting, where the union negotiated for the members alone, the conditions were in advance of any craftsmen in the engineering, shipbuilding and building industries. The union could take pride in the professional and workman-like negotiating styles adopted by both sides in negotiations – particularly as both sides had very real difficulties to contend with; non-federated employers on the one hand and purposeful militants in the big cities on the other. The flavour of negotiations is important. It is vital that both sides respect each other's integrity, power and intellect. The following discussion on the intractable problem of trying to ensure holidays with pay in March 1938 is quoted because it is typical of the growing maturity of contracting negotiations at national level. It was not a great success or a dismal failure for the union – it was just a typical late thirties contracting NJIC agenda item.

Holidays with Pay

Mr Prain said this matter had been carried forward from agenda to agenda for many years, but now the item ought to be looked upon as important. There were very few sections of the industry who did not get holidays with pay. It would be helpful if opinion could be expressed at this meeting owing to the changed conditions.

Mr Bussey expressed the view that the whole matter should be discussed and the general principle agreed. The general principle of holidays with pay had in fact been recognized throughout the country by more and more industries, but Mr Bussey did not think it necessary at that juncture to quote figures as so many industries have fallen into line. He did feel that a step forward should be made to provide a scheme which could be brought into operation which was thought desirable on behalf of workers, for holidays with pay.

Mr Cash, NFEA, stated that so far as the NJIC was concerned, both sides had expressed themselves entirely in favour of this principle. He did not think there was any reason why the matter should not be explored, but thought holidays with pay could only be achieved if a scheme similar to the National Health Insurance was adopted, so that when a man was discharged he could enter another employer's service without losing any benefit thereunder.

Mr Prain pointed out that employment in the shipbuilding and shiprepairing trades was in fact more unstable than electrical contracting, yet they had achieved holidays with pay. He appreciated, however, the difficulty of collecting the contribution from each employer when the holiday period arrived. A practical suggestion would be to set up a clearing-house for the purpose.

Mr Walton, NFEA, said, while in full sympathy with the movement, he was bound to point out that so long as members of our federation were suffering from the severe competition of non-federated firms, largely employing non-union labour, it was practically hopeless to expect our members to accept this additional burden.

Mr Riggs, NFEA, stated that although the NFEA agreed the principle, a great deal of education would be necessary among the members before any steps could be taken. The matter should remain in abeyance to see how the reaction to this suggestion is before proceeding too far.

Mr Penwill, director and secretary of the NFEA, said he thought the difficulties already referred to could be surmounted, as all sorts of movements were on foot to meet the question of casual labour. The question of non-federated firms was a real difficulty, and if NJIC could solve that problem it would do a great deal towards achieving the end in view.

Mr Haxell said if the principle was accepted surely it was possible to get down to a scheme which would overcome the difficulties. If the problems were fully discussed no doubt they would be overcome and it would only be possible to put forward a scheme provided that was done.

Mr Penwill said he thought the views expressed by Mr Cash were right. He could affirm that the NFEA side was in favour of the principle of holidays with pay. There were, however, difficulties which, so far as his side was concerned, were insurmountable except by the legalization of voluntary agreements. Mr Penwill suggested the matter be referred to the committee which was meeting Mr Leggett.

The suggestion was agreed upon.

This type of acceptance at the negotiating table was increasingly being enjoyed by the union in Scotland, where negotiations were once again underway in 1933, and reasonable rates of pay achieved by the outbreak of war. Great strides were made in other, newer, industries. Direct employment and negotiations to go with it with government departments were achieved in 1931, and progressive agreements signed with ICI at Billingham and Fry's at Bristol as early as 1927. These companies set new standards after the General Strike in negotiating from strength agreements that covered holidays, sports and social facilities, proper premiums paid for shifts and overtime and a reasonable basic rate. They turned negotiations into a wider balancing act involving 'packages' and 'trade-offs' within the totality of the working conditions of the union's members. All over Britain, new towns and all types of industry signed up with the ETU – a closed shop at the Dundee shipyard in 1929, recognition at Falmouth shipyard in 1931. Tom Stewart made a rare but successful foray southward to recruit his fellow countrymen in the steelworks at Corby in 1934. Film studios and the BBC were signed up in the years leading up to the war, with Pinewood studios finally being organized in 1937. London Transport craftsmen were organized in 1934.

All was not one long march to success, however. The link between earnings in railway generating stations and the wider industry was broken to the railwaymen's detriment, and never properly recovered ground throughout the 1930s. The union's membership in cable-making at Pirelli fell away, leaving the union recognized simply for cable-jointing, the skilled part of the business.

Relations with Other Unions: Failure in Collieries

Throughout the inter-war period, the union was conscious in many industries that its room for manoeuvre in negotiations was restricted by the priorities of other unions – particularly the bigger general unions. Frequently, in engineering, in shipbuilding, on the railways (both generating stations and the workshops), the union's leadership expressed themselves frustrated by the larger general unions' refusal to confront the employers. Morton, for instance, in October 1929, was upset by being 'dragged at the tail of those unions'. In

February 1930, the engineering unions were immobile. According to Rowan, 'the majority of trades are in favour of passive policy. Put bluntly, they desire to do nothing, only, as they think, to let well alone, and they are also desirous of keeping other trade unions in the same position.'

This difference in tactics also led to growing rivalry for membership with other unions. Rowan drew attention in 1936 to problems with:

> ... mainly, the General Workers' Unions. Notwithstanding the superficially good feeling which exists between the general officials of these unions, there is undoubtedly an undercurrent, mainly fostered by local officials, of underground poaching, and this is tending to expand, not decrease. This factor is one which wastes a lot of the time and energy of both national and local officials.

Throughout the 1930s, the union was anxious to have as many types of employment as possible open to their members. They were particularly conscious of endemic unemployment in much of traditional heavy industry, particularly in the North of England and Scotland. Equally worrying, if certain sectors of industry employed non-ETU electricians well below the definitive NFEA or electricity supply rates, the union's chances of improving *these* rates was correspondingly diminished. It was for these two reasons that the union was concerned throughout the inter-war years with the attempt to organize the collieries and the cinema and entertainment industries. Rowan had a genuine passion for the position of colliery electricians; the union expended enormous effort to organize these men, and its determination to stand up to the MFGB eventually cost Rowan his seat on the General Council of the TUC when his outspoken criticism of the MFGB roused them to action against the ETU. Rowan's respect for skill exceeded his admiration for the hewer's effort.

He wrote in 1928 that he was annoyed at:

> ... the disgraceful position of the wages of skilled electricians being placed on the same plane as the labourer, while the coal-getter, who by no stretch of the imagination can be considered to have the same degree of either skill or training, is placed on a higher grade. All talk of the danger and inconvenience of getting coal disappears by comparison with the inconvenience and danger of an electrician employed in a coal pit; while there is no intention of minimizing the difficulties and dangers of a collier's life, they are intensified in the case of the colliery electrician.

Throughout the inter-war years, the colliers' wages were awful. Ashington Colliery, for instance, in 1930, was paying electricians 6s 9½d a shift – well under 1s an hour, compared to 1930s NFEA rates of 1s 4½d in Grade D – the grade for rural areas!

These disparities grew over the years, but the coal-owners would not cede recognition. More to the point, neither would the Miners Federation of Great Britain (MFGB).

On 12 September 1929, the union's organizer, Ben Bolton, met the full executive of the MFGB. Their attitude was spelt out with brutal frankness by Herbert Smith, who, according to Bolton, 'informed us that they were not prepared to drop their opposition to us meeting the mine owners, nor were they prepared to go along with us, as suggested. Further, they were of the opinion that small unions interfering in the coalfields were a hindrance towards the Federation getting more wages for their people, and that more money to any one section meant less money for the miner.'

A. J. Cook and Rowan exchanged acid letters in September 1930, when the MFGB prevented the employers in Lancashire and Cheshire – on pain of strikes – meeting the ETU. Rowan begged to be allowed to represent 'electricians' while Cook stood firm on the MFGB's claim to represent all 'miners' – which for him included electrical workers. Cook wrote to Rowan on 5 September 1930: 'The Miners Federation will be negotiating new agreements for the whole of the workers in the coalfields, and they are the only body that can deal with the conditions of the miners.' Rowan was angry. He wrote back that not only were the MFGB not accepting ETU invitations to discuss the issue, but they were bluntly threatening to blackleg on the electricians if they took any action against the employers. He took particular exception to this, given the impeccable response of electricians whenever the miners were in dispute. 'During the whole of this period (of twenty years), we have, in every dispute you have had with the coal-owners, placed our members at the disposal of your local miners agents. Surely this merits some more serious and careful consideration from your Federation than we have yet received.'

Throughout 1931 and 1932, the TUC presided over completely ineffectual attempts to reconcile the ETU, and other craft and general unions, to the miners. There was an 'advisory council' on the organization of workers in and around pits, that met, with huge gaps between meetings, before the MFGB once again refused to allow other organizations negotiating rights. By the autumn of 1932, the ETU was accused by a MFGB affiliate, the Durham Mechanics Association, of poaching members in Bishop Auckland and the pit village of Philadelphia.

The TUC did nothing to help: Rowan was again accused of poaching, although his confidential report to the executive on 26 August 1932 said: 'At the moment, the ETU is being singled out as the organization who they claim are poaching on the MFGB, and they are using Durham as the main example. The fact is, of course, that we have in Durham about 200 members to their forty. They claim we have poached them ... which is not correct, as they were mainly non-unionists.' Finally, the two executive committees met under TUC auspices at Transport House on 27 October 1932. Jimmy Rowan's speech in support of the ETU's right to organize its craft, wherever it was deployed, reads like a personal testament of everything the union stood for: 'We claim the right to organize any electrician no matter where he works or in which industry he works. We have no industry. We are an incubus in every other industry.' He briefly dismissed the idea that because electricity had brought technical progress to the mines, which had led to job losses, the ETU were somehow to blame for that.

More directly, Rowan was insistent that 'the wages of men responsible for the safety of life and limb should not be left to the discretion of a body of men who are superior in numbers.' He explained the basis of ETU fears when he said that wages for electricians in South Wales were thirty-three-and-a-third per cent less than contracting rates. When mining electricians heard of a job paying twenty-five per cent more than they were getting in the pit, they went, dropped out of the union and took the lower rates, thus impeding organization for electricians throughout every industry in Wales. Ebby Edwards, speaking for the MFGB executive, persistently referred to 'our friend Rowan' and then attempted to humiliate him by estimating the national colliery membership of the ETU as around 900–1,000 – 'a 850th part of the industry'. The ETU had no agreements. He flatly denied that electricians' wages were set by the votes in miners' lodges. He offered Rowan the same deal the AEU accepted in 1921, where they agreed 'that the Miners Federation shall have control in all industrial matters,' even if the AEU then had to pay 1s per month per member to the MFGB. The permission of the lodge had to be sought before an AEU man could ask for his own union to represent him in an individual dispute. 'Our friend Rowan' and the rest of the executive rejected this proposal – already rejected in 1922 – and the enmity deepened between the two organizations.

By the late spring of 1933, the union was moving to a crisis on the colliery electrician issue. They had rejected the TUC's request to stop 'poaching' in Durham. Tom Stewart's organizing was paying off, and the prospects of action discussed in Durham on 8 July by representatives covering 195 members in thirty-six collieries. In South Wales, Stewart told another conference, 'our efforts have resulted in the ostracism of our members by the miners, but the men must stand together. Something will have to be done to show the MFGB that we will stand no more nonsense and propound our determination to get recognition. ... You go into the fight with your eyes open.' At the same meeting, district secretary Paul McArdle recalled the Durham coal-owners promise to recognize the ETU if they reached fifty per cent of the membership. Now, with seventy-five per cent in the ETU and the rest non-union, they had reneged on that promise. 'You will have to force recognition, even if you are one hundred per cent strong,' said McArdle.

In the midst of this, the TUC ordered the ETU to hand back twelve named members to the MFGB at the Durham Dean and Chapter Colliery. The executive submitted, but were appalled at the TUC meeting in 'secret session', refusing to believe the ETU assertion that people were telling lies.

By January 1934, the determination of the Durham colliery electricians was growing again. On Saturday, 13 January 1934, Rowan 'attended a meeting of delegates drawn from the collieries in the County of Durham. The attendance was only moderately good as some collieries, although invited, were not represented, but I was informed that this was mainly on account of the fact that there was a cup-tie at Sunderland against Middlesbrough. I am not personally satisfied with this'. (However, the delegates who saw Sunderland win would not have shared Jimmy Rowan's priorities that particular day.)

Rowan told the conference that they must rise up against a system that paid 6s $7\frac{1}{2}$d a shift to electricians – just 1d per shift more than the common labourer got, and $1\frac{1}{2}$d an hour *less* than the coal-hewer got if temporary conditions forced *him* away from the coal-face to work as a labourer!

The recognition issue would also be dealt with by a strike in support of 2s a shift increase. Each individual miner would hand in his notice and the strike would decide the issue. Further attempts to negotiate with the coal-owners and the Federation all proved useless. In July, the notices were handed in 'and immediately there was a campaign of intimidation and terrorism,' reported Rowan. The strike collapsed instantly with the first seventeen men dismissed and thrown out of their tied cottages. The executive minutes soberly reflected that 'there was no doubt whatsoever as to the viciousness with which our members have been treated by the colliery managers'. The TUC asked the union to withdraw from the dispute, and they would attempt to settle the difficulties between the ETU and the employers, and between the ETU and MFGB. The same sort of response was meted out to the Lanarkshire Colliery electricians known to be in the ETU where the membership had fallen from 200 down to twelve by 1934. The TUC's efforts were well-meaning, but utterly ineffectual. Nothing happened.

Control over the colliery electricians' destiny was as far away as ever; a dignified but piteous circular to the branches from Rowan in January 1936 underlined the union's essential weakness.

Miners' Wages Dispute

The sub-executive council have had under consideration the position of our members (electricians) employed in and about coal mines arising out of the application by the MFGB for a general increase in wages, and their desire to put in strike notices to enforce their request. In considering the position, the sub-executive council fully realize the hostile action taken by the MFGB in the recent attempts by the ETU to increase the pitifully low base rates for electricians and the threat by the MFGB to 'black' our members if they ceased work to obtain an advance. Having taken the hostile action of the MFGB against our members into full consideration ... in the best interests of trade unionism and to assist the miners ... all members of the ETU in and about mines will be prepared to hand in notices to cease work at the request of the local miners' agents.

The miners attempted something of an olive branch in that they offered the union membership of a craft committee to advise the MFGB of craft problems before they talked to the employers. However, by the end of the year, even this was rejected by the powerful local federations in Durham, North-umberland and Yorkshire who insisted they did not want an advisory committee with anyone – they wanted 'industrial unionism'.

Rowan's last card was provided by the Government inquiry into safety in mines. Rowan had raised this issue at the 1935 TUC – no doubt to confront congress with the nature of the MFGB's behaviour towards the craft unions. He should, however, have taken note of the omens. Lightning hit the new grid extension to Margate on the eve of congress, plunging the town into darkness. The appropriate motion said that electricians in coal mines should be properly qualified – on safety grounds – and that they should also be 'adequately remunerated for their skill and responsibility'. The miners actually opposed the resolution on the grounds that they alone could be entrusted with all mining questions, including electrical safety. Rowan also expressed surprise – not wholly innocently – at the miners taking the motion 'as an attack on the MFGB by accusing them of keeping the wages of electricians at a rate much below the value of their work.' He paid dearly for his bluntness. The miners voted against his re-election to the General Council, thus pre-venting him becoming president of the TUC, and he was replaced by an official of the Draughtsmen's Union, an organization a third of the size of the ETU.

The union sent in its evidence on safety in the mines to the Royal Commission. The ETU position on electricity in the mines was that it was perfectly safe if the equipment was safeguarded to withstand 'the exceptionally heavy and sometimes careless use of the electrical apparatus installed, especially trailing cables and portable switchgear'. The implications of this, though, were that the 'actual inspection, maintenance and repair of electrical apparatus in the mine shall be in the hands of duly qualified persons'. With a central workshop often servicing a group of pits, there was no guarantee of the competence of electricians in collieries; 'there is no degree of training, cer-tification or ability required ... there is no access to technical education facilities.'

All these things had to be done, said the union, which would then more than justify raising the wages of competent men above the level of labourer: and, of course, only the ETU could be entrusted with representing them.

The Royal Commission failed to pronounce on this subject, and the MFGB continued to ignore the union, despite yet more representations to the TUC. When war broke out, the colliery membership was quiescent: the Durham Colliery at Ashington had only sixteen members and Philadelphia and Horden branches had closed. The Scottish and Welsh branches in colliery areas grew slowly and the general branches in mining areas of the North-West like Wigan and Widnes were gaining members fast – outside the collieries.

Relations with Other Unions: Failure in Cinemas

The other main area of employment that attracted the union in the 1930s was the entertainment sector – particularly the cinema electricians and, later, the projectionists proper. Once again, the union was confronted with three problems – low levels of membership, brutal employers, and an opportunistic and unprincipled rival union, NATE. Cinema workers were notoriously difficult to organize. Rowan thought in 1930 that the workers themselves were pretty poor material.

The conditions the men are working under and the wages they are receiving are only commensurate with their want of backbone in sticking up for their own conditions and their inability to combine and allow someone else to improve their conditions for them ... a disgraceful position for them to be in, but not much worse than many of them deserve.

In 1930, the Mersey operators went on strike for higher wages, but the head office had to close the dispute because of massive blacklegging. The Manchester operators tried to organize properly and failed. In the spring of 1935, NATE and the Musicians Union accepted the demands of the Cinema Exhibitors Association (CEA) to drop the forty-eight-hour week, and reimpose a sixty-hour week. At the 1935 TUC Congress, the union moved a motion against the CEA. It was taken by everyone as an attack on NATE, which it clearly was.

The following day after Rowan lost his seat on the General Council for attacking the miners' obstructive attitude to electricians' problems, George Humphreys went to the rostrum. He studiously avoided mentioning NATE, emphasizing only that the industry used to have a forty-eight-hour week and twelve hours per shift in an extremely hot projection room was far too long. Jock Muir, uncharacteristically restrained, simply formally seconded the motion. Tom O'Brien, the general secretary of NATE, leapt onto the rostrum. He said that the ETU motion was exactly the same in intention as the 'safety in mines' motion – innocent on the surface and wicked underneath. His excuse for accepting the sixty-hour week was that the whole industry was poorly organized; *his* union, *not* the ETU had ninety per cent of those who were organized; and that everyone should accept that, at the moment, the employers were in the driving seat. 'The ETU membership of the projectionists and our own in London would not fill a respectable charabanc, and yet we have to come before a body of employers and expect them, with no trade union tradition, suddenly to agree to the forty-eight hour week.'

The union brought the subject back to Congress the following year. Jimmy Rowan appealed for support on the issue of long hours. This time, his seconder was the explosive Alf Coster, who urged strikes in support of the forty-eight-hour week. He also uttered some fairly provocative remarks – 'I ask you – how is it possible for a man like me, who has to meet employers from time to time, to argue on the one hand that we are attempting to secure a maximum working week of forty hours without loss of wages, when trade unions affiliated to this congress are negotiating and signing agreements which allow them to work a sixty-hour week?' Tom O'Brien again said words to the effect of 'be realistic in this set of circumstances' and finished up with a very neat barb – 'I have every sympathy with Mr Rowan in his difficulties in trying to control an organization which is manifestly communist-ridden.'

Competition with NATE – later to take on its new name of NATKE (National Union of Theatrical and Kine Employees) – was opened up again as the union organized the emerging film studios on the edge of London. Throughout 1935 and 1936, the union opened branches to take in the electricians and sound technicians involved in the new industry. Welwyn Garden City was typical for Rowan – 'a beauty spot of England with the Welwyn studios the reason for its inception. If the branch can only become as good as its surroundings, it should be one of the best in the union.'

Problems with NATKE and the cinema employers were not resolved throughout 1937. In April 1938, the union's cinema members in London, Manchester and Hull went on strike for the restoration of the forty-eight-hour week and an increase in wages and above all, recognition of the union nationally. The strike started with great enthusiasm. Six hundred projectionists rallied in Bermondsey Town Hall, undeterred by NATKE's and the Association of Cine Technicians' (ACT) refusal to give undertakings not to supply labour to the cinemas. In Manchester and Hull, the response was tremendous. On 24 May, the Bishop of Manchester himself took a hand in organizing conciliation meetings, but the London dispute was ruined by 'wholesale blacklegging' and inadequate picketing. Strike pay was increased to £1 for married men, 10s for single men. All the strikers also got a £2 national benevolent fund grant. The London district committee ordered the Gaumont and Gainsborough studios out in support of the projectionists – a reckless move that Coster initiated by simply instructing the studio electricians in clear breach of their own procedure. They were promptly sacked, and the victimization pay of £2 10s 0d a week must have been scant compensation.

By the end of May, the executive received a letter from the branch secretary of London Cinema branch – finish the strike or the members would go back on any terms. The strikers were young new recruits to trade unionism, and the best the union could achieve was a dignified return to work where their jobs had not been filled. A short, terse note from the employers, who had refused to meet the union throughout, gives the full flavour of the union's defeat. 'The men will apply for work on 3 June, and the employers will do their best to re-absorb as many of the men as possible' – no forty-eight-hour week, no increase in wages, no recognition, no guarantee on victimization.

In Manchester, the return to work was at least orderly, with the local forty-eight-hour week agreement preserved. In Hull, the strike lasted thirty weeks. This really was magnificent defeat writ large. The local Labour Party, Trades Council and membership itself demonstrated, marched and held meetings. Morale was terrific throughout, impressing old stagers like Rowan and Stewart greatly, but defeat was still the same. At least in Hull, seventeen members stuck it out until the executive closed the dispute formally on 10 December 1938. The employers, particularly in London, were harsh in their victory. By March 1939, nearly a year after the strike had started, the union had 119 members still drawing victimization benefit, unable to work in the industry, and the executive finally stopped payments in April 1939. The cinema dispute cost the union over £15,000 in strike pay and thousands more in unemployment and victimization pay.

These two failures in the cinemas and collieries were, as it turned out, not too crucial for the development of the union due to the growth in other recruiting opportunities. But the union was not to know that the future was going to be kind to them. It is hard to understand in the modern world just what an important industry the cinema was in the 1930s, particularly in the cities and London, and just how the mining industry dominated the old industrial areas. The union was fighting to raise the standards in two industries where low pay and poor conditions existed. They wanted to lift these industries to provide alternative job opportunities for electricians in the cyclical building, engineering and shipbuilding industries; they also needed to stop low wages in the cinemas and collieries dragging down opportunities to raise wages in the other centres of ETU industrial activity. They confronted the most powerful union in the country and one of the most unscrupulous. The TUC was deaf to ETU appeals. The employers concerned were hard, brutal and indifferent. Typically, the union's leadership was not frightened of the scale of the challenge. They could hardly have been surprised at their defeat.

14

DARKNESS APPROACHES

IN THE AFTERMATH OF the General Strike, the union's leadership was consolidated in power. Jimmy Rowan polled 4,067 votes at the end of 1926. Joe Vaughan, the prominent communist, got 730. Jack Lyons, London district president and a man of the left if not a disciplined communist, a derisory 291. Even in Fulham, that touchstone of revolutionary determination, Rowan polled twenty-three votes to Vaughan's six, with Lyons getting fifteen. At the same time, Matt Greenwell beat Jack Lyons by 4,453 to 403 for assistant general secretary. In the 1927 executive elections, now held by rule every two years since the end of 1925, even the militant vote in London was depressed. Harold Morton was returned to the executive council, replacing George Humphreys. Jack Lyons was the left's candidate in the other London divisions, and his paltry 171 votes just beat Ernie Bussey and Vic Needham, both anti-left station engineer candidates. Minority Movement activist Merrells came ninth out of thirteen candidates with sixty-eight votes.

Despite this electoral triumph in the wake of the General Strike, the growth of left-wing ideas – overwhelmingly led by London activists – kept the leadership under constant pressure throughout the inter-war years, culminating in two sensational confrontations that ended in the quiet assumption of control by the left during the Second World War.

The characteristics of this confrontation first became apparent in the years following the emergence of the Communist Party in 1920–21, expressed in the trade unions largely through the Minority Movement. The main tactic it used was to exploit every dispute, every complaint and every piece of employer unreasonableness. The militant activists of the left would expose the injustice, and, just as quickly, expose the union leadership's caution as proof of their cowardice and collaboration with the 'boss class'. No concern over agreements, procedures or even chances of victory should cloud the need for the union to lead workers in struggle, not lead them away from it. If trade union leaders like Rowan and Bussey were all that were standing between workers and the opportunity to smash capitalism, get rid of Rowan and Bussey and all their local apologists. The stage was set, therefore, for endless provocative feuding on industrial issues. Behind each issue, however, irrespective of the merits of each or any case, lay the endless war for the soul of the union.

The relentless dedication of the communists and their allies in the ETU from 1926–39 was the chief characteristic of their tactics. During this period, a more innocent age of political debate within the union was destroyed for ever. Behaviour in branches, at conferences, in the executive council itself began to be characterized by a rising crescendo of lying, petty violence, systematic intimidation, flagrant breaking of the rules, misappropriation of the funds and a final assault on concepts of fraternity. And that was from just the communists.

The behaviour of the left produced a reaction from Rowan and Bussey in the 1930s that led to frequent expulsions, fierce discipline against the wreckers and a cold realization that if the Leninist-left were not fought to a standstill, the union would go down.

Increasingly, the premier battleground for this war to the death was fought over the union's elections. Victory at the polls eventually gave control of the union to the Communist Party; their systematic and corrupt abuse of the same democratic procedures was to destroy them.

London provided the base for all this nonsense: it was not until the mid-1930s that Merseyside provided some support along with a handful of individuals in Manchester.

In the late 1920s, the irritations provided by the left were initially of the pin-prick variety. The executive decided to leave Joe Vaughan alone, publishing his Minority Movement newspaper *Power*.

In 1928, the London district committee actually disaffiliated from the Minority Movement following a rude article in *Power* (which horrified Harry Pollitt, who bombarded the committee with appeals to speak to them). During the elections for the London district committee, the ETU group of the Minority Movement had issued a circular, giving a 'slate' of candidates to be supported. The executive, and the district committee, agreed not to accept Brothers Croker, Clifford and Prowse as district committee-men, because they were on the list. On 16 February, Croker had to be thrown out of the meeting by president Jim Smith. On 3 March, the district committee met to consider motions in support of the three rejected men. P. Finn was of the view that, if necessary, district committee should use force to make sure that scheduled district committee meetings took place, and intimidation was therefore defeated.

Towards the end of the year, the Minority Movement had some success at the elections in London. A. V. Hermon, the leading member of the Minority Movement, was elected, along with Croker and Prowse.

The endemic suspicion between London and the executive council found further expression in 1929 when Jack Lyons was discovered to have deliberately told a hand-picked delegate conference at the Friars Hall on 25 February 1929 that the executive objected to London's wages rising ahead of the National Agreements rates. This conference voted, 86–61, to battle on for 2s an hour and not accept the employers' offer of five per cent which would raise the rate in London to 1s 10$\frac{1}{4}$d. Bussey and Morton registered their disgust at the way the delegates to conference had been 'elected'. Each branch could send two delegates; each job could send two delegates – usually shop-stewards. There was no attendance list, no names taken. Morton said the meeting was packed with 'irresponsibles'. Shop-stewards committees from huge employers like LCC Tramways or the North Met Supply Co only got two delegates, the same as A. V. Hermon's tiny job at the Grosvenor House Hotel in Park Lane. This instruction to battle for the 2s rather than pick up the 1s 10$\frac{3}{4}$d was typical of the use of industrial power for political ends. The district committee preferred the bogus conference vote to balloting the London membership. Bussey attacked front-on.

If this majority had been a democratic vote of the rank and file, about which the district committee mouths so much, we could have maintained a united front in the London area. It appears, however, to be more concerned with fantastic theories of industrialism than with the practical requirements and demands of the membership as a whole.

Disgrace and Resignation: Bill Webb's Demise, 1929

A much more serious event that turned out to have no political overtones at all stunned the London district area and the whole union during the summer of 1929. At the end of 1928, Bill Webb, London district secretary, fell ill. He had pleurisy and bronchitis and was warned by his doctor that he must watch the state of his heart. Reluctantly, and only under pressure from his friends, Bob McLaughlin and Bill Westfallen, Webb took sick leave. In January 1929, he was still ill, and having X-rays taken at the Royal Free Hospital. By March, he was convalescing in Brighton. At the same time, head office were pressing for the normal accounts to be submitted to head office by the district committee. With Webb ill, Bill Westfallen was asked by the district committee to do the necessary work. In a series of poignant letters to Webb, it gradually dawned on Bill Westfallen that the missing paperwork – particularly the missing CWS bank pass book – implied that Webb was stealing the union's money. On 18 March 1929, Westfallen went to the bank, and was shown the account. There was a discrepancy of over £600.

Westfallen eventually saw Webb on 21 March, having coldly summoned him to the office – 'Brother Webb' now, not 'Bill'. 'I first of all told him that I never thought the day would ever come when I should have to address a letter to him on the lines I had sent the previous day. I pointed out that his action in delaying meeting me in this affair was not playing the game to me, who had always had implicit faith in him. He would have known the worry and anxiety that was thrown upon my shoulders arising from his actions.' When asked if he wanted the details of the discrepancy, Webb said he already knew all that as Bob McClaughlin had been round to see him the previous night, to tip him off. 'Brother Webb admitted full liability for the deficit. He also said he would replace into the [full-time officer] fund the amount of the deficiency.'

Westfallen then wrote to Jimmy Rowan on 26 March, saying that he knew giving Webb a few days to pay the money back was 'compounding a felony'. However, he thought that given Webb's previous record, the 'disastrous effect which a disclosure of the true position would have upon the London membership' and the need to get the money back, Rowan would support Westfallen's tolerant attitude.

Rowan was cagey. 'Get a written statement,' he told Westfallen. He said he must tell the sub-executive; but he did not tell the police.

By 9 April, Webb threw in his hand. He wrote to Westfallen that the discrepancy had been accumulating over a fairly long period and was solely his responsibility. He claimed that he never intended to defraud the members, and bemoaned the fact that his friends had not come forward to help him financially. He begged that his past service and current 'broken health and broken spirit' should be taken into account, and he resigned as district secretary.

Westfallen's report to the London district committee on all these events was written on 11 April 1929. He described the whole affair as 'the greatest disaster that has ever befallen our organization in London'. He described how he and Jim Smith, district president, were 'astounded' at the extent of the loss – never realizing that Bill Webb had any personal financial problems. The report concluded:

If I might finish on a personal note; it would be that I do not know what I have done that fate should play such a scurvy trick as to place upon my shoulders the responsibility of making this report. Webb was my pal. Always honest and straight to me. As a new official, the value of his longer experience, counsel, advice and help was always ungrudgingly placed at my disposal. Nor can I forget the great work he has done to improve the rates and conditions for that section of the industry in which I worked for twenty years. . . . Nothing but a sense of duty, responsibility and loyalty to a greater body, the union, would have made me occupy my position today.

This ought to stand a sufficient summary to judge Bill Webb's contribution to the union. In 1939, Joe Wild wrote in his 'souvenir', with Rowan looking over his shoulder: 'Brother Webb was a great force, and the only regrettable point is that he could not keep a financial balance, with the result his services had, with very great regret, to be dispensed with.'

He was expelled by his own branch, Fulham, and he appeared at the police court in Manchester on 19 June, accused of the minor offence of withholding sums of money belonging to the ETU. Mr Ashworth, the union's lawyer, after consultation with Jimmy Rowan and Bob Prain, announced to a startled court before anything was said to get proceedings under way, that Webb had agreed to repay the money in fixed instalments. The hearing lasted all of three minutes. Years later, he was still remembered in London ETU circles. In August 1940, at the age of seventy, Webb was working occasionally as a shipyard electrician in London in support of the war effort in the London docks. He reapplied for membership of the union, saying: 'I do not have many years to live and would like to pass out with a clean sheet as a member of the ETU at that time.' Fulham branch accepted his application, but, under rule, had to refer it to the sub-executive council. As Fulham branch did not create any fuss, it seems that Webb was quietly readmitted. However, by 1942, he was finally retired. Although in ill health, the executive would not let branches break the rules by contributing benevolent grants to retired members. Later that year he died.

More Minority Movement Problems

The election to provide Bill Webb's successor produced the next furore. George Humphreys, ex-Electrical Winders Society secretary, ex-executive councillor in London and left-winger (but not a communist), was the most prominent candidate. A. V. Hermon, the Minority Movement candidate, was accused of sponsoring the wide distribution of a postcard from Putney branch that attacked Humphreys disgracefully. P. Winter, the Putney secretary, and Dick Homewood, Putney's branch president, had circulated a postcard throughout London, copied from a letter from Fulham, that alleged George Humphreys had worked quietly in a non-union armature winding shop. This was proved to be quite false; but by November 1930, the whole business had degenerated into executive-Minority Movement confrontation. Herman had managed to prove he was not involved in the postcard business.

However, he flaunted his Minority Movement credentials in a 'personal statement' to the district committee that was circulated to the members. 'I contest this election for the position of London district secetary on the policy of the National Minority Movement and the Communist Party; on the policy pursued by the Minority Movement group on the London district committee,

(*Above*) Jimmy Rowan, pictured here in 1904, was National Organizer (1904–7) and General Secretary (1907–40).

(*Above*) Alf Ewer, local organizer of the Union's first strike; first National Organizer (1899–1901) and General Secretary (1901–7).
(*Left*) Alex Calipé, Executive Councillor and Treasurer of the Union (1893–1907).

The first Executive Council elected on a national basis in December 1907. *Back row* H. E. Oakleigh London and the South), W. C. McKay (Manchester), J. Kinniburgh (Scotland), F. Soughton (Midlands and Wales), A. Garner (Liverpool and North West). *Front row* B. MacMillan (N.E. Coast and Yorks.), . Rowan (General Secretary), J. W. Ball (General President), H. Coulthard (General Treasurer), . Ferguson (National Organizer).

A. GARNER J. McCOUBREY P. SOUGHTON H. HAWKINS
(Birkenhead). (Belfast). (Cardiff). (Trafford Park).

W. J. WEBB W. H. CASS W. H. SWINDURNE W. NOBLE R. FRAIN P. A. IRVINE R. W. WILSON J. J. MELVILLE F. E. RELFE S. LOWE G. R. DAWSON E. FISHER A. WRIGHT T. HELM
(London West). (Leeds). (Middlesbrough). (Newcastle). (Glasgow). (Trafford Park). (Birmingham). (Glasgow). (Aberdare). (Nottingham). (Sheffield). (Manchester). (Dublin). (Preston).

A. GERARD W. G. BUCKE A. H. STEWART W. TODD J. FIDLER F. W. TRIGGS A. H. BOND E. C. GRIER T. E. FARR
(Greenock). (London Central). (Glasgow). (Newcastle). (Oldham). (Liverpool). (Sunderland). (Leicester). (Plymouth).

J. W. PRATT T. D. MILBURN T. PHILPOT W. C. McKAY J. KINNIBURGH J. ROWAN J. W. BALL H. COULTARD J. R. SEDDON F. ARUNDEL W. H. KEMP
(London East). (Manchester). (London S.E.). (Manchester). (Organiser). (Gen. Secretary). (G.E. President). (Gen. Treasurer). (Bootle). (Barrow). (Bolton).

(*Above*) The delegates to the 1911 conference in Manchester. This picture includes virtually all of the original branch secretaries who took the Union from obscurity to national recognition in the years either side of the First World War.

(*Far left*) C. H. Stavenhagen, Syndicalist and fundamental Socialist, Executive Councillor (1915–19) and Chairman of London District Committee during the First World War.

(*Left*) Bill Webb, Executive Councillor (1916–17) and London full-time official (1917–29).

(*Left*) Walter Citrine, the first elected district full-time official on Merseyside (1914–20), Assistant General Secretary (1920–4). His great career at the TUC as General Secretary, at the Coal Board as a director and as Chairman of the nationalized electricity supply industry makes him the ETU's most famous son.

Two views of the Union's growth. The first (*right*) was published in the left-wing London magazine *Electron* in 1918. The Left took an unfriendly attitude to other unions' style, preferring ETU members to take the 'right road' to emancipation on its own. The second approach, as seen in the Union's official magazine, the *Electrical Trades Journal*, in 1924, preferred growth through amalgamation with other unions. The fears expressed in the caption were well-founded.

"TOWARDS THE DAWN."

Are YOU on the Right Road?

IF NOT,

JOIN THE E.T.U.

Printed by the Twentieth Century Press (1912), Ltd., T.U. & 44 hours, 37a, Clerkenwell Green, London, E.C.

"LINKING

The Reader :—"Well, Tom, what are you going to do about it?"
Tom :—"Vote for it myself and get others to vote for it."
The Reader :—"That's the ticket. It's no use shouting for amalgamation and then not voting for it when you get the chance."

The Executive Council, 1924. *Back row* F. Morrison (N.E. Coast and E. Scotland), T. Corbett (Merseyside and Lancs.). *Standing, left to right* J. Kinniburgh (National Organizer), T. Anderson (W. Scotland), J. Smith (London), W. Minor (Wales and South West), M. Greenwell (Assistant General Secretary), W. McKay (Manchester), W. Finn (Ireland), J. Bellamy (Yorks.), T. Stewart (National Organizer). *Sitting, left to right* H. P. Bolton (London), J. Rowan (General Secretary), J. W. Ball (General President), R. Prain (Assistant General Secretary).

During the early 1930s, the technologies represented by electricity began to become all prevalent as the national grid spread. This picture shows Walter Lewis, the Birmingham District Secretary from 1923 to 1947, on the right of a display used in Lewis's successful campaign for the local council in 1932. Progressive technology was linked with the Labour Party in this way – despite the horse-drawn float.

The Union supports the Labour Party. The cartoon on the left, from 1924, interestingly pre-dates David Low's more famous characterization of the Labour movement as a carthorse. The second (*right*) is from 1929.

President Ernie Bussey (left) and General Secretary Jimmy Rowan on the seafront at Margate during the 1935 Trades Union Congress.

The Executive Council 1939. *Back row, left to right* R. C. Todd (N. Ireland), Colin Innes (E. Scotland), Willie Turnbull (W. Scotland). *Middle row* H. Thorpe (Yorks.), Alf Martin (London and West Home Counties), Harry Turner (Wales and South-West), Alf Hatton (Manchester) Gus Cole (Merseyside and Lancs.), E. R. Lee (Midlands), Frank Haxell (E. London and East Anglia). *Front row* Ernie Irwin (National Organizer), Bob Prain (Assistant General Secretary), Jimmy Rowan (General Secretary), Ernie Bussey (President), Jack Ball (Hon. Vice-President), Matt Greenwell (Assistant General Secretary), Ben Bolton (National Organizer). (Les Gregory was ill when this photograph was taken.)

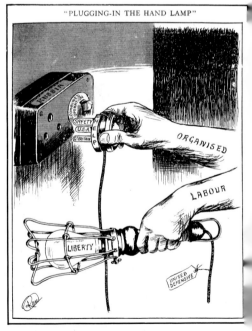

Two war-time cartoons show the Union's political attitudes to the war through electrical allusions. The cartoon on the left was published in April 1940, the one on the right following the turning-point of Russia's entry into the war in July 1941.

Until the end of 1965, Executive Councillors worked at the trade; most, however, grew to live off delegation expenses. Harry Turner, Executive Councillor for Wales and the South West (1937–44), is pictured here in 1940 at work.

The Communist-dominated Executive Council on the day Esher Place opened in 1953. *Back row* Jim Humphrey, Bob McLennan, Les Cannon, Bill Benson, George Stevens, Les Gregory, Tom Vincent, Gus Cole, Peter Snadden. *Front row* Frank Murphy, Jim Cosby, Jack Potter, Walter Stevens, Frank Foulkes, Frank Haxell, Bert Batchelor, Tommy Vetterlein.

President Ben Bolton and General Secretary Ernie Bussey stand proudly by the YMCA tea-van donated by the Union to the armed forces in 1944.

The Three 'Generals' 1959: General Secretary, Frank Haxell, General President, Frank Foulkes and Assistant General Secretary, Bob McLennan.

Walter Stevens, Assistant General Secretary (1942–8), General Secretary (1948–54).

Three Communist-supporting delegates at the 1952 Rules Revision Conference at Whitley Bay: Jack Hendy, Wally Bolt and Jack Frazer. Behind them, alone, sits Jock Byrne.

and on my activities in the workshop on behalf of the workers.' Faction politics in the raw. His supporters were discovered in the following year to have overpaid benefits, readmitted expelled members, and refused to accept executive council instructions. The executive shut Putney and Fulham branches and promptly expelled Winter, Homewood, Patrick Kennedy and S. Longish. The branches were later reopened by 'loyal' members. Hermon became ever more infamous. He got 493 votes against George Humphreys 1,156 votes in the election. He came second – well ahead of stalwarts like Fred Alford and Jack Lyons. It is clear that the communist vote was being solidified. Nevertheless, he was not allowed to go to the 1930 Labour Party conference as a delegate, having signed a Minority Movement ETU Group diatribe that the union ought to leave the Labour Party.

In early 1931, Hermon was in trouble for circulating a letter concerning the executive's alleged sell-out in the Dagenham dispute, which then appeared in the *Daily Worker*. Rowan had been accused, falsely, of going off from a union meeting to dinner with the employers. (He had been with the executive council all day and night.) Brother H. Merrells, who wrote the circular, was the organizer for the Minority Movement ETU group. He was also the delegate who could not attend the 1930 rules revision conference because he was attending the fifth world conference of the Red International of Labour Unions in Moscow. His apology was not accepted! Hermon gave the information to the *Daily Worker*. Both refused to accept the rules of the union about circulating and disclosing the business of the union. Both claimed a higher loyalty to the working-class. Both were expelled from the union in July 1931. Curiously, the executive let Hermon and Homewood back in the union less than a year later, on their undertakings to obey the executive. Merrells was made of sterner stuff. Although he reapplied and freely admitted that the allegation about Rowan was a lie, he insisted that the Minority Movement came first.

Bussey asked Mr Merrells, if, as a member of the National Minority Movement, the governing body of that Movement laid down a policy and principles which were opposed to the policy and principles of the executive council of the ETU, would he follow the principles and policy of the National Minority Movement instead of the principles and policy of the executive of the ETU?

Mr Merrells stated that any policy of the Minority Movement must be in the interests of the trade union movement.

This kind of equivocation made sure he was not allowed back in until March 1934. (On the occasion of his readmission, Rowan ruefully pondered out loud just how it was that this non-unionist had been tolerated as the only 'nonner' at Woolwich Council for ages!)

Dagenham 1931

The Dagenham strike had provided the Minority Movement with a set of highly promising circumstances. In March 1931, a contractor called B. French from Kidderminster, working on part of the huge site for the building of Ford's new car plant at Dagenham, discovered that only one-sixth of the site was actually in the London area, with five-sixths of it in Essex. Consequently, they refused to pay their electricians the London rate (1s 9$\frac{1}{2}$d and five per cent [1s 10$\frac{1}{2}$d]) and instead paid the Essex county rate, Grade 'C', of 1s 6d an hour despite the fact that other contractors were paying London rates. All members of the ETU on the site were withdrawn by the London district committee, particularly as French's were not paying any travelling expenses or country allowances, either. An aggregate meeting on 18 March in London decided, 910–145, to strike in defence of the London rate for Dagenham, and what's more, to strike in defence of the extra five per cent on the London rate that the NFEA were threatening to withdraw if the Dagenham dispute continued.

The executive council supported the constitutional behaviour of the London district committee, and made the strike official. The NFEA cut wages by five per cent. The NFEA spokesmen – Messrs Riggs and Penwill – were willing to have the issue referred to arbitration, but only if the men went back on Essex rates. Rowan and Lyons told the NFEA on 10 March that it was up to them to put French's right (they had a history of underpaying in London – for instance, on the Firestone Tyres factory site in West London). The strike commenced all across London, but was quickly settled on the basis of paying Dagenham strikers the Essex rates plus 1d an hour, and the five per cent was restored to the London membership.

The Minority Movement seized on this to denounce executive and district committee alike. For months after the strike, carefully co-ordinated protests were sent in to the executive, culminating in an invasion of the executive council boardroom on Saturday, 12 September 1931. 'Brother Muirhead, who was attending as a deputation from LSE No. 17 branch, burst into the room, and seizing hold of the back of one of the chairs adopted a "throw-me-out-if-you-dare" attitude. Brother Muirhead was asked by the chairman to leave the room. He informed the executive that he refused to leave the room until he was heard. The meeting of the executive council was immediately adjourned.' An unofficial strike committee was still trying to keep the dispute with French's going, but it quietly fell away as the London district committee did not wish to pursue the issue for fear of imperilling the five per cent at a time when the falling cost of living had brought an automatic sliding scale reduction of 1$\frac{1}{4}$d in the rate.

By the end of 1931, the union had a new president. Jack Ball had to resign to stay in Manchester, close to his job as a radiographer. In all trade union elections, the great moment of opportunity arises when a long-term incumbent of a high position retires or dies. All the candidates feel they have a chance. Factories organize with a real sense of anticipation. Jack Ball had been president since 1908, initially elected by executive colleagues, and re-elected at every election involving the whole membership since 1912. At his last election, held in December 1930, he had beaten Joe Vaughan by 5,646 to 702, with Jack Lyons getting 540 votes. Ball had won seventy-nine per cent of the vote. The nearest anyone ever came to him was in 1919 when in a huge field of fifteen candidates, Ball beat Stavenhagen, 3,552–1,646, taking fifty-six per cent of the vote to Stavenhagen's twenty-six per cent.

Ernie Bussey as President, 1931

The 1931 result in an open field of thirteen candidates was much clearer. The left had two serious candidates. Joe Vaughan got 527 votes. Jack Lyons, already on the executive for the North and North-West and East of London since January 1928, sometime president of the London district committee, got 2,009 votes. Harold Morton stood, and got 1,886 votes, winning his own South London and South of England executive division and the North-East (where he was supported by Paul McArdle, the local official, who had a special interest in supply and knew Morton well). The winner was Ernest Bussey. Bussey was born in 1892 in Poplar in East London. He came from a family of seven and his father worked in the docks. He joined the Independent Labour Party in Keir Hardie's early West Ham stronghold in 1909, and went to technical college before becoming a junior engineer at the West Ham electricity undertaking. After four years there, he joined LCC Tramways as an electrical engineer. Disappointed with the early forerunner of the EPEA, the Association of Electrical Station Engineers, he set up the first station engineers' branch of the ETU with his life-long political friend, Harold Morton, in November 1916. By 1919, he was secretary of the huge North London supply branch, LSE No. 10, and confronted the left in London who wanted to use supply workers in 1919 to guarantee the achievement of the forty-hour week for all. He was a tall, bulky man who could write well and speak in a literate and passionate way. He had suffered meeting after meeting of the London district committee's madder moments. He had endured the personal abuse and the accusations of betrayal and personal corruption since the early 1920s. He saved the 1929 conference from rejecting reform of the union's structure and moved the reorganization scheme at the 1930 conference. He won every region of the union, including the North and Eastern London division, except Merseyside (which went to Lyons) and South London (which voted for Morton). He got 2,968 votes which amounted to 32.5 per cent of the vote. Throughout the 1930s, though, he increased his vote and his margins of victory enormously.

In December 1933, he beat Jock Muir, 6,108–3,143, although he was defeated in both London executive council divisions. Again Muir was the opponent for the 1936–7 period of office and again won in London, but Bussey won overall, 7,694–3,679. He beat Joe Lane comfortably in 1937, and leading the union into war, he was elected by 15,068 votes to Alf Martin's 3,738 in December 1939, even winning two out of the three executive council divisions in London. His seventy-seven per cent of the vote in that election has to be borne in mind as the evidence of insult, fury and abuse is examined through the 1930s.

Throughout the 1930s, the rivalry between the left and the leadership gathered momentum. In 1932, branches had to be reminded that they were not permitted to affiliate to the Minority Movement or similar 'vigilance committees'.

More Trouble with the District Committee in London, 1932–6

By October, the London district committee was suspended for the umpteenth time. This time, it defied the executive over three separate issues. First, the executive would not support the London district committee's attempts to impose a closed shop at Poplar Council – mainly because the 1927 Trades Disputes Act was threatened against the union. Second, the district committee wanted to organize a conference against the means test alongside the obvious communist front organization, the National Unemployed Workers Movement. Third, yet another unofficial dispute. This time a young man called Snow had just finished his apprenticeship for G. E. Taylor's, working on a job on the Queen's Road Cinema in Bayswater. He was paid only eighty per cent of the rate, and the union tacitly accepted this – including the leading lights in London, Jack Lyons and George Humphreys, who were involved in the negotiations – while talks went on at national level with the NFEA. Battersea Power Station men came out, briefly, in support of Taylor's strikers. Rowan was angry with Lyons who had not told Rowan originally that back in March the London disputes committee had this issue well in hand. Defiance was heaped on defiance, with the district committee paying strike pay out of its 'distress fund', urging branches to pay strike pay and making arrangements to circulate branches. The executive voted 8–1 (Jack Lyons) to suspend the district committee while at the union's conference in Blackpool – and also wrote to the London officials to tell them to take their orders from the executive council. Jack Lyons resigned as executive councillor on 15 October 1932; on 21 November 1932, the sub-executive council summoned the London officials and reviewed their performance in these three crises: Rowan told them that he feared that the real target was the break-up of the national agreement in contracting with the NFEA, and he was not having it. George Humphreys had to sign an undertaking not to break the rules. This meeting encapsulated the perennial problem concerning the role of the full-time officials and explains what was behind the reorganization scheme's insistence that only by paying officials out of national funds instead of local levies, would the authority of the executive be established once and for all. Rowan was annoyed that the London officials had not disowned the unconstitutional action taken in the G. E. Taylor's/Battersea strikes. Worse still, they had not obeyed the executive instructions sent to them. Westfallen told the sub-executive that:

... he always understood that he was a servant of the members of the London district, and was under the control and jurisdiction of the London district committee, and had to carry out the instructions given by the committee to him as an official. Brother Rowan informed Brother Westfallen that he was not bound to carry out the instructions of the London district committee if such instructions were contrary to the constitution and rules of the union!... He, Brother Rowan, wished to be perfectly frank about the statements made as to the London officials telling members one thing as officials of the union, and making other statements as rank and file members ... statements made by Brother Coster at Dagenham and in the recent Taylor dispute, had informed the men on strike that as an official he must point out to them that they were entirely out of order and should return to work. He then added that personally, if *he* was in their position, he knew what he would do!

By the end of the year, the ex-district committee was meeting fairly openly as an 'alternative' district committee in London – calling itself the 'broad committee', issuing circulars and advice to branches and members. Arthur Cox, from London East, and J. F. Francis, from Fulham, were expelled when they rather unfortunately were the only ex-district committee men to admit to having launched the broad committee at the Friars Hall on 16 December 1932. Cox had been the latest left candidate to be devastated by Rowan, 5,032–1,927, in the general secretary election one year before. The Fulham branch took legal advice that the district committee 'elections' held in September 1932 were legal and got an injunction to prevent any further district committee elections. It was not until May 1934 that Fulham withdrew their legal case (which cost the members concerned £453, payable to the union). In the meantime, the executive shut Plaistow branch for readmitting the expelled A. E. Cox and circularizing branches and were then embarrassed by complaints from the Tailor and Garment Workers Union that Joe Vaughan was attending their strike meetings and breaking them up by attacking the garment workers' officials in the now conventional vernacular of betrayal and sell-out.

So much for London: early in 1934, the first signs of the conspiracy started to appear in the provinces. George Chadwick sent a report to the executive that a 'rank and file' meeting had been held at Transport Hall, Islington in Liverpool on 6 January 1934. In the chair was Frank Foulkes, chairman of

Walton branch and a shop- and money steward at Edge Lane Tramcar Works. Other Liverpool branch officials and district committee delegates were also in attendance, like Maguire, the secretary of Liverpool station engineers, and Tansley, Gordon, Comus and Brierley from Bootle. Also present was Gus Cole from Walton branch. They were going to organize a strike against the NFEA agreement in Liverpool if something was not done. Two delegates to this meeting, Townsley and Gordon, actually sent apologies to the district committee which was meeting at the same time, to say they thought the 'rank and file' meeting took priority. The executive ignored this, but the next month they received a letter from Stockport branch complaining about Plaistow being closed and Cox being expelled – particularly as he had won a place on the TUC delegation ahead of Bussey and was right in line with left-wingers Jim Smith and George Millar who had just won London executive seats. Rowan could not take this. He wrote back to Stockport in March 1934.

You are acting under a great misapprehension if you think that the voting in the London district during the past two years indicates the actual position in London. You will have to realize that during this period, the communist or Minority Movement have been visiting branches and putting forth all sorts of unfounded allegations against the executive council and in every way possible, to poison the minds of the members.

He was to reinforce this message vigorously at the union's conference in Blackpool in May. The normal business was suspended on the Friday morning to discuss the implications behind the leafleting of the conference with a handbill advertising a mass meeting in London the following week. This meeting was going to be addressed by 'rank and file' speakers, and the delegates were urged, in capital letters, to remember the means test certificate, the suspension of the London district committee, the differential treatment meted out to the broad committee, Dagenham, the five per cent cut and the Poplar and the Taylor's dispute. Frank Morrison, the lean, cigarette-smoking left-wing executive member from Edinburgh, was mellowing in his old age. He thought the circular was simple abuse of the executive. London delegate Hallam ignored the issue of unsigned, unofficial handbills and urged 'tact and a little knowledge of human nature' over Plaistow and urged 'tolerance' for the erstwhile London district committee.

Jimmy Rowan sprang to his feet. His first remarks were to the effect that if this unofficial pamphleting would stop, half the sub-executive's work would be over. He quoted Robert Blatchford, the old 'Clarion' socialist, in saying that what Brother Hallam wanted the executive to do was to 'tolerate the intolerable'. He then tried to explain to the conference that the anonymous people behind the leaflet were not interested in the means test or wages or any other issue:

... the people behind these meetings were not concerned one little bit with the good of the ETU. It was well known that a number of our members, particularly in the London area, were closely identified with the Communist Party, and all its various subsidiary committees. He referred to brother J. J. Vaughan, of Hackney branch, who, although he had not been working in the industry for about fifteen years, still retained his trade union ticket.... The only reason Brother Vaughan had for holding a ticket was so that he could carry out the avowed policy of the Communist Party.

He then reported his embarrassing story about Vaughan and the Tailor and Garment Workers' meetings and repeated that the problems in London were caused by people who 'would use heaven and earth to prevent any settlement of any dispute affecting the ETU.' The Minority Movement supporters in the conference wriggled under this onslaught. Hallam as we have seen, pleaded for 'tolerance'. Cliburn (from London) said what was wrong with meeting to talk about wages? Liverpool's Gordon said that the conference did not know who issued the circular and so they should get on with the rules revision agenda. Preston's iconoclast La Vatte wanted to talk about the rules, not communists. Glasgow's T. Carter moved, and London delegate W. Ives seconded (saying briefly that not all London delegates were against everything the executive did), that the conference 'repudiate' the circular/handbill, and they did, 22–9, with five other delegates not voting. This was not to be the last time that the role of the Communist Party in the union's affairs was to be directly debated.

On return from conference, the Plaistow branch was reopened and 'Walter Henry Homewood' as he put on his form, along with Cox and Francis, was readmitted to the union at the end of the year. Any thoughts that the war was over were cruelly shattered by the reopening of the London district committee, now in its four regional committees with a central committee. The London-wide election produced an old friend as president – Jock Muir – who also won a seat on the executive council again in December 1935. He had been absent from the executive for fourteen years. However, back in December 1934, there was near-chaos over a dispute with Drake and Gorham. They had a depot in central London. They had sites in Kilburn and Willesden and in an endeavour to avoid paying travelling allowances they opened a new office locally, and engaged the men formally from there. They promptly refused to go to the local office, signed on in central London, and walked out to Kilburn or Willesden, working twenty-three not forty-seven hours each week

The London district committee ordered George Humphreys not to discuss the issue with the London NFEA, who promptly threatened to withdraw the five per cent. The executive confronted the district committee yet again, but the dispute was settled at the NFEA by defining properly where a 'shop' was based. Jock Muir and George Humphreys were also involved in an irritating bit of defiance when the members at RACS (Royal Arsenal Co-operative Society) in Woolwich were instructed not to work any overtime or talk to the president of the union when Bussey tried to sort the problem out locally. Muir and Humphreys were summoned to the executive and told to toe the line. Humphreys was clearly uneasy at the position he kept finding himself in. 'Did the sub-executive council appreciate the difficult position he was in in attempting to carry out the decisions of his committee and the contrary instructions from the executive council? It appeared to him that he was at all times between the upper and nether millstone.' Bill Turnbull was having none of that. 'We are entitled to expect Brother Humphreys to know that the supreme authority in the union is the executive council. When a district committee decision is contrary to an executive council instruction, it is his clear duty to tell the district committee that he cannot act on their decision.' Muir was censured for urging the district committee to ignore executive instructions to follow procedures and for organizing the silence of the Woolwich Co-op men.

Still the catalogue of confrontation lengthened, with two more strikes at Poplar Council in 1935 and 1936. The 1935 strike involved sixty members who were in dispute over wages and replaced by blacklegs; Hackney branch tried to spread it from the council contracting/installation men into the electricity supply part of the council's operation. The executive did not want to fight the NJIC in supply, and it is not hard to understand their irritation with the shop-steward at the council, Ronnie Sell, when in early 1936, another strike broke out. Sell had worked at the council since 1932 as a meter reader. On 17 January, after an informal discussion with the borough engineer, he agreed that 100 meters a day was a reasonable average to read. That day, Sell went out with a book of 154 meters – many in multi-occupancy houses – and read 122 meters and brought the book back and went home. The next day, he did the remainder and started a new book – a total of 122 meters once again. The same management that had imported blacklegs a few months earlier was not having this, and sacked Sell. His action, according to Sell himself when interviewed by the sub-executive council, was 'taken deliberately with the full intention of raising the whole matter of what he alleged was an agreement between the chief electrical engineer and himself that 100 meters a day was a fair average.' The executive refused to accept the district committee's demands for victimization pay.

The London central committee was hard at it throughout the summer of 1936. They urged the union to reduce contributions so that the ETU could attract a more general, industrial membership. Then, at the same moment, they levied the London membership 'voluntarily' 1d per member to set up a 'fighting fund' to get round the lack of executive support for each and every dispute. They had to be ordered to stop a ballot for breaking away from the contracting national agreement, as it was in contravention of national union policy, as expressed by both conference and executive decision. In September, there was a dispute at Fulham Power Station, when the members voted, 22–19, to strike in defence of the need to keep a certain ratio of mates to craftsmen on a contracting job. Coster had gone down to encourage the strikers, the London central committee had demanded strike pay, some of the strikers were touring branches and denouncing colleagues who had worked. The London central committee, Muir, and especially Coster, were criticized by the executive for keeping the dispute going even though the executive quickly moved to solve the issue apparently most involved – the mates/craftsmen ratio. The significance of this dispute was that George Millar, elected on a left ticket in London, moved the executive resolution to hold Muir 'personally responsible' if any other sheer defiance was demonstrated by the London district committee.

The Dam Breaks: Earl's Court, 1936

At the end of 1936, probably the most significant dispute in the union's history took place at the Earl's Court Exhibition Centre. After this dispute, things were never the same within the union. Political change followed remorselessly in the next five years. The Communist Party influence in the union was to be in the ascendant for over twenty years after it. And all over wellington boots.

The weather was uniformly awful in October and November 1936. The main electrical contract at Earl's Court was held by Electrical Installations Ltd, and there was a subsidiary group of electricians employed by the main contractor, Messrs Hegeman and Harris Ltd, working on the whole site's temporary lighting.

On 16 December, Alf Coster and Mr Penwill met as a NFEA disputes committee to consider, belatedly, a claim for abnormal conditions money. Mr Penwill conceded that at one time, the men had been 'up to their eyes in mud' and that even Mr Coster had got water over his shoes. But that was in October and November; by mid-December, as the work progressed, the site was getting a lot easier to work on. Mr Penwill therefore offered the men £50 between the 100 or so men affected to compensate for ruined shoes, cleaning bills, the purchase of boots etc. That was Penwill's version of the disputes committee hearing, and he could produce 'minutes' to prove it. Alf Coster had a different story. His version of events was that he raised with Penwill the legitimate claim that under Clause 18 of the London Agreement, the employers should pay 1s a day for each man for the October/November period (approximately £3 each) – just as Tommy Clarke's, the contractor, had done on the Dorchester Hotel job in similar circumstances. Furthermore, Coster wrote to the shop-steward, W. Lindsell, at Earl's Court on 17 December implying that that was what Penwill was going to do, and the letter was pinned up in the electricians' mess room.

It is not difficult to imagine how the men from Electrical Installations Ltd felt cheated when the formal offer was made of £50 between them and not 1s a day. On New Year's Eve, the strike commenced. On 4 January, Penwill authorized an increased offer of £75, whilst emphasizing that the men were out of procedure. The men from Electrical Installations Ltd rejected that, but the situation was made worse on the same day by Coster persuading the main contractor, Hegeman and Harris, to pay the 1s a day for the two months to the temporary lightmen.

The whole issue turned on whether Penwill *did* agree to 1s a day, and then thought better of it, or whether Coster imagined that 1s a day – because it had recently been paid at the Dorchester – was the inevitable result of Penwill's concession that some sort of payment was going to be made. The political fall-out from this was to be enormous.

The executive were told of the dispute, by Mr Penwill, on 6 January while at other negotiations on the national working rules card. They were not best pleased when they received the London central committee's response contained in the district committee minutes of Tuesday 5 January.

The London central committee had heard from a deputation from Earl's Court, led by the chairman of the works committee, Brother Collier. He told the central committee that the Electrical Installations strikers were annoyed at the lack of help they were getting from Hegeman and Harris sparks, quite happy with Coster's work, and were determined to be paid for the time lost during the dispute! They then asked for the dispute to be made official. At this point, the issue became one between the London central committee and the executive council.

The chairman pointed out that due to the action taken, it was not possible for the central committee to approach the executive council to make the dispute official, as the committee knew from previous experience that this would be refused. The committee, however, as a committee, was prepared to back our members both morally, and as far as it was able, financially.

On 7 January, they met again and advanced the strikers £1 each from the unofficial emergency fund they controlled.

The sub-executive saw Coster, Humphreys and Muir the following day and limited themselves initially to expressing the view that no one could construe from either Penwill's minutes or Coster's letter that there had ever been a promise of 1s a day. Amongst the Hegeman and Harris workers affected on site was George Millar – executive councillor and, by virtue of being a London executive man, part of the sub-executive council. The sub-executive got Coster to return to the men to put Penwill's 4 January offer of £75 to the men. They turned it down, 71–14. On 16 January, the sub-executive council, led by Rowan, went to the Atlas Hotel in West Brompton and urged the members to return to work. They again refused, despite Rowan insisting that Coster's letter was not a sufficient basis on which to make the strike official. On 22 January, the sub-executive took over the running of the dispute, ordering the London central committee to push the issue up the procedure to them, and in the meantime, the dispute was not to be mentioned at central committee, nor was any time to be spent by the committee on it.

On the evening of 26 January, Rowan and Bussey met Mr Cash of the NFEA, who had just left an executive meeting of the ECA. Mr Cash, according to Bussey, laid it on the line.

The concern of the ECA was not with the immediate merits or demerits of the dispute at Earl's Court. They were concerned about the London district committee's role – the central committee's role – in the dispute.

Their concern was that the men were out and being actively supported by a responsible committee of the union which was party to the joint machinery for dealing with such matters. They (the employers) had been very clearly advised by our representatives that as far as London was concerned, the decision of the central committee was paramount. If that was the position, and the executive of the union had no control over its committees or members, if 'the tail was wagging the dog', then the ECA had instructed them (the NFEA) to say that the national membership of that body would protect itself against the uncontrolled membership of the ETU.

Rowan told them that they unreservedly withdrew Coster's letter and Coster had been told to do so – not least because George Humphreys was equivocal in his memory as to whether Coster had been justified in writing the letter in the first place. Mr Walton of the NFEA said that that was all right, as far as it goes, but the strikers were being supported financially by an official body of the ETU – the London central committee. He reported the veiled threat of a national lock-out in the absence of the ETU leadership's re-establishing control. Bussey gave them what they wanted. 'I stated ... that acting for and on behalf of the executive council ... I would instruct our members of the ETU to resume work for the purpose of permitting the agreement to operate and the complaint to be sympathetically considered.' George Humphreys was written to the following morning in just that vein, and George Humphreys went to Earl's Court to tell them to go back to work. A meeting was held at a cafe in West Brompton with around seventy men squashed in. Only two dissented when Collier moved that the strikers 'ignore the executive council's instructions and pin our faith on the central committee and stay as we were'.

The strike went on, and the circulars started to fly round the branches, denouncing the executive and in particular accusing George Millar and the men on Hegemans and Harris of betraying the strikers. Millar was a charge-hand for the company, and was able to bring witnesses with minutes of meetings that showed the original dispute to have been completely hatched by Electrical Installations members – they never consulted Millar's members or the forty men putting in the Express Lifts, or the handful of others working for companies installing the public address systems.

On 7 February 1937, the London central committee came before the executive council. Muir thought if only there had been joint action on the original claim, of 1s a day, then the main contractors would have paid for Electrical Installations as well as their own men at Hegemans and Harris – but the NFEA had blocked that approach. Although 'they (the London central committee) did not ask the men to go on strike, now they were on strike, and prepared to fight the issue, then he was prepared to back them'. Muir agreed with the statements current in London 'that the head office of the ETU had simply become a sub-office of the NFEA'.

Bob McClennan, a central committee man and a friend of Ronnie Sells in the same branch of LSE No. 5, just bluntly faced out the executive. He said there had been fifteen strikes in London since May 1935 and the executive had supported just one. What was the point of going through procedure or asking for the strike to be made official? He felt justified in supporting members on strike, both morally and financially: and that trying to get the London central committee to follow 'procedures' was a back-door way to getting them to accept the discipline of the NJIC for contracting. London rejected this. His aggressiveness was only exceeded by Joe Vaughan. 'In his opinion, it was all part of the class struggle, and he supported the class struggle at all times.' Percy Cliburn, the South East London district secretary, made a 'vicious' attack on George Millar. Harold Ross from London Press said that Millar had been seduced on the executive until he 'no longer gave consideration to the needs of the members'. Hallam said that if supporting men on strike 'brought discredit on the union', he was very glad he was quitting. He recalled hearing Jock Muir twenty-three years ago saying you would only get out of an employer what you could force out of him – and he still believed that. Francis, Hart and Lester were all unrepentant on behalf of the strikers, irrespective of any other considerations.

The following day, the full executive tore into George Humphreys. He had allowed unsubstantiated insults to Jimmy Rowan to go out in the minutes unchecked. He had not defended the non-striking members at Earl's Court who had followed the constitution of the union. He was complaining about overwork on the official business of the union, but could find plenty of time to get involved in this unofficial nonsense. He was issuing details of an unofficial fund – 'the fighting fund' – on official union notepaper. He was following the instructions of the central committee without demur, when his real responsibility was to the executive council.

Humphreys again made reference to being between the upper and nether millstones of the central committee and the executive council; and although he was clearly uncomfortable, he had to maintain standards of probity at the area office – not least over the fighting fund which, although unofficial, was at least, in his hands, run properly. Coster was pilloried again for his misleading letter, and then the shop-stewards from the non-striking companies gave evidence of how they had been intimidated by the strikers and their supporters.

The executive then looked at all the evidence: what was astonishing was that the charge was led by George Millar and Jim Smith. These left-wing London executive councillors were clearly moved by the intensity of the defiance offered by the London central committee. Millar said that, as an executive councillor, he could not possibly countenance unofficial action on the job he worked on personally. Jim Smith, Bill Webb's old friend, ex-London district president, was very angry indeed. 'The whole substance of the matter is that the London central committee have made up their minds to openly defy the executive council. The executive council were either the governing body of the union or they were not.' He understood the position about being disappointed at the way they were held back by the national agreement in contracting – but it was only there in the first place because of a national ballot vote of the members. Muir, of course, as an executive councillor as well as president of the London district committee, sat through all this impassively. Further consideration was postponed until 13 February.

Bussey opened that meeting by referring to the circulars that showed the central committee were pamphleteering, despite being told not to. The executive council agreed – with everyone present except Muir – that the London central committee had brought discredit on the union. At that moment, with a large number of members outside, delegates from the four district committees in London asked to be heard. They were allowed into the room. Haskell and Irvine (the old Manchester-based treasurer of the union before the First World War) from the London North-East district committee; London West branch's Bill Bryant and Les Gregory from Brixton branch, for the South West district committee, C. Bond and J. A. Lane from London North West and Eltham's H. Young and Minority Movement stalwart Merrells from South East London.

Fred Haskell was the spokesman. What he said raised the stakes even higher. An unofficial assembly of branch officials and branch committees had met the previous night at the Conway Hall on 12 February. This group had delegated Haskell and friends, not their district committees. The members present supported the London central committee. They thought the executive were puppets for the employers and were opposed to the NJIC approach to industrial relations. The final conclusion of this meeting was embodied in a resolution.

A strong deputation from this meeting inform the executive council that if any attempt is made to suspend or penalize the London central committee or the officials, then the London membership will definitely consider the formation of another union for electrical workers.

Bussey, in answering, was at his presidential best. He started by pointing out that the London central committee had condoned openly unofficial action. The union could not continue on that basis. 'The executive council were quite prepared to face up to the position; and it would be better for those people to get outside the ETU and form a union which would be carried on in the manner in which they desired.'

The executive had let the deputation in, thinking they had some ideas on how to solve the crisis. Instead, they had merely added another dimension to it. The executive would not be intimidated by anyone. Bussey demanded loyalty to the union, and the meeting adjourned at 7 p.m. that night.

First thing the next morning, they expelled Jock Muir, Joe Vaughan, Bob McLennan, Fred Lester, Harold Ross, Percy Cliburn, Hugh Young, J. F. Francis – the whole committee, and issued a fairly sympathetic warning to Humphreys and a stern one to Coster to stop being 'irresponsible' in adding to the 'chaos' in London.

In early March, Rowan sent out circulars throughout the union, reiterating that the issue at stake was not the courage or lack of it of the executive, but the vital importance of sustaining, by rule, the supremacy of the executive council over the district committee concerned.

The strike ended on the recommendation of the strike committee, made on 15 February 1937. Over the next seven days, the executive got £220 out of the employers, and made ex-gratia payments of £3 to full benefit members and £1 10s 0d to apprentices. A site visit on 22 February produced a further final concession from Penwill – wellington boots.

The strike was over; but the political war was just starting. Throughout London, branches withheld contributions, although the threat to set up a rival union was never activated. Much of the 'credit' for this, if 'credit' is the word, lay with the Communist Party. Their line was the old Leninist one that to leave the union in the hands of the 'right-wing' was 'infantile' – that for communist influence to eventually triumph, it was best to stay within the union.

Throughout the rest of the year, over a dozen London branches withheld contributions from the executive, and set up parallel branches, marking members' cards with their own small stickers. Legal action was taken against the likes of LSE No. 5 (where Ronnie Sell and Bob McLennan orchestrated the protest), Croydon, London East, North-West, North, West, Central and others. By the end of the year, this legal action was bringing the branches back into the fold. In mid-July, the unofficial LSE No. 5 gave in, at least formally. They returned the money collected and promised to behave constitutionally, especially since 'the non[-member], McLennan, no longer attends meetings'. It was not until January 1938 that Bussey himself reopened the branch, and even then McLennan and Sell were lurking about outside. Sell was confident (with some justification), that the new executive would readmit the expelled London central committee, but Bussey was angry at his presence at the meeting. The atmosphere throughout the year was vitriolic. London North East district committee attempted to ban the Poplar branch delegate, Poole, who had been a non-striking shop-steward at Earl's Court. More worrying for the executive, there was further evidence of communist-led solidarity action with the London central committee men from outside London. The Mersey district committee, on Walton branch's initiative (where Foulkes and Cole were leading lights), urged an aggregate meeting to be called. They wanted it addressed by the London central committee expellees, and refused to countenance Mersey executive councillor G. McKernan's suggestion that the executive council should provide a speaker. The executive told them, in effect, that if they flouted the executive instruction *not* to call such a meeting, the Mersey committee might get what London got!

Throughout 1937, in leadership elections, the more conventional candidates were successful. Ernie Irwin won Tom Stewart's old national organizer's job, on the second ballot from London's Hugh Young, 6,253–4,450. Nevertheless, with Foulkes now the full-time officer in Liverpool and Walter Stevens being elected in London, apparent members of the Labour Party with strong connections with the Communist Party were assuming crucial local roles.

Triumph of the Left: Executive Council Elections, 1937

The uproar in London in 1937 culminated in the executive council elections in December that year. This was the year that a significant organized communist presence appeared on the executive, supported for much of the time by non-communist left-wingers. Throughout 1938–9, votes on the executive became extremely close. It is worth looking in detail at the 1937 executive elections. It is in these elections that the analyst is struck by some branches voting in a way that is extraordinarily enthusiastic for a single candidate. Before there can be any proof of ballot-rigging, it is necessary to discount the influence of a man being voted for in huge numbers in his own branch; that is not unlikely. Secondly, some branches are dominated by workers from a particular industry or who are concentrated in a single factory that may be the candidate's industry or his old factory.

No one should be surprised if they favour a particular candidate. The union's balloting system – complained of from time to time throughout the union's history – was still fundamentally the same. Branch secretaries distributed ballot papers to each member, who either turned up at the meeting or voted by post, or via his shop-steward, if he could not get to the meeting. The possibilities of branch secretaries or shop-stewards interfering with votes was always present by the very nature of the balloting system.

There is no direct evidence of ballot-rigging in the 1937 executive elections. The combination of influences outlined above, plus the traditional left bias in London elections, plus the political background of the war in Spain may have produced – especially after the furore surrounding the London central committee – a totally straight, deliberate choice of communist-backed candidates.

In Division 1, South London and South-East England, Les Gregory destroyed Harold Morton. Les Gregory was an exceptionally young (twenty-one) contracting electrician from Brixton branch who had joined the union in 1932. Gregory got 1,480 votes to Morton's 360. Two years before, Jim Smith, who by the end of 1937 was covering for the ill Bill Westfallen as a 'temporary' appointed official in electricity supply, had beaten Morton, 727–460.

In Division 2, East and North East London, along with East Anglia, Frank Haxell was, like Les Gregory, running for the first time. George Millar had first won his seat in December 1933 and won again in 1935 by 515 votes to Fred Haskell's 406. Peter Irvine then got 112 and Joe Vaughan 120. Other prominent left-wingers on the London district committee, like Doherty, Muirhead and Turner, had also picked up a few votes. This time, in 1937, everyone on the left knew what was expected of them. George Millar's strength in 1935 had been concentrated in LSE No. 10 (Bussey's branch – with 211 votes) and his own Poplar branch (with 139 votes). However, he had picked up votes in fifteen other branches. In 1937, out of a total of 753 votes, he scored heavily in LSE No. 10 (with 558 votes) and Poplar (175 votes). He got just twenty more votes across the whole division in just five other branches. Frank Haxell had joined the union in 1919 and the Communist Party in 1935. He got a huge 1,483 votes. Erstwhile left-wingers like Haskell and Irvine barely got 200 votes between them. George Millar paid a high price for his stand over Earl's Court.

In Division 3, W. H. Bryant won by 1,023 votes to C. R. Bond's 919. This produced some interesting voting. They were both left-wingers, both very close to the Communist Party. Bond had held the seat for most of 1937, winning a by-election after the expulsion of Jock Muir. Fulham voted for Bryant by 273 votes to 13 between the other five candidates. Hayes, in Middlesex, voted with splendid unanimity, 207–0, for Bond. London West put in 150 votes for Bryant, Ealing 102 for Bond. In 1935, Bond had not stood at all, and Bryant got all of 62 votes! Bryant could not take up his seat, however, as he was a suspended branch official of London West. He was replaced in April 1938 by another good communist, Alf Martin, who beat Joe Lane, 1,241–799.

Outside of London, there were dramatic changes as well. In the Wales and South-West of England seat, the sitting member, Swansea district secretary, Frank Johns, got 990 votes. Harry Turner, Bristol district secretary, got 1,252 votes. His own branch, Bristol No. 1, had a tradition of unanimous voting. In 1935, when Turner was not a candidate, they voted 251–0 for Johns. In 1937 when Turner was a candidate with Johns as his opponent, Turner got a massive 428 votes and Johns got nought! Turner was a left-wing Labour man – very close to being a communist in his voting record and political inclination. However, he was a fiercely independent man and by no means a party hack.

In Division 5, for the Midlands, the moderate supporter of Bussey and Rowan for many years, E. R. Lee, was returned.

In Division 8, H. Thorpe, the moderate Yorkshireman, had no trouble, and the two Scottish divisions sent Rowan supporters back to the executive in Brothers Innes and Turnbull. R. A. Smyth, who left the executive to be replaced by the traditionalist Todd, gave a moderate tinge to the Irish political dimension. There were two more political gains for the left.

In Manchester, following Ernie Irwin's election as national organizer, Alf Hatton beat Bolton branch secretary George Haslam, 630–548. A Stretford man, Hatton was not a communist, but he was certainly to the left of the Manchester tradition.

In Liverpool, Walton branch's Gus Cole took the seat as a proper communist from left-winger McKernan, 761–517. The new executive council for 1938 and 1939 was therefore made up of five 'loyalist' votes (Lee, Thorpe, Innes, Turnbull and Todd), four 'communist' votes (Gregory, Haxell, Martin and Cole) and two left-wing sympathizers who were not formally members of the Communist Party group (Hatton and Turner).

1938 was a difficult year for the union's leadership politically, not least because London's district secretary, George Humphreys, had finally had enough. He resigned on 15 December 1937, citing pressure of work. He wrote to the general secretary that: 'The turmoil in London during the last few years has left its mark on me, and moreover, the life, generally speaking, of the London full-time official is a harassing one.... My doctor has told me that persisting in working under the conditions I have been will mean a serious illness, and I am not prepared to face this.' LSE No. 1 thought this was the last straw. They wrote a letter to the executive on 8 February 1938, demanding, in the wake of Humphreys's resignation, a conference of branches to discuss their concerns over:

... the absolute impossibility of a member who is loyal to the rule book and the executive council holding office with any confidence in London ... the entire lack of any trade union qualification of the horde of applicants for any full-time appointment going ... the nobbling of branch members by visiting 'scouts' who attend and misrepresent their standing at branch meetings in the interests of any particular individual who is standing for election ... a rigid investigation into the London ballot returns on the last executive council election.

This was referred to the July 1938 policy conference – and forgotten, apart from a desultory discussion about nominations for the executive. The legal saga with London branches gradually sorted itself out, and by October, the London central committee were readmitted to the union. However, it was the end of the road for Joe Vaughan, who had first run for the executive in 1917. He was unemployed and had not worked in the electrical industry for nearly twenty years. Alf Martin was still for letting him back in and Les Gregory abstained, but the other nine executive members voted not to readmit Vaughan.

Strangely, in July 1938, the energy returned to George Humphreys and he ran again for office in London. In the first ballot, a completely obscure communist called Arnold got 1,390 votes to George Humphreys 994. Arnold was a nobody. He worked at Barking Power Station. He was, however the communist candidate, on his own admission, despite being over £1 in arrears at the time of election. He stacked up some impressive branch votes. Ninety-seven branches took part in the election. Seventy branches recorded some votes for Arnold. Fulham voted for him with 188 votes, with 8 other votes between the other twenty candidates! In Kingston, Surrey, he got 80 votes with 8 spread over the other twenty candidates. In Hackney, he scored 68, with 5 votes between the other twenty.

On the second ballot, George Humphreys only narrowly beat Arnold back by 2,862 to 2,101: the machine that could amass votes for any candidate, with or without an industrial record in the union, was born. Within five years, Arnold had left the Communist Party, the union and the industry. There were many other little issues in which the new executive tried to shake Rowan and Bussey's hold: Cole innocently suggested to Rowan that the union's journal should be administered by an executive editorial board – to give it more life and relieve Rowan of the work. Jimmy Rowan outmanoeuvred Cole by suggesting Matt Greenwell could help – and this was agreed. Cole and Hatton wanted all wage deals balloted on by the members. On this, the executive decided to 'consult the members'. Jim Kearns was prevented from going to Moscow with the Manchester Trades Council – but only when his workload was proved too high. At the 1938 Torquay policy conference, there was uproar when it was shown that Arthur Stride, a London delegate, was reading a speech on the need for a low-contribution industrial section for the union from a communist-prepared brief. It had been circulated weeks before the conference, and Bussey had a copy.

The Vigon Affair: Two Years of Tumult, 1938–9

All of this was nothing compared to what happened next. The political crisis caused by the expulsion of the London central committee and the sea-change on the executive council must have seemed sensational at the time. It was nothing compared to what sprang from a dispute at Chorley in Lancashire on the site of the new Royal Ordnance Factory (ROF). This was a large job, with 467 members of the union working on it. About a third of the men were from Lancashire, with just under half contracting electricians from London. The remainder came from Liverpool. There were several other contracting and cable-laying companies working on site who were largely ununionized, but the original dispute was with Tommy Clarke's, who employed the 467 members.

This site was well known to electricians throughout the country, and had started in early 1938. It was four square miles in area, on four separate sites with dozens of different buildings under construction at the same time. The whole site was dominated by an enormous concrete mixer, near which many open-air meetings were held. Right from the start, the site suffered from comparability claims as London electricians were imported onto the site, due to the sophistication of some of the electrical work involved (the installation of solid drawn galvanized conduit). They worked three shifts originally on a site that seemed to be a permanent quagmire. The security on the site was all pervasive and very enthusiastic; indeed, so large were the buildings that on occasion electricians were accidentally locked in all night by over-zealous security men.

There was a series of small disputes throughout 1938 on the site; but towards the end of the autumn, the most serious dispute that broke out was fundamentally about the provincial electricians demanding parity with the Londoners who enjoyed country allowance *and* five shillings a week fares to their Preston lodgings.

On 9 November 1938, president Ernie Bussey was just leaving Edinburgh when he was contacted by phone by Mr Penwill from the NFEA. Would Bussey call in at Chorley on his way home and help sort out a dispute at the crucial ROF site – work that was clearly connected with the post-Munich rearmament programme? Bussey agreed to do this, and the following day went to the site with J. J. Hall, the Preston area official.

Bussey later reported to the executive that the whole issue – just like Earl's Court – had started with wellington boots. The four shop-stewards on the Tommy Clarke's contract had asked for boots – or money in lieu. They had also asked for 3s a week pay rise (completely outside the national agreements). This claim had been lodged on 4 August 1938 and nothing had happened. J. J. Hall had made the claim; unfortunately, Hall and the stewards had

exaggerated the country allowance and shift premium due to the members –
which Clarke's had paid – until the War Office contract scrutiny officials told
Clarke's they were paying anything up to 21s a week too much to certain
individuals.

Leaving aside the issue of overpayment, the employers offered Bussey on
10 December £1 for each member to buy boots, a continuing supply of boots
to new starters, and 'sympathetic consideration' to those electricians who
couldn't wear them due to 'trench feet'! Alternatively, the issue could be
referred to an emergency committee of the NJIC on 14 November, where the
question of overpayment would undoubtedly be raised.

These two options were put to the whole site's electrical workforce at a
mass meeting; by this time, Mersey district secretary Frank Foulkes and
Manchester district secretary Jim Kearns had joined Bussey and unanimously
recommended the £1/promise-of-boots option. Mr Penwill had let it be known
that he would try to get NFEA dispensation to continue the over-payment
on this site – just this once. Bussey was very pleased with this, and even more
pleased when the members voted to hold back from a strike if the boots were
provided and the over-payments continued. Bussey wrote, 'I desire to express
my sincere thanks to Brothers Hall, Kearns and Foulkes for their loyal co-
operation and advice.'

All seemed well. Still smarting from the over-payment issue, no doubt, the
War Office were furious to hear that on 25 November, mass meetings of
electricians had voted for a 'ca' canny' policy – a mixture of non-co-operation
and 'Spanish customs' as contemporary phraseology might describe it, in
support of the higher wage claim. The War Office told Tommy Clarke's that
their contract for 'priority work' was now at an end. On Wednesday 30
November, 257 men were made redundant. A mass meeting said that *no* work
would be done anywhere on the site until everyone was reinstated. Quite
coincidentally, Hall and Kearns were on site recruiting non-unionists working
for the Helsby Cable Co. They rushed to the mass meeting. 'Both Brothers
Hall and Kearns were howled down, and the shop-stewards informed them
that *they* were taking control and advised them to get off the site.' The situation
was getting out of control. The War Office, through the Ministry of Works
officials, withdrew the use of site facilities from the strikers and banned Hall
from visiting without a security permit. Penwill rang head office and told Bob
Prain that if the other 200 or so strikers did not go back to work by 8 a.m. on
Friday 2 December, they would be sacked too!

Jimmy Rowan decided to travel to Preston overnight on 1 December and
went to the mass meeting arranged at a small village hall in Euxton, just north
of Chorley. He was greeted by pickets and a 'strike committee'. He bluntly
refused to speak to them and pressed his way into the hall. He was howled
down as he tried to get the meeting under way at 1 p.m. Jimmy Rowan was

not given any opportunity of addressing the meeting and a sing-song started which lasted until 2 p.m. The strike committee came on the platform and informed the meeting they had been 'ignored' by the general secretary and area full-time official. Rowan went down into the body of the members. For over an hour he tried to get a hearing. Eventually, he was able to speak – still from the floor – and persuaded the meeting that the 'sacked' 257 should leave the hall while the 200 or so electricians still employed determined their attitude to taking supporting action – bearing in mind Mr Penwill's edict that they faced the sack as well if they did. Rowan then said that he would leave too, but the shop-stewards/strike committee were so enjoying this process of humiliating the general secretary that he was not allowed to leave. Rowan's ironic report to the sub-executive, minuted by Bob Prain, went on 'the members on the platform insisted that it would do the general secretary good to see the "solidarity" of the members of the union. The result of the vote which showed the "solidarity" was as follows: For resumption of work – 118; Against resumption of work – 56.'

Rowan then delicately describes what must have been a menagerie – familiar to all trade unionists in similar circumstances: 'The hall was then opened for the members who had been discharged, and Brother Rowan can only describe the scene which took place as "bedlam let loose". Those who had been discharged blamed those who had decided to go back to work for having let them down, and many unparliamentary expressions were used.'

It was clear that unreal expectations on the site had been raised; some men had been promised earnings by the shop-stewards of £7–9. Some wanted the union to sue to guarantee this sum. Rowan told them that the only way they would earn such money was through massive overtime and not a 'ca' canny' policy and not by breaking national agreements. Rowan stressed before he left that his only ambition was to prevent the 200 from 'making fools of themselves'.

On 11 December, the full executive reviewed Rowan's performance. Scots-man Bill Turnbull was unequivocal in his support for Rowan's actions. He said that good firms that paid proper rates and recognized the union, like Tommy Clarke's, should not be exploited in this way, and if we broke agreements when we felt like it, what was to prevent employers when they were in the driving seat from doing likewise. What was at issue here was 'an end to trade unionism and collective bargaining'. The communist minority on the executive took the opposite view. Haxell said that Rowan had exceeded his brief from the sub-executive in charging in to confront the membership. Cole said that the 'ca' canny' policy was instituted when the War Office had sought to replace the overpaid shift patterns with less lucrative overtime – and the union might as well use the dispute to enforce one hundred per cent membership on Helsby Cables and British Insulated while they were at it. This produced a further outburst from Turnbull who noted that Tommy

Clarke's were one hundred per cent and it was an outrage to penalize them as a way of forcing others to get non-unionists into the union. Les Gregory thought there was something fishy about the sudden announcement that the Clarke's contract was no longer 'priority work' and Rowan should have been more sympathetic to the members' views on this – the core of the dispute. Alf Martin thought Rowan was quite out of order in not meeting the shop-stewards, even if they were out on unofficial strike.

Rowan's actions were endorsed by the executive, 6–3. Two of the left-wing, if not Communisty Party, members of the executive, Hatton and Turner, voted with the majority. Les Gregory abstained. And there the matter was left, except to set up an inquiry into just how the whole business had arisen. The inquiry team was to be chaired by Bussey, along with Rowan, Haxell and, later, the local executive councillor, Cole.

The committee of inquiry made fairly leisurely enquiries into the origins of the dispute, concentrating particularly on the justifications for the precipitate sackings on 30 November. In February 1939, a further, more serious dispute occurred. Originally, electricians working in the huge buildings asked for 'danger money'. In particular, huge puddles all over the unmade floors of the buildings were in reality huge holes which would eventually be manholes into the floor areas designed to carry the necessary services around the buildings. Small strikes had occasionally taken place on this issue, but by the first week in February 1939, an NFEA-ETU working party had decided that such payments could not be made outside the national agreement.

On 9 February, a day when the employer (Tommy Clark's) was due to meet the shop-stewards, the members were again refusing to work in 'enclosed areas'. At the meeting, the senior shop-steward, A. Dickinson, submitted a claim in writing for all sorts of other things – facilities for the shop-stewards to meet, with pay; extra travelling time for some particularly inaccessible part of the site, Section 6 Hut; better and quicker distribution of boots; and that the foremen should stop working overtime by going round the installations at the end of each day. The demands finished with a peremptory paragraph. 'If the above demands are not met by tomorrow, Friday February 10th, dinner time, Mr Astley [the Engineer in charge for Clarke's] must appear with a satisfactory answer.' Mr Astley travelled up that day and told the office he would see the stewards at 5.10 p.m. on that Friday. The shop-stewards hung around the site office waiting to see Mr Astley, and pestering the office staff as to when he would see them. (Their persistence was not surprising. Once again, it was pouring with rain throughout the day.)

Eventually, Mr Astley appeared and sacked the shop-stewards on the spot for not clocking off before coming to wait for him! A hastily convened mass meeting decided to strike in support of the shop stewards.

On 17 February 1939, the sub-executive took a hand, and after meeting the

NFEA in London, decided to send Bussey and Haxell, to be joined at Preston by Rowan, to go to Chorley and speak to the remaining strikers. Bussey and Haxell travelled up with representatives of the NFEA and Tommy Clarke's on the evening of Sunday 19 February, and booked in at the Bull and Royal, not far from Preston railway station. The following day, they met the shop-stewards at the Euxton community hall where an orderly but unpleasant meeting ended with Rowan accusing one of the stewards, Joe Vigon, of applying for a charge-hand's job behind the backs of his mates among the unofficial strikers. The strikers responded by passing a vote of no confidence in the executive. Rowan promptly went back to London. Further meetings were held in London with the NFEA on 6 March and 21 March, and the issue took on the nature of a joint inquiry. However, the union also pursued its own lines of enquiry.

The committee made arrangements to interview the foremen and shop-stewards from the site on 29 April. One shop-steward, Joe Vigon, had, apparently, been expelled by his branch in Hackney on 14 April and so he was not present. However, the other shop-stewards arrived at Macaulay Road on that Sunday morning. Anderson, Dickinson, Pearce, Murray and Dick Homewood were the stewards – all well-known shop-stewards with left-wing sympathies, and the meeting did not *end* in uproar – it *started* in upoar. Homewood demanded the committee allow him to circularize the whole membership with his version of events. Pearce denounced the presence of the foremen – all members of the union for years – and told Rowan his views didn't count because he's 'only' the general secretary and should support the members on strike a bit more! Bussey demanded discipline, Homewood shouted and roared back at him, and Bussey threw him out of the meeting and suspended the hearing. Rowan reported to the executive council on 6 May that 'the atmosphere was deliberately created' [at that Sunday morning meeting] and 'the whole thing was engineered to prevent the enquiry committee arriving at a decision in respect to what led up to the recent strike at Chorley.'

The executive supported Bussey's action, but narrowly felt that nothing more should be done, and the enquiry team into the Chorley dispute was quietly disbanded.

All of the events surrounding the ROF dispute were but a side-show for what happened next. On 20 July, Jimmy Rowan received a letter at head office from Joe Vigon, the ex-shop-steward at Chorley and a known left-winger in London, of whom Rowan had a low view. Indeed, he was known in the past to have referred to Vigon as a 'rat', particularly when it had been revealed that Vigon had applied for a charge-hand's job at Chorley during the strike period in February 1939. Vigon's letter ran to nearly 5,000 words. It was marked 'private and confidential'. It was headed 'Chorley Job and the Working of a

Group'. It was devastating stuff. First, Vigon wrote, 'I am now in a position to expose the workings of a "group" or "militant" section of the ETU, who do nothing else but undermine the officials of the executive council and the workings of the men. This so-called "group" operates all over the country.' The letter was mainly concerned to show that the 'group' were attempting to embarrass the leadership of the union by using Chorley to expose them as half-hearted and pro-employers. Equally, the letter set out to show the co-ordinated nature of the conspiracy across the country. Most sensational of all, in naming names with a will, it pointed straight at the leading left-wingers in the union as the architects of the conspiracy against their own colleagues.

Vigon said that the events surrounding the weekend of Friday 17 February–Monday 20 February were orchestrated between Les Gregory in London who alerted Frank Foulkes and Gus Cole in Liverpool to the ETU-NFEA delegation travelling plans on the Sunday evening, 19 February.

Vigon had travelled to Liverpool on the Friday evening with another shop-steward, Pearce, after Les Gregory had apparently been told to ring the strikers. Ostensibly, Vigon and Pearce were appealing to the Liverpool district committee for support in an application to the executive to get the strike made official. Vigon's letter shows that other matters were to be decided.

Firstly, I was introduced to Brother Foulkes ... and after about ten minutes we went up ... and were introduced to the following members of the [district] committee – Brother Foulkes, chairman, Brother Turner, secretary, Brothers Cole, McKernan, Gordon, McGuire and another whose name I did not get. Before starting the meeting, Brothers Foulkes and Cole were talking together and after a little while, Brother Cole asked me if I were a member of the Communist Party. I said 'Yes'.... After the meeting, Foulkes said, 'I want you to come ... to the shop-stewards' meeting and later to a party meeting of the Communist Party ETU militants'. I said, 'What about Pearce?' and Foulkes said, 'We have to be very careful. You know we have a job of work to do in the 1940 policy conference and cannot afford to lose good men.' I said, 'He can be trusted'.... Foulkes then said, 'The men you have just met are all party members, with one exception, and they are trumps, but Gus is the governor.'

The next day, back at his digs, which were the strike committee-rooms, Vigon and the other shop-stewards compared notes – and Vigon saw telegrams from Walter Stevens, making arrangements to meet the other stewards in Crewe the following day. At the same time, Vigon and Pearce were to go to a public meeting in Manchester Free Trade Hall to get Sir Stafford Cripps to read a message of support for the strikers. At the same meeting, Syd Jenkins from Manchester Central approached them in a state of high excitement. This was the man who in 1931 had been briefly expelled for being an 'unmitigated nuisance', having been arrested for inciting disorder in the Manchester dock strikes. He said that 'Brothers Foulkes and Cole were in touch with him on the matter and . . . here is our opportunity to defeat Jimmy Rowan and Bussey.' Sunday morning saw Vigon and Pearce at the Communist Party rooms in Liverpool in the Haymarket. Vigon thought there were twenty ETU members there, and between them and Vigon they composed the strikers' case as a pamphlet and Cole dictated it to a secretary. While they were waiting for this to be duplicated, Cole addressed the meeting, and Foulkes made a bravura performance about what would happen if *he* went to the Euxton Hall meeting on the following day, Monday – 'I will wipe the floor with them.' At that moment the phone rang. It was Haxell. Foulkes explained that they had got the strikers' case ready, and they had a scheme ready to get a copy of it to Haxell that Sunday night so that he could be briefed with the strikers' case before the meeting the following day. Vigon's letter reported what Foulkes said.

'I have just spoken to Haxell,' said Foulkes, 'He wants to meet you at the Bull and Royal, Preston, where he and Bussey are staying. You must be at Preston station to meet the London train in and watch who comes off and follow. Then, after they enter the Bull and Royal, wait 10–15 minutes and then ask the porter to send in for Brother Haxell and say a friend of his wishes to speak to him, and walk towards Preston station slowly near the kerb so as he will know you.'

Vigon did not know what Haxell looked like – so Gus Cole gave him a photo of the 1938 conference delegates and marked Haxell with a cross. Later that night, back at Preston, Vigon met Haxell and handed over the copy of the strikers' case. Haxell quickly told Vigon: 'Carry out what Cole and Foulkes told you to do, and I will pass a note to you when I think fit on the platform.' Haxell then quickly returned to the hotel and joined Bussey and the employers for dinner.

The following day, Monday 20 February 1939, the meeting was held at the Euxton Hall. The note was passed and on it was written: 'Condemn them as much as you like.' At which point, Vigon started to attack the executive and the employers. In innocent retaliation for this startling abuse, Rowan brought up the matter of Vigon's application for a charge-hand's job and the meeting broke up in some disarray, if not disorder, with the strikers passing a vote of no confidence in the leadership, and Rowan and Bussey and Haxell leaving the hall, to call on the employers back at the hotel and from there to return to London. Haxell, however, stayed behind and was instrumental in getting the shop-stewards to lift the vote of no confidence.

But this was not to be the end of the story for Vigon. He left Lancashire the following Saturday and got a job as a contracting electrician in Scunthorpe. Seven weeks later, he got a note from his own Hackney branch summoning him back to London to face charges from his branch associated with his application for the charge-hand's job. He told them he could not attend. On

14 April 1939, his branch secretary, Hill, wrote to Vigon to let him know he had been expelled from the union. Worse followed for Vigon. The shop-steward on the Scunthorpe job wired Matt Greenwell for advice, and Greenwell told the steward that the company had to sack Vigon in order to sustain the closed shop with the company: if they did not, there would be more trouble with their London sites. These threats were led by other Hackney branch members like Brothers Cohen, Leaman and secretary Hill.

Leaman turned out to be a key figure. Along with Brothers McLennan and Sell of LSE No. 5, he had got Brother Hill, of the Hackney branch, to set up a 'fraction' in their part of North-East London: Vigon, as branch chairman, was invited to join and reported Leaman's advice.

Listen, Vigon; you are in a position in the branch which is very useful to us. All you have got to do is to give a lead from the chair as to what we say. You see, the members are not educated yet as to who shall be the leaders. When they hear that a certain man should be voted for and the lead comes from an official of the branch, they will all give you their support, and therefore our work gets completed because we have the man in that we want.

Vigon described the detail of the 'fraction' meetings at Leaman's house – where the main topic of conversation was the need to get Walter Stevens elected as the new full-time official in London. The Hackney 'fraction' also attended London-wide meetings of the 'group' at Marx House in Farringdon Street every Saturday at 3.30 p.m. Vigon described in his letter the last meeting of this type he attended in the winter of 1937.

I met him [Leaman] and he took me to [Marx House]. I was led to a door which had a small flap, and Leaman tapped on this and the tiny flap opened and we were then allowed in. In here, I saw about 150 men mostly known to me. Brother Hill was in the chair, Brother Sell, secretary, Brother McLennan, assistant secretary, brother Martin, propaganda secretary, Brother Breed, leader and Brother Stride, spokesman.... The meeting now started in full swing, and the first item to deal with was Brother Stevens and the area official's job. It was decided that members must attend as many branches as they can and try to push Brother Stevens name over. Second item was the industrial section – this took up about three-and-a-half hours discussion and Brothers Sell, Stride and Martin spoke on this for some time. It was then decided to leave it to the Bureau of the Communist Party to get out the findings of this committee and put it in type and to inform the provincial groups of the same. I obtained a copy of this, this being the first evidence in writing. I forwarded it to Brother Bussey for his perusal. . . .

Vigon finished his mammoth letter by saying, in support of his appeal against expulsion by Hackney branch, 'I must now come to a close, asking the officials of the ETU to take some action in the matter, and rid the rotten element that exists among these so-called "groups". Then, no doubt, some members of the executive council will be able to hear some truth of themselves and how they became officials.'

Bussey and Rowan proceeded with the utmost caution. Vigon was known to them, but he was not a confidant. Rowan was to hotly deny having anything to do with him directly. 'Brother Rowan repudiated with scorn any suggestion that he had been in touch with *anyone* attached to the Communist Party.' However, Vigon had sent Bussey the aggregate meeting's brief on the industrial section which Arthur Stride used at the 1938 Torquay conference in support of the left's demand for an 'industrial section'.

He clearly was losing his faith after his contacts with the Hackney fraction, and his close connection with the communist machine during the Chorley dispute must have finally tipped him over. Being exposed for applying for the charge-hand's job and losing his Scunthorpe employment due to pressure from the Hackney fraction could not have increased his affection for communist activity in the union.

Vigon's motivation is less important than the practical impact on the union of his sensational allegations.

The letter was received by Rowan on 20 July. Nothing was said immediately. At the sub-executive on 10 August, Vigon's appeal against expulsion was to be heard, with Hackney branch secretary Hill being in attendance. The existence of Vigon's letter was revealed – but it was not read out, and the appeal was postponed. It is important to note that Haxell, as a London executive member, was at the sub-executive. On 26 August, the full executive met. Haxell and Martin tried to flush Rowan out by demanding that if this letter was so important, someone must be charged. The full executive (by 7–3) said no – and set up an enquiry team instead of Jimmy Rowan, Ernie Bussey and strenuous anti-communists Thorpe, Turnbull and Lee along with left-supporting but Manchester-based Alf Hatton. Vigon's letter was then distributed to the executive.

On 16 October, Bussey and Hatton's investigations allowed them, as part of the enquiry team, to move the laying of charges against Hill and Haxell for encouraging 'fractions' who were 'imposing results of their discussions on the branches' by methods which Rowan described as amounting to 'underground action'. Curiously, the executive would not publish the letter, by eight votes to three, despite Rowan's insistence that the outside membership know the truth. However, the wily old general secretary got round his colleagues' desire for discretion by publishing the Vigon letter in its entirety in the November 5/6 executive minutes as part of the enquiry committee's interim report. Les Gregory was annoyed at this sharp practice, but attention quickly moved on to the report. Hill was easily dealt with. The report noted Hill's brazen admission that the activities of the 'fraction' were quite permissible because most of the other members of the branch were just 'ticket holders' who needed livening up by 'fraction' members – who were the only real 'trade unionists' in the branch.

The report then quoted extensively from three separate passages of Lenin's *Left-Wing Communism – An Infantile Disorder*, concentrating on the need for communists to battle against the 'labour aristocracy' and the 'social-chauvinist' leadership of unions while never, never leaving the unions but battling away within. For the enquiry committee, the Vigon letter was simply 'a confirmation of what is known to exist'. The work of 'fractions' like Hill's was to 'create a general feeling of suspicion and discontent against those in office both nationally and locally, who are known to be antagonistic to their policy. Secondly, to move names of members of the group for positions in the union for the purpose of obtaining control of the machinery of the union on behalf of the Communist Party and its allied groups.'

Those prophetic words were then followed by an examination of the charges arising out of the report against executive councillor Frank Haxell. The report noted that much of the evidence was circumstantial – however, it found that Haxell had been disloyal to executive colleagues Rowan and Bussey by being a party to the attacks on them at the Euxton Hall meeting. Haxell *had* met Vigon and he *had* passed a note to Vigon. Vigon still had Foulkes's calling card and the marked conference photo given to him by Gus Cole. The report was 'accepted', 10–1 (Haxell), and the only criticism of the report came from Birmingham's executive member, Ernie Lee, who thought the report was very mild considering the nature of the offences. Charges were laid under Rule 6, Clause 44 (g) that Hill and Haxell's activities 'brought discredit on the union' and the hearing of the charges was set for the weekend of 25/26 November 1939.

Hill's defence was dealt with on Saturday, 25 November. He said he was very young, led astray by Leaman and others. He was banned from holding office *sine die*, and could only hold a union position again with the permission of the executive council.

Haxell's case was, of course, the big one. Haxell had completely reserved his defence for this meeting – a sensible course which gave him weeks to analyse the case against him before he started his reply, which was written and distributed at the meeting on the Sunday morning of 26 November. His defence was vigorous, if flawed. He did leave the Bull and Royal at Preston that Sunday night, not to talk to Vigon, but to talk to two members from the Chorley site who wanted to complain about the antics of their shop-steward – Joe Vigon! However, despite having weeks to prepare his case, Haxell could not remember what their names were or where they worked at the site. He flatly denied the president's statement that Bussey had seen Vigon on the station and pointed him out to Haxell. The note at the meeting, as it happens, was not to Vigon to tell him to attack the executive, but a note for fellow steward Pearce to get *him* to stop Vigon upsetting the meeting!

Vigon himself gave evidence to the full executive that day. Gus Cole and Alf Martin said they had never seen Vigon before in their lives. Les Gregory said he had never talked to Vigon on the phone, despite Vigon's insistence that he had paid for London trunk calls to Gregory from his digs.

The executive considered the issue. Harry Turner, the new left executive member from Bristol, was a crucial vote. His view was equivocal, but decisive. He was worried about the lack of corroboration in the evidence. However, his common sense forced him to say 'that if only ten per cent of the story was true, the two concerned cannot carry on as officials of this union.' Rowan had the final word. Only a short while from retirement and by now increasingly fond of a shot of whisky from the early morning onwards, he reviewed the seriousness of the situation. The union risked disintegration via increased communist control over the union's elections. 'Very largely, the fractions of the Communist Party were concerned in dealing with nominations for official positions in the union so that they could have a stronger hold on the union and its work.'

Haxell's friends on the executive council tried to move first to limit the damage to their man. Les Gregory and Alf Martin moved 'that the charge is not proven, but we are of the opinion that Brother Haxell is guilty of an indiscretion.' Gus Cole, Alf Martin and Les Gregory voted for this. Harry Turner and Alf Hatton abstained. It went down 5–3 when Brothers Lee, Innes, Turnbull, Todd and Thorpe chucked it out. The same voting saw Frank Haxell removed from all office in the union and suspended *sine die*, only to hold office again at the pleasure of the executive council. Ernie Bussey then asked Haxell to leave the executive, and he did, without any fuss.

The executive then turned their attention during the early months of 1940 to other people's roles in the affair. Alf Martin was believed when he said he had never attended any Marx House aggregate meetings. Dick Homewood's latest application to hold office again was defeated 7–2 on the executive with only Gus Cole and Alf Martin supporting this disruptive, argumentative and aggressive communist. Throughout 1940 the enquiry committee investigated the serious implications of Vigon's accusations against executive councillor Les Gregory and Mersey area official Frank Foulkes. Charges under Rule 6, Clause 44 (g) – the same rule used to proceed against Haxell – were brought against Les Gregory and Frank Foulkes at an executive meeting held at the Crown and Mitre Hotel in Carlisle on 6 December 1940. These deliberations were coloured by the hearing taking place at exactly the same time as the election for a new general secretary at the end of Jimmy Rowan's long period of office – an election in which Foulkes was a candidate.

Both Foulkes and Gregory had plausible accounts of confusion in Vigon's mind as to dates and times of his meetings in Liverpool and phone calls from Les Gregory in London. Foulkes's formal reply, though, was a forerunner of his evidence to a more serious legal forum twenty years later. It is full of pleadings about how unjustly his case had been handled, how high his standing was in the wider movement, just what a 'mountebank' Vigon was and how impressive was Foulkes's service to the Liverpool Labour Party and wider Labour movement. However, Foulkes told a straightforward lie in insisting on his Labour Party membership. Twenty years later his membership of the Communist Party was established by his own admission in the High Court as dating from 1931. The last paragraph of his written rejection of the Vigon accusations is indicative of his capacity to declaim with conviction things he knew were just not true.

The next and last paragraph [of the enquiry committee report] does not interest me greatly. I only repeat that I am not a member of the Communist Party and have not time to attend fractions or meetings of any kind outside ordinary union business. My time is fully occupied in doing my best to further the interests of our union and serve the membership in my area to the best of my ability. I am satisfied this has been done, and in consequence, I know that I have the loyalty, friendship and comradeship of the members, the vast majority of whom will always believe me innocent of these charges, no matter what the verdict of the executive council may be.

This mixture of truth, lies, unctuous self-righteousness and defiance was to reappear in later years. During the hearings, Foulkes, in particular, shook some of Vigon's statements. He challenged Vigon's recollections of the events at his digs and the memory of a member called Beales, who held firmly to the view that Vigon talked to Foulkes on the phone from his digs in Preston. The landlady of the digs was produced to say she had never heard Foulkes on the phone at all.

However, Foulkes was trapped by Turnbull, who innocently asked if Foulkes ever communicated with other districts of the union, campaigning against executive decisions? Foulkes made a loud denial, only to be confronted by Turnbull with the recorded contacts between himself and the London central committee at the time of their expulsions in 1937. Foulkes admitted that was the case – and the executive drew the obvious conclusions.

Nevertheless, with the country at war, and two years having elapsed since the Chorley dispute started, the executive were not of a mind to pursue the issue further. Thorpe and Lee moved: 'That we, the executive council, find, arising from the charges laid against Brothers Foulkes and Gregory, that grave indiscretions by them took place during the Chorley dispute. We warn the two members concerned that any repetition of these indiscretions will be dealt with very severely by the executive council.' Hatton and Turner voted with the majority this time: only Cole and Martin voted against.

Perhaps the use of the word 'indiscretions' was a direct reference to Gregory's misplaced amendment when he tried to save Haxell when he was suspended from office. Whatever it was, it was clear to everyone that the rising tide of aggressiveness by the Communist Party in the union's affairs had forced the issue of the party's role in the union to the centre of the union's affairs. It was to remain so for twenty years and more. Vigon might have thought his letter was about saving his job and getting him back in the union. It was to take on a heavier significance than that. But for the moment, the Vigon affair was closed.

15

THE UNION AT WAR, 1939–45

THE SECOND WORLD WAR broke out just as the union celebrated its fiftieth anniversary. All members and their wives with over thirty years' service in the union, along with the full-time officers, the executive council and distinguished old boy Citrine had a dinner and concert in London at Gatti's Restaurant on 18 August 1939. The following day, there was a drive to Hampton Court and Windsor Castle, the day ending with tea and another concert at Slater's Hotel in Kensington. All attention was riveted, though, on the slide towards war. When it came, on 3 September, it could not have been a surprise to Bussey or Rowan.

The ETU and the Rise of Fascism, 1933–9

Since the rise of Hitler, the union had taken a growing interest in foreign affairs. They were already closely interested in Russia, particularly as the communist and left 'opposition' in the union was so closely concerned with the fortunes of the world's first socialist state. It was inevitable, then, that the rise of Fascism in Britain and abroad should interest the union's leadership and activists. As early as 1933, Jimmy Rowan had been sent to the American Federation of Labour (AFL) convention as the TUC fraternal delegate. (He remains the only ETU delegate ever sent by the TUC to either of their American or Canadian counterparts.) His whole speech was dominated by what the Federated Press reporter, Carl Haessler, called 'a comprehensive attack on Hitlerism'. Rowan asked the question: 'Can it be possible that Hitlerism is condoned by international capital and capitalist governments and even by the Communist Government of Russia, because Hitler is destroying democracy and liberty? My question must for the moment be unanswered.'

Throughout the 1930s, the answer became clearer. The union's leadership was unanimous and passionate in its denunciation of the various manifestations of Fascism throughout the period. They were particularly moved by the plight of Spain from 1936–9. They contributed to TUC and Labour Party appeals for direct aid, for aid to refugees, for help for returning International Brigaders. Throughout all of this work, Rowan kept the executive clear of simple-minded endorsement of the communist line that owed a great deal to the requirements of Soviet foreign policy. The Russians had changed tack. Back in 1932, the twelfth congress of the British Communist Party denounced 'the social-fascist role and policy of the Labour Party'.

Communists were expected to undertake 'revolutionary mass work in the reformist trade unions', organize against official trade union leadership by encouraging the Minority Movement, and set up party factions in the National Unemployed Workers Movement. However, by January 1935 the rise of Hitler produced the opposite policy of the United Front. When the union held its first policy conference at Scarborough in 1936, the issue of co-operating with the Communist Party as the key to opposing Fascism was the central debate. A set of related debates aired all the issues thoroughly. Firstly, Albert Oates moved a general denunciation of war, revealing that he was a conscientious objector. This was carried unanimously and it was agreed to send the sceptical Jimmy Rowan to an International Peace Congress in Brussels. The only note of caution was sounded by Clydeside's Bissell, who underlined the point that rearmament had started to turn back the tide of dreadful unemployment on the Clyde, in Belfast and on the Tyne.

The next issue was the union's attitude to rearmament. A motion calling for the union to refuse 'to collaborate' in the National Government's policy of 'piling up armaments' was neatly side-stepped by an amendment that called for the union to pledge itself to the collective security that would be forthcoming from the League of Nations. Finally, Londoners Hugh Young and Basil Trussler moved that the union's delegates to the TUC and Labour Party conference should vote for the 'affiliation of all parties to the United Front policy'.

Rowan immediately said if you did this, 'the difficulty was the danger of interference with the policy of the Labour Party from outside.' Bussey then ruled from the chair that only those delegates who were Labour Party members could vote in the debate on Labour Party issues. When Kennedy, from Fulham branch, objected, saying they were branch delegates and therefore to be heard, Bussey's ruling was supported, 25–8, with nine delegates abstaining. Communists like Syd Jenkins from Manchester claimed great things for the United Front in Spain and the achievement of the forty-hour week in France. Tommy Carter, the Glasgow delegate, was blunt. 'What is behind the present call for a United Front? It was impossible to look upon the Communist Party as a democratic party ... and any seats which had been gained by the Communist Party either in parliamentary or municipal elections had been gained at the expense of the Labour Party candidates.' Bob Prain made a rare speech on a policy issue, and was equally forthright. Practical politics demanded the exclusion of the communists, he said, because if they *were* involved, the United Front policies would suffer because many moderate Labour voters would be put off by communist involvement. The conference voted, 24–15, for an amendment that ditched the issue by calling for the parties in a United Front to satisfy the constitutional requirements of the TUC and Labour Party – both of whom banned communists.

The Torquay conference met in July 1938 in the weeks before Munich. Bussey's presidential address was unequivocal.

The lesson surely to be learned is that if democratic countries are to withstand the aggressors of the totalitarian states, they must be prepared to defend themselves collectively, and by armed force if necessary, against those nations whose government's concepts of international law seems to be contained in bombing aeroplanes and the destruction and terrorizing of the populace to gain their end.

At this conference, Rowan's allies took the initiative and moved a resolution attacking the United Front. It was cleverly worded. It called for a United Front of 'all citizens' (not parties) against Fascism and the National Government, and ended by urging people to join the Labour Party to achieve it. Bob Prain had good reason to speak for the platform on the issue. Due to the untimely death of the sitting member of Labour's National Executive Committee, just after the 1937 National Executive Committee elections, Bob Prain was summoned to fill the vacancy as the next man on the list. He retained the seat in 1938, but lost it once again in 1939. He was the first ETU man to sit on Labour's governing body and remains only one of three, since the party's birth in 1900, to do so (the others were Ernie Irwin and Frank Chapple). Ben Bolton was elected to the NEC in 1944, but illness prevented him attending. Prain echoed Labour's official policy when he told the Torquay conference: 'To form a United Front with the Communist Party would be farcical – it would be a United Front with no unity!' Barrow's delegate, W. Carter, was even more outspoken. He was 'opposed to the Communist Party on the grounds they were subject to, and took their orders from, their masters, namely the Third International.' Syd Jenkins made the same speech he had made two years before. First, the role of the communist in Spain was highly laudable, and he himself, although a known communist in Manchester, had been elected by his branch and worked for the workers in Manchester to some effect. Brother Ives from London said 'it was not possible to defeat Fascism through the Labour Party alone. As a matter of fact, the Labour Party had never been able to do anything alone.' Harold Morton finished the debate by bringing these outside, international considerations back into the heart of the union's internal politics when he made reference to 'examples of the United Front in our own union, where intimidation was carried out if one dared to differ from the opinion of some of the left-wing movement.'

Conference carried the anti-communist motion, 22–13. Rowan must have been pleased.

He was probably less pleased with the National Government's war preparations, such as they were, that took place in the spring and summer months of 1939. The executive council was convinced of the need to oppose the National Government, recollecting their fears of the 1914–18 war was on key questions like dilution and conscription.

Jimmy Rowan summed up these fears in the October 1939 journal.

There is a demand for electricians that it has been nearly impossible to cope with ... and [there is] a tendency to introduce dilution without agreement. In the light of our experiences in the last war, we shall have to be very careful of allowing semi-skilled labour to be installed as electricians in shipping to our ultimate very great loss. At the end of the last war, and especially in shipping centres, we were faced with a surplus of unemployed workers who had been introduced during the war, without any proper agreement. This resulted in the loss of tens of thousands of pounds and many thousands of members who were brought in during the war. In this respect, we shall have to be careful with even our own members, as there is a tendency in certain shipping areas to have mates upgraded to craftsmen. There is a double purpose in this: firstly, exemption certificates from the army, and secondly, a desire to prevent outsiders coming into the electrical trade.

He said the 'painful' experiences of 1918 'must not occur again'.

In March 1939, the executive voted 6–4 to reject National Voluntary Service until the Government supported the League of Nations and concepts of collective security. The recognition of the victorious Franco in Spain further alienated the executive. Just before the TUC organized a conference of executives, the executive bound themselves by passing resolutions that because of the introduction of conscription, the ETU would not co-operate with the National Government at all!

However, events were moving fast: the union's blanket opposition to dilution was undermined by the AEU, who unilaterally signed an agreement with the EEF on dilution in late August, 'thus tying the hands of the other trade unions', as Rowan put it.

Russia and Germany signed the Nazi-Soviet non-aggression pact on 23 August 1939. Rowan's question in 1933 was at last answered. He wrote in September 1939:

It has been said that Russia were only holding off Germany from getting too big a hold of Eastern Europe, but facts are stubborn things, and in this Polish war, the facts are that Russia took over 200,000 fighting men away from the army which was fighting

Germany. They took over their equipment, took over their means of success so far as they could and from this point alone, they are the allies of the Germans.... It is a very old axiom that extremes meet, and in this case the Russians and the Germans ... have come together and apparently for one purpose only, to destroy democracy and the rights of the people.

Just after the war broke out, the Nazi-Soviet pact meant the Communist Party suddenly said that Fascism was no longer to be opposed by war: Britain and Germany were just as bad as each other, and peace should be sought as soon as possible. Throughout the months of the 'phoney war', when nothing happened in serious military terms, the communists poured out anti-war propaganda. On 26 February 1940, the London central committee agreed the following resolution without opposition.

That this London central committee is of the opinion that the present war between the allies and Germany is being waged not for democracy and against aggression, but for the same reason as all capitalist wars are fought, namely, for the domination of world markets. This being so, the London central committee will fight against all so-called sacrifices for the national war effort, being convinced that such attacks upon our members conditions constitute the introduction into this country, of precisely those conditions against which the nation is alleged to be fighting.

The union did not, however, get involved in many disputes that can be clearly identified as subversive to the war effort. There were many early disputes, particularly in shipbuilding, over subsistence allowances and fares being paid to electricians despatched to shipping areas – particularly from London. Mass meetings in London demanded £2 a week subsistence payments, a complete ban on dilution while there was unemployment in the capital, and total exemption from military service for every electrician in Britain. A strike over non-unionists at Speke Aircraft works was stopped by Foulkes. Belfast's Harland and Wolff's men were sent back by the executive in early April 1940, when they went on strike over an application for 2d an hour in the shipyard.

Britain Stands Alone: The ETU Response, 1940

On 10 May, Hitler invaded the Low Countries, and by 22 June, France fell. The union's conference opened on 15 July at Morecambe. The imminence of invasion, the fall of Chamberlain and his replacement by Winston Churchill, and the entry of Attlee and Bevin into the coalition government, produced a completely different attitude to the war. If any of the union's communists and their allies still thought it was a capitalists' war, and it didn't matter who won, they were keeping quiet now.

Ernie Bussey's chairman's address was masterly. He explained first the frustration with the appeasers.

Given strong and virile leadership that itself is crystal clear in its directive ability and strong in its democratic faith, the people will always serve such leadership instinctively and unquestionably. The White Paper waved to the crowd at Heston on the return of Mr Chamberlain from Munich was symbolical of the policy which had been carried out by the Government he represented.

He then spoke, as it were, of the ETU's war aims. On the outbreak of war, Bussey said:

We had to examine the extent of freedom enjoyed under our institutions, and to decide whether these things were worth preserving as a foundation for the establishment of a larger and freer democracy.... The greatest danger to freedom that I see is that its continuation is taken as an accepted condition of our lives. So many fail to appreciate its value until it is lost. So, there can be but one answer to the threat from the totalitarian states – we believe in peace, we will work for peace, but if peace means serfdom and the loss of all we cherish and hold dear in our political and industrial life, there can be no peace for us.... If freedom is most to mankind, what else in life is worthwhile?

He now turned, almost explicitly, to the communist forces within the union when he emphasized the importance of 'bourgeois democracy'.

To those critics who would cast doubt upon the value of freedom as we have established it, I would point to this conference and many similar institutions being carried on unfettered in this country at the present time. Do not underestimate or undervalue those gifts handed to us by those who worked and suffered in this land that we might be free. The duty has fallen upon the workers of this land to be the spearhead in the defence of democracy.... In conjunction with the whole of the working-class movement, the issue is determined. We line up in defence of democracy as we understand and appreciate it, with all its weaknesses and shortcomings, against a force that has proved its intentions to destroy freedom of thought, conscience and action within its own state and within the world of mankind.... Today, at this conference, I am able to announce that the executive council of the union has decided to lend to the British Government, free of interest, the sum of £50,000 to assist in the struggle we are waging against Nazism and Fascism.

Having settled the moral basis of a just war, Bussey spelt out the practical sacrifices that the union would have to make. 'It has meant that, in the interests of the state, we, in common with other important trade unions, have agreed to relinquish many of our cherished customs, and hard-won rights and privileges in an endeavour to increase the national urge towards defence and security against the aggressor.' With nineteen out of fifty delegates from

London in the conference, the next few remarks were for their district committee's benefit.

To those who would challenge the executive with not balloting the membership on this emergency issue, I would reply 'Hitler does not wait to take a ballot vote – whilst some sections of democracy talk, Hitler jumps and Mussolini stabs.' One of the lessons the events of the past few years have taught many of us in the supporters of democracy, ... if they are to meet on an equal footing those who would destroy them, [is that] first of all we must make our machinery of government more flexible to deal with the modern trend of events and secondly, extend greater confidence to those whom they have elected to lead the fight on their behalf. We have made no bargain with the Government, nor with the employers' associations. These are not the days for bargaining. The primary duty of all is service.... It is this great mass of the workers, harnessed to the chariot of the State, imbued with the desire to serve, that all look to at the present time. I venture to believe that a new conception of values of classes in this land has impressed itself on the people, which will leave its mark upon the institution of our country when the menace of Hitlerism is removed from these isles.

The Communists Join in: The Attack on Russia, 1941

This unity of purpose in support of the nation's war aims was confirmed once and for all when the Germans attacked Russia on 22 June 1941. The communist attitude to the war had been at best equivocal, at worst, pure sabotage. But after the invasion of Russia, the energy displayed by the left in support of the war, in order to help Russia, was amazing. No one blinked at the complete volte-face in policy. In the early summer of 1941, the London district leadership moved that the union's TUC motion for 1941 should call for a review of the legislation affecting industrial relations because it was 'cutting across trade union agreements'. They also urged the withdrawal of the Labour members from a government which was 'constantly attacking the workers' rights and liberties, persistently attempting to weaken trade union organizations and is responsible for the chaotic conditions existing in various industries.' They refused to support the National Savings Movement, saying that tax increases and the rising cost of living already forced on them 'compulsory' savings!

Within a month, everything had changed. In July 1941, the London district committee urged all branches to distribute a call to action by the union's members. They must 'campaign on their jobs for the purpose of obtaining the greatest possible output' and understand 'the necessity for a tremendous increase in the production of equipment required for the purpose of bringing about the collapse of the Nazi regime.' Walter Stevens' letter that accompanied this exhortation talked of 'our gallant allies, the USSR,' and the need for 'unsparing effort to produce the equipment.' However, Stevens, at least, was not going to get carried away. 'In conclusion,' he wrote 'the district committee feel it necessary to remind the membership that they must, at all times, carefully watch their own conditions of employment, established by the trade union movement, against any encroachments which may be attempted arising from their zealous reaction to this appeal.'

The behaviour of communists within the union's internal politics during the war remained problematic, even after the invasion of Russia in 1941. However, in terms of their commitment to the war effort they were singing the same tune as the leadership. They acquiesced in dilution, supported different schemes for rewarding higher output and refrained, largely, from organizing unofficial action. Frank Foulkes knew he and others were behaving in a novel way after unofficial strikes broke out in Barrow in 1943 over a bonus issue. Foulkes wrote that the Barrow ETU men put on 'a display of solidarity that in normal times would have demanded admiration, but taking place as it did in the throes of a mighty conflict with Fascism, had to be the subject of the reverse of approbation.' Despite the strange and mannered phraseology, it is clear what he meant!

The union's members shared the British experience of the home front and the fighting war; by the end of the war, over 25,000 members were serving with the armed forces. Throughout the war – possibly because it was a 'just' war without the persistent opposition to it that characterized parts of the response to 1914–18 – young electricians volunteered to join as fighting men. The country clearly needed skilled young electricians – particularly apprentices – to work in the war industries. However, young men like Don Cook in Walsall volunteered secretly for war service and left the employer no time to reclaim him: others went as far as getting themselves sacked in order to be in a position to go to war. The union's roll of honour showed 389 members were killed during the war. Several won medals. Pilot Officer Benny Jackson, an apprentice at Trislington Colliery and a member of Bishop Auckland branch, won the Distinguished Flying Cross (DFC) when he brought back to England a badly damaged Wellington bomber in early 1944.

In the autumn of 1942, Robert Ellis got the British Empire Medal (BEM) for gallantry and devotion to duty at sea. He was invested at Buckingham Palace, to the delight of his Liverpool Corporation electrical department colleagues. Heroism was shown at home as well; Alf Jackson of LSE No. 12 also won the BEM when Quinn and Axtens, a drapery store in Brixton, was hit in December 1940. He dashed back into the burning electricity sub-station next door to disconnect the electricity supply, as the firemen playing water on the shop and sub-station were in danger of electrocuting themselves.

Even one of the union's officials won the BEM in 1944. Llew Price was the union's district secretary in Monmouthshire and the branch secretary of Blaenavon branch. On top of that, he was an important functionary with the South Wales skilled trades committee, the Welsh engineering foundry committee, the Pontypool and District hospital executive committee, the Blaenavon post-war reconstruction committee, the Blaenavon old age pensioners fund and a Labour councillor in Blaenavon town. He won a medal for service to the community which was magnificent but not unique; thousands of the union's members took part in the same mixture of industrial, political and community service. It was a special time in Britain's history.

For the electricians who went to war, their craft was often deployed in trying circumstances. Private A. W. Bridge, RASC, wrote to his area official, J. Middleton, in Sheffield on 21 January 1944.

Dear Brother Middleton

I am writing to you chiefly with a view to gaining knowledge as to present and future conditions in the trade. Have heard quite a lot re the Beveridge plans, but would appreciate a fuller report by you. For over two years, I have heard very little of the union, and two of my mates are in a similar predicament, one being in the London branch and the other in the Hull branch. Would you do your utmost to reply to this as fully as possible please?

As you may gather, I am still an electrician, but the work is confined chiefly to lorry wiring and battery repairs. Occasionally we get a break on some AC or DC supply job. Installations out here vary considerably in type and quality from those at home. Everything is run in overhead aerials or cleats, occasionally reverting to slot conduit with an insulated interior. Supply voltages are 11,000 to subs, and 550 supply for power and 110 for lighting, 3 phase, three and four wire. As I say, installations are of a very inferior quality. Overheads are protected by fuses situated on the line-insulators, and consist of a single lead or copper wire held by two nuts. Joints are situated anywhere, and all are held by a steel clamp to stop them undoing in case of excessive strains on the line. Needless to say, the supply is very erratic – on more than one occasion I have been turned out at night to find (or try to find) a blown fuse, somewhere across a ploughed field. Quite a healthy job when the natives (wogs) around here do not pay much attention to social standing and have no scruples about socking you one with a brick, so as to collect your cash, etc. But it's all in a life-time I guess.

Switchgear is of the open knife-blade type, with the exception of the breakers, which are built on modern lines.

We recently installed a 15 h.p. AC motor, driving a 50 volt 50 'A' genny to supply a cinema in the building. Also installed stage lighting with a loading up to present of 7,000 watts. Had one or two noted ENSA concert parties, and have very modern films direct from America. As you will gather, with only three actual electricians, all the above and about 140 trucks, plus odds and ends, we are kept fairly busy. There is no saying 'where's my time-and-a-half for Saturday or double-time for Sunday morning, or all day.' Just stick on 6s 9d per day. Not too bad, I guess, but could do with twice that.

For now, I will bid you *au revoir*, and trust to have a speedy and full reply if you can find time to attend to my needs. Trusting everything is progressing favourably. My regards to the boys.

Yours sincerely

A. W. Bridge

The Home Front

Although they were at home, it is probable that many of the union's members would have swapped their perilous duties for Brother Bridge's obligations – particularly the union's members in electricity supply sub-stations. During the blitz from September 1940–March 1941, they worked alone in perilous circumstances. As the city emptied in the early evening before the bombers arrived, the sub-station attendants working for London Transport and Southern Railway, along with the supply companies, waited to sustain supply in bomb-ravaged London and other city centres.

In London, the companies were peculiarly insensitive to these men's problems. It was not until January 1940 that the railway companies agreed to issue torches, steel helmets and civilian gas masks to workers working alone in over twenty railway sub-stations with blacked-out glass roofs. Just after midnight on 19 March 1941, London Transport sub-stations at Limehouse and Clapham were destroyed. Two men were killed and two injured in these two-man sub-stations. Bussey was thunderstruck when he discovered that there were no helmets at these stations, no emergency exits, no nearby shelter and no emergency phones. Worse still, no London Transport official thought to notify the members' families at the Limehouse tragedy. At 4.20 p.m. the following day, wondering why Mr Strelitz had not returned from his twelve-hour shift, his wife and daughter went to the sub-station to be told the awful news. Bussey contrasted the horror of this with the way every other member of London Transport's staff fled London in the late afternoon, or went to company-provided shelters. He at least wrung an apology from London Transport's chairman, Lord Ashfield.

Later that year, a double-manned station was hit at Streatham, on the Southern Railway. On this occasion, the members concerned escaped with their lives, but were badly injured. Southern Railway's response was astonishing. When Bussey insisted on discussing the problem with Colonel Llewellin, the parliamentary secretary of the Ministry of Transport, on 27 October, Southern Railway's representatives 'endeavoured to prove that if a one-man station had been obtained in places like Streatham, which was bombed, only *one* man would have been injured instead of two!'

The bombing intensified during the glorious weeks of September 1940, as the German bombers turned away in defeat from confronting the RAF. They took to pounding the cities of Britain, particularly London, and the war came home to the union direct. At noon on Sunday 15 September, the head office in Macauley Road, Clapham was hit by a high explosive bomb. Caretaker Tom Reed was killed, along with his wife's mother and a young friend of his son Peter, who was staying for the weekend. Mrs Reed and Peter were hurt, but survived. In the same raid, Miss Hickin, a typist at the office, was also hurt. No. 9 Macauley Road was a total loss, and No. 11 and the new board room were extensively damaged – to the tune of £5,408. The union decided to leave the building (it was later used by Wandsworth Council as temporary accommodation for bombed-out families) and move out of London. Matt Greenwell found a marvellous country seat near Malmesbury in Wiltshire where 'even air-raid warnings are almost unknown' for £18,000, but just as he was negotiating the final details, Jimmy Rowan and Ernie Bussey found a better bargain. For £7,000, they bought Ollerenshaw Hall near Whaley Bridge in Derbyshire (close to the south-eastern edge of Manchester). On 9 December, the union moved its remaining office equipment and records up to the hall and ran the union's war effort from there. The London office was also affected by the blitz. An unexploded bomb, just outside Rugby Chambers, meant a hasty departure to nearby Swinton House, in Gray's Inn Road, where the ISTC head office was situated. On 4 May 1941, the Liverpool area office was totally destroyed with all its paperwork and furniture – in fact everything, but there were no casualties.

In response to the bombing, executive councillor Fred Haskell was firmly of the view that the union ought to be able to dispense immediate aid to bombed-out members. His proposal, later validated in a membership ballot 17,250–1,215, was to make over £1,000 from the national benevolent fund and levy the members 1d a week during the war into a war distress fund. Area officials were then permitted to hand out sums of up to £25 to alleviate immediate emergencies caused by the bombing. The general secretary of the union was unwilling to publish details of the fund's expenditure at the end of the war, because of the sensitive nature of the personal problems revealed by such an audit. However, from October 1940–January 1946, the fund paid out £19,021 10s 0d.

As one phase of the blitz ended in June 1941, the fund had paid out £5,389 between October 1940 and 25 June 1941; 1,025 claims were made on the fund, by June 1941, with 538 in London, ninety-four in Glasgow, sixty-one in Liverpool, forty-nine in Plymouth, forty in Belfast, twenty-seven in Sheffield, twenty-one in Manchester, seventeen in Birmingham and 178 across the rest of Britain. Over £6,900 was spent in 1944 when serious bombing problems returned with the V1 and V2 rocket attacks. The fund was a great success, and was to form the financial basis of the union's post-war convalescent and educational work when the money was not returned to the general funds of the union, but earmarked for these special purposes.

Ernie Bevin, the TGWU general secretary, became Minister of Labour in May 1940, in Churchill's new Government. New industrial legislation was enacted to deal with three main problems associated with the war effort. First, the problem of strikes and industrial peace; second, the need to allocate the right type of labour where it was needed most; and third, the need to encourage production and output with a suitable sense of commitment and interest by the workers concerned.

Commitment to the War Effort

The incidence of strikes in the Second World War never reached the level of the First World War. In 1915, 2.96 million days were lost in strikes. By 1918, the figure had risen to 5.89 million that year. In contrast, in 1940, only 940,000 days were lost, and in 1943 only 1.81 million. By 1944, the figure rose to 3.71 million, but over half of these were unofficial disputes in the turbulent coal industry. The ETU, in the First World War, were often involved in the significant strikes of the time – particularly the 1917 engineering disputes and 1918's fight to ensure the widest application of Committee on Production awards. In the Second World War, the union was involved in one short, but significant, contracting strike, covering the whole of the Manchester region in September 1943. The members had a good case, with an arbitration award that did not help them to catch up with the earnings in the munitions industry. However, two main influences stopped that strike quickly and prevented any others from materializing with official encouragement. First, the new Coalition Government passed into law the Emergency Powers (Defence) Act on 22 May 1940, giving the Government wide powers expected in a war situation. Under the legislation, an Order in Council, No. 1305, was quickly issued. This made strikes illegal. However, it also banned lock-outs and obliged the parties to refer industrial disputes to the national arbitration tribunal. By March 1941, this legislation was refined by the 'essential work' orders, which could designate 'essential' work locations and direct workers towards them. Once again, there was a considerable sweetening effect. No worker could leave an 'essential' works, but then he couldn't be sacked without the right of appeal to a national service officer. Again, Bevin made sure that all workers would be guaranteed their week's pay so long as they were available for work. The terms and conditions of work should also be the recognized district or industrial rates normally negotiated by trade unions.

Secondly, the low incidence of strikes was assured by the left's enthusiastic belief in production at any cost. In 1943, when the spontaneous Manchester contracting strikes broke out, they wanted help from London. They received many messages and resolutions from jobs and branches that expressed no confidence in the executive and called for the resignation of the London district committee. Les Gregory told a conference of London contracting shop-stewards on 14 November 1943 that 'strikes during the war do not affect the employers so much as they hinder the Government with regard to its war production and military programme.' Arthur Stride told the same conference, 'it would be totally incorrect for the London contracting membership, even in the face of such action to obtain redress.... The London district committee in normal times would have given only one answer to the employers, but now is not the time to give such an answer.' The demand for the resignation of the district committee and the executive 'only plays into the hands of all pro-Fascists in this country, who welcome any move that tends to split the unions. ... If we think that such tactics as splitting the union, or the taking of strike action by 2–3,000 electricians are going to affect Government policy on wages, then we have to think again, and more clearly.'

The trade unions were bound into the Government's direction of labour through their guarded, but sensible, acquiescence in different aspects of the direction of labour to essential war work. First, the union thought that the ages were too high under which electricians (and full-time officers of the union!) were to lose their ability to claim deferment for military service. By the end of the war, the union, by rule, was telling branches not to nominate anyone under thirty-five for office in the union, because they might have to be called up. In March 1941, Bussey met William Beveridge at the Ministry of Labour and succeeded in showing the ministry that 265 members of the union were not being used properly in the Armed Forces – their technical skills were being ignored. Thirty-four cases were represented by Bussey and Bolton in front of the committee, and were successfully redeployed to technical work. Beveridge's committee's report accepted Bussey's case when writing: 'The trade unions have made out their case; they have shown failure to use men according to their skill in a substantial number of cases, and have proved the need to take more effective measures in the future.'

Members working at sea were delighted to have the chance of achieving petty officer status for electrical skills, in the same way as engineers had, and also introduced a regrading scheme that recognized a grade of electrical mechanic at sea.

In June 1940, the Government introduced the Restrictions on Engagement Order, which obliged employers to obtain their workers through an employment exchange or the union; and this brought further responsibility on the union to assist in the most effective direction of labour. In 1942, there was little support for furious London shipping members redeployed to Southampton. Their overtime ban was ignored. The Registration for Employment Order produced lists of all men over forty-one and all women between the ages of eighteen and forty, except people already in military or civil service work. This, too, simplified union co-operation in the direction of labour.

Dilution Wins the War

From the earliest days of the war, the union had entered into dilution agreements with the engineering and shipbuilding industries. Indeed, Jimmy Rowan was pleased with the agreement with the engineering employers of April 1940, which allowed the ETU to reclaim a dilutee job back the moment they could provide a skilled man. Dilution agreements were signed in contracting and electricity supply in early 1942, but it was in shipbuilding that the union went furthest in its determination to help the Government and the nation.

Right from the beginning of the war, there were shortages of electricians in the shipbuilding and ship-repair yards. The union entered into dilution agreements from early 1940, and attempted to direct skilled men into shipbuilding and ship-repair from London, where there was some unemployment in contracting at the outbreak of war. This industry probably faced its finest hour in terms of the demands made on it. New building, conversion of American lend-lease ships, quick turn-around of ships demanded excessive hours, working in air-raids, and working away from home. By December 1940, only the Thames and Bristol Channel could meet their demands for skilled men without dilution. Attention quickly focused on the payments system in the industry, where resistance to piece-work, PBR (payment by results), was part of the skilled man's tradition. In November 1940, the chief of the labour department at Cammell Lairds in Birkenhead, a Mr Dunham, travelled to York, to plead with the executive council directly and personally to let him introduce PBR into his shipyard. Between 1 June and 19 October 1940, with the help of Frank Foulkes in the Liverpool office, he had recruited 140 electricians. However, 146 had left over the same period, chasing the higher earnings in contracting. They could not use dilutees on the technical, naval work they had in mind, and Mr Dunham was desperate for the executive's help. The company eventually paid a flat rate war bonus to their electricians of twenty per cent on the rate. In the six weeks following the agreement, only four left. However, the Tyne and Clyde yards would not allow a general move towards PBR and the executive would not contemplate the individual basis of pay that PBR implied.

A further problem arose; it was preferred that some of the dilutees, if they were not long-serving auxiliaries or apprentices who were made up early, would be other craftsmen working on parts of the electricians' work. It will be recalled that the union fought bitter demarcation struggles at the turn of the century with carpenters and joiners over the question of casing. Electric cable or wires would run through different coverings or casings and it was perfectly possible for joiners to run the casing, even if they did not connect up the electrical equipment concerned. On the Tyne, they were happy for joiners to do this work, if they left the Amalgamated Society of Woodworkers (ASW) and joined the special section of the ETU reserved for dilutees! – the war emergency section. Proud woodworkers were hardly likely to find that an appealing proposition.

After the invasion of Russia, there was still no dilution in ship-repair and very little in shipbuilding. According to Frank Foulkes, the Mersey district were now ready for PBR, whether to help Soviet Russia or boost earnings was not quite clear; there was, however, 'an insistent demand for some system whereby they could obtain increased payments.' By May 1942, they were also offering to work an eight-day week to avoid the Sunday shut-down and rotate rest days. Minor disputes about transfer between yards, subsistence payments, travel allowances were frequent; there was even a spectacular closed shop strike in Belfast when J Mackie's set on a non-unionist called James Pim from Dublin. In 1942, the shipbuilders did not help by steadfastly refusing to move significantly on basic rates.

Other eyes were watching. In early August 1942, Bussey, now general secretary of the union after Rowan's retirement, received a telegram from Mr Maddison, the chief industrial advisor to the Government. This told of 'urgent work on naval vessels' being retarded by ship joiners not being allowed to do 'certain electricians' work'. Bussy urged local district official, Paul McArdle, to co-operate. Ernie Bevin then stepped in and summoned the ETU executive and ASW representatives to see him at the ministry on 14 August. Alf Martin, the London area official dealing with shipbuilding and repair in London, brought details to the meeting of a separate, irritating, issue. Fifty electricians and 150 other trades had just been made redundant in the London port; they were told to go north to work on the cruisers building on the Tyne. If they refused to go, they would be automatically de-reserved, and would be available for service with the Armed Forces. Bevin frankly told the ETU delegation of the huge demand for escort vessels to America and, significantly, to Russia, that the war now demanded of the shipyards. He also said that if the union's policy for a Second Front to be opened to assist Russia was to be a possibility, the ETU must help Bevin. Bussey's report of the conversation said that Bevin then put it to the delegation that the minister 'was justified in advising us, that knowing the strategy of the war as a member of the Government, the Second Front for electricians at the moment was on shipbuilding.' Bevin was pressing hard: however, he and Bussey did an old-fashioned trade union deal. Bussey agreed to accept the joiners working as dilutees immediately, as far as the two cruisers were concerned. Future ASW recruits would stay in their own union, and pay just 3d a week to join the ETU war emergency section, thus preserving the union's post-war rights to reclaim the work. In return,

Bevin ordered that the threats of de-reservation hanging over the London port electricians be withdrawn, and Martin given time to relocate the members on a voluntary basis. Bussey and McArdle worked harder still, clearly pleased to be involved in high strategic politics. By the end of that weekend, they had extended the offer of dilution beyond the woodworkers. They allowed the introduction of female dilutees, the recruitment of other auxiliary electrical workers outside the shipyards to come in as dilutee electricians, and the formation of mobile squads of contracting/electricity supply skilled men to work the weekends in the yards. Dilution spread throughout the shipyards: by December 1944, for instance, there were 315 dilutees alongside 810 fully skilled craftsmen at Harland and Wolff's in Belfast.

There remained the problem of PBR. Here, the union's leadership was ahead of the members. The leadership postponed a PBR agreement until they saw the 1942 wages deal. It was pathetic (2d an hour for maintenance electricians, nothing for the rest). The deal the union were trying to sell the employers was that they could pay the skilled electricians more for their extra skills. This would make shipyard work attractive for skilled men outside. Whether from fear of repercussions from other groups or plain meanness, the employers would not entertain the idea. At the end of 1942, the ETU shipyard members rejected PBR solidly, 3,097–2,257. Cowes, Falmouth and Southampton shipyards voted for – all the others against. On the Clyde, it was 821–707. On the Tyne, it was 211–197. Belfast voted 231–129. In London, it was 459–58. Even on Frank Foulkes's Merseyside, PBR was rejected by 650–513. The minister, Ernie Bevin, expressed his disappointment and so Bussey called a delegate conference to discuss the principle of PBR on 3 February 1943. The suggested schemes were all based on group performance – and never on individual output.

Ernie Bevin added his ministerial weight to the PBR case, urging the delegates to remember Russia in the Government's need to get a thirty per cent increase in electrical work. PBR was the only way.

Some members were genuinely anxious about whether the schemes would place too heavy a physical burden on the men. Pat McCarthy, from the Port of London, was representative of this view. 'The position of the men is that they have been working seven days a week. There is a limit to human endurance and many of these men are travelling approximately one-and-a-half hours night and morning. They are called upon as members of the Home Guard to be on duty one or two nights during the week. They want to rest on Sundays, but instead have to go out on a route march.' The conference was also addressed by Vice-Admiral Wake Walker and George Hall, the financial secretary to the Admiralty. In the end, the patriotic card was enough. The union implemented the schemes on 22 February.

Ernie Bevin paid tribute to the union's effort in these two cases – the joiners acting as dilutees, and the adoption of PBR in shipbuilding. He told the 1943 TUC:

Let me just mention two incidents in this U-boat campaign showing how, first of all, helpfulness on the part of unions, who responded without knowing all the facts, helped this campaign. I had a dispute between the joiners and the ETU. I met them. The plea of urgency was accepted by both of them. They settled their difficulty and by helping one another and us, they saved months in the fitting out of certain vital ships on the North-East Coast and the Clyde.

Then, I suddenly had to find 4,000 electricians. I think the general secretary (Walter Citrine) will agree that whatever else you can get out of an incubator, you cannot get electricians, so I could not hatch them! We met the union – indeed we met most of the shipbuilding unions in their various branches. They all helped. But the ETU – and I pay them public compliment – agreed with me to take on that pernicious thing, as they have always thought it, Payment by Results, to help us in this task. Now what was the result? The change they made at their delegate conference was worth about 3,000 to 4,000 men to us and it enabled us to put on the campaign against the U-boats at the precise date that the Cabinet had decided it should operate.

The members were probably just as interested in the 'reasonable yields' of the schemes that became apparent by the end of 1943.

This was not the end of the union's involvement in the government of Britain during the war. Bevin was keen to ensure the positive incorporation of trade union officials, local and national, lay and full-time into the network of joint production committees. These were joint union – management committees that planned the removal of production difficulties. First introduced into ROFs in early 1942, there were over 4,000 at work throughout British industry by 1944.

Bussey pointed out that they were mainly in larger firms, but their importance was not to be underestimated in terms of the self-respect and self-confidence they gave to their trade union participants.

Bussey saw that they should not be 'grouse committees', should avoid trivia, and should pre-circulate agendas with both union and management providing agenda items. Production committees should be liaising with the local Home Guard to try to get exemption for craftsmen who were already working sixty hours a week. Heating bills, saving on scrap, the layout of electrical stores and workshop areas, the staggering of factory hours to ease overcrowding on local buses, were all typical issues Bussey suggested for production committee agendas in 1944.

In March 1942, Bussey wrote:

The function of management in industry has always been viewed as a privilege of ownership. No one except the owner of an establishment, or his direct nominee, could exercise the sacred function of management. The workers were 'hands', hewers of wood and drawers of water, to be disciplined in the factory or workshop by one of their own kind in the figure of an overlooker or a foreman, but taking orders from above. Problems of workshop management were considered outside the province of the worker.... In the twenty years [since 1922] during which this agreement [the Engineering Procedure Agreement] has been in operation, not one single breach has been made in the employers' right to exclusive managerial control. There are signs, however, that this barrier of exclusiveness is being broken down.... For the first time in the history of industrial relations in this country, the right of labour to participate with the management on matters relating to production is recognized.

There is no doubt that the union's experience of joint production committees – particularly as the workshop committees linked to regional and national committees under the Ministry of Production working to a structure designed by Citrine – fuelled their growing confidence in the worker's capacity to make his own future. This feeling was to have a significant political effect in 1945.

Throughout the war, their contact with government and the controlling forces of the economy deepened and professionalized the union's leaders capacity to lead. The trade union function became multi-faceted. New legislation produced new challenges. Bussey summed it up in 1942.

The new features which the orders have introduced into industrial relations have greatly added to the responsibilities of the union, as well as calling for greater vigilance on our part.... Each day our work grows more onerous and complex. Though we never were a purely industrial organization, our activities are taking on more and more of a political and legal character. The innumerable statutory rules and orders have added immensely to the general routine of our work of negotiation and conciliation, and our activities have now penetrated to every department of state.

Collective Bargaining during the War

Indeed, 'the general routine of negotiation' did continue throughout the war. A. J. P. Taylor's view of earnings during the war is that, due to taxation policy and stricter control over 'profiteering', 'the entire population settled at the level of the skilled artisan'. It is easy to see what he means. Between 1938 and 1947 (calculated at 1947 prices) wages rose by 18 per cent in real terms, while income from property fell 15 per cent and salaries by 21 per cent. The cost of living index rose between 1938 and 1944 by around 50 per cent, while wage rates rose $81\frac{1}{2}$ per cent (21 per cent in real terms).

For the first twenty months of the war, this rise in the cost of living index, meant regular rises for the contracting membership. In 1939, in the months either side of the declaration of war in September, the National Standardized

Agreement had undergone considerable change. The new 'zoning' agreement abolished Grade 'D' and moved 'D' grades into 'C'. 'C' moved up into 'B2' grade. On the wages front, a 10-point surge in the cost of living between August and September 1939 forced the NJIC to arrange a new sliding scale to take account of the war inflation. The agreement, operational from January 1940, gave the union a 3s 6d rise immediately, with 5d a week to come for every point the index rose, reviewed every three months. The new base was to be a cost of living scale starting in September 1939. This agreement provided 'considerable benefit' to the membership in 1940. So much so, that in August 1940, the NFEA demanded the suspension of the formula: here, the union was able to utilize the national arbitration tribunal to order that the agreement had to stand for the duration of the war. They took their time, publishing the award in July 1941. The war bonus went up from 11s 8d a week to 18s 4d per week. More positively, the employers and union at last signed the national working rules card on 1 October, which was confirmed by a ballot vote, 7,069–5,049. This cut out many regional variations in the conditions of work and made the agreements truly national. However, in the summer of 1941, the lucrative wages agreement started to be undermined by the jiggery-pokery being played by the Government with the cost of living index. The index was heavily weighted in favour of food items. The Government subsidized basic foodstuffs (£72 million in 1940, £250 million in 1945) whilst 'luxury' items were left outside the index and uncontrolled. With innovations like purchase tax, the real cost of living was perceived by workers to be rising. In 1942, pressure for wages to reflect this perception grew: but the union's success in negotiating higher subsistence allowances when working away, and at last getting an agreed percentage scale for unindentured apprentices and 'boy labour' alike, kept the protests under control.

In 1943, the 1939 Wages (War Adjustment) Agreement became increasingly difficult to defend. In March 1943, the union asked for 3d an hour increase. The NFEA offered nothing except further talks on allowances and expenses. In August, the union's delegate conference of shop-stewards rejected small increases on the war bonus. Bolton's district secretary, Les Cannon, said that the offer should be rejected, and the executive supported him.

In September 1943, Ernie Bevin promised to convene meetings under his ministry's auspices. This stopped the spontaneous strikes in Manchester spreading out of contracting and into engineering and electricity supply. The same dissatisfaction with the cost of living index was also becoming apparent in these industries. The talks at the Ministry of Labour quickly produced a temporary agreement as a solution to the dispute.

This agreement scrapped the war bonus of 18s 4d by consolidating it into the rates at an extra $4\frac{3}{4}$d per hour – attracting the possibility of higher earnings on top of that from enhanced overtime rates. The members were still unhappy.

Engineering, shipbuilding and supply had had recent increases of 5d an hour, and earnings for contracting electricians were not really competitive. For a forty-seven hour week, skilled building workers got £5 1s 5½d a week. Electricians in supply were getting £5 11s 7½d and electricians in engineering were earning approximately £5 9s 8d a week. Contracting electricians were only getting £5 6s 9d a week. Les Gregory provided these figures to the London mass meeting in contracting in November 1943.

All was not lost, however. The 3d a week claim went forward to arbitration, which reported on 4 November 1943. The limits of wartime patience were seriously tried when the arbitration by Sir Hector Hetherington produced ¾d an hour for Grades 'B', 'B2' and 'C', but absolutely nothing for London in Grade 'A'. This narrowed the differential for London. Grade 'A' was 2s 3½d an hour, and Grade 'B2' 2s 0½d.

Mass meetings in London expressed their disappointment, but there were no strikes. A countrywide delegate conference of shop-stewards was held in February 1944 when a national rate of 2s 6d an hour was demanded. This was formally presented to the employers at Africa House in Kingsway on 2 May. Bussey explained, in what Mr Penwill of the NFEA was gracious enough to describe as a 'comprehensive and logical statement', that there were two main problems in the wage structure. First, London had missed out on wages at the same time as the value of the travelling allowance element in the hourly rate was falling in value. Secondly, the problems with the cost of living index, rendering the sliding scale immobile, was hurting contracting electricians, especially as they had little access to the production bonuses enjoyed by their equivalents in engineering or shipbuilding. The NFEA understood the 'urgency' of the claim, said Mr Penwill, but wanted to discuss the whole agreement – wages as part of a package that included zoning, the national working rules, travelling time and other allowances. The immediate problem was helped somewhat by 1d an hour for *all* grades conceded on 21 June 1944.

The modern observer is forcibly struck with just how long negotiations of this sort dragged on. A charitable view in looking at the contracting negotiations from 1943–5 might easily rest its case on the fact that huge strides were made in the non-wage aspects of the agreement. Where travelling time exceeded thirty minutes between lodgings and site, travelling time was to be paid after thirty minutes and actual fares for anything over 6d were paid. On 2 June 1943, after years of talks, one week's holiday with pay was assured with members paying 1s 6d a week to assure themselves of holiday credits, an agreement closely followed by the Scottish contracting industry. Zoning was improved with different towns moving up grades. In September 1944, there was a further small rise in pay, but a big step forward in getting all of grade 'B2' upgraded into 'B'. A national scheme for travelling time and fares was negotiated in 1944 for implementation in January 1945, excluding only

London, Manchester and Liverpool. 'Abnormal conditions' payments of 1s were agreed, and the conditions defined for inclusion in the national working rules. In 1945, just as the war ended, London got back the ¾d it 'lost' in 1943, and everyone got an extra 2d on the war addition to the hourly rate. Apprentice percentages were raised, an NJIC certificate of completion of apprenticeship issued and joint work undergone at last to control training content independent of the rest of the building industry. And London at long last joined its local DJIC for the industry.

There were fewer similar improvements in electricity supply, although they were far ahead of contracting in their conditions of work, if not necessarily in terms of earnings. The stability in the industry was sustained during the war. Various agreements gave small annual cost of living increases, confirming the supply authorities' preference for comparing their wage *rates* (if not *earnings*) with outside industry rather than their capacity to pay. Workers in supply became more productive. By 1944, they were supplying forty per cent more electricity than in 1939, with a workforce that had shrunk to 90,000 from 120,000. Dilutees were widespread after the 1942 agreements, with seventeen per cent of the workforce being women (particularly in clerical and meter-reading jobs). Only what Leslie Hannah describes as a 'skeleton staff' of skilled men remained by the end of the war. Indifference to trade unions was also a problem outside of big cities. Frank Foulkes went to the South of England in January 1945 to evaluate the local official's problems in organizing an area from Brighton to Penzance. He discovered, while looking at the organizational problems, that there were twenty-five electrical undertakings in that huge area – but the average trade union penetration (by all unions) was no more than thirty-five per cent.

Engineering during the war produced much the same picture as shipbuilding. Small bonuses were paid throughout the war after regular trips to the national arbitration tribunal – 1941's settlement of 3s 6d on the bonus was 'scandalous', according to Jimmy Rowan in his last annual report. Shipbuilding's similar sum produced 'bitter resentment in the unions'. Both industries, however, produced a small extra payment for maintenance electricians, distinctive from other grades, and in engineering, in 1944, the EEF signed a formal procedure agreement to allow the union to represent women workers and continued to understand at least a little of the case for paying skilled men more by advancing extra money to electrical testers working on main test beds.

The war increased considerably the range of negotiating responsibilities undertaken by the union. Throughout the first fifty years of its existence, most negotiations were involved in long-drawn-out justification for 1d/hour claims or offers. With the war coming to a close, the union was represented at national level in contracting, electricity supply, shipbuilding and engineering (through its membership of the CSEU and the Joint Wages Movement). Talks took on a growing sophistication also at the Admiralty, the Air Ministry, the War Department and the Office of Works. The railways, the cablemaking industry, the new radio and radar industries, London Transport, ICI, Courtaulds, the Chemical Industries Federation – even the seed-crushing industry – all now signed lengthy, multi-issue agreements with the ETU. The union was helped here by its new research department, where Joe Wild produced careful analysis of every industry, particularly in servicing the union's post-war reconstruction committee. His prolific output after his appointment in 1939 by Rowan (although he was an acknowledged supporter of the left) helped the union's leadership immeasurably in the establishment of their intellectual bona fides with the growing corporate state that was the nation at war.

Membership Growth, 1939–45

The Second World War produced enormous growth for the union, just as the First World War had done. Once again, the union's co-operation in the war effort brought influence and prestige that was rewarded in the perceptions of non-unionists, who saw the union as something that delivered the goods. Union officials were crucial to the success of the union's growth in the war, but in a novel way. Now they supervised and organized the work of shop-stewards. The days of Kinniburgh and Stewart personally recruiting everyone was gone. Frank Foulkes was aware of the change when he started work as national organizer in 1942. 'Although I am designated "organizer", the area form of organization and the efforts of the active shop-stewards and the members on the job have reduced the actual recruitment by a national organizer of male members to an absolute minimum.'

Table 3 shows the change in the membership figures, along with the different percentages of the various grades of membership.

Table 3

Section of the Union	1939 No.	1939 % of membership	1945 No.	1945 % of membership
Full Benefit	42,165	60.17	67,555	50.78
Trade Protection	97	.14	482	.36
Auxiliary	18,648	26.62	23,586	17.72
Apprentice	9,155	13.07	27,688	20.82
War Emergency	—	—	10,706	8.05
Female	—	—	3,016	2.27
TOTALS	70,065		133,033	

The union's membership nearly doubled in the six years of war. Although the percentage of the membership that was 'skilled' – the full-benefit members – fell to just over fifty per cent, the huge increase in apprentice members kept the 'skilled' percentage, taking the full-benefit and apprentices together, at virtually the same level of seventy-two to seventy-three per cent of the total. The regulation of apprentices' working conditions by the union effectively started with the 1939 contracting agreement, which really came into its own during the war. Before 1939, the employers had vigorously insisted that the apprentices' terms and conditions were between the company, the parents and the boy himself – nothing to do with the union. That all changed in the war. Equally, with the union's insistence that all dilutees join the war emergency section of the union, from 1940 onwards or the female section after 1944, there was new growth amongst people entering industry under wartime conditions. The union's dilution agreements generally looked to the employers 'making-up' auxiliary members to skilled status as a first step, and then bringing in women and untrained men as semi-skilled or 'mates', 'assistants' and 'labourers'. Throughout the war, retired skilled men returned to work. In June 1941, for instance, Tom Hollywood, a seventy-eight-year-old Irishman, returned to the Govan shipyard as an electrician. As we have seen, Bill Webb worked in the London docks during the blitz, at the age of seventy.

Unofficial pressure on employers to set up or maintain the closed shop was a powerful way of making sure that dilution was not a back-door to the end of organization. This was particularly galling to the Admiralty who often had to send Admiralty dockyard electricians into civilian dockyards to fine-tune or check work on navy ships. By the end of the war, they were careful to make sure they sent trade union members. The union also signed agreements with many other unions to allow other tradesmen to be adopted to electrical work. Such men paid 3d a week to the ETU, and were promised a return to their unions at the end of the war. There was no such gesture from the MFGB, even when 'Bevin boys' were sent to the mines later in the war – some of whom were members of other unions.

Throughout the war, the union's finances grew stronger. In 1939, the union's general fund balance stood at £203,062. That year, income was £139,623 and expenditure £94,100 (with unemployment benefit costing £15,863 and strike pay of £3,485).

In 1945, the balance had risen to over £700,000. Income was £244,288 and expenditure £165,451. There was a small amount of unemployment at the end of 1944 as some munitions industries were run down and this cost the union £1,599. There was no expenditure on strikes at all as legislation effectively banned official strikes. These were huge balances for the union compared to their hand-to-mouth finances in the inter-war years. The leadership was acutely aware, however, of how the industrial collapse of 1921–2 had devastated the balances built up after the First World War, and they were fearful of the return of unemployment.

The wartime increase in union membership, allied to the enormous extension of the union's negotiating and administrative burdens, produced considerable structural change in the union's constitution. Equally, the political war in the union that had reached a pre-war crescendo in the Earl's Court and Vigon issues started to resolve itself in the left's favour, despite a spirited rearguarded action carried out by Bussey and his allies on the executive.

It is not fashionable to attribute historical change to the attributes of 'great men'. However unfashionable it may be, it is difficult not to note the fact that the union could never have been the same after Jimmy Rowan retired as general secretary on 30 April 1941. His period of office expired on 31 October 1941, but he suggested that the election for his successor should take place in December 1940; he would then stay on for a while as 'advisor' to the executive council and retire at the proper moment. Rowan was by now old and tired; he did not have long to enjoy retirement. He died at Flixton on 5 January 1944.

Jimmy Rowan

Jimmy Rowan's record speaks for itself. When he became general secretary in 1907, his three predecessors had run off with the union's funds. There were less than 1,500 members. When he retired in 1941, the union had over 80,000 members. From an obscure, ill-organized, incoherent organization, he had guided it towards independence, respect from other unions and employers and a general fund balance of £265,000. He wrote the fiftieth annual report for 1940, his own thirty-fifth, just before he retired in April 1941. He was characteristically laconic about his own contribution. 'I have had a remarkably good run.... At least I have done my duty with the union during this long period.' His Scottish ancestry and Mancunian reserve produced a cool, determined and occasionally unpleasant ferocity in his relationships. However, he could be tremendous company, with or without a glass of whisky in his hand. In his earlier years, in particular, he was much in demand at smoking concerts and branch socials. His friends' tributes were not simply conventional tributes; the man's character shows through. Bob Prain, assistant general secretary from 1912–42, probably knew Rowan best. 'In his prime, Brother Rowan was not excelled by any trade unionist in the country as a negotiator. ... He was a man of strong opinions. He was a good friend, a great general secretary and at all times, a "bonny fetcher".'

Ernie Bussey was his close political ally as the left grew in power in the union in the 1930s. Apart from saying how deep his debt to Rowan was, he noted that his friend 'could be stubborn and intractable to the point of exasperation ... often blunt and to the point, his forthright manner never left a doubt as to his meaning.' Rowan's political opponents felt his tongue. He was profoundly anti-communist, and told new executive councillor George Haslam that after voting with the left at his first executive meeting, he would never get elected again! Jimmy Rowan would see to that! Les Gregory long remembered the fur that flew when he confronted the left caucus at the 1938 Torquay conference. Yet the left recognized his qualities – not least when he used his own money to guarantee the union's loans just after the General Strike. He was obsessed with the union's funds, no doubt as a reaction to the persistent corruption in the period before he became general secretary. It was his administrative genius that set him apart.

He rescued the finances, organized the recruitment of members into the union, dealt with the crises of war and still led the negotiations from the dawn of the organization in three main industries – contracting, electricity supply and engineering. He tried all his life to achieve unity among the engineering trades with his favourite aphorism – 'There are too many trade unions and not enough trade unionists'. He served on the FEST, and its later reincarnation, the CSEU. He was on the General Council of the TUC from 1921–35, when he lost the chance to be TUC president at the 1935 congress. He would not turn away from confronting the MFGB and the Entertainment Union. They had electricians in their unions who were ill-paid and poorly regarded by their contemporaries and Rowan couldn't stand that. Joe Lane was branch secretary of LSE No. 17 and senior committee man of the London district committee in 1944. Later that year, he was its president. A man of the left, his tribute to Rowan is significant. 'Despite the fact we had many disagreements, we are conscious of how much we owe to his wise administration. Permeating the whole fabric of our organization, as a monument, can be traced the guiding hand and genius of Jimmy Rowan.'

Jimmy Rowan's final triumph was to do much more than simply build a trade union for electrical workers – huge as that achievement was. He was inspired by the desire to raise the standing of the electrician in the society in which he lived. He was not alone, but was supreme in his advocacy of the separate and, yes, superior skill of the electrician. This drove him on equally against the employers who would deny that, and against other trade unions who would deny it. Rowan's monument is the separate, indestructible and indispensable skill of the electrician.

The war years saw death take other pioneers. Bill Webb died in 1942; Jock Muir in 1940. Jack Ball died in the spring of 1943. Bob Prain retired at the end of 1942. He was appreciated by all factions in the union for his scrupulous honesty and administrative talents. His health and dedication must have been exemplary, for he only missed one executive council meeting in thirty years. Fellow Scotsman and staunch ally of Rowan, executive councillor Turnbull, retired with his four volumes of Burns. The communist-supporting Alf Coster died in early retirement in Southend. George Humphreys retired in early 1944, one of the earliest beneficiaries of the new pension rights enjoyed by the union's officials and staff since December 1940.

Structural Change during the War

These changes in personalities at the top of the union were accompanied by structural change to the organization itself. First and foremost, the union was determined to separate out the dilutees from the traditional craft core of the union. There were two main ideas behind this. First, the union felt profoundly obligated to 25,000 members who served in the forces. They had to have their jobs back when the war was over, even if the implication of that was unemployment for the dilutees. Second, the union remembered 1919–21. At the end of the First World War, thousands of auxiliary members and dilutees were thrown out of work, but were entitled to draw comparatively huge amounts of unemployment benefit without ever having any prospect of return-ing to the electrical industries. Once their benefit was exhausted, thousands drifted out of the union. Consequently, the union introduced in 1940 the war emergency section for people who had never worked in the electrical industry before. They paid 6d a week contribution for no benefits, beyond industrial representation and legal representation. This was altered to accommodate the eight skilled unions who provided electrical dilutees – pre-eminently the carpenters – whose members paid the ETU 3d a week on top of their contribution to their own union, but still did not receive the range of usual benefits. By 1944, there were 15,609 members in the section.

In 1943, the executive made a more sensitive reaction to the problem of dilution by setting up the female section of the union. By April 1943, it was estimated that the section had around 5,000 members. Most of them were not dilutees working instead of skilled men away at war. Most of them were working either in semi-skilled capacities or on jobs associated with the radio and radar industries that just did not exist before the war. They worked in ROFs, aircraft electrical sections and coil winding. Consequently, the new section had a low contribution – 6d – compared to the auxiliary section's 8d; but it had a range of modest benefits. There was no intention of throwing these women out of the industry at the end of the war. They would receive 5s unemployment or accident benefit for six weeks, a maximum funeral benefit of £5 and strike pay of 10s a week for six weeks.

They were clearly restricted to obscure branch offices like doorkeeper and branch committee member, and could be shop-stewards, but only for fellow female section members. The new section was approved in a ballot in July 1943, 16,500–5,135.

The 1940 conference made several other changes of note. First, the general president's position was made a full-time position within the union at the same wage of a little over £10 a week that the general secretary was paid. The London district committee organization was again redrawn. The 'quadrant' approach was abandoned, being replaced by a central committee, elected in industrial constituencies with sub-committees acting as trade committees from the leading industries. The quadrants had overlapped and bickered with the central committee. The new district committee would have a president elected by all the London membership.

The 1940 conference also narrowly rejected the suggestion that there should be an elected lay appeals court, placed above the executive council, that members upset with executive decisions could complain to. The proposal was supported by delegates who thought that the executive council should not sit in judgment over people the executive might have dealt with under their interpretation of the rules – that they were judge and jury at the same time. One of the London delegates from the Ilford area, D. Evans, opposed the suggested new appeals court on the grounds that the executive council were lay members of the union, and having been elected, it was ridiculous to impose an appeals court on top of them that implied a lack of confidence in the people just elected. Jimmy Rowan saw the politics behind the suggestion. Leading supporters of the proposal were Merrells and Lester – regular communist and Minority Movement supporters, up before the executive council at different times in the 1930s. They wanted an appeals court to continue their war against the properly constituted authorities in the union. No wonder they were in favour of an appeals court. It was narrowly defeated, 25–24.

One other wartime conference looked at the structure of the union and how it had to adapt to the huge increase in membership. In May 1944, a special rules revision conference looked at the growing confusion in the district committee structure. One hundred and three out of 398 branches were not affiliated to the thirty-five district committees. Some district committees had full-time officers to serve them thoroughly – some did not. The conference, therefore, redivided the country into eighteen separate areas, with every branch tied up with an area committee, and every area with full-time official coverage. Ernie Bussey was sure the union could afford it, and urged the provision of decent offices in each area that the members would not be embarrassed to enter and in which the employers would be prepared to do business with the union. The executive council would expect the area secretary – the full-time official – to lead the area committee in such a fashion that the district/centre arguments of the 1920s and 30s would be over for ever. The preparation of the new scheme had been largely undertaken by the new assistant general secretary, Walter Stevens, who saw in the scheme the opportunity to improve not just the organizational performance of the union, but also its negotiating impact. He estimated that over half the country, geographically, was effectively unrepresented by the old type of district organization. The area scheme would help enormously in giving the weaker and scattered centres of membership access to the union's negotiating officers. The scheme was carried into the union's constitution, 36–12.

Throughout the war, the union's problems with the communists changed from the crude confrontations of the late 1930s, not least because the London district committee was determined to help Russia through zealous commitment to greater production and industrial peace. There was no time for Earl's Court-style disputes with the leadership. In any case, during the war, many leadership positions fell vacant, both regional and national, and were often won for the first time by communists or their supporters. One obvious exception to this lay with the elections at the end of 1940. With Jimmy Rowan retiring, and Ernie Bussey a candidate in the general secretary election, held on December quarter night 1940, there was once again a moment of high political struggle in the union. Bussey, as the union's sitting president, was expected to win. However, the left's vote was maximized by enthusiastic voting in the usual 'communist' branches, as well as a self-righteous campaign by Frank Foulkes who claimed he was being hounded over the Vigon affair for electoral reasons, In the end, all would depend on the third candidate – dependable, experienced, London-based assistant general secretary Matt Greenwell. He got 4,645 votes. Foulkes got 5,723 and Ernie Bussey, 8,261. Greenwell's disappointment was assuaged by his victory in the election for his own job as assistant general secretary when he got 12,608 votes to Fred Haskell's 948. Jack Lyons, the once dominant ex-London district president, got just 216 votes.

In April 1941, the political excitement must have been even more intense. The second ballot for general secretary was run at the same time as the initial ballot for the first full-time general president. Bussey beat Foulkes, 12,665–9,791. Ben Bolton got 8,927 to Walter Stevens' 6,000 with Newcastle official Paul McArdle getting 3,460. In the second ballot in July 1941, Ben Bolton was elected by 12,854 votes to 8,772 for Walter Stevens. Bolton had a long record in the union. Born in Birmingham, but brought up in London, he had come out of London West branch and the London district committee along with Webb and Stavenhagen. He had been national organizer since 1925, but there is no evidence of him ever receiving the affection and respect that was clearly showered on Jack Kinniburgh and even Tom Stewart. Nevertheless, he had struggled to discipline the London situation throughout the 1930s and had been Rowan's number two in electricity supply negotiations. He was nearing retirement age in 1940–41: indeed, it is believed by many that he underestimated his age by one year in order to qualify to run for one full term as general president of the union! He retired soon after the end of the war, and Foulkes was elected president of the union on the first ballot by 13,571 to Ernie Irwin's 4,496 and Paul McArdle's 2,298. Foulkes's old job as national organizer was cleaned up by his old Merseyside district committee and political friend, Gus Cole, who got 11,344 votes to an obscure Scottish area official called Jock Byrne's 1,903 votes. When Bob Prain retired in 1942, the assistant general secretary's job fell to the left when Walter Stevens beat Paul McArdle on the second ballot. This was a curious election, at least statistically. McArdle got 8,688 votes to Stevens's 8,687 in the first ballot. There were twenty-one other candidates who came nowhere. However, on the second ballot, Walter Stevens beat McArdle, 14,385–13,068. Throughout the war, the left's control of the executive council grew stronger, partly because robust anti-communists like Glasgow's Turnbull and Yorkshire's Thorpe retired or were defeated, partly because of outright left victories. By the end of 1945, the communists and their knowing allies held the post of president, but not general secretary (Bussey). They held one of the two assistant general secretaryships in Walter Stevens, whose youth and vigour could possibly be compared with the increasingly illness-prone Matt Greenwell, who had won the OBE in the 1945 New Year's Honours List. Gus Cole was a left-winger, balanced, perhaps, by Ernie Irwin.

The really significant change had occurred on the executive. To start with, there were virtually no votes on issues on the executive by late 1945–early 1946. Affiliation to the British Soviet Friendship society was carried 10–1, with only Jack Potter from Yorkshire voting against. In January 1946, the new executive voted to end a particularly sensitive 1942 decision of the previous executive council with only three votes against. The general secretary had been empowered to prevent interference by the Communist Party in the union's affairs by sacking staff who were communists or helped the party by disclosing ETU affairs. These three anti-communists in January 1946 were the Glaswegian Tom Carter, the Birmingham-based Ted Haynes and Yorkshire's Jack Potter. The other executive members who were present that day were the London executive members, Les Gregory, Ted Breed (a small, sprightly man with a reputation in the union for serious Marxist scholarship) and Frank Haxell. Suspended from holding office as a result of the Vigon affair in November 1939, the ban on Haxell was removed in October 1941. In December 1943, he had been re-elected to the executive over two London left-wing but non-communist stalwarts, J. Millo and C. Thursby. By the end of 1945, he held the seat over left-wing Pat McCarthy, by 1,175 votes to 864, having chaired the 1945 rules revision conference at Cardiff during Foulkes's absence at an International Labour Organization meeting in Copenhagen, to which he had been nominated by the TUC. New on the executive at the same election was Les Cannon, at that time an energetic young communist from Wigan. These four were almost invariably backed up by Ed Morrow, from Northern Ireland, who moved the end to Bussey's powers over communist staff members, and Jim Deans, the left-winger from East Scotland and the North-East Coast. George Stevens from Manchester and Llew Price from South Wales completed the executive and voted almost invariably with the majority.

The picture was different among the area officials with the exception of London. The capital had approximately 40,000 members at the end of 1945 and needed six area officials. All were on the left, but one, C. Thursby, was narrowly elected against a prominent communist, Bert Batchelor. After Walter Stevens became assistant general secretary in 1942, the London area secretary became Alf Martin, and the colleagues and political friends that joined him at Swinton House in 1945 were Messrs Benson, Turner, Haskell and Stride.

Outside London, the main centre of the left remained Liverpool – Area 9, then, as now – and it had two officials who were both successors to Foulkes's politics and not Citrine's. Fred Turner and Cec Bibby were the officials concerned. In Manchester too, R. Tyldesley was a supporter of the Communist Party, although Alf Hatton was not. The other great manufacturing centres of England and Scotland were largely led by local full-time officials who were anything but communists. Pre-eminent among these was Walter Lewis in Birmingham, who had been mayor of the city in 1942–3. Paul McArdle, the Newcastle area secretary, and Rowland Penrose, in Leeds, went back almost to before the First World War as district secretaries. They shared their Labour sympathies with newer officials like Jock Byrne in Glasgow (first elected in 1942), Harry Madden in Middlesbrough, Jim Middleton in Sheffield (who had replaced Albert Oates, who had died from a heart attack at the early age of fifty while out driving with his family). Harry Turner had left the executive and become the area secretary in Bristol. He was, by his own revelation in a 1941 election address, 'a socialist by conviction and training'. However, he 'paid my dues to the Labour Party' and distanced himself from the communist line at the time of the Earl's Court and the Vigon affair.

Political Change during the War

Political questions came to the fore during the war in a way that they never quite managed to do beforehand. In the aftermath of the 1927 Trades Disputes Act, the union's political fund was made up of members contracting-in to the fund individually. This never produced much cash. When members contributed their political levy of 1s per year, the branches retained half of it for local political activity – activity eventually restricted to support for the Labour Party on the insistence of the executive council.

During the war, the union's concern with matters parliamentary took on a more relevant and intense nature. As concerned citizens, they were anxious that the social security system and the full employment envisaged by a resurgent Labour Party should come to pass after the war. From the late 1930s, and at every union wartime conference, the union urged the nationalization of electricity supply – particularly given the large private companies' demands to undermine the rights of municipal electricity supply in the early days of 1945. It is impossible to underestimate the sheer authority of collectivist ideas in wartime. Everybody's daily experience of shared discomfort in the face of shortage, hard work and personal tragedy produced a willing acceptance of uniformity, equality of sacrifice and shared objectives that has arguably never been equalled in British society before or since. The Labour Party's acceptance of the responsibilities of government, along with the convincing and honest performance of men like Attlee, Bevin and Morrison, reflected well on their trade union supporters like Ernie Bussey. The union, therefore, resolved to do something about its political work. By early 1944, only 44,000 of the union's 130,000 members paid the political levy, despite the influences outlined above, the radicals in London, and the exhortations of the union's leadership. However, because of the split allocation of the levy, the head office could only afford, on a national level, to affiliate to the Labour Party on the cost of 16,000 votes. This meant they had to say no when Walter Lewis was offered the parliamentary nomination in both Aston and Yardley in 1943 (although the financial excuse may have been trotted out by a leadership anxious not to lose a powerful friend and brilliant, influential organizer). This lack of money dated back to 1937 when the membership voted against any increase in the levy, 3,528–2,967. In the spring of 1944, the union organized a new fund – the '100,000 shilling' fund, specifically earmarked to support the new political sub-committee of the executive in its work of forming a parliamentary panel of members and getting them round the country until a member of the ETU won a parliamentary seat. The new fund, and a unanimous conference decision to support this new determination to get the union to punch its weight politically, then had to be put before the membership. They voted, 4,933–3,622, to increase the political levy from 1s a year to 1d per week. This did the trick, and Tom Cook became the first ETU-sponsored MP at the 1945 General Election. He represented Dundee, but came from Rutherglen in Glasgow where he was secretary of the constituency, and director of the Rutherglen Co-op. He worked as a maintenance elecrician and had held local branch office in the ETU. The union's political sub-committee could only allocate funds to support two candidates. Cook was chosen and won Dundee, but the other candidate, C. J. Hurley of Hull, did not get a nomination and was to complain that selection conferences preferred to choose Oxford-educated friends of the party leadership rather than good working-class lads like him.

The 'communist' issue would not go away. Most of their effort went into war work – and as such earned individual communists enormous regard from the community, employers and fellow trade union leaders. Equally, everyone was profoundly aware of the Russian contribution on the Eastern Front, where sacrifice and pain endured in the Great Patriotic War were an inspiration to a Britain that had once stood alone. British communists got some of the reflected credit for that, especially when collecting vigorously for Mrs Churchill's Red Cross Fund for Russia and supporting (as the executive did with a gift of £100) the Veterinary Fund for the Relief of Horses in the Soviet Army in 1942. The London district committee sent weekly sums to an Aid for Russia Fund, collected every week on sites and jobs across the capital. This activity was reflected in good union election results for communists and their friends, particularly in London. Some of their progress was due to this tenor of the times; some due to their youth, vigour and application.

Some was due to less appealing influences. During the war, bells were rung in warning against ballot-rigging. Barrow branch had voted, 402–0, for McKernan in the 1941 executive council elections, but then wrote and said the secretary had got the names mixed up, and could those votes be transferred to E. G. Davies. Although this was nothing to do with the communists, the executive asked to see the ballot papers but were told by the branch that 'due to the limited space at the disposal of the branch, they are not able to store what they considered to be unnecessary paper.' At Belfast Central in May 1942, the local scrutineers were appalled when the caretaker at the Belfast office brought in a bundle of seventy-three votes from area official Lowden's office for the branch to count in the Frank Foulkes election for national organizer. The votes all had identical paper marks. Lowden claimed they had been separately brought to the office by members' wives and the shop-steward at Belfast corporation. The executive would not allow the ballot to stand. *If* this was a corrupt ballot, it has enormous significance in the light of the 1959–61 crisis. It shows that extra ballot papers were available to people *outside* the branch structure to feed in at branch level. There is no proof in this case, but it does highlight a possible contributory factor to the enthusiastic support for left candidates from an early period, in certain parts of the country.

In May 1943, Leigh branch complained of Wigan's habit of casting a 'bloc vote' at the branch that tended to swamp anyone else's nominee at elections for delegates to conference. These elections used to group a handful of branches together to form a 'division' from which the conference delegates would be elected. Normally, each branch put up its own candidate – a local man – and normally voted for him. The communists would work hard to legitimately win the nomination for their man in one branch and then get their supporters in the other branches to cluster round the party nominee. Few 'favourite sons' of individual branches could stand against a 'political' machine that could produce insufficient votes in each branch, taken separately, but could produce the goods – sometimes honestly – across a group of branches. It is admittedly little to do with democracy – that either the nominee of the largest branch won or the nominee of the best organized faction won – but that was how it was done in the days before each branch sent a delegate to the rules revision conferences.

Eccentric electoral practices were even used to attempt to elect people to area committees. Brother Ellis of Rhos branch in North Wales complained in January 1945 of 'goings-on' in the Caernarvon branch (a branch famous for its unanimity of view voting in the 1942 assistant general secretary election for Walter Stevens (110) and Paul McArdle (0). Ellis was quoted by the executive council minutes as reporting:

> It was stated that members of the organization were approached in a public house and signed a blank scrutineers' return form, which was completed at a later date. On examination of the scrutineers' return form which was submitted by Caernarvon branch, it was noted that their representative had polled 190, whilst three other nominees had not received a vote. Two hundred and sixteen members had been privileged (to vote – they were paid up), five members had attended the specially summoned meeting and 185 votes had been received by post and through the shop-stewards.

The Wigan incident led to the decision to refer the whole issue of balloting procedures to the 1944 conference which, in its turn, postponed the issue to 1946.

Communist Party Interference: The Conway Hall Conference, 1943

The subject of communist influence in the union was, however, tackled head on. At the 1940 and 1942 conferences of the union, the issue of banning communists from holding office in the union was debated but rejected. In October 1942, however, the St Marylebone Communist Party circulated a questionnaire to ETU branches enquiring as to their attitude towards the Communist Party campaigns for the Second Front in Europe, the repeal of a TUC decision to exclude communists from trade councils and freedom for India. More pertinently, it asked what attitude branch officials had towards the Communist Party and what were their names and addresses. On 14 October 1942, London Railway Shopmen No. 1 branch in Paddington sent the circular to Bussey. He put it before the executive council. Bussey demanded the executive back him in stopping this type of 'interference' from spreading from the branches into district or head office. The executive said yes – and Miss Hilda Vernon was sacked from Macauley Road. Bussey pressed on. He demanded the whole issue be reviewed by a special rules revision conference, with a view to establishing the evidence of Communist Party interference, and then to discuss the need for banning communists from holding office in the union. This was only carried 5–4 (with Haskell, Haslam, Cole and even Turner voting against. Les Gregory was away ill). Consequently, under the rules, if the executive were not unanimous, they had to ballot the membership for permission to hold a rules revision conference. In December 1942, this authority was granted by the members, 11,343–6,662. This ballot shows the strength of the left minority in the union, presumably all campaigning like mad to prevent such a conference from being held. Caernarvon, as usual, knew where it stood – 150–0 said *they* didn't need a conference. Wigan, too, was unanimous, 207–0. Nevertheless, there was a clear majority in favour, and the fifty delegate conference duly convened at the Conway Hall in London from 9–10 May 1943.

Ben Bolton's introductory remarks set the tone from the presidential chair:

> We cannot stand by and permit the whole of the union's structure, the whole of the inner and outside lives of the branch, district and national officials, to be interrupted for a political treatise. I am, personally, very reluctant to ever see the industrial movement handed over to the mercy of any political party.

Ernie Bussey then addressed the conference. He spoke for nearly an hour. He started by outlining the reasons for calling the conference by analysing the St Marylebone circular. But he was clearly anxious to broaden his attack to encompass many other aspects of communist 'interference' in the union's affairs. Jimmy Rowan, sitting in at the conference as a guest, only a few months before he died in retirement, must have been pleased with what he heard.

Ernie Bussey told the conference that the Communist Party could not be tolerated in the union. There was:

> ... not a scrap of honesty or reliability in the statements of its officers, from the general secretary [Harry Pollitt] downwards, and that by its interference as a political party in the machine of an industrial movement, it is destroying the whole basis of mutual trust and confidence between the membership, upon which this society has been built.

According to Bussey, the party would ensure branch nominations by sending people round to branches, reading from lists. During the elections, there is 'mass canvassing of branches, in which motor cars travel from town to town with the candidate around the branches in the area ... now developed to a fine technique.' Look at the candidates they put up, too, people with no industrial record. T. J. Arnold in the 1938 come-back election that saw a 'straight' man like George Humphreys narrowly successful in London was a good example. Arnold had spent very little time in the union and was one year in arrears with his contributions. By 1943, he had left the Communist Party (and been persecuted for it on certain jobs in London) and eventually left the union. 'His Communist Party membership was more important than his ETU membership.' Or take the 1938 conference at Torquay, where Arthur Stride's speech on the need for an industrial section of the union (to turn the ETU away from its craft base) was being circulated by communist sympathizers weeks before the conference. Bussey had been sent two copies! The Reading branch secretary, in 1942, had been sent a letter enclosing a list of suggested Communist Party causes on which the branch might like to submit conference resolutions. The Motherwell branch and other Scottish branches had been circularized by the Scottish district secretary of the Communist Party. At the height of the Earl's Court affair, the editor of *Tribune* had taken Harry Pollitt's advice to ring Alf Coster concerning the likely anti-executive line Coster would take – as he was 'if not a member of the Communist Party, was in the closest association with it for many years.' And just recently, Bussey had 'intercepted' a letter to R. Tyldesley in the Manchester office when he was in the union's office there, which came from Pat Devine, a Communist Party organizer and central committee member. Devine wrote, and Bussey read to the conference, 'I am very worried at the fact that I do not seem to be able to get a word with you regarding the very important questions that are being discussed in your organization and trade.' Bussey brushed aside queries as to how he 'intercepted' this letter, and Tyldesley flatly denied ever having heard of Devine – but could not deny the authenticity of the letter.

Bussey broadened the attack by pointing out how vindictive the Communist Party had been to their own heroes who disagreed over the war before Russia's entry in 1941. International Brigaders who had fought Fascism in Spain were expelled for supporting the war against Fascism at home by organizing and supporting units of the Home Guard! All of this was typical of the party which was attacking the ETU's constitution and should be publicly exposed as 'interference' in the union's affairs.

He was supported by W. J. Smith, who had been associated with the union for many years in South-East London, near New Cross. He was the secretary of the South-East branch for many years, and had seen the development of the problem in the district committee's personnel.

Speaking with the experience of twenty years of South-East branch ... one remembers the interference by the party which ran the old contingent fund. We have had the interference of the vigilance committee. We have had the interference from the National Minority Movement. What I object to is those individuals who put a hammer and sickle button in their coat ... who come to the branches and disrupt our organized meetings. Let me give you an instance. On one occasion, we were taking a ballot vote. Certain individuals were there at the back of the room ... there was a rush to the table, they emptied water over the ballot papers, and at the conclusion of the meeting, a bundle of ballot papers was found outside.

Walter Lewis supported this view about different forms of bad behaviour at meetings. 'Young fellows came in and they don't even know how to spell the name of the man they are moving. Look at the national ballots which have taken place – and the sooner we inquire into the system of ballot voting in this union, the better. It is the biggest swindle ever known.' Fellow area official Harry Madden was equally blunt. He recalled the sabotage of factory building in Middlesbrough in 1940. Shouting back at hecklers, he told them, 'You endeavoured to have a strike every day.' They sought to control the union through winning elections, and they even came to see him at his house to ask him what he was going to say at the conference. Harry Turner, a man of the left, but no communist, told the conference that when it became known he was running for full-time official, letters of complaint were sent to the executive council and the district committee in Bristol, complaining about his lack of negotiating skills. When he tracked down the complainant, he turned out to be a member who had been in the union two months. He said that it was the wish of the Community Party to run someone else, and if he stood aside this time, no doubt the party would support him next time. Agreeing with Walter Lewis about fiddling in ballots, John Bull, from LSE No. 1 branch, was an interesting if fundamentally titillating witness. He frankly told the conference that in the early 1930s, although not now, he had been the London secretary of the ETU section of the National Minority Movement. The 'interference' had been going on since 1927 and he knew how plenty of people in the conference had got elected. He would say no more.

Needless to say, the communists and their supporters had answers to all this. Gus Cole, an executive member, said that the St Marylebone circular was a simple mistake by over-zealous local Communist Party men, who had been told not to do it again by Harry Pollitt himself. Bob McLennan came next. He had been at the centre of the Earl's Court dispute, having been on the London central committee. He had been associated with the uproar in LSE No. 5 branch when they refused to pay contributions to the union after the dispute. He had organized the Hackney 'fraction' revealed by Vigon. And yet he spoke at the 1942 Trades Union Congress in the debate about the TUC banning communists from trades councils in the following terms. He told Congress he had joined the union aged eighteen, and the Communist Party shortly afterwards. 'He did not think anyone could point the finger of scorn at him and say that at any time during his work as a trades unionist, he had been concerned about disrupting the trade union movement or his own particular organization.'

Despite all that, he told the Conway Hall conference that solidarity with Russia demanded the defeat of Bussey's proposition, that the communists' support for PBR in shipbuilding had helped the war effort tremendously and that the branches of the union weren't 'soft' – they passed things because they believed them!

Fred Lester, of Croydon, always emphasized he was not a communist; but he always supported their line, sneering at '£100 a week' Ernie Bevin and 'Sir' Walter Citrine who were clearly behind the whole issue.

Other more sophisticated arguments were advanced to deflect the thrust of Bussey's remarks. Townsley, from Liverpool, urged the conference not to confuse Communist Party activity with Communist Party disruption. The union needed young Communists, full of activity and commitment. Arthur Stride said what about Catholic interference in the union in the way they advised members on whom to vote for. Harry Madden was furious here (as was Paul McArdle, who had suffered from a whispering campaign in Belfast when he ran against Communist Party-supported Walter Stevens for assistant general secretary in 1942 on the basis that he was a Roman Catholic). Madden jumped up and said that Catholics, unlike communists, had never broken the rules of the union.

Stride was of the view that this type of disunity only helped the cause of Fascism. Ted Breed, the new executive member in West London, insisted that the Communist Party did not invent packing meetings. Real disruption was being caused by non-communists and there was no proof of communist authorship of the circulars complained of. Jack Hendy, a young communist from Willesden, expressed pained disappointment at Bussey's apparent hysteria. Surely the union was big enough to take all this? 'To say that because certain individuals ring up certain individuals on the phone, that we as a society should behave like some coy female, is absurd.'

The first part of the debate was over – and the conference voted decisively 31–19, in favour of the proposition that communist interference was certainly established.

The atmosphere changed, though, when Bussey wanted to pursue the second part of the issue – that communists should be banned from holding office in the union. Non-communist delegates, like Ted Haynes, summed up the feelings of many when he said that the provisions of the rule-book concerning disruptive behaviour were quite sufficient. There would be difficulty in identifying communists from any other type of extremist disrupters – or, indeed, any type of disruptive influence. 'In my branch, we don't get a lot of this, but we do get plenty of disruption. They are not communists – they are contracting lads wanting some more money. How do *I* know? They might be *worse* than communists!' Bussey himself could feel the mood. He readily admitted that banning the communists would present problems of identification, expelling them and then there would be rows about victimization. And then there was the war card. Arthur Stride said how he got letters from a sergeant air-gunner on active service in the Middle East – a member of his

Gray's Inn branch who also happened to be a communist. 'Are we to say to this sergeant air-gunner, a comrade of ours, when he returns, you cannot be a shop-steward anymore? Why is that, brother? A certain conference was held ... what a state we are getting to.' Further, great pioneers of the ETU would be insulted. 'Our tried old friend, Jock Muir. He was run out of our society with all his communist views. Never was there a bigger fighter on behalf of the ETU.'

Even president Ben Bolton suggested the proposition was 'a little severe'. Bussey withdrew it, in 'the spirit of unity'. It was to be another twenty-one years before the proposition saw the light of day again. More immediately, there was a war to win and the communist contribution was not wholly negative. Bussey left it there.

Towards the end of the war, the union's politics were dominated by concepts of 'a new dawn', of 'something over the horizon', of expectation of a better life for all, in stark contrast to the workers experience of 1918–19. Indeed, all were looking forward to the armistice. So much so, that many companies signed agreements with the union as to exactly what would happen on VE Day. Courtauld's signed an agreement on 7 December 1944 that the men could have the day off after the official announcement and a three-day holiday as soon as it could be arranged. 'The company and the union have taken into consideration the distinct possibility that all operatives will want to celebrate this outstanding occasion.' The Ministry of Supply was a little more school-masterly in their similar agreement, 'There shall be no loose play with explosives and other dangerous articles; all maintenance men, policemen and key personnel shall remain at their posts.'

In his presidential address to the union's 1944 conference, read for him by Harry Turner in Bolton's absence due to illness, Ben Bolton summed it all up in, forgivably, wholly appropriate Churchillian tones.

The outlines of victory are taking shape. After five years of sacrifice, toil, blood, sweat and tears, we can see the end in sight. In building up the framework of victory, the common peoples have made a major contribution. It is their sons and daughters who are manning the battle fronts. They have stood up – and still stand up – to the terrors of air bombardment of the Fascists, while yet fulfilling every demand of the armed forces. They have given unstintingly of their meagre leisure hours to the home defence of their country – in the Home Guard, the Auxiliary Fire Service, as fire guards and Civil Defence workers. Never was so much asked of them, and never was so much given. They were the first fighters against the foul hordes of Fascism. Their sons were the first to fall in the fight ... Our rulers asked much and they were given much. By their sacrifices, their toil, their blood and their tears, the common people have earned the right to a fuller, freer life than they have ever known before.

They do not ask for the earth. But they do expect at least, a guarantee of reasonable employment with decent conditions, good homes, efficient medical and hospital services, a chance for their children, adequate allowances in case of sickness or accident and security in their old age. These things ... are the essential minima of a decent, civilized existence. If these things cannot be obtained because monopoly, vested interests, landlordism, private ownership, privilege and caste stand in their way, then, I say, they must be swept away. I am hoping that our great trade union and Labour movement will be strong and powerful enough to see to it that these minimum demands of the people are adequately and fully met with the shortest possible time at the close of the war.

And they were. By the late summer of 1945, Labour was in power with a huge majority in the House of Commons for the first time. The ETU saw that victory as 'the consummation of generations of working-class struggle and trade union endeavour.' Brave New World, indeed.

16

ANTICIPATION AND DISILLUSION,
1945–54

THE ETU HAD BEEN brought enthusiastically into the national war effort for 1939–45. After the war, that experience was to change for ever the priorities of the union's leadership and raise issues with the membership that went far beyond the pre-war collective bargaining priorities that then dominated the union's concerns. The existence of Attlee's Labour Government with a workable majority took socialism out of the realm of fantasy and into the daily concerns of trade union bureaucracy. The union now gained a direct access to Labour Party policy-making. Bob Prain had served on Labour's National Executive Committee in 1937–8, largely as the result of his filling a casual vacancy due to the death of a sitting committee man. In the summer of 1945, just after the election, the same thing happened again. Ernie Irwin was next on the list, and became a National Executive Committee member from 1945–55. He was the first National Executive Committee member *not* to be elected chairman of the Labour Party on the principle of Buggins' turn. He was overlooked in 1955 due to 'ill-health'. It is more likely that the party's grave concerns about the communist leadership of the union had plenty to do with it. Ernie Irwin was a regular attender at National Executive Committee meetings, although he rarely contributed to the committee work in a decisive or influential fashion. However, it mattered what trade unions thought about the Government's performance – 'their' Government's performance. It is hard to do justice to the sense of anticipation in the union movement of the mid-1940s. For the leadership of the ETU, there was the extra dimension of 'left talking unto left' – with a Labour Government in Britain and the Soviet system triumphant in arms throughout Europe. This feeling that there was a new place for trade unions in the *political* life of the country began to dominate the internal life of the ETU. Issues that were a million miles from the minutiae of the membership's economic problems began to dominate the agendas of branch, area and national meetings. The communist leadership of the union had a further self-appointed responsibility. They had to present to the wider movement at the TUC and the Labour Party their responsibility to the Communist Party and their Russian allies. The ETU became the conduit down which passed the hopes and fears of the executive committee of the Communist Party of Great Britain into the counsels of the wider Labour movement. There must have been a sense of triumph and pleasure, too, in the leadership's political control over the union. For years, the communists had steadily undermined Rowan and Bussey's leadership until, during the war, they had come into their inheritance through success in union elections. In any event, the communists were the masters now. Despite wartime devastation, despite fears of the return of post-war unemployment, despite shortages, the housing crisis and rationing, the union was initially determined to support the new Government. From 1945–7, the union's leadership pledged itself time and again to the new 'war' for productivity in British industry. Exports had to be dramatically increased in order to pay for the new social services and the literal rebuilding of Britain. Gus Cole understood that the new Jerusalem had to be earned by the workers' efforts. He wrote in early 1946 that the workers were not only interested:

> ... in such articles as wireless, television sets, refrigerators etc., but also a means to increased leisure ... the organized workers will have to appreciate that you cannot 'get blood out of a stone', and consequently, increased leisure must be worked for by increased production per man hour. ... It is therefore necessary to retain or reintroduce joint production committees to organize improved methods in the workshop or on site, not only to introduce new methods and counteract obstruction, which in some cases may amount to political sabotage, but to ensure proper welfare arrangements and special provision for part-time workers. All labour will be needed.

One of the candidates for the executive council in Lancashire, Les Cannon, had a letter published in the journal at the time of the union's elections in November 1945. He called for a change of attitude by workers to increase production – particularly in the soon-to-be nationalized industries. 'These industries can become a shining example of efficiency and high productivity, which in turn will have a tremendous political effect in the fight for socialism.' At different times throughout the first two years after the war, the union's circulars and conferences rang with declarations of loyalty to the Government, paralleled with policy decisions in favour of PBR; no opposition to the continuing wartime controls over the direction of labour, and the ban on strikes. Cartoons in the union's magazine denounced the unofficial striker as throwing a spanner in the works of Great Britain and Co Ltd. Despite a gradual rise in disillusion with the Labour Government and the TUC's support for its central pillars of policy, the union continued to give its encouragement in the war for production. As late as September 1947, despite its rising concern at the Government's determination to restrict wages, the executive placed a motion before the full-time officials' conference at the Ambassadors Hotel in London which was still strongly supportive.

The key to the crisis lies not only in the necessity for a change in Government policy, but in the degree to which [the members] support the Government in raising output by a greater individual effort and the removal of restrictive practices. We therefore call on all our members to make a greater contribution to industry, to assist in the development of joint production committees, and to make every effort to take the lead in the factories where they are employed.

The union strongly supported the Government during the appalling fuel crisis in 1947 which reduced a freezing Britain to near-disintegration in both home and factory. The chaos was the fault of the 'past inefficiency and neglect of the coal-owners' and the union pledged the 'maximum assistance possible' in the power stations to deal with the crisis.

By the end of 1947, the picture started to change. The union's leadership was steadily falling out with the Government and its TUC allies as the Cold War deepened and the isolation of Soviet Russia began. At home, majority opinion in the Labour movement supported this condemnation of East European 'people's democracies'. Further support was expressed for Labour Government policies to restrict the rate at which wages rose. This, too, was opposed root and branch by the ETU. In the last two issues of the union's journal in 1947, the concern, the criticism, the worry, crystallized into fairly obvious opposition. In the December editorial, Walter Stevens wrote about the great Fabian pioneer, Sidney Webb, who had recently died. According to Stevens, Webb had realized that the Fabian dedication to 'the inevitability of gradualness' in the march towards socialism had been wrong. Writing with wife Beatrice in 1935, his book *Soviet Communism – A New Civilization?* had shown the modern way forward. Stevens commented:

We have now reached a stage in our development when, as the Webbs wrote, the object and purpose of the workers, organized vocationally in trade unions and professional associations and politically in the Labour Party, comprise nothing less than the reconstruction of society. For we have reached that stage, when, without such reconstruction, the primary functions of trade unions cannot be fulfilled.

Stevens had looked at the Labour Government's King's speech for the opening of Parliament in the autumn of 1947, and his verdict was harsh. 'Nowhere in it is there to be found anything which in any way reflects the need for drastic political and economic changes.'

Domestic opposition to the Government and their TUC allies lay fundamentally in their attitude to pay. The union was convinced in the late 1940s that profits were rising and being retained or distributed by capitalists while at the same time workers were being urged by government White Papers to restrain or freeze wage increases. All of this was happening against the background of a rising cost of living, with the official index of prices failing to reflect the consumption patterns of workers. Wages policy in isolation from control over investment and the direction of capital was a nonsense. Price control was perfectly feasible through a government-appointed commission, but the country needed an overall socialist plan in which these different elements would be so balanced that the workers would not pay the price of post-war reconstruction on their own. There was a tie-in with the fortunes of Soviet Russia. First, Russian exports to Britain, particularly of raw materials like wood for the building and housing campaigns, were being restricted on the orders of America. (This issue produced a voluminous correspondence with Harold Wilson MP, then the President of the Board of Trade, who advanced the more plausible reasoning that the devastation of Russia prevented the reconstruction of the export trade with their own country in ruins.) Second, American capitalism was dictating the nature of the Labour Government's economic policy in its cold war with the Russians. They simply could not let socialism succeed in Britain for reasons of economic and military strategy.

As early as March 1947, Les Gregory had presented to the executive council a comprehensive report headed 'Wages, Prices and Profits'. With little change, it was to be the basis of the arguments that the union presented to its own members and the outside world for the next fifteen years. It relied on the work of a statistician from the London and Cambridge Economic Service, Dr Tibor Barna. He had judged that prices had risen fifty-seven per cent from 1938–45, while wages had only risen by forty-nine to fifty per cent. Productivity had risen, with the national income rising by twenty-five per cent, along with a slight fall in the numbers employed. Looking at the distribution of the output of industry, rent, interest and profit's share had risen from 32.4 per cent to 38.8 per cent. The share enjoyed by salaries had fallen from twenty-three per cent to just under nineteen per cent. The share taken by manual worker's wages had fallen, too, from 44.6 per cent to 42.4 per cent. 'A greater share of the product of industry has gone to the capitalists and a smaller share to the workers.' Retail prices had risen faster than wages: industrial prices had risen faster than wages, with the employers maintaining the rate of profit per unit of production in an environment in which productivity was rising. Wartime experience in production methodology had increased standardized product runs and there was a much higher capacity working of plant than before the war.

The Government was not imposing price control vigorously. Some goods were not affected by fixed price (utility) schemes at all, like some household items and most capital goods in industry. Many controlled prices allowed too high margins for many monopoly suppliers, particularly in iron and steel. Les

Gregory's paper admitted the beneficial effect of subsidies on key foodstuffs and tobacco. However, the Government's policy seemed to freeze the present allocation of resources between the capitalists and the workers. If they were really interested in higher production, they should make sure the workers had the incentive to work for the higher productivity when needed, at the expense only of record profits. Equally, workers' conditions could be alleviated if more attention was paid to the level of maximum controlled prices, extending the range of 'utility' goods and opening up the ROFs for peace-time production of goods that would set good examples to private industry.

On 31 July 1947, Morgan Phillips, the general secretary of the Labour Party, wrote to the union to express just how far the Government, the party and their leading trade union supporters dissented from this analysis.

First, the Government were doing all that was practical by imposing new rates of 'super-tax' on those who enjoyed huge incomes, and had introduced new taxes on profits. As for price control, eighty-five per cent of food prices were controlled in one way or another, as were eighty per cent of clothing prices. The country could not impose further price control without taking yet more productive workers into the bureaucracy to supervise it and, more seriously, further price control would produce the real danger of hugely increased black market activity. The whole basis of the Government's appeal for restraint implied in the 1948 White Paper, 'Statement on Personal Incomes, Costs and Prices', was the fear of inflation. Arthur Deakin, the general secretary of the TGWU, told the 1948 Labour Party conference:

> It is all very well for people to say, 'Tackle prices, tackle profits first.' When you come to look closely at this delicate economic question, you have some difficulty in knowing where you are to start – which comes first. Some of the applications we have made could not possibly be met out of profits. It follows that if wage increases were conceded, that the increased cost must be passed on to the customer.... In 1919–20 there were soaring prices, with wages lagging behind and never able to overtake them, and there was considerable depression that followed. If we have not learnt by experience the effect of an inflationary tendency of that character, we have just lived in vain.

Sir Stafford Cripps had said in his 1948 budget speech that wage deals would be left to voluntary agreement between the parties, but 'the country cannot now afford any general rise in personal incomes of any sort.' Allowances would be made for productivity improvement, but Stevens's fears were well placed. With the wartime controls of the national arbitration tribunal and Order 1305 still banning strikes, it was surely more likely that the arbitration machinery would pay attention to Sir Stafford Cripps's White Paper and effectively keep down wages. Stevens spoke at the TUC on this subject for three years from 1948–50, eventually winning the Congress to his proposition that wage increases could be paid for out of profits, not by raising prices. Each time he made the same arguments.

Each time he argued against a simple appeal for increasing the size of the national cake, arguing the essentially political case that profits were so enormous as to be able to find wage rises in the here and now. It was *his* issue, and it brought him prominence and a national role as leader of the left unions on the economic front. He moved the composite motions against the General Council platform time after time until the policy changed in 1950.

Throughout the late 1940s, the pro-restraint policy of the TUC and the Labour Government was thrown in the union negotiators' faces by the employers, exemplified by Mr Penwill's quoting large chunks of government exhortation on wages during NJIC negotiations in the contracting industry in October 1947. The EEF did the same throughout the period. Frank Foulkes's presidential address to the 1948 policy conference emphasized this aspect of disillusion with the Government. 'There was to be a complete freezing of wages, with no increases, while all other incomes and profits were to be left to the goodwill of the recipients and to private arrangements of a purely voluntary character.' The union's leadership was also not disposed to support moves to higher productivity while this remained their interpretation of the Government's attitude to prices and profits. They opposed the early introduction of work study schemes which were being tried out, particularly by ICI. They were suspicious of the various productivity-sponsoring councils that sprang up. In July 1948, the union attacked the newly formed Anglo-American advisory committee on productivity.

The British trade union movement will be wise to remember that it will be dealing with the most ruthless and predatory groups of monopoly capitalists in the world today. The strong-arm methods of dealing with their own employees have made American employers notorious throughout the world. Having managed to manacle the American trade unions by the Taft-Hartley Anti-Trade Union Act, they will not hesitate to extend the principle to any country where their influence becomes predominant. Nor must it be forgotten that Fascism is the institutional structure of monopoly capitalism, the initial act of which is the destruction of trade unions.

Despite this sombre warning, the union let this body pay for Peter Snadden to tour high-productivity American factories towards the end of 1951. His report recognized the high standard of living of American workers, but denounced their mistaken impressions of Britain.

The union's disappointment at the Government's wages policy, and their consequent reluctance to accept what was later to be called productivity bargaining, was closely related to the Government's failure to impose a levy on capital, direct investment and produce a comprehensive economic national plan to ensure the transformation to a socialist society.

However, at local level, Labour Party loyalists were prepared to support the TUC and Government view; the Birmingham area committee and its full-time officials, Bolas and Haynes, were threatened by the executive with suspension in the early spring of 1950 for accepting the TUC policy on wage restraint. In 1951, the union's conference was debating a motion that congratulated the executive council on the overthrow of the White Paper, 'Statement on Personal Incomes, Costs and Prices', as a vindication of the union's policy. George Scott from Kirkcaldy branch defended the Labour Government's defence of social security in a turbulent world, and said that the end of wage restraint would herald a 'scramble' for more wages, and would not help the Labour Government in its attempt to 'shift the burden onto the spivs and drones'.

After the return of the Conservative Government at the end of 1951, the union's opposition to wage restraint became less problematic and more routine. It remained a regular, almost monotonous feature of its submissions to outside conferences, and was generally passed on the nod when the Tories were in control.

Negotiations and Wages, 1946–54

The communist leadership of the union – particularly Frank Haxell – would in later years luxuriate in the word 'militant'. The communist leadership would frequently boast that they fought harder than Rowan and Bussey ever did for higher standards of living for electricians, and, in later years, than Chapple and Cannon were prepared to do. It is important therefore to try to examine the Walter Stevens years (from approximately 1946 to his death in 1954) to examine the genesis of this delight in apparently successful industrial struggle. This claim was most clearly applied to electrical contracting, where the employers were private capitalists and the union the only negotiating body on the union side. Negotiations in engineering and shipbuilding were dominated by other unions; *whatever* the union's posture in negotiations, it had little influence over the final settlements in the face of opposition from the general workers' unions – or 'the bloc vote democrats', as an angry young Frank Chapple referred to them at the 1950 policy conference at Ramsgate.

Different considerations apply in looking at the union's performance in electricity supply. Here the position was totally transformed by nationalization, and despite many reservations about the nature of the new industry, Frank Foulkes, as chairman of the five supply unions, was not going to use the negotiations just to prove what a powerful, demonic negotiator he was.

It was in contracting, then, that the union's leadership 'hung its hat'. After the war, the union's negotiating team on the special or standing committee of the NJIC was led by Ernie Bussey, and supported by Les Gregory, Ted

Haynes, Manchester's executive councillor George Stevens, and Wally Stevens. Frank Foulkes would chair meetings on a rotation with the NFEA's negotiators, who were dominated in everything by their director and secretary, L. Penwill. The union's claims now ran to over a dozen pages of closely argued statistical analysis, supported by various comparisons across the building industry. These claims were initially the work of research officer Joe Wild, who throughout the war had produced the wage claims and the statistical back-up for eventual presentation to national arbitration tribunals on every imaginable national and local dispute.

In early 1946, there were 30,145 people working for electrical contracting companies: 23,358 of these were electricians, 5,270 were mates and the rest spread over a dozen other specialist building trades – the most significant of which were 486 plumbers and glaziers. In round terms, 7,000 were working on new houses and flats, 6,000 on other new buildings, 4,000 on war damage repair work and nearly 13,000 on other repair, maintenance, demolition and debris clearance work. Although 1,839 of the electrical contractors did not directly employ anyone, a further 3,067 did; but they typically employed very few.

Of the 3,067 firms with directly employed workers on the payroll, 571 employed only one; 838 firms employed between six and nineteen workers; 254 between twenty and ninety-nine; and only thirty-six companies employed over 100 and under 500 electricians.

The union had ambitious plans to change the wages structure for those companies, the majority of whom were organized in the electrical contractors negotiating body (NFEA) with a further 350 organized in the Scottish ECA. First, they sought to abolish what they called the 'fodder' basis of paying wages – where the whole determination of wages was based on the scale of movement of the official cost of living index. The union sought instead to persuade the employers to pay electricians on the basis of their skill, having due regard to the industry's profits (which were hard to find out about, and the employers were not telling) and the industry's productivity record (which the NFEA insisted was only sixty per cent of pre-war levels without being able to present any accurate figures at all to justify the assertion). The union sought to introduce extra holidays with pay beyond one week, payment for bank holidays, a reduction in hours from forty-seven, a guaranteed working week to be confirmed now the war was over and the reduction of geographical zoning for payment purposes. They wanted just a London and a provincial rate – not London, Merseyside and the two provincial rates for 'B' and 'C'.

The first task in negotiation – which often proved languid and time-consuming – was to keep wages rising while progress was attempted on the structural changes that the union's claim on 10 October 1945 first outlined. From 1945–52, small increases were granted, grudgingly, by the employers and accepted with various displays of bad grace by the union's negotiators. Every year, Penwill complained about the sixty per cent productivity figure; every year he refused to explain where he got the figure from or make allowance for the shortage of materials or even the ravages of the weather. The negotiations were often waspish. Penwill was sceptical about the union's claims of rejuvenated workers producing more from a shorter working week. They had not got fifty-four hours' work when the hours fell to forty-seven in 1919 he said, and he was sure they would not get forty-seven hours' worth from a forty-hour week. Equally, he frequently rejected the union's claims for a second week of paid holiday by referring to 'massive' but unspecified numbers of 'moonlighting' electricians working for themselves whilst supposedly on holiday and robbing the employers that way, or taking the holiday allowance and working for someone else during the holiday period. The negotiations dragged on interminably from 1945–7, relieved only by a tiny increase on the war bonus. In December 1946, negotiations broke down altogether, and there was no official pay agreement from January 1947. The employers were adamant that wages must be 'stabilized' by being linked to a cost of living index – the newly constituted 1947 one would do nicely. The union wanted to see some form of PBR on building sites – but this was, and remained, notoriously difficult to measure for electricians. The union rejected completely the concept of grading operatives by their skills and therefore paying them more; however, around fifteen per cent of all operatives were given 'merit' awards on an 'individual' basis – no doubt where other building workers were earning bonuses that led to jealousy amongst electricians and overwhelming pressure on employers to raise wages.

On 27 November 1947, a comprehensive deal was at last finalized, but only because recent increases in the building industry forced the employers' hand. There had been no increase for electricians since April 1946, although the abolition of Grade 'C' had elevated a tiny number of rural electricians into Grade 'B' rate. The new agreement produced an hourly increase for London of 4d, and for the provincial grades of $3\frac{1}{2}$d. The working week was reduced from forty-seven to forty-four hours, with an average of 49.2 hours per week being worked. It still proved impossible to design a PBR system. They granted the five-day week, at the sole discretion of the employer – despite Ted Haynes's patient explanation that, given the amount of work that ever got done on a Saturday morning, it was probably in the employer's best interest to end the five-and-a-half day week. The employers listened carefully to his description of the problems associated with travelling time, laying out of tools and assembling materials, but were convinced that the ending of Saturday working would only lead to even more 'moonlighting' by electricians which had reached, according to Penwill, 'alarming proportions'.

This agreement effectively broke the automatic 'sliding scale' approach to wages based on the cost of living index, and, in return, the union promised not to re-submit a wage claim for at least eight months. The London rate was 3s 1d an hour, the Mersey rate 2s 10½d and the 'B' rate 2s 9½d. The Scottish negotiations fixed a fairly strong future association with the 'B' rate and, back in England, mates were to be paid seventy-five per cent of the craftsmen's rate. In September 1948, the union's claim went straight to the National Arbitration Tribunal, given the background of Government policy urging employers not to concede wage increases that were unrelated to productivity improvement. The result was a lecture from the tribunal on the strange absence of incentive schemes in electrical contracting and the fabulous award of one whole penny on the rate. The employers' main thrust that year was to attack apprentices' earnings. Despite the fact that they were, on average, two-thirds of other building trades apprentice rates, the employers proposed to reduce the younger boys' wages by ten per cent and to reduce the eighteen to twenty-year-olds by twenty-five per cent! They would prefer much higher utilization of Category III boys – virtually casual labour. This suggestion produced nearly two years of negotiation and reference to the National Arbitration Tribunal. On 1 September 1950, to the union's great delight, Category III boys were abolished, with the tribunal setting a final date for their employment of the 31 December 1951. All apprentices now were either indentured or Category II – a recognized apprenticeship. Parents paid 10s into a training fund, and the union and employers operated an apprenticeship and training council. The employers had to release the boys for forty-four days' technical school instruction up to the age of eighteen, and then pay for the fees for apprentices to attend night school until they qualified. The union settled for 'realistic' percentage rates of pay in order to achieve this breakthrough in raising the standard of skilled entry to the trade. All boys, of whatever age, were to be paid a third of whatever bonuses came the craftsmen's way. The basic rate percentage was linked to age as follows.

Age	%
15	12
16	16
17	22
18	27
19	40
20	60
21	60

Ideally, the apprentice should do his five years' apprenticeship between the ages of sixteen and twenty-one or, if essential, fifteen and twenty.

Wage rates in the late forties proved more difficult to shift. The union claimed in 1949 parity with electricity supply whose rates were between $\frac{1}{2}$d–1d an hour more than contracting, although supply conditions (sick pay, holidays, pensions) were so far in advance of contracting as to be worth a further 4d an hour, the union claimed. On 31 October 1949, once again the National Arbitration Tribunal had to pronounce in the face of the employers' completely negative response. Their award was to 'defer' a decision for six months and to tell the industry to come up with an incentive scheme. They finally met again on 21 June 1950, only to hear that it was impossible to arrive at an incentive scheme due to the employers' unwillingness to let the ETU anywhere near negotiations about contract prices. This information would be vital to work out the basis of incentives based on early completion of work or some such obvious measure of achievement that would sustain a bonus scheme. The NFEA were not going to let the union know such intimate details at any price. In the end, the union signed a long-term wage deal. The London rate was to be 3s 4d for 1950, and 3s 8d from 5 March 1951. The Mersey rate would rise in two stages to 3s 4d and Grade 'B' to 3s 3d. There were small rises in the country allowances and travelling time payments. In February 1952, the union quietly accepted 2d on the rates. But 1952 provides the watershed: from 1945–52, improvements were made, but as the result of painstaking – even painful – patience in negotiation. By 1952, contracting members in London in particular were beginning to get angry: they did not take their disappointment out on the union, despite the fact that their *comparative* hourly earnings position had been devastated since 1948. Just before the war, seventeen industries had higher average hourly earnings than contracting. By 1952, that figure had risen to seventy-five!

From the spring of 1952 to the summer of 1954, the contracting industry was racked with strikes, Government courts of inquiry, employer refusal to negotiate. Accusations were made of basic political motivation behind the union's claims: it was at this time that newspaper interest in the union as a communist conspiracy became regular and repetitive.

The fundamental problem in the industry was that as the building industry generally improved its position – particularly in London – the non-electrical sectors of the industry paid both craftsmen and labourers frequent bonuses. These bonuses were sometimes wholly legitimate and related to measurable output. Frequently they were not: they were simply extra payments to retain labour in boom conditions. The electrical contractors were frequently unable or unwilling to adapt their payment system in a similar way. The result was genuine frustration at earnings levels (if not basic wage rates), which often fell behind general labourers on building sites.

Early in 1952, two sharp little disputes set the tone for bitter wage bargaining and highlighted the difficulties caused by things going on in the building industry generally. In February 1952, the union took action at Olympia. The employers had been reluctantly paying 2d an hour at the three exhibition centres in London – Earl's Court, Olympia and White City – an allowance that had been extended to the Festival of Britain site on the South Bank. The employers now wanted to stop making extra payments for exhibition work altogether. Their evidence to the Industrial Disputes Tribunal gives a good flavour of the relationships at the time.

The Association contended that the union had never been prepared to argue that any special skill is needed; that in fact there are many types of work in the electrical contracting industry for which the standard rate is payable which demand the continuous exercise of a high degree of skill – e.g., the maintenance of complicated industrial machinery. Exhibition work is carried out in congenial surroundings in heated, well-lighted and well-ventilated halls as opposed to the far less congenial conditions experienced, for example, on building sites. The need for improvisation, upon which the union has laid some stress, occurs no more frequently than on other types of work. The conditions of rush, which the union alleges are characteristic of exhibition work, do not exist to any greater extent than in other sections of the industry. In fact, the operatives regard exhibition work as easy and when employed on other work have shown a tendency to resent the fact that additional payments were made for exhibition work.

The union, however, was on strong ground. The other trades in the exhibition industry had a plus payment of 2s 6d a day – nominally a buy-out of long-forgotten entitlements under their national agreement, but in reality a straightforward payment to workers who held a gun at every exhibition organizer's head just prior to the opening of one important trade show after another. This factor alone made it impossible for the employers to withdraw the 2d an hour (which worked out less than 2s 6d a day). The tribunal so found and the 2d was retained at the three sites.

The second dispute was nastier. In April, the management of the Festival Gardens site at Battersea decided to dispense with their directly employed workforce and award the contract to an NFEA member contractor, Barlow and Young. The men went on strike on 17 April, and were supported with strike pay of 16s a day plus 4s if they were married and a further 2s per child.

Pickets were posted, and the NFEA took this to imply unwarranted interference in the contractor's work and so suspended the negotiating machinery on 28 April, just before the important meetings to discuss wages were scheduled. The union summoned a meeting of contracting shop-stewards from all over London. Their unanimous recommendation was to strike in pursuit of the restoration of negotiations: 3,000 members attended a mass meeting at Central Hall, Westminster, with many more outside, unable to get in. The strike started in London on 28 May, and following meetings at the union's conference was extended nation-wide for the first few days of June. Sir Robert

Gould, the chief industrial commissioner at the Ministry of Labour, summoned everyone concerned to the ministry on 4 June, where the NFEA were convinced the strike was a pre-planned gesture in favour of direct labour as opposed to contractors: the union stoutly maintained it was simply a dispute over the redundancy affecting twenty-three members of the union. However, the two parties agreed to discuss it further. The negotiating machinery was restored, the national dispute called off by telegram on 5 June. The London strike continued, highlighted again by a massively theatrical rally on Friday 6 June at Westminster's Central Hall and Church Hall simultaneously. They decided amidst huge applause for the executive, to return to work on Monday 9 June. The successful resolution read:

This meeting of the ETU members in the contracting section of the industry congratulates the executive council on the successful conclusion of the dispute. We recognize that only the first round of the battle has been won and pledge our full support to the executive council in any action they deem necessary to win our claim for a substantial increase in wages, two weeks' holiday with full pay and a sick pay scheme.

The actual dispute had finished weeks before. On 6 May, Barlow and Young employed all the men previously working directly for the Festival Gardens management. Mr Penwill agreed to drop the subject at the 10 June NJIC meeting: but not before he got Walter Stevens to acknowledge that the union did not wish contractors ill when they managed to increase the maintenance contract areas of their business. However, the union could not let employers sack the union's members and see another group of members appear on the Battersea site two days later.

The 1952 wage negotiations then took place against this fractious background of Olympia and Battersea, culminating in the first national dispute in the industry since the war. The negotiations were firmly on the 'fodder' basis so disliked by Ernie Bussey in those post-war attempts at redefining the basis of the union's entitlement to a post-war higher standard of living. The argument was temporarily suspended when the employers refused to continue negotiating because of the union leadership's apparent support for an unofficial dispute in Newmarket. However, its main ebb and flow is instructive of negotiations in this period.

Wally Stevens made the union's case, armed as ever with graphs and statistical tables provided by Joe Wild. He told the employers of 'rapidly deteriorating standards' of electricians' wages.

Between February 1951 and April 1952, the cost of living index had risen by seventeen points or over 14.4 per cent. The January 1952 settlement of 2d had fallen well short of the 6.3d it should have been in London and well short, too, of the 5.6d it should have been for the provinces. Mr Penwill said that unfortunately everyone had to take into account the new Tory Government's appeals for wage restraint as witnessed by meetings between the employers' federations, the TUC and the Chancellor. Walter Stevens said that he was not going to allow the employers to get away with that: they used to want automatic linking to the cost of living index. Suddenly they had other priorities. However, Mr Penwill could juggle with the 'fodder' index as well. He urged that the union should look at earnings in relation to the index since 1947, when the index was reconstituted. This had increased by thirty-five per cent, while there had been increases of thirty-nine per cent in London electricians' earnings and a thirty-seven per cent increase in provincial electricians' earnings. That wasn't the point, argued Stevens. The actual rate for the provincial electrician had risen from £5 17s 6d to £7 10s 4d for the forty-four-hour week. This was only a twenty-eight per cent rise, and so the provincial rate should rise by at least 2¼d an hour.

Mr Penwill then suggested that average earnings figures from selected industries showed the electrical contracting industry way in front. Contracting's average rates of earnings amounted to £8 7s 6d a week – with electricity supply only managing £7 19s 9d, the building industry £7 17s 3d and only piece-work engineering doing better at £8 12s 3d. Income tax was coming down with the new Government and the introduction of family allowances had all helped family budgets considerably since 1947. Furthermore, the industry was facing a recession if the costs, from wage increases, rose any further, and the NFEA would lose many members. Curiously, a new danger threatened the industry. Cheap work was being done by moonlighting colliery electricians and Post Office engineers!

Stevens wasn't having any of this, either. Earnings were not the same as rates, and the union had to think of the rate. In any case surely the employers did not want to lose their independence by constant reference to other earnings. The industry should lead, not follow. Secondly, talk about future income tax cuts could be easily offset by quoting rises in national insurance contributions, prescription charges and the ending of food subsidies.

The talks dragged on into November 1952, when the deal was finally struck in a hurry, following a 2d rise in electricity supply. The employers granted a 2d rise on all rates and conceded the 'principle' of two weeks' paid holiday to be initiated in 1954.

The union thought this too represented simply an 'interim' payment, and resubmitted a claim for increased wages in May 1953. Stevens started this time with a new set of comparisons. He used 1948 as the base year, because that was when the forty-four-hour week had been introduced. On this basis, by February 1953, the cost of living has risen by thirty-four per cent, but the London rate had only risen by thirty per cent and the provincial rate by twenty-eight per cent. Mr Penwill's sarcastic reply to this was the suggestion that the figures would be improved to everyone's satisfaction if the union accepted an immediate return to the forty-seven-hour week! In any case, they couldn't afford any rise at all.

By the summer, the NFEA were still refusing to put any suggestions to the union at all. On 10 June, they wrote at last, but only to underline their attitude of 24 March – no increase at all was justified.

In reaction to this response, the union's executive inaugurated a subtle and planned approach to the inevitable dispute that was brewing. On 28 July, the executive finalized its plans. It set up an organizing committee, consisting of Foulkes and Stevens, with executive councillors Les Cannon, Peter Snadden (the new executive councillor from the Midlands) and Tom Vincent, along with assistant general secretary Bob McLennan. This committee looked at where the union's biggest sites were in operation – they chose the following ten sites (see table 4) from a list provided by each of the union's areas who nominated four sites each for the committee to choose from. The sites were then chosen – later it was alleged because of their national defence implications; it is clearly possible that just that aspect would have impressed the employers and members alike. These contracts were also lucrative, enormous and read like a *Who's Who* of the employers in the industry.

Table 4

Site Location	Electrical Contractor Affected	No. of Members
Leyland	F. Hancock	140
Capenhurst	N. G. Bailey	132
Ellesmere Port	Ass. Ethyl Co/W. H. Smith/ D. C. Engineering/W. J. Furze	200
Longbridge	Walker Brothers	88
Trostre Steel Works	F. H. Wheeler	70
Margam Steel Works	W. J. Furze/J. Morris/ Drake & Goreham	88
Aldermaston	Matthew Hall/Edmundsons/ Troughton & Young/ Reid & Partner	39
Isle of Grain	Matthew Hall	110
Coryton Terminal	Electrical Installations	60
London Airport	Rashleigh Phipps/ Electrical Installations/ Troughton & Young	70

These sites, plus a further 200 members working at Earl's Court and Olympia, were to make themselves ready for a strike starting on 24 August.

A voluntary fund was to be organized among non-striking workers to enable the strikers to be sustained in some comparative comfort. On 23 July, the general secretary wrote to Mr Penwill, underlining the union's claim by reference to further rises in the cost of living and a 1½d settlement in electricity supply.

There was complete silence from the NFEA, apart from a formal acknowledgement of Stevens's letter. By 25 August, the ten sites and Earl's Court/Olympia were on strike with around 1,300 members out. The ministry immediately stepped in, and arranged for the parties to meet on 31 August. In the meanwhile, the union ordered a resumption of work.

At the meeting, Stevens updated his cost of living figures. Penwill started by talking about income tax reductions being taken into account but had to change tack when Stevens showed that the reduction for a man earning £10 a week was the princely sum of 1d a week! There were then hours of 'corridor meetings' with Foulkes and Stevens attempting to persuade Penwill and the president of the NFEA, W. T. Trace, that some movement was essential. All the NFEA negotiating team would offer was further talks after consulting their ninety-three local branches, or, alternatively the whole dispute should go to arbitration. The union's leadership was incensed, and promptly ordered all the previous sites back on strike and added to it any site they could find where the NFEA's negotiating team companies were working, and ordered them out too, 'because of the scant regard shown by them to their fellow members of the Association who were directly involved.'

The strikes went on throughout September, until the Government stepped in with a court of inquiry. The strike stopped on 17 September, and the court deliberated for four days towards the end of the month, chaired by a Queen's Counsel, John Cameron QC. The first problem was why the union would not go to arbitration. Stevens told the court that the union had no principled objection to arbitration – indeed twelve disputes with other employers had been settled in this way in 1953 alone. The union *did* object to arbitration as far as the NFEA were concerned. In February that year, arbitration had recommended certain improvements in apprentices' wages that the NFEA had point-blank refused to implement. The employers were represented at the court by Mr Phillimore QC. He said the union would not go to arbitration because they knew they would lose. The union's leadership was determined to smash the negotiating machinery and affect the nation's defence interests for political reasons.

The court summarized the low pitch to which the negotiating machinery had fallen. It was clear to the court that the union accused the NFEA of not being sincere in negotiations; they tried constantly to delay them (there was advantage to the employers in doing this; settlements at that time were rarely back-dated); the employers would ignore arbitration awards that didn't suit them; and their constant reference to silly political matters sought to undermine the union's leadership authority over their members.

The court characterized the employers' views of the union as based on their view that the union was causing disputes for purely political, not industrial, motives, and so they would not settle disputes rationally – and that was why they wouldn't accept arbitration. The court's final report, published on 14 October, did not recommend any settlement. Instead, it urged the two sides to formally incorporate arbitration into their machinery and to settle mutually on various sets of cost of living figures before negotiations start. Penwill was not accepting advice from anyone. Two areas' DJICs were suspended because of the union's 'vindictive' actions against NFEA negotiators after the 31 August meeting. Throughout November, meetings were held throughout the country, sometimes of members, sometimes of shop-stewards, sometimes of both. Two hundred and fifty-three branch officials and 138 shop-stewards attended a meeting in London; there was also a mass meeting of 1,200. In Plymouth, twenty-three branch officers, three shop-stewards and ten members got together. In every area, all the meetings pledged support for the executive and contributed money to the voluntary fund. By 9 December, the employers were still refusing to make any sort of satisfactory offer, so the executive reconstituted the organizing committee to develop a further round of strikes. The strikes were further refined on 31 December. The committee was to select sites for a series of sporadic disputes, of varying duration including a national one-day token stoppage.

The ministry tried again to intervene; under their auspices the employers at last came up with an offer of 1½d an hour. However, they also wanted a reduction in the overtime rate from time-and-a-half to time-and-a-third for the first six hours of overtime worked! Stevens was caustic about this. 'No trade union, with the slightest regard of the living standards of its members, could have treated this "final" offer seriously.'

The union responded by finally losing patience with the employers' delaying tactics – behaviour that Stevens later characterized as carrying 'procrastination to fantastic lengths'. In the first few days of January 1954, the organizing committee again laid plans for a mixture of strike events. A final appeal to the employers to make a more 'realistic' offer than 1½d and reopen negotiations was ignored. The executive planned some strikes of indefinite length which would attract strike pay of 12s per day, augmented by a further 4s from the voluntary defence fund. This eventually raised £28,600 in 1954. The strikes started on 11 January 1954, and included a national one-day strike on 18 January. At Scunthorpe, the members working for F. H. Wheeler and W. H. Smith initially showed some reluctance to stop work on the Appleby-Frodingham steel works contract. Seven members of the auxiliary section were so upset they left the site completely and four apprentices were allowed to return to work. The skilled men went on strike, as they had done the previous year, but the newspapers made hay of Frank Foulkes's 'instructions' to them to join the strike.

In that first week, strikes took place at Sellafield, Caenarvon, Pembrey, London, Rugby, Oldham and St Helens. On the 13th, they were joined by members at Capenhurst and Aldermaston. The new oil refinery being built at Coryton in Essex also came out. By the end of the first week, over 1,000 members had been involved, and the union claimed that 20,000 members attended the fifty-three meetings held on the national strike day of 18 January. The newspapers became distraught in their fury with the union, first suggesting that support for the strike was way below the near one hundred per cent the union claimed and then concentrating on the communist angle. On 19 January, the Cassandra column in the *Daily Mirror* said:

Foulkes was issuing taut, crisp orders that would have sounded better had he been a platoon commander at Stalingrad than a boastful agitator fermenting trouble in Scunthorpe. But I'll tell you who does profit (from the deadlock in negotiations) – the Communist Party. Who helps them to profit? The union leaders. Who are these people? They are Messrs Foulkes, Stevens and Haxell, a powerful, hectoring triumvirate of self-avowed communists who have by their industry, by their ant-like and purposeful toil climbed to complete control of the ETU. Today they are in their element – leading the gnawing, wasting attack on British industrial life that brings glee to all who support the Soviet Union and joy to all who welcome bitterness and strife as a means of weakening and sapping British productive power. 'YOU ARE REQUIRED TO REPORT,' snaps this Kremlin jackanapes (Mr Foulkes), 'TO ANY ONE OF THE FOLLOWING MEETINGS'. Then follows a list of the meeting halls and rooms where the sheep will dutifully assemble to be shorn.

The *Daily Mail* added to this sort of approach by saying: 'Freeborn Englishmen refuse to dance to tunes played by men who derive their inspiration from a slave country. All honour and praise to the rebels (in Scunthorpe). It takes courage to have done what they have done.' The *Daily Express* even printed a letter from an electrician in Glasgow headlined 'Ban My Union'. It turned out the man concerned was not even a member of the ETU! The strikes were extended. The Abbey steel works at Margam in South Wales were hit. In the second week, members were withdrawn at atomic energy establishments, oil refineries, steelworks and airfields. Indefinite strikes started at the nuclear sites of Capenhurst, Sellafield and Aldermaston. The Hotel and Catering Exhibition at Olympia was affected. The NFEA were now offering arbitration and a promise to abide by it; but the strikes went on.

On 25 January, a one-day dispute all over London brought out 7,000 members, affecting power station building, TV studios, docks and the House of Commons. In a curious historical echo, the management of the Albert Hall got its own back on the union for its activities in 1918 by refusing to let it hold a report-back meeting at the Albert Hall. The day before the one-day strike, on Sunday 24 January, thousands of electricians marched through London in filthy, wintry weather. Many of the slogans concentrated on the press abuse and distortion of the strike.

The following week, Liverpool became the centre for the strikes, with one-week disputes started in early February. Huge mass meetings at the Picton Hall pledged support for the disputes which covered Liverpool and other Merseyside towns like Runcorn, Widnes, Northwich, Warrington and St Helens. One thousand five hundred were involved and on the third day, joined by highly visible delegations from London, marched through the city in company with supporters from the local CSEU and the Building Trades Federation. The contemporary accounts all emphasize the solidarity, the meetings, the atmosphere. Jock Byrnes's Glasgow notes to the union's journal gave a hint that despite the complete answer to the one-day strike call, very few attended the 'mass' meetings and in the Stafford region, contributions to the voluntary fund were 'very poor'. There were a few reprisals after the 18 January strike, notably in Manchester where W. H. Smith sacked their Shepley works members of the union, only to take them back without much fuss four days later. Walker Brothers in Birmingham docked one hours' pay as a punishment for not giving notice of lightning strikes during the dispute. Ted Haynes got this refunded and organized large recruitment meetings after the dispute was over. This was a feature of the dispute – even in the unpromising territory of Ramsgate, twelve contracting electricians joined the union, having been impressed with the dispute.

From 8 February, the focus of the disputes shifted to Manchester. Forty-seven firms were affected and another huge rally left the Salford Co-Operative Hall to march through Manchester. The strike at Olympia produced the cancellation of Cruft's Dog Show. Six hundred members went on strike for a week starting on 15 February in Northern Ireland. Two big contractors in Birmingham were picked out for strikes starting on 17 February. The previous day had already been decided upon for another London-wide one-day dispute. This strike produced the most marvellous propaganda presentation of the whole dispute. At 1.30 p.m. at the Empress Hall in Earl's Court, 6,000 members filled the huge concourse in front of an enormous floodlit platform, filled by the leadership of the union, the London contracting trade committee and the whole of the executive, the London officials and the national officers. Walter Stevens's rhetoric was rapturously received. He finished his storming address by saying:

We are engaged in an epic struggle. It is perhaps our union's 'finest hour'. We are carving a crusade to maintain and improve the standard of life which will develop and grow among all the workers of our country. Your magnificent solidarity, your splendid discipline behind the executive council is a source of admiration for all working people. It is a cause for rage and dismay by all the employers and all those other elements who support them.

The carefully staged rally was followed that evening by a torchlit parade of thousands of members throughout London. The march was led by six apprentices carrying illuminated boxes which spelt out the key political message: 'We all agree with our EC'. There were bands, the union's great Walter Crane banner and carefully marshalled contingents from all the sites in the country who had been on strike since 11 January. A forest of posters was carried by the demonstrators, and down each side of the column every man carried an electric torch. Floodlit lorries carried effective attacks on the NFEA. *Reynolds News* described the marchers: 'The electricians were well-dressed, self-confident and healthy looking. And they were marching in order that they should stay that way.'

The strike took new forms in the capital. All the men employed by Phoenix Electrical came out on indefinite strike, as did the 400 members employed by Troughton & Young. This was one of the few companies to publish figures about its economic performance. They had made £206,000 profit in the year 1952–3: the union thought this figure represented profits of £8 6s 0d per employee per week.

As the strike entered its ninth week, there were signs which the executive made the most of) that some of the employers were weakening. At the Coryton oil refinery site, the main contractor, Lummus, threw the strike-bound Electrical Installations Ltd off the site and directly employed over 100 members; they settled for a $4\frac{1}{2}$d increase per hour, plus extra money on the country allowance and a bonus of £5 each.

In early March, Sir Robert Gould managed to bring the two sides together at the Ministry of Labour. By 9 March, the union was able to put to the members on indefinite strike the following package.

After nine weeks' strike, the offer amounted to 2d an hour with effect from 15 March and the NJIC was to meet on 12 March to further discuss the claim. The four mass meetings held at Port Talbot, Liverpool, Belfast and London were not unanimous: indeed, there was a strong feeling that 2d was not enough after all the effort deployed, particularly by those who had been on strike since 11 January. The aggregate vote at the four meetings was to return to work, 1,600–900. On 12 March, there was a huge rally at the Albert Hall – at last – to hear a report-back on the NJIC negotiations. These were, in effect, simply an offer to meet again. The men returned to work on the 15th, and the employers started their prevarication again. This time, the union quietly allowed the issue to be referred to arbitration. The Industrial Disputes

Tribunal added a princely $\frac{1}{2}$d to the interim settlement of 2d on 5 April 1954, making the London rate 4s 2$\frac{1}{2}$d, Mersey 3s 10$\frac{1}{2}$d and the provincial rate 3s 9$\frac{1}{2}$d.

The judgment on this dispute has to be equivocal. The union's leadership and fan-club in the branches thought it had been wonderful. The union's policy conference at Margate at the end of May gave its verdict. Walter Stevens thought it was 'a story of struggle which will go down in the annals of history as one of the most important demonstrations of militancy and solidarity that the trade union movement has even known.' The union had faced down the employers who were supported by a Tory Government anxious to beat the electricians before imposing wage freezes throughout the working-class. The union's victory had therefore struck a blow for everyone. He suggested that as it was everyone's battle, the TUC and other big unions might have done more to help the electricians who 'bore the brunt of the struggle, bore the sacrifices and prevented any breach in the solid front with which we faced the employers.'

Eric Elsom from Grimsby took up this theme, congratulating the 'wise and courageous leadership' saying that it was not, in general terms, 'the rank and file trade unionist who is not prepared to struggle, but some of the leaders who lack the courage to lead.'

Although few hands were raised against the executive, two voices were heard during the debate. Ernie Hadley, from Sheffield Central, brought up the initial unwillingness of the Scunthorpe men to come out. He was followed by W. E. ('Tubs') Lawrence from London Central No. 2 branch, who was associated with a growing group of left-Labour delegates – characterized the moment he sat down by Frank Chapple as a 'suicide squad for fighting some vague ideological battle'. Lawrence was *not* impressed with the settlement.

So far as a large section of contracting members are concerned, they are very disillusioned and greatly disappointed at the increase, which, as you know, went on record as a 'substantial' one. They realize that their efforts and all their solidarity during this dispute finished up with a couple of packets of fags a week.... Is there going to be another fight, and, if there is going to be another fight, is it going to take another two years for, say, another 2$\frac{1}{2}$d? Are we going to say that is another 'grand and glorious victory'?

The positive side of the dispute was the actual organization of the industrial action itself. The variety of activities earned the title of 'guerrilla strikes'. There was an element of swashbuckling romance associated with the careful planning that called national, local and company strikes for indefinite, weekly and one-day periods. Other groups of members could feel good by helping with the voluntary fund. This, though, was variable in its effect. London Central told the executive in January that their members would not cough up. However, a young shop-steward working for Wimpey on the Isle of Grain,

Eric Hammond, collected £65 from the other tradesmen in mid-January on the site and organized weekly collections thereafter. Wilmslow branch got really excited. The hand of international capitalism was clearly behind this dispute. They wrote to the executive in January that 'real trade unionists were one hundred per cent behind the strike in spite of Penwill, Monckton (the Minister of Labour), Churchill and Eisenhower etc.'! Caernarvon branch, too, knew what was at stake. 'The executive council were fighting for their existence against a dirty monster and another Black Friday.' Although the final result must have privately disappointed many, the union's leadership did set new propaganda standards in the conduct of this dispute. If the rallies and marches looked and felt like East European extravaganzas of a similar sort, they carefully used these events to maintain control over the dispute, enthuse the troops and keep up attacks on the external enemies – the employers, the Government and newspapers. From this time on, every mention of the ETU would include reference to 'Reds'. After this dispute, everything the ETU did attracted press attention. This attention was eventually to undo the communist leadership when interest was diverted from contracting strikes to the union's internal affairs.

Electrical Supply: Nationalization and Negotiations, 1945–54

Throughout this period, the negotiations in the electricity supply industry became even more interesting to the union, given the nationalization of the industry in 1948.

The union had been dedicated to the cause of nationalizing the electricity supply industry since the 1930s. It was their advocacy for the issue that made it national policy for the TUC and the Labour Party. Curiously, the union took little vocal part in the pre-Labour Government discussion on the nature of workers' representation within a nationalized industry. They were to put that right when they challenged the Morrisonian model. This put competence before class credentials, and the leaders of the new industries were not usually chosen on their known record of socialist devotion. Nevertheless, the union supported the Government's plans, even so far as paying for pro-nationalization posters to be put up on the London underground. When the private power companies demanded equal access, though, London Transport had them taken down.

The public ownership of electricity supply created no real disappointments in terms of the types of negotiations, their structure and their representation rights, with one exception, which we shall look at later. On Vesting Day, 1 April 1948, the new British Electricity Authority (BEA) quietly absorbed over 541 authorized supply undertakings in Great Britain, both municipal and privately owned. The negotiating structure involved a NJIC, and fifteen

DJICs dealing with the newly created area boards throughout the country leaving out the North of Scotland. At each undertaking, there were to be works committees for both local negotiations on the implementation of district and national agreements, and also to make sure the chain of command received considered responses to these decisions. In parallel to the negotiating committees, there were to be advisory committees which were concerned with education, training and social facilities in the industry, guaranteed by section 53 of the Act of Nationalization.

The union itself duplicated this in big cities like London with quarterly meetings of shop-stewards in the industry. Since the end of the war, the industry had conceded small hourly wage increases – 1d in 1945, raising the bonus in 1946 to 8d an hour, improving the electricians' basic rate to 2s 6d an hour in 1947, and giving 1½d raise just before Vesting Day. The wages were beginning to fall slightly behind contracting and earnings were behind engineering, but the conditions of employment were well in advance of other industries. By 1948, there was a forty-four-hour week, a sick pay scheme that paid thirteen weeks at normal pay and two weeks' paid holiday (with a further week advanced to shift workers). Trade union membership density had risen throughout the war; by Vesting Day it was approaching eighty per cent without a closed-shop agreement. On 31 March 1948, the NJIC reissued an agreement on trade-union membership which first set out the view that:

> The joint negotiating machinery has operated successfully during the past thirty years. Its value as a means for the just and amicable settlement of wages, conditions of service and matters in dispute, can best be maintained by the full support both of electricity boards and trade unions. The NJIC are therefore of the opinion that it is in the interests of every manual worker that he should be a member of a trade union which shares with the employers the responsibility for negotiating the wages and conditions of service in the industry.

The employers were not going to get involved with disputes over membership or non-membership of a union.

First, any such issues were not subject (as wages were) to reference to arbitration in the event of disagreement; they had to be settled internally. By December 1948, there was a procedure in place should members of unions refuse to work with 'nonners'. A non-unionist was to be interviewed by the men's shop-steward. If that failed to do the trick, he would be formally presented to both sides of the works committee, the DJIC and, theoretically, the full NJIC.

By June 1949, the employers were willing to pursue to the end the logic of their declaration concerning the importance of joint negotiations with trade unions. Non-unionists had no access to the joint machinery beyond the reference of any complaint to their immediate superior. The ETU sustained the tradition set by Jimmy Rowan since 1919: they retained the chairmanship of the workers' side of the NJIC, athough they only had three out of the twelve workers' seats, sharing the rest with the GMWU, the TGWU, their affiliate the Enginemen, Firemen and Electrical Workers and the AEU. A similar allocation of workers' seats was arranged for all DJICs. Frank Foulkes led for the workers' side at the NJIC.

The chairman of the BEA was Walter, now Lord, Citrine. From June 1947, when he joined the organizing committee before nationalization, Ernie Bussey left the general secretaryship of the ETU to be the BEA member responsible for the health, education, training and welfare aspects of the authority's work – what would today be called the personnel director. Ernie Bussey formally left the ETU on 13 September 1947. He had been the branch secretary of LSE No. 10 from just after the First World War until 1941, including his years as general president from 1931–41. He succeeded Jimmy Rowan as general secretary and presided over the explosive growth of the union during the war. Membership had more than doubled to over 170,000 and the general fund was worth £800,000, compared to £265,000 by the time he left in 1947. He was an important part of the TUC hierarchy during the war: he was elected to the general council in 1941 and served on numerous government bodies – most significant of which was the national advisory committee at the Ministry of Production.

His reputation suffered by comparison with the pioneering energy of his predecessor, Jimmy Rowan, and his more flamboyant, left-wing successor, Walter Stevens. In going to the BEA, where he showed little sympathy for the union in its struggle to establish contracting rates in supply, his erstwhile colleagues were unlikely to be well disposed towards him. After a serious illness in 1950, he was never the same man and died in 1958 leaving £7,194 in his will. He ought to be remembered as well as the resolute opponent of using power workers as an unwilling revolutionary battering ram. He inherited Rowan's fears of the consequences of communist domination of the union, and in 1943 nearly stopped them dead in their tracks at the special conference at Conway Hall. His war service and leadership brought nothing but credit on the union's reputation at a moment of supreme national trial. He could speak well and wrote better, particularly when making a case with research officer Joe Wild at his side. If his sudden departure to the BEA in 1947 looked like running away from facing up to communist control of the executive, it is up to anyone who makes that criticism to show they have done more in the same fight. Very few can.

The new industry also took into itself some of the most impressive non-communist officials in the union. Right from the start, Walter Lewis gave up his political ambition and his job as Birmingham area secretary to become the chairman of the Midlands Electricity Board, thus following his friend Bussey into the higher echelons of supply management. Paul McArdle, the experienced Newcastle area secretary of the union, left on 3 April 1948, to become the labour relations officer of the North-Eastern office of the BEA. He remains one of the great 'might-have-beens' in ETU history. He was the only man ever to beat Walter Stevens into second place in a full-time official election. In July 1942 he lost the election for the assistant general secretary's position eventually on the second ballot, having beaten Stevens by one vote in the first ballot. He came desperately close in July 1947 to beating the communist, McLennan, for a post as national officer. His running mate in that election against another communist, Bill Benson, was Harry Madden, the acid Middlesbrough area secretary, who did not hold himself back from attacking the leadership in public at the union's conferences throughout the 1940s. Harry Madden took a little longer before he, too, decided to leave. In April 1949, he became the secretary to the North-Eastern Board's DJIC. These men now gave their energies to making the industry a success. The union's leadership was probably glad to see the back of them in political terms. And it was the politics of the new nationalized industries, including supply, that the leadership did not like.

First, the union objected to what they saw as the generous value of the compensation paid out to the old owners of the industry. More seriously, they immediately spotted that the fundamental relationships between employer and employed in the industry had not altered. Frank Foulkes told the Margate policy conference of the union in May 1947:

Workers' control and participation in management are reduced to a minimum. The national boards and control authorities are over-represented by monopoly finance. The status of the worker in the industry remains unchanged. The relationship of the employee to the employer is continued. Therefore, the primary function of the trade unions will continue to be that of collective bargaining to safeguard and improve the workers' standard of living.

Although the Minister of Fuel and Power, Emmanuel Shinwell, was warmly welcomed at the conference and spoke energetically about the benefits that would flow from the parallel advisory and consultative machinery, the conference rededicated itself to the workers' control of the industry. Walter Citrine was also warmly welcomed to the same conference; Frank Foulkes even cheerfully looked forward to Citrine being chairman of the new authority-to-be in supply. He was not to say that again after Vesting Day. At the 1948 conference in May at Great Yarmouth, he returned to the attack on the basis of the terms of compensation and the lack of workers' control, and threw in for good measure the Government's failure to nationalize the heavy engineering industry that manufactured equipment for the suply industry. Still, Bussey was greeted like a long-lost friend and nice things were said about the consultation process and the training schemes. By 1949, at Worthing, with one year's experience of the newly nationalized industry behind them, the union's communist activists had a field day. Foulkes was 'disappointed'; executive councillor Les Cannon was appalled by the financiers and retired military figures that appeared to make up the majority of the area boards' members. Frank Chapple, the young delegate from Bussey's old branch, LSE No. 10, was fiercely dismissive of the miners' similar experience in the coal industry. He quoted Harold Davies, a Labour MP 'who said that the only difference between the National Coal Board (NCB) and Old King Cole was that Old King Cole knew how many fiddlers he had!' Harold Morton had returned to conference from LSE No. 1. The old executive councillor, the prime agitator in the organization of supply in 1916, was ruefully in support of the executive's dismissive attitude to nationalization. His complaint was strangely prophetic. No one in the new set-up would make a decision. Conflict was arising from the frustration emerging from the constant buck-passing. No supply manager would give a decision without referring every issue back to the centre.

Nevertheless, in April 1949, the NJIC unions had issued over Foulkes's signature a list of eighteen 'major improvements' in workers' conditions after the first year of nationalization. Their circular insisted that the changeover to the BEA and its fifteen area boards, rather than 541 different undertakings had 'a great and beneficial significance' for the workers in the industry. Some of the eighteen benefits were fairly small beer – like the ex gratia payment of an extra shift for shift-workers working at Christmas in 1948. But the cumulative list of improvements in pay for shifts and special duties, coupled to a series of significant general advances in sick pay, payment for meetings, works committees, the guaranteed week, the abolition of the lower-paid geographic zones, lodging allowances, the absorption of Central Electricity Board men into the system – all meant real progress for the workers concerned in the here and now of 1949.

Even so, the union's political objections to the way that nationalized industry was structured became more strident as both their experience of the new industry and their political objections to the Labour Government's wages policy and foreign policy poisoned the initial support they had given the Government. Once Shinwell was replaced by Hugh Gaitskell, the political divide was always going to affect the union's relationship with the Government and the BEA alike. In May 1949, at the Worthing conference, Gaitskell got what his biographer, Philip Williams, described as a 'chilly and unresponsive reception'. Gaitskell confronted the conference with the classic justifications for rejecting directly-elected worker directors in the industry. If men were full-time worker directors, they would lose touch with their membership and their representative integrity would be lost. If they were part-time, the other directors and the industry's bureaucrats would have every opportunity to overwhelm them. Fundamentally, they could not represent the men and manage the industry; they were two different responsibilities and the industry and the country must know who was responsible for the industry. Again, management had to be as tough as it had to be; management could not featherbed nationalized industries because the political opposition to nationalization was just waiting to criticize the take-over of private enterprise.

The new managers must be promoted from within the industry and within the working-class – which means that trade union activists must stop denouncing as class traitors bright young people who get on in the industry. Finally, one last home truth was rammed home. Gaitskell finished his speech with these words.

You are concerned, ... and inevitably concerned, with the repercussions of nationalization on your own conditions. Nevertheless, I, as the minister, I also have to have regard to the public attitude to nationalization. And do not forget we shall be fighting a General Election in a year or so, and that one of the issues of that election will be nationalization. It will not be judged ... on the basis of whether it is benefiting the worker in the industries ... [but] on whether [the public] think they are getting a better service out of it as well ... the service they require and the service they deserve.

The status of the official unions in the first couple of years of nationalized control was much enhanced. The immense increase in trade union membership penetration was due to management encouragement; other public service unions like the National Union of Public Employees (NUPE) were kept out of the industry. By 1950, most of the regional bonuses and plus payments had been absorbed into a truly national wages structure. Cheerful and amusing to everyone, Foulkes was liked by the management of the supply industry. He was sought out as an entertaining companion by the national newspaper industrial correspondents. He was also tolerated by the other unions' leaders who recognized him as an informed and effective negotiator. In return, Foulkes was hardly a revolutionary agitator. He left that to the unofficial shop-stewards' movement which arose in the industry in 1946–7, complete with its obligatory news-sheet *The Power Worker*. Earlier, in the summer of 1946, the London electricity shop-stewards' committee had organized disputes at Barking and Littlebrook power stations over the issue of non-unionists, only to be told to behave 'constitutionally' by the executive council. The most melodramatic of these disputes, involving Barking and Littlebrook once more, was to occur in mid-December 1949, involving 2,750 workers, and yet no mention of it appeared in the executive council minutes or the union's journal. It was an embarrassment to the leadership. Three power stations in the capital were hit by unofficial strikes on 12 December in opposition to the merging of their bonuses, negotiated by Foulkes. Hugh Gaitskell saw the politics of the dispute in stark terms, and with Citrine's full backing, put troops into the stations. Barking power station joined the dispute in opposition to the troops. The strike only lasted a few days as the troops, along with the EPEA members, provided some sort of service and the strike collapsed. The official unions – including the ETU – denounced the strikers, but this didn't altogether convince Gaitskell. He had little time for the union. He wrote of the ETU in his diary on 27 January 1950 that:

> ... although it denounced the strikers officially, we are perfectly certain the unofficial elements are largely guided and controlled by the communists as well. ... The Ministry of Labour were concerned almost wholly with ending the strike; whereas we were concerned with smashing the strikers. I wrote a long minute to the PM ... but ... the fundamental issue is still unresolved. ... It is quite possible that the Communist Party would not mind in the least landing this sort of thing on us just before the election. When the election is over, the Government ought really to face up to the issue of power station strikes, and decide whether they can afford to treat them as ordinary industrial disputes. In my view, they cannot.

This issue highlights one of the curiosities of the union's behaviour in the late 1940s and early 1950s. Its power in the electricity supply industry was rarely, if ever, deployed to render civilized life impossible. Unlike the early 1920s, when the London district committee attempted to use the power workers as a revolutionary instrument, Frank Foulkes was circumspect to the point of anonymity. The most serious dispute in the industry during the years of Labour Government centred on a particular aspect of trade union recognition, where the possibilities of using the industrial power of supply workers to achieve political aims took very much a back seat. It was an argument that found total support throughout the supply membership and the union's committees and executive council.

Since the earliest days of the industry, electrical contracting companies had done the installation work for many electricity supply undertakings – both privately- and municipally-owned. Before 1926, there was competition between private contractors and other undertakings to do the consumer's installation work. After the 1926 Electricity Supply Act, municipal authorities started up their own contracting departments and decided to pay NFEA–ETU contracting rates. At the huge 1932 inquiry into supply wage cuts, Mr A. H. Banks, the industrial adviser to the supply NJIC, told that inquiry that '[the rate] is negotiated by other parties, but we say we are in the market competing with you not as supply undertakings, but as wiring contractors, and we will pay that rate.' During the war, essential works orders lumped supply contracting workers together with other contracting men rather than with other types of electricians working in other parts of supply. In May 1946, a little before nationalization, the supply NJIC had written to the Government in another context concerning the wages of supply installation workers. 'The rates of wages and working conditions applicable to electricians wholly or mainly employed by electricity supply installations undertakings on electrical installation work ... are those prescribed in the agreement of the NJIC for the electrical contracting industry.'

During the run-up to nationalization, it was agreed to put the issue off, so that it did not delay the setting up of the new machinery. Bussey himself, in his last days as general secretary of the union, had made clear the union's stand on this issue. He led the BEA side during many meetings from 1948 to the end of 1950 at which this subject was discussed. Even Sir Robert Gould, at the Ministry of Labour, could not persuade the union to accept the BEA solution. The union wanted a separate negotiating committee not unlike the building craftsmen enjoyed, which dealt with building workers engaged by supply companies who were negotiated for by the National Federation of Building Trade Workers and not the NJIC unions. Bussey would only offer a sub-committee of the NJIC which would have a 'preponderance' of ETU representation on the workers' side, but whose decisions would be subject to the oversight of the full NJIC – a position the union could not accept alongside its exclusive claim for negotiating rights.

This issue was not really about money. The rates between 1934–51 were virtually interchangeable. In October 1934 the hourly rates for London electricians in both supply and contracting were 1s 9¼d. By 1951, the contracting rate had risen 4d to 3s 8d in contracting, but the supply rate of 3s 4½d, when they settled later in the year, was expected to catch up with contracting. In the provinces, the rates tended to keep pace, although contracting had taken a small lead over supply rates by the end of the war. Access to overtime on contracting sites probably ensured higher earnings than supply, where overtime averaged two-and-a-half hours on top of the forty-four-hour week in 1948. But the conditions of employment in supply were very attractive. Sick pay, two weeks' holiday and a host of other allowances were in existence in supply, which of course was permanent work unaffected by the opening and closing of building sites.

On the face of it, it seems strange that the union should object to a gradual changeover, by their contracting members working in supply, to full supply conditions. Indeed, many local officials negotiated such changes across the country. However, the union would negotiate the claim for the supply contracting men *outside* the DJIC machinery.

They would not allow other unions into this area of negotiating, for fear they would attempt to spread from there into the heartland of ETU exclusivity – the electrical contracting industry itself. Frank Haxell revealed this in May 1954 when answering a conference debate concerning installation electricians working in supply. He started by making public his political concerns about the ex-ETU men (Citrine and Bussey) running the industry.

There are ex-members of this union who are in rather important and influential positions in the BEA ... we can only suggest their motive ... is because they believe that, if they are able to create the circumstances in which this union is compelled to negotiate with other unions, then those other unions will be able to weaken the fighting spirit of this organization in its efforts on behalf of its members.

However, there was the further, fundamental point. The union wanted the nationalized supply industry to eventually grow by absorbing the contracting industry itself.

If, in the light of *that* policy, we accept other unions on the machinery [for installation in supply], we shall then be inviting a situation for the future whereby electricians in the contracting industry will have their rates and conditions negotiated by a number of unions instead of by this union only.

In early 1951, it is difficult to avoid the conclusion that the authorities in the industry and at least two of the other NJIC unions – the general workers' unions – wanted to bring this issue of the electricity supply installation departments to a head.

The inevitable confrontation eventually happened at the Digby Street depot in Bethnal Green in East London. This depot of eighteen workers was almost exclusively concerned with the installation contracts won by the London Electricity Board (LEB) for the connecting up of domestic appliances in consumers' houses. On 5 February 1951, a labourer called Backman was promoted from his job in the mains department and transferred to Digby Street as an electrician's mate. This was especially provocative as ETU mates had been made redundant the previous month. He was a member of the TGWU, entering a one-hundred-per-cent ETU depot to do the type of work – installation contracting – that the ETU claimed exclusive negotiating rights for nationwide. A shop meeting that day said that Backman must join the ETU.

The local TGWU official said that his members elsewhere in the Bethnal Green area would take action if Backman was forced into the ETU, irrespective of Backman's willingness to transfer. The ETU official, Arthur Stride, was down at the depot on 9 February to tell the LEB that the ETU men would not work with Backman if he did not join the ETU. The LEB issued instructions on 13 February to a skilled electrician, Holbrook, to take Backman out as his mate. Holbrook refused. He was suspended without pay. By 23 February, all 200 ETU men in the Bethnal Green area were on strike.

On 24 February, the strike committee at Bethnal Green were quite clear about what the strike was about. 'It is the considered opinion of ETU members that the LEB has provoked this strike by deliberately introducing a non-ETU member into a contracting department in furtherance of the policy of the BEA to deny the right of the ETU to obtain a unilateral agreement on behalf of their members employed in contracting departments.' By 2 March, the LEB were attempting to get the work done by contractors (who no doubt were paying contracting conditions – ironically, the very cause of the dispute). Pickets were despatched by the central disputes committee (whose local chairman was C. Rogers and secretary, J. F. Huxtable). The area committee met on 27 February and gave its full support to the dispute; the executive council met on 3 March and gave their full support. At that time, the wartime legislation governed by Essential Works Order 1305, banning strikes, was still in force. Therefore the executive granted 'ex gratia' payments to the 1,075 members in London who were on strike. Skilled men got £3 a week, auxiliary section men were paid £2 8s od and apprentices got £1 4s od.

On 13 March, the deputy chairman of the LEB, E. A. Mills, wrote to the strikers and posted notices throughout the LEB area professing to be appalled that ETU activists were threatening members with disciplinary action by the union if they didn't join the strike. Mr Mills said the strike was the ETU's fault for not using the NJIC/DJIC negotiating machinery and refusing to talk to the board and the TGWU about the issue. Ted Ward, the ETU official who was the No. 1 (London) DJIC secretary, had refused to attend a meeting in mid-February 1951 that *he* had not convened, but that the other unions attended and joined the management in ordering the ETU members back to work. On 14 March, the NJIC met, and commenced their agenda with an endorsement of the DJIC minutes – including this London decision. Foulkes led an ETU walk-out from the NJIC, which then decided to form itself into a special emergency committee with Citrine and Bussey now lined up against their old political opponents in the ETU. The chief industrial commissioner of the Ministry of Labour, Sir Robert Gould, attempted to mediate, but the ETU were adamant that they would not discuss the strike and the issue behind it – installation contracting – at the NJIC, because the whole core of their case was that installation contracting was the exclusive concern of the ETU.

There was a vocal and well-attended demonstration outside the LEB offices on 16 March, and on 20 March, the executive raised the 'ex gratia' payments to £3 10s od for every striker, irrespective of section of the union, along with an extra £1 10s od if the member was married with a further 5s per child. On 21 March, a 1,000-plus march paraded down Fleet Street to protest about the predictably anti-ETU coverage of the dispute. That night, the strike had spread to seventeen depots on the outskirts of London that were owned by the Eastern Electricity Board, and the Orpington depot of the South-Eastern Board was also out in support of the forty-one LEB depots on strike. A total of 1,888 men were in dispute. By mid-April, 2,161 were on strike, with three depots from the South-Eastern Board, one from Southern, seventeen from Eastern and forty-six LEB depots involved. The union attempted to counter the board's propaganda about irresponsibility by volunteering their installation services free to anyone who bought an appliance while they were on strike.

Meanwhile, at the national negotiating level, meetings were arranged to which the ETU officials were invited when, quite clearly, the employers and the other unions had already had pre-meetings to present a united front to the ETU.

The new Minister of Labour, Aneurin Bevan, saw the union's leaders on 8 April and again on the 9th when it was agreed to set up a court of inquiry under Sir Charles Doughty KC, which was urged to consider the wider question of the ETU's claim to exclusively organize installation electricians in supply along with the immediate causes of the dispute. On this basis, a mass meeting agreed to return to work on 17 April, with the exception of the men at Bethnal Green who remained on strike.

The inquiry met on 23, 25 and 27 April – and by this time the union was put under greater pressure by writs served on behalf of seven members from the Croydon and Tooting branches. These members sought legal help in getting strike pay – the 'ex gratia' payments – declared illegal, along with further declarations that the union must not penalize LEB members who worked during the dispute.

However, at the inquiry the union put up a spirited defence of the fundamental case for exclusive negotiating rights. Foulkes directly confronted Bussey once again as he quoted the historical precedents for the contracting industry conditions for supply installation work. He emphasized that although the Bethnal Green men had supply conditions, they were negotiated locally – initially by George Humphreys in 1940, outside the NJIC structure. Why else, the union asked, would the BEA maintain separate installation departments to 'compete' with contractors? Why else would supply officers write to Bussey at the ETU in 1947 to complain of not being kept up to date with the NFEA circulars that were used to set conditions in supply installation departments?

The inquiry listened to Bussey speak against the ETU. He explained that there were 9,000 electricians involved across the country, over two-thirds of whom worked at supply rates on supply conditions; 1,750 other men worked sometimes at 'supply' and sometimes at 'contracting' work for the boards. Only fifty of them were on contracting rates. Less than ten per cent overall had the lesser contracting conditions (holidays, lack of sick pay, etc.).

The assistant general secretary of the TGWU, Tiffin, also spoke against the union. The ETU should have requested the transfer of Backman, not threatened the employer with a strike. Even if the TGWU had refused the transfer, the union should have used the TUC Bridlington inter-union

procedures before taking action that hit the consumers and other trade unionists alike. The TGWU would never accept the installation side of the work
being an exclusive preserve of the ETU. In the future, there might be
redundancies in the supply side of the board's work, and Tiffen wanted his
members to have access to any contracting work that was going. This was
supported with vigour by R. Cook, the GMWU official who was the NJIC
workers' side secretary.

The inquiry's conclusions were published on 7 May 1951. They thought
that the LEB were perhaps a little premature in sending Backman out so
quickly as to make confrontation inevitable; however, the ETU should have
used the Bridlington procedures to sort out the union membership problem.
Nevertheless, Sir Charles Doughty's tribunal of inquiry was conscious that
this was not the issue. The whole case turned on the ETU's assertion that the
electricity supply installation departments were 'integral' to the electrical
contracting industry. Two arguments were 'fatal' to this contention. First,
the overwhelming majority of men were paid supply rates and conditions
throughout the country. Second, inter-changeability between supply and
installation tasks rendered the ETU's distinction futile – even at Bethnal
Green – where men went backwards and forwards between 'each side of the
consumer's terminals' as the distinction between supply and installation was
described. The inquiry totally supported the BEA's view that the sub-committee, already offered, of the NJIC would provide all the influence the ETU
needed in negotiations.

The executive council rejected the findings of the inquiry completely, and
raised the Bethnal Green members' strike pay to £7 for skilled workers, and
£6 for auxiliary workers and apprentices alike. The union's conference that
year skilfully avoided making a messy situation worse. D. W. Fido, the Tooting
delegate who worked in supply, some of whose members were suing the union,
was no friend of the executive council's general political approach. He agreed
to withdraw his motion denouncing one and all at the conference. In return,
the speech he would have made was published in the executive council minutes,
which were and are, nominally, private and confidential to members of the
union. Fido wrote what was the lesson of Bethnal Green for him.

Overshadowing all other questions that face Britain's trade union movement is the
terrible twins; the two large general workers' unions. With a finger in every industrial
pie, dominating by means of their huge bloc vote every TUC or Labour Party
conference, when, as is usual, they march hand in hand ... these unions are a reminder
of the time when the skilled worker was contemptuous of the less skilled. Now with a
low contribution, they have taken full advantage of the fact that in these days it is
numbers that count as far as representation on joint bodies is concerned, and not the
quality of the membership or its skill at the industry. ...

Throughout the summer, the union prepared for the court case to be brought by its seven members whose legal fees were paid by the LEB. In July, Stevens and Foulkes saw the minister, and the BEA tried to get the issue raised at the NJIC. In September, the BEA were persuaded not to impose Backman elsewhere; on 17 September, all the other Bethnal Green men returned to work when the skilled man Holbrook was reinstated. The Digby Street installation workers remained on strike. The court hearing was on 2 October. By this time, Arthur Deakin, the TGWU general secretary, had met Stevens and said that although he would not order Backman to join the ETU, he would not stand in his way if he chose to do so. The court proceedings ended with the reserved judgment published on 31 October. The £50,000 paid out in 'ex gratia' payments was illegal, because the union had not followed its own strict rules about balloting before strikes. However, the union could not sensibly be proceeded against under Order 1305, because that had been effectively abandoned by the Government in August 1951. In any event, the dispute, too, was already over. The judge ordered costs against the union, as well as predictable orders against victimizing the seven LEB employees. He pointed out that the union ought to change its rules if it wanted to continue what it was doing at Bethnal Green.

A special rules revision conference was convened on 2 December 1951, to do just that, and retrospective endorsement of strike action by the executive was introduced to the union's rule-book. This, as one delegate, J. E. Hobday, pointed out, was not a wholly unalloyed good thing. 'There is a great deal of feeling that although official strikes should be financed from the union's funds, unofficial stoppages should not be encouraged by the knowledge that ex gratia payments are there for the asking.' It was not until 1957 that the union's conference accepted the need to throw in its hand, and quietly accept the Doughty award of a sub-committee of the NJIC for installation departments in supply.

Wage rises in supply throughout this period were modest. They were rarely, however, as a result of strikes. Arbitration was the most used method of resolving disputes, even though Walter Citrine thought arbitration was an unwelcome sign of management incompetence.

From the start, the nationalized industry emphasized the importance of national standard rates of pay. Much effort was deployed in absorbing the many plus payments, benefits and lead rates involved in the previous 541 undertakings. Foulkes led at the NJIC in insisting on trade union discipline as the structure evolved. There was no support for unofficial strikes from the ETU. There was not even any support from Foulkes for negotiating percentage increases for skilled men. He did not want to upset the delicate trade union balance on the NJIC and went along with the general union's insistence on flat rate increases – 1½d an hour in 1949, 1½d in 1950, 2d in 1951, 2d in 1952,

1½d in 1953 and 3d conceded in 1954, payable from 1 January 1955. There is a case to be made that says were it not for Citrine telling successive governments that he would not tolerate the interference implied by government pay policy, supply workers would have got even less. Be that as it may, these negotiations make one pause when measured against the post-1962 rhetoric of 'the fighting union' in the fifties. Throughout the war years and just after, electricity supply workers' position in the wages league had fallen to fifty-ninth out of ninety-five by 1947. In the first ten years of nationalization, settlements kept ahead of inflation to the extent of producing over the decade, a fifteen per cent improvement in living standards. This did little, however, for their standing in the wages league. By October 1954, average weekly earnings in supply were nearly £9 10s 0d compared to the all-industries average of £10 4s 8d. Their position in the earnings league was at an all-time low of ninety-six out of 132 industries.

Nevertheless, the industry did possess better conditions than most industries. The consultative and advisory machinery was genuine and its integrity was insisted upon by Lord Citrine, often in the face of management scepticism, most typically from the aggressive Harry Randall, chairman of the LEB. Sick pay, holidays and superannuation schemes were well in advance of other industries. However, the national rates were nothing to write home about – roughly the same as contracting. There was virtually no room for local bargaining to reward productive labour. The only uncontrolled element was overtime. The trick, therefore, from the workers' point of view, was to fiddle around with demarcation and other restrictive practices in order to build in extra overtime. Although this was only averaging two-and-a-half hours per employee in 1948, it had risen to nearly five hours by 1954 along with large increases in the number of men employed.

The absence of disputes over wages in supply did not mean that controversy was totally absent from the industry. We have seen the issue of contracting departments on supply/contracting conditions at Bethnal Green in 1951 escalating into a large dispute. It was finally settled in 1957 on the management's terms. A further dispute broke out in London in January 1952. On Tuesday 1 January 1952, meter readers working for the LEB at the Hammersmith depot in West London went on strike, having discovered that two temporary workers at the depot were in fact sons of the sub-area commercial manager, home on holiday from university, going round checking the numbers of meters read the previous day by ETU members. A settlement was reached locally to withdraw the students, but Harry Randall, the chairman of the LEB, would not confirm the settlement since the whole business raised the 'principle' of management's right to hire whom they liked for whatever purpose. Furthermore, he would not accept the DJIC recommendation to suspend the accompaniment of meter readers with proper supervisors, and pending a review, the men would go back to work. Randall would not have it. The men had to return unconditionally and the management would insist on supervisors accompanying meter readers as planned. Randall threw in some well-publicized remarks about the 'Red menace' for good measure. By 9 January, meter readers were out all over London until 22 January, by which time the dispute had become less about 'snooping' and productivity and more about the LEB's rights to make people redundant. Foulkes drew the depressing lesson that it was a sad truth that a great nationalized industry could behave in just the same way as the worst private employer. Foulkes was specially pained about the emergence of the 'Red menace' angle. He was to remark years later in a conference aside. 'You remember the meter readers' case. A perfectly simple, innocent case ... [but] it was suggested that I was putting meter readers on the barricades, starting a revolution with a strike of meter readers!'

If the union's performance in contracting and supply was uneven, it cannot fairly be judged either way in engineering and shipbuilding where they were considerably beholden to the general workers' axis on the one hand and the desires of the AEU on the other. Post-war negotiations had conceded by 1948 a guaranteed week, increases in war bonuses and the forty-four-hour week. A court inquiry under the chairmanship of Sir John Foster had introduced for the first time the characteristic, modern wage structure in engineering with a skilled national, minimum time rate of 66s a week and an unskilled rate of 51s (plus the national bonus of 41s). The union was, like all other unions in the industry, quick to build on these national minimum rates through company negotiations, taking advantage of the era of full employment and skill shortage. The executive had taken a policy decision in October 1946 to stop claiming contracting rates in engineering, tacitly accepting that this would restrict their negotiating options in engineering on a company-by-company, plant-by-plant basis. On 28 November 1949, the EEF made further concessions, rather than refer the union's claims that year to arbitration. This consolidated the war bonus, added 11s and gave a minimum skilled rate of £5 18s od for forty-four hours. Steady progress was made with a rise of 11s, and a second week's holiday in 1951 on top of six paid bank holidays. By 1952, the EEF was looking to R. A. Butler, Chancellor of the Exchequer, to provide Government support for EEF resistance to the 1952 CSEU wage claim.

On Friday 8 August 1952, one week before the CSEU met at York, the union called a conference of forty-nine shop-stewards to consider the EEF's rejection of any wage claim. This conference showed the modern preference for consulting shop-stewards, not branch officers. Jim McKernan from Belfast said that the members would have to strike or submit to arbitration, which usually failed the workers. The union should demand £2 a week, and in so doing, smash the Government's pay policy. Only four out of the forty-nine stewards preached caution; they talked of apathy, high earnings on piece-work, massive overtime earnings. The rest supported strikes, if need be. The CSEU correctly judged an overtime ban and restrictions on piece-work to be sufficient. They successfully refused to accept the EEF's eventual offer of arbitration. The employers climbed down in the end, and gave 7s 4d on all rates, although the ETU thought the CSEU should have pushed for more – certainly closer to their £2 target. This was a regular feature of ETU voting at the CSEU. They would always take a proudly militant line in the vote, knowing that the conventional reactions of the other unions would usually mean that militant gesturing would not be called in.

However, in 1953, there were some fireworks, not least because the new director of the EEF was to be Ben Macarty, the previous director of the Manchester EEF, although the president, Yorkshireman Percy Mills, handled early response to the 1953 claim. This was for a fifteen per cent wage increase, tabled in May. In October and November there were large demonstrations in favour of these claims, and on 2 December, there was a national one-day strike, supported by eighty-five per cent of the workforce. Just before Christmas, the CSEU decided to operate an overtime ban and piece-work restriction from 18 January 1954. The employers were persuaded to accept a court of inquiry: in February it gave advances of 8s 6d for skilled workers, 7s 6d for semi-skilled and 6s 6d for labourers – approximately eight per cent. Foulkes thought that the CSEU had let everyone down once again, but was heartened that it showed growing solidarity, particularly if considered alongside the struggle in contracting.

Throughout the period, the shipbuilding negotiations generally ended up with exactly the same settlements as in engineering. In other industries, the union had become signatory to literally dozens of company and industrial agreements. In inter-union relationships, peace, on the National Union of Mineworkers' (NUM) terms, had been made with the miners. They occasionally 'consulted' the ETU about colliery electricians' wages. The union also settled its long-standing rows with NATKE when, along with ACT, definitive film studio agreements were signed, setting out the areas of work reserved for ETU members. The union gave up its claim to represent electricians in theatres, music halls or cinemas. The union's last redoubt of cinema electricians in Glasgow objected to this – but to no avail. They also conceded to NATKE the right to organize studio projectionists. In return, the ETU was the sole union for contracting electricians working temporarily in places of entertainment and the union could organize all other electrical workers in studios and film laboratories. Sound engineers were handed over to ACT.

Ever since the end of the war, when a series of shop-steward consultative conferences were held at the Filey holiday camp on the Yorkshire coast, the union had tried to map out areas of organization and recruitment. They tried to organize the emerging servicing industries in radio and television. They particularly targeted women electrical workers. This reflected an aggressive desire to spread the union's net wider. Jack Hendy spoke in 1955 of the need to improve the union's recruitment record. He was proud that the ETU's rate of growth from 1939–55 was 350 per cent compared to the overall trade union growth figure over the same period of seventy per cent. However, there were over 800,000 non-unionists in the electrical engineering industry alone. Jack Hendy knew what had to be done if the union was to fulfil its slogan of 'On to the quarter-million!' Membership had not actually exploded in the era of full employment. The massive gains were in the war. From 1939–46 membership had risen to 161,943 from 70,065. Then the yearly rises thereafter were 8,000; 11,000; 6,000; 5,000; 5,000; 6,000; 8,000; and in 1954, they reached a December total of 215,596 with a 4,000 increase. Frank Haxell admitted in 1954 that in 1948, the union was expecting an annual growth of 10,000 per year. Jack Hendy was convinced that there was 'beyond all doubt ... one answer – 'a strong, virile leadership. . . . Not for us the boss-class policy of the Cold War and the wage freeze.'

He also resurrected all the key elements in that eternal argument about just who should be in the ETU.

If, however, we are to continue to make progress, we must take the initiative now and begin to get away from the idea that our society is one mainly catering for craftsmen in the electrical contracting industry and their associates in electricity supply ... we have got to ... cast away all the dead conservatism of the narrow craft attitude which still hampers recruitment. We have to make it clear that craft sectarianism has never protected the skilled man. . . . Only when our union is not only strong and tough, but BIG, will we be able to enforce on the employers the policies that will give the members the standards of living that they want and deserve.

Some progress had been made by 1954. Over 2,836 women were recruited towards the end of the year in a special campaign.

Policy Making and Communist Influence, 1945–54

The union's membership was probably more interested in the detailed developments, or lack of them, in their terms and conditions of work. It was ever thus. However, the union's activists and leadership were increasingly concerned with national and international political issues. This concern was clearly inspired by where people stood politically, particularly in relation to the tactics and policies of the British Communist Party and its relationship with the more conventional bodies in the Labour movement, the Labour Party and the TUC.

We have noted how the ETU took some pride in its leadership of the economic debate about wage restraint, culminating in Stevens overturning the general council's policy in support of the Labour Government in 1950. This could not have endeared Stevens to the TUC. When Bussey went to the BEA in 1947, the congress did not elect Stevens to fill his place on the general council, despite the established significance of the union in the industrial community. No ETU representative was to serve on the General Council until 1965. Given the relentless series of issues over which the ETU challenged the TUC, it is not surprising that the union became increasingly estranged from the TUC.

In 1949, the TUC issued a circular entitled *The Trade Union Movement and Communism*, followed later in the year by two pamphlets called *Defend Democracy* and *The Tactics of Disruption*. These documents did not mince words. Written at the height of the cold war, they were unequivocal in their aims. They called upon affiliated unions to 'counteract every manifestation of communist influence within their unions.' Walter Stevens wrote to the TUC rejecting the drift of these pamphlets. He claimed that the best way to deal with 'outside interference' by anyone in a trade union's affairs was to democraticize the union. (Throughout his argument, he was clearly, if unspokenly, contrasting the new ETU constitution with the more closed, authoritarian structures of the big general unions.) Since the communists took power in the union, the union's conferences had been extended, a right of appeal had been established against executive decisions and all officials were elected and re-elected every five years. This system gave the membership the opportunity to complain about communists or anything else; if they did not choose to exercise that option, what had it got to do with the TUC? 'My executive council,' Stevens wrote on 8 March 1949:

... are of the opinion that the document issued by the general council constitutes an interference with the freedom of individual members of affiliated organizations, insofar as it attempts to influence them in exercising their conscience in determining the constitution of their own organization.... This document, if acted upon, can only result in splitting the ranks of the trade union movement, at a time when it is vital to maintain and strengthen to the utmost the unity of working people in defence of their living standards.

Not a single member of the executive council voted against the endorsement of this reply. Continuing disagreement flowed from the TUC's banning of communists attending trades councils and the vigorous suppression of the big city trades councils like Glasgow and London which Congress House thought had fallen under the sway of the communists. At the 1953 policy conference of the union, the executive council decided to make a set-piece of the whole problem. They put up a special motion which was entitled 'Democratic Rights'. It was carefully worded.

This conference deplores 'witch hunts' of all kinds and reaffirms its democratic right – a right which it believes must be applicable to every trade union – to formulate its own policy to suit the needs and aspirations of the majority of its members. This conference recalls with pride the fact that in this organization, any member duly qualified in accordance with its rules may be elected to any office in the union, without regard to the candidate's sex, race, religion or politics, and calls upon the executive council to endeavour by all means at their disposal to extend this principle to all organizations to which this union is affiliated.

This skilful appeal to libertarian principles masked the reality of communist behaviour in both Britain and the world outside. Frank Haxell, though, insisted in his speech that the motion was an expression of the need for 'unity'; as everyone knew, bans and proscriptions in working-class organizations had never helped the movement's progress towards the abolition of capitalism. Indeed, such a policy led to McCarthyism, Fascism and police attacks on innocent people at public meetings where people assembled to hear the noted 'progressive', Paul Robeson, sing. Even in Britain, it was the same train of thought that had led to the banning of communists from trades councils. It was the same train of thought that had led to the Labour Party's proscribing over seventy organizations for their communist connections. The result had been the 'expelling of loyal members of the Labour Party, many of whom had given many years of service; much more service, in fact, than some of the Oxford dons who have climbed on to the bandwagon and are parading themselves as socialists. Their only crime is associating themselves with local peace organizations.' The motion was seconded by J. E. Hobday from Nottingham who had nearly been sacked because the local authority management thought, mistakenly, he was a communist.

The motion was opposed by Tooting's delegate, Dave Fido. With a name like his, it is not surprising that several of his conference contributions in the 1950s were greeted with left-wing catcalls of 'Woof! Woof!' He had a slightly pompous manner about him, but the sincerity of his contributions when confronting the communists on their own ground is impressive. He said that the motion's sting was in its tail – 'to extend this principle to all organizations to which this union is affiliated.' For Fido, that meant the Labour Party, as well as the relatively insignificant trades councils. He deplored the talk about 'unity', when the communists ran candidates against the Labour Party – the party to which the union was affiliated. In Aberdeen, the union's branch secretary had run for the local council for the Labour Party, only to be opposed by his own branch president, a local communist! Frank Haxell had referred to McCarthyism – but what about Stalinism as manifested in Eastern Europe, Poland and Czechoslovakia in particular. No, said Fido: 'The brothers of the Communist Party are entitled to their political opinions, but they are not entitled to take advantage of the affiliation of this union to the Labour Party and use that for the purposes of the Communist Party.'

His mainstream appeal was impressive: the debate then revealed the tip of the fratricidal iceberg between different shades of left-wing delegates. Dave Finch was the Brixton delegate, and he urged the executive to stop trying to get into the Labour Party. The motion was not necessary if people were genuinely interested in left-wing ideas. 'Inside the Labour Party at the present time is developing a left-wing independent of Moscow and, just as important, independent of Washington ... this left-wing has an attraction not only to members of the Labour Party within the trade union movement, but even to members of the Communist Party.' Frank Chapple was the very next delegate; he appears to have reserved most of his early conference contributions for attacks on the left-wing adventurists that were emerging at this time. He told Dave Finch straight 'if members of the Communist Party, and the Communist Party itself, had any ulterior motives in mind in relation to the Labour Party, they would do what the Trotskyites have been doing for years; namely, concealing their identity and calling themselves loyal members of the Labour Party.'

However, despite predictable repetition of the 'unity' argument from Eric Elsom, and Sid Maitland, the conference took Fido's view in a vote, 165–151. This narrow defeat for the platform produced a revealing, spontaneous response from Foulkes in the presidential chair. 'The motion is defeated by fourteen votes. The press thank you for the headlines they will use tomorrow morning – "First Defeat of the Communist-Controlled Executive Council".'

These disgreements with the TUC were writ much larger as the union's leadership turned increasingly to foreign affairs. Their obsession with Soviet Russia's foreign policy imperatives was to provide endless controversy between the union and the outside bodies to which it was affiliated. Alongside their unflagging enthusiasm to support Soviet Russia ran an extremely vitriolic view of post-war America.

The union was genuinely appalled at the spread of paranoiac anti-communism that culminated in the witch-hunting hearings of Senator Joe McCarthy at the House Committee for Un-American Activities. The union struck up relationships with leading entertainment figures who suffered at that time. In 1953, messages of goodwill were read to the conference from Charlie Chaplin, who also wrote to the union congratulating the executive on the attractive nature of the *Electron* magazine. Several years earlier, in 1949, Paul Robeson had visited the policy conference, to speak on the need for solidarity between the oppressed negroes in America and exploited workers in Britain. He also sang to the conference, concentrating on Labour movement songs like 'The Ballad of Joe Hill' and read a poem, 'The Freedom Train'. The sort of response this produced in the *Daily Express* is interesting.

Why was Paul Robeson, a foreign political agitator, invited to attend the electrician's conference? His tear-jerking interlude had nothing to do with the conference's problems, which are concerned with work and wages in Britain. Was it because of his reputation as a highly paid singer? Or was it an impudent attempt to foist propaganda for international communism on the delegates? The delegates should ask their communist president, Frank Foulkes, what was he up to?

However, this concern about the fate of 'progressive' forces in America was often overlaid with sheer political vituperation – the equal of the *Daily Express* – emerging from their communist-inspired rejection of everything America stood for. America was a 'fascist' state. It was planning war. It was preventing the spread of socialism world-wide. Wholly typical of this profound hatred of America is this passage from Frank Foulkes's presidential address to the Margate conference in May 1954.

Those in control in America have no love of Britain – they may approve of the form of government we have at the moment, but if we changed our form of government, if we elected a socialist government, we have no guarantee that hydrogen bombs would not be used against the people of this country if Eisenhower or Dulles considered that America's vital interests were involved.... American vested interests are afraid of socialism. American vested interests are afraid of peace.... America only tolerates Britain for what she considers to be her own safety.

Clearly, though, the targets for attacks of this genre were fairly phlegmatic when they received the appropriate letter from the general secretary after each conference resolution piled on the insults. Typical of the cool reaction is the following reply from the American Embassy in London in October 1951, addressed to Walter Stevens.

The receipt is acknowledged of your letter of October 4th, 1951, forwarding a resolution passed by your Annual Policy Conference of the Electrical Trades Union, calling upon the Government [presumably the government of the United Kingdom] to take certain steps to ensure that United States armed forces in Great Britain be withdrawn.

Your courtesy in forwarding a copy of the resolution for the information of this Embassy is appreciated.

Very Truly Yours,
For the Ambassador,
Herbert F. Propps
Second Secretary of the Embassy

And that was that.
The executive submitted a motion on foreign policy to the 1946 TUC. It

would no doubt have been welcomed by what were euphemistically called then, as now, 'progressive forces' round the world. It read:

This Congress views with concern aspects of the Government's Foreign Policy. We note that the policy pursued in Greece has strengthened the hands of the reactionary forces, instituted favourable conditions for the return of the Monarchy, and led to the suppression of the progressive forces. In Spain, the continuation of economic and diplomatic relations with General Franco assists in maintaining a Fascist state of society.

In Germany, the failure to de-Nazify the country and establish democratic institutions and economic control is in opposition to the agreement reached at Potsdam. The relationship between the Soviet Union and this country has deteriorated during the past twelve months, due to the policy of Anglo-American domination and the isolation of the Soviet Union, along with the tying of the economy of Britain with that of capitalist America, [which] is, in our view, extremely dangerous and one that may prejudice the fulfilment of the Government's progressive programme outlined in 'Let Us Face the Future'. [the Government's 1945 election manifesto].

This motion was not the idea of Ernie Bussey. The general secretary urged the executive to withdraw it as late as the Sunday night delegation meeting on 20 October. He told them that the direct attack on America and the insinuation that the Government supported the isolation of Russia was likely to be 'very badly misunderstood'. Bussey also told the delegation, no doubt having attended a fairly warm meeting of the general council of the TUC or its senior officers, that the motion's similarity to others submitted gave rise to the idea that it 'was inspired from channels outside the union'. It is a real measure of Bussey's isolation within the leadership by the end of 1946 that his advice was ignored. The motion stood, and was due to be moved on the Thursday afternoon of Congress by Foulkes after Prime Minister Attlee had addressed Congress.

Attlee spoke at length on full employment and the need for greater productivity effort. Eventually, he turned to the Government's attitude to Russia and other foreign policy issues. He got his retaliation in first. He was ferocious in his denunciation of the communist view of British foreign policy.

Everyone who does not take orders from the communists is described as a Fascist. ... I notice on your agenda that the only resolution on foreign affairs is one [and here the ETU sponsors of the motion must have sat up straight in their seats] which seems to me to be filled with the kind of misrepresentation to which we have become accustomed from the members of the Communist Party, their dupes, and fellow-travellers.

There was no chance to challenge Attlee in debate: the union's delegation issued a press release the following day. It is worth quoting in full to illustrate clearly Bussey's quandary. It also illustrates the union's skill in deflecting the real point about communist foreign policy in the unions on to a series of plausible points about civil rights in the unions, which Attlee's remarks had never even referred to, but it made good newspaper copy.

The executive council of the ETU, responsible to the trade union movement for 150,000 workers, is neither an adjunct of the Communist Party nor will it permit anyone, including the Prime Minister, to classify it as a dupe of, or a fellow-traveller with, the Communist Party. A ballot of its membership on the question of affiliation of the Communist Party to the Labour Party rejected the same by a two-to-one majority. The trade union section of the annual conference of the Labour Party has elected a member of the ETU to the executive of the party. It is true there are communists in the ETU and on its executive as there are in every other trade union. When the trade union movement seeks to put a political ban on its membership we will approach the breaking up of the trade union movement as we see it in the country today. I would, further, add – the day the annual congress of the movement ceases to be the sounding-board of the variety of opinions of the rank and file of the movement, as expressed in resolutions constitutionally submitted by the executives of affiliated unions, and only tolerates majority opinions, it will become stagnant in ideas and sow seeds of decay.

The executive council of the ETU, in submitting its resolutions to congress, conscientiously believed it was expressing the concern of a large section of the trade union and Labour movement at the deterioration of the relations between the great powers and that this deterioration had its roots in the economic policy being pursued by the Government. It had a right to express that point of view and to ask Congress to discuss it and determine the same in a constitutional manner.

The intervention of the Prime Minister in attacking a resolution still before congress for discussion was not only a breach of the standard of courtesy normally expected from fraternal delegates on these occasions, but, if persisted in, is bound to pollute the wells of democratic thought and action by stifling free and frank discussion of problems of public interest.

Finally, I would add, the executive council of the ETU, whom the Prime Minister chose to attack, is exactly the same personnel as that which was thanked at the 1943 trades union congress by Mr Ernest Bevin for their special contribution to the war effort, and who had been specially mentioned by ministers and heads of government departments for their services to the nation both during the war and in the post-war period. The union offered its fullest co-operation to the Government in respect of the nationalization of the electricity supply industry, which has been welcomed by the ministers and Government representatives. If the price to be paid for loyalty is that free and honest discussion is to be suppressed and supporters of the Government are expected to become 'yes-men' to Government policy, then I am bound to declare the ETU will never sink to such a low level in the political or industrial fields of our movement.

The original ETU motion was eventually defeated at congress by 3.5 million votes to 2.1 million.

The union's leadership did not leave the issue alone, returning to the foreign policy arena at the union's first policy conference at Margate, from 5–9 May 1947. The 1947 conference had one extraordinary feature about it that was never to be repeated. At the 1946 Hastings rules revision conference, the union had decided to have an annual policy conference. The initial basis of representation was to be one delegate per branch which had over 400 members. The rest of the branches would be clutched together to form multi-branch constituencies of around 725 members. The total number of delegates expected for the 1947 conference – the first new policy conference – was around 170. However, for the multi-branch constituencies, proper ballots would be required, and each branch normally nominated someone for the multi-branch constituency it was part of. The elections were due to take place in the dreadful winter of 1946–7. There were shortages of everything, including paper for ballots. The executive therefore decided to hold the conference with 343 delegates, not 170. Every branch nomination was accepted as the paper shortage prevented the elections taking place!

Foulkes set the tone in his presidential address. 'Our foreign policy must be divorced from American imperialism. . . . Truman's philosophy will inevitably result in permanent crisis, mass unemployment and hunger, and must eventually lead us into another war.'

Alf Wallis was a left-winger from the Bradford branch; he moved a foreign policy motion that urged 'wholehearted' support for the union's 1946 TUC motion and the general secretary's press release in response to Attlee's 'unwarranted' remarks. Wallis made some interesting connections between domestic political problems and foreign policy issues. He was convinced that a shortage of building materials in Britain was due to the political decisions to refuse to import timber from the 'new democracies' in Eastern Europe. (This point was strongly denied by Harold Wilson MP, President of the Board of Trade, in a voluminous contemporary correspondence with Walter Stevens.) Wallis went on to denounce the return of royalism in Greece, the failure to 'de-Nazify' Germany, British assistance to an oil-hungry USA in Palestine, relations with Spain, the compulsion attached to the dollar loan from America and the retention of known Conservatives as British ambassadors. He also fulminated against 80,000 Poles who were being kept 'in idleness' in Britain. These men were accused by some in the union of being Fascists who had fought for Hitler, rather than refugees from both Russian and German tyranny. For two or three years after the war, it was often difficult for Polish war veterans who had fought for Britain – particularly aircrew or aircraft maintenance men – to get jobs in Britain. It was especially difficult to persuade left-wing branch secretaries like Wallis to place Polish veterans in jobs. But he was not the only one. The executive council and Walter Stevens were firmly of the view that all Polish citizens in Britain should return home to help build socialism. The executive resisted for months Government appeals to use Polish labour as a form of dilution in crucial export industries. The union's resistance proved ineffective as the Government and employers were taking them on anyway, and they became absorbed into British society. Even Alf Wallis's branch at last stopped preventing Polish war heroes from working in the power industry in the West Riding of Yorkshire.

In any case, the debate at Margate was supposed to be a parade of congratulation for the line the executive had taken in standing up to Attlee the previous October.

The first and most telling contribution that upset this scenario came from a young delegate from Dagenham branch, Bill Sullivan. He told the conference – the largest in the union's history:

I was in Greece for nine months. During that time, the plebiscite and the General Election took place. Our friends do not refer to the communist reign of terror that took place in Greece in December 1944. . . . I was engaged to a girl, and I will admit this, who was a royalist . . . and her brother was a royalist, and he fought in the guerrilla groups against the Germans. Because he refused to accept the Communist Party's policy, that man has been dead for two years. That is the Communist Party policy in Greece – the same as in all countries – to wipe out any opposition to the Communist Party.

Bill Sullivan was no Conservative. He was unhappy about Spain and the dollar loan to Britain. It was just his open-mindedness that made his next sally on the question of Yugoslavian refugees so powerful.

Whilst in Italy, I was on a squadron, and on that squadron were many Yugoslavs, and they were fine chaps: chaps who I am pleased to know, but they were what we call 'Conservatives'. Those chaps today are refugees in Egypt, in Italy, trying to get to England or to France. The reason is, that though they may have fought on the side of the Allies in the war against the Germans, they are not the allies of Tito, and cannot go back to Yugoslavia unless they want to die.

Bert Batchelor and Charlie Corcoran attempted to make loyal declarations of support to the executive. But worse was to follow for the executive. In what was to be his last speech to an ETU conference, Walter Lewis, the Birmingham full-time official, really got stuck in. First, he said that the offending resolution had been a pretty strange way to demonstrate loyalty to the Labour Government. He then raised another point. 'Who decided to send these resolutions to the TUC or the Labour Party? The executive council. How many of them, though, are actually members of the Labour Party?' He was applauded when he described Ernest Bevin, the foreign secretary, as 'the most popular man in this country today'.

Frank Foulkes could see the way the wind was blowing. He suddenly said, 'Does the conference want to vote?' A delegate called out that they wanted to hear an executive council spokesman. Foulkes dourly replied: 'The executive made all its statements at Congress.' Poor old Alf Wallis! He had to answer the debate. He talked of Labour's foreign policy being dedicated to the freedom of all peoples – and threw in an attack on Dutch imperialism in Indonesia for good measure.

The conference defeated the motion congratulating the executive, 166–107. The next resolution was clearly originally scheduled to build on the expected confirmation of the attack on Government foreign policy. That support had just failed to materialize. Nevertheless the next motion believed, 'our future well-being is bound up with the Soviet Union and the new democratic countries on the continent, and deplore our present line-up with the policies emanating from American imperialism.' Tommy Vetterlein urged the meshing of our planned economy with those of Europe, Asia and the Dominions to avoid the coming slump. J. A. Benjafield wanted to end our 'trade dependency on America'. Les Cannon, for the executive, was not too aggressively pro-Soviet, saying that Britain would be better off outside either an Anglo-Soviet bloc or Anglo-American bloc. Ernie Bussey then intervened on the same balanced line and got the motion referred to the executive, making a pledge in passing that motions submitted in future to outside bodies would not be done without consulting the membership. Having said that, he was preparing the ground for another potential embarrassment for the executive, if not for Bussey.

Jimmy Dougan from Cambuslang, and a close friend of Jock Byrne's in Scotland, produced a proposition that said that major resolutions governing policy should be submitted to the branches before being sent by the executive council to outside bodies. Dougan interpreted Bussey's pledge of consultation to mean ballot votes and he warmly welcomed it. Foulkes jumped down his throat.

I must interrupt here. The general secretary did not say there would be a ballot vote. The general secretary said, after consultation with me, that the executive council ... would have to devise some ways and means of consulting the membership. That was said deliberately by me to the general secretary. A ballot vote may take too long to conduct ... it may be through the shop-stewards we shall act.

Tommy Vetterlein opposed the suggestion as it 'was a definite slight to the executive council who have given great leadership, initiative and drive to the policy of this society.' Les Tuck, the delegate from London Central, took the same view: the executive council was elected – let them get on with it.

Ted Breed answered for the executive: he started with emotional anecdotes about his own fear of the bombing of London, the deaths caused in the invasion of Germany and the atomic devastation caused at Hiroshima. These were the real issues, and it was to deal with these issues that the executive sought to affiliate the Communist Party to the Labour Party and sent its motion of criticism on the foreign policy issue. He then said, in defence of the executive: 'We have the right to anticipate the membership. I want to say, frankly and honestly, that we did not take our motion to the TUC just as an isolated little group. All the indications at that time, I beg you to believe, pointed to the fact that the membership were dissatisfied with the foreign policy.'

He then began to ramble over Spain, Russia and America, only to be interrupted by Foulkes, having run out of time. Dougan, in his reply, mercilessly pointed out how Breed's emotional appeals had nothing to do with the question in hand – that the executive should stop committing the union to issues outside the union to which the membership were known to object. His motion was carried. Little changed.

It was always the Communist Party's great ambition in the post-war era to achieve their ambitions by affiliating the Communist Party directly to the Labour Party.

From the communists' point of view, the advantages were obvious. They were also aware that their wartime record (if only the Nazi-Soviet pact could be left to one side) had gained them something of a reputation as active, energetic anti-Fascists. Their immediate post-war effort in the struggle for exports and the rebirth of Britain under a Labour Government showed again a positive side to their character. They had even wrung from the anti-communist Harry Madden, the union's official on Teeside, the following post-election tribute. 'I consider our communist members especially need mentioning because of the hard work they carried out so unselfishly on behalf of the Labour Party.'

At the February 1946 meeting of the executive council, the executive council decided to send to the Labour Party conference a motion calling for the affiliation of the Communist Party to the Labour Party. The motion was moved by Frank Haxell and seconded by Les Cannon. No one at all opposed it.

Outside the executive council, things were very different. By the April meeting of the executive, the protests from branches gave the non-communist executive members, Jack Potter and Llew Price, the opening to persuade the executive to submit the proposal on amalgamating the Communist Party into the Labour Party to the membership in a ballot.

It was a strange ballot; the arrangements reflected the leadership's recognition of the opposition to the proposal. It also showed their attempts to get it through the members despite the opposition. First, they restricted the ballot to those members paying the political levy. In April/May 1946, the effects of the Labour Government's repeal of the Trades Disputes Act were yet to be felt. Members still contracted-in to paying the levy. Consequently, there were 41,419 ballot papers issued, as only approximately twenty-eight per cent of the membership paid the political levy. It was only reasonable to presume that this active core of politically-conscious members, including all the communists and their supporters in the union, would vote for the Communist Party policy of affiliation. Clearly, there might have been a difficulty if all the union's membership had been consulted, when non-Labour supporters votes would have been included. The leadership departed from precedents associated with all the other ballots conducted by the union. They set out the executive council motion from February on the ballot paper and asked the members to vote for or against the resolution. The completed ballots were to be sealed and returned to head office not later than 29 May 1946, rather than counted in the branches.

Over forty-five per cent of the political levy payers voted. The result was clear. It must have come as a shock to the executive: 6,030 voted for Communist Party affiliation to the Labour Party; 12,899 voted against. The motion was withdrawn from the Labour Party agenda in some considerable embarrassment, and the delegation was forced to vote against a similar proposal.

Throughout this period, the executive council gave vast amounts of time and resource to obviously communist-backed causes and organizations that would have made Jimmy Rowan cry. An attempt was made to invest in the *Daily Worker*. The *Daily Herald* was denounced for printing Michael Foot's comments on the Russian leaders. Michael Foot had attacked the show trials prosecutor. 'Mr Vyshinsky, who has had some experience of trials, has never shown any special respect or tenderness for those who confess crimes of which they are not guilty.' Alf Martin, ex-executive councillor and London district secretary, in June 1946 wrote, 'This can only mean that Mr Foot considers Bukharin, Zinoviev and the rest [victims of Stalin's purges] who were condemned to death for treason, Vyshinsky prosecuting, and who finally confessed, were, in fact, not guilty. This is the most foul insinuation that could possibly be made against Soviet justice.' This sort of blind 'fan-club' type of Russia-worship was widely displayed in hosts of other ways. Money was regularly donated to causes like Czechoslovak Film Week, League of Democracy in Greece, Canadian Seamen's Strike and sending delegations to Eastern Europe (including Russia itself in 1950). Typical of the returning delegation's reports from the period is the following assessment of East Germany in 1954.

The delegation were convinced by what they learned from their visit that the GDR was quickly establishing a socialist economy and that the ordinary working people were playing a real and enthusiastic part in the rebuilding of their country, in the management of their industries and in all aspects of the life of the country.

The union's growing concern, almost obsession, with the communist interest in world affairs becomes wearisome after a while. But it was never wearisome to the leadership of the ETU. They took a particular interest in the fortunes of the World Federation of Trade Unions (WFTU). In the last months of the war and up to October 1945, trade unions throughout the world wanted to set up an international body to bring together trade unionists in defence of the peace so hard won by the workers in the recent war against the Nazis. The AFL would not join, casting doubt on the Russian unions' independence from their government. Nevertheless, the WFTU was inaugurated in Paris in October 1945, with Walter Citrine as its first president. The unity of the WFTU was always fragile; steadily, it echoed the requirements of Soviet foreign policy. With Ernie Bevin taking a very close interest, the British TUC and the American Congress of Industrial Organizations (CIO) called for a WFTU executive meeting in February 1948 to decide a positive attitude to the disbursement of American aid to a war-torn world via the Marshall plan. By the autumn, the Eastern bloc trade union centres had made their opposition very clear. By 18 January 1949, the new president of the WFTU, the fiercely anti-communist TGWU general secretary, Arthur Deakin, urged the suspension of all WFTU activity and the ETU were banned by the TUC from sending 'observers' to the Milan conference of the WFTU. The communist majority said 'no' to Marshall Aid and the TUC, the CIO and many other Western trade union affiliates left the WFTU in dramatic circumstances. In November 1949, now including the powerful AFL, the seceders set up the International Confederation of Free Trade Unions (ICFTU) with a Belgian president.

These events appalled the ETU leadership. They supported the WFTU with great enthusiasm and criticized the TUC on every occasion that the WFTU looked threatened. After the TUC left, in 1949, the union's machine went into action. Foulkes said on 15 May 1950, 'Our vision of five years ago has not materialized ... working-class industrial leadership should ceaselessly concentrate on finding a basis of common understanding with the workers in other lands.' At the 1950 policy conference, the debate on the international trade union question nearly produced another massive rebuff to the leadership's communist ambitions. One motion was moved by the Bootle branch delegate,

Arthur Shannon, and it applauded the WFTU, as its policy of international trade union unity would lead to the prevention of war. On the other hand, A. Taylor, from a group of Manchester branches, moved a motion that was seconded by Sheffield Central's, Ernie Hadley, that welcomed the ICFTU on the basis of its avowed independence from government control. The executive's standing orders committee preferred the WFTU motion, but were wary of its possible failure and laid contingency plans. Frank Haxell was put up to support the WFTU motion and call for the defeat of the ICFTU motion. But only one vote was going to take place – either for WFTU or ICFTU. Haxell started to develop a case full of quotes that sought to establish just how the TUC had never had any intention of meeting the WFTU half-way. He said it was 'a deliberate lie' that the WFTU policies reflected the Russian trade unions' subservience to the Soviet Government. However, it was as plain as a pikestaff that the ICFTU was not founded 'for the purpose ... of bringing about real international trade union unity, but is for the purpose of pursuing the policies of America which are the dominant feature. ...' At that stage, he ran out of time and the conference refused the suggestion that he be allowed to go on. The vote was taken. The ICFTU motion was preferred, 190–103. The executive now deployed their next card – an amendment to the successful ICFTU motion which had just been carried: this was skilfully worded to urge support for and co-operation with all the national and international bodies that were independent of government (which formally would include WFTU), and to urge the ETU to support all trade union organizations which were fighting for their members' wishes 'towards the ultimate object of true socialism' (which in the minds of the executive could also be construed to include the WFTU). Colin Whittombe, who moved the amendment, attacked the AFL in America, the non-representation on ICFTU of Greek and Malayan unions, and Arthur Deakin. 'Has Arthur Deakin, the sponsor of the walk-out from the WFTU, shown any sign of solidarity with the rank and file of his own union? Go and ask the dockers ... their action in support of the Canadian seamen ... was an expression of international solidarity which Arthur Deakin attempted to break down.' It was always good stuff to attack Deakin – as E. F. Philips had already said, 'We do not support Arthur Deakin – in or out of the World Federation.' The emerging Trotskyist faction in the conference was represented by Birmingham Central's Sam Goldberg who attacked the Soviets and Americans with equal alacrity, and he supported the amendment.

Delegates in the conference, like the determined D. Fido, tried to accuse the platform of rerunning the case for the WFTU. The mover of the ICFTU motion wanted to accept the amendment which seemed fairly bland. Ernie Hadley would not let him. He had to plough on, unenthusiastically. Foulkes ruled all the complainants out of order and brought in Wally Stevens to insist that the amendment ought to appeal to conference because it preserved the ETU's independence. In the confusion, the amendment was carried, 169–103, thus freeing the executive from the potential check on their international ambitions that the defeat of the pro-WFTU motion had looked like providing. Throughout the 1950s, the union was able to justify its contacts with Eastern Europe through such permissive conference decisions that allowed them to visit and consult with the 'trade unions' in Eastern Europe. The British TUC was always anxious that their decision to ignore WFTU and support ICFTU would not be undermined by individual affiliates virtually setting up their own relationships with the East. We have seen how they threatened the ETU with discipline under Rule 13 of the TUC ('bringing discredit to the movement') for suggesting the ETU might send 'observers' to the 1949 WFTU congress. At the end of 1952, it was made clear to the ETU that they were not to send delegates to the 'People's Congress for Peace' in Vienna. Seven ETU members did attend, but not as a formal 'delegation'. In 1954–5 a similar threat was made by the TUC when it was discovered the ETU were organizing an international conference for electrical unions which would include Western WFTU affiliates as well as Eastern Bloc trade unions. On both occasions, the executive stepped back from confronting the TUC.

All this may seem bizarre to contemporary, non-political readers. What was an industrial trade union doing debating arcane matters like this? A further thought might occur to delegates today. What use was any sort of international trade union body? In great contrast, it cannot be emphasized enough that the whole issue was central, vital, crucial, to Frank Foulkes's conception of what he was in trade union activity for in the first place.

When the amendment was carried, Foulkes told the conference:

I just want to say that we three (meaning Foulkes, Stevens and Haxell), anyhow, put a lot into that discussion. We felt very keenly about it, and if you had not carried that amendment, we would have had to look at our position in this organization ... it meant so much, not only to this organization but to the international working-class solidarity to which I referred in my presidential address.

The union's leaders were convinced of their own case. The Labour Party, the TUC, the Government, the press, and, of course, the employers, were all against them. The whole thing was a conspiracy. And yet, American capitalism, working flat out on rearmament and war plans to avoid the inevitable slump, was driving the world towards a more certain totality of destruction, given the nuclear dimension to the American war-machine. The issue of 'peace' became another front on which to fight for Russia and Britain alike. It took on a desperate dimension, given the background of the Korean War. The British peace committee came into existence and launched a petition that all communist activists and other left-wingers spent great energy in getting people to sign. In June 1950, the union's executive endorsed the petition and circulated it round the branches.

It was then that branches started to write in on the basis of a round-robin campaign protesting about the nature of the British peace committee and the growing scandal, as they saw it, of the executive's support for communist front organizations and 'friendship' societies.

On 21 October 1950, the union held a special delegate conference at St Pancras Town Hall with one delegate invited from every branch – a total of 600 delegates. So fearful were the leadership of the embryonic campaign against them, they issued strict instructions that no delegate was to come to the conference mandated by his branch, and each delegate had to sign an undertaking to that effect. A handful did not and were refused admission to the conference in acrimonious circumstances, including Ernie Hadley and A. Taylor from Hulme, the two delegates responsible for the defeat of the pro-WFTU motion at the May policy conference the same year.

The conference was to be asked to endorse, or otherwise, the executive's support for the British peace committee and its circulation of their petition. Walter Stevens, though, in a long, rambling speech, brought out everything in a subconscious rerun of the 1943 'communist interference' conference; only this time, it was to be others who were to be accused of distorting and perverting the union's democratic life.

Walter Stevens started by explaining that the union had always been in favour of peace. To prove this, he then read to the conference the motion drawn up by Jimmy Rowan in 1914 on the eve of the First World War. Stevens emphasized that the union's conference in May 1950 had gone on record as being in favour of peace and against nuclear weapons. On that basis, the union was entitled to send a motion on peace to the Labour Party conference, 'request' all the members to sign the peace petition and affiliate to the British peace committee. These decisions were taken on 22 June 1951. Then, the Canterbury branch started circulating the union, and by mid-July, the union was awash with circulars and controversy. It was the duty of the conference to pronounce on these matters. Stevens was then heckled when he rather waspishly told the conference that the leadership would have been quite within its rights to 'instruct' the membership to sign the petition. After all, the 1950 policy conference had declared itself in favour of peace. However, Stevens said that the executive did not want to impinge 'on the personal opinions of our members'.

Walter Stevens asked what was wrong with affiliating with the British peace committee when they already affiliated to the national peace council and the United Nations Association. They should ignore the TUC whose rules, apart from poaching membership, held no power over the ETU.

It would be a sorry day indeed for the membership of our organization if this were not so, because what it would really mean is that the policy of the membership of our organization could be determined by the bloc vote of the general workers' unions operating at congress.

He then dealt with the opposition to the peace committee because it was presumed to be a communist front organization.

It is recorded in publications by both the TUC and the Labour Party that the British peace committee emanated from the World Congress of Culture in Defence of Peace, which, they assert, was conceived on the instructions of the Cominform. There is not one single shred of evidence which justifies this allegation. ... The opposition to the world peace committee is inspired by the capitalists of Wall Street. ... We see building up before our very eyes a revival of Franco Fascism and Hitler Nazism in the United States of America, and no matter how they try to disguise it by shouting freedom and democracy, the evidence is there for all to see.

He was disappointed at the Labour movement in Britain, as represented by the TUC and the Labour Party, who had 'abandoned the teachings of Keir Hardie and seek to conceal the unassailable historical fact that capitalism breeds war.'

Stevens then did a very strange thing: he leapt from this rarefied, international political rhetoric to a five-point examination of what he called 'subversive intrigue' within the union.

First, he revealed some correspondence from Northern Ireland indicating an attempt to organize the votes of ETU members in support of a member called W. Rose. These letters were written on behalf of the 'Ulster Unionist Labour Association' to influence the election for the successor to Joe Lowden (who had retired quickly, upon discovery of a £600 defalcation in his name).

Second, he read extracts from the Catholic newspapers, the *Universe* and the *Catholic Worker*, illustrating their concern about the 'Red menace' within the union: Bill Sullivan and A. Campbell rose to inquire what this had to do with peace, but were told to sit down.

Third, it was revealed that the Council for Conservative Trade Unionists had been sending propaganda to branch secretaries.

Fourth, a pamphlet had appeared in the huge engineering works in Manchester – Metropolitan-Vickers – publishing a slate of moderate candidates for the area committee elections, headlined 'Oust the Communists Now!' Stevens deplored the circulation of this pamphlet in the company's internal mail and noted 'many of you will recall that the so-called "Blackwell" case was centred on this particular establishment, from which, you are, of course, entitled to draw your own conclusions.'

The Blackwell case had proved to be an early example of the communist leadership's concern to use the constitution of the union to silence anti-communist activists. In the summer of 1948, Chris Blackwell was the union's senior shop-steward at Metropolitan-Vickers works in Manchester. He was a well-known Catholic, and was at daggers drawn with the communist-dominated AEU structure in the works, as well as their left-wing sympathizers among the ETU shop-stewards. The AEU were about to ask the left-dominated ETU area committee to withdraw Blackwell's credentials for not supporting two ETU stewards in the factory. Blackwell had written to Charlie Robinson, a member of the area committee, asking Robinson to speak for him at the area committee and insinuating that area official Alf Hatton might well support the AEU line if he could get away with it.

This letter became known to the area committee, who suspended Blackwell's credentials. The local and national newspapers made Blackwell a martyr and his case was written up as evidence of communist terror and circulated as a pamphlet. A mass meeting was held at the Co-op Hall in Downing Street, Manchester on 17 October at which all sorts of allegations were made. Foulkes talked piously of the constitution; members at the meeting reminded him he had not been so delicately disposed towards it at the time of the Chorley ROF dispute! The depth of the Catholic-communist divide was bitterly revealed; the issue of talking to the press became quite secondary. Eventually, Blackwell's appeal to the executive concerning his credentials was lost; then further revelations and accusations were published as a pamphlet, *The Blackwell Case* – which now included allegations of a political supporter being given a job at head office as a maintenance man and more attacks on Les Cannon and local official Dick Tyldesley. On 31 January 1949, Blackwell was expelled from the union.

Back at the 1950 'peace' conference, Stevens left the Blackwell connection to attack the fifth subversion – a routine attack on the national press who were speculating on the morning of the conference that Foulkes and Stevens had 'had it'.

All of this was against the background of members in the Canterbury branch setting themselves up as a 'Canterbury members committee' in a feeble attempt to avoid internal discipline aimed at their circulating the union's members. These people had co-ordinated the sending to head office of seventy-eight letters complaining about the peace committee – forty-two of which directly quoted the offending Canterbury circular. Stevens was furious that all of twenty-six branch secretaries had written back to these people! Equally, the opposition were whipping up complaints – a further forty branches had written in to complain that the executive had convened a special conference and not held a ballot on the peace issue. Curiously, after going on for over an hour, Stevens finished abruptly: 'I exhort you to ignore the splitters, to answer the disrupters who stand revealed today, by standing four-square behind your executive council in the certain knowledge that they are activated alone by an immense desire to improve the standards of living of the membership of the union.'

Most ordinary delegates were undeterred by this strange rag-bag of international, national and internal political tirade. They ranged far and wide of the peace committee also. Supporters of the executive, like Eric Elsom from Grimsby, said that the executive were perfectly entitled to interpret the members' wishes on the subject in hand – for the policy conference delegates had signed the petition. Anyway, Stalin had promised that Russia did not want to impose socialism on anybody and President Roosevelt had said, just before he died, everyone must live and work together. A rambling contribution by S. McVicker about how he had met Keir Hardie as a boy was followed eventually by some of the Communist Party's big guns amongst the delegates. Jack Frazer, from London South-West said that the conference was a really good democratic way to make decisions – wicked Arthur Deakin's Transport and General ignored conference decisions and denied dockers and busmen a forum. Anyway, the executive's support for the peace committee's insistence on a pledge of no first use of nuclear weapons was clearly right. Bradford delegate Tynan was insistent that Russia spent less of its gross domestic product (GDP) on arms than Britain. LSE No. 9's O'Connor hated war; and he advanced the view that the TUC were only opposed to the ETU's support for the peace committee because Walter Stevens had successfully overthrown the TUC policy in support of wage control! Sid Lyons from London Press backed the executive after conversations in the local near the union's new convalescent home, where members were apparently willing to give the executive the benefit of any political doubt because they were clearly on the right lines in providing such a marvellous facility at Rustington. The final speaker for the executive, G. Lavine, was the youth conference delegate and his contribution urged support on the basis that atomic war would be devastating. Walter Stevens knew that, and he must be supported, even in arguing with the TUC. After all, Walter had been right over wage restraint. He was right over peace.

The opposition to the executive were not going to be overawed by this sort of thing. Jimmy Irvine of Falkirk was the first to oppose Stevens. If Russia was sincere, what did she need a standing army of four-and-a-half million for? He was of the view that the Russian and British Communist Party support for the world peace congress was aimed at softening up the democracies' desire to resist totalitarianism. Further Scottish voices were raised against the executive. Dougan of Cambuslang reminded Stevens of the Nazi-Soviet pact and George Scott of Kirkcaldy widened the scope of the attack to insist that if the executive had balloted the members rather than called a conference, the executive would have been defeated. He urged support for the TUC and

Labour Government's approach and quoted Aneurin Bevan's suggestion that the union ought to refer its demands for peace to the Kremlin. P. Partos, from Manchester, had complained vigorously about the non-admission of delegates who refused to be mandated: now he criticized the executive for not recognizing the interference in the union's life exercised by the *Daily Worker* newspaper. Once again, he was interested in peace. He had fought in Spain and Germany. But the executive's refusal to call a ballot and hold the conference showed that they were once more trying to keep the rank and file away from decision making. A. Cooper, of Small Heath in Birmingham, wished 'to protest about the executive council using this sort of method as a vote of confidence.' Sam Goldberg produced a good example of labyrinthine left-wing nit-picking. He objected to the executive's decision on the grounds that the world peace congress had refused to admit the Yugoslav delegation. Tito had just fallen out with Stalin. More to the point, he was of the view that the petition would not prevent war, so why bother irritating everyone on its behalf!

Stevens's reply was brief, almost desultory. He explained the Nazi-Soviet pact by quoting Sir Stafford Cripps's justification that it had bought time for the democracies. He denied the conference was a vote of confidence, but admitted that it was not binding on the executive in the way, by implication, a ballot vote was. The vote was taken by roll-call, where each delegate rises and casts his vote individually. After this long process was over, the executive had been soundly defeated: 335 had rejected their attitude to the peace committee and its congress; only 178 were in favour.

The real significance of the 'peace congress' conference was the shocking jolt it gave to Stevens and Foulkes. They could not guarantee the results of large conferences with delegates from every branch. Members of the union who were communists at the time are convinced that this defeat led to the realization that communist control of the union could not be assured by normal electoral means. Extra efforts would have to be made.

Throughout the period 1945–54, it is therefore clear that the executive did not have it all its own way, particularly on policy issues that suggested the union lined up with Eastern Europe. The WFTU, the British peace committee and opposition to Ernie Bevin's foreign policy were all issues dear to the leadership's heart on which they were defeated at the union's new policy conferences.

The wholly political obsession of the union's leadership was best revealed when the Labour Government fell in October 1951. The TUC moved quickly to let the world know that much as they regretted the demise of the Labour Government, they would of course seek to work with the Conservative Government in the interests of their members. The ETU executive was not having any of this. They got Frank Murphy and Peter Snadden – the non-communist executive members – to move and second the following motion.

The General Council had disaffiliated from the WFTU on the grounds of the trade unions collaborating with the governments of their countries, and were not, therefore, independent. The General Council has issued their statement that they would seek to work amicably with a Tory Government, saying this was not a new principle, but maintained that they were completely independent of the Government.

A sharp note was sent to the TUC, telling them that 'whilst it was necessary for the trade union movement to negotiate with the employers in order to obtain increased wages and better working conditions for their members, it was altogether a different matter to state that the trades unions would work "amicably" with a government which represents the capitalist class of this country.'

One last aspect of foreign policy took up much of the activists' time; it was probably the one issue that ordinary members did feel strongly about. Throughout the period, the union was strongly opposed to the rearming of the defeated West Germans and their incorporation into a European defence force, the North Atlantic Treaty Organization (NATO). Many in trade unions and the Labour Party took this view, and were not all enthusiastic communists. Many opposed German rearmament because of their own and their families' experiences in the all-too-recent Second World War. Typical of this view was Edinburgh delegate Bill Blairford's outburst at the 1955 conference.

It is, to say the least, fantastic that ten years after the defeat of German Fascists, the Tories, and unfortunately some of the Labour leaders, welcome with open arms, clasp to their breasts, the destroyers of Clydebank, Coventry and London ... the men and women, if you can describe them as human, who deliberately set out to destroy peoples and nations ... the political leaders of the Tory Party care nothing for the promises made to the millions who lie dead and the millions who fought against Fascism. They are concerned only with the need ... to preserve their interests to stem the spread of communism. ... What guarantees are there that this second Frankenstein that they are building will not again attack its Master?

This, and much more, was greeted at the conference with 'loud applause'.

Throughout the period 1945–54, the union's relationship with the Labour Party remained fragile and ambivalent for the leadership, but important and rewarding for the union's activists who were not communists. Throughout the country, the explosion of Labour success in local elections brought many members on to local councils for the first time; ninety-eight members sat on local authorities in 1946 and throughout the period several key towns produced ETU members as leaders of councils or mayors of important towns – like Peter Renwick in Newcastle or Tom Merry in Wigan.

The leadership's aim to affiliate the Communist Party to Labour was thwarted by the overwhelming ballot vote in 1946. Most significant in that ballot was the revelation that approximately twenty-eight per cent of the union's membership paid the political levy when they had to make a personal commitment to Labour and 'contract-in'. When the abolition of the 1927 Trades Disputes Act took effect in 1947, 'contracting-out' produced an enormous improvement in the number paying the political levy. By June 1947, the number paying the levy rose from 65,874 to 126,845, representing eighty-four per cent of the total membership – a percentage that held remarkably constant as the union grew in the 1950s.

Throughout the period, there was one permanent embarrassment hanging over the union. It was conventional for the president of the union to lead the union's delegation to the Labour Party conference. Just after his election to succeed Ben Bolton, the executive also nominated Frank Foulkes for the National Executive of the Labour Party in February 1945. On his own admission, Foulkes had been a member of the Communist Party since 1931, a fact revealed at the High Court in 1961, but not known in 1945. He wrote to Bussey saying he would like to decline nomination because he wanted to concentrate on his industrial responsibilities. Bussey pursued the issue, drawing attention to the rules of the union. Foulkes then had to have minuted two embarrassing revelations – 'since I have for some years disassociated myself from active participation and individual membership in the Labour Party, my political leanings are towards the Communist Party,' and, again, in a letter to Bussey, 'I would refer to our conversation concerning my nomination for the National Executive Committee of the Labour Party, when I informed you of my intention of making application to join the Communist Party. . . .' This problem only got worse as the decade unfolded with the president, general secretary, assistant general secretary and four out of the five national officers all communists. The union had Ernie Irwin as the delegation leader and National Executive Committee member – but it still rankled with Labour Party activists in the union that their national leadership could be construed as having turned their backs on the Labour Party.

Relationships deteriorated with the union's sponsored MP, Dundee's Tom Cook. Initially, Cook was a conventional left-wing Labour MP, but as the difficulties mounted for the Labour Government and when he became Sir Stafford Cripps's parliamentary private secretary, a policy gulf started to open up between Cook and the leadership of the union. These difficulties culminated in early 1952 when the union wanted Cook to protest about the LEB's behaviour over the meter readers' dispute. During the campaign to get London MPs to protest about the issue, several refused to help because 'the ETU MP' would not. In April, the union's political sub-committee met in considerable frustration. This committee included Ernie Irwin 'ex-officio'. The full members, Stevens, Haxell, Batchelor and Cosby, were all communists. Referring to Tom Cook, the sub-committee minutes read: 'The whole idea that members could accept nomination or sponsorship by an organization and then regard themselves as free agents with no responsibility to the organization to whom they owed their position, was completely unthinkable.' Something would have to be done about 'the present unsatisfactory position regarding this union's relations with Brother T. Cook MP.' The implications behind this produced from Ernie Irwin his most determined example of opposition to the communist leadership – an opposition that the records of the union rarely otherwise reveal. As a member of the Labour Party National Executive Committee he had minuted his insistence that 'as he was elected by the joint membership of all the trade unions, and not solely by the ETU, he could bear in mind the policy of the ETU in its relationship to the issues before the Labour Party Executive, as, indeed, he always had done. However, he could not give any undertakings and there could be no pressure from the executive council on these lines.' In the end, the political sub-committee satisfied itself with simply requiring reports from Irwin and the union's sponsored candidates.

The new strength of the political fund allowed the union to raise the affiliation of the union at the party's conference. In 1946, the union was affiliated on the basis of only 17,615 members. By 1948, that rose to 30,000. By July 1954, the union's affiliation to the Labour Party had risen to 140,000. Affiliation fees cost £3,599 a year and there was over £60,000 in the political fund.

In addition to Tom Cook MP, the union had another member in Parliament, Stan Tiffany, the MP for Peterborough, who was, however, sponsored not by the union, but by the Co-op. Ill-health forced him to stand down in the summer of 1950. Charley J. Hurley, from Hull, had come within five votes at the Smethwick selection conference in 1946. He was the candidate for the Lancashire seat of Heywood and Royden, while Jim Finnigan, from Plymouth, contested Cheltenham for Labour. The union paid for their travelling and subsistence to the constituency – £84 for Hurley in the period June–December 1950, and £110 to Finnigan in the same period. The union budgeted £13,000 in an election year like 1951, with £3,000 on affiliations, £3,000 to support the three candidates, £1,800 for election expenses and £4,075 to be paid on delegations fees and 'education'. At the election in 1951, the union's executive contributed £10,000 – a good sum for the time.

Post-War Rules Revision

Between 1945–54, the union held rules revision conferences in 1945, 1946, 1947, 1948, 1951, 1952 and 1954. The experience of war and readjusting to its aftermath produced enormous strains on the union's structure. This structure had evolved by 1945 following the Bussey-inspired reorganization committee's work in 1930–31. But after the war, the huge leap in the union's membership demanded virtually an annual 'fine-tuning' to come to terms administratively with the post-war world. Not all the rule changes were simply administrative – many had very serious political implications.

The most sensational proposition put to the series of rules revision conferences in this period was the resurrection of the idea of amalgamating with the AEU. No one could call the executive over-hasty, although few doubted their enthusiasm for the project.

On 3 December 1942, the AEU had written to twenty-six other unions in the engineering industry, and the first meeting of seventeen of them was held in August 1943 in Manchester: between May and November 1944, eight unions retained a serious interest in the talks, and on 15 February 1945, an organizational plan was published. On 27 April, the following unions recommended the plan to their executives: the AEU itself, the Foundry Workers, the Draughtsmen, the Constructional Engineering Union, the Patternmakers, the Scottish Brassturners, the Scalemakers and the largest (apart from the AEU) the ETU.

Ordinary members would have been impressed with the contribution level of 9d (compared to the ETU's 1s 2d, 8d for the auxiliary section and 4d for apprentices). The benefits would have been comparable – strike pay a little more, unemployment benefit a little less. For an extra 3d a week, members could have an extra 10s unemployment entitlement. For a further shilling per week, a pension was promised of 10s per week after forty years' contributions. The political levy at 2s a year was less than the ETU's 1d per week.

The suggested structure of the new union was interesting. Each union would retain its separate branches. Each union would retain its separate equivalents to the ETU's area committees, and call them district trades committees. Each union would retain its national executives and call them national trade committees. The union would be administered by a national joint executive, with four AEU nominees, two ETU and one each from the other six unions. In that sense, the new union would not be dominated by the AEU, although they were much the biggest union involved.

The amalgamation would really come alive with each district trade committee sending an undecided number of delegates to one of fifty-two district joint committees. They would each send delegates to a national joint council, which would be the policy-making body – a sort of annual policy conference, although its frequency of meeting was not specified in the plan.

In strict terms, the post-war conferences should not have considered the subject at all: the 1944 conference had already dealt with it. It was clearly both the head office and communist policy to amalgamate with the AEU. Both groups had long advocated it. Back in 1936, Jimmy Rowan and Ernie Bussey had both been flatly ignored when they spoke in favour of it. In 1944, it was almost as bad. Les Cannon moved a general pro-amalgamation motion that urged closer unity to face a changing world. He had laid down his marker on the subject in a series of letters to the union's journal in the early summer of 1944. 'Anyone working in an engineering factory [can see] that the section of the trade union movement covering that industry is unscientific, and is, in its present form, an obstacle to the closer unity of the workers.' One united engineering workers' union would quickly realize 'our ultimate aim, which is not the control of the *electrical* industry, but the control of *all* the means of production in the interests of the working-class, or, in one word, socialism.'

A very old and long-retired Archie Stewart wrote in to the magazine in reply to this. He had been present at the 1919 talks which led to the founding of the AEU. He remembered the controversial circumstances in which the ETU didn't join up in the new union. Archie Stewart was scathing of the results of the amalgamation in engineering where throughout the pre-war period engineering workers had been forced to accept a situation where 'the wages and conditions of labour deteriorated to such an extent that their wage status reached the level of corporation labourers'. Amalgamation was 'another furtive pursuit of a mirage'. Cannon was not dismayed; he wrote again to the journal and duplicated his argument at the September 1944 conference. Amalgamation was necessary to handle the post-war blurring of sectional demarcations. It would provide the necessary unity behind the leaders of the working-class who would be helping with the planning of the post-war world. It was necessary at the factory level where the multiplicity of unions might work against the unions when the employers would inevitably reassert themselves after the war. Jack Hendy seconded the motion. He drew on the example of George Humphreys, the recently-retired London district secretary who had in 1917 amalgamated the Electrical Winders Society into the ETU, sacrificing at the time his own position as general secretary. He rammed home the point that to be in the ETU was not an end in itself, but a means to widespread working-class emancipation.

His opponents were subtle; they were keen to absorb other electrical unions (unspecified) and other electrical workers. John Bull – the ex-syndicalist from London – openly acknowledged he had been wrong before the war. The growth of the electrical industries made it imperative that the energies of the executive should be directed towards building the ETU and not amalgamating with anyone else. The point was clearly made by Walter Lewis. The Birmingham district secretary said that in his thirty-three year membership of the union, he had known many amalgamation 'stunts'. What good had it done engineering workers, he asked, and then contrasted their experience with the Birmingham district of the ETU which had grown from 778 to 10,000 members since he had been district secretary without any amalgamation talk at all! The union would lose an effective leadership who had all worked at the trade in return for the possibility of being bullied by people who had not. 'Our Union is comparatively young, and in spite of this, we have got one of the most efficient machines in the country, and, I believe, if after the war we organize all the electrical trades workers, we shall be a still more important union.' Ealing's J. Crabb, no right-winger, was equally anti-amalgamation. First, he started with plain rudeness about the AEU being in great need of a 'damned lot of new blood', particularly given their careless administrative attitude where arrears of contributions could rise to £25 per member resulting in 40,000 men being expelled from the union at a single time! Bill Benson, a communist area official in London, talked some more about unity, with the different twist that they ought to want to deploy the union's obvious intelligence on a broader stage for electricians and everyone else's mutual benefit. Ken Alban – the Barrow delegate – was another whose close industrial experience with the AEU in his shipyard had not impressed him. He contrasted his closed shop for twelve years covering 700 electrical workers with AEU levels of organization as low as fifteen per cent in certain parts of the shipyard. He felt he was in a position to deride the proposition that amalgamation would strengthen his hand. 'At the present moment, we are a strong bottle of vintage wine, and we are talking about amalgamating with a barrel of very poor beer!'

In the face of such cheerful self-confidence based on real experience, Frank Haxell was pushing a large stone up a big hill when he spoke next. He talked of a post-war world in which strikes would only be effective if they came from amalgamated unions; it was vital for the ETU to stop asking simply what amalgamation could do for them. Ernie Bussey reaffirmed his commitment to amalgamation by reading out great slabs of his 1936 conference contributions, forgetting that the conference had rejected it then. They continued to reject it in 1944, 27–19.

By the time the issue came up again in 1946, the amalgamation plan, outlined above, had been published for nearly a year. The executive were anxious to avoid a direct vote on the AEU: so the motion put up was a general one urging the conference to permit the executive to keep talking to anyone and everyone about the subject. Jack Hendy supported that; this time *he* read Bussey's 1936 contribution to the conference. He supported the idea of a wider loyalty to the class, but was quick to distance himself from the specific plan that the amalgamationists had come up with over the previous two years. Foulkes guaranteed that there would be no amalgamation with anyone without a ballot. Once again, the familiar arguments were rehearsed. Those who *really* wanted to amalgamate with the AEU (Bob McLennan, Ernie Bussey) couched their arguments in terms of a dedication to the higher unity of the workers: those who spoke in favour of tying the executive to amalgamation *only* within the electrical industries were really opposed to any sort of amalgamation with anyone.

Joe Lane was against the AEU. It clearly gave him enormous pleasure to tell the conference that his branch had been suspended over twenty-five years before for not distributing amalgamation ballots! He spoke the truth when he said: 'Although we talk about notions of amalgamation, in our hearts, none of us really want it.' Frank Murphy, from Glasgow Central, a moderate socialist who would eventually be elected to the executive council in 1949, repeated the point. 'I have never, at any time, heard any expression of opinion, in any branch, in favour of amalgamation.' Harry Madden was opposed. The AEU had stolen our members at Billingham. ETU men had withheld their contributions. They thought that the executive was letting new members have easy access to the union's skilled section. During this petty row, the AEU had moved in. 'Do we want to amalgamate with people like that?' asked the outraged Madden. Walter Lewis repeated his confidence in the ETU without help from others. It took assistant general secretary Walter Stevens to save the day for the executive. He appealed, in some desperation, that the rules revision conference should not effectively ban the executive from discussing amalgamation, full stop. He made a clear point of the pace of technical change demanding organizational flexibility in the union's approach. Perhaps, he mused, within two years' time, the union ought to be better entitled 'The National Union of Atomic Workers'. His final point, that nothing would be done without a ballot, enabled the executive to hang on, 25–24. Nevertheless, the plan was quietly dropped and the prospect of amalgamation with the engineering workers' union cooled for some years more.

The November 1945 conference at Cardiff was interesting in several ways. First, Frank Haxell was in the chair as Ben Bolton was ill. It remains to this day the only national delegate conference held in the principality. It saw the emergence as a national figure in the union of Jock Byrne. It illustrated once again the political war that was never far from the surface, even when an apparently innocent practical subject was under discussion.

The practical subject under discussion at Cardiff was how to adapt the union's structure so that the union could accommodate the returning 25,000 members from the war and also deal with the huge numbers of dilutees who had entered the industry.

Ernie Bussey recognized the two main problems the union had to face. First, the returning members were in everyone's minds. Secondly, new skills had emerged in the war – especially radio, radar and electronics – and many dilutees had become forces-trained to high levels of skill. Both problems were confronted with the dreadful experience in 1918–21 still fresh in the memory. After the First World War, returning men faced periods of unemployment, and dilutees, as they were discarded, nearly bankrupted the union. They drew their unemployment benefit before disappearing from the union's books for ever. Bussey knew that 'in the final analysis, we are bound to protect the interests of our fully skilled members, those who have built up this industry, and are the bulwarks of our industry – we are bound to protect them.' However, the union did not want to be undermined by 'drifting' demobilized men or rejected war emergency section dilutees. They would cut the rates if they remained unorganized, augmented by thousands of military-trained electrical ex-servicemen like torpedo gunner's mates and leading torpedo operators.

The executive council proposed the setting up of a resettlement section of the union. All dilutees in the war emergency section and all demobilized skilled men and all war-trained electrical ex-servicemen would go into the resettlement section. They would pay a slightly lower contribution – 1s (compared to 1s 2d) and receive slightly lower benefits: each member would then be transferred to the full benefit section if he obtained skilled work at the skilled rate of pay. Alternatively, if he reverted to semi-skilled status, he would be transferred to the auxiliary section. As sometimes happens in trade union conferences, the arguments were all on one side: the silent votes largely on the other. Jock Byrne, the area official from Glasgow, made a biting, opinionated and forceful contribution. This was not surprising, given the nature of the man. Born in 1902, he had joined the Clydebank branch of the union in 1927. In the 1930s he held many branch offices and was a shop-steward in the Yarrow shipyard, the Elderslie dockyard and Yoker Power Station. He was regularly returned to the Clyde district committee, becoming district secretary before being elected as the area official in 1942. He was crucial to the war effort in the last three years of the war as the district secretary of the CSEU, co-ordinating the munitions industries and handling the problems of continuity of production and dilution. His toughness and his determination to battle against the odds were demonstrated in his youth when he was an accomplished half-mile runner. He ran at unofficial meetings organized in Glasgow in the depression that paid appearance money and attracted betting. He was a Celtic supporter and a declared Catholic. This was to provide him, no doubt, with the personal inspiration to oppose communism – an opposition that was to deprive him for years of high office in the union and kill him prematurely.

In his speech to the 1945 rules revision conference, he was scornful of the executive's plan, objecting in passing to not being called in the main debate on the subject. 'Our first responsibility is to our members in the forces – it is still our first responsibility. No, Mr Chairman, the dilutees must go out and they must stay out. Why play upon our fears? Are we, as an organization, afraid that the AEU is going to dictate to us?' (By recruiting ex-dilutees.) 'In shipbuilding, what did we do for the dilutee during the course of the war? We placed him in a position much more favourable than our own members, *and* he got deferment from the Armed Forces. He had a damn fine time, very often not doing fully skilled work by any means. Now we have got to tell the executive council where they get off here. I am not going back to our members and telling them that we are going to accept dilutees.' He was supported by fellow Clydesider Hardie who was furious that another craftsman (a stone-mason) working as a dilutee electrician could join the war emergency section, transfer to the resettlement section and get skilled employment. A proper ETU apprentice, however, had to wait for the expiry of his five year appren-ticeship before he got his full benefit card.

Harry Madden broadened the debate, suspecting the executive council of wanting to introduce the London mates system of acquiring skill in contrast to the northern apprenticeship route to the full benefit card. The union had 'to be able to restrict would-be interlopers into that section – the full benefit section.' Barrow's Ken Alban also saw the anti-craft London hand in the suggestion. 'We are going to have industrialization, camouflaged under the ETU. ... we have treated the dilutee honourably, and saw he got a fair deal ... his place now is to go back where he came from.' The arguments in favour of the resettlement section were slightly more uplifting and would have found some support in Aldershot, at least. In that town, a furious group of auxiliary members wrote to the union's journal in defence of their 'dilutee' fellow-workers. 'May we point out that 22,000 dilutees cannot, and will not, be cancelled out simply by wishful thinking and childish antagonism of self-styled experts. We accuse the trade unions, and the ETU in particular, of snobbery and class distinction far more vicious in intent and results than that of the social élite!' This letter was later published in newspapers, forcing Bussey to promise sympathetic resettlement for all war-workers, skilled or dilutee. Alf Martin supported the new section when he said the union must not restrict the rapid growth of skilled labour in the new war for production in support of the Labour Government. Les Cannon thought Jock Byrne's speech was 'a disgusting shame'. The union must organize the dilutees as they either stayed in the war industries or dispersed elsewhere, because if the union didn't, they would work outside organized industry for anti-union employers. The second full-time official elected in Birmingham, Jack Bolas, emphasized the shortage-of-skill problem in Birmingham where all sorts of people were calling themselves skilled workers. The resettlement section would allow the union to recruit widely and then review which section of the union people should eventually work in. This was the telling point emphasized by Walter Stevens in his summing-up. He was disappointed that still people didn't realize that electricians entered the industry, and always had, from other sources than the indentured apprenticeship. In defence of everyone, the union could not restrict the types of electrical skill it chose to organize. The resettlement section was going to filter everyone into the appropriate section of the union in the branches, and in that way, the sanctity of skill would be protected. The section was passed, 35–11, with four abstentions. Women members of either the dilutee sections would be transferred to skilled or female sections. Then the executive tried a sharp one.

For years, the apprentices in industry had been divided into three types of boy labour – particularly in contracting. There were indentured apprentices (called Category I in contracting) who had a legal entitlement to the training that their parents had signed for. Category II were also called apprentices, but did not have a legal, individual right to training. They were usually employed as junior helps who were given training or not, as the company or the individual craftsmen decided. After periods of time – typically five years – the boys were taken on as craftsmen because they had gradually assimilated the skills of the men they worked alongside. Category III apprentices were the most exposed group. They were little more than young, cheap casual labourers, who were sometimes employed only for the duration of a particular contract. They rarely got any training, but hung around the industry depressing earnings and providing a pool of labour for unscrupulous employers – particularly in big cities.

The executive's proposal was to take in all young boys into the apprentice section, irrespective of what type of youth they were, in an effort to organize the casual youngsters and introduce training and welfare elements into their employment. The opponents of the executive were not having this. J. Hardie summed it up by emphasizing 'we wish to get rid of boy and young labour within the electrical industry. We want apprentices, people who work at a skilled job.' Jock Byrne was persuasive when he objected to the contradictions in the proposal. The union would end up giving a young storekeeper a full benefit card at the age of twenty-one, and yet we would still be trying to insist that we were organizing all youngsters in an attempt to protect the skill from its dilution by growing numbers of youngsters! There was no substitute for apprentices being defined by proper training. The executive were forced to accept this, and took the proposal back. In the end, they set up a junior auxiliary section to accommodate youths who were clearly not receiving the proper grounding in the skill. The 1948 rules revision conference decided not to admit any further members into the resettlement section; but it had done its job of providing an orderly re-entry to civilian work and control over dilutees. It is probable that most branches quickly despatched returning members directly into their correct sections. In 1946, the skilled section grew by over 14,000 and the auxiliary section by over 16,000 with only 4,669 remaining members of the resettlement section.

The Hastings rules revision conference held in July 1946 addressed the post-war world with some seriousness. First, they decided to ballot the membership of the union on setting up separate education and convalescence funds, initially resourced, if the members were willing, by the £47,529 left over from the war distress fund. (Legal advice required any individual member who wanted to, to ask for his contributions back: only eighty did so.) Specific proposals were brought forward to the 1947 rules revision conference at Bournemouth. Two separate funds were set up for education and convalescence, to have two per cent of general fund income and five per cent of general fund income per annum respectively. The conference approved, and the final proposition was agreed by the membership by an enormous majority – 45,752–2,693 – in the summer of 1948.

It was agreed to have an annual conference to discuss the policy of the union. The delegates would come from every branch over 400 members plus one delegate per 725 members from groups of smaller branches, eventually producing policy conferences of around 300 delegates in total. Rules revision conferences would be held separately as large seminars – with delegates elected from just fifty divisions, to meet at six-yearly intervals (although they met more frequently in the post-war upheaval).

The thorny question of piece-work was considered. During the war, an enthusiastic leadership had led an unwilling membership into the acceptance of piece-work as part of their war effort. In the aftermath of war, the Labour Government needed even more effort on behalf of exports and productivity-led economic expansion. The toleration of continuing piece-work schemes was only narrowly endorsed by the 1946 conference, 28–21. The first policy conference at Margate in May 1947 only allowed the executive to convene a specific conference on the subject, 162–144. At the Bournemouth conference in December 1947, the rules revision conference – a much smaller conference – voted 35–14 for PBR. The argument was largely carried on the basis of the union's insistence on group schemes, not individual schemes. Even so, one delegate, H. Meek, said that PBR would result in the end of the comprehensively skilled craftsman as the job was broken up into specialisms that could attract measurement and output bonuses. The Scottish and Midlands delegates were fearful of the system, thinking that it would lead to less men doing more work, and therefore lead to unemployment.

Two key propositions with interesting implications for the future development of the union were defeated in 1946. The moderate delegates from Manchester, Fox and Roddy, were keen that the executive council should become a full-time body. It would be more professional and provide an oversight of the work of the permanent officials. Harry Madden, the Middlesbrough area official, did not mince his words in contrasting the general level of competence amongst the area officials with the executive council – two of whom in his opinion *were* as good as area officials. Without a full-time executive, the quality of candidate for executive would not be high enough. Jack Potter, the Yorkshire executive councillor, made one of his rare conference speeches in support of the proposal. He knew from personal experience that the pressure of work required a full-time executive. The leadership of the union was not so keen. Walter Stevens urged an increase in the number of national organizers to four, retitled national officers. With Matt Greenwell's retirement, it was also decided to have just one assistant general secretary from 1947 onwards. Stevens was also keen to send the head office back to London and increase the frequency of dealing with routine business by the sub-executive council (the body composed of general secretary, president, the assistant general secretary and the two executive councillors who lived closest to the head office). The argument about a full-time executive was also linked to the suggestion that the union's internal discipline should be subject to a final appeals court. There would be a small group of lay members, voted for by the whole membership, who could overrule the decisions of the executive. The executive council met that suggestion by introducing a right of appeal against executive council decisions in the event of ten per cent of branches – amounting to around fifty in 1946 – asking for a ballot vote of the members. Therefore, there was no need for a rank-and-file appeals committee (defeated 33–9) and it was therefore important to keep intact the rank-and-file nature of the executive council – so the full-time executive proposition was defeated, 43–6.

The Scottish delegates again attempted to introduce reform into another controversial area of the union's life – ballots. We will examine later the different types of dissatisfaction with the union's balloting systems. Suffice it to say at this stage that concern was starting to shade towards scandal by 1946. Frank Murphy of Glasgow Central urged the adoption of secret postal balloting, with the union paying the postage on the returned envelopes. 'There had been many complaints [at past conferences] regarding ballot voting, of apathy, of irregularities; indeed the word corruption was used.' Stevens said it couldn't be done for less than £500 for a national official's election. He did admit, however, that cost was the only consideration. 'This question has received the earnest attention of the ballot committee, arising out of the reference back at Blackpool [when the 1944 conference asked for a review of balloting procedure] and it has been found that while the method is practicable from the point of view of administration, it would be virtually impracticable from the point of view of cost' and would of course involve an increase in contributions. (This threat from the platform of any trade union conference is usually the kiss of death for any proposal.)

Frank Murphy was not dismayed. 'I think it would be cheap for £500 to get a true consensus of the opinion of our members. At present, the money is being wasted. Are you prepared to spend more money and have a fair return or spend less money and have an unfair return. The number of ballot papers will be increased if there is a postal ballot system.' These arguments would return, more powerfully armed, to haunt the communists. In 1946, only eight delegates saw the force of them.

The 1947 rules revision conference was largely called to authorize the general acceptance of PBR schemes, and did so. It also paid attention to the abolition of the trade protection section (in which skilled but over-age or infirm members joined and were therefore not entitled to funeral benefits etc.). It retitled the old full benefit section, now to be called the skilled section of the union, reintroducing the 1930 definition of skill. This allowed any member, male or female, or any applicant, to join the union on as wide a basis as was compatible with the union's craft tradition. A skilled section applicant would be admitted if he had served a recognized apprenticeship, worked five years at the trade or was recognized as skilled by his employer's action in paying him the skilled rate of pay.

However, no conference was complete without a communist–anti-communist confrontation. 1947 was no exception. The 1946 conference had abolished the requirement for the executive to ballot the members before deciding on individual investment decisions – a minor but acceptable administrative reform. However, the executive brought forward to the *next* conference, in 1947, a new set of rules for governing executive investment decisions. The rule would be altered to allow the executive to invest in 'any public stock of British *or of any foreign government or state* in any undertaking of any kind whatsoever which exists in order to further the interests of the Labour and trade union movement.'

Jimmy Finnigan from Plymouth was instantly suspicious that the new rule did not restrict such investments to causes and organizations approved by the Labour Party and the TUC. Jock Byrne was not put off by platform sneers at 'Red menace' scaremongering. Byrne spoke plainly.

I suggest there are no bogies, or communists under the bed – but some are within the trade union movement. We have two sets of people contending for power within the movement, and at this stage it is obvious that they may have ignored the demands of the membership. . . . we can say we recognize the Communist Party are out to frame their particular affairs in the light they see them.

He thought the issue should be the subject of a ballot vote. He, like others, was of the view that the whole thing had been set up to allow the union to invest in the communist newspaper, the *Daily Worker,* who had recently set up the People's Press Printing Society to publish the paper. Ted Breed had attended the various meetings that set the paper up, and was predictably enthusiastic about its importance. However, they were also held back by Labour Party's secretary, Morgan Phillips, who had told the executive council that investment in the *Daily Worker* 'constitutes a clear case of association with the Communist Party; in conflict with oft-repeated (conference) declarations.' The amendment was carried, 30–19, and became the basis in rule of

various donations and investments in the future that were to become controversies in their own right, although there was no immediate investment made
in the *Daily Worker*.

More decisions were required of the only conference in the union ever held
in Scotland, a rules revision conference at Ayr in 1948. This conference finally
sorted out the administrative details of the union's convalescent and education
effort. It was made clear that the union's education courses were going to
concentrate on its own administration, history and industrial relations problems. Walter Stevens explained that the executive thought they could afford the
very first trade-union-owned college in Britain for around £25,000 (courtesy of
the war distress fund). The annual expenditure on the college-based courses
for around 200 students a year was to be £9,000. With a further £4,000 spent
on affiliations to the National Council of Labour Colleges and the Workers'
Educational Association along with three scholarships to technical universities
and colleges, twenty-five £10 apprentice awards and an annual scholarship at
the London School of Economics (which Jack Hendy of Willesden was the
first beneficiary of). All sides thought this was a good package, and the search
began for a suitable college and suitable convalescent home. Harry Madden
congratulated Walter Stevens while seeking reassurance that political education
would be exclusively in support of the Labour Party!

Part of the union's organizing priority was to recruit and politicize 'youth'.
In July 1947, the young and brilliant executive councillor, Les Cannon, was
delegated to attend a World Festival of Youth in Prague, organized by the
World Federation of Democratic Youth. His co-delegate, whom Les Cannon
met for the first time on this trip, was Frank Chapple. The conference lasted
for nearly five weeks; Les Cannon used his charm with one of the girls acting
as an interpreter to make sure he and Frank Chapple ate well and met many
leading communists of the era. Equally, the same interpreter was to eventually
introduce Cannon to his Czech wife Olga the following year. Les Cannon's
report of the conference to the executive council mentioned nothing about
girls or communists. Rather, it drew attention to the fact that at the opening
ceremony, 'Brother Chapple led the British contingent in the field, with the
miners delegation behind, and Brother Cannon made a speech of greeting on
behalf of the delegation.' This report led to the setting up of a 'Youth in the
ETU' committee, with Les Cannon, Foulkes, Stevens and Scottish executive
councillor Tom Carter, which eventually recommended to the 1948 rules
revision conference a new structure for 'youth' in the union. There was to be
a delegate conference in each area of young members under twenty-three, and
a national conference of around 100 delegates with a young chairman and old
executive councillors in attendance. Frank Chapple wanted the union to go
further, with youth councils in each area, or, a slightly different idea that he
advanced in 1952, a youth committee in each branch. However, although for

hand-picked militants in the London area like Eric Hammond, Harry Woolf and Seymour Moss, the youth structure produced some opportunities for early contact with the leadership of the union, the overwhelming experience of the youth conferences was the complete indifference of young members – particularly to the area level of activity, despite the fact that apprentices who were enticed to attend often received more in one day's delegation fees and travel expenses than they received in a week's wages as an apprentice. On 29 March 1951, the youth committee reported to the executive that 'generally speaking, the branches have little or no interest in the problems facing the young members of this organization or in any way encouraging the young members themselves to adequately express the matters which affect them or in any way encouraging them to play a part in the life of the organization.' By the 1952 rules revision conference, Les Cannon was describing the whole structure as 'disappointing in the extreme', with most areas apart from London only able to assemble four or five young delegates for an area youth 'confer-ence'. The 1952 conference decided to retrench, effectively abandoning local youth conferences, rather than adopt Frank Chapple's suggestion of youth committees in every branch.

The 1948 rules revision conference changed the financial administration of the union alongside other administrative changes the union had made. Much of the impetus for this was undoubtedly due to the election of Walter Stevens, replacing Ernie Bussey, as general secretary in January 1948 by 30,202 votes to 11,484 for Jock Byrne. Stevens was born in Woolwich in South-East London in 1904, the eldest of five sons. His father was a labourer, and died when Stevens was only ten-and-a-half. By the age of thirteen-and-a-half he was working full-time as an apprentice in the electrical department of a film renting and production company. After some time in contracting, he became a respected sound maintenance engineer, being closely associated with the sound installation system at Denham Studios. He joined the union in 1929 and helped organize the film studios in the mid-1930s. He served as a shop-steward and branch secretary before being elected as an area official in London in January 1938 as part of the leftward swing in the union in the aftermath of the Earl's Court affair. Two years later, he was the senior official in the five-man London office, and in 1942 was elected, very narrowly, on the second ballot, over Paul McArdle, as assistant general secretary in succession to Bob Prain.

He was nominally a member of the Labour Party, although the frequency of the mentions of his name during the Vigon affair showed that he was trusted, relied upon and supported by the union's communists. He formally joined the party in 1947: some still say under a degree of pressure from the Communist Party majority amongst the union's leadership. Analysis of his post-war speeches in defence of communists within the union, his loathing of

America, and his love for the WFTU would tend to indicate his membership of the Communist Party was no imposition on him at all.

However, there was another side to Walter Stevens. He was an innovative administrator. He reformed the union's record-keeping systems, which had not changed since Citrine's work in 1921. He revised accounting procedures to accommodate the huge increases in membership. The Ayr rules revision conference in 1948 accepted a new system of what amounted to budgeting. He took the previous year's income and allocated it proportionately to different funds – administration, capital, financial benefits, legal, education, con-valescence, development and the separately financed political fund. He organized a financial committee and called conferences of branch secretaries (which had never been done before). He did not want to go back to a basic contribution with extra 3ds for extra benefits. He retained the all-in-one contribution and introduced a novel way to settle the level of benefits. The rules revision conference would set a minimum, and every six months, after looking at the health of the funds, the executive would leave it at the minimum or announce a percentage increase for each benefit, such as unemployment and accident (although due to legislation they had to make ex gratia 'distress' payments, not strike pay, before the end of 1951). Walter Stevens was a genuinely popular man. Political opponents respected his administative skills even when they did not like his politics. The staff at the union's head office thought the world of him. He was a great devotee of boxing, played snooker frequently and supported Arsenal – all part of a capacity he had to reach people irrespective of politics.

One of the 1948 reforms did not work out well. The union's growth demanded an increase in areas and area officials. There was no difficulty with that, and the union split further into twenty-six separate areas: the previous year, the basis of executive council representation had been changed, and the area reorganization fitted more closely into the eleven executive divisions. The whole arrangement reflected the changes in the union's membership figures.

Scotland now only had one executive member with 16,439 members out of the union's total of 181,775 (including around 9,000 in the Forces). The rest of the eleven members were roughly the same geographically as before, but the extra Scottish seat was given to the London and Home Counties area who now shared four seats between nearly 70,000 members.

The areas were each, of course, to have an area committee. It was decided to elect them on the basis of trade committees, not one delegate per branch. Typical would have been the substantial Birmingham area of the union. Twenty-three branches could nominate for an area committee that was made up of three supply delegates, three contracting, four engineering, one transport and one miscellaneous trades, producing a total of twelve with the area secretary to organize the committee's administration. However, no branch could have more than one member per trade grouping. Birmingham supply branch, for instance, would probably have taken all three supply seats, but under these rules, other branch nominees had to take up the other two seats, irrespective of how many votes they got.

This was to produce a decade of confusion and muddle as area committees, particularly out of London, struggled to ensure that each trade section of the committee was up to strength. Loyal communist supporters of the executive spoke feelingly against the platform at the 1952 Whitley Bay rules revision conference – particularly from Merseyside. Although the system survived until 1957, the practical difficulties were enormous. First, in the event of an area committee man resigning, it often proved impossible to get a suitably qualified replacement. People changed jobs and became ineligible for a particular trade section. The second major problem was that many smaller branches ended up with no representative in any section and therefore no representation on the full area committee. Plymouth, for instance, in 1957 had nineteen branches, but only nine were represented on the area committee.

The 1952 conference produced in Stevens's mind the 'finishing touches' to the post-war restructuring of the union that he had in mind. His summary of the conference finished with the assessment that the rule-book ought to last nicely until the next rules revision conference scheduled for 1961. A lot was to happen in the intervening period to render that judgment completely awry.

Nevertheless, Stevens had a great deal to be pleased about, if he looked at his own performance from 1945–54. The union's administration was fast modernizing as Walter Stevens took more of the administrative responsibility in his latter days as assistant general secretary just after the war. In February 1946, the union's officials became motorized. At the end of 1944, thirteen were running their own cars while seven were still getting round the huge new areas by public transport. In 1946, the union paid £400 each for 10 h.p. Austins from Messrs Kennings Ltd. The new offices and ever-developing clerical support brought the union into the modern age. Stevens was also exceptionally conscious of the use of propaganda. The union's magazine was retitled in 1950, and called the *Electron* (possibly, sub-consciously, resurrecting Stavenhagen and Westfallen's radical magazine of the early 1920s). It rapidly introduced colour, photographs in abundance, women's pages, film reviews and endless, if well-presented, left-wing propaganda articles. These were to draw a series of repetitive and unsuccessful motions at conferences that decried its political bias.

The most spectacular propaganda gesture was the production of the union's own film, *A Power in the Land;* The project was hatched with the film technician's official, Ralph Bond, who produced the film and commissioned the script from a young Ted Willis. It was directed by Terry Bishop. It featured the role of electricity in every facet of modern life – steel rolling mill, an atom-splitting cyclotron, post office electronics, television, domestic gadgetry and medical electrics – all leading to an uplifting address about the union's democracy and structure which featured pictures of the post-war executive council in action. The film cost the union a staggering £10,158 19s 10d, but it had a wide showing in early 1948 as a commercial 'short' film. *The Cinema* magazine thought that the film's treatment of its electrical subject matter was 'interesting' and praised its direction and its sensitivity to the non-technical audience. It rather wryly noted, however, that the film is 'linked by a commentary based on [the membership files] of the ETU, for whose members the film concludes on a plea that brings an unfortunate propagandic touch to the whole.'

Walter Stevens's most lasting contribution to the union's whole life was his skilful property dealing. He determined that the union should try, wherever possible, to buy its offices and facilities rather than rent them. His first success was the union's head office. After the war, property in London was scarce because of war damage and virtually unrepairable because of scarcity of materials and restraints on new building. Instead, the union's leadership looked for office accommodation on the edge of London in order that they could return to the capital from their north Derbyshire wartime retreat of Ollerenshaw Hall. A large old house in Redhill fell through, before the executive decided to buy Hayes Court on 2 May 1946 – by six votes to three. The purchase was confirmed in November 1946 and the £19,000 required paid over. There was considerable repair work to be done to the house that had once belonged to Pitt the Younger. Damage caused by army occupation during the war had to be repaired, often by the union's senior officials and the first secretaries who moved in before most of the head office departments arrived by the end of 1947. Either side of Christmas that year, the union spent nearly £10,000 on houses and property round about the estate, to house key workers returning to London from Ollerenshaw Hall. The first executive council meeting was held at Hayes Court on 25 August 1948, and the offices were officially opened by Frank Foulkes on 28 April 1949, with distinguished guests in attendance – the Minister of National Insurance, Jim Griffiths, and the deputy chairman of the BEA, Sir Henry Self. Just over sixty people worked for the union and the total cost of purchase and refurbishment had come to £24,000. A large proportion of this outlay was recouped in the spring of 1949 by the sale of much of the surrounding 'estate' at Hayes Court for £7,500 and the sale of Ollerenshaw Hall and its farm for a further £10,900.

Nineteen forty-nine saw Walter Stevens busy in the property market again. The union's decision to use the war distress fund as the basis for the purchase of a convalescent home and the first trade union college was now to be realized. The convalescent home for a weekly intake of around twenty recuperating members was purchased. Rustington House, near Brighton, cost £12,500 and was officially opened on 7 October 1949 by a Mr F. J. Lawrence, the chairman of Rustington Parish Council. Famous guests present included the union's old friend Sir Robert Gould, the chief conciliation officer at the Ministry of Labour, Herbert Bullock, that year's president of the TUC and Morgan Phillips, the general secretary of the Labour Party. For Les Cannon and Frank Haxell, however, the day was ruined by their involvement in a fairly serious car crash at Horsham on their way home. At the same time, Stevens was trying to purchase a building for a trade union college at Shortlands, close to the union's head office, near Bromley in Kent. There were difficulties with council planning permission to allow a change of use – no doubt politically inspired. Another problem was dry rot in the next building the union attempted to buy. Most members of the union would probably say in retrospect, thank goodness for that. On 20 January 1952, the executive eventually decided to buy instead Esher Place, at Esher in Surrey, for £22,500. This house was magnificent, with genuine connections with the ruling class that made the irony of its purchase by the left-led ETU absolutely perfect. The union had already employed in 1950, as the union's first 'warden', even before the college was purchased, J. O. N. Vickers. Vickers was related to the engineering company and a Cambridge graduate in Modern History and English Literature, who had also secured the Diploma of Education at London University. He worked at the union's head office in the research department with Joe Wild and Jack Cramp while waiting for the purchase of a suitable college. He occupied part of his time in writing course notes for every session of the range of one-week courses he was designing. Even before the eventual purchase of Esher, John Vickers had presided over the first course for exclusively ETU members when he ran an event at Beatrice Webb House in the Surrey hills near Reigate from 7–14 July 1951.

Throughout 1952, Esher was refurbished. Murals were painted on the walls depicting general working-class landmarks like the Tolpuddle Martyrs and the General Strike. They were painted in the classic 'socialist realism' style by Cliffe Rowe, who had studied art in Moscow, and were displayed in the lounge at Esher. Frank Haxell took such a close interest in the murals that while they were being completed he ordered the deletion of a defeatist soup kitchen scene in the General Strike mural, and its replacement with heroic workers standing up to snarling policemen. The other murals depicted ETU scenes – the significant strike at Bolton electricity department in 1899, a curiously obscure sympathy strike with dustmen employed by Fulham Council in October 1923 and the considerably more sensational removal of the Albert Hall fuses by Brother A. J. Leggett in November 1918. The first course at Esher was in June 1953, and the college was an instant success. It was the first trade-union college in Britain and the mixture of its charm as a place and the skill of Vickers's innovative teaching style, mixing group discussions with formal lectures, brought nothing but praise for Stevens. The whole venture was a 'tribute to the imagination and enterprise of the general secretary', according to Frank Foulkes, who opened the college formally on 9 May 1953. The union's magazine, on this occasion, could be forgiven a rhetorical flourish.

We know that from now on, week by week, there will be marching from Esher Place an army of trade union advocates for our union, an army of propagandists for the British trade union movement; an army well equipped with facts, with reason, with logic; an army who will play a vital part in the struggle for the emancipation of the working people. We understand the concern that our venture has caused in those circles who are solely activated by the profit motive. For them the future is indeed black. For us a new day is born.

17

COMMUNISTS IN CONTROL: FINANCIAL CRISIS AND COLLECTIVE BARGAINING, 1954–9

DESPITE THE UNION'S MEMBERSHIP marching on beyond 210,000, details began to emerge in the summer of 1954 of impending financial difficulties.

Walter Stevens's approach to the union's finances was a contradictory mixture. He improved the professional efficiency of the union's administrative machine. However, he was, on the other hand, always in support of the politically-inspired expenditure that prevented the union enjoying the benefits of administrative reform.

On 18 May 1954, Stevens reported to the executive the bare bones of financial crisis; the union's expenditure was running ahead of its income, capped by the thousands spent on the contracting strikes. The union was fast running out of the patiently assembled Rowan/Bussey surpluses. Stevens suggested that there was a need for a rules revision conference to discuss administrative reform of the accounts, the possibility of a rise in contributions and a twenty-week levy of 6d (for skilled men) to replenish the strike-hit finances. (Especially as the voluntary strike fund closed with around £40,000 in it – just a quarter to a third of the expected final costs of the guerrilla strikes.) The 1954 policy conference was alerted to the problem. On 15 August, Stevens spelt out to the executive council the problem and its solution, as he saw it.

By 1953, the expansion of the union's expenditure was fast outstripping the expansion of the union's income. Between 1945–53, the union had increased the number of areas from fifteen to twenty-eight, the number of area officials from twenty to thirty-seven, and by 1954 the number of national officers from four to five, along with their administrative support. Wages has risen from £32,947 to £81,398. Total expenditure had increased by £310,712 and income had increased by only £141,192. Benefits had risen four-fold, from £21,146 in 1945 to £86,864 in 1953. Printing and stationery had risen nearly four times from £26,549 to £96,572. Affiliations had gone up from £5,556 to £21,408.

Branch officers' expenses had gone up from £39,445 to £74,284. Costs per member had risen to £2 6s 0d in 1953 compared to £1 5s 0d in 1945. Income per member was falling; it was down to £2 0s 3d by the end of 1953 from £2 4s 1d in 1947.

The executive council decided, however, to cancel the plans for the levy. There had been 'massive interference' from the press; more to the point, there had been awful administrative mistakes made with the printing of ballot papers and so the levy ballot was cancelled. The rules revision conference was due for October 1954, when the August executive minutes would be available, along with the conference documentation. The executive endorsed Stevens's administrative and financial changes for presentation to the conference. Stevens's popularity and reputation for administrative excellence were about to be sorely tested. However, he never had to face that test.

Just before the conference opened on Sunday 24 October 1954, the radio announced at 8 a.m. that morning, that Walter Stevens had been killed in a car crash in South-East London at the age of fifty. He had been elected in 1948 with a large majority over Jock Byrne, and returned unopposed in 1952 with over 400 branch nominations. His funeral at Honor Oak Park cemetery in South London on 2 November was attended by over 1,500 mourners, led by the union's ancient banner. His political friends gave him a solemn and dignified send-off. Arthur Horner and Abe Moffat for the miners were there, as was Jim Gardner of the Foundry Workers and the whole of the AEU's executive council. Lord Citrine led the main column of mourners, and the funeral ovation was given by the Communist Party's Harry Pollitt. The 23rd Psalm and the hymn 'City of God' were followed at the end of the service by the singing of the 'International'. Stevens's reputation remains high in the union. He was general secretary for only six years, although his administrative hand in the union was clearly the dominant one from the moment he was elected as assistant general secretary in 1942. In his short time as general secretary, he established his own reputation as the leading opponent of wage control, and a leading anti-American and pro-international trade union 'unity' speaker in the wider movement. He laid the foundations of the union's institutional strength in terms of the purchase of Hayes Court, Rustingdon, Esher and several regional offices, with the new London office at Highbury being the most substantial. His personality was to stand particularly favourable comparisons with his successor, Frank Haxell. The legend goes in the union that if he had lived, the disgrace that engulfed the leadership at the end of the decade might have been avoided. That may be so; it is just as easy, and just as inconclusive, to argue that he was a beneficiary himself of dubious electoral practice. All Haxell and his friends were to do was refine the machine. The final conclusion about Wally Stevens is that he was genuinely admired in the union way beyond the Communist Party and their fellow travellers. He was a stirring conference speaker, an imaginative administrator and a decent, natural man. He was cremated and his ashes interred in a rose garden at Esher Place.

The rules revision conference was devastated by the news of Stevens's death which naturally overwhelmed the opening niceties at the Linden Hall Hydro in Bournemouh where the conference was due to be held. Nevertheless, the conference started eventually, and Frank Haxell presented other shocks to the delegates – the details of the financial crisis.

The union's financial policy since the Ayr rules revision conference had been based on three main propositions. First, the union would live on the previous year's expenditure, divided up proportionally between various funds – administrative, educational, benefits, convalescent, legal, capital and the separate political fund. The advantage of this would be that it was a form of budgeting, as each year the individual funds would be allocated a fixed proportion of the previous year's income. The other two presumptions were nominally sensible. The union expected to grow decisively. Full employment and the start of a new surge in electrically-based industry (consumer goods, atomic power, rebuilding British and world industry) gave this hope some basis in fact. Women and young workers were to be specially targeted. The second presumption was that administrative reform at head office would dramatically attack the growing problem of arrears in contributions. All union's count as a positive element in their income the nominal sums of money they are owed by members who have not quite managed to pop down to the local branch and pay up. There is no getting away from the fact that those members kept on the books are very often non-existent altogether; they have died, gone to Australia or changed jobs and are working in non-union areas. The growing arrears problem did not necessarily shroud a growing casualness by individual members in the matter of contribution payment; rather it betrayed a refusal to write people off the books which in itself would have underlined the true failure to recruit sufficiently well in this period.

Haxell admitted as much at the conference.

If we look at the achievements we anticipated so far as organization was concerned, . . . we estimated that there would be a minimum increase in membership at an annual rate of 10,000 from 1948 onwards. They were our minimum targets. This of course means that by the end of 1952, our membership should have stood at 222,000, whereas, of course, it reached the figure of 203,000, 17,000 below the target.

The effects of this admitted shortfall were then further accentuated by the arrears problem. There was some progress made in this problem between 1947–53. On 31 December 1947, the total membership was 169,967. They contributed in 1948 £335,812, with the 90,406 skilled members producing £242,922 (exclusive of political fund). This was eleven-and-a-half per cent short of what you would expect 90,406 people paying £3 0s 8d for a full year to produce. The whole membership was thirteen-and-a-half per cent short on this basis (around £52,291).

By 1953, the arrears of the skilled section were falling. On 31 December 1952, the union had 203,344 members, expecting to produce £476,164 in 1953. The larger (113,231) skilled section now produced, paying the same contribution, £323,970 – just five-and-a-half per cent short of the notional amount. But the other sections of the union were just not paying. The auxiliary section (nominally 54,692 strong) were ten-and-a-half per cent light; the 24,778 apprentices a staggering thirty-three per cent light. The union overall, though, were only 9.3 per cent short (£44,241).

The arrears problem showed up the highly uneconomic turnover of membership. In 1947, there were 32,170 people recruited into the union, but 24,686 were excluded, leaving a net gain of just 8,024.

In 1953, the numbers were different, but the pattern was the same: 28,410 were admitted, and 23,024 were excluded, for a net gain of 5,380. This constant coming-and-going was costly to administer and prevented any effective assault on the arrears problem.

However, at the start of this period everything had gone well. In 1949, the union were using 1948's income for 1949's expenditure. And 1948 had been a good year. Membership rose by 12,000 – comfortably over the 10,000 required by Stevens's planning framework. Income for the year exceeded expenditure by £14,500 in 1949. By 1953, eighty-six per cent of total income was available, with five per cent already earmarked for education, five per cent for convalescence and four per cent for the benevolent fund. Because of the comparative failure to recruit and the related failure to rectify the arrears problem, there was insufficient money in the eighty-six per cent allocation of income – a figure for 1953 of £366,188. Expenditure plans, meanwhile, had been laid that led to an astonishing expenditure for 1953 of £474,740 – an overspend of £108,552.

Expenditure had risen sharply, comparing 1953 with 1949. Branches spent £13,000 a year more. Area offices cost £40,000 more. The head office cost £21,000 more. Salaries for the extra officials cost £12,000 more, their staff support £23,000 extra. Everything else had risen in cost – printing and stationery by £36,000 per year. Benefits had risen from £37,000 in 1949 to £85,000 in 1953 – £45,000 of which was disputes benefit. Haxell must have known that a large bill was coming for the contracting strikes – and large it was; the overall cost of dispute benefit in 1954 was to rise to £190,645. However, the leadership's justifications were ready, Haxell laid it down clearly. 'Now one has to recognize the fact that if we are going actively to pursue the policies that we have democratically decided; if we are going to fight for those things we think are proper, right and just ... dispute benefit is bound to take a fair proportion of the union's funds.'

The solution was simple – raise more revenue and cut expenditure. The leadership put a package of suggestions to the conference that was, of course, the original work of Walter Stevens, although it was presented to conference by Frank Haxell. It seems incredible, but there had been no contributions increase since 1935. The 1s 3d a week (including the political levy of 1d) was demonstrably the cheapest skilled union contribution – the nearest other was 1s 6d. Few other unions had the convalescent facility the union had; no others had an equivalent of Esher Place for a trade-union college. The auxiliary contribution of 9d (including political levy) was slightly ahead of the general workers' unions, and it was a particularly sensitive matter in electricity supply. The great fear here, where the union was close to being an industrial union, was that semi-skilled new starters would join the TGWU or GMWU if the auxiliary contribution became comparatively expensive. The female contribution of 7d (including political levy) was roughly comparable with other unions, as was the apprentices' 5d. The proposal was to raise £90,000 a year by raising the skilled contribution to 1s 7d a week and £10,000 by raising the auxiliary contribution to 10d. Female section and apprentices were to be left alone. The political fund was reduced by now charging the first two weeks' contributions each year as the political fund – not one penny per week, irrespective of section of the union. This effectively raised the general funds of the union, particularly from that fifteen per cent of members who had contracted out of the political levy – they no longer got 4s 4d back: the maximum would be 3s 2d for a skilled man.

It would appear to modern analysts, used to bouts of considerable inflation, that the union's leadership should have raised contributions long before 1954, particularly if they were going to expand services and benefits *and* deliberately make a virtue of supporting strikes financially – especially by making retrospective payments to unofficial strikers. The 1954 rules revision conference did not make that criticism, although Jimmy Finnigan implied it. He pointed out how the pre-war contribution of 1s 3d came close to the pre-war contracting rate of 1s 6d an hour. By 1954, the rate was 3s 9½d and the contribution was still 1s 3d! The conference did raise other issues. First, several delegates would have preferred the more convenient sums at the branch treasurer's table of 1s 6d skilled, 1s 0d auxiliary and 6d for apprentices, females and junior auxiliaries. Foulkes was able to show that that happened to be actuarial nonsense; the only section of the union that really paid for the rest was the skilled section – and so it must go up to 1s 7d. If the auxiliary contribution rose to 1s, it would be so far ahead of the general workers' – particularly in supply – that the union was bound to lose members and income. More seriously, J. E. Gill, from the Darlington–Bishop Auckland area and the Darlington branch secretary, produced some noisy political points. He thought the contribution increase put all the burden on the ordinary member although he later voted for the increase. He had a critical but vivid image of the leadership's attitude to spending the union's money.

To my mind, over the past few years, our executive council have been prepared to spend all of our money. They put me in mind of a man who gets his wages at the end of the week and when he is going home he meets Tom, Dick and Harry and says to them: 'Come on, lads, have a drink with me,' all hale, well-met and hearty. He stands them a drink and spends all his wages. Then he goes home to his wife and six kids and places 30s on the table and says, 'I'm sorry, lass, but that's all I've got left, because I have met some pals and given them a drink'.

He wanted to know what was being done about the 'enormous' expenses of the full-time officials – on average, £500 a year. He thought £16,000 would be well saved by abolishing the policy conference. £23,000 could be saved by suspending the use of Esher. Who could justify £2,200 spent on a delegation to China?

Two delegates from East Anglia – H. Gascoyne from Norwich and Les Chittock from Ipswich – were also opposed to the rise in contributions. Gascoyne made the effective point that if arrears was the main problem, how was it going to improve by raising the contributions? Les Chittock agreed with this, and also had sympathy for the money stewards collecting the money, particularly in electricity supply where recruitment might be harmed.

One of the most effective communist delegates at conferences throughout the 1950s was West London's Sid Maitland. He congratulated the executive on not asking for a contribution increase before, due to their excellent administration. He was on more persuasive ground when he said how other unions applauded the college, the convalescent home, the annual conference; and he posed the question, knowing the answer – 'Are we to continue to give the British trade union movement the character of militant leadership which we have been given over this last number of years, or are we to degenerate? That is the issue.' The contribution rises were agreed, 45–5.

There was more opposition to some of the other proposals. First, there was some pleasure taken in the modernizing of branch financial returns. Each branch would send in on one form a fortnightly balance of income and expenditure that would be checked by head office with the use of £10,000 of new machinery. Every item of expenditure was to be authorized by the branch secretary and branch treasurer, and a copy sent to head office on the fortnightly statement. The head office would return a statement of account to the branch, read by the president to the branch and checked against the copies of the fortnightly statements retained in the branch. This allowed continual auditing to take place at head office, and obviated the need for branch auditors, who would be replaced by a spot-check of calling in twenty-five cards each quarter.

Slightly more controversial was the suggestion that the total amount paid to branch officers should be frozen by reducing their percentage 'take' of the contributions. Up to 1954, branch secretaries got seven-and-a-half per cent of the total contribution income and treasurers got three-and-three-quarters per cent. Assistant branch secretaries got a third of the branch secretary's percentage – two-and-a-half per cent. The executive proposed to reduce the percentage to secretaries to six per cent of the income from skilled members, seven per cent from the other sections. For treasurers, their percentage would fall to one per cent and three-and-a-half per cent according to section. This would save £13,000. Much more controversial, the leadership urged the abolition of the post of assistant branch secretary altogether, which, along with the abolition of branch auditors, would save £11,000.

This proposal produced genuine concern from otherwise staunch supporters of the executive. Frank Chapple led the opposition, particularly for branches with large memberships. His own, LSE, No. 10, was the largest in London with just over 1,000 members. He was concerned that branches might have a secretary who would often be involved in other Labour movement duties like local councillor and might occasionally be absent. He also did not believe that the reforms in branch accounting, including changes in the banking bureaucracy, would materially affect the need for assistant branch secretaries. He did not believe that the branch committee could help here – they were more likely, 'something in the fashion of the executive council,' to decide what ought to be done and get the branch officials (like the full-time officials) to implement the decisions. He knew the union ought to save money and recommended reducing the various delegation fees back to their 1952 levels. He was seconded by Ernie Hadley, not at that time a political friend, who gave a vivid picture of life in a busy branch room in the 1950s – and Sheffield Central, his branch, was the fourth largest in the country with approximately 1,400 members in 1954 (just behind Birmingham Midland with 1,640, Stretford with 1,667 and the largest, Liverpool Central, with 1,727 members).

Ernie Hadley spoke of the problems associated with taking £100 in one-and-a-half hours at the branch meeting.

There is a long line of members, including twenty-eight money stewards and that means the branch treasurer is absolutely unapproachable during the meeting, because you cannot stop his work; he is too busy ... The branch president or branch secretary, on the same night, may have twenty to thirty proposition forms to deal with. Room has to be found for the new branch entrants. Their history sheets have to be made out there and then and the contribution book and the cards also have to be made out. The secretary cannot conduct the meeting and also carry out his work ... The place you need good administration is in the branches, not head office.

Other speakers added the problems of ballots and arrears notices to support the retention of assistant branch secretaries. Sid Maitland toed the loyal line –

saying that branch committees should do more; Jack Hendy thought assistant branch secretaries should do it for nothing. Arthur Attwood said that excessive concentration on the entitlement of assistant branch secretaries to payment only highlighted the fact that shop-stewards got nothing – and they did a far more important job for the union. Such was the breadth of opposition, though, that, in the end, the executive allowed the rule to be amended to retain assistant branch secretaries, where required, for one more year and thereafter each case would be judged on its merits by the executive. That proposal was carried.

The 1954 rules revision conference was significant in that it raised questions for the first time publicly about the communists' administrative priorities; it showed that the union faced real problems once its historical surpluses had been raided nearly to extinction. It threw the first few beams of light on the leadership's lifestyle – the question of expenses, delegations and a sense of extravagance when a touch of austerity might have been more appropriate. Trade union members always hate contribution increases; it makes them wonder out loud – sometimes unkindly – about what the union ever does for them. The 1954 increases raised questions of that sort.

From this time on – from the end of 1954 – the union's internal affairs began to take precedence over its negotiating responsibilities. All trade unions – as living institutions – actually give much of their time and resources to internal considerations. These priorities – so very real to the participants – have generally been ignored by academic analysts of trade union affairs. For the union's leadership in the mid-1950s, the concentration of press 'attacks' and the emergence of coherent internal opposition began to take more of their time, more of their propaganda effort, more of the union's resources.

On the face of it, though, early 1955 was the high-water mark for the union's communist leadership. In terms of conquering the significant decision-making institutions in the union, their control was virtually total, although their influence in the wider movement was diminishing into isolation. There was no ETU representative on the General Council of the TUC, no sponsored ETU MP and, when Ernie Irwin retired, no national Labour Party executive member. The compensation, though, was that the three main offices in the Union were held by communists. Frank Foulkes had been re-elected unopposed in 1954. In April 1955, Frank Haxell beat Jock Byrne in comfort, 27,935–14,924, to replace Walter Stevens as general secretary. It was not a good year for Jock Byrne. In November, Bob McLennan beat him by an even larger margin – 28,779–13,426 – for Haxell's vacant assistant general secretary job.

At that time, the executive council was formally a lay body of working electricians. It was important to be on the executive council, but it was not the highest aspiration for a union activist. The pinnacle of achievement was rather to get a national officer's job, which was full-time. In 1954, it was decided to raise the number of national officers to five. Les Gregory had been first elected to the executive in December 1937. He sat on the executive continuously until getting elected to the newest national officer vacancy in 1954 by 22,312 votes to Bill Sullivan's 4,286. With the exception of Ernie Irwin, all the other national officers were communists – Gus Cole, Bill Benson and Bob McLennan. Third in that election was Kirkcaldy's Scottish standard bearer, George Scott, who got 3,198 votes. Scott had opposed the executive council with some vigour: he had often spoken at conference against the platform to some effect. This guaranteed his electoral defeats in national officer elections in 1952 although it has often been said that he was seduced into his later apparent role as a fellow-traveller while on a delegation to Poland at the end of 1951. Whatever the truth in that, in 1952 both Benson and McLennan beat him by around 22,000 votes on each occasion. He was no right-winger like the Scotsmen who grouped themselves round Jock Byrne. He had opposed Frank Murphy in the December 1949 executive elections at the same time as opposing Bill Blairford, then the communist-backed candidate. He received a derisory 432 votes against Blairford's 757 and the successful Frank Murphy's 1,370. There seemed little future for a left-wing non-communist Fifer in the ETU. He had some success in the Labour Party as a local councillor and contested Edinburgh North, unsuccessfully, in the 1955 General Election.

By 1955, though still maintainng his Labour Party membership position with some passion, he had thrown in his hand with Haxell. He was helped in this by the impending retirement of Ernie Irwin and Bob McLennan moving up to assistant general secretary. Irwin had become an historical curio – a leftover from the pre-war Jimmy Rowan Manchester-based era. He fulfilled one useful function for the union: he sat on the Labour Party's national executive committee and led the delegation at the conference from within the hall. (The senior communist officers of the union had to sit in the visitors' gallery, but, just like their complete willingness to deliberate on Labour Party matters within the political sub-committee of the executive, they also joined the delegation meetings at the Labour Party conference.) The communists were going to run Bert Batchelor for the other national officer vacancy at the end of 1955 – another communist. It was therefore imperative that a sym-pathetic left-wing Labour man should be chosen in order that at least one national officer could get in the Labour Party conference. George Scott got the nod. Bill Sullivan was his opponent and now it was *his* turn to get around 6,000 votes and George Scott's turn to get over 23,000 – an increase of 20,000 in just over a year. This is dramatic evidence indeed of the power of the communist's national electoral machine – however they actually achieved the result.

Again, in late 1954–5, the communist grip on the executive was total. In London, now with four executive councillors covering the capital and the home counties, all four were communists. Jim Humphrey was a particularly dedicated crony of Haxell's. Bert Batchelor was from a film studio background, a long-time source of left strength in the union. Tommy Vetterlein had an attractive personality that was as well known in his native East End as were his convinced communist views. These three all had around seven years' experience on the executive when they were joined in September 1954 by Jack Frazer, replacing Les Gregory on his 'elevation' to national officer. Frazer was already being groomed to replace Frank Foulkes as the communists' preference for president when Foulkes was due to go in the mid-1960s. Frazer was a good conference speaker, but his dedicated committee work as the secretary of the national advisory committee of communists in the ETU was his real power base in the union.

He was also canny. He loved fast cars; but he would apparently travel to meetings by bus or tube having left the shiny red sports car one stop away. The members would not have understood. He would be more willing to tell the story of how he was arguably the only electrician in history to have received a royal 'bollocking'. Frazer had been sunbathing on the roof of Buckingham Palace in the early 1950s when he should have been working on the Palace electrics. King George VI himself spotted Frazer reclining and took immediate steps to get him back to work! By mid-1955, Peter Snadden in the Midlands had been replaced by Sam Goldberg. Goldberg had been a Trotskyist critic of the executive in the early 1950s. Like George Scott, though, he too had mended his fences with Haxell. The rest of the executive were either straightforward communists or the most un-argumentative fellow-travellers. When Frank Murphy, the Scottish Executive Member, died on 26 January 1955, the only genuinely anti-Communist voice was stilled; and he had been ill for a long time in 1954. He came from mining stock in the village of Baillieston, and was a Lanarkshire county councillor, speaking there and inside the union with some authority on housing issues in particular. His concern over the possibility of the union's ballots being corrupted by rigging and his consequential support for secret postal ballots were ahead of their time.

The executive's most powerful intellect, Les Cannon, was returned, unopposed, for the period 1954–5. In fact, after winning his initial excutive election in December 1945 for the Merseyside and North Lancashire seat, Cannon was returned unopposed at every election afterwards. Les Cannon was a literate and well-read communist, something he inherited from his father. From 1945–51, he was invited by the executive to be their spokesman on important issues – peace, Eastern Europe, amalgamation, youth. Foulkes, Stevens and Haxell must have known how well the Communist Party leadership thought of Cannon. Harry Pollitt was a family friend. Willie Gallagher, MP for Fife, actually travelled to Czechoslovakia to be best man at Cannon's impulsive, romantic wedding to Olga in August 1949. Nevertheless, this impeccable contact with the centre of Communist influence probably worked against Cannon in the minds of his intellectual inferiors at Hayes Court. Steadily, out of sheer jealousy, or fear of his undoubted ambition to sit in their chairs one day, the leadership gradually dropped Cannon from his conference and committee responsibilities. Steadily, he lost the lucrative sub-committee work and union delegations that rendered academic a lay executive member's reliance on his pay packet. As one illustration of just how important this was to any executive councillor, it is useful to look at Les Cannon's employment record with the North-Western Electricity Board where he worked from 1 September 1946 to 6 October 1948. This period totalled 626 working days. Cannon had thirty-two days' holiday and turned up for work on only seventy-eight days of the remainder!

From 1 January 1948 to 6 October 1948 (when he was dismissed at last for unauthorized absence), he had only worked seven days that year! He had enjoyed 204 days' absence with permission and 312 without. All his absences were due to union business. Les Cannon was not by any means unique in this. From the time of *his* election to the executive in 1954, Jack Frazer apparently never worked at the trade; he supplemented his income from delegations by filling in as a temporary local official in Middlesbrough, Coventry, Leicester, Southampton and London. Often local area elections took months to organize – from nomination through to a possible second ballot. This gave weeks of lucrative employment to favoured executive councillors. Cannon could feel it slipping away; by 1951, he was arguing with other members of the national advisory committee of communists within the ETU over nominations for union positions. He became 'unreliable' and irritating to the union's leadership in early 1952. He was now working for a living again, this time for English Electric in Liverpool. In February 1952, two shop-stewards and eleven other trade unionists were made redundant. Cannon was one of the stewards. Just before Christmas, he had been negotiating with the employers to sustain the bonus earnings of women coil-winders. He was adamant that the company's retiming of the women's jobs should allow them to improve their bonus earnings, not further depress them. As soon as he and the others were made redundant, 107 members, soon to rise to 233, came out on strike in protest at this victimization. A resumption of work was achieved while the union, represented by Frank Foulkes and Frank Haxell, tried to persuade the factory management to reconsider the 'redundancies'. It was unheard of for the union's president and assistant general secretary to intervene in this way; the result of their deliberations was pretty surprising too. They failed to convince the EEF to describe the dispute as victimization, which could be pursued through the procedure, rather than 'redundancy', which could not – that issue was down to managerial prerogative. Consequently, the same two national officials held a mass meeting of the strikers to tell them it was going to be difficult. On 3

March, Foulkes told the erstwhile strikers that it was not in their interests to strike anymore: 181 were present. They voted 129–29 to reopen the strike, but the executive backed Foulkes and Haxell, refused to order a new strike, paid victimization benefit to the nine ETU men concerned and left Les Cannon in the lurch. He got a job soon after at a Merseyside power station, but never forgave the executive for their abandonment of him and the others at English Electric. Nevertheless, he remained an executive member until a fateful change of job in 1954.

Early in 1954, John Vickers, the union's education officer at Esher, had established with the executive council that he needed an assistant to help with the growing number of courses the union planned. This job, along with every other ETU job of substance, was discussed at the national advisory committee. This committee, duplicated at the local level, was a committee of prominent ETU communists who were usually joined by Communist Party functionaries. Their existence, and the leading communists' flat denial of their existence, was to become an issue some years later.

In early 1954, Les Cannon was a member of the national advisory committee. John Vickers's assistant, on Haxell's insistence, was to be the colourless factotum, Jim Humphrey. Haxell understood the political importance of Esher, and he wanted his man there. Cannon rang John Vickers and told him the bad news. Vickers went to Walter Stevens and told him that he had heard on the grapevine that Humphrey was likely to be his assistant. If that was so, Vickers would resign. A startled Stevens registered Vickers's objections; no one made the connection at the next national advisory committee when Cannon volunteered to help everyone out of a hole by doing the job himself. It meant leaving the executive, and he had to promise not to run for election from the college. Significantly, he was no longer an official of the union – he was a member of staff appointed by the general secretary. This decision was endorsed on 15 August by the executive, and the September minutes noted Les Cannon's 'consistent and conscientious' service on the executive and sent him 'warm wishes for his happiness and success' at Esher. More mature reflection would have made many of those who endorsed such sentiments wish Les Cannon had stayed in the comparative obscurity of Liverpool. His presence at Esher from September 1954 to April 1957 was to give him an unrivalled network of local ETU activists when the time came.

From 1954–9, the union's affairs were to be dominated by internal problems, culminating in the crisis surrounding the general secretary's election in 1959. Back in the real world, though, negoiations went on. After the excitement of the 1954 guerrilla strikes which finished with $2\frac{1}{2}$d settlement, it is not surprising that contracting negotiations in the late 1950s did not degenerate into the sort of national disputes that had dominated 1952–4 inclusive.

In 1955, the acrimony was gone and the employers paid an extra 3d an hour from 15 March. Once again, the union recognized that the *rate* was comparable with others, but the *earnings* were not. In 1938, they had been thirteenth in the earnings league; by 1947, they had fallen to thirty-sixth. By 1954, they were fifty-first.

The NFEA and Mr Penwill had not lost their feeling for the intellectual fight, however. How was it that the union always emphasized *earnings* in their contracting negotiations and yet, in engineering, where electricians' rates were also above others and in order to resist piece-work, the *rate* had a holy significance. In engineering, it appeared, the union always argued on the sancity of the *rate*, not earnings. If the same respect for the rate existed in contracting negotiations, the industry's London rate was fifth in the league table and the provincial rate still a comparatively high sixteenth!

By March 1956, in an era of no unemployment in the industry, a further 4d was granted without much fuss: London and Bristol mates were to get eighty per cent of the rate and Mersey and provincial mates seventy-five per cent. Country allowance was up to 8s and abnormal conditions money to 2s per day. However, several very real problems continued to be incapable of solution. There was no PBR scheme capable of being designed for the industry. 'Anomalies' with other building workers were rife. In Birmingham in 1956, although the rates for electricians were higher than bricklayers or carpenters, electricians' average hourly earnings fell short of the other crafts by over 6d an hour. All the men earning 'merit pay' in the town were in reality receiving a bogus bonus. Haxell suggested to the employers in November 1955 that individual companies or area JICs could pay site or company bonuses, and the NJIC itself should look at big national sites like Windscale or Television House in Kingsway where there was always resentment at other craftsmen's earnings potential.

Penwill was fundamentally opposed to any of this. The NJIC must decide rates for the whole country as it had done since 1919.

Electricians' dissatisfaction arose, not from the operation of their own agreement but because of the abuse of other industrial agreements by some of those who were party to them. For the contracting industry to alter its fundamental principles because a section of the building industry broke its own laws was very unsound and not a foundation upon which to base industrial agreements.

It was all very well for Mr Penwill to take this principled stand, but anecdotal evidence deployed by Haxell painted a picture of employers with an abundance of work being forced to bribe people to come and work for them. Still Penwill was not convinced. He feared that introducing job and company rates would only lead to electricians – with the union's encouragement – leaving one job at the drop of a hat in order to turn up at a newly opening site paying some fabulous bonus or another. By the end of 1956, the union was introducing a new strand of powerful argument into contracting negotiations. Not only were other building craftsmen and even labourers getting more than electricians, but the knack had spread to engineering maintenance workers as well. Imagine the frustration of contracting electricians doing a maintenance contract or installation in a factory. Male adult workers in vehicle manufacture in April 1956 were getting 74.7d an hour, compared to electricians 56.7d. The average hourly rate for all adult males in engineering and shipbuilding was 61.5d.

Still the NFEA would not relent beyond the customary 'fodder' adjustment. On 3 April 1957, the London rate rose 2½d an hour to 5s an hour. The provincial rate rose similarly to 4s 7d an hour. However, the NFEA would not countenance any reaction on the basis of overpaid labourers elsewhere. They were unskilled, but working under supervision on building sites, they were productive. This could be contrasted with the position of the electrician's mate, who, the NFEA implied, was what his title described – an unproductive electrician's private assistant working under no supervision save that of his craftsman. Engineering earnings may well have been high in April 1956; but look at them in October, when short-time working, redundancy and insecurity did not compare well with contracting. Incidentally, Penwill argued forcefully, with his usual lack of specific instances, what about the moonlighting, the evening work, the spare-time electrician? What was the union doing about that? They were not anxious to concede a sick-pay scheme either. As the worker was only actually at work for twenty-five per cent of the week, why should his employer feel obliged to support his whole outgoings while he was sick?

The union had other problems in negotiations. Overtime was routinely denounced; Eric Hammond regretfully told the 1956 conference that his members working for Malcolm & Allen's at Tilbury Power Station were loath to give up the overtime today in return for some promise of higher rates and shorter hours tomorrow.

At the 1957 policy conference, held at Folkestone, Dick Allum, from Reading, criticized the union's performance in contracting. On most sites, the conditions were disgusting. There were no washing facilities, toilets, lock-ups or canteens. There was no sick-pay. Travelling time allowances and fares were useless; country money way below other trades. Two weeks' holiday pay was still not being paid. They had to pay for tools and work in ghastly conditions for a miserly two shillings extra a *day*! They had just accepted a four-and-a-half per cent wage increase without a whimper. In engineering, however, they were denouncing the other unions for selling out the great strike in return for six-and-a-half per cent in that industry! Hours of work were still nowhere near the forty-hour ideal. Bill Sullivan seconded this powerful attack on the union's great negotiators and directly blamed the executive council. Washing was still in a bucket and the paper towels now provided by Rashleigh Phipps were an unusual innovation. The following painful barb was wholly excluded from the printed summary of the conference proceedings and no wonder. Bill Sullivan said:

Brothers, this is the contracting industry, the one industry in which we have sole negotiating rights. How many times have you heard it said that in this industry, or that industry, if only we had sole negotiating rights, we would do this or that? Why, you heard our general president, only yesterday morning, thundering our defiance to the engineering employers about wage freezes, increases with strings, etc. It is a pity that when the cry came from the contracting shop-stewards, representing a most militant section of the organization, for a battle on wages, for a rejection of wage freezes, for no strings, our sole negotiating body was apparently in silent solitude, immune from the cry.

There were genuine problems in the industry. London South-West's delegate, Pat O'Neil, emphasized the unique problems in contracting of organizing each site afresh and the amount of time wasted on trivial, short disputes to get small matters put right. The employers knew full well of the union's difficulties in organizing the industry. T. Hall of Bexleyheath queried the union's activists' depth of commitment. He described the embarrassment of the London contracting shop-stewards' conference, over 100 strong, deciding to picket the NFEA headquarters and only thirty stewards actually turned up! Len Tripp from Fulham was still sceptical of the gap between rhetoric and performance. 'I was told at Esher last year ... that we live in an era of jungle economics. If that is so, then it is time we employed some jungle methods in our wage fights, and not guerrilla tactics, which are called off at the point of complete victory for a mere $2\frac{1}{2}$d an hour. ... It has been said we are a power in the land. Unfortunately, this is only true in a technical sense. If we were a power in a trade union sense, this would reflect itself in our wages today.' In 1958 an industrial disputes tribunal rejected the union's appeal that Clause 8 – the individual merit pay clause – should be broadened to allow more flexibility payments.

By 1959, a crisis was looming once again. The talks broke down with the NFEA once again point-blank refusing, on 14 May, to consider any increase at all on the basis of the claim submitted at the end of 1958. Overtime bans were promised to be followed by an all-out strike at the end of June 1959. The rhetoric soared at the policy conference: on 19 June, just afterwards, the claim was settled for 1d an hour in London and $1\frac{1}{2}$d in the provinces. The London rate stood at 5s $3\frac{1}{2}$d, the provincial rate at 4s 11d.

A dispute at the end of the 1950s highlighted everything that was frustrating, and unresolved, about the contracting payment system. One of the biggest jobs of the decade was the Shell Mex site on the South Bank of the Thames.

The site started life with the discovery of an enormous unexploded bomb. After that had been dealt with, several groups of electricians began work. As the project progressed, electricians directly employed by the main contractor, Sir Robert McAlpine & Co, were in receipt of two extra payments above the NFEA rates. They were paid an extra £2 10s od a week for skilled men and £2 5s od for mates. In addition, they were paid a 'radius allowance' of 5¾d per mile from the employment exchange nearest the electrician's home address. These payments were made simply to approach the bonuses being paid to other craftsmen which ranged from £2 15s od to £15 a week in the case of steel erectors.

Ninety-nine electricians arrived in March, working for the sub-contractors F. H. Wheeler & Sons. When they heard about everyone else's bonuses – particularly the McAlpine electricians' payments – they made a claim to the company for a 'special site' allowance of 5s a day on 26 March. The company were apparently sympathetic, but referred the claim to the NFEA. Time dragged by. In September the employers' representatives on the area DJIC did not judge the site 'special' in any way. On 5 October, a full meeting of NJIC was held. The union sustained its claim for the average bonus of craftsmen on the site, given the payments being made there to one and all – including McAlpine's directly employed electricians. The NFEA representatives thought that as only seventeen per cent of building workers were paid piece-work and bonuses, it was not sensible for contracting to start to introduce bonuses on a general basis. Apart from its size, there was nothing 'special' about the Shell site, either. There were sixty other buildings under construction in London that might feel they operated in similar circumstances and might therefore make similar claims. They recognized that the industry did, rarely, make exceptional payments due to abnormal conditions or lack of amenities or the isolation of a site – but never because some builder was paying someone else a bonus. The employers expressed sympathy about the 'human' problems faced by ETU members in these circumstances, but there was nothing the NFEA could do. All electrical labour employed by F. H. Wheeler stopped work on the site on 21 October 1959.

This empty-handed approach of Mr Penwill was further accentuated by his not attempting to organize any meetings to resolve the problem, beyond a formal notification to the Ministry of Labour. It was this aspect of the problem that annoyed McAlpine. They wrote to the ministry to complain. 'The delay in settling this dispute is having repercussions which are rapidly gathering momentum in that tomorrow we shall be forced to dismiss no less than 162 workmen, comprising joiners, scaffolders, steel fixers and labourers because we are running short of work for them, directly attributable to the stoppage of work by the electricians.' By mid-November, Mr F. T. Claro at the ministry was successful in fixing up further talks which took place on 23 November.

The employers refused to make any interim payment; the union refused to go to arbitration. The ministry set up a committee of investigation. They deliberated in mid-January 1960 and found themselves unable to recommend any payment until the national agreement was altered. They therefore thought the men should return to work, and that the NJIC should negotiate a fixed sum for operation on those sites where other people were working piece-work or bonus systems; this should not vary according to the level of other people's bonuses etc. It should not be so high as to produce problems on sites where no extra payments would be achievable. This fixed bonus would also help employers who were tendering for fixed-price contracts.

The men went back to work on 10 February. The NFEA the next day accepted this idea of a fixed bonus but made an unsatisfactory offer: consequently the union threatened a national overtime ban and selective strikes. Negotiations quickly resumed with a novelty. The NJIC was chaired by a Ministry of Labour-appointed QC, Mr G. G. Honeyman. Having knocked heads together, Mr Honeyman put forward the figure of 4s a day bonus to be paid where other trades operated bonus or productivity schemes. Still paranoid about the payments spreading throughout the industry, the NFEA eventually agreed to a 5s payment to 'operatives employed on the initial construction of buildings reasonably comparable with the Shell building on the South Bank, London, and the petrochemical buildings at Urmston, Manchester.' The agreement was for six months only, and any extension to the sites covered was to be by agreement between the chief officers of the ETU and NFEA.

In electricity supply, the same period of 1954–9 saw the same unspectacular but conventional rise in wages, once more dependent on cost of living claims, despite Foulkes's oft-repeated statement that a nationalized industry should endeavour to improve the workers' standard of living, not just occasionally raise wages in a catching-up exercise with prices. Nevertheless, increases of 3d an hour were paid in January 1955, 4d an hour in January 1956, and from 1 March 1957, a further 2½d. Supply workers at this time were concerned about wages and only slightly mollified by the knowledge of their better conditions. They were already irritated, however, by the better holidays, sick-pay and allowances enjoyed by staff workers in the industry, the refusal to pay overheard linesmen working on lower voltages the skilled rate, and, not for the last time, the differential meal allowances paid to other supply workers. Jim Smith, LSE No. 5's branch secretary and later area president in London, was interested in this issue and also in the need to retain the inspection of installations by area boards in the hands of their own inspectorate. By the end of the decade, the industry was storing up problems for itself as the genuine rises in productivity were based on improved efficiency of investment and not workpeople. The industry was constantly pressurized by the Treasury to hold down wages in supply, where increases were quoted in every other industry;

to buy peace, the supply authorities granted an 8s 3d 'productivity' allowance in 1958 and followed that up in 1959, to become operative in 1960, with a reduction in the working week to forty-two hours. This had the effect of increasing overtime earnings for everyone, but did little to head off the major demands of skilled people in the industry to improve the differentials between them and others. This problem of rewarding skilled people and improving productivity by dealing with overtime was to dominate the following decade. At the end of 1959, Foulkes still led negotiations which comparatively benefited the general workers more than his own skilled élite. It was to be left to others to reconcile these interests by confronting the problem.

Throughout the late 1950s, the union's collective bargaining effort spread into new industries, reflecting newly important industries like television – both in the studios of the BBC and the Independent Television companies and in servicing the brand-new televisions that started to be rented by working-class homes in large numbers. Early in 1958, TV engineers working for Rentaset in Wales were being paid £13 a week and the Scottish Co-op were paying £12 10s 0d. Television manufacture and other consumer industries provided the union with a potentially huge field of new recruitment. In these industries, the union's determination to recruit women electrical workers seemed most promising, particularly as they comprised twenty-eight per cent of the total electrical engineering workforce.

From November 1954, there was a specific organizing campaign, with a personalized letter sent by Foulkes to each female member urging their help in recruitment. Each area was to identify target factories and specific leaflets and campaign material produced for each target area. In the first six months, 2,836 members were enrolled. By the end of 1955, 13,424 members were women assembly workers, 3,300 up on 1954's figure. London alone had added 1,400 with healthy rises in Liverpool, Teesside and Manchester. However, by late 1959, the campaign had run into the sand, and the female membership had fallen back to just below 13,000. Some notable factories were organized in this period. The Ekco factory in Southend raised its membership to over 450 in 1955. The Pye, Lowestoft, factory was organized at last. They had opened two subsidiary companies in the area called TV Manufacturing and Pye Marine in 1951. By September 1954, the union had recruited only eighty of the 1,400 employees spread over the two factories. In mid-March 1955, the women at TV Manufacturing heard that the company were paying charge-hands and foremen production bonuses of between £5–£50: when they suggested something similar should be advanced to the people who actually made the sets, the management sent them away saying that what they paid charge-hands and foremen was nothing to do with the union. On 17 March, and for three days following, there were demonstrations round the factory, leading to the suspension of six ring-leaders and strike action by 375 women at the factory one hour before finishing time. The women were on strike for five weeks during which time the union recruited 475 members between the two Lowestoft factories and won negotiating rights and recognition from the company in April 1955. Over 500 new members were recruited at the EMI factory in Hayes in Middlesex in the same period, and pitifully low levels of organization at STC factories at Foots Cray and Basildon started to improve. What is difficult to judge today is the effectiveness of some of the recruitment techniques deployed by male full-time officials. Cec Bibby, the Liverpool area official, organized the Mullard factory at Southport in the summer of 1955. His report on the organizing campaign at least showed initiative.

We have been present at the factory gates during the midday meal break playing records of a type which are attractive to the teenage girls employed in this establishment. In between records of Johnnie Ray and various jazz experts, we have exhorted the girls to join the ETU. It is not possible at this stage to say how successful those tactics have been, but there can be no doubt that the ETU has been well advertised at this factory.

Not a lot about the evils of international capitalism in that message.

The expansion of the electrical engineering industries throughout the 1950's produced a new family of problems for the union associated with automation and productivity-based payment systems that relied on different types of work-measurement techniques. The union faced this problem with some equivocation, some good sense and much political rhetoric. Typical was Bob McLennan's considered response at a conference organized in the summer of 1955 by the Institution of Production Engineers. He had attended the whole conference, including an exhibition of electronic devices and he said he could not 'fail to be struck by the enthusiasm of the engineers for the new technical devices.' However, he was of course concerned about the human problems associated with automation. 'The aim of production in our present form of society is profit for private employers. If commodities cannot provide profits then their production ceases.' The aim of automation in the abstract was to 'increase productivity and total overall production'. Such success would reduce labour unit costs. Employers must not reduce wages or sack workers. They must keep up wages and increase leisure hours for their employees. He was worried that increased production meant over-production, leading to collapsing prices and therefore lower wages and unemployment. He then set out the union's policy on the subject in a handful of paragraphs that demonstrated, behind the natural concern about change, the union's understanding that technical innovation in electronics was to be more of a boom than a hindrance to the union in the years to come.

My union has a very great interest in this question. Our members as skilled maintenance workers in industry will be called upon to solve new intricate problems in order to maintain in good working order those new machines, whose control is mainly done by electronic devices and equipment. Also, more maintenance workers will be required. At the same time, we have many members working as production workers whose jobs will be in jeopardy.

We therefore consider that there should be a national economic plan for the country, integrating and controlling developments in the field of automation; that full responsibility must be borne by automated industries, factories, works and offices for the full maintenance at previous wage levels of those workers who cannot be absorbed; and for the safeguarding of the existing rights of those transferred to other jobs due to the new techniques.

Those managements seeking the advantages of automated processes shall accept the responsibility for solving problems of labour displacement and the retraining of existing employees ... national wage agreements, which take time to adapt themselves to the new developments in particular factories or industries, should not be used to hold wages at a minimum, but local freedom should be exercised to negotiate higher returns to labour where automation is introduced. The introduction of automation ... should also result in the shorter working week.

These basic principles, minus perhaps the East European type of faith in a 'national plan', were to be the core of the union's policy towards the increased use of automated production control techniques for the next thirty-five years. McLennan knew that new technology would augment the comparative import-ance of the maintenance electrician, and he gave a prophetic word of warning that national agreements must not stand in the way of higher earnings for specific groups of highly skilled workers associated with looking after the new machinery. New technology must benefit the workers through shorter hours and higher wages. Displaced workers had to be retrained in mid-life career. With these protective policies for the workers concerned, there was no sugges-tion that technology could be stopped.

The union had an uncomfortable time putting these policies into practice. A highly significant dispute for all trade unions occurred in July 1956 at the Standard Motor Company, a part of the new British Motor Corporation (BMC). The important part about this dispute was that a 'rationalized' British motor industry was trying to invest rapidly in order to compete in car markets that were expanding world-wide. It had announced 6,000 redundancies with one week's pay in lieu of notice. The managing director of the company had announced: 'We are not installing £4 million worth of equipment in order to employ the same number of men. We can't carry people for fun.' This sensitive statement was made in an era when consultation with the unions was unheard of, let alone negotiating severance payments. There was no national minimum redundancy payment guaranteed by law. Four hundred and two ETU members came out throughout the BMC at the end of July (although the majority of maintenance men at Austin's at Longbridge stayed in). Eventually, in mid-August, the unions won a modest redundancy payment and a negotiating procedure to deal with the issue at local level in any future difficulty. The involvement of shop-stewards in such matters was a crucial change and reflected the union's awareness that shop-stewards had effectively become the central figures in the union's real task of collective bargaining. There was great uneasiness, however, expressed at the 1956 conference. It was all very well to have a 'no sackings' policy in the face of technology-based redundancy: the final settlement at the Standard Motor Company did not save the jobs involved, even if it ameliorated, slightly, the effects of the abrupt dismissals and granted welcome negotiating rights to a newly relevant shop-steward organization. This quandary would confront many trade unionists in the future. Certainly the communists had no clear view on how to prevent it either.

If the negotiating of wider issues like redundancy was an increasing indicator of the relevance of workplace organization, so were the increasing number of disputes that arose locally, were led locally and settled locally. Here the union's policy of retrospective endorsement of strikes (except Les Cannon's at English Electric) recognized the reality of growing self-confidence, an end to deference, and sheer trade union strength represented by the shop-stewards, particularly in manufacturing.

Throughout the late 1950s, the union was involved in dozens of such strikes every year. One factory in Hemel Hempstead provides a good illustration of this trend. Hemel Hempstead was a new town beyond the northern fringe of London, near to Watford. A company called Rotax (part of Joseph Lucas), had a successful engineering works there, making various components for the motor car and aerospace industries. In March 1955, 240 members were on strike for three days in support of a sacked AEU setter operator who had refused to operate two separate machines. In January 1956, they were on strike for eight days in support of the reinstatement of allegedy redundant AEU shop-stewards at the company's Beaconsfield works. In November 1957, the shop-stewards in the works engineering department wanted to discuss the bonus-rate fixer's report, the revision of base rates, merit awards and changes in work practices in the boilerhouse. The management delayed meetings, and a sit-down stoppage produced the desired meeting. However, the superintendant told the stewards to raise the individual issues with their individual foremen first. A sit-down strike was recommended in the works engineering department and a one-hour stoppage took place across the whole factory in support. In May 1958, there was a twelve-day strike by twenty-nine skilled members against the company's 'arbitrary' decision to let certain work be done by auxiliary members. Thirty-two members in the test department were on strike for three weeks in October 1958. Earnings in the test department were linked to the average earnings in the assembly shop. However, earnings were falling in the assembly area, and the test department resented the fall in their linked bonus from 120 per cent on the base rate to eighty-five per cent on the rate. They refused to use procedure – works conferences and local conferences under the enginering procedure – because the delay only helped management to further put off reviewing the test department's bonus scheme – although going to local conferences *was* the eventual solution adopted.

In February 1959, three ETU members who were inspectors were on strike for a week, also wanting a revision of their bonus scheme and also eventually settling for using the negotiating procedures. In early 1960, 109 ETU members in the assembly stores also went on strike after eighteen months' frustration at renegotiating *their* bonus scheme. So much for one typical engineering works in the late 1950s.

The union was also involved in strikes where their own negotiating position was in question. They would often support closed-shop strikes. They drew considerable attention to themselves in the spring of 1955 in a short strike that shut down the London national newspapers in pursuit of recognition for the AEU and ETU to negotiate outside the precedents set each year by the Print Unions Federation, to which the skilled maintenance unions did not belong. Frank Foulkes told the Ministry of Labour, when the union reluctantly agreed to refer the issue to a court of inquiry, that following along behind the Print Unions' negotiations 'ignored the special claims of different categories of workpeople in the industry. It precluded from consideration any claim for additional payments based upon a higher technical requirement, additional skill and responsibility which were consequent upon the introduction of new methods of production and the adoption of new processes and techniques.' That dispute provided high-profile evidence of the 'fighting union'; so did another dispute in 1958, at British Overseas Airways Corporation (BOAC) at London Airport. A wage claim was submitted on 3 June, but not even replied to until 17 September. The offer was rejected and talks resumed. They got nowhere, and an overtime ban was imposed by the maintenance engineering workers. Twenty-seven men were ordered to work overtime and the rest of the workforce went on strike in protest at their impending dimissal. This was Sid Maitland's finest hour as the chairman of the shop-stewards' committee and the London Airport local engineering 'panel' (negotiating body). The Jack committee of inquiry report hinted darkly that Sid Maitland and the shop-stewards were running the dispute on behalf of communist ideas and con-demned the national officer, George Scott, for not disciplining the stewards who were leading a strike, out of procedure, before anyone had been sacked. Needless to say, both got a hero's welcome some months later at the 1959 policy conference.

It is often said, particularly with the rosy afterglow of nostalgia, that in those days the union was not only courageous but effective – effective because it was a 'fighting union'. This is difficult to measure comprehensively, although there was nothing particularly effective in terms of earnings about the union's performance in contracting or supply. Evidence is hard to come by, but here is one interesting, little-quoted source of information regarding the union's standing at the end of the 1950s. Hugh Clegg, early in his career as an academic analyst of industrial relations, wrote a book, with A. J. Killick and Rex Adams, on *Trade Union Officers*, published in March 1961. Most of the research for this study of trade union officials was done in the late 1950s. The research, at one stage, questioned seventy-two personnel managers from a number of large private multi-plant companies. Four unions were mentioned often enough to be included in the analysis – the TGWU, the GMWU, the AEU and the ETU. Forty-one personnel officers dealt with sufficient unions to make a comparison of 'all-round competence' of the officials. The ETU officials were chosen by the personnel officers as the most competent they dealt with in only four replies out of forty-one possibles. Twenty-two out of the forty-one placed them last on this subjective 'competence' measure. Clegg goes on to say:

There is no doubt about one reason for the poor score of the electricians, for several respondents added comments to their questionnaire to explain that the union would have stood higher had it not been for its political affiliations and their industrial consequences. One quotation will illustrate the point.

'The fifth choice, namely the ETU, would on competence alone be head and shoulders above any. The local officer is a most able man in every respect, but like his colleagues in this union is a communist and a troublemaker. His ability and intelligence, however, are far more than average.'

This somewhat sketchy analysis remains tantalising and inconclusive. If the above quotation is representative, then the leadership's delight that they frightened employers appears justified. They *were* a 'fighting union'. Whether this produced results for the members of the union remains a moot point. Would personnel officers like the above feel predisposed to concede points to the electricians, sympathize with their pleas for different, better treatment despite their lack of numbers, recommend to colleagues in an unorganized or green-field site to recognize the union? Probably not.

More direct, immediate implications for the union were to follow on out of the crisis in the engineering and shipbuilding industries in the spring of 1957.

The CSEU justified a late-1956 claim on the basis of the industry's workers deserving a higher standard of living, particularly given the profits earned by the industry (with the exception of the vehicle sector). Minimum time rates were still vital to large numbers of engineering workers; and they were lagging behind the cost of living. The skilled minimum time rate had risen by sixty-five per cent between 1946–56. However, the cost of living index overall had risen by seventy per cent and the food prices index by one hundred per cent.

On 29 November, the EEF point-blank refused any increase whatsoever. Meetings in January and February 1957 produced no movement from the employers;. On 23 March, all engineering works affiliated to the EEF in marine districts came out on strike. On 30 March, the strike was extended nation-wide. The parallel claim in shipbuilding finally broke down on 5 March, and the strike started in shipyards on 16 March. On 25 March, the shipbuilders offered 8s 6d a week to skilled workers and pro-rata amounts to other grades, and the EEF offered 6s 0d to skilled engineering workers the next day. On 27 March, the largest union involved, the AEU agreed, on the casting vote of president Bill Carron, to go back to work pending a government court of inquiry into the dispute. This view narrowly prevailed at the CSEU's meeting: the AEU were supported by the GMWU, the Woodworkers and Shipwrights. The ETU opposed the settlement and were joined by a newly radicalized TGWU. The previous year, the election of Frank Cousins as the TGWU general secretary had been heralded by Frank Foulkes with the phrase 'a new light is shining in the TGWU'. Foulkes was certain the court of inquiry was designed to stop the strike and not to give engineering workers justice. The members returned to work on 4 April 1957. The court of inquiry made hopeful noises about the industry adopting a national joint council, arbitration methods and a national wages policy board. All that had to wait. In the meanwhile, the skilled time rate rose by 11s, intermediate grades got 9s and unskilled workers 9s. Foulkes's criticism of this settlement was merely going through the motions. The development of plant bargaining meant that many skilled maintenance workers would use the six-and-a-half per cent increase in the minimum time rates as their starting point for local talks.

The real significance of the 1957 engineering and shipbuilding dispute lay elsewhere for the ETU. It dealt a shattering blow to the union's finances and, furthermore, responding to the crisis produced solutions which led directly to the end of communist control of the ETU.

The executive council met on 13/14 April 1957. The decisions taken at that meeting were further explained to the private session of the union's policy conference at Folkestone in early June.

Haxell gave a review of the union's financial policy since the war. In 1946, the union's leadership expected full employment and recruitment to allow the union to add £71,500 to reserve every year until by 1949 there would be around £1 million in reserve. Sixty per cent of their income went on administration, so the union could, if it avoided major catastrophe, clearly afford the highly desirable new benefits of education and convalescence. In summary, Haxell repeated in 1957 the arguments that had justified the 1954 increases in contributions. The union had not recruited at the rate it expected (10,000 per annum). The membership at the end of 1956 was still only 228,158, and the arrears problem remained acute. The contributions had gone up in 1954 to

1s 7d for skilled men. The administrative savings had produced £49,372 in 1955–6 and the rising income produced surpluses of £73,000 to go into reserve over the same two years. Steady progress. However, Haxell said, 'We knew we were living on a close margin. We knew that if a major dispute took place, we would need to take special steps ... nobody should be surprised to hear that as a result of a major dispute, special measures have in fact been taken.'

The position at the start of 1957 was that the total worth of the union was £572,405 (£204,586 in liquid assets, £367,819 in fixed assets). At the outbreak of the engineering/shipbuilding strikes, liquid assets only amounted to £148,945, with fixed assets of £417,819. The cost of the fortnight's strike was £187,000, more than enough not only to plunge the union into a current account deficit but also to wipe out its assets. The executive on 13 April had been confronted with a range of unpalatable options. Should they have sold investments? They had originally cost £141,438 but were only worth £107,684. Should they borrow the necessary £500,000 to keep the union going? At six per cent bank rate? Should they cut or suspend benefits like unemployment, accident or dispute? No. They decided to cut what Haxell called the 'fringe' benefits – convalescence and education, the union's magazine and the youth conferences. The youth conferences had never done what was expected of them back in 1948; their suspension, never to reappear, was mourned by few. The union's magazine, *Electron*, was reduced in size by a half. The convalescence facility would be suspended, as would the union's college. The mothballing of Rustington and Esher would save £50,000 per year.

These instant economies saved the union from taking out an expensive loan or having to sell investments. The rebuilding of the finances was to be achieved at a rules revision conference held at the end of November 1957 at the Agricultural Hall in Knightsbridge in London. The conference voted, 36–13, to raise the contributions for skilled members from 1s 7d to 2s 3d; for auxiliary members from 10d to 1s 2d and for apprentices, junior auxiliaries and females to 7d from 4d or 5d; it was expected to produce £810,000 per year.

The general fund of the union could be built up over five years to £600,000, with the adoption of further reforms on top of the huge increase in contributions. First, they wanted to build up special funds for dispute benefit and unemployment benefit by allocating extra sums – for disputes, by allocating £100,000 per year for five years (£44,000 per annum *more* than the average over the previous eleven years), so that in five years they should be able to achieve a dispute fund of £200,000 whilst still maintaining average levels of strike pay while they did it. The same would be done to raise an unemployment benefit fund. They proposed to reopen the convalescent and education facilities as soon as possible, but not in their former state (only eleven courses for shop-stewards were to be run in 1958). Funeral benefits were to rise to £20 for skilled and £10 for auxiliary members; unemployment benefit was to be a minimum of £1 10s od and accident benefit £2. There was to be no unemployment benefit for female section members; if they wanted it, they would have to join the auxiliary section.

The conference would not link the contribution to the contracting rate, believing that the non-contracting sections of membership would resent it. They finalized strike pay at 12s a day. The executive in future would not be bound to allocate money to different funds on a percentage basis, but on the basis of need. Branch officials' payments were altered: secretaries got six per cent, irrespective of which section the contributions were paid into. Treasurers, on a similar basis were to get four per cent and money stewards five per cent.

In a move that infuriated Scottish delegates Jimmy Duggan and Jock Reynolds, the executive put in front of the conference several other rule changes that had not been discussed in the branches and, as they were executive council propositions, could not under rule be amended. First, they altered the basis of area committees. The trade sub-committees had never really worked properly; instead, every branch was to have one delegate to the area committee. That committee would set up industrial sub-committees from amongst its number and co-opt people when a negotiating body, to which the area committee sent delegates, was short of sufficient expertise on the committee. The increase in travelling expenses would be countered by the savings in not having elections anymore, although the area president would be elected as in the past. The new rule would provide seven area committees of around twenty-five to thirty delegates with an enormous area committee in London of 127! Further savings would accrue by reducing executive meetings from twelve to eight a year.

The conference turned its attention to the arrears problem. The union had grown: it had grown faster than virtually all other TUC unions. It had recruited 142,000 members in the five years from 1952–6 inclusive. But it had lost 112,000 members for a net gain of only 30,000 in six years (remembering always Stevens's ambition to recruit at least 10,000 members net per year). The arrears amounted to 9s 2d per member! The collection of contributions was in chaos. A single factory might have had three or four money stewards trying to collect contributions from members who belonged to three or four different branches. Sid Maitland emphasized this point when he explained that the thousand or so members at London airport belonged to thirty-four separate branches.

The suggestion Haxell favoured was to set up an appointed bureaucrat, paid somewhere between a research officer and an area official (£600–£1,000), called an area treasurer (or debt collector, as one delegate shouted out from the hall). This suggestion was completely novel and wholly unexpected. Albert Mearns, the Bolton delegate, was so confused he refused to vote. 'I want to say that I do not agree with any of it. I cannot make my mind up on this issue either way. It is not so much that I am neutral, but I just did not bother to vote on something that nobody seems to understand.' The proposal to allow the executive to institute area treasurers to attack the arrears problem by supervising the accounts of groups of branches was carried, 26–13, with eleven delegates in Mearns' position.

There was more clarity about a determination to recruit foremen. The conference set up the technical and supervisory section, at an increased contribution of 2s 6d a week, to organize foreman and others separately from the craftsmen they supervised. The conference finished by making several detailed changes to ballot and discipline rules, and listened to Haxell talk about the controversy currently exploding in the union.

The union had become of great interest to the media and one fateful decision of the April executive, discussed by both the rules and policy conferences in 1957, was the suspension of Esher College. This single decision produced a focus for protest that had been missing; it also produced the one person whose indomitable will was to inspire the creation of an effective, organized anti-communist alliance. On the evening of 17 April 1957, Les Cannon answered the phone at his Chessington semi-detached home, close to Esher Place where he was the acting education officer – John Vickers had left some six months before. A correspondent from the *Daily Express* asked Cannon if he thought that his sacking from the union's college had anything to do with his having left the Communist Party the previous November? It was the first Cannon had heard of it. It was not going to be the last Haxell heard of it.

18

THE END OF THE BEGINNING: AN OPPOSITION EMERGES

WHEN LES CANNON PUT the phone down on the *Daily Express* reporter on the night of Tuesday 17 April 1957, he must have been devastated. There was a deep personal sense of disappointment. Jack Hendy had been helping out at Esher in the months after John Vickers's departure. Hendy had always been friendly with Les Cannon, probably based on their mutual respect for the attempts they had both made to educate themselves in Marxist and political ideas. Both were convinced intellectual communists, not opportunists. Both had sat on communist advisory committees together as well as the union's executive council. Correspondence survives to show the political relationship between them to have been warm and based on attempts to outmanoeuvre Haxell and his cronies. Hendy was no doubt upset when Cannon left the Communist Party in the late autumn of 1956, disillusioned at last with the role of the Communist Party in Britain. The reason for Cannon's special disappointment, though, was that Jack Hendy had been at the executive council meeting the previous weekend, had taken part in the decision to 'suspend' Esher on financial grounds, had been with Cannon at Esher since, and had not said a word.

Les Cannon was on the verge of being cut adrift, alone. Alone, even in his opposition to the executive. The central point about the opposition to the leadership in the spring of 1957 was its complete lack of co-ordination. This is not surprising, given the four separate groups involved. Throughout the post-war period, the largest and most persistent group were the moderate Labour men loosely grouped round Jock Byrne in Scotland. There is no doubt that much of their anti-communist inspiration sprang from a profound Catholic belief. Branch activists like Jimmy Dougan, Frank Murphy, Jock Reynolds, Jimmy Irvine and the new executive councillor for Scotland, Colin Walker, persistently opposed the executive council. Elected in February 1956, after Frank Murphy's death, Colin Walker beat the communist candidate, Bill

Blairford, 2,012–1,954. From then until early 1958, he was the only anti-communist vote on the executive, rendered ineffective even as a focus of protest by his inevitable failure to secure a seconder for any controversial proposition. There were other members throughout the early 1950s who presented consistent, if circumspect, opposition to the executive. In Yorkshire, particularly round Huddersfield and Sheffield, opposition to the communists was vigorous. One such individual opponent in the South-West was Jimmy Finnigan in Plymouth, who was a member of the Association of Catholic Trade Unionists. He was to run, unsuccessfully, for area official in the area, and at one stage, in 1952, was charged by the executive with bringing discredit on the union through encouraging the Association to canvass support for him. His vigorous denials of this partly convinced the executive not to proceed against him. He was a sceptical conference delegate, but he also did something few other ETU men could do in that era: he got himself nominated to run for Parliament in two constituencies, Cheltenham in 1955 and later in Bridgewater in 1959.

His opposition to the executive was personal; he knew that in Gloucesteshire his political ambition was held back by his association with the communist ETU. He lost Cheltenham in 1955 by over 7,600 votes. He discreetly reported to the executive: 'Violent personal attacks on me in connection with my membership of the ETU may have persuaded some electors to abstain from voting.'

These Catholic trade unionists aroused enormous fear and loathing amongst the union's leadership; even when Foulkes was in front of the TUC in September 1961, appealing against the union's expulsion from the TUC, he spoke for five minutes on the iniquity of the *Catholic Herald* recommending particular executive council nominees to the faithful. He even mentioned from the TUC rostrum the very close interest in the union's affairs revealed in the local parish bulletin of Father William Mena of St Edmund's Roman Catholic Church at Loughton in Essex!

These Catholic trade unionists were overwhelmingly stalwarts of the Labour Party. In their opposition to the executive council's communist policies, they would be joined by other Labour Party men whose first inspiration might not have been religious conviction, but rather an overwhelming dedication to the Labour cause. This second group had no real sense of organization, except that which arises quite spontaneously at conferences and committees in the pub or hotel after the debating is done. These people were particularly affected by the leadership's dutiful obsession with the Communist Party's foreign policy imperatives. Men like Ernie Hadley from Sheffield, Dave Fido (who changed his name to Dave Chalkley) from Tooting, Peter Renwick from Newcastle, Robert Fenwick from Jarrow, John Bull from London Transport, and Bill Shippey from Plaistow in East London often opposed the anti-Labour

Party implications of the leadership's pro-Soviet pronouncements. They were joined at different times by more Catholic or Labour stalwarts, particularly from the Manchester region; men like H. Fox, P. Portos, A. Taylor and R. Roddy made articulate and heartfelt protests at conferences or through branch correspondence and then slipped into inactivity in sheer frustration. Arguably the most persistent, informed and determined opponent of the communist leadership throughout the post-war period was Bill Sullivan. Bill Sullivan was elected Dagenham branch secretary in the spring of 1957, but he was the branch's delegate at policy conferences from 1947 onwards, with the exception of 1950 and 1953.

His branch bombarded the executive council and the London district committee with complaints and protests. Their lack of effectiveness never dissuaded Dagenham branch from keeping up the pressure. Bill Sullivan was never a communist, having been irreversibly put off the communists by direct experiences of communists during the Greek Civil War at the end of the Second World War. However, he was well known throughout the London contracting industry. His branch and conference activities gave him at least a skeleton outline of relationships with dissident elements inside and outside London that was to prove useful when the determined and tireless ex-communists joined the battle against the leadership.

By April 1957, Les Cannon was in a position to move from disillusioned intellectual distaste to personal crusade against the leadership. He was not the only communist in danger of losing his faith at the time. The events in Hungary in November 1956 closely followed the revelations of Khruschev's speech to the twentieth party congress, revelations that showed that Stalin was a common thug rather than an all-seeing divinity. Les Cannon would always insist in later years that it was the twentieth congress speech of Khruschev that finally tipped him away from the party. The revelations that the Soviet beacon – 'the future that worked' – was founded on mass murder, personal corruption and terror deeply disturbed Cannon. Married to a Czechoslovakian, Olga, he was there in August 1956 when he decided to leave the Communist Party. Cannon was a Marxist scholar, and never forgot or abandoned the economic and sociological insights of Marx. What he now rejected clearly was the Leninist adjunct to Marx's thought. In the context of trade union activity, Lenin's contribution was to deny the possibility of working-class progress through democratic change in parliament, based on a mass working-class political party. Lenin demanded a small, coherent, disciplined political party. The vanguard of the working-class would 'debate' issues, but once the decision was taken by the appropriate committee, dissent and continuing argument could not be tolerated. Party members would not be tainted, in their iron discipline, with the soppiness and toleration expected of mainstream democratic parties like the Labour Party. Communists knew that any stratagem, any illegality, any trick would be perfectly legitimate if it hastened the day when communists were in a sufficient number of strong positions to seize power in Britain, the only sort of handover of power that capitalists would understand. Lenin's famous advice to British communists in the trade unions in 1920 bears repeating here.

It is necessary to combine the strictest loyalty to the ideas of communism with the ability to make all necessary practical compromises, the 'tack' to make agreements, zig-zags, retreats and so on ... to resort to all sorts of devices, manoeuvres and illegal methods, to evasion and subterfuge, in order to penetrate into the trade unions, to remain in them and carry on communist work in them at all costs.

By 1957, Cannon no longer believed any of this; this was not the way for Marxists to make progress in Britain. He now thought, just as his father, Jim, had advised him in 1939 when he first joined the Communist Party, that the Labour Party was the only vehicle for progress that the organized working-class was prepared to work through.

Other communists like Mark Young, chairman of Finchley branch, though an exile from Newcastle upon Tyne, were also losing their faith at this time. Frank Chapple, then working at Vauxhall's in Luton, along with Mark Young and Lew Britz, another contracting electrician in Finchley branch, were struggling to keep their belief: and they had personal experience of communist control in the union to further undermine their sagging faith in the splendour of the Soviet example. Frank Chapple was always friendly with Tommy Vetterlein, the East London executive councillor. Vetterlein had been a communist since 1924 and on the executive since April 1949. In the spring of 1957, the friends of Frank Haxell in London were first of all angry that Tommy Vetterlein won the communist advisory committee backing to run for a vacant London area full-time official's job in place of Haxell's place-man supreme, Jim Humphrey. They must have been equally irritated when Frank Chapple got the 'left' nomination to replace Tommy Vetterlein as the executive council nominee later that year instead of Alf McBrowse. These two men, along with others in the party, paid close attention to E. P. Thomson's journal for dissident communists, *The Reasoner*. The central argument within the party, fuelled by *The Reasoner*, sparked off by Khruschev's revelations and Hungary, was how far was the British Communist Party capable of distancing itself from the palpable wrongdoing by communists in Hungary and elsewhere? Typical, at the grass-roots level, of this concern is a private letter written on 10 November 1956 by communist electrician A. Holliday to Frank Chapple, presenting his apologies for not attending a forthcoming London advisory committee. Gray's Inn branch stalwart Holliday wrote:

In relation to events taking place at the moment, I, like most party members, am very disturbed. On Hungary, I feel that we must fight to explain to workers the danger of the Soviet forces withdrawing and allowing reactionary elements to set up a Fascist government on the borders of the Soviet Union; nevertheless, I cannot excuse the blunders made by the party in the Soviet Union and Poland and Hungary, re the People's Democracies.

I also consider that the use of power politics (i.e. threats) by the Soviet Government within the last few days has lost us many sympathizers and has destroyed the arguments used by us for many years. We even have now the ridiculous situation of the Soviet Union supporting a military dictator in Egypt (Nasser) while our party comrades are imprisoned in that country!

Few ETU communists left the party in the wake of Hungary directly; they drifted away as the arguments between communists within the union became more divisive.

The fourth group of anti-leadership elements emerging in the spring of 1957 was an increasingly lively group of genuine Trotskyists, largely based in London. They were Marxists and Leninists, too; however, they opposed Russian imperialism and its state-capitalist refusal to press on with the march towards communism. They were among the first people to see the extraordinary contrast between alleged communist ideals and the personal corruption of the ETU leadership. In their disapproval of Russian foreign policy, they were quick to criticize the executive on other grounds. They were fond of 'adventurist' exposure of the ETU's leadership caution. There were good grounds for this caution from Haxell's and Foulkes's point of view. The Communist Party were always urging the ETU leadership not 'to go out on a limb', as Les Cannon later recalled it. The ETU was needed by the communists to give it access to the TUC, Labour Party and CSEU agendas. This influence must not be thrown away. Trotskyists associated with Gerry Healy's Socialist Labour League had no such inhibitions. They gleefully chased after the executive for lack of *real* militance in wage bargaining – particularly in contracting and supply negotiations. They were to expose Foulkes's denunciation of American rocket bases as a sham when he refused to order strikes against the rocket sites to stop them being built. This communist-Trotskyist sparring was to find a fairly nasty but typical expression in the affairs of the Clerkenwell branch in 1956. Harry Woolf, an energetic young communist, accused the excitable Trotskyist, Alan Courtenay, of being in arrears when he sought nomination for the 1956 policy conference; and what was worse, he had falsified his own contribution card to try and disprove it! The whole running of the branch was held to be 'unsatisfactory', Courtenay censured and Harry Woolf ended up elected as branch secretary. When this episode was up for confirmation at the executive, three executive councillors actually voted against the findings of the area sub-committee enquiry. Colin Walker and Tom Vincent were joined by ex-Socialist Labour League supporter Sam Goldberg. Goldberg had been refused access to the 'A' list of Labour Party candidates and later, in 1956, refused national executive committee endorsement of his candidature for Labour at the Nottingham South constitutency. Goldberg was not suitable as a Labour candidate, according to national agent Mr A. Williams, referring to Goldberg's Socialist Labour League associations. 'The decision concerning Mr S. Goldberg was due to his past political associations and it was felt that insufficient time had elapsed since he had broken these associations.' As we have seen earlier, Goldberg, like George Scott, certainly preferred the communist leadership to the emerging anti-communist opposition, Trotskyist or otherwise; his vote for Courtenay may have been for old times sake.

Les Cannon Enters the Lists

Les Cannon originally fell out with Haxell and Foulkes in late 1951 when they refused to support strike action in support of Cannon, who had been sacked by English Electric in Liverpool. For a long time, they put Cannon's inspiration down to thwarted ambition, particularly as he disagreed with the ETU leadership at the national advisory committee of the Communist Party and other party meetings in front of senior communist functionaries like Peter Kerrigan, the party's industrial organizer, Harry Pollitt and the new secretary from 1956, John Gollan.

After Cannon left the Communist Party in November 1956, he was marked out by Haxell. The first attempt to hound him was trivial. Cannon had used Esher's van before he could drive, had had a slight accident, causing around £5 worth of damage, and then got one of the college's workers, Gunn, to sign the insurance forms that he was in the van when he wasn't. Nine months after the event, Gunn stood firm by this small lie to protect Cannon when Haxell summoned the man to head office, clearly trying to use this against Cannon.

On 17 April 1957, the day Cannon was to hear of his sacking at Esher, he wrote to Haxell on another subject, in a tone that would have made the general secretary bristle. He reported a conversation with an old friend in the Fire Brigades Union, who, like Cannon, had recently left the Communist Party. This man had told Cannon that a Mr L. Howie, chairman of the Surrey district of the Communist Party, had been talking about Cannon.

The phrases used were that this Howie knew Cannon 'was all sewed up', that there 'were many ways of getting rid' of Cannon – that at the opportune moment, Frank Foulkes was going to 'arrange it'. Cannon finished the letter by saying: 'I take an extremely serious view of this matter and shall be very glad if you will take steps to stop this person interfering in the affairs of the

ETU.' McLennan replied saying there was nothing he could do; the following week, though, Cannon was directly concerned with his own position. On 24 April, after the Easter break, he was summoned to head office, at 4 p.m., along with Sam Simkin, the domestic arrangements man, or warden at Esher and his Rustington equivalent, Alan Woodcock. The other two were given jobs as caretakers of the two buildings: the rest of the staff and Les Cannon were sacked. Cannon suggested he continue his educational work by lecturing in the branches. Haxell said this option had already been dismissed by the executive (they hadn't even discussed it). Haxell was stone-hearted: he wrote a formal letter to Cannon on 26 April, telling him he would get three months' pay for a redundancy payment. He then added how Haxell 'would like to take this opportunity of expressing the sincere thanks of the executive council for the services you have rendered whilst acting as education officer at the college, and our deep regrets at the circumstances which have arisen.' Cannon pressed on; he demanded the right of appeal to the full executive. This was denied him on the cruel grounds that acting education officer was a 'staff' appointment, not like a full-time official or executive councillor, and 'staff' had no right of appeal to the executive council. After seventeen years' service to the union, its clearest, best-read, most forceful mind was supposed to get a job elsewhere.

Finance was the reason behind the suspension of Esher and Rustington. In the wake of the engineering strikes, it was expected to save £37,000 by suspending Esher, although Haxell eventually kept a staff of three on to keep the building ticking over; the union also spent more than £9,000 on alterations. Cannon kept up a bitter correspondence with Haxell; later on, on 1 April 1958, Haxell wrote: 'I did, as you know, advise you when you were pressing for confirmation of your appointment as education officer, that I was extremely doubtful as to your suitability and whether you had the necessary qualifications for the job.' He admitted Cannon knew all the ins and outs about the union, but his attitude and approach were 'dictatorial'. Haxwell went on: 'In my view it was psychologically necessary to have someone in charge of the college who was understanding, tolerant and prepared to listen to and take account of the student's point of view. In this regard, I always felt that a trained person, such as a Cambridge or Oxford graduate, would be most suitable for that very important aspect of our educational work.' Needless to say, this last remark drove Cannon up the wall. He got testimonials from John Vickers (Cambridge), and the well-known socialist writer, Henry Collins (Oxford), to say how good Cannon was at trade union education. John Vickers's recommendation stirred the pudding a bit by emphasizing just how highly Walter Stevens had thought of Les Cannon's ability. Cannon's savage personal reply to Haxell's deliberate slight drew attention to how nasty Haxell had been to Cambridge graduate Vickers; how he left sessions early with no explanation to the branch officers concerned and how he visited Esher to look at building works and ignored the shop-stewards. All this was proof of a 'dictatorial' attitude on Haxell's part. Haxell put a stop to the correspondence in May 1958, by which time Cannon was in deep battle with the leadership over the wider issues of ballot rigging and campaigning within the union. The issue of Cannon's dismissal, which he always felt was primarily a political act, not the consequence of a financial act, is interesting for several reasons. It fired Cannon up to fight. It shows, in the length and ferocity of the correspondence just how obsessive, mocking and brutal he could be, irrespective of the apparent grandeur of his opponent, the general secretary. Secondly, it shows Haxell to be supremely relaxed, unflummoxed and willing to trade insults. If Cannon had not been so angry, it is possible to think they both rather enjoyed it.

If the issue of Cannon's dismissal was of great importance to him, it would be of minor relevance elsewhere. It was raised at the policy conference in May 1957, in private session, and Haxell said, 'It was just one of those things'. When Ernie Hadley got up to debate the issue, Foulkes moved on to debate other things. However, Les Cannon had another front on which to fight; this time on battle-ground that would invite others to join him. At the June quarterly branch meetings in the South-West London and South of England executive council division, Division No. 9, Jack Frazer was up for re-election. Fraser was a special target for Cannon at the best of times; he was Foulkes's nominated successor by the communist machine (a job Cannon knew he ought to have) and he was Haxell's most effective travelling henchman.

Cannon went to Folkestone to the policy conference, and sat in the gallery during the public sessions. He was looking for ex-students at the college among the delegates from Frazer's executive council division to support his nomination on their return from conference. He took extra encouragement from the executive's financial embarrassment, and took even more from their foreign policy humiliation.

To start with, the executive decided to discuss Cyprus, Poland and Hungary in private session. Cyprus had proved an embarrassment for the leadership when they sent £20 to help imprisoned trade unionists arrested during the Cyprus emergency in 1956. The *Daily Mail* had encapsulated the vulgar but powerful feelings held in certain quarters on this subject: 'Union Split by Terror Gift – Bullet in Back for Cyprus Britons by Red-Run ETU'. The executive rode out that storm; they even took action against twenty members who wrote to the press to condemn the policy. Some had organized collections for injured British soldiers at work and wanted the world to know it. Equally cool, their response to the Poznan riots in Poland was to politely request the Polish authorities to bring the accused to trial promptly. After the invasion of Hungary in the first few days of November 1956, the executive of the union remained silent. On 14 December 1956, they at last responded with a resolution that 'deeply regrets that owing to past mistakes of the Hungarian and Soviet

Governments, a situation arose in which the Hungarian Government requested the intervention of Soviet troops ... the Soviet troops should be withdrawn ... we reaffirm the [executive's] belief in the principles of non-interference in the internal affairs of sovereign states ... and the withdrawal of all foreign troops from all countries in Europe, both East and West.' They also attempted to buy internal peace with a £1,000 gift to the TUC Hungarian refugees' distress fund. Consequently, they only had to answer for the policy at the Folkestone conference nearly six months after the executive's resolution.

Motion No. 144 at that conference 'welcomes the financial assistance and solidarity shown by the executive council towards our Cypriot brothers, but is disturbed by the executive council's attitude towards the shooting down of the workers at Poznan, and its belated protest against the attempt of Russian troops to suppress the workers' revolution in Hungary'.

It was moved with a delicate caution by the Luton branch delegate Gonshor, who revealed he had been under great pressure from the standing orders committee to take out all references to Cyprus, Hungary and Poland and congratulate the executive simply on its giving financial assistance and solidarity! Gonshor was also clearly got at in the suggestion that actually the Hungarian workers on the streets were born-again Nazis. Bill Sullivan was, however, an inspiring seconder.

I recall the demonstration at Trafalgar Square on 4 November against the war when Egypt was invaded. I then recall the reaction of the working-class to the brutal intervention of Russia to smash the workers' revolution and install a puppet regime. This action weakened the anti-war struggle and strengthened imperialism.

Where was the protest of our leadership? I reject their trick resolution on Hungary, six long weeks later, which, in effect, condoned the intervention. Let the executive council tell conference now: do you condemn the two Russian interventions? Do you condemn the death penalty for striking workers? Why have you not protested at the execution of the revolutionary workers in Hungary? You know, there was an electrician executed for his part in that revolution. . . .

The same people who had called Tito a Fascist were defending 'Rákosi and his murderous henchmen' in Hungary.

Les Tuck, the London lift and crane delegate, at that time was a communist loyalist. His interpretation of events in Hungary was different. Talking of the original protests against shortages '. . . to this just and progressive movement of the working people, there soon adhered forces to exploit the dissatisfaction of a section of the working people in order to undermine the foundations of the people's system in Hungary and to restore the old regime of landlords and capitalists.'

A further motion, No. 146, was moved by Jim Duggan from Cambuslang branch, and it called on the conference to denounce the invasion of Hungary on the grounds that such condemnation was in line with existing union policy on anti-colonialization! Duggan asked the conference 'to compare the action of the executive council in relation to Hungary, as against their action in relation to other countries. Why have they failed to carry out union policy?'

R. Beech, from LSE No. 3, gave the official line. Hungary's economy was devastated in the war; they were encircled, fearful of invasion from the West. They therefore had spent too much money on capital reinvestment, and not enough on consumer goods. Consequently, there were fertile grounds for protest. However,

... superimposed on this great economic strain were the criminal activities of some officials, many ex-Fascists, who had jumped on the band-wagon after the war. The brutalities of these criminals, on top of the economic tension, created a passionate desire for change, only to be exploited by those hostile elements ... White terror in Budapest had converted lamp posts into gallows, not only for security police, but for any known communists or social workers.

The Welwyn delegate, Jenkins, refused to condemn the executive when America had never done anything for the workers. McLennan, replying for the executive, gave the conference more of the same. He regretted the 'mistakes' made in the building of socialism. He blamed rather the propaganda of Radio Free Europe subverting Hungary. He put it to conference squarely.

I would ask all genuine socialists, would it have served the cause of socialism if reaction had triumphed in Hungary? Would it have helped the cause of world peace if the reactionaries had conquered and if Hungary had been made a hotbed of capitalist intrigue, poised ready to strike at the Soviet Union and start a world conflagration? I would ask, when in history have we witnessed such a demonstration of the most reactionary circles in the capitalist countries expressing their solidarity with a working-class revolution?

Bringing it closer home, McLennan finished by saying:

Are the movers of the motions genuinely interested in the faith and future of the Hungarian working-class? I suggest quite sincerely, that the opportunity has been taken once again by Brother Duggan to come to this rostrum and to this conference in order to convey his nearly pathological hatred of the Soviet Union and to use Hungary, on this occasion as the beating stick.

This type of attack could not save the platform. The Luton motion was carried narrowly: a vote was taken; it was carried, 177–154. Jimmy Duggan's motion on Hungary was carried comfortably – Foulkes didn't even bother to count.

With this bit of politicking done, and encouraged by the debate on Hungary, Les Cannon started his campaign against Jack Frazer in executive council division No. 9. Les Cannon knew a bit about executive council elections; even more pertinent, he knew a bit about communist tactics deployed to win them.

19

CAMPAIGNING AGAINST THE COMMUNISTS, 1957–9

LES CANNON GOT MORE than enough nominations to contest the executive council election against Jack Frazer in the summer of 1957. Cannon had contacts in fifty-six of the sixty-one branches, and adding up the results he knew, plus taking the results from the 1955 election from the five small branches he didn't know, Cannon concluded by the end of September that he had won by over 300 votes. Nevertheless, he was wary. At meetings he attended, 'visitors' had made it clear that some pro-Cannon branch results would be challenged.

Haxell always thought that Cannon leaked his estimates to the press there and then in order to intimidate the executive council into accepting the result. Particularly vitriolic were the articles by Preston Benson in the London evening paper of the time, *The Star*. Haxell wrote to Bill Blair, the Ruislip branch secretary, in March 1958, on this point, concerning the genesis of the press campaign. He wrote:

I would remind you that the campaign started on 7 October 1957, before the specific job of investigating the returns of the two branches [LSE No. 14 and Mitcham] had begun ... the press in that intervening period [between the end of the election and the end of the 'inquiry'] had tried various methods of influencing an election within the union: it was first suggested there should be a Government inquiry and questions were asked in the House; it was suggested that there should be an enquiry by the TUC. It was later suggested that an independent authority such as the Proportional Representation Society should examine the results of the ballots. Then it was suggested there should be a rank and file enquiry into the ballots. Finally, when all these various angles had been pursued and did not seem likely to succeed, the suggestion was made that in order to be completely 'fair' about this matter, a fresh election should be held.

On 19 October, the date the results were to be declared, Division No. 9, Les Cannon's division, was stated to be under investigation. 'Irregularities' had been revealed in certain branches, and needed investigating. London Jointers, like many branches throughout the division, had been visited on the night of the election by hawk-eyed protagonists of both sides. Normally, they chose the heartland of their enemy to invigilate in this way. Les Cannon himself noted at London Jointers that in the absence of the proper scrutineers, the doorkeeper had been opening the ballots until the scrutineers arrived at 8.30 p.m. The executive minutes registered Brother Sullivan's protest, from Dagenham, three weeks later, and London Jointers' votes were rejected. Haxell, though, had been well represented at two key pro-Cannon branches. LSE No. 14 met in Wimbledon Labour Club, and the secretary, Harry Gittins, was a well-known anti-communist.

Their election night was observed by Wally Bolt, from Peckham branch, an equally prominent supporter of the executive. His report to the executive resulted in the disqualification of the branch returns. First, there was a green box in the Wimbledon Labour Club for members to pass by and put their votes in. These ballots therefore had no postmark and were invalid, as they were not brought to the meeting personally or by an accredited shop-steward. Second, there was no motion to accept the scrutineers' returns. Third, the branch treasurer had helped count the votes. The later investigation showed a degree of confusion in the branch books. The branch thought 932 members were entitled to vote; and distributed that number of ballots. Close examination of the branch's books at head office on 11 February by the leadership, Harry Gittins and his branch committee, showed that actually only 797 were in benefit and entitled to vote. The eventual number of votes cast was 125–106 for Les Cannon and only 19 for Fraser. A survey had revealed that sixty-eight members who were entitled to vote had said they'd never received a ballot. The whole thing was very confusing. On 18 March 1958, secretary Harry Gittins tersely gave the required undertaking to abide by the rules of the union.

The communists sent national officer Bert Batchelor to Mitcham Electronic Engineers branch to watch their 1957 quarterly September branch meeting. Here, allegedly on the suggestion of Bert Batchelor, the communist-supporting president of the branch, E. S. Chesterman, discovered an extremely detailed breach of rule. He refused to sign the scrutineers' form on the grounds that Harry Marshall, the branch secretary (and well-known anti-communist), had brought to the branch large numbers of ballots from the Philips factory where he was senior shop-steward. The breach of rule alleged that Harry Marshall had brought not only *his* section's votes from the factory, but several other shop-steward's piles of votes as well. Cannon had visited many branches himself, to keep watch and learn the results first-hand. What really upset him about the Mitcham case was that nothing similar had happened to others – who needless to say had voted for Frazer. In writing to Haxell on 13 October –

before the decision to disallow some of Cannon's branches had been announced – he wrote that he wished:

... to raise the same question in relation to Gosport, Shirley, Winchester, Clapham, LSE No. 12, London South West and London Jointers branches where the respective secretaries, as in the case of Mitcham, brought in the great preponderance of ballot returns. In my view, none of these branches, including Mitcham, violated the rule in question, but if it is argued Mitcham did, then I aver they all did.

This branch return was crucial to Cannon's expected '300' vote majority. It had voted for him decisively, 410–35. When Cannon realized the potential danger of Mitcham's disqualification on Saturday 19 October, he agreed to contact the press, taking Harry Marshall and branch committee-man (later branch president) Dennis Kingston with him. They met Geoffrey Goodman of the *News Chronicle* and Len Jackson of the *Mirror* the following day. On Monday 21 October, the story appeared in these two papers, as well as the *Daily Herald*. Dennis Kingston allowed himself to be directly quoted.

Haxell's 'investigation' demanded the branch books. Harry Marshall refused to answer letters. On 22 October, Gus Cole and Jack Hendy went to his house, and Harry Marshall sent them away without the books. A couple of days later he relented. On 22 January, the branch officials went to Hayes Court to examine their own books in the presence of Bob McLennan and Jim Humphrey. They appeared to be in an appalling state, by mutual agreement. There were 1,353 names on the contribution ledger at June quarter night, 568 of whom were apparently in arrears. 1,084 ballots had been ordered, and 460 used. Later in the year, it was at last clear that there was £108 8s od more on the members' cards than in the branch ledger. On 28 January 1958, Harry Marshall wrote to Haxell admitting how the extent of the 'chaos' in the branch books 'really shocked me'. He put it down to the movement of Philips from Mitcham to Croydon, and the organizing of the part-transferred, part-newly-recruited workforce amounting to over 500 changes of membership. This recruitment exercise at work had taken priority over his branch administrative duties. He freely admitted he should have been more efficient, and should have called the branch committee together more often: however, the abolition of assistant branch secretaries and the much-vaunted head office, instead of branch, audit of his accounts had ruined his capacity to keep on top of a difficult situation.

Harry Marshall gave undertakings to abide by the rules. Dennis Kingston and E. S. Chesterman were told not to talk to the newspapers again.

These two branch disqualifications were excellently undertaken by Haxell. He had chosen the necessary two large pro-Cannon branches and exposed the chaos in their books. They were disqualified on technical grounds. However, to have been entirely legitimate, *every* branch in the division, all sixty-one, should have been torn apart administratively.

Other branches were disqualified. The press got to hear of Reading, which had voted, 50–12, for Cannon. They were disqualified for not electing their branch scrutineers, as required under rule, at the meeting before the quarterly meeting at which the vote was taken. (Incidentally, they were ruled out by Haxell personally and not referred to the national scrutineers.) What really hurt in Reading was that Reading supply had voted for Frazer, 135–81. Reading Supply's returns were late in being sent to head office. However, as it was the first offence of a single person – the branch secretary – Haxell unilaterally allowed these figures to stand. His later excuse was that Reading's returns had to be disqualified because the failure to elect scrutineers properly at the right meeting was the *whole* branch's fault, in contrast to Reading Supply's which was one man's fault and therefore they were excused disqualification. Jersey and LSE No. 17 were disqualified on the same grounds as Reading and there was an interesting twist at Southampton Docks branch. Local communist supporter Dickie Gibbs was one of the two scrutineers. Most of the Southampton branches had elected their scrutineers on the night of the quarterly meeting for years, despite the rules, as their shiftworking members could not guarantee to be at the quarterly meeting. Dickie Gibbs could not have been pleased when the vote went 17–9 to Cannon. Four days later on 21 September he approached the branch officers. He then raised his 'mistake' at the branch meeting on 1 October. On asking head office for guidance, the branch was disqualified for electing a scrutineer on the wrong night.

On 16 October 1957, Les Cannon received a letter from Bruce Howard, the Woolston (near Southampton) branch chairman. His letter shows the type of man who was effectively joining Cannon's campaign, but not without some heart-searching. He wrote:

Well, Les, I am writing to you as an ordinary individual member of the ETU, and not in any way connected with branch business. I am employed in BTC with Stan Withecombe (the Southampton Docks branch secretary) and he has shown me a letter that he has received from the executive council regarding the recent ballot for executive councillor. I am, by the way, chairman of Woolston branch, and was very disappointed when you were gagged by the executive council from attending our branch.

I will be going to Docks branch as a visitor, but I cannot be too conspicuous, because I rarely go there except in exceptional circumstances, such as affect this job (as I am also senior shop-steward here), and most members of Docks branch are in this department.

My reason for going to Docks branch is to know just 'the ins and outs' of this business, as you see my own branch adopts the same procedure, and nominates its scrutineers on the night of the ballot. And as it happens, Brother Frazer received most votes, by about seven over you [the vote was actually 18–9 for Frazer].

As far as I'm concerned, if one branch is out of order according to rule, well, every branch which adopts the same procedure must be treated likewise. I'm only sorry I could not raise this matter last night, but of course it was strictly Docks branch business. . . .

I feel wheels within wheels have been turning nationally, as well as locally, to spoil the chances of a man, and I am referring to you, Les, who feels that he cannot support a regime or system that is not strictly in line with the dictates of his conscience.

Personally, myself, Les, I am strictly a socialist and I feel that I could never support anything that would restrict both my religious and political freedom, and although I think we have a good executive council, I am always suspicious of them as their political leanings leave me that way . . . Don't think me a sentimentalist or a preacher as I am a trade unionist, but the methods adopted by the Communist Party – I can never put my cross on a ballot form to back anyone who will betray my trust in them.

Well, Les, I have seen from one national newspaper that you have received most votes for the executive council vacancy. I only hope this is right, so I will close now, hoping your return to the executive council is assured, so all the best for the future and a long seat on the executive council.

His good wishes were premature. On Friday 15 November, the result was announced. Jack Frazer had beaten Les Cannon, 2,023–1,451.

With the disqualification of Mitcham, LSE No. 14, LSE No. 17, Jersey, Reading, Southampton Docks, London Jointers, and Walton and Hersham, Les Cannon had lost. The result was uproar. First and foremost, Cannon made sure the newspapers knew the story of the selective branch disqualifications and investigations.

The press had been occasionally interested in the 'Red-baiting' type of stories in the few years before the end of 1957. In 1955, Woodrow Wyatt, the wholly unique Labour MP for Aston (1945–55) and, later, Bosworth (1959–70), had already written on the affairs of the ETU. In 1955, he had published a pamphlet about *The Peril in our Midst*, which had concentrated on the suspicious circumstances surrounding the 1948 Haxell–Byrne election for assistant general secretary. In January 1956, a series of articles in the *Daily Telegraph* had concentrated on the union's elections: the paper then refused to publish Haxell's 1,500-word reply because it was too long. Other papers, like the *Daily Express*, attacked the union's election system that year, and Woodrow Wyatt returned to the subject with an article in *Illustrated* on 8 September 1956. The article was headed, 'How Communists Fake the Ballot Box'. Branches wrote in to Hayes Court to urge taking legal action. However, the executive decided that the publicity surrounding the case, the costs, the further excuses for abuse, would not be in the union's wider interests. The uproar over the Cannon–Frazer election had to be seen in that context. What really sent the executive into paroxysms of rage was Woodrow Wyatt's

Panorama programme that went out on BBC television on 9 December 1957. Here, in a darkened studio with their identities concealed, branch officials revealed all sorts of irregularities with the union's elections that were the result of communist machination. One, Sidcup's E. J. Murphy, later publicly regretted his participation in the programme. The union's magazine was furious that the BBC had allowed 'the notorious communist baiter Woodrow Wyatt' to attack the union, and justified the refusal to debate the issue with Wyatt on a subsequent programme because they 'were not going to give Woodrow Wyatt or the BBC an opportunity to film the interview and then cut the film to suit their purposes.'

The union's official view on what lay behind this 'unprecedented' press campaign was clear. 'A member, or members, of this union, presumably with vested interest and/or political axes to grind, sought and obtained the use of the press to air publicly their views.' This was a clear reference to Les Cannon. However, the leadership sought to turn people's eyes away from the details of particular elections in 1957 or any other time by showing what wicked purposes Cannon's complaints were being used for. The real aims were to interfere in the AEU elections, persuade the TUC to get involved and stimulate the increasing demands for the Government to step in and 'impose shackling legislation on the trade union movement which would put the clock back'. As far as the union was concerned, it rejected 'public concern' for its affairs when the press never inquired into the meetings of newspaper directors, the appointments of editors, the affairs of boards of directors and the internal workings of the Freemasons. Central to the whole thing was the fact that the ETU was a constant challenge to the capitalist interest represented by the millionaire owners of the press. The leadership were slightly mollified in an article that was published in the *Daily Worker* on 14 December 1957 by George Scott, national officer, the substance of which was repeated by Frank Foulkes, live on *This Week* on ITV, that same night. George Scott was so angry that he asked Haxell if he might write for the *Daily Worker*. He thundered about the press, thwarted ambition and so on, but his major point was that it didn't really matter anyway – all this fuss about the Cannon–Frazer election. 'The decision to declare invalid the votes of branches referred to by the press was taken before those voting figures were known. The fact which blows the press fantasy to smithereens is that, even if those votes had been included, the result would have been the same.' George Scott, the one Labour Party man in a senior national position in the union, was anxious to defend his colleagues. They were not so anxious to help him. Proper emphasis in Scott's article was given to the phrase 'referred to by the press' – the branches mentioned in the critical articles. One further branch had been disqualified for a late return of the scrutineers' form but NOT MENTIONED BY THE PRESS OR TV – Walton and Hersham. If *their* votes were included,

Cannon had won by thirty-four votes. Either Haxell did not tell George Scott that, or George Scott deliberately wrote what he did in the *Daily Worker*. In any case, Foulkes was involved too. He sat on the sub-executive council which saw *all* the returns – those accepted and those rejected. He, too, knew that if *all* the rejected branches were included, Cannon *had* won.

A circular from head office was to further extend the lie in early December by saying: 'It is not without interest to note that had all the votes of the branch mentioned been accepted, then it would not have made any difference to the result of the ballot.' Again, in writing to the Director-General of the BBC, the lie was repeated. 'Whatever figures other people may have, in this office we have the actual voting returns from each of the sixty-one branches in the No. 9 division and we repeat, that if every branch mentioned in the broadcast and by the press as having had their votes disqualified were to be included, then it would make no difference to the result.' Four years later, in the High Court, Walton and Hersham's votes were taken into account by Justice Winn. Les Cannon *had* won the election after all, by thirty-four votes.

One of Les Cannon's less noticed skills was the way he could handle the press. Before he turned his attention to writing and speaking to the press, the anti-communist opposition, such as it was, was terrified of the press. This was partly because all trade unionists, of every political dimension, have an inbuilt suspicion of the motives and competence of journalists in roughly equal measure. Most active trade unionists have been directly involved in a dispute or a controversy at work and not recognized it at all in the version it appears in the media. More particularly, 'talking to the press' was a capital offence as far as Hayes Court were concerned. Colin Walker could not risk being caught. He was constantly under suspicion anyway, being the only opponent of Haxell on the executive. During Colin Walker's lonely year on the executive, 1956–7, he would attempt to guide such journalists as Blake Baker (*Daily Telegraph*) and Keith Mason (*Daily Herald*) for a few minutes at Euston station before returning north to Scotland after executive meetings. He would also speak to *Telegraph* reporters in Glasgow, often with Jock Byrne at the meeting. After the Frazer–Cannon election, it was all going to be different. Les Cannon had a skill in knowing just which parts of complex trade union minutiae could be presented to a wider newspaper audience. He formed genuine friendships with journalists he met from this period on. As far as Keith Mason was concerned, he came to appreciate 'over a long acquaintance, he was the greatest man I ever met. He was great in the sense that he had both the intelligence to see what needed to be done and the dogged persistence and courage to go ahead and do it. He was thus able to do what few of us are ever able to do – actually influence the course of events.' His colleague at the *Daily Herald*, Geoffrey Goodman, was also much struck by Cannon and drew close to him. Goodman knew what the ETU was like. He had covered their conferences for a few years previously. In 1952, at the Eastbourne policy conference, he even moved the reply to the vote of thanks to the press, revealing in the middle of amusing stories and some gentle advice about not being paranoiac about the press, the information that at national level, the ETU leadership was ahead of all other unions in its willingness to be available to the press. This is of passing interest, given the contemporary obsession about revealing the union's affairs outside the union. Throughout this period, and to the present day, it is true that all industrial relations journalists are under considerable pressure when reporting the activities of 'dissidents' inside unions. Too much apparently favourable coverage for such people leads to less easy access and even exclusion from the confidence of the current leadership. Such considerations try the personal integrity of all journalists.

At the end of 1957, Les Cannon failed to get on the executive council. However, someone else did – Frank Chapple. He was the left candidate for the East London/East Anglia division and still a communist. He beat the increasingly credible Bill Sullivan, 2,239–1,527, when he inherited his friend Tommy Vetterlein's seat. Tommy Vetterlein was running for a London full-time official's post. Two years previously, Vetterlein had won the executive council seat by 2,953 to Bill Sullivan's 971. The electoral tide was on the turn. Tommy Vetterlein and Frank Chapple organized throughout the East End of London to make it impossible for Haxell at the national advisory committee of the Communist Party to overturn their nominations. They got the over-whelming number of branch nominations; Haxell's preference for both or either nomination, Jim Humphrey, was quietly withdrawn.

Frank Chapple came from Hoxton, in the East End of London. His father was an illiterate shoe-mender, though he had been a painter and decorator before the First World War. His mother's family kept a greengrocery stall in Hoxton market. When his uncle opened a new greengrocer's shop, the electrical contracting company doing the wiring of the new premises took the young Chapple on as an unindentured apprentice: he spent much of his time with a wheelbarrow, transporting electrical equipment and supplies on foot to the various contracts in London being run by the company. At the age of sixteen he joined the union. Just before the war, in company with Ted Willis, the author and playwright, he left the Labour League of Youth (on its dis-bandment) and joined the Shoreditch Young Communist League. Like Les Cannon, his main inspiration to join the Communist Party was its determined willingness to stand up to Fascism, in Spain, in Europe and, more directly, on the streets of the East End of London.

During the war, he associated with all the leading communists in London, just as they were on the brink of taking over the union. He was an electrician's mate to Arthur Stride, at one ROF, a member of a strike committee with Dick Homewood, a militant communist who made George Humphreys's life a misery just before the war. He struck up in the wartime docks a friendship with Tommy Vetterlein and got to know the other leading communists and their sympathizers who spent most of the war on war-exempt work in the docks and ship-repairing industries on the Thames. While spending eight months as a Young Communist League organizer, he was drawn into the rigorous study of Marxist and Leninist theory – one stopping-off point in a lifetime's respect for books and learning that ranged far beyond politics, encompassing philosophy and economics. Such intellectual rigour was to stand Chapple in good stead in the years of battle with the communists. Not only did he know most of the personalities concerned; not only had he been a participant in the committees and organizations of the communists; he knew the way they thought; he knew the 'holy texts' of Marxism. He was as 'scientific' about political ideas as they were.

He saw military service in the war and just after. From April 1943 to early 1947, he served in the army. Recently married to Joan, he was on the Normandy beaches twenty days after D-day in 1944 with a Royal Electrical and Mechanical Engineers (REME) active service unit. When the war finished, he was in Germany and witnessed first-hand the devastation of Germany and the obscenity of the concentration camp of Celle. Before being demobbed in early 1947, he spent some months in Lübeck on the Baltic Coast, often in contact with the German Communist Party and was a witness to the unwillingness of Russian and Yugoslavian prisoners of war to return to the socialist paradise further east.

On his return from military service, Frank Chapple rejoined union activity by becoming assistant branch secretary at Ernie Bussey's old branch, LSE No. 10. By this time, in late 1947–early 1948, he was earmarked for useful communist activity within the union. Working now in contracting, he attended his first union conference in 1948 – the rules revision conference at Ayr. His first contribution was to directly contradict Jock Byrne, who was trying to prevent members expelled at the time of Earl's Court in 1937 from being rehabilitated in the union. He returned to the rostrum to attack Jock Byrne again, this time adding a wholly characteristic remark about 'comedians who became officials'.

Throughout the period 1948–56, he was a member of the London advisory and national advisory committee of the Communist Party. However, he never liked Haxell, or Foulkes. He was never interested in conspicuous consumption himself; he was always unimpressed by those who were. The leading communists in the Union, in contrast, were very impressed by the good life. Even before the anti-communists in the union from 1958–60 were to make much of the lifestyles of Haxell and Foulkes, Frank Chapple was disappointed by such things as silk shirts for the president or sumptuous banquets for fraternal delegates. It was the convention that, after a union conference, the fraternal delegates would be entertained before they went home. There was nothing unusual or, indeed, immoral, about that. However, in 1958, the union entertained just one fraternal delegate (all the others had gone home) at the Waldorf Hotel in London – an Italian fraternal delegate who could not speak a word of English. He sat quietly at the top table while the rest of the leadership got stuck in.

Chapple did everything asked of him up to 1956, although his spiky personality never reduced him to the status of one of Haxell's henchmen. Haxell delighted in slighting him – even when he was still in the party. He was elected to the executive in October 1957, to take up office in January 1958. He was curtly told that he could not attend the November 1957 rules revision conference, and that was that!

During the latter part of 1956, Chapple's attitude to Hungary had not endeared him to his communist associates. He had taken the attitude that the Communist Party in Britain must reform itself, particularly in terms of distancing itself from its previous role as the leading apologist for Soviet foreign policy. Throughout 1957, he argued the case within the party, rather than leave the party outright. It was in this frame of mind that he watched Les Cannon's campaign get underway. There was no doubt which way he would fall in early 1958. He became central to the reform of the union as he fought a minority position on the executive council; at least he got the official papers for the reformers to work on. From early 1958–60, he was under threat of disciplinary action for revealing union business (eventually activated in December 1959) and was careful not to talk direct to the press – because it would have got back to Haxell from his friends in the newspapers.

Just as Les Cannon's crusade about the Fraser-Cannon election was quietening down, another flurry of articles in the press kept the issue alive. Bill Sullivan had a letter published in *Tribune* on 7 February 1958 in reply to Sam Goldberg's 'explanation' of the Cannon–Fraser election. This followed up another characteristic volley from Woodrow Wyatt in the *New Statesman* on 18 January 1958. This article elicited an enormous reply from Haxell which the magazine would not print on grounds of length. It was later published as a pamphlet and attacked the union's persecutors for saying that low polls due to apathy let communists into power; and that if there was a high poll to let communists into power, it must have been rigged!

Throughout 1957–8, Les Cannon toured the union, trying to interest branches in these problems. He also sent out scurrilous roneoed circulars to all the 675-odd branches. But others were becoming increasingly active. Bill Sullivan, again, attempted to raise the unconstitutional conduct of his own executive council ballot against Frank Chapple in the Southend Electronic Engineers branch. In May 1958, the policy conference met at Morecambe. Again, Bill Sullivan put the executive on the spot by calling for the withdrawal of all troops from Europe – Germany in particular – in a process started by the unilateral withdrawal of British troops. He was seconded by Ipswich's Eric Clayton, anticipating Sid Maitland's amendment that rejected the unilateral withdrawal of British troops in favour of four-power negotiations. Eric Clayton, though, was using international politics to attack the Communist Party position.

I believe that the mover of the amendment and the executive council speaker do not give twopence for real internationalism. They will cry out in horror when imperialism strikes in Cyprus and South Africa, for example. I applaud them for it, because I hate imperialism too. But if they are silent – and so far they have been – when a Stalin or an Ulbricht or a Kádár imprisons or kills, they cannot be expected to be taken seriously when they protest at imperialist actions. The amendment may satisfy the *Daily Worker*, but it should not satisfy the membership.

The conference was quiet in terms of controversy at the rostrum, but outside the conference hall, the anti-leadership forces were meeting; they were consolidating their contacts, introducing themselves to new delegates like Tom Breakell from Preston, Ken Griffin from Swansea and Alf McLuckie from Motherwell. By this time, they had some sort of organization throughout each of the union's areas, and had met at Birmingham on a national basis. Frank Chapple and Bill Sullivan were crucial in this conference hand-shaking.

By mid-summer 1958, a further focus of protest was to be provided. In January 1958, Les Cannon had been nominated to run for the TUC delegation and for the post of London area official, with Bill Sullivan withdrawing in his favour. As the 1957 executive council elections had shown, Bill Sullivan was getting close to defeating the communists' machine. Both in 1958 and 1959, when he allowed Frank Chapple a free run at the executive seat, Bill Sullivan made real practical sacrifices for the reform group. The communists decided not to run a straight-up party member. Instead they ran Labour Party member, but executive supporter, Tommy Symms from Woolwich. Symms had, as we shall see in the next chapter, a deep scepticism about ETU elections that had never been satisfactorily answered. However, he must have known where his support was coming from in a high-profile election against Les Cannon. The leadership's nominee could only have been helped by the secretary of LSE No. 10, Edward Nash, running as a third candidate. The practical effect of this would be to take votes away from Cannon; the left always know who *the* candidate is.

With the heightened sense of excitement at election times in the union, the actual voting meetings, particularly in London, were usually visited by observers from one political camp or the other within the union. This may be why many elections of the late 1950s do not appear to have such a high turn-out as those of the early 1950s. Some of the cruder fiddles were not being used so often. In earlier elections, some branches would vote, say 35–10, for a particular candidate. Unscrupulous branch officers would not read the results to the branch on the night; it was not recorded in the minutes: it would appear in the executive minutes months later as 335–10 and never read to the branch. The branch secretary had given his candidate a bit of a boost before posting the scrutineers' forms! Visitors to branches tended to put a stop to things like that by simply asking to know the result and ostentatiously writing it down.

The simplest and most regular method of fiddling ballots hinged on the branch secretary. He would receive the ballot papers for the membership he had indented for. He would keep some back, particularly if he'd deliberately over-ordered ballots. He would then send out a ballot paper and an election address to each member of the branch. They could vote by either bringing their ballot to the quarterly meeting, vote and ask the shop-steward at work to take it to the meeting, or vote and post it back to the branch secretary, who would take it to the meeting. The unscrupulous branch secretary would then post completed ballots to himself. This was the main way ballots were corrupted and was the most difficult to prove. This was a key point that Cannon's circular to the branches in March 1958 hammered home. He wrote: 'At least their fiddling has now been narrowed down to the postal vote – perhaps the members will observe these phenomenal postal ballots in future elections.' In another circular, the point was also emphasized by comparing the voting record of London South-West in the early 1950s, when Jack Frazer was secretary, with the middle 1950s when a non-communist, Sam Adams, became secretary.

London South-West branch. Brother Frazer himself used to be the secretary of this branch. In his day, the branch often used to have a ballot of 250–300 votes, as was the case with communist George Tilbury before him. After he was defeated for the secretaryship by Sam Adams (Labour Party member) the vote dropped to proportions common to a branch of this size and composition in the union generally.

Typical of the ballots during Sam Adams's term as secretary are as follows (see Table 5) (total votes of all candidates given).

Table 5

Year	Ballot	Votes Cast
1954	Area 27 full-time officer	65
1955	National officer	69
1956	Area 27 full-time officer	69
1957	Area 27 full-time officer	48
1958	Area 27 full-time officer	72

At the March 1958 quarterly meetings, the candidates and their supporters 'visited' branches as usual. Les Cannon himself was present at London Electronic Engineers No. 2 branch at the community centre in Hayes, Middlesex, at 5.30 p.m. on the evening of 28 March. This branch was largely based on the EMI factory at Hayes, with a large female factory membership (over 1,000) that rarely attended the branch. There were thirteen members present, including secretary J. J. Maling, who was known to be an admirer of Haxell's and whose branch had for years produced enormous majorities for communist nominees. Les Cannon estimated that there were over fifty ballots brought in by shop-stewards and then the branch secretary himself gave to the scrutineers around 200 ballots from a carrier bag, saying they had been posted to him.

The branch meeting was discussing at the time the press campaign against the union and Les Cannon spoke in the debate, as a visitor. During the course of his remarks he drew attention to the branch secretary's bag full of votes and contrasted it with the Mitcham business the previous year. The official branch minutes recorded: 'Brother Cannon declared he would report the secretary. Brother Cannon remarked that he did not believe that the number of postal ballots was correct and that the secretary posted them.' Les Cannon's own submission on the subject said: 'For example, if the same investigation was held in regard to the Mitcham ballot, it might be found that the membership had not posted these ballot papers. It might, indeed, be found that the secretary had posted them to himself.' When the scrutineers totted up the result it showed 243 votes for Tommy Symms, three for Edward Nash and five for Cannon! Cannon's own branch, Kingston-upon-Thames, demanded an investigation. At the June executive meeting, the executive decided there were no grounds for an appeal. Kingston branch started the appeals procedure on 18 July 1958, calling a special meeting to challenge the executive's refusal to investigate London Electronic Engineers No. 2 (and Hayes branch, too). Haxell wrote back on 19 August 1958 to say that the executive's decisions 'were taken in connection with the [election] scrutineers' report, and such decisions are not subject to the appeals procedure within the union.'

This apparently plain, bureaucratic matter was, in reality, one of the deepest and most deliberate tricks played by Haxell on the membership of the union. After the 1957 rules revision conference, and before the new rule-book appeared from the printers, the executive's powers to set out the boundaries of executive council divisions for electoral purposes without them being appealed against, was extended – WITHOUT THE KNOWLEDGE OF THE CONFERENCE OR EXECUTIVE – to everything to do with the scrutineers' reports on elections. This issue was exposed at some length in the High Court in 1961.

Seven weeks after Cannon's remarks at London Electronic Engineers No. 2, the branch secretary, J. J. Maling, wrote to E. J. Turner, the London area secretary, initiating a charge against Cannon under the catch-all Rule 38, Clause 11, that his remarks about 'posting ballots to himself' brought injury upon Maling and discredit upon the union. Maling felt that the wide circulation of these allegations in unofficial circulars and his own branch committee's insistence made it necessary for him to proceed against Cannon.

This proved exceptionally convenient for the leadership. At the same election for full-time official in London (which Cannon lost to Tommy Symms, 3,951–2,856, with Edward Nash getting 608), Cannon *had* won election as a TUC delegate to the September congress.

On Thursday 24 July, the London area sub-committee met to consider the charges: there were three out of the five people at least who could not be considered Les Cannon's friends – Sid Maitland, Bert Gray and Charlie Corcoran. Their recommendations were endorsed by the full London area committee on 28 August 1958, with only Sister Walker (an active member of Mark Young's Finchley branch), J. E. V. Campbell (the long-time opponent of the communists from LSE No. 18) and the indefatigable, politically-experienced Johnnie Bull voting against. On 29 August, with the TUC due to start on 1 September, Haxell wrote to Cannon. He had been informed of the area committee's decision. Les Cannon had been fined £5 and it had also been decided that:

> you be removed from any office you may hold in or on behalf of the union and that you be disqualified from holding any office in or on behalf of the union for a period of five years.

> In the light of this decision, it is not possible for you to act as a delegate at the forthcoming TUC, and I have therefore taken the necessary steps to withdraw your name from the list of delegates representing the union at congress.

Cannon noted later that all the delegates had had their credentials despatched by post on 21 August: he never received his. Haxell knew what was coming from Turner's area committee on 28 August. Cannon was already in Bournemouth on holiday and knew nothing, deliberately, of the letter on his front doormat back in Chessington. He therefore turned up at the delegation meeting at 10.30 a.m. on Sunday 31 August in the Royal Exeter Hotel, Bournemouth (where incidentally Haxell's and Foulkes's drinks bill came to over £192 for the week). Cannon's own note of the embarrassing conversation that then ensued ran something like Les Cannon saying he had no credentials or information about the Congress. Foulkes replied, 'In that case, you'd better go home and find out.'

By this time, another prominent communist was drifting out of the party. Bill Blairford, the Edinburgh man who gave Cannon his letter sent with the credentials to prove what date they were sent, urged caution on Cannon. After all, if they would suspend him from office for making remarks about J. J.

Maling at a London Electronic Engineers No. 2 branch meeting, what would they do if he made a fuss on the eve of the TUC.

Les Cannon held a press conference at 8 o'clock, attended by all the newspapers and television and radio companies. His initial statement went straight for the main targets.

I have decided to make this statement to you after eighteen months of consistent provocation, resulting from a continuous campaign by the Communist Party inside the ETU to discredit me, and ultimately to deprive me of my democratic rights inside the union ... I am in no doubt that such a vicious penalty [over the J. J. Maling business] would not have been initiated by the communists unless it was a well-discussed decision of the national ETU advisory committee of the Communist Party, of which Mr Haxell is chairman.

He then pointed out that three out of the five on the area sub-committee were party members, as were eleven members of the area committee.

These sensational accusations were repeated in all the papers the following morning. To Foulkes's complete fury, Walter Padley, the shopworkers's leader, asked, on the opening of Congress, if the general council could do something about it? They could not; each union was responsible only to itself concerning the make-up of its delegation. The whole business could only have added to Foulkes's hatred of Cannon and an intensification of the war within the union.

Cannon could no longer run for office. It was difficult to continue to make the focus of the whole campaign his election performances. Interestingly, just like the left in the late 1930s, Les Cannon's steadily growing group saw elections to office as the obvious key to changing the political complexion of the union. This avenue was now closed to them; this was particularly frustrating as Les Cannon could not run against Les Gregory at the end of 1958 for national officer, as he intended to do.

In the late summer of 1958, just before the TUC, a further front was opened against Haxell. Mark Young had at last been expelled from the Communist Party on 20 July 1958. He was expelled for failing to read the *Daily Worker*, not supporting communist candidates in local elections, and for defending Les Cannon in late 1957, outraged at the obsessive support mobilized for Jack Frazer. On 9 August 1958, he wrote to the *New Statesman*, tenuously picking up the Woodrow Wyatt articles eight months earlier as a peg to hang his political credo on. The letter remains one of the most succinct accounts of the position within the union at the end of the summer of 1958.

Sir, Earlier this year, you published articles and letters discussing the role of communists in the ETU. As chairman of the ETU Finchley branch for five years, and as a communist for nine years, I would like to make some further observations on this subject.

On 20 July, I was expelled from the Communist Party for 'political activity incompatible with party membership'. It is true, as I conceded in a written statement to the London district committee, that I disapproved of the Soviet intervention in Hungary and of 'the crimes exposed throughout the communist-controlled countries'. But my views on these subjects were known and I frankly discussed them with party officials. This disagreement was not the reason for my expulsion. As I pointed out at length in my written statement, my 'hostility to the party' was to the party leadership within the ETU, which, to my knowledge, had persistently rigged elections to union office.

It is now four years since I first raised this issue within the union. I have raised it at all levels in the Communist Party, and at a personal interview with Peter Kerrigan, the national organizer, as much as three years ago. Nor have mine been solitary efforts. At least two executive councillors of the union – both of them communists – have expressed complete disagreement with such practices, one before the London district secretariat of the party and the other at a meeting with Harry Pollitt himself, called for that very purpose. Criticisms of this kind are met either with disbelief, or, if the evidence is found irrefutable, with the argument that the anti-communists fiddle union votes on a bigger scale.

How the controlling Communist Party group rigs elections may be illustrated by a consideration of the votes cast by the various union branches in the March elections for a London area official. Following the irregularities in elections, the *opposition* vote in certain branches decreased significantly. But in a number of branches where the Communist Party is in control (and where, therefore, there is no danger of an inquiry) the vote actually increased, despite a lower membership entitled to vote. Furthermore, one is asked to believe that over sixty per cent of the members in these branches posted their vote, whereas previously never more than ten per cent of the members did so. The reason for this, of course, is that under the new rules only posted votes can be given to the scrutineers by branch secretaries. Thus in one branch in which approximately 250 members were entitled to vote 179 votes were cast, 159 of which the secretary gave to the scrutineers as posted votes. In another branch in which 200 members were entitled to vote 131 out of 137 votes were again posted votes.

The Communist Party maintains its control of the union through factions called 'advisory committees' at the national and local level. At the last advisory committee I attended, in February 1958, the only topic of discussion was how to defeat our ex-comrade Cannon in the pending March election. We were directed to make contacts in each branch that had nominated Cannon and to undermine him principally by describing him as 'the candidate of the capitalist press'. I challenged that allegation. No evidence was produced then or since to support it.

In December 1957, there was a press campaign concerning the result of the Cannon–Fraser election in Division 9 of the union for an executive councillor which had taken place in September. The Communist Party spared no efforts on behalf of its candidate Fraser. The whole union machine was placed at his disposal; there was unprecedented activity around the branches by union officials; by smear and defamation the communist machine raised the atmosphere to fever pitch. Nothing for example, of the December press campaign could explain a communist union official's statement in a branch in Division 9 during a discussion on its nomination which linked Cannon to the Economic League! For this statement was made six months prior to the press campaign.

It was this activity, plus the inquiry by the general secretary after the election and the delay in announcing the result, that led to the press maintaining in December that branches were being disenfranchised in order that the communist candidate Frazer might be declared elected. In due course the union leadership announced that Frazer had won the election and that a number of branches had been disenfranchised, if branches *mentioned in the press* had been counted the result would not have been affected. No figures wer given. In February 1958 the voting was announced in the executive minutes, together with a list of disenfranchised branches whose votes were not given. It then appeared, however, that an extra branch *not mentioned in the press* had been disenfranchised. When the general secretary was asked what the voting was in this branch he eventually replied that he did not know and that it was not his business to know the vote of disenfranchised branches!

Finally, however, it was announced by the union leadership that there was, in any case, a right of appeal by the branches into its rulings. I know of at least thirty branches which appealed against the minute which dealt with the disenfranchised branches and the scrutineers' report. The general secretary calmly decided that this minute could not be appealed against and the matter did not even go before the elected executive committee of the union. It was possible to appeal on only one minute – that dealing with the general secretary's inquiry into the election. Appeals against this minute were at first permitted and according to procedure the general secretary, the president, and other national officers of the union went to the appealing branches and stated the executive's view. Two branches persisted in voting for their appeal, however, and procedure required that their appeal should now be published: if ten per cent of the branches agreed with it a national conference or ballot would be held to settle the matter. But the appeal was never published. Instead a solicitor's opinion was sent to the appealing branches stating that their appeal was not legally in order. And there the matter rests.

The Communist Party had gone to great lengths to obtain the executive position in Division 9 for its candidate Frazer. The ultimate significance of these efforts can only be appreciated, however, if it is known that Frazer is secretary of the national advisory committee of the Communist Party, i.e., of the leading body of communists in the ETU and furthermore is the party's intended candidate for the office of general president whenever it falls vacant. Despite the rule that executive councillors of the union are working men (not paid officials), Frazer has not worked at his trade for four years but has been employed in one capacity or another by the union, thus he has been a union official in Middlesbrough, Coventry, Leicester, Southampton and London. It is evident that the party intends that its candidates for the office of general president will be well known to the members!

To conclude, I must explain why I find it necessary to bring my views to public notice. The first is that I learn from Communist Party contacts that the Communist Party group is planning disciplinary action against Les Cannon. Secondly, my branch has requested a visit to discuss the question of elections with its executive councillor. The general secretary has refused our request and wishes to send us a union official. In desperation we sent a deputation to our executive councillor; we discovered that on most of the issues which we had referred to the executive council's attention he had either no information or was misinformed. The communists win elections; it is up to the members to win the fight for union democracy.

(signed) MARK YOUNG

By the end of 1958, the reformers were taking on the appearance of a proper group. Les Cannon was writing the pamphlets and circulars and bombarding Hayes Court with correspondence via the Kingston branch. Bill Sullivan was once again the electoral focus for the reformers: in a national officer's election, Les Gregory beat Bill Sullivan, 12,253–7,837. However, four years earlier the gap between the two had been 22,312–4,286. So progress of a sort. The two executive members, Chapple and Walker, were feeding the reformers sufficient information to keep the circular factory in Chessington going. Even so, despite a growing sense of organization, it was hardly a mass movement. There were less than a hundred members involved throughout the country; however, some of these individuals had sufficent courage and personality to make up for the lack of committed adherents. By the end of 1958, the reformers were boosted by the return to London from South Africa of Dick Reno; Dick Reno was fearless and opinionated – opponents described him as 'volatile'. He was originally a communist in the early 1950s, but not impressed by the oppressive atmosphere of the union.

This is best illustrated by an incident that happened towards the end of the Korean War in 1952. Fulham branch was meeting and a young apprentice member, John Coventry, was attending the meeting. It was a special meeting in so far as the assistant general secretary, Frank Haxell, was there to give an address; Haxell concentrated on the wickedness of capitalism, as evidenced by the Korean War, and insisted that British troops should be brought home, and should not be involved. This incensed the young apprentice, whose friend, like him an electrical apprentice, but non-indentured, had been killed in Korea. The apprentice leapt to his feet and, completely unaware of who Haxell was, shouted at the meeting: 'Who the ... is this ...?' Dick Reno came to the rescue, grasping the lad's arm to pull him strongly down into his seat and addressing the meeting. He appealed on behalf of the apprentice's youth and inexperience, and urged that a fortnight's suspension from the branch was quite sufficient in all the circumstances. Two weeks later, the apprentice returned and went on to build a long career within the union. Dick Reno, meanwhile, left the Communist Party in 1953, and became a member of the embryonic Trotskyist sect grouped round the *Militant* newspaper. As such, he initially approached his criticism of the executive from a left-wing viewpoint. Nevertheless, he was well known through London's contracting and film studio trade-union world where his uncharacteristic (for a Trotskyist) sense of fun made him good company and a welcome ally of Les Cannon's. He was a brilliant cartoonist who would draw caricatures of actors and directors while in the lighting gantries on set, which he would flutter down from above on to the people he had been drawing. The Ruislip branch, too, with its prominent conference delegate Bill Blair to the fore in the discussions, had protested about the Cannon–Frazer election. Throughout 1958, the branch, and Blair privately, carried on an extensive correspondence. Their restrained suspicion was turned to disappointed opposition by two main head office reactions. First, they were unconvinced by executive councillor Jack Hendy's visits to the branch. Second, Haxell actually took legal advice to impress upon the branch that they had no right of appeal over the Cannon–Frazer election result. Bill Blair had a wider audience than Ruislip and West London's suburbs. He had been a delegate to the policy conference and as such was widely known in the union. Throughout the 1950s he was elected on to the union's TUC and Labour Party delegation by nation-wide elections. He was tall, well-dressed and good-looking, with an impeccable ETU background that dated all the way back to his militant activity at Chorley before the war. His conference speeches were often on non-predictable subjects – urging the abolition of capital punishment in 1954. He was a constant target by the leadership for seduction into the communist camp, particularly when he made moves towards their general policy stance, such as when he moved the nationalization of the engineering industry in 1956. From 1955 onwards, he was regularly elected to the union's TUC and Labour Party delegations with some measure of Communist Party support. In 1952, he had got 1,405 votes for the TUC: in 1953, he got 10,659 and missed the delegation by just 200. By 1955, he was in receipt of 20,389 votes – coming second in the poll. This flirtation never led anywhere, though. By 1956, he was able to retain just half that vote, 10,981, although still remaining on the delegation. The same in 1957, although he was now attracting a different style of support. By 1958, his vote had gone down to 7,858 for the TUC. Cannon had received 9,286 and seven Communist Party supporters between 9–11,000 votes. Throughout the period, from 1955, he did maintain a steady vote for the Labour Party delegation, usually being the last or second last on the delegation. All this activity brought him a national status in the union. The irrevocable distancing of Bill Blair from Haxell during 1958 was to provide the reformers with an added dimension of mainstream credibility.

At the end of 1958, yet another source of pressure on the leadership of the ETU opened up. It is plain that the TUC was not anxious to publicly discuss the uproar inside the ETU. Indeed, they had effectively ignored Woodrow Wyatt for years. Some TUC unions were communist-dominated themselves. Some had communist groups in a powerful minority who needed to be placated. Some took the view that the TUC *never* interfered in the internal affairs of *any* union on *any* subject; if it were otherwise, where would the TUC intervention end? George Woodcock, TUC general secretary by 1961, partially admitted the validity of criticisms of tardiness when he said in September 1961:

> Accusations were made against the General Council of timidity, and of inability to deal with its own domestic affairs, but we remained patient throughout the whole time. We were driven, even as early as 1959, to report to Congress our very serious doubts about the intentions of the ETU to deal seriously with the questions we brought to their notice.

To Les Cannon, this reticence and this patience looked like cowardice, certainly towards the end of 1958. The continuing press campaign, the Fraser–Cannon election backwash and the hullabaloo at the 1958 TUC congress itself over Cannon's candidacy had apparently failed to agitate anyone at Congress House (with the exception of Vic Feather, who was to later prove, anonymously, a good friend of the reformers).

Vincent Tewson was still TUC general secretary when he wrote to the ETU on 17 December 1958, asking for the ETU to comment on 'public allegations of the manipulation of elections and of the influence of the Communist Party (which) have become so widespread and persistent that it is increasingly difficult for the General Council to ignore the possible effect on them on the prestige and public reputation of the trade union movement as a whole.' Later in the year, in November 1959, the TUC General Council was to complain of the 'evasive nature of the replies sent by your union's leadership in answer to the comparatively simple questions put to them by the General Council and their persistent habit of seeking to delay the General Council in reaching a conclusion.'

There can be little argument with this analysis. The executive replied to the TUC's initial inquiry on 23 January 1959, saying they too were concerned about the press campaign and flatly denying the existence of communist control over the union.

On 18 February 1959, Les Cannon wrote to every member of the TUC General Council to repeat his allegations about communist control of the union and Mr Haxell's 'abuse' of the appeals machinery, and his non-reporting of issues to the executive. He had legal advice that he had a case for conspiracy, but in order to avoid encouraging Tory Government legislative intervention on the back of such legal moves, he would prefer the TUC to investigate. He also drew attention to the paradox of his anticipating further action against himself and Bill Sullivan and Mark Young for talking to the press when no action was taken against the leadership for divulging the union's business to communist advisory committees for twenty years.

Further pressure from the TUC produced a decision to set up a committee of inquiry into the whole series of allegations that Les Cannon had made after the 1958 TUC and Mark Young had made in his August 1958 *New Statesman* article. The TUC agreed to step back and wait for the result.

The three-man inquiry team was George Scott, national officer, in the chair, the executive councillor for Wales, Tom Vincent, and the new executive councillor for the Manchester region, Harry West. All were Labour Party members. All regularly voted with the communists. In the meantime, on 4 April, the executive merely 'censured' Cannon and Young for their aggressive press 'revelations'. They did not even charge them with bringing discredit on the union under the infamous Clause 38 of the rules.

The committee of inquiry was a bizarre farce. The executive had put ostensibly non-communist dignitaries on the inquiry team. Tom Vincent, although a virtual recluse in terms of ever saying anything at all on the executive, had been a member of the union since 1916 and a member of the Labour Party since 1921. Ever since 1955, he had received the huge, unexplained leap in his vote for TUC and Labour Party delegations that revealed his total acquiescence in the doings of the communist leadership; unlike Bill Blair, he had continued to enjoy that patronage. Cannon and Young refused to develop their accusations on the grounds that actually the committee of inquiry was up to their eyes in the substance of their accusations. Furthermore, the committee might not be communists – at least nominally – but the secretarial staff servicing the committee were! There were long-drawn-out hearings on 11, 12, 26 and 27 May 1959. Scott would say, in a thousand different ways, 'Give us this evidence of communist interference you are on about.' Les Cannon and Mark Young would reply, 'No – you are not impartial, because you, personally, are the beneficiaries of the conspiracy we are on about.' Mark Young summarized the position by saying:

After eighteen months of complaints which arose over the executive council division 9 ballot, my letter to the *New Statesman*, the refusal to allow appeals, the refusal to have a branch delegate conference or an enquiry by impartial members, only now, after having found me guilty on a charge relating to my letter to the *New Statesman,* is the need for such an inquiry accepted by the executive council. The time has long passed when the executive council could pose as a body capable of conducting an impartial inquiry....

Part of the evidence I would provide an impartial body, would concern how Brother Scott and Brother West came to occupy their present positions as national officer and executive councillor respectively. In Brother Scott's case, I would bring witnesses to testify of national and London advisory committee meetings that discussed Communist Party support for him for the position of national officer. These meetings discussed a report in the Scottish Communist Party which spoke in glowing terms of brother Scott's co-operation with Communist Party councillors in his position of being a Labour Party councillor. The report went on to outline that in view of the necessity of building and maintaining unity it was necessary to fill the vacancy caused through the retirement of Brother Irwin with such a Labour Party candidate as Brother Scott afforded. The national and London advisory committees agreed arising from that report to support Brother Scott for the job. So, from being in a position of an 'also-ran' in such national elections before that date, he was elected on the first ballot over several other candidates, subsequent to the support the Communist Party afforded him. It will be noted, too, that many of the branches whose votes are now being questioned, on that occasion polled heavily for Brother Scott.

In Brother West's case, I would bring witnesses to testify how he came to hold the position of executive councillor. These would testify that Brothers Haxell, Fraser and Hendy, accompanied by Mr Peter Kerrigan, the Communist Party's national industrial organizer, journeyed to Manchester on two occasions. The purpose of these journeys was to meet the Manchester ETU communists who had decided to support a communist, Brother Turner, for the post of executive councillor.

The national advisory committee had decided that they wanted 'in the interests of unity', to run a Labour Party member, Brother West. These visits by members of the national advisory committee were on the instigation on the first occasion of the national advisory committee, but on the second visit it was on the direct instigation of the political sub-committee of the Communist Party, who had endorsed the view that Brother West should be the candidate. It was only subsequent to the Hungarian events of 1956 that the Manchester communists were prepared to change their candidate from Brother Turner to Brother West.

Since, therefore, two members of this committee are implicated by the evidence I could bring, I have no intention of bringing my evidence before any enquiry committee on which Brother Scott and Brother West form a part.

The committee of inquiry report was presented to the executive council on 18 July 1959 and sent to the TUC in the middle of August, just before Congress. The committee of inquiry's report, having haughtily denounced Cannon and Young's 'non-co-operation', came to the following wholly predictable conclusion.

No evidence has been produced to show that the Communist Party has interfered in the affairs of our union. Nor was there any evidence to show that even if there had been such interference, it would or could have affected the democratic processes by which our union elects its officers and officials and carries out its business, including the important internal matter of conducting appeals.

They were of the view that Cannon and Young's unsubstantial allegations, their 'hectoring and insulting' innuendos at the committee hearings were indicative of a deeply laid plot to discredit the union and sow doubt in its members minds. They even went on to the offensive.

The committee considers it necessary to take this opportunity to express their unanimous view that the executive council have been excessively lenient in connection with the continued activities of those members who, in our opinion, have abused their democratic rights. We wish to impress upon the executive council that if they continue to act with such leniency, there is a grave danger that considerable harm will be done to the union. It is our view that the executive council have displayed this leniency in an attempt to effect the greatest possible unity, but a continuation of the present undesirable atmosphere will make this laudable intention impossible.

The TUC invited the full executive council to come to Congress House to discuss the matter. Haxell quickly said yes to the suggested date a month or so later. Five days before the meeting was due, the leadership wrote to the TUC saying it was wholly unreasonable to invite the whole executive council (in reality, probably because Messrs Chapple and Walker might have spoken out of turn) to talk to just the finance and general purposes committee of congress – it ought to be the whole General Council (on which presumably sat at least a handful of Haxell's pals). Anyway, everyone at Hayes Court was now busy and the date was inconvenient. At this point, the TUC wrote back on 25 November (nearly a full year already since their first tentative request) saying that 'the present leadership of the ETU is more concerned to evade than to deal adequately with the questions put to the union by the general council' and that they were driven to the conclusion that the leadership of the ETU were behaving as though they were 'aware that there is so much substance in the charges that they are unwilling to have them thoroughly investigated and unable to specifically and unequivocally to deny them.'

The TUC had challenged them, like LSE No. 5 had done back in 1957, to take legal action against the liars and charlatans in the press. Haxell added a dash of cheek to his normal reticence in his reply.

We have already explained that our reluctance to take legal proceedings is born of our experience, the experience of the movement generally, the fact that such actions are used by the press to adversely attack the unions, and the costs involved. However, if the General Council does not agree with our view, and still hold that the reports of the newspapers and journals on the affairs of the ETU are harmful to the movement as a whole, then providing the General Council are prepared to finance the legal action and accept the consequences of any adverse publicity on the movement as a whole, my union are quite willing to co-operate with the General Council in taking such action.

By Christmas 1959, that was where the TUC left it, refusing to pay Haxell's bills and emphasizing their refusal to enter into any more silly correspondence. All that Woodcock had in mind was to report the whole pathetic episode to the 1960 congress some ten months later and see what they said. The crisis that emerged out of the Haxell–Byrne election reactivated their interest in early 1960. Meanwhile, the reformers were thrown back on their own resources.

In June 1959, the union's policy conference met at Bridlington. It met amidst unprecedented suspicion and unpleasantness. For one resolution, critical of the executive, only seven out of 380 delegates voted against the platform. Les Cannon sat alone in the gallery like a leper, although he told journalist Keith Mason that one day he would sit in Foulkes's chair. It was not as though all the executive's opponents had disappeared from the conference. Bill Blair was particularly vigorous in support of his motion deploring the growing rift between the Labour Party and the union. He said how dreadful it was to be the only union at the 1958 Labour Party conference to vote against British membership of NATO. 'No one in this conference will blush when I say that on issues of this kind, the policy of the ETU is synonymous with that of the Communist Party.' Charlie Hurley from Hull – forty-seven years in the union and the Labour Party and veteran parliamentary candidate – seconded. 'I recognize the fact that the ETU has always been a militant organization; that some of the things you say here are being said within the Labour Party itself. But to level a constant stream of criticism against the Labour Government or against the Labour Party is not exactly playing the game.' Laurie Hancock from Scunthorpe and Jim Smith from Hayes branch moved an amendment that pledged support to the '1945 policies', not the 1959 Gaitskellite 'revisionism'. Hancock did this by quoting previous speeches by Bill Blair about the 'spirit of 1945'. Jim Smith did it by insisting that deteriorating relations with the Labour Party was not caused by the union. It was caused by the Labour Party rejecting Sam Goldberg at Nottingham South, accepting wage restraint and watering down policy. This view narrowly prevailed, 184–165, showing that mainstream Labour support still existed. There was the usual parade of overwhelming majorities for the usual parade of policies: East-West trading, peace, socialism, anti-wage restraint, pro-forty-hour week, international trade union unity. However, the real excitement, as expected, came in the private session. It was the culmination of over a year's work by Les Cannon, Bill Sullivan and Dick Reno on the union's finances and the personal financial affairs of the union's leading officials. The rules of the union allowed members to consult the books at Hayes Court; despite bureaucratic impediments and the usual delays, key figures began to emerge, leading up to the 1959 conference. These enquiries were carried out against the background of financial crisis engendered in 1957, when Esher was shut for financial reasons. Some strange things began to emerge. First, the drinks bills at the TUC Congresses for the union's senior officials to entertain their friends – £315 16s 3d at the Bedford Hotel in Brighton in 1956, for instance. The communist official, Colin Whittome, was lent £1,147 on 11 June 1958, quite against the rules – a clerical error, according to Haxell, easily rectified. Arthur Stride had gone to Warsaw, but not as an elected member of an official ETU delegation – the union paid the £80 air fare. In 1957, four executive councillors were effectively working full-time for the union, living off delegation fees. Les Cannon's favourite man, Jack Frazer, received £1,700 in this way that year when £15 a week was a good wage for an electrician at work. Frank Haxell got expenses of £1,800 in 1958 over and above his salary of £1,158. In 1959, he never submitted expenses regularly; he also ignored the detailed expenses form (so much for petrol, so much for rail fares, so much for delegation fees etc.). He would obtain cash from the union's accounts department, leave scruffy paper IOUs for the amounts and every now and again submit claims for huge round figures that paid off his clutch of IOUs and then some!

When branches like the persistent Kingston asked Haxell to visit the branch to talk about the union's finances, he refused. It was left to Dick Reno to directly accuse Haxell and the executive in frequent branch visits of financial malpractice. Frank Foulkes did not escape the spotlight. He used to claim expenses of £3 10s 0d delegation fees for crossing the corridor to attend the sub-executive council at Hayes Court. He would claim £9 10s 0d for a full executive council meeting, a sum that included an overnight delegation fee as if he were still residing in his native Liverpool. The fact was that his marriage had long broken down and he had been living in a flat near the head office for the previous ten years! Lastly, Dick Reno accused Haxell and Foulkes of using the union's employees from the estates department to improve the homes they lived in and, in Haxell's case, renovate it for him so that when he resold the house he garnered a nice profit of over £3,000.

Frank Haxell had no time for all of this. He told the 1959 conference straight.

I say to you very clearly, very definitely and decisively that not one penny of the union's funds has been used in costs involved with either this property, its repair, building of garages or decorations. When I say 'the funds of the union' I mean cash, time, or labour costs. I think, quite frankly, that this is one of the most low and despicable stories ever put round this union.

He later wrote that this statement drew great applause from the conference who knew full well that Dick Reno 'was present at the meeting and was one of those who had put around the story to which I had referred'. For his pains, Dick Reno was banned from holding office in the union for *ten* years and fined £10. Reno took out a legal case against this in later years, as we shall see. It is appropriate, though, to contrast Haxell's 'definite and decisive' statement above with his eventual admission in the High Court on 13 March 1964 in a formal apology to Dick Reno.

'It was necessary to correct' his statement to the 1959 conference. 'I now find it necessary to state to my deep regret that the funds and labour of the union had been involved in a substantial extent in the repair and improvement of No. 57 Clarence Road, Bromley ... the allegations are substantially true.'

By the end of the summer of 1959, the protests were reaching into every branch of the union, a fact recognized by Foulkes when he said in his presidential address

During the twelve months since the last conference of the union, branch rooms have been used to discuss questions that have no connection whatsoever with the working conditions or living standards of the members. Questions upon which the whole of the union's membership should be concentrating its undivided attention have been neglected. A tremendous amount of time of officials and staff at the head office has been diverted in defending the union against slander, vilification and abuse....

Foulkes himself was up for election at the September quarter night. The scrutiny, the 'visiting' of branches was on an unprecedented scale. As a consequence, the conduct of the election was comparatively fair. Les Cannon was impressed that only twelve branches nation-wide were disqualified; even so, places like London South West (now back in the hands of a communist secretary, P. O'Neil) and LSE No. 11 voted with enthusiasm for Foulkes at hugely increased levels over the 1959 Les Gregory election turn-out (up 300 per cent in London South West and 600 per cent in LSE No. 11 – mostly 'postal' votes brought in by the branch secretary). The 1959 Foulkes election was curious in many ways. There is no doubt at all that Frank Foulkes was an extremely popular man in the union. His chairmanship of the conferences was always widely enjoyed and respected by political friend and foe. He paid great attention to the 'hail-fellow, well-met!' part of a trade-union leadership. He gave out gold badges and long-service awards at endless branch functions. He never concealed his communist views but was forgiven them across the country as people enjoyed his cheerful personality. The reformers clearly felt that an attack on Foulkes, personally, might rebound on the gathering campaign. The candidate they ran against Foulkes was Bill Blairford, the Edinburgh man who had until very recently been a keen, active communist, but who, like many others, had started his slow slide out of the Communist Party after Hungary.

The result was astonishing. Bill Blairford would not have objected to being called a comparative unknown. The result was declared at the October 1959 executive meeting. Foulkes got 18,100 votes; Bill Blairford 15,311. The most popular electable communist had nearly been beaten. Blairford either won or ran Foulkes close in some of the 'touchstone' branches in a fair ballot. Fulham voted for Blairford, 41–31. London Central did, 31–23. He only lost London Press 143–140. Blairford won all three Southampton branches, did well in the North-East and did very well in London. This election, though, was felt at the time to be a dry run for Christmas 1959, when Frank Haxell was up for re-election. The reformers argued about who the candidate should be. It could not be Cannon – he was banned.

However, Frank Chapple was now out of the Communist Party and firing on all cylinders. Indeed, by the end of November 1959, he asked for permission to circulate the union with his own denial of Haxell's repudiation of communist interference in the union. Not only did he do that, but he wrote to the TUC along the same lines – which was the same as publishing it in the papers – at the end of the first week in December 1959, just as the quarterly meetings got under way. It could have been Bill Sullivan. Dick Reno had just got over 1,800 votes in a brave attempt to carry Cannon's flag and defeat Frazer in the executive council elections. It could have been the energetic Mark Young.

After some discussion, all were agreed. Only Jock Byrne had the truly national standing to run against Haxell. He had first 'lost' to him in 1948. Surely his time had come.

20

THE END OF THE TUNNEL: THE 1959 GENERAL SECRETARY ELECTION

THROUGHOUT 1957–9, THE POLITICAL struggle between the communist leadership and their adversaries focused evermore on the stream of allegations about the corruption of the union's votes.

It is a fact that concern over fiddling ballots had been implied and expressly suggested long before the communists made what Frank Chapple was to call a 'science' out of it. For decades, some members' desire to see themselves or their friends in office within the union led them to cheat in branch ballots. Jack Ball implied this as early as 1916 when he bemoaned the intense competition for the first generation of full-time jobs in the union. Glasgow Central branch had suggested at the end of 1915 that the executive council should investigate every branch that apparently reported more than fifty per cent of the members voting.

'The discussion arose by some members drawing attention to the large number in certain branches voting in one direction, and the opinion was expressed that if the voting was all genuine, some branches displayed a great amount of activity at election times.' The sanctity of fair ballots was originally a left cause. In the London area, in 1922, the anti-executive syndicalist magazine, the *Electron*, ran a debate about low turn-outs in union elections which had averaged twenty-five per cent in 1919. LSE No. 6 sent in their ideas.

Many members think that the postal ballot is the most democratic manner in which to ascertain the verdict of the members, especially as a large number of members are prevented by work from attending the branch . . . Others argue that this method places a veto in the hands of the 'deadheads' . . . the confidence of the rank and file will only be retained by giving to each the knowledge that he will receive the same power of registering his opinions as another.

Minority Movement activist Merrels told the 1929 conference that they should adopt postal ballots with stamped addressed envelopes used to return each member's vote. He 'suggested that by allowing shop-stewards to hand out and collect ballot papers, abuses of the ballot took place.' By 1944, Ernie Bussey was aware of just how damaging fiddled ballots could be.

It must be appreciated that there are very few trade unions holding as many ballots as this union, which may be to the good, and may be in the interests of democracy as we understand it. But democracy can be of no value, and those elected through a democratic machine can have no value in representation unless the procedure by which they are elected is clean and wholesome in its operation.

Frank Murphy, the Scottish executive councillor from 1949–55, as we have seen, spoke to the 1946 rules revision conferences urging postal ballots. It was turned down by Stevens because it cost too much. Jock Byrne's election address was altered in 1959, under the rule that restricted election addresses to the candidates' 'industrial record', on just this point.

With almost all ballots there is a surfeit of complaints about the conduct of the ballot. This is not a happy state of affairs, and I would advocate the scrapping of the present system, and its replacement by a postal ballot where each member entitled to vote would receive a stamped return form which would be subject to scrutiny by independent scrutineers.

Perhaps the most revealing discussion about the union's ballots took place at the 1952 rules revision conference at Whitley Bay. Tommy Symms, from Woolwich, urged that shop-stewards should no longer be able to bring in ballots to the branch count. Only individual members should be allowed to do this. 'Woolwich branch asks you to support this amendment, because we believe that for a long time past, wholesale fiddling has taken place in connection with ballot returns ... our ballot machinery is wide open to roguery and corruption.' He had clearly thought about this issue in some detail. He took his own branch, for example. Woolwich had 700 members, with over 350 at the Woolwich Arsenal alone. The ballots went out fourteen days before the ballot. For several years, he had organized the eight shop-stewards and the one money steward, plus himself, to approach and badger each member at the Arsenal about the importance of voting. Never, over many years, had more than 130 out of 350 Arsenal workers voted. He could not recall over many years more than 200 out of the branch's 700 members voting. He told how he had visited other branches to see how it was that others seemed to get a eighty-five to ninety per cent turn-out. Foulkes interrupted to say it was not fair to attack other branches' procedures in their absence. Tommy Symms then drew attention to some branches that voted with absolutely no votes on one side or the other.

I do not know whether we have peculiar individuals in the Woolwich area, but human nature being what it is, I must say this. From our experience in and around the Woolwich area ... [they could not understand] where two people go to a ballot, one man can get ... almost the total return in a branch and the other two cannot get a vote at all. It is something contrary to all the teachings of human nature.

Sid Maitland was pomposity itself in reply. The shop-stewards were the cream of the membership. It was inconceivable they would fix ballots. Sid Lyons, from London press, said that their huge votes were as a result of great activity by the local branch officials. Walter Stevens recognized that in the past there had been ballots where branches had voted with more votes than members. He also admitted cheerfully that postal voting was feasible, but would cost too much. Tommy Symms's amendment and the implications of his thinking out loud, based on his own experience, sank out of sight. He eventually became an area official in 1958, beating Les Cannon. There is, unfortunately, no record of his concern about the balloting system then.

The election for general secretary in 1959 must have reminded Byrne of the 1948 assistant general secretary election where he had clearly beaten Haxell. He had then got 27,586 votes to Haxell's 25,361; a third candidate, the Northern Ireland full-time official, Lowden, got 2,184, just sufficient to deny Byrne outright victory by 221 votes. It is still believed, given Lowden's resignation soon afterwards over a small matter of £600, that Lowden was forced to stand in order to attract votes away from Byrne towards the Irish favourite son, in return for not being prosecuted over the alleged theft. Anyway, that is in the realm of legend. The realm of fact was that on the second ballot, Byrne's vote rose to 28,732 but Haxell's went up to a record 33,399. Careful examination of the two voting returns shows a surge in extra support for Haxell in fifteen or so branches by 100 votes or over in each branch. Liverpool Central voted for Haxell in the first ballot, 251–27, and in the second, 481–25. Walton voted 180–15 and then 272–17. Wigan voted 355–1 and then 462–6 in the second ballot. Blackpool was 595–1 and then 695–5. Tommy Symms must have been astonished by all this. His branch then voted 114–42 for Haxell and 237–46 for Haxell in the second round. Perhaps it was this result that still nagged in his mind at Whitley Bay four years later. Fifty branches were disqualified in this election, thus probably robbing Byrne of outright victory in the first ballot. There was even the amazing Swansea result that defies analysis. In the first ballot they voted 498–0 for Byrne. In the second, 497–63 for Haxell! Byrne won 299 out of 483 branch votes in the first ballot, compared to Haxell's 172. He still beat Haxell in terms of branches (257 or fifty-five per cent) in the second ballot. But the huge increase in votes in those branches where Haxell got over 100 votes (up from seventy to ninety-five branches) was decisive.

This election in particular, along with further, if less spectacular, defeats by Haxell in 1953 (assistant general secretary) and 1955 (general secretary), fired in Byrne and his supporters a deep sense of resentment, purpose and determination. The campaigning was huge, the 'visiting' of branches on a nation-wide scale.

But for the communists at Hayes Court, the prize was equally valuable. They knew that their relatively plush lifestyle was at stake if Haxell went down, never mind the damage to the Communist Party's prestige. They could not help themselves. They had to win.

The key to understanding just how the members of the union were deceived in this election is to look at the election process in three distinct phases. First, crucial frauds were initated before the ballots went out, in a 'pre-voting' stage, largely coming out of the union's head office.

Secondly, at the moment of voting, there was widespread malpractice throughout the union, particularly in branches whose branch secretaries were active communists.

Thirdly, the most spectacular fiddles were reserved for the 'post-voting' period when it became apparent to the union's leadership that Byrne had won the election, despite the comprehensive fiddling that had gone on in the first two phases of the election.

Firstly, then, what chicanery went on before the moment of voting? The printers for the ballot papers were the Express Printing Company in Manchester. In previous elections, there had been complaints of slow delivery of ballot papers to the branches. For the 1959 general secretary election, therefore, Norman Swift at the printers required the head office to let him know the numbers of ballots required, per branch, before the September membership figures could be collated at head office to produce an up-to-date picture of the union's paid-up membership.

Jim Humphrey, the office manager, was responsible for telling Mr Swift how many ballots per branch were required. Humphrey had served for ten years on the executive on the union throughout the 1940s and 50s. He had been a branch official himself for years. He joined the Communist Party in 1950. He understood elections in the ETU and had spent six years at Hayes Court – nominally as executive councillor – but in reality as office manager until his formal appointment earlier in 1959.

Because of the apparent time-constraint identified by the printers, the figures per branch were estimated by Humphrey and sent to the printers. The 'method' he used to estimate the numbers required per branch was frankly bizarre. He looked at three separate figures. First he looked at the March 1959 and June 1959 figures. He then checked to make sure there had not been any higher branch membership returns and then added extra figures 'in order that it would not be necessary, once we had the numbers printed . . . to go back to the printers again to have more printed.' However, the printers were given estimates that gave a completely bogus impression of precision.

Belfast Municipal, for instance, was estimated to need precisely 691 ballots. Jim Humphrey's explanation for this figure was, 'I must have said "Well allow about six hundred and fifty and add forty-one," or something like that.' Why he added forty-one and not fifty or 100 was never properly explained in court, to the obvious puzzlement of the judge.

Then in early November, Bob Oliver, the recently retired office manager went to Manchester to supervise the despatch of the *exact* number of ballots indented for by each branch. The branch secretary would then receive his requirements for the election, and it was up to him to distribute them to the members of the branch.

Belfast Central demonstrates how the system worked. Jim Humphrey's unconventional estimate was 591. Express Printers, printing in sheets of four, printed 600. Bob Oliver's final figures for the branch's requirements, however, came to 502, and this number was duly despatched to the branch. This left ninety-eight spare Belfast Central ballot papers.

All of the branches with a similar surplus had their ballots bundled up and sent to St Pancras Station in twenty-seven separate parcels between 12–20 November. They were not sent to Hayes Court, the union's head office. They were not destroyed at the printers. They went to St Pancras Station, marked 'to be called for'. There were 26,833 surplus ballot papers. They were called for by Jim Humphrey over several days. He denied that anyone else was encouraged to 'call for' a parcel in the same period.

At Hayes Court, they were locked in a room to which only Mr Humphrey had access; they were burnt, on Mr Humphrey's instructions, at the 'end of November' over a period of nine to ten days. For ten days or so, they remained undisturbed – except for twenty-six branches who claimed not to have received any ballots from the printers, and Mr Humphrey took out and despatched the required numbers to these branches out of this store of 'spare' ballots.

It is almost certain that this huge over-ordering of ballot papers was a deliberate and central part of the overall fraud. There was great encouragement to fraudulent use of these ballots printed on the form itself. Before the 1957 rules revision conference, branch secretaries had to stamp each ballot with the distinctive branch stamp before sending them out to the members. After 1957 each branch had a code number placed on all its ballots at the printers. This meant that ballots could be returned by post to branch secretaries direct from the surplus papers deposit at Hayes Court, without having to have each paper stamped by the branch secretary. This meant that postal votes would be counted in all innocence by branch secretaries, unaware of the true source of the ballot. Clearly, under the previous system extra ballots could be made available to systematic 'fiddlers' to put the stamp on. However, after 1957, fraudulent votes could now be easily placed in innocent branches as well. The experiences of three branches in the Southampton area supports this judgment.

Charles Saunders was the secretary of Woolston branch. On the evening of Sunday 13 December, Mr Saunders went round to his branch treasurer, Mr Sullivan. The two men checked and found correct the branch's allocation of ballots – 175. They checked who was entitled to vote – who was paid up – and filled the envelopes with notices calling the quarterly meeting for 22 December and the necessary voting papers to those entitled to receive them. There were eleven ballots left over, and Mr Saunders handed them in to George Scott at the subsequent enquiry. The work was finished at around 10 p.m., and the envelopes posted. They would catch the first post at 9 a.m., on the following day, Monday 14 December.

That Monday evening, Charlies Saunders got in from work at 7.30 p.m. The day's post had brought him four returned ballot papers. They were postmarked 6.45 p.m., Sunday 13 December, the previous day! At that time, the branch allocation was still being sorted by him and brother Sullivan, prior to being posted at 10 p.m. Charlie Saunders's *own* ballot paper – posted just like all the rest – arrived at his house on the Tuesday morning, 15 December. That night, the ordinary branch meeting opened the four premature ballots. Charlie Saunders letter to Haxell, of 15 December, says it all.

Our meeting tonight decided to open these envelopes, and found that they each contained a vote for Brother Haxell – apparently by the same person, as they were similarly crossed with identical type markings. I am prepared to swear on oath that I have not previously seen or handled these ballot envelopes prior to receiving them individually by post last evening. The branch number of both envelope and ballot paper completely corresponds with this branch's official issue, and we are at a loss to understand how it came about. The branch feels that the fullest possible investigations should be made, as there appears to be a deliberate attempt by a person or persons yet unknown to carry out a forgery ... We feel sure you will regard this as a serious matter in view of recent publicity on this union's ballots.

Exactly the same thing happened to Eric Storrer at Southampton Central. He had five ballot papers sent to him which could not possibly have been from his branch allocation, arriving on Monday 14 December. Six votes were involved at the Hythe branch where Edgar Dew, the secretary, received his bogus votes for Haxell at his house before he had even sent out the branch ballots to the members at all! He was to recall his involvement on 2 February 1962 in this way.

I received my packet of eighty-nine ballot papers from the printers and I checked them, I put them in the cupboard, and I left them there. On the following Monday I came home at dinner-time to go to town with my wife, and I found six ballot papers already returned to me through the post. At the branch committee meeting I produced my ballot papers. The branch committee checked those, and made the correct number of eighty-nine. I then produced the lists with the members' names on which were entitled to the ballot papers. The branch committee checked those, and made the correct number of eighty-nine. I then produced the lists with the members' names on which were entitled to the ballot papers. They counted them and they corresponded. *I then insisted that they re-check the ballot papers and the members' names again, which they did and made the correct number correspond. I then produced the six ballot papers which I received by post from my pocket. To this the committee did not know what to say.*

George Scott was sent by Haxell to investigate. He exonerated the branch officials. All three branches were to vote for Byrne, 136–40 between them, and the best Scott and the executive could later come up with was that friends of Les Cannon must have somehow got hold of ballot papers and sent them in like this to produce evidence of fraud to undermine the executive!

It is much more likely, and was the considered view of Justice Winn, that the Southampton branches were just the tip of the surplus ballot paper iceberg. We will never know how many branches got such an extra, if modest, push to Haxell's eventual vote. This was not a case of communist branch secretaries being able to post themselves large numbers of extra ballots. Four or five extra votes in hundreds of branches, pro-communist and anti-communist alike, would have produced at least 2,000 extra votes for Haxell.

While the events in Southampton were unfolding – from 15–17 December – Bob McLennan asked Jim Humphrey, 'what the position was about the Hythe and Woolston ballot papers'. Jim Humphrey told him that only 'the correct amount had been sent to those branches from the printers'. Gerald Gardiner then asked Humphrey at the trial if he had told McLennan that he had stored 26,833 ballot papers, including spares for the Southampton area, in the downstairs office at Hayes Court for the best part of a fortnight. Humphrey said it had not occurred to him to tell McLennan this.

Justice Winn was to say:

... my judgement of this matter, expressed with full appreciation that it involves a grave finding against Mr Humphrey, is that he deliberately ordered substantial excess quantities of ballots for branches where he expected that fraudulent votes could be registered, if need be, for Mr Haxell, intending that the excess quantities could be sent to head office, or could be caused earlier to be sent to branches.

Many branches had received extra ballot papers, claiming that despite Mr Humphrey's estimating and Mr Oliver's supervising the despatch of the ballots, they were still short. Justice Winn rightly emphasized that all the suspicion in the world did not add up to proof. LSE No. 1 provided a typical example of suspicion without proof in this regard. An executive-supporting branch, its secretary Albert Aitkenhead had indented for 443 votes and only received 400. He rang head office for the 'missing' forty-three and received them within three days. His branch books revealed later that only 408 were entitled to vote in the first place and he stoutly maintained that he did not know that the printers had been told to provide 522. Around fifty per cent of the branch's true financial membership apparently voted, over twice the national average.

This first phase of fraud involved the printing and distribution of surplus ballots, presumably from the union's head office or St Pancras Station cache.

The second phase of the fraud was at the moment of voting. Each member was sent a ballot paper with a pro forma envelope addressed to the branch scrutineers. The member would either attend the quarterly meeting in December 1959 and hand in his ballot inside the sealed envelope, or he would post it to the branch secretary (at his own expense), who would take it to the quarterly meeting or he could hand the ballot paper to his shop-steward or money steward at work to take to the quarterly meeting on his behalf.

The extent of individual rigging in branches is again a matter of informed suspicion, rather than obvious proof or, even less, subsequent admission of guilt by communist-supporting branch officials.

However, high postal votes in certain branches gave much cause for concern. East Ham, for instance, had had thirty-two members at the meeting, but the postal votes received produced a result of 114–58 in Haxell's favour. There were 169 out of 179 votes for Haxell in the Peckham branch. Eighty-five per cent were by post. At Tottenham – where Hill, the secretary, was a well-known executive supporter – 122 out of 185 votes were for Haxell, with seventy per cent voting by post. LSE No. 9 had 126 out of 203 financial members vote by post. Other pro-Haxell branches like London Jointers (seventy per cent), Gray's Inn (eighty-five per cent) and London North-West (154 out of 282 qualified members) had high postal votes. In some cases, they proved decisive. Belfast Central had supported Jock Byrne in national elections back into the 1940s. No previous candidate had got more than thirty-two votes against Bryne in all those years. The branch had nominated him for general secretary. Imagine their suprise when ninety postal votes arrived (compared to the previous highest ever postal vote in the branch of twenty-five) with forty-eight bearing an identical postmark and date stamp. Given the branch's voting and nominating preference for Byrne in past elections, the eventual result of 127–41 in favour of Haxell was an even bigger surprise. Gerald Gardiner thought there was a 'legitimate inference' that Bob McLennan had posted the extra votes himself on a twenty-four-hour visit to Belfast during the period in November when the extra ballots were at Hayes Court. If this was so, and contemporary sources have privately confirmed this episode with the author, then it surely proves that a wide distribution was intended for the surplus ballot papers, in non-communist branches as well as in those branches where the branch officials could be relied upon to use their initiative – or do what they always did. There is less evidence in the 1959 election trial for the abuse of the electoral procedure at the moment of voting by shop-stewards; however, it was widely believed at the time that communist shop-stewards would collect *some* votes from a large site or factory membership and produce at branch meetings a pile of ballots suitably augmented from the Hayes Court or St Pancras Station cache.

The most breathtaking frauds were reserved for the third phase – after the voting was over. This involved careful manipulation of the obtuse and confusing 1958 rule-book on the one hand, and spectacular melodrama on the other. First, the Preston branch produced a grotesque fiddle when the scrutineers' return of Haxell's majority of 101–52 was improved by the time it reached the executive minutes to 191–52. This result was challenged in the branch by branch member Tom Breakell, and the branch books were sent for by the head office, only to completely disappear, without trace, post office receipt or head office acknowledgement.

The supreme melodrama was played out in the last few days of 1959, deceiving the national scrutineers, Rengert and Shipman, who were exonerated at the trial from any suggestion of responsibility for the events that were to follow.

After its quarterly meeting, each branch would send in to head office its scrutineers' return form which gave the election result in that branch. The form would contain the names and signatures of the branch scrutineers, secretary, president and the appropriate figures and dates of meeting etc. These returns had to be returned to head office within five days of the quarterly meeting to which they referred, irrespective of whether a weekend intervened or not. However, since 1953, an informal system had grown up that resulted in minor infringements of the bureaucracy associated with this procedure being excused for a 'first offence'. If, for instance, the branch president's signature was missing from the scrutineers' return form, or the branch had met on the wrong night to conduct the election or was, most significant of all, late in its returns, it was conventional to warn the branch for a first offence, and refuse to accept their returns thereafter. It was therefore of crucial importance that the branch scrutineers' forms from 703 branches should be presented to the national scrutineers honestly. Only Jim Humphrey could open the pro forma branch election returns envelopes as the returns started to come in. He would then place them into two files – 'All Right' and a file which listed the various infringements (which had been entered on a card index, for future reference). They would then be processed by Mrs Lilian Higgs for the attention of the national scrutineers. Gerald Gardiner put two devastating sets of questions to Mrs Higgs, whose honest answers further isolated Jim Humphrey. First, four branches in Liverpool (South, Central, East and Instrument Makers) had voted, two branches for Byrne and two for Haxell. All four met on 21 December. All four arrived late on 28 December. The two that voted for Byrne were disqualified, and the two that voted for Haxell were in the 'All Right' file and escaped disqualification.

Second, all the *envelopes* went first to Jim Humphrey before going to Lilian Higgs to be sorted into various groups of infringements. Gerald Gardiner showed her thirty branches whose envelopes showed they were late; yet not one had been listed as late by Mrs Higgs as she made up her files. Clearly, by the time they arrived at Lilian Higgs's desk, they were in the 'All Right' file and therefore not examined at all. Later on, Gardiner showed Humphrey a list of branches whose meetings were on the 14 and 15 of December, and their receipt stamp was the twenty-first. A further batch had met on 16, 17 and 18 December with a receipt stamp of 23–24 December. All late. Every single one which had voted for Byrne was disqualified. Every single one which had voted for Haxell was allowed. It was clear from the evidence of the national scrutineers that *their* work was largely examining the branches over which there was to be some argument – *not* the branches in the 'All Right' file. In any case, the national scrutiny amounted only to a single ninety-minute examination of the branch scrutineers' returns.

Despite his protestations to the contrary. Jim Humphrey was opening the envelopes as they came in and must have been aware by Christmas Eve that despite all the other 'rigging' that was going on with the surplus ballot papers, the high postal votes, the shop-stewards' satchels of votes and his own manipulation of the infringements file, the election was going badly for Haxell, sitting uneasily along the corridor.

Contemporary figures produced for the trial, by the communist leadership itself, but rarely examined in detail, show clearly what must have become apparent to Humphrey on Christmas Day. On 21 and 22 December, branch totals covering over 12,000 votes were received at head office, to be added to the 11,000 received since the first returns came in on 8 December. This was the surge of branch returns that would make the difference. On Christmas Eve, while head office was busy with seasonal departmental parties, the figures were reviewed in Haxell's office with his strongest political supporters. Byrne led, 11,423–10,565 – a majority of 858. The office was open, briefly, between Christmas and New Year. On 1 January, the next surge of returns showed Byrne to lead, 22,861–20,650, an unthinkable majority of 2,211. Legitimate disqualification of branches, manipulation of the 'All Right' file, the steady supply and use of surplus ballot papers, exceptional postal vosting and legitimate votes had not been enough. It was then that Haxell and his closest supporters decided to perpetrate the crudest fraud of all. In order to achieve the desired result, a large number of branches would have to be disqualified.

This was done by replacing legitimate branch envelopes that had arrived on time with branch envelopes that were apparently late – beyond the five-day limit.

An astonishing 109 branches were disqualified in this election. Three of them had voted for Haxell – with a majority for Haxell in each of just one vote! The other 106 had all voted for Byrne! The trial evidence managed to produce 40 disqualified branches who disputed their disqualification on this substitute envelope controversy. Judge Winn was very strict with this allegation. He said that before he, 'sitting without a jury, decides such an issue as this one of "substitution" he has the lonely task of debating it with his conscience.' He found twenty-seven out of the forty established to his 'complete satisfaction' and a further four were very probably substituted, too.

Supporters of the Haxell regime at the time have told the author that the decision to substitute the envelopes – a trick that had worked in the Cannon-Frazer election in 1957 – was made on Christmas Eve at Hayes Court. The judge was convinced that Haxell was involved personally as was Jack Frazer, who had drawn petrol for a range of 400 miles between Christmas and New Year. He told a wholly implausible story about travelling between Kingston (where a new area office was to be opened), Hayes Court and the London office at Highbury. The paperwork he was involved in was apparently so important that he could not pop in to the committee at Highbury which was meeting at the same time, and of which Jack Frazer was a member. He might have cast his net wider had Bert Batchelor been capable of giving evidence in relation to his petrol expenses in that end-of-year period. Batchelor was excused on medical evidence of ulcers and even finally excused by the judge that 'by contrast with those of other defendants, the evidence and the inferences to be drawn therefrom do not come up to the standard required to establish so grave a charge.'

Les Cannon discovered the strongest symmetry within the disqualified branches. Many of them had been disqualified for posting their branch returns late. Most of these vehemently denied it, having a hundred and one anecdotes about how they had posted the returns following the branch meetings. Some remembered the company they were in on the evening they posted the envelope. Some remembered popping out to post the envelope at the same time as buying cigarettes and sweets. Some remembered being in Scotland for the New Year holiday on the date they were supposed to have posted an obviously bogus envelope. Some frankly remembered the sheer political pleasure reflected in their branch's pro-Byrne vote that they were sending, posthaste, to the big count at head office.

Les Cannon made several lists of disqualified branches, stretching out from London in westerly, north-western and north-eastern directions. He then compared the real posting dates of the envelopes with the dates (now late and so disqualified) on the envelopes produced at head office. There is a random scattering of dates in the real list – a suspicious symmetry about the second.

Take the north-eastern route for instance, illustrated in table 6.

Table 6

	Byrne Majority	Real Posting Date	Substitute Posting Date
Peterborough	50	23 December	30 December
Boston	33	24 December	30 December
Spilsby	10	19 December	30 December
Brigg	32	20 December	30 December
Doncaster	88	23 December	30 December
Barnsley	33	26 December	31 December
Huddersfield	42	18 December	31 December
Whitby	11	21 December	31 December
Bishop Auckland	85	24 December	31 December

Someone had driven north and north-east, posting the pro forma envelopes back to head office, now with dates that rendered them disqualified because they were over five days late. A private detective, William Cobbett, proved that this could be done by posting a similar batch of envelopes. This sensational allegation of methodical posting was slightly weakened by the argument of Neil Lawson, the union's QC at the trial. He pointed out that it would have been easier, if people *were* substituting envelopes in the methodical way Mr Cobbett implied, to substitute in towns where the pro-Byrne majorities were much higher. The judge, and most opinion since, has taken the view that the panic on Christmas Eve which led to people leaving Hayes Court after Christmas with a list on the 'back of a fag packet', as it were, probably prevented a more leisured assessment of where the substituting could be done to better effect. In any event, seventeen of Justice Winn's twenty-seven *certain* substitutions were on Mr Cobbett's list. Equally, if some of the envelopes were sent to other loyal branch communists to post back, that would mean that *some* of the branch disqualifications were done by these car tours, *others* by local activists. The pattern would then be dictated by where the 'friends' were rather than exclusively where the branches existed at which large pro-Byrne majorities had been recorded.

There is a curious footnote to this story. At Christmas time 1960, one year after the Haxell-Byrne election, but before the trial took place in June 1961, the communist leadership issued letters to Communist Party, supporting full-time officers throughout the country. They were required to post to Hayes Court letters from certain places at certain times over the Christmas period.

It is simply speculation to wonder what they were up to. Perhaps it was an attempt to show that the substitute envelope itinerary would have been impossible. Whatever it was for, the results were never produced at the trial, so the experiment could not possibly have helped Haxell's case, or dented Byrne's and Chapple's contentions.

This was the most spectacular 'post-voting' fraud. However, the communists then had up their sleeve several manoeuvres based on the rule-book that helped to prevent the full story coming out. Needless to say, no one was going to be told the result of the election until the executive council accepted the national scrutineers' report. The anti-communist reform movement, however, knew something was happening when in early January, pro-Byrne branches started to receive letters from Bob McLennan stating: 'The national scrutineers at their last meeting decided they could not accept your branch quarterly documents in view of an infringement of Rule 21 Clauses 65 and 74 (the clauses about late posting).' Many branches, separately and furiously, wrote back complaining and demanding access to the envelopes. In early March, many complainant branch officials were summoned to head office to be confronted by Bob McLennan and Jack Frazer with the *substitute* envelope, and required to sign an intimidating undertaking that the envelope was theirs. If the branch persisted in its criticism, as so many so courageously did, they were then told that the whole issue was *sub judice*, following the issue of writs for fraud on 10 May. Consequently, there was no appeal allowed to the executive for each individual branch.

There were other interesting weapons in Haxell's armoury. After the 1957 rules revision conference was over, and unbeknown to the executive council, he sent small detailed changes to the union's rule-book to the Registrar of trade unions and friendly societies. He merely altered the numbering of the clauses. The effect of these changes to Rule 11 was to now prevent branch appeals against national scrutineers' decision on elections, rather than, as the conference thought it had voted, prevent appeals on the less contentious area of the boundaries of electoral divisions.

There could be no appeal against anything the executive did until it appeared in the executive minutes. Haxell delayed the publication of the minutes of the 6 February 1960 meeting, at which Haxell was pronounced general secretary, until May 1960. During this time, no one was certain just how many branches – and which ones – had been disqualified. In Les Cannon's March 1960 reform group circular, the reformers were aware of the result. They thought, from their soundings, that Byrne had won by nearly 5,000 votes. They were appalled to discover that forty-seven branches had been disqualified. What is interesting here is the fact that they only knew of forty-seven of the 109 invalidated branches. They had not been helped by the executive council meeting of 6 February. Transcripts survive of that meeting; the executive and Haxell's phone calls were systematically recorded. It is worth quoting the transcript concerning the announcement of the result in full. After an acrimonious discussion on the validity of Foulkes' own re-election, he suddenly said:

Foulkes	Ballots. December Quarter Night 1959 Results.
	General Secretary.
McLennan	Full-Time Official. General Secretary. We the undersigned have scrutinised the above mentioned ballot and declare the results to be as follows:
	Byrne J. T. 18,577
	Haxell F. L. 19,611.
	F. L. Haxell elected.
Foulkes	Brother Fraser and Brother Sell. All those in favour – Against.

It was to be shown at the trial that the instant response to get 'move' and 'second' done so quickly, before the question of disqualification was discussed, was intended to avoid embarrassing revelations. It also prevented Frank Chapple, Ernest Hadley and Colin Walker from noting anything more than a small fraction of the disqualified branch names. It was the last play in the post-voting fraud.

Frank Chapple was not going to be intimidated by this.

Chapple	I would like to ask some questions on this before you take such a motion. We are entitled to have a scrutineers' report which includes the ... [no doubt he was about to say 'the number of disqualifications'].
Foulkes	Just a moment – who was against the motion?
Chapple	I was against the motion.
Foulkes	Brother Walker and Brother Hadley are against the motion.
Chapple	Now I want to ask a question about the scrutineers' report if I may. This is the second election that has been rushed through in this manner.
Foulkes	The second?
Chapple	The second one. Yes. The first one was yours.
Foulkes	There could be 2,000 as far as I am concerned.
Chapple	No alright. I am not worried about the rest. I am only worried about these. Can I have some report of the scrutineers as an executive councillor?
McLennan	Well, you have had the usual report, Mr Chairman. If anybody wants to raise anything in relation to the report of the scrutineers, it is always dealt with.
Chapple	I wish to ask Mr Chairman were any branches disqualified in this ballot?
Foulkes	The answer is yes.
Chapple	Can I know how many there were and who they were?
McLennan	Well there was a whole number of branches as there usually is, probably more so on this occasion because all kinds of people seem to be having circuses round the country trying to find out votes and ballots and

	inevitably you are bound to get involved in more disqualifications as a consequence.
Chapple	I would like to know, Mr Chairman, the names of those branches disqualified in this ballot.
McLennan	Abertillery.
Walker	Just a minute. I want to know something more about this too. I do know that in my own particular division there has been an investigation into a branch as it happens to be within the area which I am looking after from time to time, and I understand there was a fairly substantial vote. I understand also that Brother Scott was up in Glasgow last Monday dealing with this branch. I want to know whether their results are included in this or not.
McLennan	There are some branches that are still being investigated but in any case whatever the results are of these branches it makes no difference to the final result. That has always been the position so far as any investigations are concerned. There is not going to be any difference in the result as the result of investigations does not alter the scrutineers' report.
Chapple	Can I have them slowly, please, because I would like to make a note of them. If you don't mind.
Foulkes	Just read them in the normal way. We are not giving press publicity.
McLennan	Abertillery, Aldershot, Altrincham, Aston, Ayr, Barnet, Barnsley, Bath, Bedford, Bideford, Billingham, Birmingham Jointers, Birmingham Traction, Blackburn, Blaenau Ffestiniog, Bishop Auckland, Boston, Bourne, Bracknell, Brigg, Bristol, Bromsgrove, Burnley, Burton, Bury, Cambuslang, Cardigan, Cirencester, Coleraine, Colchester, Crewkerne, Cwmbran, Doncaster, Eastbourne, East Kilbride, Exeter, Fakenham, Galashiels, Gillmoss, Glasgow N.W., Kendal, Larne, Leeds Central, Leicester, Letchworth, Liverpool East, Liverpool Instrument Makers, London Station Engineers No. 4., London Station Engineers No. 8., London Station Engineers No. 18., London Station Engineers No. 20., Long Eaton, Luton, Market Drayton, Mildenhall, Mitcham Electronic Engineers, Neath, Newport No. 1., North Shields, Nuneaton, Okehampton, Oldham No. 1., Penrith, Port Talbot Supervisory, Peterborough, Pontypool, Prescot, Reading No. 1., Reading Supply, Rochdale, Rogerstone, Salisbury, Scunthorpe, Seaham, Silloth, Solihull, Southend, Spilsby, Staines, Stanley, Stevenston, Stirling, Sunderland, Swindon, Torquay, Totnes, Treorchy, Twickenham, Wallingford, Wellington, Welshpool, Whitby, Widnes, Wisbech, Woking, Yate, Yeovil.
Hadley	Can I ask how many that makes, Mr Chairman, because I could not possibly follow the list.
McLennan	It is round about a hundred I think.
Chapple	There are one hundred branches disqualified?

Foulkes	Full-time officials.
Chapple	Alright, I am still asking questions out of the scrutineers' report.
Foulkes	No, you can't.
Chapple	I have got several more to ask. I want to know now if any branch ballots were sent to head office on this occasion and were counted by the national scrutineers.
McLennan	There were a number.
Chapple	Thank you. Are you prepared to give me the names of these?
Foulkes	No, it is not in the scrutineers' report.
Chapple	Right ho. It's alright.
Hadley	How many branches were not disqualified, Mr Chairman, after complaints had been received?
Foulkes	About twenty.
Walker	So that is about a hundred branches still to be investigated?
Foulkes	No, they have been investigated and the scrutineers have decided they are not valid.
Foulkes	Full-time official area No. 1.
McLennan	We the undersigned have scrutinized the above mentioned ballot and declare the results to be as follows: Cosby J. 1,347 Pyke 285
Foulkes	Brother Cosby declared elected five years, etc. All those in favour? Against – one. Brother Chapple.
Chapple	You have got me down as against in the other one haven't you, General Secretary?
Foulkes	Yes. Brother Walker voted against.
Walker	Yes.
Hadley	Mr Chairman, I voted against.
Walker	While I am only getting part information I intend to vote against them all. I want more information on the whole of those ballots.
Foulkes	What information do you want on that one?
Walker	I am told there were a hundred branches being investigated. I am asked to accept the returns. I am not told what type of investigation or why it was decided that there was no longer any cause to debar them.
Foulkes	I don't know where we are going to. You elect two scrutineers. You give them the job of scrutinizing and this particular scrutiny was conducted with the general secretary absent and I presided over the scrutiny and then you want to do it all yourselves.
Chapple	That must seem unfair to you.
Foulkes	I would suggest that you do not be cheeky all the time.
Chapple	Well, I have had plenty of it, Mr Chairman.
Foulkes	I would suggest that you be your age for once.

That then is how they did it. Surplus ballot papers, altered rule-books, fraudulent postal voting and factory voting, deliberate suppression of enquiry and protest and spectacular substitution of inconvenient branch returns. Justice Winn said at the trial that but for these fiddles, Jock Byrne 'would in my judgment have had a majority of at least one thousand one hundred and fifty, but probably of the order of fifteen hundred'.

Waiting for Justice Winn: Christmas 1959–June 1961

It is easy to forget that all of this evidence of wrong-doing in the 1959 election did not become apparent until the case came to the High Court on 17 April 1961, with the verdict finally being handed down on 28 June.

It is vital to remember the pressure that all the participants were under – the reformers were desperate to discover the detail of the fraud; the union's leadership were desperate to conceal or destroy the evidence. Green huts appeared in the grounds of Hayes Court, where papers were sorted and, on occasion, shredded.

After the election campaign in December 1959, there was an uneasy calm. Les Cannon's propaganda war was stepped up with a leaflet that in forecasting victory for Byrne by over 5,000 votes, warned that the communists might try to prevent Byrne's victory: they might disallow it on the grounds of 'press interference', and following on from that, increase pressure on Frank Chapple for revealing things to the TUC and the press. Before they knew the result, Les Cannon's circular emphasised his suspicions of Hill of Tottenham, Barker of Gray's Inn, Hart of Lewisham, Monti of London North West, Aitkenhead of LSE No. 1, Dudman of LSE No. 3, Lambert of London West.' The same circular honed in on Harry West, the Manchester executive councillor, accusing him of the basest personal motives in being the fellow-traveller Haxell liked to use best – particularly in giving credence to the Cannon-Young 'Inquiry' and the Jarrow 'Inquiry'. This inquiry took nearly a year (December 1958– October 1959) to express itself completely nonplussed by the most obvious and crude postal vote swindle possible. The Jarrow branch secretary, Carr, had voted for himself for area president. The inquiry circulated 279 members in the branch: 257 replied, of whom only six had voted by post. However, Carr had produced sixty-three postal votes, sixty-one of which had the same postmark (10 a.m., 22.9.58) over an Empire Games 3d stamp. All the votes were for him. Harry West didn't mind that, according to Cannon, as he stood to gain support for his nomination for the TUC delegation.

On 6 February, the executive council met to announce the result, as we have seen. Frank Haxell had won by 19,611 to Jock Byrne's 18,577 votes. Even at that meeting, the reformers knew that branches were being invalidated on the grounds of late posting. Gillmoss on Merseyside had heard as early as

8 January 1960. They were still astonished to hear that 109 branches had been invalidated. The atmosphere was electric at that meeting, with Frank Chapple snarling at Foulkes and Haxell and them giving it back with interest. Colin Walker, too, was disdainful and the new Yorkshire anti-communist executive member, Ernie Hadley, asked the questions and voted with the two rebels. As if the election 'result' announcement was not enough for the nerves, it was at that same executive meeting that Frank Chapple was fined £5 under Rule 38. His letter to the TUC on 29 November 1959 (circulated to influence the election then going on) brought the fine upon his head, along with a menacing rider that if he did it again 'the executive council would give consideration to imposing the maximum penalty under the rules.'

Now the reformers had to face the question of legal action. Les Cannon, during his years in the wilderness, had spent much of his time studying law and the legal process. It held no perils for him; others, including Chapple and Byrne, were initially against using the law. But the rules forbidding appeals against the scrutineers' reports and the refusal to hold a special delegate conference pushed the reformers towards the courts. On 8 February, Ben Hooberman, from the solicitors Lawfords, began the preparation of writs against the union. On 10 February, he submitted the papers to Gerald Gardiner QC (later Lord Gardiner and Lord Chancellor in the Labour Government). On 26 February, Ben Hooberman finally convinced Frank Chapple of the viability of conspiracy action. By the end of February 1960, events gathered speed. On 15 February, the *Panorama* programme interviewed Eastbourne branch secretary Satchwill, London Lift Engineers' J. Collins, and veteran campaigners Harry Marshall and Dick Reno. All bluntly alleged ballot rigging. The following programme featured a sensational, and in retrospect, pathetic, interview with Frank Foulkes. John Freeman (who as a junior minister in the Labour Government had been introduced by Foulkes to the 1948 policy conference) asked Foulkes all the right questions, which Freeman had been thoroughly briefed on by Les Cannon the previous day. No one has to be prejudiced against Foulkes at all to note how evasive and shifty he was; later analysis of the interview was to prove him as an outright liar as well. He accused branch secretaries of incompetence and negligence. He did not think that high postal votes were peculiar; there were no such things as 'communist branches' or branch secretaries. He didn't know exactly which branches had been disqualified, and so on. The most effective questioning by Freeman took place while the camera filled the screen with Foulkes's face, with John Freeman's steady barrage of questions heard off-camera. It was an early example of 'trial by television' that was emotionally highly charged for the participants and proved too much for many contemporaries at the time. Even George Brown MP specifically complained about the 'loaded prejudiced atmosphere' when he protested about Freeman's interview with Foulkes –

whom he referred to as 'an old friend of mine' – and George Brown was no communist!

On 8 April, Gerald Gardiner expressed the view that writs should be issued promptly, and that they had every chance of success. In these first few days of April 1960, Les Cannon was writing to all his contacts throughout the union, still trying to establish exactly who had been disqualified and who had not. Typical of these letters was one he wrote to J. E. Gill, the foreman mains supply electrician who was Darlington's branch secretary, who had spoken out against the leadership in 1954 on the grounds of finance. Les Cannon wrote:

Dear Brother Gill,
We are anxious to find out the actual branches which have come under the guillotine in the recent hullabaloo, and we wondered if Darlington were among the unfortunate. We would be glad for any information you can let us have in confidence as soon as you can.

All best wishes.

Les Cannon.

As it happened, they had not been disqualified. Cannon used his network to tie in with their own contacts. In this way, Dick Keill of Gillmoss, Liverpool, quizzed Tommy Rooney at Prescot branch, and Scunthorpe's Bill Wright wrote to contacts at Stocksbridge among the fellow steel workers there. However, he felt it inappropriate to ask questions in the Brigg branch, 'too near to the Grimsby regime and his followers' (a reference to Eric Elsom's communist credentials in that part of Britain).

The die was nearly cast. On 12 April 1960, Les Cannon wrote to Jock Byrne, who obviously could not be seen to be popping up and down to London to talk to the lawyers. He wrote:

Sorry I didn't write earlier. You can imagine things are requiring more and more time these days. We had a very good meeting last Friday. Gardiner is very happy with the case and absolutely confident about it. The statement of claim, tentatively, is for a declaration that Haxell didn't win the election; further, that you did win the election, with the alternate claim that the ballot be declared null and void.

It is fairly certain that as the pleadings are bound to allege that there was a conspiracy, that the outcome can be very serious for them. The defendants will be the union in the first place (this is absolutely necessary for otherwise it is not possible to obtain an order for discovery of all the relevant documents). In addition, it is suggested that there be individual defendants because of the element of conspiracy. These have not been finally decided. They are bound to include Foulkes, Haxell, McLennan and the six party members on the executive council. Have you any other ideas?

On 4 May, Jock Byrne did come to London, and the fateful decision was taken. On 10 May, at noon, the writs were issued by Frank Chapple and Jock Byrne. The previous day, the two men issued a joint statement to the press that incidentally brought to a halt the demands for action from an increasingly irritated TUC. The statement itself paid a sideways-looking compliment to the TUC, apologizing for preventing the TUC investigation and recognizing the dangers of suspension from the TUC facing the union. They concluded that suspension

would deprive our members of the prestige and privileges of affiliation to Congress and would leave all questions unresolved. We are proceeding [however] at this stage because we believe that the very considerable and important issues involved can only be resolved in the High Court. We feel that the membership will understand that we are left with no alternative but to act in this way.

Throughout 1960, the fight broadened across other fronts: every piece of evidence the plaintiffs needed had to be legally forced out of Hayes Court. However, Les Cannon was working full-time as clerk to the solicitors, and he knew roughly what to ask for. The problems continued, though. 'Discovery' of documentation took time. The shredders in the green huts meant some specific and 'juicy' documents weren't available! Les Cannon toured the country in June and July 1960, trying to persuade branch secretaries to give statements and promise to be available when the case came to court. He would often be followed by trusted lieutenants of the leadership – men like Harry Woolf and Sid Lyons – who would test the commitment of the people Cannon spoke to and write an evaluation of their likely evidence for Haxell's lawyer, Maurice Tarlo. Equally, they were looking for evidence of compulsion on Les Cannon's part. At certain stages, the reform group would be augmented by contacts made. The Gloucester branch was upset at its disqualification and a branch activist, R. J. Stevens, was telling everyone so in early 1960 on a course at the newly reopened Esher College. Overnight, his brand-new car was scratched with some sort of metal object. Stevens was furious and drew the obvious political lessons. He was to be invited to help Cannon and the reform group. However, he changed his mind about the political implications. His wife suggested that Les Cannon was 'using him as a tool', when Cannon stayed at their house; he would stay there as a base for visiting Bath and South Wales in the company of Gloucester branch chairman Pat Collins. Stevens was even invited to Les Cannon's house for a reform group meeting on 3 September. At about that time, he was in touch with the union's leadership over what he knew about Cannon's activities. For instance, he was to become aware of just what Frank Chapple was up to over the assistant general secretary's job.

In March 1960, nominations were required for Bob McLennan's job. The reformers met in a pub in the Borough High Street in South London at

Sunday lunch-time. It was clear that Eric Clayton would run against George Scott for national officer. For assistant general secretary, after an amicable discussion, in which Les Tuck's name was also mentioned, everyone agreed that Bill Blair was the nominee with the widest national reputation who could challenge McLennan. When he got home, Blair's wife, Doris, flatly refused to countenance it. Bill Blair had to get in touch with Frank Chapple quickly, and explain that he could not now stand. The reformers, meanwhile, were all primed to move Blair's name in the branches. That was no problem; Blair could just withdraw his name, but that would leave McLennan to fight either an unknown or be re-elected unopposed. Frank Chapple's friends spent the next few days scurrying round mainly southern branches to move Chapple's name for assistant general secretary and he just squeaked on to the ballot paper. He then set about raising the tension further through the controversial nature of his election address. Since April 1948, the executive had insisted that 'election addresses of candidates must be confined to their industrial record and the work they have performed and propose to perform on behalf of the organization within the constitution of the union.' This was decided upon after Jock Byrne's election address in the late 1947 general secretary election against Walter Stevens had concentrated on the political nature of the communist support for Stevens. An election address committee was set up; it originally included Les Cannon.

Frank Chapple's address in 1960 was carefully prepared. The key sections read: 'I pledge myself to work for the application of the constitution without discrimination. I have little time for those who never tire of boasting about our union's democracy, yet lay an ever-ready tongue to slander those who dare to take advantage of this democracy in offering themselves as candidates for office.' He promised to 'get at the root' of the union's 'present difficulties', to end the building of unity on 'prejudice and intrigue or the intimidation of those with whom I may not agree', and denounced the suppression of criticism as 'a short step from totalitarianism'. Wholly predictably, this sort of thing was rubbed out by the election address sub-committee at its April 1960 meeting. A solicitor's letter threatened to go to the High Court. On 25 May, Frank Chapple got an injunction to prevent the election going ahead. Justice Danckwerts ruled that the election address 'all dealt with the work that the plaintiff proposed to perform on behalf of the organization.' On 28 May, the executive council accepted the implications of this, published the election address and proceeded with the election to be held later that year. (As it happened, the court action on 29 August offered a further deferment of the assistant general secretary election due to multiple breach of rules. By 5 November, McLennan's mandate had run out, and a legal challenge was filed to that: however, the executive council appointed him 'acting assistant general secretary' on 17 December, pending an election McLennan was never going to take part in.) Frank Chapple got £30 damages out of his election address campaign and had to undergo ever-increasing spitefulness at each executive meeting. Much more valuable than the £30, though, was the mid-year boost to the reformers' morale, proving that the monolith could be confronted head-on.

By late 1960, everyone was at it: Les Cannon just failed in his own case, conducted by himself, attempting to get an injunction to restore his rights to run for office. Les Tuck took out a writ alleging illegalities in the executive's choice of groupings of branches for the 1961 rules revision conference constituencies. Ken Knight, a moderate candidate in the south-west of the country for an area official's job, took legal action to get his election address restored. Early in 1961, Harry Gittins was in the frame, expressing his concern over the apparent election as area official of communist Arthur Attwood. Finally, Dick Reno (under his real name of T. R. Odlin) was suing the union over the punishment meted out to him for telling the financial truth about the regime.

Most spectacular of all, Haxell nearly ended up in prison, sharing a cell with George Scott. On 28 October, Scott addressed a mass meeting of shop-stewards at the Conway Hall, urging members not to help Byrne and Chapple's lawyers. Frank Haxell's circular went to every branch on 30 November 1960, urging all officials and branch officers not to co-operate with representatives of Byrne and Chapple in their attempts to 'discover' evidence for the forthcoming trial. This was the clearest possible contempt of court. The Lord Chief Justice said that it merited imprisonment, but that would only further delay the hearing of the case. The leadership sent out another circular, contradicting the one of 30 November, freeing the path towards the trial.

The court case itself was held in Divorce Court No. 4 at the Royal Courts of Justice in the Strand. It started on 17 April and finished on 16 June, after forty-two days in court, the speaking of 1.4 million words and the shuffling of over a ton of ETU papers. Justice Winn heard the case, without a jury, and reserved judgment, which he eventually gave on 28 June 1961. On 3 July, he made his final pronouncements on the implications of the judgment, but it was Wednesday 28 June 1961 that was victory day for the reformers. Frank Chapple described it as an 'amazing triumph' and 'an incomparable turning-point'. Despite his own huge efforts, and along with Jock Byrne's courage, he always acknowledged that the verdict was the 'total vindication of an unrelenting dedication to a cause' by Les Cannon.

For both of them, it was their previous involvement with the Communist Party 'conspiracy' that had given them the key understanding of the mechanics of the scandal. Frank Chapple was challenged on his past associations in the High Court hearing and he boldly admitted it. 'I am saying, not only that I was a member of that conspiracy, but that I am heartily ashamed of my part in it.'

The immense detail of this closed trade union world rarely daunted Gerald Gardiner QC and his 'junior', Jonathan Sofer. These barristers were opposed by Neil Lawson QC and his 'junior', Ralph Milner. Each day the court was full of interested observers – on some days, such as the last day when Frank Foulkes gave evidence, it was packed with supporters of each side anxious to avoid confronting each other in the court-room visitors' gallery. The evidence has been summarized in a book, *All Those in Favour?* (1962) published quite soon after the trial by a legal journalist, C. H. Rolph. The only thing missing from that book is the tension in the court-room as the story unravelled. The extraordinary thing about the cross-examination of the main defendants, Haxell, Frazer, McLennan, Hendy and Foulkes, is just how weak and unconvincing their replies were. The best they could do was flat denial of the various accusations. The judge was to evaluate their respective contributions with considerable irritation – with the exception of Jack Hendy who was slightly more straightforward than the others. Justice Winn was irritated by 'the sorry figure in the witness box' that was Haxell, dissatisfied with Frazer's 'thoroughly unsatisfactory' account of his movements while the envelopes were being substituted. Justice Winn thought the pair of them 'blunt, unsubtle and ruthless'.

The most bizarre part of these extraordinary proceedings came from the last witness, president Frank Foulkes. His defence, which he maintained with great determination, was that even if the election had been rigged, *he* knew nothing about it. As it happened, he was part of the conspiracy by virtue of his lies in 1957, over the Cannon-Frazer election, and by virtue of his rushing through the announcement of the result. Most serious of all, Foulkes for many years had *not* done what any honest man *should* have done. He presided over so many suspicious incidents and complaints without doing a thing. Lord Justice Sellers, at Foulkes's appeal on 31 January 1962, said that Foulkes's 'complete failure to have the position thoroughly investigated, either at the scrutiny or perhaps more particularly when under pressure at the executive council on 6 February, provides its own evidence of guilty complicity.' Lord Justice Donovan, soon to preside over the famous mid–1960s Commission into Trade Unions and Employers Associations, supported this view on Foulkes's complicity with some enthusiasm. He said 'the evidence not merely justified the judge's (Justice Winn's) finding against Mr Foulkes, but compelled it.'

Nevertheless, at the original trial, Foulkes had finally come up with a theory. The election *had* been rigged after all. This astonishing statement produced an interesting reaction from Frank Haxell. Eye-witnesses in the court saw Haxell sink his head into his hands in despair. He need not have worried. Foulkes didn't think he'd done it. He thought Les Cannon had been 'the brain behind it'.

My theory, or at least my bad thoughts, if you like, is that Cannon and the other defendant (Chapple) did not want Byrne as the general secretary. Byrne was determined to stand because he had done so previously against me, quite rightly; he is entitled to stand ... Byrne decides to stand. They decide to adopt him, but they do not want him as the general secretary. What they want to do is continue the atmosphere that has been prevalent in our organization from four years ago when Cannon was discharged from the college because we had to close the college down on financial grounds. ... I have had reports from various parts of the country – north, south, east and west, from people who do not meet each other – that Cannon has made statements that he would spend every penny he had to smash Haxell. [He had been impressed with the evidence of substituted envelopes.] So I personally think that somebody other than my colleagues has been guilty of late posting in order to create a tremendous number of votes that were not valid in order to keep this atmosphere going; they are my honest feelings – only feeling; I cannot prove a thing!

Quite so. The judge was gentle with him and quickly passed on to less fantastic aspects of his evidence. Foulkes left court that day on his own, unaccompanied by the other defendants. He was finished in the union of which he had been an official for twenty-five years.

The leadership of the union were particularly anxious to conceal one main area of evidence. They were desperate to conceal the client relationship of the union to the Communist Party. They had to deny that the party's 'advisory committees' met with outside communist dignitaries like industrial organizers Mr Allison and, later, Peter Kerrigan, being present to effectively give the party's instructions to leading ETU activists. These advisory committees at national and local level would discuss conference tactics, policy issues, and, above all, nominations for elections. Throughout the trial, Haxell, Frazer and Jack Hendy, in particular, attempted to draw a picture of advisory committees summoned to advise the Communist Party on industrial matters – feeling in the building industry and details of the construction problems highlighted by the post-war housing crisis. That far alone they would admit, but flatly denied that meetings of the national advisory committee were held on the last Wednesday of every month, and often on Communist Party premises.

Despite the fact that the defendants had had the whole period from May 1960–April 1961 to get ready for these accusations of communist interference through advisory committee decisions, their eventual denial of them was weak and uncertain. Justice Winn thought that all the defendants told lies about the advisory committees. All of them wriggled and ducked questions; Justice Winn was rather reluctantly impressed by Jack Hendy's 'wonderful performance of adroit side-stepping and circumlocution'. He was less impressed by the denials of Fraser and Haxell, amounting to nothing less than 'puerile mendacities.' They were primarily exposed by the survival of a letter Jack

Hendy had written to his erstwhile friend Les Cannon on November 23rd 1951. It summed up the whole atmosphere of advisory committees. It showed conclusively that advisory committees were keenly interested in the internal affairs of the union – nominations in this case for the ETU delegation to the TUC. All of this was to be discussed in the presence of Communist Party officials. These were not simply gatherings of Communists in the ETU to discuss industrial policy and developments. They were in reality, the government of the union.

Hendy told Cannon that a full meeting of the committee had taken place the previous evening with Peter Kerrigan in the chair who had pointed out that though he had not yet been appointed he would be definitely taking over the following month.

It was very clear from the beginning that Haxell and Co. had already established close and friendly relations and were all set to serve up the mixture as before.

In view of that Hendy had to reconsider the blunt statements he had intended to make. It was just as well. It was always Hendy's desire that the communists within the union should have a greater say over the policies adopted by the Hayes Court communists, Walter Stevens, Frank Foulkes and Frank Haxell. According to Jack Hendy, the meeting had dealt with the contracting departments first – the first time the matter had ever been discussed at all. It was agreed to recommend all-out transfer to contracting conditions. This decision dealt with the long-running saga over the Bethnal Green dispute much earlier in 1951.

The next item was to consider the selection of the three officials and seven members to attend the TUC. In view of George Stevens [the Manchester executive member] ill-health possibly causing him to decline, it was agreed by the committee to consult him.

At Hendy's suggestion Peter Kerrigan opened by reading the suggestion sent by Arthur Shannon (in which Hendy's name *did not* appear.) [Shannon came from Bootle, and was a leading Merseyside communist.]

Whittome and Vetterlein moved that his name go in, in the room of Benjafield. Frazer suggested they dealt with the removal of Benjafield first and *then* deal with the vacancy. This was done, and the vacancy made. [Benjafield had become persona non grata after a visit to Yugoslavia and was no longer totally reliable, being a possible 'Titoist'.]

Again Whittome and Vetterlein nominated Hendy. Then Haxell said that in view of the *educative* aspect of congress a new man should go and he proposed [Sid] Maitland. This move – which Hendy told Cannon he could not but admire for its adroitness – received general support and was carried. Frazer then suggested that if G Stevens doesn't run they leave it at that and make no nomination. Haxell supported this view.

That however proved too much even for that meeting, according to Hendy and it was agreed that if Stevens didn't run, Hendy should. So Jack Hendy did win something even if he thought it was only the wooden spoon. His guess was that Stevens would then be persuaded to attend – even on a stretcher. Hendy then told Cannon of further tighter controls exercised by the Committtee.

A proposal came up to have a committee to look at the two forthcoming conferences. Hendy made a heavy attack on the failure to have proper consultations in the past, and in spite of counter attacks, he was generally supported.

He then suggested a meeting before 2 Dec – preferably the first as Les Cannon had suggested. It was turned down flat as having no useful purpose etc.

In other business Hendy asked that machinery be set up, i.e., by regular meetings, to enable people to draw attention to letters from the provinces. Kerrigan demanded to know how Hendy came to be doing this work and not the secretary Frazer. That gave Hendy the opportunity of doing some explaining which he seized with both hands.

Kerrigan apparently thought the matter needed further consideration and the letters were handed to Haxell though Kerrigan kept Shannon's to take up with the local organizer the need to ensure that future correspondence is less obvious and more personal.

It was agreed that the next meeting be on 20 Dec. Hendy was keen that Cannon would be there as it was his intention to tackle the whole set-up and, if Cannon agreed, to fight to recover the secretaryship. [While Hendy had been at the LSE, Frazer had taken over as secretary of the national advisory committee.] He then pointed out that they had a long hard fight in front of them, but he was confident in the eventual victory of those who fought to the true line of the party.

Jack Hendy was known as 'Honest' John – the legend has it, because he actually objected to Kerrigan and Pollitt about ballot-rigging. At the trial, he claimed the epithet was coined by Walter Stevens because he argued with the leadership, rather than being overawed by them. Justice Winn judged Hendy to be 'a man of intellectual honesty as well as intellectual power', although his dedication to the Communist cause left him 'inspired if not possessed by a fervent faith that the Communist creed is the Ultimate Truth'. It was this letter that rather 'pinned and cribbed' Jack Hendy on the existence of the advisory committees. Justice Winn thought Hendy must have known about the ballot rigging, but the high standard of proof required to establish his complicity in the conspiracy was not quite good enough, and Hendy escaped. The letter, along with other agendas and references, supported in particular by the evidence of Tommy Vetterlein, was conclusive. Vetterlein was an official of the union. Despite the hold the leadership therefore had over him, his exposure of the communist advisory set-up was particularly vivid and particularly brave. The proven existence of the advisory committee structure was conclusive evidence to add to the fact that the communist executive councillors were put into every area as a 'stop gap' before area officials could get elected; that the conferences, particularly the rules revision conferences, were communist parades; that the election addresses were curtailed; that there was frequent suppression of appeals on elections; that there was intimidation of members who 'revealed' the union's business to 'outside sources' (an admonition not applied to the advisory committees). All of this led to Justice Winn's two most memorable conclusions.

The substance of the matter is, I find, that not only was the ETU managed and controlled by communists and pliant sympathizers, but it was so managed in the service of the Communist Party of the United Kingdom and the ideas of the party.

He had an equally memorable set of phrases to hand when he came to muse out loud on what had made them all do it.

Only a recluse in an ivory tower would fail to appreciate the tendency of all forms of single-minded devotion to an ideology, whether religious, political or economic, to degenerate into fanaticism, and a state of obsessive delusion that the only criterion of good and ill in conduct is utility for the achievement of chosen ends.

21

INFLICTING THE MORTAL WOUND: JUNE 1961–JANUARY 1962

IT IS NOT IN the nature of communists, on suffering a defeat, however significant, to fold their tents and creep away into the night. When Jock Byrne went to Hayes Court on 4 July 1961 to take up his position as general secretary, he was hardly surrounded by friends. The executive had decided on 2 July (the last meeting Haxell was to attend) to appeal against the various judgments. The executive was still firmly in the hands of the communists. McLennan, despite being a convicted fraud, was the acting assistant general secretary, and it was he who had to escort Byrne round Hayes Court, introducing him to a bewildered and often hostile staff. Numbers of the senior officials' secretaries were also party members and were as appalled as the officials at the outcome of the trial.

Jock Byrne could have been forgiven for wondering whether it had all been worth it. He had left his family back on the Clyde to live in digs in suburban London; he had no friends at work. He reacted promptly to this state of affairs, and immediately suspended office manager Jim Humphrey. He then appointed Les Cannon and Frank Chapple as special assistants. He had to appoint them as 'staff' members, as this alone was within the general secretary's remit under the rules of the Union.

On 10–11 July 1961, the executive council met with Jock Byrne at the president's side for the first time. The communist counter-attack was swift. Les Cannon's appointment provoked the communists beyond all measure. To have Cannon walking round Hayes Court again must have been appalling for Foulkes, in particular, who had long cherished a hearty loathing of Cannon. The executive council expressed itself 'seriously concerned' at Humphrey's suspension and Cannon and Chapple's appointments. Its 'concern' of course, was nothing to do with the political fall-out from the High Court case. No; the executive 'could not admit the union's members or staff to entertain a suspicion that staff changes are to be determined by patronage or prejudice'.

This remark is breathtaking in its hypocrisy after years and years of 'patronage and prejudice' displayed by the communist leadership in support of their policies and friends, in and out of the union. Byrne was unmoved by the resolutions and the bluster; he stood pat on the rule-book as regards 'staff' at head office. He was not going to be moved, and indeed used the situation by telling the TUC that this incident just showed how the communists were unwilling to accept the verdict of the court. He saw general secretary George Woodcock on the evening of 3 July, the day of the final judgments from Justice Winn. The general secretary of the TUC 'advised Mr Byrne to go carefully, to avoid provocation wherever possible, . . . make sure that he was not likely to be challenged legally'.

More serious for Byrne and his two lieutenants was the other prong of the executive's attack. Again, in a breathtaking example of double-think, the executive accepted *one* of Justice Winn's admonishments. They *now* entirely agreed with his evaluation of Haxell's position, which had amounted to 'a rank abuse of power by the general secretary and illustrates the danger always inherent in the establishment of a quasi-full-time permanent post in such a body of part-time members [the executive council]. It is trite that usurped power corrupts even more absolutely than power duly conferred.' Ignoring completely the context in which Justice Winn said this (attacking Haxell's cavalier attitude to disqualifying branches and his failure to put things to the executive council), the executive used these sentences to justify the assertion of a new exercise of executive council authority. From now on, the union's ballots, its publications (including the *Electron*), its establishments ('staff' appointments and the treatment of officials), and litigation were all going to be run by executive council committees, not by the general secretary!

At the end of the court case, the executive would not commit themselves, despite Justice Winn's clear recommendation, to a system of secret postal ballots. However, they did make certain changes in line with undertakings given in court. A classic case, at the very best, of closing the stable door after the horse has bolted. Equally, it was a telling admission of the faults of the previous system which the executive council had done nothing to alter or criticize in the decade beforehand.

First, all branch returns were now opened by the national scrutineers – not the office manager with his highly selective 'All Right' file. Chartered accountants would supervise the printing and distribution of ballot papers. Branch secretaries would only open the ballot parcels and distribute the individual ballots in front of the branch committee, and those meetings would be certificated. The chartered accountants would be present when the national scrutineers opened and tabulated the branch returns.

These undertakings were to prove vital in ensuring a reasonably fair set of executive council elections in the autumn of 1961. On June quarter nights, nominations for the executive elections were being taken; it was still vital to win branch nominations because their appearance on the ballot paper was often influential with members who knew little of the personalities or politics involved. Each executive area had its own campaign and the reform group sent letters of encouragement and even 'visitors' to branches to build a genuine movement throughout the union. Frank Chapple wrote to a supporter in Lincolnshire on 22 February 1961 – even before the court case was finalized – emphasizing the endless nature of the battle and the need to sustain an organized group of activists. Chapple wrote:

> The odds always favour those who control the machine. It is fortunate, indeed, for us, that they only control the union and not the state.... I am glad you liked the [1960 assistant general secretary] election address. It has an outstanding place in our union's history as the one that undid communist censorship of non-communist election addresses. I hope those who follow me in seeking election to office take full advantage of it. I don't know how busy you are, or how interested in doing battle with the Communist Party you may be, for it's a tough and often unrewarding task. It is absolutely essential, whatever the outcome of the court case, to build a fighting force wherever we can. The only way I know of doing this is to visit branches in the same area and build up contacts in this way.

Les Cannon was in contact with the same activist in Scunthorpe. On 31 May, he wrote:

> I am very pleased that you are able to make contacts in the branches you mention. In the case of Lincoln, we have already had assurances that the secretary will be supporting us.... If you are able to get the Scunthorpe nomination, it will also be of great help as it is one of the bigger voting branches in the area. We have two good tours in other parts of the executive council division No. 6. Our joint efforts should bring us a greater number of nominations than Goldberg will get. I am in no doubt that we can win this seat. Please keep me informed of how things go with the nominations. It is essential to know this so that we will know what they are up to when they start their usual invalidations.

The securing of nominations went on apace. The court case verdict was announced at the end of June. The executive's riposte was to denounce Byrne's appointments and the suspension of Humphrey and to strip him of his powers through the four executive sub-committees. All this was to be put before the conference, due to open at Portsmouth on 17 July.

The reform group now came out of the shadows. They announced at two 'open' meetings of delegates (the first attended by sixty-five delegates, the second by seventy-two) that they were now the 'the ETU reform movement', set up to openly oppose the Communist Party within the ETU. The secretary was Mark Young and his pamphlet after the conference was clear in its determination to continue the battle, particularly with the September executive council elections imminent.

The conference itself reached new heights of tension. Jock Byrne was given plain-clothes police protection. There were demonstrators from the South Bank site in London picketing the conference which included communist activists, in and out of the union, who all gave vent to their hatred of Byrne and Chapple. For some delegates, they were learning the hard way of the violence and spite that lay behind much of the communist's frustrations with the result of the court case. Mark Young estimated that there were 120 communists and sixty fellow-travellers amongst the 363 delegates. The conference assembled in silence. There was no response to the arrival of the platform party. Frank Foulkes took the chair. He introduced the fraternal delegates and ignored Byrne, save to say that the boilermakers' leader, Ted Hill, was sitting 'the other side of the general secretary'. He finished the introductions by adding 'and Frank Haxell is in the gallery'. Instant, emotional applause.

Foulkes was at his most unctuous. 'I face a conference of those I have served under a cloud of suspicion.... I am completely innocent.... I have never told a deliberate lie during the whole of my career....' He called for 'unity' and an end to 'personal feuds'. He set in motion the manifesto for communist apologists for the next decade. Ignoring the proof of ballot-rigging and grotesque personal corruption, Foulkes was 'justifiably proud of the record'. Since 1936, when he became a full-time official in Liverpool, the union had grown from 48,000 to 242,000. There were now forty-six areas with fifty-five area officials rather than ten areas with thirteen officials. Annual conferences met to decide policy with over 300 delegates instead of biennial fifty-delegate assemblies. There was a printed report to conference and a right of appeal against executive decisions (although Foulkes did not mention how outrageously these rights were set aside by Haxell during the election disputes). Over 15,000 women had been recruited, convalescent, educational and old age holiday benefits introduced. Wages for electricians had risen faster than average over the twenty-five years he had been in office. Frank Haxell's budgeting had boosted the general fund to over £1 million. He ended by quoting Joe Hill, the American revolutionary shot on the orders of the copper bosses in Utah – he said the day of his execution: 'Don't mourn, organize!', to which Foulkes melodramatically added, 'Don't retreat, mobilize!'

There was going to be no apology, no regret, no change. The usual parade began. First, Harry Woolf joined in the contracting wages debate, congratulating the executive for the genuinely huge increases won at the end of 1960 – 1s an hour. Frank Haxell and Mr Penwill had personally come to the deal, confirmed unanimously by the executive at its meeting on 6 October 1960. Harry Woolf knew what had to be highlighted here. 'This wage increase of one shilling per hour. We know it's an unprecedented wage increase for manual workers in the history of the trade union movement in this country ... and I think we should give credit to Frank Haxell on this question.' Dave Gregory saw it as a breakthrough for everyone else's negotiations, giving his own talks in civil air transport as a good example. Bob McLennan thought it a 'momentous agreement'. Mr Penwill, quoted in the executive council report to conference, was equally fulsome. 'History in their particular field of industry had that day been made ... a new era in the industry's negotiations would be started ... the goodwill of both sides to get an era of peace, something which money could not buy.' Mr Penwill knew he would have difficulties on his side ... 'it was an undreamed of and spectacular increase' but he was prepared to take the responsibility. After decades of parsimony, here was Mr Penwill with his arm round Frank Haxell, handing over 12d an hour – a whole shilling!

It took Seymour Moss to puncture the euphoria. It was a huge increase, and so it ought to be, given the electricians' position in the wages league. BUT it was a two-and-a-half-year agreement, which could only be opened up again if prices moved five per cent one way or another. If that wasn't wage restraint and 'fodder'-based negotiations, Seymour Moss wanted to know what was. Furthermore, the big sites allowances that had solved the South Bank dispute were abolished. Many men were going to lose £3–4 a week from these. Overtime rates for the first two hours were now to be time-and-a-third, and the forty-two hour week was to be introduced, although there was no further progress to forty hours, and there was still no sick-pay scheme in the industry.

Throughout the conference, the internal issues kept surfacing. Jock Byrne eventually spoke – on the momentous issue of improvements in apprentice training – and got an extremely good hand from his supporters. The Trotskyist-left revealed that it would stand by the communists in preference to throwing in its hand with the 'right'. The Camden Town delegate and part-time Socialist Labour League organizer, Alan Courtenay, knew what had to be done. 'This conference is going to stand shoulder to shoulder in the fight against the right-wing, who are, in fact, whether they like it or not, whether they are conscious of it or not, whether they are insincere or sincere, are in fact, representatives of the employing class.' This political stand was occasionally spiced by pure invective, fresh from the demonstrations outside the hall. Tommy Searle could not contain himself. In referring to the unilateralist Aldermaston Campaign for Nuclear Disarmament (CND) marches, he said, 'At the last march, Frank Haxell was with us, in the forefront of the ETU, and I would say this,' he turned from the rostrum, gesturing at the platform: 'When is this puppet-appointed general secretary going to give us a lead on this matter? Or is he going to adopt the same Hugh Gaitskell line that we make the policy decisions and he reverses them?' There was great applause for that.

The highlight of the week was the Wednesday afternoon private session.

Conference was asked to give a vote of confidence in the leadership and to endorse its decisions critical of Byrne in the matters of his appointments and powers. The vote of confidence and the attack on Byrne was carried, but only by 216–145. Here was a reasonable base on which to build.

There was to be no respite for Foulkes and his friends. On 24 July, the whole executive council was summoned before the finance and general purposes committee of the General Council of the TUC. Following the court case and the conference, following the persecution of Byrne and his attempted isolation; the TUC at last got tough. They were not going to be put off by Foulkes's request that as they were appealing, the whole issue was *sub judice*. The meeting on 24 July was later described by George Woodcock. 'I have never in my life had a more miserable experience than the experience we had in meeting the whole of the present ETU executive council in Congress House. We were there for five hours, in the course of which we got from them precisely nothing. There was not the slightest willingness on their part, if they could have avoided it, even to admit there had been a court case, much less that it was of any significance.' Their whole approach was to refuse to do anything while appeals were under way – including dealing with the accused office holders and the branch fiddlers. However, they were anxious to misapply a part of the judgment – the bit to do with clipping the general secretary's wings. The replies of Foulkes amounted to 'constantly meeting stone-walling'. The TUC demanded the union ban from office Haxell, McLennan, Frazer, Hendy and Humphrey for at least five years. Given that Foulkes was only involved, probably, in what modern parlance would describe as the 'cover-up' rather than the direct original fraud, the TUC demanded he resubmit himself to the members in an election. Thirdly, the union's executive should drop the sub-committees to control the general secretary and let Byrne get on with it.

On Friday 28 July, the executive rejected the whole package. It was 'wholly unacceptable and unwarranted interference. The TUC is more interested in changing the policy and leadership of the union than ensuring the efficient continuation of its administration.' The TUC therefore had no option but to recommend congress to expel the ETU on the first day of congress; this was done, once more in Portsmouth, on 4 September 1961. Danny McGarvey of the Boilermakers spoke against, as did representatives from the Draughtsmen's Union (the forerunner of TASS, the Technical and Supervisory Section of the AUEW) and the cine technicians (ACT). Four ETU representatives spoke. Foulkes made the main 'defence'. The TUC should not throw the ETU out, said Foulkes, because it weakened unity in the fight for higher wages and avoiding war. The appeals had yet to be heard – and then he could not help himself. Perhaps he knew how the votes were already stacked up – one usually does at the TUC. Foulkes then attacked the democratic bona fides of the General Council – eleven of whom were appointed for life and a further thirteen of whom were elected once and that was it. The press was behind it all, and Congress ought to take into account 'for four years, an individual with frustrated ambition has been employed by somebody or other travelling the country, spreading a mixture of half-truths, lies and innuendos ... successfully carrying out a personal vendetta'. Les Cannon's ambition was supported by the Catholic Church, the Economic League and the Conservative Central Office. The ETU had been badly treated at Congress House, particularly given that they were appealing and only one member of the executive was found guilty in court. The TUC should condemn the anti-communist group as well as the communist group in the ETU and it also ought to condemn all communist groups in all the other unions. Finally, he repeated the assertion that the whole thing was got up to get at the ETU's policies within the movement. Sam Goldberg objected to the lack of 'investigation' by the TUC! He ignored the 1958–61 inquiries that had been sidetracked and ignored. He insinuated that the judge's methods of establishing conspiracy on the basis of the balance of probability and the demeanour of witnesses was somehow inadequate – as though nothing could be done unless Haxell and friends had filmed themselves filling in someone else's ballot papers. He also claimed that there was another form of ballot-rigging – by implication as bad as that he said had not taken place in the ETU – 'the coercion and intimidation of electors'. And this was what the TUC was doing – intimidating ETU members in the run-up to the executive elections. This line was pursued with wholly typical unpleasantness by Jack Frazer.

What it is all about is intimidation by this General Council in the hope that they get your support to influence the forthcoming elections in this union, where they hope that they can replace a militant and progressive leadership with a leadership which will be more servile to the line which is at present being pursued by the Selwyn Lloyds and the Tory Government's economic planning within a capitalist system of society.

With equally typical courage, Jock Byrne took the rostrum. He blew away Foulkes's appeal for 'unity' by exposing the existence of the 'defend the union' campaign – an amalgam of communists and Trotskyists pledged to Byrne's removal. Danny McGarvey had suggested that perhaps the ETU should ballot on the General Council's recommendations. Byrne called out in genuine concern, 'What, again?' He was not optimistic of a conventional rules revision conference doing the decent thing either, comprised as it was 'of something like forty communists out of fifty'. The TUC adjourned for ten minutes to consider what they had heard. They voted, by over ten to one, to expel the union. The Labour Party took the same view: just before conference met, Len Williams, the party's national agent and deputy general secretary, tersely informed the union that the national executive committee had expelled the union 'on the grounds that it is a communist-controlled organization'. Goldberg's appeal at the Labour Party was ignored, particularly as he again used the argument that the expulsion was only brought forward to influence the ETU executive elections. Charlie Pannell MP, the secretary of the Parliamentary Group of Trade Union Sponsored MPs, had been in court and denounced the ETU's clear communist connections. The union was expelled by 5.3 million votes to around 640,000.

All of this was of no real concern to the communists. They regrouped, as Byrne had told the TUC, under the *ad hoc* organization 'Defend the Union'. They met at Central Hall, Westminster, on 15 September and 9 December, pledged to support the old executive council for its fine record as a fighting union. At a packed meeting, Lew and Jack Britz, as well-known reform group members, embarrassed the conference into letting Lew Britz speak. Amidst uproar, he told the assembly of communists, Trotskyists and fellow-travellers that the executive's record was comparatively modest and what there was of it was based on fraud and electoral cheating. Lew Britz, shouting above the storm, urged the group to study the record. Surrounded on all sides by shrieking opponents, the Britz brothers were insulted, jostled and finally chased at full speed into the Westminster evening. They were followed in their car through the City of London. However, the Britz brothers eventually reached Frank Chapple's home in north London. Chapple was sitting quietly in front of the television. 'How many of them were there?' asked Chapple. The excited Lew Britz told him there had been over 1,500 in the hall. 'Is that all?' said Chapple. 'They need 5,000 in London. They are finished. We will win the elections now.'

Voting in the executive elections went on throughout September. The count started on 9, 10 and 11 October by the national scrutineers with their chartered accountant supervisors. On 17 October, disaster struck. Jock Byrne failed to turn up for work. Les Cannon went round to his digs to discover that Jock Byrne was being rushed to hospital, having had a stroke. It was not fatal, and he recovered, after a fashion. However, it allowed the executive to appoint acting assistant general secretary McLennan as acting general secretary! But by then, they knew the game was up. The counting of votes had been postponed until 10 November in deference to Jock Byrne's illness. He was not to return to the executive until 2 January 1962 – but he would have been at *that* meeting if it had killed him. The 10 November count announced at the executive on 12 November 1961, showed that the communist reign was over. Never before had six sitting executive councillors been defeated; the nearest had been the five overturned in the post-Earl's Court swing to the left at the end of 1937.

The September 1961 executive elections remain the crucial turning point in the union's history. The court case was spectacular, dramatic and understandable in its impact. However, the behaviour of the party in reaction to

Jock Byrne's arrival shows that, on its own, the overthrow of Haxell was not going to do the trick. Look at what was stacked against the reformers. The 'Defend the Union' campaign regrouped the left, and brought into the communist ambit its erstwhile Trotskyist rivals and a new generation of fellow-travellers untainted with a ballot-rigging reputation. The executive's pursuit of Byrne, ignoring the expulsion from the TUC and Labour Party, was continued even into the rules revision conference at the end of November 1961, where changes in the rule-book enshrined the emasculation of the general secretary's powers. Finally, the standard bearer, Jock Byrne, was very ill and recuperating on Clydeside.

The executive elections are worth dwelling on, not least because they were basically honest and took place amidst a storm of pamphleteering on both sides – whatever the rule-book said!

In total, 29,115 members voted, around thirteen per cent of the membership – with one executive member, communist-supporting Jim McKernan, returned unopposed from Northern Ireland. In Scotland, the turn-out of votes rose by thirty-one per cent. Bill Blairford, the anti-communist who was first elected to the executive in July 1961, to replace Colin Walker, increased his vote from 1,300 to 2,115. Yorkshireman Ernie Hadley, who had supported Frank Chapple on the executive since he succeeded the pliant Jack Potter in late 1959, improved his vote from 1,668 to 4,170, with the total turn-out up thirty-six per cent on the 1959 figures. On Merseyside, where a communist had been on the executive council since 1937, Tom Breakell, from Preston, beat communist Jim Feathers, 1,827–1,334. Feathers's vote had fallen by just ninety-two votes. In 1959, he had been opposed by G. W. Cooper, who got 666 votes. The total turn-out, then, was up fifty-one per cent. In Manchester, where the malleable Harry West had been unopposed in 1959, he just hung on by 2,215 votes to J. Webb's 2,030. In the West/East Midlands seat, there was a real sensation. Sam Goldberg got 1,588 votes – just sixty-six less than in 1959. His opponent, Frank Sharman, from Northampton, got 4,043 votes compared to 1,013 two years before. The total turn-out was up a fantastic 111 per cent. Les Cannon's work was paying off handsomely. ETU branches were now voting politically, not quite so parochially. Leaving aside the rigging aspects; in 1959, the Aston branch in Birmingham had voted for Birmingham boy Goldberg, 135–18. By 1961, that vote was now decisively in Sharman's favour – 231–65. Birmingham Central had turned round from 43–8 in Goldberg's favour in 1959 to 40–23 to Sharman after the court case. Coventry Central had voted for Goldberg 72–36 in 1959; voted for Sharman 96–80 in 1961. The other side of the Midlands was quite certain it had changed. Derby in 1959 voted 37–37. In 1961, it voted for Sharman by 215 votes to forty-three. In Nottingham South, the branch secretary was J. E. Hobday, a supporter of the old executive; he would have been satisfied in 1959 to watch his branch vote for Goldberg by fifty-two votes to sixteen. He must have been shocked to see it vote 110–65 for Sharman in 1961. Les Cannon's friend in Scunthorpe turned up trumps as well. In 1959, the branch had voted, 39–34, for Goldberg. In 1961, it was 167–56 for Sharman. The twist in this division was going to be that on many occasions Sharman voted with the communist apologists once he got to the executive, particularly where Frank Foulkes was concerned whom he had always held in high regard.

In Wales and the West Country, in 1959, the obscure communist, Ivor Davies, had beaten Ebbw Vale's Ivor Parton, the Bristol area's supply worker from Portishead, branch secretary, Jim O'Neil and Torquay's secretary, R. J. Lawrence. The communist vote was 1,857. In 1961, the total vote rose forty-nine per cent. This time, Jim O'Neil's vote went up from 710 to 2,862. The communist vote fell by just over 200.

And so to the four seats in London and the Home Counties – for over twenty years the bedrock of left power in the union. Frank Chapple had been unopposed in 1959, despite the fact he had left the Communist Party and was representing parts of east London where the party was nominally strong. In 1961, the left backed Alf McBrowse. McBrowse was not a communist but usually attracted their help.

Compared to the last time in 1957 when the left candidate, then Frank Chapple, of course, won, this election too was a disaster for the left. Alf McBrowse got 2,435 votes (compared to Chapple's 1957 vote of 2,239). Frank Chapple, though, improved on Bill Sullivan's 1957 total of 1,527 votes to a winning score of 3,776.

In Ronnie Sell's division, like in the Midlands, the same two candidates opposed each other. South London, Kent and Sussex increased its turn-out by seventy-three per cent. Ronnie Sell's vote rose from 1,382 to 1,795. Dartford, for instance, voted for him in 1961 by 108–29 over Les Tuck, compared to 52–17 in 1959. London Press increased its pro-communist vote for Ronnie Sell from 172–101 in 1959 to 274–236 in 1961. But all across the division, the huge increase in turn-out swept Sell aside. Les Tuck's vote rose from 824 in 1959 to 2,014 in 1961. In Division 9, where Jack Frazer had cheated Les Cannon in 1957 and probably cheated Dick Reno in 1959, the turn-out rose by a mere forty-five per cent. Frazer's vote fell just over 100 to 2,189. Harry Gittins, the secretary of LSE No. 14, disqualified amidst controversy in 1957, got a thumping 3,880 votes. It was the same story in West and North West London. Jack Hendy's vote rose by seventeen votes. The turn-out increased by forty-six per cent. 'Honest' Jack Hendy was destroyed by Bill Blair. His vote rose from 926 to 2,213. The man who might have been general secretary of the union, if he had sustained his reform group nomination for assistant general secretary in 1960, was elected to the executive. He achieved this in the heartland of the Communist Party's 1960s support (based on London Airport) and by defeating the party's most straightforward (if verbose) candidate in Hendy.

No one could say these men were necessarily vastly experienced in union affairs, although they had all held branch and other local posts of responsibility. These lay men, all with normal jobs to try to hold down, now had to come to London in January 1962 to set right the years of communist fiefdom, as they saw it, with little executive trade union experience. It was to be a daunting prospect, and they needed more than ever the clearly developed sophistication of Les Cannon and Frank Chapple. No one likes to admit dependence, and these new men had just won the most closely fought public elections in trade union history and won them handsomely. They were not going to be easy to order about, even if anyone had wanted to. However, with Jock Byrne ill, and Les Cannon back at Esher as education officer (and reading for the Bar at the same time – studies he never finished, but which he started under Gerald Gardiner's tutelage), the new executive council were not out of the wood by simple virtue of their election victory. It was still going to be a bumpy ride. It is never over.

The decisions taken at the first two executive council meetings in January 1962 heralded the break-up of the communist empire. They sacked McLennan. They sacked the left-sympathizing lawyers, Seifert and Sedley. They sacked the union's own solicitor, Maurice Tarlo, whose speciality was charging legal fees on top of his salary.

They limited Foulkes and Scott's legal aid to restore their positions on appeal and defend a cross appeal respectively. (There was a strongly held view that Justice Winn had been excessively generous in letting George Scott off.) They reallocated executive council responsibilities. (What the Anglo-Soviet Friendship Society made of Les Tuck's appointment one can only guess.) They threw the national officers out of the executive council room; they were never to return. Byrne was of the view that they ought to be out negotiating, not listening to the strategic government of the union; it had the added advantage of removing five communists and their sympathizers from the executive council boardroom. The prestige of the executive council had to be established with plain, obvious insistence. Frank Chapple urged on the executive a new role for the executive councillor. From that day, they were to visit branches at their own discretion, and not solely on the invitation of branches and with the permission of the rest of the executive (requirements that had long been used to prevent him touring his own division). Area committees were to be addressed by the executive members; national officers had to tell executive members if they were visiting their divisions. The members would reclaim their own union through boosting the position of the individual executive councillor.

These sensational meetings then set aside the decisions of the 1961 rules revision conference which had attempted to hamstring Byrne's role as general secretary; and decided to ballot the members on a special conference, with a delegate from each branch, to reshape the rule-book. (This permission was later granted by a huge majority, 26,458–6,206.)

They finally agreed to co-operate in making a television documentary on the whole ballot-rigging story, which was shown on 2 February, and issued a press statement that outlined their new intentions.

We are deeply conscious of the fact that the exposure of fraud and conspiracy, directed against the democratic desires of our members, is the chief reason for our being elected. . . . We will not hesitate to take decisions to deal with fraud and conspiracy in the light of existing evidence if it should ever become manifest in the future.

After years of political ambition, this new executive had a new priority – to 'seek to advance the lot of electrical workers to a position commensurate with their industrial importance to the community'.

22

CHANGING THE UNION'S STRUCTURE
TO CHANGE ITS PURPOSE

THE ELECTION OF A committed anti-communist executive council was the single most important political change in the union since the war: however, it had only a two-year period of office in front of it, the presidency was still occupied by Frank Foulkes and the national officers were all supporters of the previous regime. Throughout the country, many prominent area officials were communists or fellow-travellers. The London office was devoid of executive supporters with the great exception of Tommy Vetterlein and the London area committee was still dominated by communists. Jock Byrne was ill; the communist machine had already started a new life, building a propaganda image of contemporary pygmies following Frank Haxell's giants. This approach was slightly knocked aside by the Communist Party's own belated admission that something had gone wrong.

Peter Kerrigan had attended the court hearings on behalf of the Communist Party, and did not like what he heard. He and fellow members of the Communist Party's executive committee pursued their own investigation, using, Frank Chapple always said, borrowed copies of the union's own transcripts of the trial. Kerrigan was less than impressed with the evidence of high living that close scrutiny revealed; Foulkes was particularly at fault here. In early December 1961, the executive committee of the Communist Party received Frank Haxell's resignation. Witnesses to the scene were struck how Haxell was completely unapologetic. His attitude, delivered forcefully to the committee by Haxell standing up and never once removing his raincoat, was blunt. He would not apologize for trying everything to keep the ETU within the party's control. He would accept the responsibility for what had gone on but not the blame.

On 4 December 1961, the Communist Party published its considered response: 'The general secretary, Frank Haxell, must, as the leading official in charge of the administration of head office, accept the responsibility for the situation which has brought discredit on the union and its executive ... [the party] unreservedly condemn all such practices' as ballot-rigging and have accepted Haxell's resignation from the party.

However, the Communist Party could discover some mitigating circumstances. The newspapers hated the ETU leadership because of its opposition to incomes policy, the guerrilla strikes of 1954, its opposition to German rearmament and the watering down of Labour Party policy. This drove the leadership at Hayes Court to fiddle the presentation of the results. This had been stupid because Les Cannon's group was 'the darling of the monopoly capitalist press ... it was more than ever imperative that all the actions of the Communist Party members connected with the election should be fair and above board ... We believe that the conduct of the election at head office gravely compromised the Communist Party.' They were bewildered that if the ETU leadership could admit on the first day of the trial that the result was unsustainable, why had they not said that months before and rerun the election? They knew that 'the handling of this election will be presented by reaction as a normal feature of communist trade union activity'. So it would be.

The new executive had to fight on several fronts at once, but each issue led back to the core argument. Which broad set of political ideas would triumph? Which broad set of political ideas would underpin the union's industrial relations responses in the 1960s? Which broad set of political ideas would govern and inform the union's contributions to the broader Labour movement's deliberations?

The 1960s were dominated by two main industrial relations problems – the question of the role of rising wages in inflation, and the growing interest of government in the trade unions' perceived capacity to weaken a declining economy through 'irresponsible' strikes and other industrial action.

The two issues became inseparably linked as the Labour Government returned to office from 1964–70 sought to use legislation to control both inflation and trade union 'excesses'.

For the ETU, their response to these challenges was conditioned by the perpetual attack from the left on the leadership. It cannot be emphasized too strongly that the attacks from the left on the leadership of the union throughout the 1960s were relentless, skilful and unforgiving. The communists' first success was to convince other left-wingers in the union – Trotskyists and Labour left-wingers alike – that foregiveness for the ballot-riggers was morally better ground to stand on than the risk of being associated with right-wingers and establishment apologists. From 1962 onwards, the distinctions in the left in the ETU became more blurred; there can be little doubt, though, that the strategy, the planning, the thought, all still came from the Communist Party. The foot soldiers and resolution movers may have come from other political factions, but the Communist Party was determined that it was to be the beneficiary of change in future executive councils.

The union had to cleanse itself of the ballot-riggers first. A tortuous set of expulsions and branch appeals dominated the executive council's proceedings in the first half of 1962. For much of the time, Foulkes was absent. He now added backache to his other problems and had to undergo X-ray treatment for a spinal condition. In his absence, the executive set about unpicking the myriad of communist threads that ran through the whole of the union's structure. On 20 March, Frank Haxell was expelled from the union by eight votes to nil. Jim McKernan, Harry West and Frank Sharman all abstained. Exactly similar votes were recorded for McLennan, Frazer and Humphrey. Jim Feathers was banned from office for three years, and Ronnie Sell for five. (Sell had been party to an extra, if minor, deception. When Humphrey was lining up the office manager's job in 1959, he well knew he would have to resign from the executive. Only Sell and the Communist Party knew of his intentions. Humphrey allowed branches to nominate him, withdrew, and left Sell to inherit the executive council seat having secured the nominations of branches 'in the know' about Humphrey's impending resignation.) Branch secretary Pat O'Neil – London South West's strong communist supporter – was easily exposed as a ballot-rigger during the elections *after* the court case for rules revision conference delegate in late 1961. In his branch, 355 had voted for him and only two for Dave Chalkley. Only 259 out of London South West's 372 members were eligible to vote. Of those 259, over 100 testified to *not* having received a ballot paper at all. Only fifty-four of those who did had voted. O'Neil was expelled.

Sam Goldberg was banned from office for seven years by six votes to four. This time Jim O'Neil wanted to give Goldberg the benefit of the doubt, attaching less blame to his 'cover-up' machinations than to the actual fraud-sters. The appeals procedure was taken most seriously by Jack Hendy. He told the executive council that:

> ... he admitted fraud and conspiracy had been committed, but mentioned that he had never suspected it had been perpetrated by members of the executive council. He said he had done his best to defend the interests of the Communist Party in court ... it was not part of Communist Party policy to cheat. He admitted that Communist Party meetings to consider ETU elections were held and were still being held.

He produced letters from senior officials of other unions saying what a good fellow he was; one of these was Clive Jenkins, a youthful general secretary of the Association of Scientific, Technical and Managerial Staff (ASTMS)'s forerunner, the Association of Supervisory Staffs, Executives and Technicians (ASSET), who wrote of Jack Hendy's 'diligence and integrity'. Despite this support from a man who was thought to have organized fund-raising for

Haxell's legal costs – or perhaps because of it – Hendy was banned from holding office for seven years by seven votes to three. Harry West was charged, mainly on the basis of his complicity in the Mark Young/Les Cannon 'court of inquiry' in 1959 and the post-1959 votes on the executive to accept Haxell as general secretary. He threw himself on the mercy of his fellow executive councillors. 'Brothers Cannon and Young had refused to produce any evidence in support of their allegations [at the inquiry] and he could now understand why ... Brother West concluded by saying ... in the light of subsequent events, his views had changed, and he was now convinced he had been misled and used.' The executive's decision was to merely 'reprimand' him, as Harry West had been 'honest and frank. He realized he had been used in the past and now had the courage to admit it.'

George Scott was found not guilty by the court. The executive's cross-appeal to prove conspiracy failed even after his report, which whitewashed the Southend Electronic Engineers' branch voting, mysteriously 'turned up' at Hayes Court. Nevertheless, the executive were determined to get rid of him. His role in the court of inquiry into Cannon and Young, his article in the *Daily Worker* over the Frazer–Cannon election and his organizing of financial support for Haxell and the others' appeals led to his being banned from holding office in the union *sine die*. (He was to show what he thought of that by travelling to Kincardine power station 'in a private capacity' to advise the strikers there who were on strike against the executive's advice.)

His national officer colleague, Bill Benson, had already resigned in June 1962 on 'medical advice'. Benson is remembered primarily for his conference organizing – where delegates were paid expenses out of an enormous roll of banknotes kept in Benson's inside pocket. He was also responsible for the union's car fleet which, when it needed changing, was assembled in the Hayes Court car park and sold for cash to second-hand car dealers. His special pleasure was snuff and snuff boxes were often given to him by officials collecting cars.

The greatest difficulty lay with Frank Foulkes. He had convinced himself that it had been a gross miscarriage of justice to link him with the fraudsters. The fact was, he had done absolutely nothing to expose Haxell and Humphrey and had deliberately obstructed those who for years had complained about ETU elections; but this meant nothing to Foulkes. He was the senior negotiator in the electricity supply industry, the president of the CSEU and the president of the ETU since 1945. He had not actually fiddled a single vote himself and so it was nothing at all to do with him. His legal appeal along these lines had failed on 31 January 1962. Due to his back problems, he did not return to the executive council until June. The executive asked him, directly, what was he going to do now? His appeal had failed and he was a convicted fraudster. Even so, they offered him a deal. If he resigned now, two years before his final term of office ran out, he would be paid his union pension early and for ever. Foulkes refused point-black. He was given twenty-four hours to reconsider. He still refused. On 7 July 1962, he was expelled from the union by seven votes to four (Jim O'Neil again joined McKernan, West and Sharman) because, as the executive judged it, 'even allowing that he was not part of the conspiracy, it was certainly dereliction of duty and a breach of trust placed in him by the membership.' Even so, the executive paid a pension of £757 7s od per year to Foulkes up to his entitlement to come on to his union pension. Tragically for Foulkes, this decision was legally challenged. As an expelled member, he could not receive a union pension. He passed into retirement quietly and in disgrace although he was often a guest at social events organized by the re-emerging left at the Deptford Engineers Club in south-east London. Ernie Hadley was eventually appointed temporary president until the elections could be organized for a new president in 1963.

Expelling and disciplining the handful of prominent communists responsible for the ballot-rigging was the relatively easy bit. The rest of the year was spent in confronting furious party activists on a thousand fronts. Firstly, members of the executive had to visit hundreds of branches and area committees to explain the executive's view and to explain their policies for the future. The atmosphere at these meetings was generally appalling. On 23 January, Harry Gittins and Tom Breakell went to the Croydon branch where Bob McLennan turned up, Tommy Searle was insulting and they would not let Les Cannon in because he had forgotten his membership card! On 11 January, there was a bitter debate between Les Cannon and Frank Haxell at Coventry Auto branch. Harry Gittins was shouted at in the Shirley branch. Frank Chapple was annoyed at Romford branch on 1 May when local communist official Bert Whittome turned up and advised the local hecklers that they were asking Chapple the wrong questions and proceeded to advise them of questions that were 'difficult' for the executive councillor. Brentwood branch invited Frank Chapple, but did not tell him they had also invited local communist sympathizer Bill Eason, from the Harlow branch, to oppose everything Chapple would say. Out of the twelve members present, Frank Chapple identified seven members of the Communist Party. With a well-chosen phrase or two to the branch officials, he left! He also had to go all the way to Gorton branch, where the communist presence was so strong that they only voted 13–12 to reapply to join the Labour Party.

The main features of these meetings, though, were the fairly small turnouts, the travelling circus of committed communists (particularly in London), and the steady growth in self-confidence of the anti-communist members as well as the anti-communist executive councillors taking the meetings. Les Tuck went to London Central No. 2. There were twenty-five there, but seven were 'visitors'. The usual criticisms were voiced by the 'visitors' while the members sat in silence. When Les Tuck had finished debating with his tormentors, he was delighted that 'when the vote of thanks was moved and accepted, it was also accepted by the clapping of branch members present.' Similarly, Bill Blairford got used to it. There were only fifteen out of 900 members present at Paisley branch. He had a good night at Edinburgh West in April 1962. 'The chairman called for a vote of thanks to me, and whether or not they were in agreement with what I had said, all applauded except the three party members. As I said about the Paisley branch [in his report to the executive council], the more meetings the party organize for us, the better we like it. We always come out on top!' There was still much to be done. Even in defeat, though, Les Tuck took pleasure from his visit to LSE No. 1 on 6 April. There were forty-nine members at this ancient supply branch with a communist voting record. Fifteen were visitors, including nine well-known left-wingers from LSE No. 9 who should have been at their own branch meeting which met the same night. The meeting dragged on, until at 10.30 p.m., the left moved a vote of no confidence in Les Tuck and the executive council. The vote was carried 7–2. Les Tuck was delighted: 'Over thirty did not vote at all!'

Out of this endless round of noisy, personal and unpleasant meetings, the executive councillors drew further reserves of courage and determination to press on against the communist disrupters. And this disruption and intimidation was not restricted to specially summoned branch meetings.

On Saturday 24 February the executive met at Hayes Court. The Area 25 area committee was meeting in Croydon the same day, and after a few introductory items of business, abandoned the meeting and set off to Hayes Court to speak to the executive council.

They arrived at Hayes Court, and demanded to be met. Frank Chapple and Tom Breakell spoke to the ten members present, and as voices were raised 'profane' language was used in a 'most disgusting exhibition', according to Tom Breakell, and 'attempts were made to provoke Brother Chapple to violence'. Tommy Searle, from Croydon, was the leading demonstrator along with the veteran Dick Homewood. Tommy Searle demanded to see Tom Breakell's card during the uproar. Eventually the protesters left. Eight members were later fined £3 each – including a youthful Peter Adams – and Tommy Searle was banned from holding office for his part in the swearing and jostling. Dick Homewood clearly knew the ropes. He demanded his own shorthand writer, verbatim copies of the executive council minutes and refused to answer questions if he didn't get them – all of which he had done in 1939 when driving Ernie Bussey up the wall at the height of the Vigon crisis. He, too, was suspended from holding any office in the union. He finally retired to Littlehampton from where the branch occasionally sent Frank Chapple revolutionary resolutions with Homewood's hand clearly behind them.

Area 25's area committee protest at Hayes Court indicated just how intensely excited area committees could get. One further example will suffice. On 25 January, the communist-dominated London area committee wanted to criticize executive council decisions; area president Jim Smith (elected by ballot in London) ruled that only branches could appeal to the executive. Area committees merely had jurisdiction over terms and conditions of employment. In the ensuing uproar, the delegate from Bethnal Green branch banged constantly on the table, and refused to sit down when ordered to do so by the chairman. To increased uproar and the complete astonishment of the rest of the shouting delegates, Smith closed the meeting.

This determination of certain area committees not to implement the policy of the executive council forced the executive to instruct all area committees to restrict themselves to their own responsibilities and not spend time on issues that did not concern them. The executive meant what they said. They threatened to take 'a more serious view' of the London area committee's resolutions on the Cuba crisis in October 1962, even if the London area committee thought they were entitled to take a view on the likelihood of the Third World War breaking out. The executive took an equally dim view of the London area committee attempting to impose a ban and permit system to control overtime in the capital when so few members were unemployed.

More significantly, as 1962 shaded into 1963, the executive could look back on certain other policy changes which were in direct contrast to the previous executive's attitudes. First, the union's finances were to be built up. Although the union's general fund had returned to its late 1940s level, there was only £3 19s 9d per member at the end of 1961 compared to £4 19s 10d in 1949, the year of the Ayr conference 'reforms'.

Money would be saved in Scotland by not opening up separate areas for Glasgow and the countryside round it (which was originally thought up by the communist leadership to isolate Jock Byrne in his area official's job – his supporters were largely out of town; his enemies based in central Glasgow). Equally, the Edinburgh area was not split up. The printers of the *Electron* were changed to another firm, the Belmont Press in Northampton. Professional advice was sought concerning investing the union's balances of account in more lucrative places: £407,000 was taken out of bank accounts and invested in CWS Development Bonds at five per cent.

By 1965, the era of keeping large sums in the bank was over. On 9 December 1964, the executive had appointed its first professionally qualified accountant, Martin Diamond, to advise the general secretary on a more entrepreneurial approach to maximizing the investment income potential of the union's cash balances. He started a review of the union's properties; and the process began of selling off the houses originally bought for officials and rented out to them at the laughable rents of around £2 per week. (Les Cannon, for instance, bought his house at Chessington for the market rate of £3,000.) In January 1965, the chairman of the newly-formed Trade Union Unit Trust (TUUT), Mr D. Hirchfield, addressed the executive. They decided to invest £100,000 in the TUUT then and there; a further £100,000 went into TUUT units in July 1965, and another £150,000 by June 1966. By January 1989, just over £500,000 had been spent on TUUT units, but they had a market value of £4.27 million, producing an income in 1988 of £141,870. The TUUT investment amounted to thirty-six per cent of the union's £11.76 million investments as it entered its centenary year.

Local authority loans and government securities had actually declined in value, and the union no longer saw them as an exclusive priority for investment. From 1963 onwards, particularly after 1965, the union was going to make its money work for it.

Not only did the investment policy become both more adventurous and more professional: closer scrutiny revealed further substantial deficiencies in local branch and, worse, in area officials' accounts. An Edinburgh official owed £1,880 at the end of 1962. The Carlisle official could not account for a missing £690 the following year. Ex-union solicitor Maurice Tarlo was driven into bankruptcy as the union discovered that in addition to receiving a salary of £1,500 a year from the union, he had also pocketed the costs from every successful accident case and then charged the union an extra £15,000 for his other legal services in the period 1959–61. Financial probity was returning to the union and small details were not overlooked, either. In September 1963, Camden Town branch were told to repay to the union's funds 16s 8d they spent on a pompous telegram telling Harold Wilson to demand a General Election as soon as possible!

Political points and financial savings went hand-in-hand over the question of affiliations, too. Within a year, the union had cancelled its affiliations to the British-China Friendship Society, prevented branches from affiliating to CND (although they sustained a nominal £25 national affiliation) and cancelled affiliation to the Haldane Society and the Labour Research Department.

Policy changed, too, on support for strikes. The new executive were not against supporting disputes. They paid out £90,312 in dispute pay in 1962, twice the 1961 and 1960 levels. However, as early as 1962, they gave clear indications that for a strike to have official backing, the cause must be just and the procedures properly followed where the members were initiating action rather than simply reacting to employers' unjustified provocation. They took several months to establish the legitimacy of a BEA lock-out pay entitlement at Heathrow in early 1962. Typical of this new attitude to 'supporting our members in struggle' was the executive's response to a strike at Halewood in early October 1962. Two members of the union, working for Lee, Beesley and Co Ltd at Ford's plant at Halewood on Merseyside, were caught working on their motor car in working hours. They were sacked. Strike action was taken by around 500 other members of the union, and although the management offered to find the two men alternative work in the Birmingham area, the strike continued. Gus Cole was 'requested to visit the site for the purpose of instructing our members to return to work.' He did this successfully on 11 October and the members went back to work. There was to be no more automatic 'support' for every and any strike undertaken by the members.

As we shall see, the opposition to the executive council in the 1960s was to find its feet more successfully in exploiting opposition to the radical new initiatives the union was to take in the two big sets of negotiations in contracting and supply. As far as the union's constitution was concerned, their road back was to be made infinitely more difficult by the constitutional changes in the union between 1962 and 1965.

First and foremost, the special rules revision conference which met at Margate from 8–12 October 1962 initiated the fundamental reform in the union's election systems that the events of the previous twenty years cried out for. The conference was chaired by Frank Chapple and a challenge to the acceptance of the conference rules of debate (standing orders) was made by two members of the new generation of leftists, Charlie Montgomery and Alf McBrowse, who were not communists themselves, but had often supported much of the policy of the old regime. They persuaded conference to allow speakers as long as they liked on the rostrum. Such an issue may be insignificant in itself, but a successful challenge on the subject shows the platform who is boss in any trade union conference. As such, it takes on a huge significance, and the left at Margate wanted to show Frank Chapple that he could not have it all his own way. The reference back of the standing orders was carried, 364–271, at the conference.

However, a more even, sober temperament quickly settled over this unprecedented rules revision conference. There was a delegate there from every branch – not the usual fifty-delegate event. Bill Blair moved the new Rule 21 to end forever the system whereby 'to steal [the member's] vote is to steal his opinion'. Elections in future were to be for five years for all – including executive councillors (whom the executive wanted to be converted at last into full-time workers for the union). It was quickly obvious that the conference was probably going to object to a five-year full-time executive; in mid-debate, Chapple announced that the executive were withdrawing the five-year period of office suggestion and sticking with the two-year period of office for executive councillors.

Bill Blair laid out the reforms in voting procedures, The union was going to replace branch ballots with the single transferable vote in a secret postal ballot. Members would vote for candidates in order of preference on the same ballot paper. If one candidate did not get fifty per cent of the vote immediately, the person who initially came bottom of the poll had his votes redistributed. Each of that bottom candidate's second choices were then allocated to the remaining candidates until one candidate got fifty per cent of the final vote.

Such a system would be administered by an independent returning officer (the Electoral Reform Society). On 28 April and 28 October, each branch would send in a list of all members less than thirteen weeks in arrears (not five weeks as pre-1962). Nominations would be made at branches at March and September quarter nights and voting would take place in June and December. Most innovative of all, the candidates would be allowed to attend the actual counting of the votes at the offices of the Electoral Reform Society. A minor triumph for sanity was achieved by changing the method of election to the TUC and Labour Party delegations. In future, they would be elected by the regional groups of delegates to the biennial delegate conference, instead of in national branch ballots, which typically would confront members with a ballot paper containing thirty-five names for nine places for the TUC delegation. Equally, the ballot paper would no longer contain the suggestive lists of branch nominations, garnered in by enthusiastic political factions at poorly attended nomination meetings.

The aborted 1961 rules revision conference had actually abolished election addresses. These were to be reintroduced and members allowed to state their industrial and political records, along with what they intended to do for the union in the future. Blair justified this by saying 'No one wants interference in our internal affairs by an outside body, but if members cannot obtain the information they want about a candidate from his election address, they have no alternative but to turn to the national press where they will undoubtedly obtain the information they seek.'

The opposition to all this was muted. Trotskyist Alan Courtenay was opposed to farming out the elections to an 'outside body' and thought allowing people who were up to thirteen weeks in arrears to vote was a bad move. R. A. F. Davenport, the speaker for the left, disapproved of the thirteen weeks' arrears limit, objected to 'politics' in election addresses (mainly because he well knew that candidates stating they were *not* communists always seemed to attract more votes more readily than candidates who announced they *were* communists – if such a candidate could be found). He wanted to keep branch nominations on the ballot papers and wanted to keep electing TUC and Labour Party delegates nation-wide.

There was no open objection from the left to the postal ballot, and Courtenay aside, no apparent objection to outsiders running the mechanics of the election. Jock Reynolds was not satisfied with this tacit approval. He rounded on the left in an emotional speech in which he said they were picking on details to justify voting against the fundamentals of postal ballots and independent scrutiny. Bill Blair's reply to the debate was equally punchy. The new executive council were elected to reform the election system above all else, and they were going to do it.

The conference knew that. Whatever fun they had had from turning Frank Chapple over on the reference back of the standing orders, they knew their responsibility now. The majority in favour of the new system was so decisive it didn't need counting. Frank Chapple was to be the first official elected under the new system. The long-delayed assistant general secretary election was counted and announced in March 1963. The first thing to notice about the new system was the increase in turn-out. The previous system had produced a turn-out in Bert Batchelor's July 1961 national officer election of around ten per cent. The sensational executive council elections in late 1961 polled around twenty per cent. Chapple's election in March 1962 was the next national ballot, and twenty-six-and-a-half per cent of the membership voted using the new secret postal ballot. He got 26,338 first preferences. Yorkshire official, Albert Wallis, got 12,477, with communist support (although he wanted to sue the Conservative Party trade union groups for suggesting so in contemporary leaflets). Three other candidates got over 4,000 votes each, Alan Courtenay, George Cooper and Bill McCreedy. When McCreedy's votes were the first to be redistributed, Frank Chapple immediately had well over the fifty per cent required and was declared elected.

In modern times, secret postal ballots in trade union elections have been attacked by largely academic writers. First, it is said that voting at home in front of the member's living-room fire, or, more insidiously, his television set, is anti-trade union. He ought intead to go to a branch meeting or a canteen meeting to openly discuss with his fellow workers the attributes of candidates in a trade union atmosphere. An argument closely allied to this is the one that says that the ordinary member will place himself in the hands of the biased media who will name the 'left' candidate and abuse him. These twin objections have no substance as far as the EETPU are concerned. First, if a member votes at home, and posts the vote in, it is likely to be secure: it is certain to be more secure than branch meetings or canteen meetings where votes are placed in hand-made cardboard boxes and stored, occasionally, in dubious circumstances. Second, a member who votes at home always has sufficient knowledge of working life to spot the main drift – both politically and industrially – of the candidates, even if he has never met them. Third, he will still discuss the election with concerned shop-stewards and other members at work, but outside the potentially intimidating atmosphere of meetings harangued by enthusiasts of any sort. Finally, if members vote against the left candidate in the elections after having the candidate's politics identified in newspapers, two things must be borne in mind. Time without number, left candidates are described in periodicals and pamphlets as the 'progressive' candidate and their 'right-wing' or 'reactionary' opponents abused. Equally, the objection may just be based on the frustration felt by the left that the majority of trade union voters often (but not always) vote *against* the left candidate. Paddy McMahon, a national officer of the EETPU in the 1970s and 1980s, once effectively ridiculed this argument about the members being influenced by newspapers when he said at Esher Place: 'In 1872, the land-owners of that time denounced the growth of democracy by saying you must not give the vote to workers because they cannot read. Today, the left insist you must not give the vote to workers because they can!'

The 1962 conference dealt with the need for urgent change in other rules. First, other ballots of the membership were also to be carried out by secret postal ballot. Second, the conference turned its attention to the union's conferences. The annual policy conference, with its direct representation for large branches and others represented in groups, was replaced by a biennial policy conference with a delegate from every branch. In between the new policy conferences, there would be industrial conferences of shop-stewards, concentrating on the collective bargaining problems of specific industries like electricity supply, contracting and shipbuilding. Smaller industries were not to be ignored, and indeed the first one held in early 1963 was for lift engineers.

There were two grounds of left-led opposition to this proposition. However, everyone recognized that the role of branches was declining in importance compared to the emergence in the 1950s of the role of the shop-steward. It is arguable that no union has a greater reliance on the skills of shop-stewards than the EETPU. Its typical group of members is usually small and exposed to the potential intimidation of both employers and other groups of workers. With branch attendances falling (down to five-and-a-half per cent according to Tom Breakell at the 1962 conference) the union depended on shop-stewards more than ever: it was at work where the union now lived and the most important communication line was between the leadership and the shop-stewards, rather than the leadership and the branches. Tom Breakell described this shift of ground. 'The shop floor is the only place you can measure the temper of the membership and the desires of the membership.'

Roy Sanderson was insistent that annual policy conferences should remain and, what's more, their decisions should be binding on the executive council. The communist leadership had not taken that view when *they* were in power: they understood, as the new leadership thought then and think today, that the union's leaders, elected nation-wide, are far more representative and accountable in finality than any conference of delegates. These delegates are usually elected at branch meetings with an average five per cent turn-out – not all of whom vote for the successful delegates – a fairly thin mandate.

The second basis of criticism was one which still finds occasional echo in modern times. The idea that each branch, irrespective of size, should send a delegate to the biennial policy conference was rejected by the left. They thought it was more 'democratic' that larger branches should cast extra votes – perhaps a branch bloc vote. Tom Breakell also rejected this on relatively sophisticated grounds. First, big branches do not necessarily attract huge attendances at the meetings. Consequently, delegates from such branches often only represented small cliques, not the vast number nominally associated with big city branches. Secondly, small branches often produce talented individuals who ought to have the chance to come to conference in order to develop their contribution to the union. Thirdly, it was more important to get the widest possible geographic spread in the conference, because its democratic virtue had to be recognized as limited. Compared to the executive elections, shop-steward conferences and pre-eminently, ballots of the membership, policy conferences were useful and necessary but not supreme. This view prevailed quite comfortably.

The conference stopped electing area presidents directly (which had the effect of replacing Jim Smith in London with Alf McBrowse), and made all area committees have one delegate per branch. Most significant of all, they set up a final appeals court of eleven delegates, one from each executive council division, elected by the conference, to oversee the appeals from the numbers of highly-charged disciplinary cases. This was expected to be accompanied by the move to a full-time executive council, so that there was a lay element of 'shop floor commonsense' in discipline cases. However, the executive withdrew the proposal for a full-time executive council, because with only a two-year period of office, it was unrealistic to expect people to give up their jobs for that short period of time. Ernie Hadley, however, made a statement about the necessity for a full-time executive. Part-timers could not get to grips with the multiplicity of issues in modern trade unions. The union now had over three times the number of agreements it had in 1945, and it was increasingly difficult for the executive to supervise the work of the growing number of officials who were responsible for those agreements, let alone the head office full-time officers.

Although still unwell, Jock Byrne turned up at the conference to speak to the delegates at the end of this significant conference. To considerable applause, he said: 'This has been a most memorable conference and has made a tremendous contribution towards restoring the rights of the membership and the pride of being a member of the ETU, throughout the country. I wish to record my heartfelt thanks to the delegates here who have accomplished the freeing of the members.

The new leadership was further strengthened when Frank Sharman resigned from the executive for health reasons, and returned to Northampton. He was replaced by Derby branch secretary Jack Ashfield, who beat the Rugby branch secretary, Norman Leuty, in a labyrinthine test of the single-transferable vote. In a field of six candidates, Jack Ashfield was forty-six votes in front of Norman

Leuty on the first count. On the fourth redistribution, Leuty edged in front, but was still short of the necessary fifty per cent. After the final redistribution, Jack Ashfield took it, 1878–1810. He was the quintessential East Midlands skilled man. He kept quiet unless angry. He would then jab his forefinger to emphasize a point. His claims of military and technical prowess in the war were often to be the subject of hilarity amongst his colleagues – so long as they were out of earshot. He was a fierce defender of craft privilege and relished fight after fight in Midlands engineering works to establish it. He normally voted steadily with the anti-communist majority, but his prickly personality made him not wholly 'reliable' in his voting habits and he fell out with Frank Chapple on occasion with relish.

In July 1963, Mark Young was elected as a national officer, beating the communists' most active member not in disgrace, Sid Maitland. Maitland had become an area official in a one-man office near Heathrow at Hounslow in an unopposed election in June 1960, and although Mark Young got 15,036 votes to Maitland's 10,869 in the first ballot, the transferable vote gave him some anxious moments. Blackpool's George Cooper and Coventry's Vic Blundell both got over 7,000 votes. By the time they were redistributed, Mark Young only beat Sid Maitland by 22,257 by 20,530. The communists were not dead yet: they girded their loins for the late 1963 elections. First, the presidency. It would seem in retrospect that the new leadership would automatically and enthusiastically run Les Cannon in triumph. Nothing of the sort. It is a curiosity of human nature that people resent being dependent or beholden to others, however much they recognize their intellectual calibre, their tactical awareness, their capacity for strategic thought. Several members of the executive council thought that they had done enough to be entitled to carry the reformers' banner into the presidency of the union. They were encouraged by the knowledge that Jock Byrne did not fancy having Les Cannon as his partner at the top of the union; they resented the fierce spotlight of publicity always illuminating the intelligence, the sparkle of Les Cannon, rather than the provincial determination of an unwell Jock Byrne. Bill Blairford was an obvious 'compromise' candidate, although his candidacy was never pushed with enthusiasm by Blairford himself. Other names were in the ring, occasionally on their own behalf. Harry Gittins even went as far as seeking branch nominations in June 1963, and was appalled to read in the *Daily Telegraph* on 24 June that he did not want to run, thus discouraging branches which were meeting at the end of the month from adding to the seven he received – leaving him five short of getting on to the ballot paper. Mark Young now did not fancy Les Cannon for the presidency, and had apprently got the support of Jock Byrne. Les Tuck and Harry Gittins were suspicious of Cannon's motives and resentful of his energetic and opinionated personality. Most people who met Les Cannon were in awe of his intelligence. Few claimed that he invited affection or friendship. He suffered fools badly and his constant fear was that the new union would not be defeated by resurgent communism but buried beneath a mound of mediocrity. Worse still, he let everyone know that was what he thought.

At the first biennial policy conference at Scarborough in May 1963, one whole night was spent arguing about who the reformers' candidate should be. The discussion was personal, unpleasant and anything but fraternal. Frank Chapple believed it was the effective end of the reform movement as their comradeship fell apart in a welter of personal recrimination. The situation was helped by Bill Blair, Tom Breakell, Frank Chapple and Bill Blairford making clear their preference for Les Cannon. It was decisively changed by Cannon's insistence that he would run whatever any of the others did.

His opponents were Les Gregory, who by now had left the Communist Party, although he never lost his fundamental sympathy for the left cause; that would not have helped him deflect the 'official' communist candidate, Eric Elsom, the experienced area official from Sheffield who incidentally helped negotiate the full-time officials' wages with the executive each year. Whether that made the officials get out and support him, or oppose him, is not clear. What is clear is that there was no denying Les Cannon. Skilfully building on the thousands of early evening conversations at Esher, as he explained the detail of the court case to hundreds of key shop-stewards in 1962–3, he came into his inheritance. Eric Elsom got a derisory 9,213 votes. Les Gregory got 11,263. With sixty-three per cent of the vote on a twenty-seven per cent turn-out, Les Cannon polled the highest vote in any election in the union to date, 34,978.

At the end of the year, the members were asked to vote once more on a new executive council. They had to give a verdict on the reformers' work. Jock Byrne put it square to the membership in an editorial in the *Electron* in November 1963. He said that the new executive had 'vindicated themselves in the most creditable way' – so much so that the *Daily Worker* was issuing lists of anti-executive candidates. Jock Byrne was proud of its negotiating record as well as the way it had set the members free by reforming the constitution. The results were a delight to him. Jim O'Neil, Tom Breakell, Bill Blair, Harry Gittins, Ernie Hadley, Bill Blairford, were all comfortably returned in around twenty to twenty-four per cent turn-outs. Eric Clayton won Frank Chapple's old seat by 600 votes from Alf McBrowse's perennial challenge. Harry West and Jim McKernan hung on to their seats. The only disappointment for Byrne and the only delight for the *Daily Worker* was the election in South-East England of Eric Hammond. In a 24½ per cent poll, this West Thurrock power station shop-steward, Gravesend branch secretary and conference delegate, beat Les Tuck, 2,140–1,703. The *Daily Worker* made much of this crumb of comfort. Eric Hammond's result was 'a significant victory, and a shock for the right-wing establishment of that union.' Eric Hammond, went on the *Daily Worker*, 'was known for his progressive views'. The result was indeed 'significant'. Eric Hammond's views were to be 'progressive' – but perhaps not quite in the ways the *Daily Worker* had in mind. His new colleagues were irritated by Eric Hammond's election address which replaced the old right to print the branches nominating him with a phrase in his election address that said the same thing – 'I am encouraged by the support that the majority of branches in the division have given to me by their nominations.' He was censured by ten votes to one for avoiding the spirit of the rule change.

The new leadership was effectively consolidated in power with its leading conceptual thinker in the president's chair and its leading administrator effectively running the reforming head office from the assistant general secretary's office, as Jock Byrne was only capable of effective work in fits and starts.

The last vital links in the political chain after the 1963 elections were the decisions to ban communists from holding office in the union and the structural changes wrought by the 1965 rules revision conference. In the summer of 1964, the union's branches were asked to submit changes to rule for the 1965 rules revision conference agenda. Over ninety branches produced identical motions, calling for the reintroduction of the annual policy conference that could instruct the executive council, rather than advise it on all policy matters. The left now understood that its last redoubt was the union's conference, where a delegate elected by each branch gave them a better opportunity of organizing support at thinly-attended branch meetings. The fact that policy conferences under the communists were advisory was neither here nor there; this was the way for the left to regain control of the union now that relatively honest elections appeared to deny them total access to the executive council and senior positions in the union. Les Cannon said on 12 July 1964: 'At first we thought it was rubbish and didn't take much notice of it, but then the amendments put forward by branches arrived and the wording was identical in ninety cases to that of the circular.'

Les Cannon was convinced that the whole thing was organized by the Communist Party itself, demonstrating for the umpteenth time the party's outside interference in the union's affairs. This was it. This leadership was not going to make Ernie Bussey's mistake and refer the issue to a conference; the case for the Communist Party was distributed in the *Electron* by the publication of the Communist Party executive committee statement on the union's decision to ballot the whole membership on the issue. In the ballot, published on 10 September 1964, over twenty-nine per cent of the membership voted – the highest turn-out of members in any ballot since the war. They voted, 42,187–13,932, to ban communists from holding office. At the same time, Sid Maitland was decisively beaten by Scotsman Jock Reynolds for a national officer's post – 30,129–21,742. All communist officials were asked to leave the party or the union's employ by 1 January 1965. Twenty officials did leave the Communist Party, which, according to those who were involved at the time, insisted that the individuals concerned had to choose between their union job and their party membership. It would be naive to think that these officials changed their politics overnight, although for some it may have been the opportunity, the stimulus they needed to start a new life politically. The Communist Party apparently was quite firm that it would not 'nod and wink' at those who could give up their formal membership but stay inside the party's embrace. It was one or the other. Sid Maitland and Bert Gray, officials in the London region, nearly chose to hold their membership of the party more dear than their jobs with the union – nearly but not quite. Arthur Attwood, the union's official in the Surrey area, was the only official to leave the union: as late as 1981, he had left the modern Communist Party and joined its unashamed Stalinist offshoot, the New Communist Party, for whose magazine he wrote justifying the record of the Haxell years.

Further crushing blows were dealt to the prospects of the communists' returning to office by the rules revision conference at the Isle of Man in May 1965. This conference was carried for the executive council by the titanic performance of Les Cannon, chairing his first huge biennial delegate conference, which also perfected its new rule-book. The debates on the key issues were close, passionate and pure theatre. On issue after issue, Cannon had the last word from the president's chair on behalf of the executive. Each narrow victory can be attributed to his mixture of logic and inspirational rhetoric that dominated the conference proceedings.

Cannon's presidential address set the scene. 'We now have probably a once-and-for-all chance to reform the internal structure of the union. If we fail in this task ... we will for a time stagnate in organizational mediocrity, waiting at a later date to be rescued by some other union which has been able to grasp hold of history and move along with it.' He outlined how the union's administrative and recruitment potential had suffered in the previous years. He had a vision, published in December 1963 and widely distributed throughout the union, that the union's structure should radically change. He told the 1965 conference what most of them were aware of, following this huge consultation process on the basis of the December 1963 Discussion Paper.

At the present time we have a three-tier organization structure and committees at these three levels with continuous functions to cater for the needs of approaching 300,000 members employed in virtually every industry in the country. There is the branch, the area committee and the executive council.

There are no rules at all to determine that any of the committees at these three levels shall represent a proper weighting of the membership of the union. If a branch, area committee or the executive council at any time is representative of a cross-section of the union's membership, it is by pure chance and not by design of the rule-book itself. Our rules also provide for a biennial delegate conference for policy-making. Here again, the weighting of the industries in which delegates work needs bear no relation to the weighting of the membership of the union. Until recently the whole of our organization was miscellaneous in character. Our committees are sprawling horizontally over all the industries in which our members work. At the same time, such an organization is the bluntest instrument imaginable when urgent tasks peculiar to the separate industries await the union's attention.

Recently there has been a departure from the miscellaneous principles of organization. In 1962, on the initiative of the executive council, it became obligatory under the rules for the union to call biennial industrial conferences in the major industries, and such other industrial conferences as are necessary from time to time.

Recently, the executive council decided to set up industrial sub-committees of the executive council in order to develop specialized knowledge and treatment of each industrial problem.

Everybody has welcomed these latter industrial developments, but experience has shown the executive council that their existence is incompatible with the other forms of organizational work in the union and that for them to be fully effective they must be regarded as part of the broader pattern we are placing before you at this conference.

I now wish to say something about the life and work of our branches. I do not want to repeat matters in the document which it is hoped you have read and studied. In that document, circulated to delegates, we refer at length to the problems of branch administration: those concerned with the growth in membership; the collection of contributions; the tortuous lines on communications; the divorce of the branch from the job and the problem of communications in that respect; the maladministration in many branches; the difficulty in getting new officers elected; and the increasing pressure on existing officers. The passage of time and deeper examination of branch administration methods – such as calling in ledgers for detailed audit – have served to add great force to these arguments.

This problem is urgent as it is grave. I think, however, it is necessary to adopt as a principle, that each member of our organization, whatever his branch, should have administrative services and facilities at the level of the best. It is my view that it is only possible to do this by a radical reorganization of the branch structure of the union. The conference will know that the executive council took certain measures within the existing rules to rationalize branch organization in certain parts of the country, and has learned a great deal from that experience. It is in this regard, more than any other, that it has modified its approach.

The circulated document speaks of a direct transference to industrial branches from our present branch structure. It suggests a different line of approach in the smaller cities and major towns. It is our view, though that there are many outstanding cases for the setting up of industrial branches and, in some cases, factory branches – and such branches should be set up – that in the majority of cases, we should pass through a transitional stage before reaching this objective. This transitional stage would involve the rationalization of branches to such a size as would make it economically viable to elect a full-time administrative officer who would carry out the functions of both branch secretary and branch treasurer. I will give you examples later.

This review is based on the possibilities arising from the proposal for increased contributions.

... Other changes in the rules – such as notification of quarterly meetings, as well as some far-reaching improvements in administration methods – will serve still further to eliminate the tedious part of branch administration, thus releasing the time and energy of all our branch officers, full-time or otherwise, for the more interesting work of branch leadership. It is also our intention, following the introduction of better and, more important, standard practices in branch administration, to establish courses at our college where training will be given by our chartered accountant and an organization and methods man in the new standard administrative methods.

Our proposals will permit, on the basis of sound economics, the possibility of full-time administrative offices in branches of 1,400 and upwards. This means not only the major cities – such as London, Manchester, Liverpool, Glasgow and Birmingham, with a membership of 10,000 and above, not only Sheffield, Edinburgh, Leeds and Bristol with a membership around the 3,000 mark – but also smaller cities and the large towns such as Swansea, Portsmouth, Preston, Bolton, Bradford, Wigan, and so on, might have the service of a full-time administrative officer.

I should now like to make some comments about area committees and the middle levels of union structure. The most striking and challenging part of our original document was where we questioned the usefulness of area committees. I stress again that successive rules revision conferences have been trying to alter one ineffective form of area or district committee after another. The question these conferences have been trying to answer is: 'How can we improve the composition and functions of our middle organizational committees?'

District Committees were made larger, and then they were changed into area committees. Since then, on five occasions in the post-Second World War years, we have changed the character and functions of the area committees. Everyone knows that we are no nearer the answer to that question today than we were at the beginning. Not until now has any executive council had the courage to say that we are trying to find an answer to the wrong question. This executive council has put the matter before you with courage and realism. It has said that before you seek an answer to the question, 'How can we improve the composition and functions of our middle organizational committee?', you should first answer the crucial question, 'Are such miscellaneously-composed committees necessary at all?' We, on the executive council, with a vast amount of experience of area committee work – for some of us reaching back to the old district committees – have faced this question squarely and have unanimously answered that they are not necessary. More than that, we unanimously agree that they are rapidly becoming an impediment to efficient organization and an obstruction to speedy communication down the line to our members in the various industries.

We would, of course, be deluding ourselves if we did not recognize that this proposition has run into some opposition. At the same time, we are happy to add that the original opposition has been diminishing gradually over the months, as the inescapable logic of our case has become more appreciated. I am bound to say, as one who has been all over the country discussing this with our members, that I am at a loss to understand the substance of the argument of those who remain opposed. I have even spoken to some area committee members who confess that they are bereft of any argument against our case; indeed, they admit that the logic of our argument is unanswerable and yet, at the end of our chat, they nod their heads sideways and continue in mute opposition. One delegate, immediately on being elected at the March quarterly meeting, blandly announced, 'That's one vote the executive council will not get!' It is saddening and it is dangerous. I tell this conference that if the long debate which has gone on had proved the executive council wrong, it would have changed its views with the greatest speed and flexibility. It would have done so because the thing at stake here at this conference in the decisions we take is nothing less than the union itself – the union to which all of us have devoted so much, not only of our time and energy but also our affection.

The basic decision taken by the executive council, affecting all the major amendments before you, was that we should abandon horizontal lines of organization within the union and replace these with the vertical structure corresponding largely to the collective bargaining machinery within industry.

You will see a simplification of our activities in the union. You have the executive council and the sub-executive council, which will be a general purposes committee. Then you have the industrial sub-committees, the national industrial conferences, the area industrial conferences, and so on.

Before briefly describing the general substance of the amendments which go to make up this new type of structure, I want to make it clear beyond peradventure that these are alternative proposals to the existing state of affairs. It is impossible to graft our amendments on to an otherwise unchanged rule-book. Our amendments, for example, introducing area industrial conferences and the facilities for area shop-stewards' meetings, cannot be placed before conference as additional to area committees. This, we believe, is inconceivable and would lead to an organizational hotch-potch.

It is proposed that the executive council shall be on a full-time basis. I merely want to say at this point that it is impossible in these days to continue in an organization of our size and importance with a rank-and-file executive council; indeed, as the majority of delegates already know, it has been impossible during the whole of the post-Second World War period. Again, as most delegates know, for most of that time many members of the executive council were full-time, even though the rules provided – and still do – that they should be part-time.

The industrial sub-committees of the executive council have already been established. From there, the line structure goes down the national industrial conferences held in accordance with the rules introduced in 1962. Those who attend these conferences will testify that, in spite of all the shortcomings, the first of such conferences was amongst the most useful in the history of the union. The executive council has more than honoured the provisions of the same rule to call industrial conferences in other miscellaneous industries, and it also intends to extend this to include industrial conferences for those of our members working in combines with enterprises in different parts of the country.

I spoke earlier in my address of the industrial conferences being incompatible with the other provisions in the rule-book, and this became manifest when trying to elect delegates to the national industrial conferences in a democratic way. Our present middle structure did not provide any easy way in which this could be done, even though our original instructions were that our middle-level structure should do it.

It was clearly imperative that we should continue this principle of union structure right down the line. Therefore, you now see the provision of area industrial conferences which will be held every year. The area industrial conference, which precedes the biennial national industrial conference, will submit matters to the agenda of the national industrial conference and will democratically elect its delegates to that conference.

Continuing this structure, we are providing for area shop-stewards' meetings as and when necessary but with different facilities from those which exist under the area committee procedure.

I have only this to add. We live at a time when every thinking person in the country is anxious to see Britain modernized as quickly as possible. Governments will be elected or rejected depending on the fulfilment of their pledges to do just this. Surely every man in the conference shares this view. But for Britain to be modernized, it means not only our economy but our ideas and our institutions, including the trade union movement. One of the most important organizations in this country is the union which organizes workpeople in the electrical, electronics and telecommunications industries. So many people are all for modernization except when it affects themselves. However, I am confident that in this crucial moment in the history of our union, this conference will show that when it speaks of the new, modern Britain it recognizes the need for a new, modern electrical workers' union.

The financial rebirth of the union was built on the back of increased contributions, which rose to 3s per week for skilled men, 2s for auxiliary workers, and 1s for female and apprentice members. There was little argument over this, the proposition being carried, 558–47. Standards of probity were improved, too, with the abolition of the rule that allowed the general secretary to hold cash in his office: in future, the union's professional accountant would supervise the head office petty cash.

The first major item on Les Cannon's list was converting the executive council to a full-time body, elected by secret postal ballot every five years.

This was a fundamental change, elevating the role of executive council beyond that of regional representative of the shop floor – supervising the general strategy of the union and its implementation by full-time officials. A full-time executive council would add to *that* obligation the capacity to more closely scrutinize the head-office officials and give a local, regional lead to the business of the area offices – in that sense to be the union's national representative in each separate region of the union.

The opposition claimed in speech after speech that the full-time executive council was preventing 'rank-and-file' control over the union. Bill Eason of Harlow even invoked the pioneers of the union – oblivious to *their* long fight to secure a national leadership role for the executive council of the union. A new voice emerged for the left from its stronghold at London Airport. Fred Gore was opposed to a full-time executive because the need had only arisen due to the executive's 'interference' in negotiating duties – duties that should be undertaken by national officers. If taken in conjunction with the industrial structure, the growth of full-time officered branches, the abolition of area committees, it spelt 'complete domination from the top on all policy questions'. Ernie Hadley replied for the executive, emphasizing the plethora of committees and obligations in and out of the union that the executive councillors had to do, and could only do, on a full-time basis. The conference agreed, just – 321 votes for and 297 against.

The votes on the abolition of area committees were to be close as well: so was the balance in the arguments. As Cannon explained in his presidential address, it was the leaders' view that industrial branches with their own full-time secretaries, local committees of shop-stewards and national conferences of shop-stewards provided a better consultative process on the basic industrial responsibilities of the union than any type of branch-delegate-based area committee. The proposal to abolish them was moved by Bill Blairford in a lively and illustrative way. Some delegates were well aware of how fatuous and time-consuming they could be. The opposition was intense. Charlie Montgomery thought they were terrific for offering 'a proving ground' for new talent in the union. Fred Gore thought there was no evidence that area committees let shop-stewards down with their decisions. He also thought this 'middle-tier' of representation was a splendid form of consultation between the leadership and the branches. Jim Smith and Harry Marshall pointed out the huge amounts of time and unpleasantness associated with the area committee's disciplinary role.

It still needed Les Cannon, in what by common consent amongst those who knew him well rate his greatest ever speech, to win the day. The area committees were abolished, and replaced by the industrial structure outlined in Cannon's presidential address, by 325 votes to 292. These huge changes in the government of the union were not accompanied by the proposed change of name. The union's leadership wanted to broaden the attractiveness of the union to potential recruits by renaming it the Electrical, Electronic and Communications Association (ELECTRA). The idea barely got started. It was overwhelmingly defeated.

By the summer of 1965, the future structure of the union we know today was firmly established. A national executive, elected by secret postal ballot governed an industrial union that was moving away from branches towards its shop-stewards in the factories as the key focus for union activity. Its leadership was firmly anti-communist, encouraged to be so after the 1964 ballot result. The finances were being reformed. The negotiations were going to be inspired by different criteria as well, as we shall see.

23

CONTRACTING AND ELECTRICITY SUPPLY: REVOLUTIONARY YEARS, 1962–6

IN ANY ACCOUNT OF trade union life, it is difficult to untangle for the reader the internal politics, the external labour movement relations, the demands of employers, the manoeuvres of government. At all stages, a mixture of these forces is working on any trade union leader; similar cocktails are at work on shop-stewards and local officers.

From 1962–5, the influences pressing in on the new leadership of the ETU were enormous. We have seen how they attempted to deal with the profound hostility of their internal opponents on the political left. We must now turn to the new leadership's attitudes to collective bargaining in the 1960s. These events were tumultuous in their own right. The massive changes in philosophy behind the negotiators' minds led to new deals in crucial industries. These deals affected all the members, the political and the apathetic alike. Here was the most dangerous ground for the new leadership to step upon. They had to hope that the new image fostered by their anti-communist clean-up of the union would produce enough tolerance, enough trust to sustain the membership-leadership relationship through stormy times.

It is important to understand that throughout the early sixties, culminating in the wage freeze of July 1966, attempts were made by Government to impose limits on earnings in fear of inflation, and in fear of people spending too much on imported goods. Such spending was creating a balance of payments deficit that reached over £800 million by 1964. The world economy was losing faith in the British currency as the right money to do world business in.

The first attempt at such wage control was Selwyn Lloyd's 'pay pause', announced on 25 July 1961. Areas of employment where the Government was directly concerned, like the nationalized industries, were not supposed to give any pay rises for several months. On 5 July 1961, the electricity supply unions, still led by Frank Foulkes, although he was clearly more interested in the court case outcome at the time, submitted their claim for £2 a week.

The electricity boards' members offered two-and-a-half per cent and further movement on increments. However, following Selwyn Lloyd's diktat, they would not pay up anything until 1 April 1962. Given that the contracting industry had just been awarded the famous shilling on the rate, the comparable supply rates were now 7¼d an hour behind.

Feeling in the industry – particularly in the power stations – was strongly for action if there was no decent settlement, particularly over the proposed late settlement date of 1 April 1962. In mid-November 1961, they got 2d an hour. The settlement date satisfied the union's desire to poke two fingers at the Government – it was to be 28 January 1962. However, the unions had not had a rise since August 1960, and they were still being paid under national average earnings. The Prime Minister, Harold Macmillan, deplored the settlement. The NJIC statement included a crucial sentence: 'Early in the New Year, the National Joint Industrial Council will consider the question of productivity in the electricity supply industry and means of improving the status of the manual workers employed therein.'

The industry's negotiators started formal talks on what was to become known as the 'status agreements' in June 1962 and on 4 October 1962 the employers gave the unions a formal memorandum which had two main aims. It is easy to be sceptical of the first. The employers expressed themselves concerned at the lack of 'status' enjoyed by electricity supply industry manual workers. With the zeal of Fabian social engineers, the employers were determined to do something about that. Sir Ronald Edwards, the chairman of the Electricity Council, wrote a pamphlet in collusion with R. D. V. Roberts, the Electricity Council member for industrial relations and the true architect of management initiative throughout this period. This pamphlet, published some years later in 1967, described this intention to help the manual workers in the electricity supply industry.

The so-called manual worker was treated as slightly different from, and slightly inferior to his colleagues – clerical, administrative and technical. We regarded this as an anachronism. Many so-called manual jobs carry as great a responsibility as office jobs.... Should a senior plant operator of a vast turbo-alternator have lower status than a girl operating a ... typewriter? ...

The annual salary would bring with it the right of not inevitably having to take a cut in income every time a few hours were taken off ... to cope with a critical domestic problem, to attend a family funeral or to have an interview with a child's headmaster. In these respects our industrial staff were to be treated in the same way as the rest of the staff.

Holidays and hours of work were not be equalized with the technical, clerical and administrative staff, but sick pay, pensions and the annual salary would be exactly similar. This was a bold move to offer the eight main earnings groups in eighty occupations being paid twenty-five different hourly rates of pay in mid-1962.

The second main aim of the 'status agreement' was to do away with overtime. By April 1964, average hours among the 150,000 manual staff amounted to forty-nine, seven hours over the weekly basic. Some large groups were working sixty hours per week, and the average on the generation side was fifty-one hours for the 52,000 Central Electricity Generating Board (CEGB) employees. The employers knew why it had got out of control. They were not paying competitive hourly rates, and the 1961–2 settlement had not helped matters, particularly where the industry competed for skilled labour in places like the West Midlands. In Coventry, for instance, in 1962, average earnings were over £5 per week behind the car industry, despite average levels of overtime exceeding fifteen hours. Only overtime maintained any sort of level of weekly earnings (forty-seventh in the league table), as the hourly rate plummeted to sixty-eight in the league tables. Sensitive senior managers identified huge management problems associated with runaway overtime. Work was spun out to get particular jobs into overtime periods. Different groups of tradesmen (and there were over 40,000 of them in the industry) were easily tempted to insist on mutually beneficial rigid demarcation to get more men offered more access to more overtime. Groups of workers would insist on the equal availability of overtime, bringing in men who had no real function to perform on certain tasks. The higher financial obligations being taken on by the workers in the early 1960s made the creation of overtime a science in an industry that would not pay bonuses and piece-work rates like the lucrative engineering industries. Worst of all, from the management's perspective, the first line of supervision – the 3,500 foremen – were becoming slovenly. They had to take part in the conspiracy to create overtime to raise earnings. In so doing, they tended to lose control of the work.

In return for 'staff status', the industry's leaders wanted to abolish overtime. They wanted to do this by increasing shift working, 'staggering' the working week and the working day and the working year, so that overtime could be avoided, and increasing the mobility and flexibility of maintenance workers, linesmen teams and cable jointers. Finally they looked forward to the comprehensive planning involved, the operations research and the use of work study methods that would lead to much better utilization of labour.

All this was all very well, but the ETU had a problem – or rather a series of problems. Jock Byrne had to lead for the union in 1962–3. Harry Gittins and Jim O'Neil joined him on the NJIC and both had worked in the industry – formally, still did. With the disgrace of Frank Foulkes, however, the trade union side of the industry was now led by Bill Tudor, general secretary of the old Enginemen, Firemen, Mechanics and Electrical Workers Union who were loosely affiliated to the TGWU. The trade union secretary of the NJIC was

Jack Eccles of the GMWU. Bill Blairford identified this structural issue in the negotiations as a major problem for the union in establishing any sort of policy in the industry. He told the first conference of electricity supply industry shop-stewards, summoned after the 1962 rules revision conference at York, on 26 January 1963:

> Approximately 50,000 workers in supply are members of this union, and they constitute twenty per cent of the membership of the ETU. The remaining supply workers are divided among four other unions, including the TGWU, the National Union of General and Municipal Workers (NUGMW), and the AEU [and Bill Tudor's 30,000 strong Enginemen]. They constitute a very small minority indeed of these great unions, each with a membership of about a million. So what to us is a dispute of the greatest possible importance is a relatively minor issue to the leaders of these big unions.

For historical reasons, the union was just not represented in some power stations, although it was the dominant union in the distribution network of the area boards. Whatever their priorities were to be in the famous productivity deals to come in the mid-1960s and beyond, in late 1962–early 1963, the union was almost totally interested in money.

They had claimed, in December 1962, along with the other unions, 4d an hour for everyone, despite needing 9d to catch up with contracting. In the summer of 1962, led by Jock Byrne and Frank Chapple, the union had reopened the contracting negotiations to deal with the unacceptable two-and-a-half year deal Haxell had signed. They achieved a further $2\frac{1}{2}$d an hour on the provincial contracting rate, thus creating *more* pressure on the supply negotiations which were dominated by unions who were *not* influenced by the contracting rate at all.

The December claim, then, demanded 4d an hour, a productivity bonus divisible amongst all workers and a reopening of the 'Status' talks. The employers rejected this and offered arbitration which the NJIC negotiators rejected. To the fury of the ETU leadership, the general secretaries of the AEU and the GMWU publicly expressed their support for arbitration: this fatally undermined the ETU's official overtime ban. Its effectiveness was already being rivalled by the widespread unofficial work-to-rule, leading to power cuts (at the height of the worst winter in memory since 1947). On 16 January, the NJIC met and voted, on the trade union side, by four unions to one (the ETU) to accept the employers' final offer – $2\frac{1}{2}$d on the rate every February for three years, a productivity bonus based on an average 1s 6d a week for every half per cent fall in the pay hours needed to generate 1,000 units of electricity nation-wide, and the reopening of status talks.

The union's executive met on 20 January and reported to the 200-strong shop-stewards' conference at York on 26 January. They rejected the deal in a torrent of abuse for the Government, the employers and the other unions;

however, they had to end the overtime ban because the other unions were not bound by it and were making it inoperable. The basic pay rates for a three-year deal still left the craftsmen on £12 a week; this was no basis for a three-year deal and the union rejected it.

The union forlornly sought the reopening of negotiations and increased NJIC representation for the ETU. However, they first had to deal with the unofficial elements who were keen, of course, to upstage the ETU's official rejection of the January 16th NJIC deal. Their work-to-rule, particularly in power stations, had led to the cuts in supply which had given the political and public relations initiative back to the Government and the employers. Their chief spokesman was a Scotsman from Coatbridge in Lanarkshire, who had emigrated to America, from where he had returned in 1953. Charlie Doyle was interviewed by the sub-executive council (now including a provincial executive councillor, Tom Breakell) on 18 January. He would not withdraw from the national shop-stewards' committee he apparently ran. He would not give assurances that he would stop talking endlessly to the newspapers. He admitted cheerfully to being the editor of the unofficial paper *The Power Worker*. In March, he was expelled from the union. In the House of Lords, Lord Morris demanded his deportation to America. The executive council had to be kinder; in December that year, they let Charlie Doyle back in the union, courtesy of the Final Appeals Court, chaired by Bill Banning.

It was in this unhappy frame of mind that the union joined in the 'status' discussions in the first three-quarters of 1963. Between April and November 1963, there were nine meetings of the special status sub-committee of NJIC. Much theoretical progress was to be made on what we shall see was to be the full set of status agreements.

However, the employers insisted that the whole deal was going to be self-financing. The $2\frac{1}{2}$d was already being paid (on sufferance, as far as the ETU were concerned). The unions may well have four 'priorities' as their price for continuing talks – improvements in holidays, the forty-hour week, extra recognition for skilled men and increases in increments. The employers stood rigidly firm.

On 23 March 1964, the trade unions implemented a national work-to-rule: they called it off on 31 March in order to put their case to a Government court of inquiry, chaired by Lord Pearson, in mid-April 1964. Fundamentally, Pearson said that it was unrealistic to expect the unions to co-operate in the status agreement unless the boards were willing to come off their high horse about the inviolability of the three-year deal: things had to be conceded that led to financial gains for the members.

The boards quickly realized they would have to do this; and they were now dealing with the ETU's new president, Les Cannon. Cannon knew the industry; he knew all about work study methodology. He, above all, understood the need to get real improvements in the members' earnings that would prevent any fantasizing about Foulkes's performance for supply workers.

On 11 June 1964, agreement was reached, to operate from 1 July 1964. Manual workers in supply would now receive their wages as an annual salary, not an hourly rate, with all the benefits Sir Ronald Edwards had in mind. Of more financial benefit was the twenty-six-week sick pay scheme. Of significant financial interest, in the middle of the three-year deal was the 'co-operation bonus' of between £30–£80 per annum, depending on grade, plus £24 per annum for craftsmen. The 'Joint Statement on Employee Co-operation' urged both sides of the industry to get down to more efficient working locally, particularly with regard to the ending of overtime.

On 14 January 1965, stage II of the status agreement was implemented. This obliged workers in the industry to work into the first hour of overtime to get things done for an annual payment of £25–£35. However, extra payments were going to be paid for the revolutionary assault on overtime: £8–£48 per year was planned to be paid to those workers who worked the desired 'staggered' working week that cut out overtime at the weekend. They got the money each time they worked a 'stagger' that included one Saturday or Sunday per month. On some occasions, the boards needed shorter staggers, involving hours, not weeks: £1 10s 0d was the payment for each week that used staggered hours. Occasionally, the boards needed people at winter or summer peak periods: those 'staggers' attracted 25s each. The great fear was that members standards of living would collapse between the abrupt ending of overtime and the start of new systems of work. There were transitional allowances paid to cushion the lack of overtime. Shift workers' flat allowances of £41 per annum were increased on a range from £57 10s 0d to £70, depending on grade. The holiday remained at a basic two weeks: but workers were entitled to an extra day for each year of service from two to six years, instead of seven to eleven years. Finally, the forty-hour week was at last introduced with effect from 5 July 1965.

Stage III of the status deal, reached in September 1965, agreed to encourage the mobility of maintenance teams between power station locations. Attention continued to be paid to the allowance of temporary up- and down-grading of workers, the pooling of mates, the use of smaller jointing teams, an increased willingness of craftsmen to drive vans and a greater flexibility in just who would attend, particularly, domestic customers' premises instead of a clutch of different grades. Much of this came out of the 'joint statement' period, but wholly of stage III was the increase in service increments and the agreement in principle to introduce work study into the industry.

It is important to jump just one moment from the week-by-week scepticism, the political opposition, the sheer confusion of this enormous sea-change in industrial relations spanning the two full years from 1964–6. The results were quite spectacular. During these two years, sales of electricity rose by 6.7 per cent, and the workforce rose in total by just 1.7 per cent, despite an average fall in overtime work of just over six hours in the area boards (from forty-nine to forty-three per week) and a sensational fall in generating (from fifty-one to thirty-nine per week). Ninety per cent of CEGB staff were on weekly 'staggers'. Twenty-five per cent of area staff went on to 'staggers', usually staggered hours. The 'employee co-operation' was judged by the Prices and Incomes Board (PIB) in 1967 to have provided 'significant though not uniform advances in inter-craft flexibility'. The best part of the whole thing was the 'decisive break with excessive overtime'. Average weekly earnings rose by ten per cent, a modest total in itself. Average hourly earnings, however, were up a massive thirty per cent, and the new sick pay and traditional pension entitlements had to be considered by commentators as part of the wages package.

Les Cannon assessed the impact of the deals at the national industrial conference of shop-stewards at Colwyn Bay in North Wales in May 1966. The deals had been 'a substantial success', marred, perhaps, by two main considerations. First, some managements were far too arbitrary in attempting to impose flexibility rather than negotiate it. Secondly, a small minority of workers put up 'unreasonable resistance' to better methods of work. Two years earlier, Battersea's Tom Cox had told the 1964 conference what the priorities were. 'The overriding consideration with status must be the financial considerations that we are bound to get from it. It's the lolly, brothers! It's the pounds, shillings and pence which is the overriding interest of members of this union and the executive must realize this, and this alone.' By the autumn of 1964, Harold Wilson was in Downing Street; for Les Cannon, the supply status agreements were the 'fragments' that the industry was contributing to the 'scientific revolution' on behalf of the modernization of Britain. He wanted desperately for the union to contribute to Labour's success – but not at the expense of underpaid electrical workers. But his fiercest pride in the electricity supply industry agreements was the comparison he directly invited with the previous leadership. He told the 1964 industry conference: 'The people responsible for some of the best electricians in this country working in power stations on maintenance in hazardous conditions on £13 a week were praised as much as *we* have been *criticized* for increasing those rates by eighteen per cent in one year!'

Contracting Negotiations 1962–6

The same problems faced the negotiators in contracting. They had to improve conditions for the union's members in the face of hostility from the left, and deny the growing myth of the 'shilling' rise in 1961. Being in the private sector, there was not quite the same scrutiny of the industry by the Government. The employers were always willing to quote Government admonishment on wages, of course, but the NFEA had a new leadership in parallel with the ETU. The redoubtable Mr Penwill had been replaced by Geoffrey King as director and secretary of the NFEA. We have seen how in 1962, Frank Chapple and Jock Byrne led talks that raised the London rate to 6s 9d an hour (8¼d ahead of supply rates) and the provincial rate to 6s 4d an hour. On 1 March 1963, they signed a three-year deal, every bit as sensational as the supply deal, although it stuck to conventional ambitions. There was a 'productivity' element, however. The union agreed that tea breaks should not be excessive; stopping and starting times should be punctually observed; and spare-time working should be discontinued. (It would have been amazing if the union had *not* put its name to all this!) The deal produced hourly rate increases for 1963, 1964, and 1965 of 4d, 3d, and 2½d per hour. A sick-pay scheme was at last to be in place by 1 January 1964. Later that year, the forty-hour week demanded by C. H. Stavenhagen in 1919 was granted. There was remarkably little agitation against the deal. The next three years were well used to think of real changes in the industry that were to provide the epoch-making agreements of 1966.

For some years, Frank Chapple and members of the executive council – in particular Eric Hammond – were thinking of just how to improve the whole stadard of living of electricians in the contracting industry. These members had for decades been the backbone of the union; most of the union's activists came from the industry originally. Like much of the rest of the construction industry, contracting was a rough, tough, young man's game, with more than its fair share of sharks and tearaways among both employers and workpeople. With the opening and closing of sites, it was in perpetual turmoil. The industry had no stability at local level. The quality of supervision was a lottery. Frequently, the sites were not properly organized, with shop-stewards difficult to elect. Often known shop-stewards found it hard to work due to a fairly effective blacklising of 'militants' by employers.

With the contracting agreement up for renewal in 1966, the opportunity was to be taken to change the whole culture of the industry.

Just before the agreement was signed at the NJIC for the industry on 30 June 1966, it was discussed for a full day at Colwyn Bay by a national industrial conference of shop-stewards from the industry. Frank Chapple was in the chair and Eric Hammond presented the draft agreement to the conference. It was a presentation style that was to become familiar in the next two decades, and probably was the final blow to that *Daily Worker* industrial correspondent who had hailed his election to the executive council at the end of 1963.

The ideas in the agreement had been under discussion since April that year round the industry. All branches and over 700 shop-stewards were sent the outline proposals in the middle of the negotiations – an unheard-of consultation process. However, many jobs had no steward; many stewards were no longer working in the industry. The executive council were going to have to decide. The consultation process, enormous as it was, still could not hide the fact that the new agreement would be a huge change in the industry's procedures. Eric Hammond told the conference: 'The executive council do not underestimate the emotional resistance to change, and compounded as this emotion has been by distortion of those who want to take a factional, opportunist line in this matter, many have been inviting me this morning to enjoy the traditional hearty breakfast given to a condemned man. I reject their concern.' He went on to show the steady logic that led to the new proposals. He did it by exposing the hopelessness of the alternatives. First, the traditional 'fodder' basis of negotiating rises on the basis of the cost of living. What would that produce? Three-and-a-half per cent, in line with the prevailing incomes policy. On some big sites, there might be action to secure more. But no one should underestimate the difficulty of organizing nation-wide action when the backward state of the union's organization in the industry left it 'a bike in the jet age'. Part of the *general* lack of militance, outside of big sites, could be explained by the actual levels of contracting electricians' earnings. The *national* averages showed them earning the highest rates, with the second highest earnings in construction (13s a week behind heating and ventilating craftsmen who had to work four-and-a-half hours more for that 13s). Of course, particular sites might be able to do better than £19 for 46.4 hours in constructional engineering as well – but the union had to aim higher than three-and-a-half per cent for the generality of construction members.

He looked back, with some feeling, on the basis of his own direct experience. What had this 'golden age' of contracting between 1945–63 amounted to? Two-and-a-half pence an hour per year averaged out over the whole period. He even admitted to the difficult personal experience of explaining the $1\frac{1}{2}$d achieved in 1959 as the limit of achievement to his own members as a shop-steward in the industry.

He also knew that PBR was a virtual impossibility in the industry; it was also undesirable because PBR schemes *do* depress the basic rates in an industry – and that is of special significance to the contracting rate that was, and remains, a vital touchstone in other members' negotiations.

All of these options were rejected; the only way to get more than cost-of-living adjustments was to increase the productivity of the industry. The only way to do that was not to fiddle about with exhortations about tea breaks. 'We could only increase productivity without a direct reward-to-effort relationship by raising the level of skill in the industry and this can only be done by rewarding and thereby encouraging workers who attained and exercised greater skills.'

The agreement was due to be implemented in September 1966. Eric

Hammond started with the money. Every electrician would get a thirteen-and-a-half per cent rise – a full shilling. For most electricians in the three-year period up to September 1969, hourly rates would rise by thirty-three per cent – 2s 6d an hour. For the top rated electricians, a rise of sixty per cent (4s 6d) was in line over the three years and for mates regraded to electricians, a forty-three per cent rise (2s 8d per hour). What was proposed was a whole new structure. The NFEA and the ETU together would form a Joint Industry Board (JIB). This body would supervise the sick-pay scheme and the holiday scheme on an industry basis, but most vital of all, it would eventually grade all employees on the novel basis of technician, 'approved' electrician, electrician and labourer. Each of the grades of electrician would be dependent on the initial grading by employers, subject to appeal, and eventually subject to City and Guilds certification. Starting at the bottom, as it were, most mates with four years' experience would become electricians. Others would stay in the industry as labourers. Most electricians with five years in the industry and two with a current employer would be 'approved' electricians. The 'technicians' would be effectively foremen.

The real lurch into the future was to be provided by the national and area JIBs which would mutually control, after the second year, the grading, the training, the supervision of overtime, disputes and the provision of rights of appeal outside the industry. This was the thrilling part of decasualizing a jungle. Eric Hammond quoted one of Frank Chapple's descriptions to the employers of the type of industry they had presided over for too long. 'Our industry was one that workers came to with distaste, endured with protest and left with pleasure.' The JIB would make the contracting industry 'the brightest jewel in the crown of the ETU'. Certainly the rates were attractive, as were the increases, illustrated as follows.

Table 6

September 1966–7		September 1968–9	
Charge-hand	9s per hour	Technician	12s per hour
Journeyman Electrician	8s 6d per hour	Approved Electrician	10s per hour
Mate	6s 11½d per hour	Electrician	9s per hour

On 20 July 1966, Harold Wilson's Labour Government imposed a total wage freeze and blocked the deal.

Incomes Policy in the mid-1960s

The steadily deepening impact of incomes policy tried the patience and loyalty of the new leadership of the union. They had wanted to be associated with the restriction of higher-earning workers in return for action on prices and a clear understanding that higher wages could be paid to those workers who improved their productivity. However, even before the advent of Wilson's Government in October 1964, the new leadership made its position clear. They would not simply give up their attempts to put up wages. Frank Chapple told the first biennial policy conference at Scarborough in May 1963:

> We can and we will, by the use of our organized strength, ensure our share of current productivity. We will be asked if we wish to challenge the whole of society with our wages policy. The answer is no. We will leave such challenges to the political wing of the movement. . . . We have made it clear that we are not opposed to improving production techniques or increasing production, but that we do believe that it is essential if such efforts are to succeed that the workers receive a more equitable share of increases.

Les Cannon saw the issue in April 1965 as risking the 'ousting of the last social-democratic Government from power in Britain', leaving the trade union movement with the awful prospect of 'a succession of Conservative governments for many years'.

Harold Wilson's new Government identified the need to avoid worsening the balance of payments crisis by only paying wage increases in line with improvements in productivity and efficiency. In a White Paper in February 1965, the machinery of ensuring this basic aim was outlined, backing up the famous Declaration of Intent of December 1964 in which the unions, the employers' associations and the Government jointly signalled their support for the policy that would encourage productivity. There was to be a PIB under the chairmanship of Aubrey Jones. From April 1965, the PIB was to frown on pay settlements that exceeded the anticipated three-and-a-half per cent growth in the nation's productivity, unless workers were among the lowest paid or could show genuine productivity improvement. Les Cannon spoke to the conference of trade union executive councils that approved this policy on 30 April 1965. He had a wider vision of just what incomes policy could give trade unionists. 'In accepting a planned policy for incomes, we lose nothing in the short term; we secure full employment and in the long run strengthen our power by demonstrating that we are able to exercise that power with responsibility.' The ETU supported the policy so long as it applied to everyone, that productivity increases should be allowed and only the genuinely low paid get non-productivity related rises and that prices, profits and rents should not escalate unchecked.

However, the plan went awry. Earnings were rising by eight per cent a year by October 1965. Retail prices were rising by five per cent. The Government started up an 'early warning' notification of pay claims; the TUC got Congress to agree that *they* should vet the claims first in order to hold back further legislation. Les Cannon did not support this; neither did the union's executive. However, it didn't stop Les Cannon becoming the first ETU member of the TUC General Council since 1947.

He was elected, uniquely, against the wishes of three out of the top four unions affiliated to Congress. He could be allowed his initial response: 'It looks like the end of my Rake's Progress. I can't help smiling when I remember in 1958 the communists in my union would not let me take a seat as a delegate to Congress – now I am on the General Council!'

The vetting of wage claims went on throughout 1965 – by the TUC – including the supply claim, and in September 1965, the national plan was published, anticipating an annual growth rate of 3.4 per cent. The Government won a huge majority in the March 1966 General Election, but wages were still rising at seven per cent compared to prices at three-and-a-half per cent. The seamen's strike finally 'blew the Government off course'. On 20 July 1966, all prices and incomes were to be frozen till 31 December, with a six-month period of severe restraint to follow. Even agreements already signed could not be implemented before the end of 1966. One such agreement was the contracting deal that had been so long in the making.

The PIB report that examined the deal was published on 22 December 1966. It allowed the payment of the September 1966 first stage of the contracting agreement, but would not allow it to be paid until six months after the due date for payment (March 1967), rather than six months after the date of the agreement – which would have led to the new payments starting in January 1967. There were further knock-on effects. For instance, in Glasgow, the local authority electricians got caught by their contracting-linked wage deal being done on 21 July 1966 – one day after the freeze started. Then the six months' 'severe restraint' for local authority wages postponed the payment until July 1967! By mid-April 1967, 1,500 electricians were on strike with local shop-steward John O'Brien in trouble for 'jostling' the Secretary of State, Michael Stewart, on a visit to the city.

The union's leadership were deeply angered by this postponement of the rapid payment of the higher earnings that would please the average member, making him more amenable to the change that the JIB would be expected to institute. This result was bad enough; far worse was the actual way the PIB went about dealing with the reference of the deal. To start with, Aubrey Jones, the chairman, accused the NFEA and the ETU of 'collusion', on television (which was now becoming the regular medium for arguing about trade unions: Cannon was ever anxious to use it to let members know what the JIB deal was all about). One of the PIB investigation team was Robert Willis, the leader of the print union, the Typographical Association. The ETU were appalled that the representative of unproductive compositors was passing judgment on the genuinely productive JIB deal. Detailed criticisms of the report followed. In the six months after the deal was referred to the PIB, the board saw ETU and NFEA representatives for only three-and-a-half hours. Some PIB members signed the report without even attending the hearings!

Other employers, like ICI and the CBI, gave evidence in camera – no doubt complaining about the knock-on effect of the huge rises in the JIB deal. This conduct was 'nothing short of outrageous', thundered the executive council press release. The recommendation that the deal should be renegotiated produce a public repudiation from Les Canon after he met Michael Stewart just before Christmas. 'I told Mr Stewart there will be no renegotiation. This incompetent meddling is running the risk of smashing the whole industrial relations machinery in our industry.' The NFEA were quite willing to be seen and heard jointly supporting the union's position. A new era had dawned in the union-management relations at the top of the industry. Les Cannon and Frank Chapple were in the audience at the ECA annual dinner on 14 February 1967, when the president, Bill Speed, spoke of this new relationship.

> The successful conclusion of our previous wage agreement over the last three years, during which the union demonstrated its integrity in standing by the agreement, even when the cost of living had greatly increased, created a desire by both sides to build a structure for the future ... [and] culminated in the desire to create a Joint Industry Board which is a new concept in management-labour relations.

The row with the PIB was particularly poignant for Les Cannon, who had always been the most enthusiastic leader in favour of incomes policy as a broader social concept. Other leaders of the union and the mass of its skilled membership have always been sceptical: it is an enormous challenge to convince skilled people that unquantifiable social advance is worth more to them than the likely rise in wages their skill, often in short supply, guarantees them. This feeling is particularly accentuated when he cannot get exemption for his productivity improvement that incidentally benefits the whole economy. This feeling becomes almost overwhelming when the whole drift of incomes policy appears on the other hand to do nothing about prices, while whatever 'goodies' *are* going appear to go to the unskilled and unproductive. There is much, of course, in this caricature that is unfair: that does not stop it being widely held. As the status agreement and the advent of work study in supply arrived, and the Joint Industry Board came closer to starting up for business, these widespread feelings among skilled men would be fertile ground for political opposition to grow upon. And it did.

24

THE ETU IN THE WILSON YEARS

THE NEW LEADERSHIP OF the union met the challenges of incomes policy and trade union legislation presented by Harold Wilson's Labour Government head on; but first, the union had to adapt to the retirement of Jock Byrne, the general secretary. The titanic struggle associated with Jock Byrne's struggle against the communists destroyed his health. He had suffered a stroke in late 1961 and throughout the early 1960s he was forced to work intermittently due to ill-health. He last attended the executive on 23 February 1965 and prolonged sick leave failed to restore him to health. He formally resigned on 30 January 1966. Frank Chapple wrote in the *Electron* of the man with whom he had shared the court case limelight, 'Jock Byrne was not a man who had greatness thrust upon him; he achieved greatness in his devotion as an official of the union, and in his relentless struggle against those forces who would subvert the democratic organization of the trade union movement to doctrinaire political purposes.' Jock Byrne as general secretary is not associated with any dramatic personal initiatives to change the union. Frank Chapple and Les Cannon were more 'creative' in that sense. However, Byrne set standards of political courage within the union that have provided generations of EETPU moderates with sufficient determination to carry the battle to the politically-inspired activists of the left.

Daily Mail columnist Bernard Levin recognized this when he wrote on 1 February 1966:

It was Mr Byrne who year after year single-handed waged war on the men who had stolen his union from its members. He faced a wall of forgery, cheating, suppression, invention, threats and lies. Again and again he threw himself against the wall. Again and again he was repulsed. He was hampered, restricted, discriminated against, and the vilest slanders were spread about him. Through it all, he stuck, determined that he would drag the truth to light and force the communists to relinquish their illegal hold on the union and its activities, attitudes and funds. In 1961, he succeeded ... Seventeen years of the prime of a man's life is a long time; if you throw in his health, it is a high price for doing other people's work for them. I would like to recall the nature of Mr Byrne's achievement and salute a gallant Christian gentleman who for seventeen years – from 1944–61 – fought the good fight on behalf of us all, and won it, and got precious little thanks for it.

Quite. He returned to Clydeside with his wife but his health continued to deteriorate. He died on 4 December 1969. The TUC obituary was cagey. 'He was a candidate for the general secretaryship of the union in 1961. It was announced after the ballot that he was the losing contestant, but a legal action ensued and the High Court declared him to have been elected.' Even making allowances for the TUC's need to be non-controversial in its obituaries, that description of Byrne's contribution to honest trade unionism is parsimonious to a fault.

In September 1966, the result was announced of the election of his successor. The candidates included three left-wingers of different types: there was Charlie Montgomery from Scotland, who got 3,805 votes; and Tom O'Neil from Islington in London, with 2,668 votes. The main left-wing candidate with some sort of organized left-wing support was the senior area official in London, George Tilbury. He secured a dismal 5,391 votes. Frank Chapple, who as assistant general secretary had been effectively running the organizational side of the union's affairs since 1963, got 20,907 votes in a low turn-out of twenty per cent.

He joined general president Les Cannon at Hayes Court with the two top jobs in the union now filled by the most impressive combination since Jimmy Rowan and Jack Ball's tandem performances. In some respects, the relationship was strikingly similar. Frank Chapple, like Rowan, was the organizational power-house in the union. He was pre-eminently interested in the efficient delivery of trade union services to ordinary trade union members. He wanted better officials, more support services, better administrative procedures and, above all, stronger finances with which to modernize the union. Les Cannon, like Jack Ball, was the more visible leader, chairing the conferences and committees, leading the negotiations (although Frank Chapple was the acknow-ledged expert in contracting), and increasingly media conscious – appearing on television and radio frequently. He contributed to all the great debates about the nature of trade unionism in Harold Wilson's Britain. The two were friends, steeled in the fight against the communists. They made a fearsome pair of enemies to the left-wing critics of the leadership. They were helped by the first full-time executive, elected for five years, who took office in January 1966.

The turn-out in the elections varied just slightly. In Manchester, a nineteen-

and-a-half per cent poll saw Don Sheasby just beat the ailing Harry West (he was to die in mid-1967). Don Sheasby was the branch secretary of Manchester Central No. 1 branch. Although he was to take a fairly liberal line on some of the expulsions from the union in the late 1960s, and although he voted against the final form of the JIB (along with Jack Ashfield), he voted with the moderate majority on the central political issues. Otherwise, the executive council remained the same. However, Jim O'Neil, in the biggest turn-out of twenty-seven per cent, was hard pressed by Ivor Davies. O'Neil won by 150 votes, with the votes polarizing on a Wales–South-West England axis as well as on a conventional left–right political basis. Eric Hammond's majority was now over 1,200 votes, Eric Clayton's nearly 1,000. Exactly the same executive was to win again in executive council elections in 1970, with one exception. This time, Bernard Clarke's Welshness outpolled by 153 votes Jim O'Neil's power as the sitting candidate, despite his vote rising by over 1,300. An era of stable executive direction with Frank Chapple and Les Cannon jointly at the helm was assured.

The full-time executive councillors now underwent a profound change in their role within the union. They were no longer the 'ordinary Joe' at head office, keeping the full-time officials under review. They were now to become the eyes and ears of the head office in the regions. They were regional barons whose main function was to ensure that the local area offices and area officials delivered the goods to the members. They also took on head-office administrative functions in managing the area offices, thus rendering it unnecessary for the post of assistant general secretaty to be continued after Frank Chapple replaced Jock Byrne. By being full-time, the executive council now had the status that befitted the body that had been formally charged with guiding the union's strategic direction since its earliest days. Jack Ball would have been delighted.

The left were by no means impotent in this period. At the time, it must have seemed that their activities threatened an early return to power for the communists and their allies. They could not win executive or general official elections. However, they did not do badly in elections for national officers. Gus Cole and Bert Batchelor were due to retire in 1968. In late 1966, two separate national officer elections were held and the moderate candidate, Frank Townsley, was beaten on each occasion in a huge field after the losing candidates' votes were redistributed. In the first place, George Cooper from Blackpool, in his day a vocal defender of Foulkes and Haxell, won. He was to look after negotiations in government departments. In the second place, Harry Bould, a shop-steward from the aircraft industry in Manchester, won the election with only 6,263 first-preference votes. His election address was written in the canteen of Hawker Siddeley's by left-wing supporters. Harry Bould's election from an engineering background showed that it was still possible to elect a national nominee of the left in an ETU election. This understanding gave the new leadership much food for thought. The last election ever held for national officer saw Les Gregory win a national election yet again. In 1969, he got 20,379 first preferences. His challengers were H. Bond, who got 11,488, energetic Trotskyist Jimmy Dormer, who got 10,323 votes, and Jack Varty, a moderate from the Lake District, who had given evidence at the trial, who got 9,807 votes. Les Gregory fought his first election, for a London executive council seat, in late 1937. Altogether, he fought nine executive elections and won every time. In 1954 he won his place as a national officer. He won four national-officer elections out of four. The only election he ever lost was the 1963 presidency to Les Cannon.

Mark Young had to work hard against a relative unknown from Belfast, H. Chicken, in 1968, although he did win 18,995 first preferences to Chicken's 13,845 and Albert Hodgson's 9,158.

Among the area officials, there were few significant electoral changes: in London, George Tilbury won his last election in December 1967 against the ubiquitous Jimmy Dormer. Tilbury now enjoyed 'establishment' support against the then Trotskyist, and won by 4,683 votes to 2,634. Alf McBrowse at last made it. He won a London area official's election when Arthur Stride retired by 2,129 to Jimmy Dormer's (again!) 2,047 votes, but needed the redistributed second preference votes of the unfortunate Frank Townsley and Bert Hunter to do it. In late 1966, Ted Ward won re-election as an official in London; his largely electricity supply supporters beat Bert Hunter, a contracting man, 3,817–1,865. Ted Ward had a subtle electioneering strategy. A month or so before nomination nights at the branch meetings, discreet friends of Ted Ward's would noisily declaim in key, large branches that some minor aspect of Ward's stewardship of supply negotiations was disgraceful. As if by sheer coincidence, Ward would dutifully turn up at the next branch meeting to answer his 'critics' – a branch meeting that just happened to be nomination night for full-time officials. Ward would then reply comprehensively to the 'criticism'. So impressed would be the planted 'critic' that he would leap to his feet, profusely thank Ted Ward for his totally satisfactory answer to the query and with great enthusiasm move Ted Ward's nomination for full-time official out of sheer gratitude!

Elections continued to be problematic in the union. The need for total confidence in their probity saw occasional expensive postponements when the electoral reform society and the branch administration got the electoral registers wrong and ballots had to be rerun. Secondly, there was constant difficulty with election addresses. Since 1962, candidates could give details of their political and industrial record and intentions; few could resist the temptation to impugn the integrity of their opponents. The executive's legal advice was that the distribution of slanderous election addresses would bring legal action on the individuals concerned *and* the union for distributing them. In 1966 there was a classic case. One candidate suggested that the executive's decision to award a twelve-and-a-half per cent increase to officials – including themselves – was somehow corrupt. Later, he had to sign a public apology saying he realized it was the result of perfectly proper undertakings given to the union's conferences and committees on the subject of officials' pay. However, a good number of candidates seemed to perversely enjoy confronting this necessity to avoid abuse and slander. Perhaps they were breaking the rules in order to highlight the apparently suspicious nature of the role in the first place. Perhaps they thought that if they undermined confidence in the secret postal ballot by implying unwarranted 'censorship' of election addresses, the leadership's clean electoral reputation would be tarnished.

In any case, voices started to be raised in the union that challenged the whole idea of electing area officials and national officers. No one suggested the executive council should not be elected; but many other unions appointed their local and national negotiating officials and made them accountable to the executive. Those executive councillors then sought election or re-election on the basis of industrial policies that they supervised the appointed officials in implementing. This argument took on even more force when the executive councillors presided collectively and individually over national and local conferences and committees of shop-stewards – men and women elected directly from the shop floor. The election of the union's 'civil servants' – the officials – was therefore unnecessary and could be unhelpful if they opposed the desires of the shop-stewards and the executive council. The first recognizable kite on this issue was flown in the January 1966 *Electron* by Shotton branch activist Brendan Doyle. He thought that the challenge to the union provided by huge multi-nationals and the use of 'modern management techniques' (work study and job evaluation) demanded a closer scrutiny of full-time officials' competence. This seemed to him to demand the appointment rather than the election of full-time officials. 'We are doing a disservice to ourselves, our union and indeed democracy itself, if we use democracy as an excuse for inefficiency. It is futile to depend on our present ballot procedure to produce a highly-trained negotiator of the calibre required today.' He thought 'promising' shop-stewards should be trained properly, and after a probationary period, be confirmed as officials. This would do away with the 'distraction' of elections and the officials would remain accountable to the members through the executive. He also urged on the union the adoption of 'check-off' schemes – where employers deducted trade-union contributions from employees' wages on behalf of the union and the adoption of the closed shop with the right of appeal to an independent body in the event of a dispute. No one was interested in that, but the left instantly spotted the political impact of Doyle's first 'modernization' suggesting the appointment of officials. In the April 1966

Electron, Enfield branch's E. Woodcock thought Brendan Doyle's letter was a 'feeler' for the leadership. London Press's J. McLoughlin gave the essence of the anti-appointment case. 'The appointment of officials would eventually lead to the so-called "professional" negotiators, who might even be recruited from outside our ranks. Appointments by an executive can lead to the dangerous position of jobs for the boys, plus the added danger of choosing people inferior to themselves so that they (the executive) can remain in power and appear to be brilliant.' In the January 1967 *Electron*, Frank Chapple declared his own personal view. He was upset about the low turn-out (twenty per cent) in his own successful election for general secretary. Part of the reason, he thought, was election weariness with the union electing general officials, executive members, national officers, area officials and an increasing number of full-time branch officers. (Cost was also a factor. In July 1967, it was emphasized that ballots cost the union £4 per member.) For Frank Chapple:

> ... it is about time a kite was flown questioning the exercise of ballots for all official posts ... It is a sufficient safeguard to the basic internal democracy that ballots should continue for the election of the executive council and other senior officials ... The question is, can we afford the waste of time and money involved in producing ballot results whose only virtue seems to be to demonstrate that a mere handful of people have any interest in the organization?

He returned to the subject in July 1967. He expanded the argument to cover the proposition that the union could afford more officials, if they were appointed; their work would improve the efficiency of the support given to the members at work. This process would have a distinct effect on the members' capacity to influence their own working lives, which would be a real improvement in their democratic rights. He was particularly scathing about the argument that elections provided 'rank-and-file' control of the officials.

> I do not know any trade union whose rules permit such control. I believe that an official who allows himself to be controlled by rank-and-file members on every job on which he appears is either weak or incompetent. In any event, the role of the official is not that of a mandated puppet, but of a representative of the union as a whole, using its policy and his judgment in the interests of the members in the particular circumstances with which he is dealing. Under the rules of the Union ... the executive council has responsibility for controlling the work of the officials.

In July 1969, as we shall see, the executive council decided to ballot the members on the question of the final appeals committee. They balloted the members at the same time on this question of appointing area officials and national officers. There was considerable disagreement on the executive itself, however convinced Chapple and Cannon were of the need for change. Jack Ashfield, Jim McKernan, Don Sheasby, Jim O'Neil and Eric Hammond were against the change. Five ETU executive councillors were in favour – Tom Breakell, Bill Blairford, Bill Blair, Eric Clayton and Harry Gittins. However, since the amalgamation with the Plumbing Trades Union (PTU) in 1968, there were three plumbing section executive councillors, Charlie Lovell, Dave Fraser and Fred McGuffie. They tipped the scale to give an 8–5 vote in favour of balloting the members on the issue. On 28 September 1969, the members showed no similar hesitation at all. They voted for the appointment of full-time officials, 47,560–14,725. The decision took immediate effect. Les Gregory was the last national officer to be elected, at the end of 1968. Joe Williamson, a plumbing official in Lancashire, was the last plumbing area official to be elected on 27 August 1969. Joe Thomas was elected an official in the Luton office on 3 September, and became the last elected ETU official.

This was an immense change in the union's affairs; the way it was done was even more significant than the decision. No one could deny it was a controversial change; equally, no one could deny the mandate that a ballot vote of the members gave to the executive council. There were other dramatic changes at Hayes Court itself during this period. On 26 October 1965, the union had decided to buy a computer to store its membership records. The original decision allocated £110,000 to purchase an International Computers and Tabulators 1902 computer installation that would cost £13,000 to run per year. Computerization came in the wake of a professional consultant's examination of the union's administrative procedures. It was primarily designed to relieve the clerical imposition on branch officers so that balloting would be more straightforward and branch finances better supervised by the professional accountant, Martin Diamond, and his staff at head office. On 23 June 1967, the computer was switched on by Lord Citrine, the union's most distinguished member, whose reputation in the union had been assured just after the First World War with his contemporary reform of the union's administrative structures. By 30 March 1967, virtually all the branches had registered their membership on the new computer – a massive exercise.

In the middle 1960s, attempts were made to improve the approach to recruitment. Cannon and Chapple were both convinced that the communist leadership of the union had failed the union through its lack of real success in recruiting the new industries of the 1950s. Some growth was achieved, certainly at a faster rate than most unions. It was also true, for example, that traditional unions for the mining and railway industries were actually in steep decline. However, this progress was thrown into proper perspective when it was revealed in mid-1968 that the union's success in gaining 31,000 women members had to be set against a total unorganized female workforce in electrical engineering and electronics of over half a million.

From January 1965, the union tried to rectify the situation by setting up a proper recruitment department. Nine recruitment officers were initially appointed. Among the first to use the new recruitment vans, acting as mobile union offices, were Jim Cahill, Mike Nelson, Arthur Pickering, Seymour Moss, Mick Kearns and Frank Chapman – who was to be congratulated by name in the executive minutes for recruiting the English Electric factory at Winsford in Cheshire.

The significant feature there was the recruitment of the staff grades, which was still unusual territory for the union to invade. Towards the end of the 1960s, Frank Chapman was to preside over one of the union's most spectacular recruitment coups. The union signed a single-union deal for all the production and craft workers on a new site on the Isle of Anglesey. BICC, Rio Tinto Zinc and Keyser set up a new aluminium smelter in the rural peace of Anglesey. Les Cannon designed the agreement and Frank Chapman was sent to the island to provide the necessary recruitment and full-time trade union service until the agreement could stand alone. It had a virtual 'no-strike' clause in the agreement, as the union realized as much as the company that if the smelting furnaces once went cold, they would be ruined for ever. It was a technological nightmare, to impose a new, physical, continuous hot metal process on a rural community, even if many workers were initially imported from the closed-down British Steel works at Irlam in Manchester. Frank Chapman had to handle the recruitment and negotiations for this strange 'mixing-pot' of different types of men – some of whom were so resentful of American multi-national culture that they took to wearing a late 1960s slogan, 'Viet-Taff', on their safety helmets. Out of all this struggle, particulary under the local leadership of senior shop-steward Jim Smithurst when Chapman's organizing work was successfully done, has emerged arguably the best single agreement the union holds. National officer Eddie Linton's annual negotiations set wage levels, terms of employment, social benefits and advantages for the union in terms of representational facilities that are second to none.

Specialist recruitment is part of every trade unionist's job. Ever since the union began, thousands have had to be recruited every year merely to replace those who have left the union. Jimmy Rowan and Walter Stevens were both plagued by the lack of progress in the union's membership growth due to people slipping back into non-unionism, after their initial recruitment.

Recruitment officers, however, have other problems, It is difficult enough to get people into the union in the first place; but having done that, a relationship springs up between the recruitment officer and the first generation of activists in a factory. The recruitment officer gets involved in the first set of negotiations. It is difficult to hand over the plant to local officials who may have had little to do with the triumph and pain of the original struggle to organize. The members trust the man they already know. Within a short period, an effective recruitment officer becomes a local official himself by way of promotion. Although recruitment is everyone's responsibility, it is tempting to hand the job over to specialists. Such specialists often get drawn into the wider obligations of representation.

Jim Cahill went on to be an effective area official in the union's Cardiff office: in 1965 he wrote a piece concerning the recruitment officer's challenge which is a splendid and timeless account of the first priority in any union's life – recruiting members.

It is unbelievable that there are manual workers in industry who have an unreasonable hatred of trade unions, but they exist. Their hatred is sometimes much more insidious than some employers', who might have better reason for it. Furthermore, they appear to have sown this notion in their minds and then built a protective wall around it, resenting and resisting any attempt to dislodge it with logic or reasonable argument.

They believe unions to be unpatriotic organizations, holding the public up to ransom, making them walk to work through strike action 'just for the hell of it', threatening to cut off essential supplies to hospitals as a means of blackmailing more money from the unfortunate employers and that their officials live high on the funds of the organizations with whose affairs they are entrusted.

Such is the power of the Tory press, some say – I'm not entirely convinced. I often think it is a form of masochism; explanations, however, I leave to the 'eggheads'; sufficient is it to say that this type can make things extremely difficult for the recruitment officer. It can be said for them, however, that there is some kind of twisted virtue in their adherence to an idea.

There is another type who listens patiently to what you have to say, with a kind of detached air, as if you were propagating on behalf of some obscure religious sect and, at the end, tells you that he has no objections to unions 'but it's no good unless everybody joins' – implying thereby that he will be the last, so that if there be one of the type I have just described working alongside him, you can write him off completely. This type usually have the virtue of good manners and courtesy.

There is one type of worker, however, who has no virtue whatsoever. This one is the 'boss's lackey' who uses every loud-mouthed device he can muster to interrupt, disrupt and make your job almost impossible, in the hope that his efforts won't go unnoticed by the managerial set and, as a result, he may get promotion in his department, or will be favourably considered in the event of redundancy. Sometimes there is no motive, other than a cringing servility to authority. You don't meet many of this type, I need hardly say, but 'gimlet eyes' was one of them.

He had his back against one of the gate piers of the factory entrance when I arrived. I had done a 'recce' the day before, so he probably saw me and had all his despicable ammunition ready. I could smell trouble when I saw those 'peepers' boring into me, The defiant and questioning grin told me what to expect. I loathed everything about him but no mother could trace any kindness or benevolence in his mean countenance, so I may be forgiven for my uncharitable feelings towards him so early on this inhospitable morning.

It was leaflets on this occasion, and as I began handing them out to the workers as they arrived, my efforts were accompanied by his cheap, stupid jibes, aimed in particular at the female workers.

'Come on girls, free pictures of the Beatles.'

'Free trips to Moscow.'

'You know what to do with that, Sadie,' suggestively, with a kind of laughter from Sadie and her companions, be-jeaned and pony-tailed.

Control your Irish temper, I tell myself, this is nothing to what you'll have to endure when he starts to heckle at lunch break. Oh! for the placid temperament of the Anglo-Saxon!

He appeared again, after a hurried lunch no doubt, just as I finished rigging my sound equipment.

'It took a lot of workers' money to pay for that rig-out.' His voice raised here, because heads were appearing at the office windows. I let that go. At least the sun is shining.

They began to come in groups and sat along the dwarf wall fronting the factory; so I started my routine. So did he.

'What can you do for me?' he asks.

'I admit you look a hopeless case, mate, but we can try,' I reply, and get a quiet laugh. I get on with it and he keeps coming, but his patter seems to help me more than him.

'That's a lot of big talk – you'd have us out on strike in no time.' This is one we get often; so I reply: 'If your brain was as big as your mouth, you'd stop talking.' This gets a more hearty and encouraging laugh; so I warm him up a bit. He keeps at it but his chirpiness is begining to wane and he is running out of material.

'What have the Labour Party done since they got in?' he inquires. He's gone off the union and this must be his last salvo.

'I didn't come here to discuss politics, mate,' I say. 'In this union we have Tories, Liberals, Labourites, the lot. We don't discriminate, in fact we would even take you in, and if that's not democracy, I don't know what is.' They're laughing now and he has shot his bolt.

I finish all I have to say and then there's that loaded silence our other recruitment officers will know about. Have I made it or not? Then over she comes, followed hesitantly by her companions. 'How much is it to join?' she asks.

Good old Sadie. To hell with Dior! You look wonderful in your jeans and what must be your small sister's sweater. A few of her male workmates follow.

Who says there's anything wrong with the younger generation?'

Jock Reynolds was the national officer initially responsible for the recruitment officers, and in his first annual report in 1966, he attributed the recruitment of 7,267 members directly to the new recruitment officers. Overall, from mid-1965 to mid-1966, 13,000 were recruited; 2,500 firms were visited and over 250 shop-stewards elected in new locations.

The union pressed on with financial reforms. Here, the computer allowed a much more effective management of branch funds; Martin Diamond eventually moved on in 1969 to the BBC. He was replaced as the union's accountant by Andy Cunningham, whose background in accounting covered local authorities in England and the mysteries of the accountant's trade in darkest Africa! By the early 1980s, his management of the union's finances had earned the union rare praise from the Institute of Chartered Accountants concerning the high standard of the union's accounts: they were a match for any public company – which is not the case with most unions. By the end of 1970, the union's general fund stood at £3.3 million, compared to £1 million at the end of 1961. The membership had risen in the same period from 252,673 to 420,588. The amount of money per member in the general fund had risen from £3 19s 9d to £7 18s 5d. Even at constant 1945 prices, the same nine years saw an improvement from £2 1s 6d per member to £2 16s 10d. This was the true measure of the improvement that Frank Chapple presided over with his accountant's specialist advice to hand.

These internal changes were important at a time in the union's life when its commitment to the wider counsels of the Labour movement had never been so extensive. Les Cannon was on the TUC General Council; Frank Chapple was on the national executive committee of the Labour party – 1966–1970 was not a good period to be on the national executive, given the endless left-right war over the tumultuous problems facing the then Labour Government. The collapse of national planning in the face of devaluation, the Middle East war, incomes policy, trade union legislation, Vietnam, Rhodesia were just a handful of the major problems that split the movement in this period. Nevertheless, the union's active members were pleased to be back in the mainstream of Labour Party affairs. By 1970, they had *three* sponsored MPs. David Stoddart had worked in the supply industry, and he was now MP for Swindon after being unsuccessful in the 1969 by-election. He joined Tom Cox, the new MP for Tooting, who had also worked in supply, and Walter Harrison, MP for Wakefield, and a foreman electrician first elected in 1964. By January 1970, the union's commitment to the party was underlined by its affiliation on the basis of 350,000 members. Ken Griffin, the energetic young official in South Wales, was seconded to Tony Benn's Ministry of Technology. Les Cannon was appointed a board member of the Industrial Reorganization Corporation, which attempted to use government finance to assist British companies in restructuring to face the growing inter-nationalisation of the world economy. Deputy Prime Minister George Brown spoke to the 1965 conference: Prime Minister Harold Wilson was helicoptered down to the union's 1967 conference at Margate on the day the six-day war broke out between Israel and Egypt. Tony Benn spoke as Minister of Technology to the 1969 conference and wished the union well. All of this gave the union's Labour Party connections new vigour and new status in the eyes of the active membership. At conference after conference, leaders of the ETU pledged the union to the Labour Government. Time and again the union's leadership appealed for support for Wilson, not criticism. Time and time again they attacked the left in Parliament and in the union whom they saw as betraying the Labour Government. Les Cannon, in particular, equated the survival of democratic socialism with the survival of the Labour Government. He was always hopeful that Labour would succeed on behalf of skilled men and the genuinely deprived alike. The need to support the Government in the face of internal ETU critics on the left was also paramount. Quite predictably, they would use executive council support for 'discredited' Labour Government policy as a big stick to bash the leadership with, for internal political purposes. In denying the validity of that, the union's leadership was cool and sanguine in public over issues with the Government that in private had made them extremely angry indeed. They were particularly angry about the 1966 contracting deal, as we have seen. The support of the union could never be total, and Frank Chapple was more willing to say so publicly than perhaps Les Cannon was. In January 1967, Frank Chapple wrote in the union's magazine what he had been saying in private on the national executive committee and elsewhere behind closed doors. Still smarting from the run-in with the Government over the contracting deal, Chapple wrote: 'The hand and word of a friend and partner has been mistaken for the fealty of the vassal and the plea of a suppliant. The credit and goodwill afforded the Labour administration is not limitless and cannot extend to involving the union in self-destructive attitudes and actions.'

It was in this period that the union spoke out about the central trade union dilemmas, particularly in its evidence to the Royal Commission on Trade Unions and Employer Associations, chaired by Lord Donovan (one of the judges, incidentally, who had rejected Frank Foulkes's appeal in early 1962). The evidence drawn up by the union echoed with the firm views of Les Cannon. He had been given further recognition for his massive intelligence by being made a visiting fellow at Nuffield College and, later, through the granting of an honorary MA degree by the University of Oxford. The union's evidence to the commission was well-received by the pundits – in stark contrast to the TUC's evidence, which was felt to be a mite complacent. Lord Citrine noted 'with care, enjoyment and pride' the ETU's evidence. He knew that public opinion was shifting against trade unions. Press accounts of unofficial strikes, particularly in the car industry, were giving the impression that trade unionists were out of control, and neither the Government nor the union leaders seemed to know what to do. Academic research was to show this view to be a travesty of the truth; however it does not matter what *is* true: what matters is what people *think* is true. It was a widely held belief that Britain's economic performance was being held back by irresponsible, greedy and old-fashioned trade unions.

The union's evidence was first concerned with the large number of trade unions in Britain and the possibility of co-ordinating their negotiations more rationally. It was cool about the possibilities of amalgamations: groups of union members would continue to argue with each other and in any case, the main problem was to encourage structural arrangements to facilitate better decision-making between unions. Nevertheless, the union itself was engaged in constant merger discussions throughout the late 1960s.

One set of these talks paid off handsomely. After a long courtship, ballots in mid-1968 in both the ETU and the PTU voted for an amalgamated union. The PTU had around 55,000 members in 1968. It was the craft society with the longest traditions, even pre-dating the mid-Victorian ASE. Local societies of plumbers existed before 1800. By 1850, the organization of plumbers had spread throughout the northern counties of England and Scotland in several local societies. Pre-eminent amongst them was the Manchester Operative Plumbers Society. In December 1865, these local societies met in Liverpool and formed the first, and enduring 'United Operative Plumbers Association of Great Britain and Ireland'. At the time of the birth of the ETU, in late 1889, the plumbers already had over 5,000 members. By 1925, the plumbers had 24,000 members compared to the electricians 29,000. By the end of the Second World War, there was no comparison. The electricians had 133,000 members and the plumbers 41,000. From 1946, the union had been known as the 'Plumbing Trades Union', and they celebrated their centenary in 1965. John French's history of the PTU, *Plumbers in Unity* published to celebrate their centenary, has dealt with the long and honourable trade union traditions of the plumbers, particularly in construction and shipbuilding and, latterly, in public services like the Health Service, the gas industry and the local authorities. But by the mid-1960s, they had been running the union for several years at a deficit. They had two main financial problems – sustaining a small superannuation scheme for members and a growing problem with members falling into arrears. The only solution was to raise subscriptions, leading to further arrears problems and the risk of further fragmentation of the union as other societies took bits and pieces of what remained.

The amalgamation terms were generous. The executive council of the union would have eleven seats for the electrical section of the union representing 300,000 members and the plumbers would have three seats for the 55,000 plumbers, along with a non-voting national plumbing secretary. The general president and general secretary would be elected by all members of the union. In addition, the plumbers would run their own section of the union and control their own negotiations. They had their own left-wing who viewed the prospect with horror.

The 'Plumbing Trades Democratic Defence Committee' opposed the merger. 'This is not amalgamation – it is crude empire building without in any way strengthening the fighting capacity of either plumbers or electricians against the boss.' The PTU members ignored all this and voted for amalgamation, 10,699–4,645. There were very real structural problems following the amalgamation in 1968. Endless rows were caused by agreeing twenty key rules for the amalgamated union in 1968, and then running the 1965 ETU rule-book and the 1963 PTU rule-book for everything else, pending the 1971 rules revision conference. As we shall see, attempts to sort this out at the 1969 first biennial conference of the new union produced considerable ground for disaffection.

The ETU paperwork that accompanied the amalgamation ballot papers was very cool – even distant. It claimed that amalgamation would give 'greater influence and authority in negotiating councils and ... resolve any conflicts of an inter-union nature.' The amalgamation would 'substantially reduce costs' and should have been supported 'by all those members who desire our organization to strengthen its Power in the Land'. On 16 April 1968, the ETU membership voted, 45,452–42,621, to amalgamate with the PTU. This was a high poll and a close result.

Throughout the next couple of years, the new union, indigestibly called the Electrical, Electronic and Telecommunication Union–Plumbing Trades Union (EETU–PTU), took steps to make the plumbers feel welcome. In January 1969, 175 plumbers were in dispute at the Vickers shipyard at Barrow with the Engineering Workers' union over access to certain pipework: the executive threatened all concerned with the withdrawal of the electricians in the plumbers' support.

Attempts were made to secure representation on the NJIC for the gas industry. The union's nominee for the 1969 TUC gold badge was the plumbing section nominee, T. A. Butler, from Ealing. At the 1969 conference, Hugh Campbell, the secretary of the Birkenhead Lodge, became the first plumber to win the amalgamated union's gold badge.

The union talked to other unions in the late 1960s and early 1970s. Joint working parties of executive councillors took place with the GMWU (led by the conservatively moderate Lord Cooper) and the Amalgamated Union of Engineering Workers (led by the fashionably left-wing, at the time, Hugh Scanlon). Approaches were also made over the period to the heating and domestic engineers, the boilermakers, the sheetmetal workers and, in 1966, attempts were made to tempt away from the TGWU the virtually autonomous Enginemen, Firemen and Electricians' Union. None of these initiatives came to anything. By 1971, the electricians and plumbers rationalized their name into its modern title, the 'Electrical, Electronic, Telecommunication and Plumbing Union' (EETPU).

The union's evidence to Donovan looked more towards confederation of unions and the stiffening of trade union negotiating teams in important industries. Two years earlier, Les Cannon had put a paper to the ETU executive in which he outlined his thoughts. First of all, the CSEU. The CSEU had a representative executive and an organization in the districts. However, it never took decisions and imposed them on affiliates. It would always refer controversial matters to conferences of executives. It had no way of communicating directly with shop-stewards of all or any union in the factories direct. It had the structure of an industrial union without the will to actually behave like one. Worse still, the York memorandum held up the resolution of disputes to a dangerous extent. In engineering, a factory dispute that could not be resolved locally left the factory on a tortuous procedural path that eventually ended up at a national level meeting between unions and the EEF at the Station Hotel, York. Time after time, central conferences simply returned the problem to the factory of origin for local resolution. Time after time, local union activists realized that unofficial action brought swifter responses from all concerned than the York procedure which could take nearly three months to resolve issues.

For Les Cannon, the structure of the supply industry offered a model that could be useful throughout industry. Large companies should have national trade-union negotiating bodies, who would have plenary powers from their executive councils to deal directly with employers and the joint memberships of the union concerned. Each of the NJIC trade union groups should have their own research and secretarial facilities. They should finance their own trade union company journal. There should be annual conferences of the company's shop-stewards from all the unions concerned. Meetings of members of all unions should be encouraged at the workplace, and communications between them and their national negotiators improved. The ETU was in favour of plant bargaining, but was aware that 'leapfrogging' and 'wage drift' among engineering workers was leading to unacceptable gaps opening up between craftsmen who happened to work in different factories – never mind what it was doing to other differentials. The way forward was to make disputes procedures local; to 'beef up' company-wide bargaining by encouraging the development of genuinely representative national negotiating bodies, and to encourage the growth of productivity-based income growth.

We have seen how the union's attitude to incomes policy emerged in the first year of Labour government. It stood by its two-pronged approach. It was in favour of increases being restricted to the expected growth in the economy for all, except where they were lowly paid and except where their productivity improvement could happily absorb higher increases than the norm. Les

Cannon had some difficulty with the concept of 'low pay'. If the phrase was to have anything to do with justice, it could not merely apply to those workers, usually unskilled, at the bottom of the heap. It had to include comparative low pay within occupational groups. It was not unusual for some electricians in 1967 to be earning £30 a week. Against that background, Cannon would try to get over the concept of the low-paid skilled man: 'I put the proposition to one such trade union leader that a skilled man on £15 per week was much more "lowly paid" than the unskilled worker on £13 10s 0d – to which he replied, "Why?"' This question produced a falling-out with the TUC whose incomes policy committee had the responsibility in 1967 for 'vetting' union wage claims. In November 1967, the TUC committee 'vetted' an ETU claim for AEI workers at Blackbird Road in Leicester. It rejected the union's claim as not being 'in conformity with the requirements of incomes policy'. However, it would allow negotiations to proceed for an increase of £1 a week to those workers who earned less than the TUC definition of low pay – £15 per week.

Les Cannon wrote to the TUC general secretary, George Woodcock, on 27 November.

As you know, I have tried on one or two occasions to get some clarity on this alleged Congress policy. I would put a hypothetical case to you. If an electrician or any other skilled worker is earning £15 10s 0d a week and a labourer is earning £13 10s 0d per week, is it Congress policy that the labourer could receive an increase of up to £1 per week on the criteria of being 'lower paid', whilst the craftsman is stuck at £15 10s 0d per week?

George Woodcock confirmed that definitions of low pay related to absolute levels of pay and not correct levels of pay for a given job. Cannon feared for the relationship in pay scales, and the executive formally withdrew their support for TUC vetting 'based on their existing criteria'.

The union was facing up to the problem of pay policy's biting off more than it could chew. Wages had to react to market forces. In an explicit reference to the market, the union's evidence to the Donovan Commission grasped this nettle.

The possibility of the Government or other body (PIB) going further than [delaying and reviewing and investigating wage claims] is not only objectionable because of the unwarrantable limitations on human freedom and injustice it is likely to create. It is also likely to be grossly inefficient. In a mixed economy, such as we have at present, and are likely to have for some considerable time, one of the guides for the best use of our resources is the force of the market. This is not necessarily the best guide and not always the fairest. But it is the one that we have and we must use it. One of our most natural assets is our manpower. This being so, we must never reach a situation in which we are moving directly contrary to market forces. . . . To move against the market is to run the risk of draining manpower into sectors of the economy in which it cannot be productively employed and to deprive other sectors in which it could be put to good economic use.

The union was in favour of a government norm related to annual growth and it approved of the PIB review procedures (whatever its fury with the contracting reference). It insisted that productivity should be encouraged and therefore rewarded in excess of the norm, and it demanded social justice for groups like agricultural workers whose phenomenal productivity increase in post-war Britain had been rewarded with poverty-level wages.

As we shall see, the union was not opposed to strikes as such. The Donovan Commission reported in 1968 against the background of public concern concerning unofficial strikes. The ETU's attitude to strikes was that procedures, particularly in engineering, were responsible for much of the frustration that led to strikes. Equally, a full-blooded embrace for productivity bargaining would minimize the incidence of demarcation and inter-union disputes as unions 'sold' their old protective customs for real monetary gain. Les Cannon reacted to the publication of the report in the August 1968 edition of *Electron*. He was scathing of the report's analysis of the 'two systems' of British industrial relations – the formal, national, written procedures and the informal, factory-based, custom and practice-based procedure. As far as Les Cannon was concerned, there was no 'system' at all in Britain – particularly in the troublesome engineering industry. He thought Donovan missed a chance to analyse the necessity for company-based framework negotiations in companies like GEC, Plessey and British Leyland with plant bargaining reflecting the variety of such multi-industry conglomerates as GEC/AEI. Their power engineering factories at Trafford Park had nothing whatever in common with their television manufacturing operation in South Wales. However, Cannon welcomed the suggestion that agreements should be registered in public and made the subject of prescriptive analysis by a new body, the Commission on Industrial Relations. The union was opposed to the legal enforcement of collective agreements as a way of preventing strikes – not least because many strikes arose out of the frustrations and procedural delays associated with the agreements themselves. He was in favour of adopting American practice to minimize the incidence of strikes.

It seems to me that the trade union movement might have to give serious consideration to the type of collective agreements we conclude. There are a few agreements (I believe they will increase in number) which do not exclude strike action at the time of negotiation of a fixed period contract. But when the contract has been agreed, there is mutual agreement written into the contract that there should not be any strikes during the lifetime of the contract. All problems arising during the operation of the agreement are subject to negotiations and then arbitration. The right to strike is resumed again when the contract expires and negotiations are taking place for a new contract.

The union was also pleased with Donovan's recommendations to establish legal protection against unfair dismissal, including dismissal on the grounds of trade union membership.

The union also took advantage of the Donovan Commission's hearings to set down its attitude to 'workers' participation' which was an increasingly interesting aspect of trade union debate in the 1960s and 1970s. The union's policy again was the result of its practical experience of accommodating the pace of change in industry. Throughout the 1960s, the increased use of productivity bargaining involved the union in selling new ideas to its cautious skilled membership. The worst scenario for the union during these types of negotiation was for the members to think that the union was doing the personnel manager's job for him; any benefit to the company had to be fractionally less than the benefits accruing to the union's membership. The union could not risk giving the impression they were the employer's agents. The union started with an emphasis on the inevitability of argument and conflict between managers and managed at work.

There are conflicts within industry. Where these are damaging to the interests of both parties, they should be limited if at all possible. It is neither possible nor desirable, however, to eliminate all conflict. Conflict, properly contained, can be creative. The aim of a good system of industrial relations is not to blur the lines of conflict, but is rather to contain it within an institutional framework, so that it may be fought over without spilling over into other areas. Almost by definition, employers and employees cannot have an identity of views on every subject. Clearly, there *are* many things on which they ought to be, and indeed are, united. On other matters they must differ.... A line must be drawn, however, at participation by workers in management. It is our view that little can be gained by such participation.

If trade union representatives are in control of an undertaking they will require, quite properly, to take into consideration the views of other interests in the process of decision-making. They will, in other words, be acting as managers. They will, therefore, no longer be acting as trade unionists. If, however, they are in a minority they will have no control over decision-making and there is a danger that, due to their membership of the decision-making body, they might be inhibited in the use of their countervailing force as trade unionists. The likelihood is that they would receive the odium of being obstructionists from their management colleagues and the odium of being collaborators from their trade union colleagues.... It is not the duty of trade unionists to participate in management. Their duty, quite clearly, is to protect and advance the interests of their members.

The union was all in favour of extending and modernizing the scope of collective bargaining. It would not 'wear two hats' by supporting ETU members joining a board of directors that employed ETU members.

The final philosophic issue that the union's leadership had to grasp in the late 1960s was the advent of law into the world of industrial relations.

After the publication of the Donovan Report, with its cool, lengthy and academic analysis leading to the judgment that nothing precipitate, let alone legal, could be done to stop unofficial strikes, public opinion was left uneasy and a little flat. Their prejudices, fanned by newspaper comment, found further cause for justification in the Girling brakes strike where twenty-two men in an inter-union dispute managed to lay off thousands throughout the motor-car industry. For the first few months of 1969, the Government laid its legislative plans on the back of its White Paper, entitled 'In Place of Strife', published on 17 January 1969. Barbara Castle's legislation raised three issues not found among Donovan's proposals. There was to be a 'conciliation period' of twenty-eight days for unofficial strikes. The Secretary of State could impose, in the last analysis, a solution to inter-union disputes and the Secretary of State could impose the requirement for a ballot in strikes or threatened strikes in crucial industries. Harold Wilson saw these proposals as crucial to the country's economic future. He told the parliamentary Labour Party on 17 April 1969: 'The Bill we are discussing tonight is an essential bill. Essential to full employment. It is an essential component of ensuring the economic success of the Government.' On 18 June 1969, the Government withdrew the proposals in return for a 'solemn and binding undertaking' that the TUC would take powers to intervene in unofficial disputes and inter-union wrangles with the threat of congress discipline in the background for those who would not conform.

For the EETU–PTU, 'In Place of Strife' produced something of a disagreement between Frank Chapple – who did not believe the legislation possessed anything like the economic significance Harold Wilson and Barbara Castle believed it to possess – and Les Cannon, who wanted to examine the legislation clause-by-clause and comment to the Government accordingly. Chapple's autobiography, *Sparks Fly* (1984), makes it clear that witnessing the arguments on the Labour Party's national executive coloured his thinking. For him, the whole business was unwarranted meddling in the union's affairs, reminded him of the PIB debacle and was further proof of socialist intellectuals' profound dislike for genuinely proletarian creations, like British trade unions.

Cannon's domination of the executive, however, won the day, and a cautious approach emerged from the union's executive.

The left in the union were opposed to all of it. At the 1969 conference, Wilmslow's delegate, Ken Taylor, who was a key member of the left in the

Manchester region at the time, working at Hawker Siddeley, gave the mirror-image to Harold Wilson's point about the economic significance of the proposed legislation.

> We believe that this White Paper was born to further the demands of international financiers because they saw that the prices and incomes policy is not doing its job in deflating the living standards of our members. . . . 'In Place of Strife' is comparable to the prices and incomes policy in so far that the paragraphs on management responsibilities are very ambiguous, but with trade unions . . . the paragraphs are very specific. 'In Place of Strife' is the modern financiers' method of shattering the trade unionist.

Tom Rice, the delegate from Maidstone, who worked in the paper industry, but was a veteran of the London contracting industry and a supporter of the previous executive council, was also opposed to the White Paper. His specific angle was the exaggeration of the effect of strikes on the economy. In addition, wartime experience of strikes in disobedience of legislation showed the law did not even work in the area of stopping strikes. Bill Wright from Scunthorpe had had enough of all this. He got up to defend 'In Place of Strife' and could not resist a side-swipe at the organized nature of the left opposition in the conference.

> I am in favour of the White Paper, and my following conclusions, I might add, have not been reached or influenced by the unofficial scribes who occupied cabin No. 6 on the boat coming over [to the Isle of Man] complete with typewriters and duplicating equipment. . . . It is an insult to the executive council and the more responsible delegates that the so-called stalwarts of the working-class have the temerity to question the intelligence of conference, suggesting they are not capable of arriving at a responsible opinion without their assistance!

Tom Breakell introduced the cautious executive council statement. This drew attention to the need to get at Britain's long-term economic problems through accelerating economic growth and reforming trade union structure and method in collective bargaining. The union was recommended to take a step-by-step approach to the Government's proposals. They welcomed the Commission on Industrial Relations, which could disseminate advice on the reform of collective bargaining machinery – itself a major cause of contemporary strikes. It approved of the Government's refusal to make all collective bargains legally enforceable. It rejected the forthcoming experiment in the appointment of worker directors. It welcomed the proposition that unions could take recognition disputes to legally binding arbitration, but rejected legal interference, ministerial diktat or anything other than persuasion in interunion disputes. Reflecting Frank Chapple's concerns, the executive's policy statement denounced the White Paper's aim to eventually establish 'one union for one grade of work within one factory'. This, the union feared, would prevent its expansion. Crucially, it was opposed to the twenty-eight day 'cooling-off period'. There was no certainty that the law would be obeyed, which would only create even more serious confrontation. Equally, disruption could just as easily be mounted short of a strike. Lastly, energy spent on organizing the twenty-eight day cooling off period could be better spent on resolving the essence of the dispute. The executive were not against the strike balloting procedures, believed it reasonable that they should be enforceable and demanded the Government pay for them! It also warmly welcomed the other positive features of the proposed legislation – the rights to membership of, and recognition of, a trade union, unfair dismissal protection, disclosure of information, the registration of agreements. Tom Breakell claimed that these proposals were already benefiting the union as Heinz management in the North West unbent in their previous refusal to recognize the union in advance of the legislation. The executive's statement was carried by a three to one majority in an otherwise fractious conference.

On 5 June 1969, the TUC held a full special Congress at the Fairfields Halls. There were two events that made this Congress memorable for the ETU. The first was the reporting to the executive of Tom Rice and Ray Jones for upsetting Bill Blair on the delegation by laughing and horseplaying around. The more substantial was Les Cannon's unconventional and thought-provoking contribution. He emphasized that government, employers and the public at large all had a legitimate interest in trade union affairs: it was not just a matter for the unions. Having said that, the economic importance of strikes was being exaggerated. The Government should be criticized 'for elevating this matter above its importance'. Nevertheless, that was nothing compared to the conventional trade union reaction. The 'penal clauses' were 'a tiny intrusion on the enormous power of sections of the trade union movement'. Unions could still destroy the economy or government, if that was their wish. No one should forget how vulnerable other sectors of the workforce, like bank employees, were. Vindictive employers would be brought up short by 'In Place of Strife's insistence on the right to recognition and membership of a union.

Negotiations 1965–70

It is in this period that historical comparisons about wage increases start to become bedevilled by incomes policy restrictions and the gathering escalation of inflation rates into the 1970s. It remains important to emphasize, however, that during this period the union finally broke with the past in negotiating style and a steady, steel-eyed determination emerged to ensure that electricians got involved in productivity bargaining and then got properly paid for it.

Electricity supply provided the largest set of negotiations when the union advanced the cause of work study and job-measurement techniques to support its desire to raise wages on the back of productivity improvement. There was real urgency to expand the number of supply workers covered by productivity schemes based on work study, as their conventional earnings in the glare of the incomes policy spotlight were not keeping pace with the more discreet wage rises happening in manufacturing industry. In 1967, the union's claim had been referred to the PIB, who had estimated productivity improvement under the 'status agreements' to promise a 4.8 per cent improvement in 1968. Therefore the industry could pay 4.5 per cent on scheduled salaries from 1 July 1967. However, the PIB recognized that others were doing better than that. Adult male manual workers in supply had weekly earnings in October 1963 of £16 14s 0d. The all-industries index had a shilling a week more; manufacturing industry had 12s more with a weekly total of £17 6s 0d. From 1963–7, as we have seen, the assault on overtime, the 'co-operation' agreement, the status agreements had raised supply *hourly* earnings very close to manufacturing industry and in advance of the 'all-industries' index. However – and it was a big 'however' – *weekly* earnings were falling further behind. Adult male manual workers in supply earned £19 14s 0d in October 1967. The 'all-industries' index was £21 7s 0d and the manufacturing index had gone up to £21 18s 0d per week – a huge gap of 44s per week.

The PIB report No. 42 could not be gainsaid when it noted: 'It cannot be regarded as a good advertisement for a closer relationship between pay and performance if those who have been amongst the first to co-operate in such a relationship are seen to be falling behind others in their earnings.'

It was this problem that led Les Cannon to get the NJIC unions to cajole the industry into the widespread and enthusiastic adoption of rigorous productivity schemes based on work study. NJIC agreements in September 1967 and March 1968 introduced the schemes. It was an enormously complex task to work out just how to measure output in the industry. Fundamentally, the industry took two ways of measuring work: on the distribution side of the industry, they set 'norms' or 'equivalent units' for twelve activities that could be used as yardsticks of performance. First developed by the South of Scotland Area Board in 1965, this set standards for functions like cable jointing (joints per man day), meter readers (no. of readers per 100,000 credit consumers), garages (no. of vehicles per man) and so on. In generating, the same sort of approach saw 'equivalent units' framed from measuring the performance of power stations in a 'steady state' and then producing an index of productivity index on the input of men given a constant level of non-labour aspects of production (revised once a year). The two indices would then be combined to give a National Labour Productivity Index in the industry. All of this was backed up by data banks of best practice distributed round the industry with the union's full co-operation.

The payments from the productivity schemes were based on measuring a standard performance of 100. Bonuses were paid on a sliding scale from sixty-five to 100, ranging from three per cent to thirty-three-and-a-third per cent of the schedule salary. It took time to implement the schemes. By December 1970, only nineteen per cent of the NJIC grades were receiving productivity payments. However, the schemes were paying out at ninety to ninety-five per cent of standard, producing average payments of over £4 15s 0d per week. The 23,000 NJIC grade workers receiving the payments were growing at the rate of two per cent of the total workforce per month by the end of 1970. Nevertheless, by April 1970, the earnings gaps still remained. Weekly earnings for electricity workers were stuck at £26 12s 0d, despite the productivity schemes, a five-and-a-half per cent settlement in 1968 and a ten per cent deal in 1969. Engineering workers were getting £29 18s 0d, as were gas workers. For craftsmen (who, it will be remembered, comprised a third of the workforce), the position was even more stark. By October 1970, the gap between supply craftsmen and general manufacturing craftsmen was over £4, with the figures in engineering being even higher. The traditional comparisons of the rate with that of contracting was even more galling for ETU members who could remember the ½d here, the 1d there, differences of the early sixties. The JIB was now producing a contracting rate in September 1970 of £22 16s 8d, compared to the electricity supply industry rate of £19 17s 9d.

During the late sixties, contracting rates had risen from £20 in 1968 to £22 16s 8d in September 1970. The JIB had commenced the work of grading the workforce, often in the face of considerable opposition. In engineering, the union's skilled membership were starting to realize the potential that electronics would create for them in establishing their capacity to earn more than the common craft rate that then applied to all craftsmen in most engineering locations. Negotiations at national level in the industry bore less and less relationship to the earnings of electricians in the company or plant-based negotiations that set their standards. Hence Cannon's scorn for the industry's procedures that was such a feature of the union's evidence to Donovan and their response to 'In Place of Strife' and the problem of unofficial strikes. During this period, a new industry began to come within the ambit of the union that was to produce around 20,000 members by 1972. From early 1965, the union had turned its attention to the organization of television rental shops. As long ago as 1957 the union had signed a national agreement with the Scottish ECA. In England and Wales, the larger companies organized in the Radio, Electrical and Television Retailers Association (RETRA) were keen to resist the union through setting up house unions. By 1965, the industry was expanding and expecting a boom associated with the start of colour television in Britain. The union looked forward to it, too. 'The advent of colour television is bound to cause a tremendous boost to the rental companies because nobody in their right mind would ever buy a colour TV receiver.' In November 1965, there were fierce recognition strikes in the Home Counties in Radio Rentals. The company initially dismissed the strike as only involving seventy out of 600 employees. In January 1966, a national agreement was signed with DER; and local agreements with Surevision, Robinson Rentals and a host of local businesses started to fill the pages of the executive minutes. By April 1967, Radio Rentals/Rentaset had signed a national agreement with the union that paid a skilled engineer grade 'A' £19 19s 6d. The newest 'electrical industry' was born and one in which the EETPU was to dominate to the exclusion of other unions who tried and largely failed to be the union for television engineers.

Throughout industry, whether it was in electricity supply, at the Greater London Council (GLC) in the great pre-Upper Clyde Shipbuilders Fairfield's shipyard experiment, in engineering, brewing, all process industries, or textile manufacture, the union took the initiative in raising wages through productivity bargaining backed by training courses at Esher Place that were unique in their time. Management and shop-stewards studied together the complexities of modern management techniques under the tutelage of Jock Haston, another ex-Trotskyist from the late 1940s who had made his name in adult education in London. He was an inspirational teacher who applied his charm and offered his Glenfiddich whisky to all-comers.

The union preferred joint study of intractable problems at Esher Place. However, its attitude to disputes remained pragmatic. The union would not flinch from 'struggle', though it approached the issue in a disciplined way. It rarely paid strike pay to unofficial strikers acting in defiance of the procedures. However, the union took to supporting strikes over key principles with organized bellicosity and enhanced strike pay. Everywhere men went on strike to retain the link with the contracting link, they were supported. Typical was the dispute at Selfridges in April 1967 where Seamus Behan (playwright Brendan's brother) was one of the strikers in receipt of double strike pay in defence of the NFEA rate. Earlier the same year, the Dorchester Hotel recognized the union and paid their house electricians the contracting rate as well. In Scotland, the Scottish ECA were confronted in the summer in pursuit of higher wages and the demand for a Scottish JIB. Twenty sites were hit with one-week strikes (eight were being worked by James Scott & Co and a further six by James Kilpatrick's). The final settlement achieved a 10s rate, a four-year apprenticeship scheme, three weeks' holiday and talks on the foundation of a Scottish JIB. A jubilant leadership sent messages of congratulation and a £2 per week bonus strike pay to the members involved.

On 11 August 1969, sixty-five members went on strike at the Scottish factory of Rolls-Royce at Hillington. The management had conducted a 'job evaluation' scheme without consulting the union and furthermore, they refused to show the results to the EETU–PTU shop-stewards. Semi-skilled operators of numerically controlled machines, whose output was pre-determined by tape controls, were earning more than the electricians required to maintain this new generation of complex electronic machines. The company ignored the electricians; the executive organized local appeals and doubled strike pay. The strike dragged on. On Friday, 28 November 1969, the company conceded and a famous victory was assured. The settlement gave the men £150 each. The consultants Urwick Orr (who were constant visitors to the union's job evaluation courses at Esher), were commissioned to 'review' the scandalous job evaluation scheme. Their recommended improvements were to be back-dated to 11 November 1968. The union's shop-stewards were to be trained in job evaluation techniques by the union and the union's members given training to allow them access to a higher grade of pay associated with the electronics work. The union would have a veto over just which of its members was to receive the training. This dispute was notable for its length and for its subject matter. The union was going to fight for recognition of skill in the future. Disputes in high-profile companies like Rolls-Royce got the same message across to the union's members, other unions and the employers alike.

New Structures and New Protests

After the 1965 conference, the union's new structure started to bed down. However, everything the executive did attracted opposition from a newly confident re-emerging left in the union. The opposition did not feature most of the 1950s leaders: they were either too old, retired, dead or expelled. A new left was establishing itself, based on the Communist Party's leadership exercised from a distance.

The first focus of protest came when the executive council altered the branch structure in the union. There was a wholly innocent part to this. The union was in favour of organizing branch life in an industrial basis with full-time branch secretaries giving better professional services to the members direct. There is no denying that many branches were amalgamated or closed in order to minimize the parade of communist supporters who could still be found at the union's conferences, elected by a laughably small number of members, but holding supreme power in the union when constituted as the rules revision conference. It was particularly important to do this in London. Consequently, Lift and Crane amalgamated with Lift Engineers branch. Lambeth branch replaced Brixton and Clapham. London Airport replaced Feltham directly, but had numbers of active members who worked at the airport transferred to it from out of local branches like Slough and Windsor. These developments sustained the political awkwardness of branches like Fred Gore's London Airport, but it had the attraction for the leadership of concentrating heavyweight political opposition in certain branches whilst others would have the chance of joining the moderate camp. Islington branch was the result of an amalgamation between London North and Gray's Inn and LSE No. 5 took over Poplar's members. Thirty-three of the eighty-one branches in London were reduced to 15 in 1964. The industrialization of the branches produced West London Supply and the concentration of London Transport members at Chiswick and London Railway. When the plumbers amalgamation occurred, the same process started with the lodges. In August 1970, seven lodges were amalgamated in the city of Liverpool. The largest single exercise, in London, took from January 1969–January 1971 to achieve. The four executive councillors with members in London published a re-organization report in January 1969 that was finally implemented in early 1971 after massive consultation with all the branches affected. The report was largely drafted by Eric Hammond and the consultation exercises organized by Lew Britz.

When the process started, there were 53,013 members in London organized in eighty-one branches – only three of which (West London Supply, Lift and Escalator, and London Press) were industrial branches. This administrative machine was serviced from the Highbury office in North London. Yet recruit-ment was static: from 1964 to 1967 membership fell in London by three per cent compared to a nation-wide increase of seven-and-a-half per cent. £26,000 a year was being spent on branch officers' expenses, and yet the head office computer was the real driving force in branch administration. The solutions were painstakingly assembled: full-time officials would become the secretaries of large industrial branches. The clerical work was much better done anyhow by office staff at the Highbury office, and later at the refurbished South London Clapham office, rebuilt at a cost of £90,000. The full-time officials would then be close to the branch's negotiating priorities with their employers and the branch could form part of the consultation chain that would be directly useful to the members. Extra officials would be paid for out of the savings in branch expenses. (It took £5,200 to put an official in the field, inclusive of his wages, car and secretarial support.) All across London, branches were amalgamated into a series of new industrial branches or into a core of geographical branches. In the process, some historic branches of the union changed their identity. West London Contracting branch was to be made up on the basis of the old Fulham/Putney branch, with further contracting members from Ealing, Willesden, London Railway and Chiswick.

Tower Hamlets branch absorbed London East, Hackney and East Ham. LSE No. 10 received the membership of Tottenham, Walthamstow and LSE No. 24. Following these amalgamations, Tower Hamlets and LSE No. 10 gave up the appropriate members to form a Contracting branch for North-East London and a Supply branch for North-East London. The same process happened all over London, and reorganization on industrial lines happened in all the big cities of Britain.

The issue was opposed by the left, as was every single change of substance suggested by the leadership. We have seen how the political opposition to the leadership understood only too well the dangers posed to the prospects of their return. The structural changes of the 1960s made it difficult for them. Pre-eminent among these changes, of course, was secret postal balloting. So the left shifted its ground. To gain control of the union, they could not rely on seizing power through elections for the leadership, especially now that leadership was organized by men of the stature of Les Cannon and Frank Chapple. However, the rule-book was revised at regular intervals by a delegate conference of branch delegates. This was a much more fruitful base for left activity because branch attendances were low. Here the left's fire was concentrated on the reforms of branches and access to the conferences – particularly the rules revision conferences. Following the decision to have a full-time executive council, the union had instituted a lay final appeals committee that was elected from among conference delegates on the basis of one per executive council division. Such an appeals committee looked at executive decisions on discipline in the late 1960s. And there were plenty of decisions to look at.

The new agreements in contracting and supply produced an unprecedented storm of organized abuse of the leadership, culminating in a series of demonstrations and protests that directly confronted the leadership physically.

In contracting, two aspects of the JIB deal particularly infuriated the left. First, the issue of grading. There was an easy line of exploitation that insisted an electrician is an electrician – not 'approved' or graded by an essentially hostile employers' organization. This ignored the evidence of their own lives that even in contracting the demands made of electricians in terms of skill varied. In the future, the union was going to get the employers to pay for skill. Even more emotive than the grading issue was the question of 'penal clauses'. The employers were to be fined up to £1,000 for abrogations of the JIB agreements. In return, the union acceded to the employer's demand that individual workers who persistently disobeyed the agreements could be fined £100.

The protests of the 1960s were nothing to do with the net results of the JIB agreement as the ordinary members understood it. Before the JIB in 1966, the provincial electricians rate in contracting was 7s 6d an hour. By September 1971, the rate for an approved electrician was 11s 11d; an increase of fifty-nine per cent. Ninety-four per cent of electricians had become 'approved'. Compared to other crafts in the building industry, electricians' earnings had increased in the same post-1965 period fifty per cent quicker than the other crafts in the construction industry. On top of the improvement in wages, there was the end to Saturday working, the sick-pay scheme, improved overtime rates, the increases in country and lodging allowances, the abolition of site recruitment and the recognition of shop-stewards' role in a disputes procedure that had a joint review element in disputes. The argument was never about the results of the negotiations: it was always about the politics of the negotiators.

As early as May 1963, Jack Hendy had written to the union's journal demonstrating how the political leanings he and his friends identified in the new leadership would poison their evaluation of the results of negotiations. 'One can, of course, understand the difficulties of giving an appearance of radicalism while remaining always well to the right of centre.... A union leadership which commands the unqualified support of the *Daily Telegraph*, the *New Statesman* and the Economic League is hardly likely to storm the bastions of the capitalist establishment.' *That* was what upset the left about the new executive. *That* was what inspired them to protest with unremitting enthusiasm about every single deal the union signed in this period, however effective in terms of the ordinary member's standard of living it may have proved to be. This was the time when the unbridgeable gap opened up in the union. The leadership strove to impress the largely apolitical, non-active, less exclusively trade union-obsessed members with real benefits to the average, the normal, the straightforward member. The basis of the left opposition was that they saw the union's role as part of a socialist vanguard in the eternal war against Jack Hendy's 'capitalist establishment'. Their criticism of negotiations had as its main purpose the exposure of the executive's apparently unambitious political role for the union. The executive's criticism of the left was to be that they had no right to criticize a leadership whose negotiating successes were endorsed by the menbership of the union through elections and membership growth.

Protest turned savage in 1967. On Tuesday, 10 October, at about 11 a.m., 150 people turned up at Hayes Court, apparently to complain about the JIB three-year deal and its particular application to the exhibition industry. After some considerable doubt as to whether some of the people concerned were even members of the union, Frank Chapple and Eric Hammond agreed to meet the demonstrators in the staff canteen after lunch. The protesters were primarily Londoners, with a handful from Brighton, Corby, Leicester, Coventry, Nottingham and Buxton. Les Cannon himself later submitted a report on what happened next.

At about 2 p.m., the general secretary, together with Brother E. Hammond, executive councillor, entered the room. They were immediately greeted with a storm of booing and abuse. Brother Chapple attempted to speak to the meeting and to point out that, although it was unconstitutional, he was prepared to listen to any views and give answers to any questions on the agreement. His attempts to speak to the meeting were, however, opposed by what appeared to be an organized group, including Brothers

Candy [who was later cleared of any involvement], Doyle, McKeown, Clapp and Morgan. This group insisted that they should first be allowed to appoint a chairman for the meeting who would then decide whether or not the general secretary should be allowed to speak and for what period of time. The general secretary tried to explain to them that they could not elect a chairman as the meeting was not taking place in accordance with the union's rules. This advice was rejected with shouts for the general secretary to do what he was told, to sit down and shut up. After some fifteen to twenty minutes of almost continuous abuse and threatened violence, during which time one demonstrator had to be forcibly restrained to prevent him from assaulting the general secretary, Brother Chapple became convinced that in no circumstances was he going to be allowed to speak about the agreement, nor were those members intending to ask serious questions being given any consideration by their unruly colleagues. As he turned to leave the room he was prevented from moving out by a considerable number of demonstrators who hemmed Brother Chapple and Brother Hammond in from all sides. After a little while he once again reaffirmed his refusal to allow one of the demonstrators, Brother Morgan, to be the chairman of the meeting and following this a group which included Brother Doyle ... began once again to abuse and threaten violence to the general secretary. As he attempted once more to leave the room this group together with others forced him and Brother Hammond into a corner where, although the members of the staff present were able to partially shield the general secretary and prevent him from being dragged back into the main body of the hall, he was punched, and several demonstrators grabbed hold of his jacket in order to prevent him leaving the meeting. Brother Hammond and a member of the staff were also assaulted by members during this period.

At this point a police constable who had been summoned on the general secretary's instruction entered the building and managed, with the help of staff members, to secure a passage for the general secretary and Brother Hammond by way of the adjoining kitchen. As they left the canteen, however, cups and other implements were thrown from the body of the hall.

In January 1968, after a short holiday to recover from his injuries, the general secretary knew what was behind all this.

> The plain fact is that every major election in this union since 1961 has seen the political groups who supported the ballot-riggers using any situation as a platform to defeat the present leadership. The organizers of the demonstrations have made it abundantly clear that their target is the defeat of the general president in the election that will take place this year (1968).

The protests gathered steam, despite a head office circular warning all branches about the undesirability of attending 'unofficial meetings'. On Teeside, a local member by the name of Wood, who was permanently in arrears, booked the local Co-op Hall eight times between October 1967 and 1

February 1968 for anti-JIB protest meetings. Poole branch secretary Ray Barnes organized meetings in the Southampton area in October 1967. The Hayes Court protesters were going to hold their next meeting at the Matrix Hall in Coventry on 19 October 1967 to 'discuss' the contracting deal and invited the executive council to participate (albeit only through the columns of the *Morning Star*). An obscure member who was closely associated with the Communist party, Alfred Clapp, was the chairman of this meeting, despite the fact that his self-proclaimed militance did not extend as far as paying his union contributions. He had not paid into the union since June 1966, and at the time of the meeting, he was £12 1s 6d in arrears. Eric Hammond was all for going to the Matrix Hall. He had already spotted the contradictions in Clapp's position and eventually printed an effective exposure of this originally 'auxiliary' member for the January 1968 *Electron* entitled 'Portrait of a Militant'. Les Cannon could see why Hammond wanted to go to Coventry, along with Jack Ashfield: however, Cannon vetoed the idea on the ground that the presence of executive councillors might make it difficult to take action against the organizers of all these demonstrations. The Coventry meeting took place and was indeed provocative, urging members not to fill in their grade cards for the embryonic JIB grading process.

The sub-executive council took the view that an organized communist conspiracy was being set up – particularly as a large meeting was planned for 7 November at St Pancras Town Hall and a march and demonstration in London for 10 November. The weather was unkind to the left that day. *The Financial Times* thought there were 'hundreds' on the march. The *Guardian* thought 1,500 and the *Morning Star* was certain there were 1,500–2,000. They marched to the headquarters of the NFEA in Charing Cross Road and dispersed. The contracting area industrial conference in London was disrupted at the end of November. On 9 January 1968, there were further demonstrations at Hayes Court, where an executive council meeting was interrupted by parading demonstrators tapping on the windows of the executive council's meeting room. They later moved off on to Hayes Common and held an impromptu meeting at which Fred Morphew, from Dartford, was 'nominated' to be the 'progressive' candidate against Les Cannon in the early summer election that year. These demonstrations had a lighter side. When the hearings were later held at Hayes Court to discipline men like Fred Morphew, their supporters and friends turned up in huge grotesque masks to conceal their identity from a 'vindictive executive'. Most of the demonstrators found it difficult to conceal gales of laughter at the sight of a short, round, instantly recognizable Jimmy Dormer concealed only by a flimsy Lone Ranger eye-mask!

Throughout 1968, the executive council hit back. The organizers, platform speakers and men of violence associated with the Hayes Court demonstrations, the Matrix Hall meetings and the provincial anti-JIB rallies were suspended from holding office or expelled from the union. The hearings and then the appeals dragged on throughout 1968 and into 1969. Lawrence Braithwaite, the secretary of London Studio and Entertainment branch and the organizer of the January 1968 Hayes Court demonstration, took the union to court and succeeded in winning an injunction preventing his expulsion. His expulsion and many of the other penalties were set aside by the union's decision to change its disciplinary committee approach after the 1969 conference.

Opposition and non-official activity was not restricted to contracting. Even erstwhile supporters of the anti-communists like Dave Chalkley fell foul of the leadership. In October 1967, Dave Chalkley was censured when he wrote an article in the left magazine *The Power Worker*, criticizing the 1967 electricity supply agreement. He claimed he did not know that *The Power Worker* was an 'unofficial circular'. Charlie Doyle was back at it in late 1967, organizing unofficial meetings on 18, 20 and 21 October against the supply agreements. In his case, the executive were mellowing – he was near to retirement and they took no action. Tom Spellman, from West London Supply, was suspended from holding office for being the 'chairman of independent representatives' from the supply industry on 18 October at Harold Laski House in Fulham, although he later apologized and was quickly back as a conference delegate and shop-steward.

If all this activity was aimed at unseating Les Cannon, it did not work. He was comfortably re-elected on a reduced turn-out as president on 10 June 1968 by 25,747 to Fred Morphew's 9,616 votes. The ever-present Jimmy Dormer got 7,482 votes. Nevertheless, the 1969 biennial policy conference, attended for the first time by delegates from the plumbing section, produced some fair succour for the left as they attacked the leadership of the union – a union which in Les Cannon's judgment was now 'sodden with political conflict of a most negative character'. There was pandemonium over the adoption of the standing orders of the conference: Charlie Montgomery objected to the executive bringing forward rules revision propositions that had not been before the branches. Les Cannon said from the chair that such a complaint had nothing to do with 'standing orders' which were simple rules of debate about how long speakers spoke for and the times of the day the conference would sit, etc. Without standing orders, the conference could not start, and no one could complain about or support any issue until the framework of debating rules – the 'standing orders' – was adopted. No one listened to him. A parade of left-wing supporters came to the rostrum to be ruled out of order, including a gently spoken Irish plumber, claiming to be ignorant and unknowledgeable about procedure. Les Cannon told the conference he knew this plumber – Bill Gannon – and he was not as dull as he was pretending to be! The standing orders were eventually carried at around eleven o'clock in the morning of the first day by 281 votes to 212, indicating that the organized left were determined to fight the platform to a standstill on every or any issue.

They had genuine victories that week: they defeated the executive on detailed propositions about the trustees of the union, the retention of district committees for the plumbers and consequent refusal to allow them to attend the electricians' area and national industrial committees, and on the basis of the plumbers' representation at the biennial conference. With these defeats in mind, the executive withdrew their main proposal for reform of the final appeals committee.

Elected at the conference and dealing with discipline cases – largely associated with 'unofficial' protests at executive council policy – this committee had become the focus of left-wing organizing activity within the union. The elections themselves became the centre-piece of bar-room conversation and reception arm-twisting. What with that and the difficulties associated with Braithwaite's case, the executive put to the membership that the final appeals committee should be half of the executive council – while the original case should be heard by the other half of the executive. The membership endorsed the abolition of the old final appeals committee in a ballot of the members, 49,194–11,299, in September that year.

In June 1970, a statistical 'blip' reversed Roy Jenkins's success with the key political totem-pole, the balance of payments, leading to narrow defeat for Harold Wilson's Government. At Hayes Court, though, a more dreadful disaster confronted the union. In May 1970, Les Cannon fell ill with cancer. By August 1970, he had resigned from the supply NJIC (and Frank Chapple took his place). The last meeting he attended was on 4 November when he went to the National Economic Development Council to defend the Industrial Reorganization Corporation against Tory Government determination to abolish it. On 9 December 1970, he died, aged fifty.

Les Cannon was certainly the most brilliant, intellectual, determined and inspirational leader the union ever produced. No one would argue that he was solely responsible for the changes in the union from 1959–70. Equally, no one would deny that without his initial thought and prodigious capacity to carry the arguments to hundreds of union meetings up and down the land, few of the changes would have occurred.

His work finally exposed the ballot-riggers. His work changed the basis of the membership's standard of living from 'fodder' basis cost-of-living negotiating. He launched an innovative leadership role that improved the electricians' place in the world through his championing of productivity bargaining. He led the fight against the revanchist left in the union at a time in the Labour movement's affairs where elsewhere the will to fight the left was demonstrably weakening. He developed the union's reputation for training as the key to handling technical change. He showed how trade unions could be partners with management without becoming alienated from their members. A student of the law himself, he urged that unions should not fear the law in its affairs as a matter of principle. He knew the weaknesses in trade union structure in Britain and sought to radically change them. This massive intelligence had a darker side to it. Few people loved him where thousands admired him. He could be short-tempered, even arrogant. People were occasionally appalled at his table manners. He could not bear mediocrity. But these are trivial weights in the balance. He was simply the greatest trade union leader the ETU ever produced.

ELECTRICAL TRADES UNION   BALLOT PAPER

ELECTION OF
GENERAL SECRETARY

The following members have been duly nominated in accordance with Rule :—

Name	Branch	Age	Trade	Section	Years in Society	Vote with a X
BYRNE, J. T.	Clydebank	56	Elec. Fitter	Skilled	31	

NOMINATED BY :—

Aberdare, Abergaveny, Aberdeen, Altrincham, Aldershot, Ayr, Banbury, Bathgate, Barkingside, Barnet, Barnsley, Barnstaple, Bath, Belfast Cent., Bethnal Green, Bishop Auckland, Blackwood, Blackburn, Blythswood, Bolton, Bolton Elec. Engrs., Bournemouth, Bracknell, Bristol Cent., Burnley, Burton, Bury, Bury St. Edmunds, Caerphilly, Campbeltown, Camborne, Cambuslang, Canterbury, Chingford, Chiswick, Clydebank, Cirencester, Colchester, Corringham, Consett, Cwmbran, Dagenham, Darlington, Darwen, Devonport Elec. Engrs., Doncaster, Dorking, Dounreay, Dukinfield, Durham City, Eastbourne, East Kilbride, Eastleigh, Edinburgh East, Edinburgh Super., Elstree, Enfield, Epsom, Erdington, Finchley, Fleetwood, Gillingham, Glasgow N.W., Gloucester, Grays, Guildford, Hamilton, Hartlepools, Henlow, Hertford, Hoylake, Huddersfield, Hulme, Ilkeston, Jarrow, Keighley, Kensal Green, Kingston, Kingswear, Kilmarnock, Lanark, Leatherhead, Ledbury, Leeds Cent., Leigh Leicester, Leyland, Leven, Lincoln, Liverpool East, London Cent. No. 1, London Lift and Crane, London Lifts Engrs., London Railways No. 1, London Stat. Engrs. Nos. 5, 14 and 18, London Tele. Engrs. Nos. 1 and 2, London Studio No. 2, London West Cent., Luton, Ludlow, Market Drayton, Manchester Super., Maesteg, Mitcham, Motherwell, Motherwell Supply, Montrose, Musselburgh, Newcastle Cent., Newbury, New Milton, Newport Nos. 1 and 2, Northampton, North Shields, Nuneaton, Penrith, Peterborough, Perth, Peterhead, Plaistow, Plymouth, Portishead, Portsmouth Elec. Engrs., Redditch, Rogerstone, St. Helen's, St. Neots, Sale, Saffron Waldon, Sheffield No. 2, Silloth, Solihull, South Bank, South Benfleet Stat. Engrs., Southampton Docks, Southend, Stanley, Stevenage No. 1, Stirling, Stoke, Taunton, Torquay, Tredegar, Wallingford, Wallsend, Wednesbury, Wellington, Westhoughton, Wetherby, Weymouth, Whitby, Widnes, Worksop, Woolston, Yeovil ... ...

	Trade	Section	Years in Society	Vote with a X

Plymouth Supp., ... Preston, Purley, Putney, ... dale, Rosyth, Rotherham, Rothesay, ... thorpe, Sheffield Cent., Sheffield Elec. Engrs., Shemeld ... Sleaford, Slough and Windsor, Small Heath, Smethwick, Southam... ford, Stretford, Sutton, Swansea, Swansea Super., Swansea Supply, Swindon, Swinton and ... Tenby, Thetford, Tooting, Totnes, Tottenham, Trafford Park, Twickenham, Urmston, Uxbridge, Wakefield, Wallasey, Walsall, Waltham Cross, Walthamstow No. 1, Walton, Walton and Hersham, Warrington, Watford, Wealdstone, Welwyn Garden City, Welwyn Elec. Engrs., Wembley, West Drayton, West Ham, Weston-Super-Mare, Weybridge, Wickford, Wigan, Willesden, Wilmslow, Winchester, Woking, Wolverhampton, Woodbridge, Woodford, Woolwich, Worcester, Workington, Worthing, Wrexham, Wythenshawe, Yate, York ... ...

MEMBERS CAN VOTE FOR ONE CANDIDATE ONLY

Counting ballots in Bristol at an Area Official's election in 1960, just before the system changed.

The 1958 TUC delegation – minus Les Cannon. *Back row* Sam Goldberg, Bill Blair, Jack Frazer, Bill Sullivan, Sid Maitland, Bill Blairford, Jack Hendy, Albert Owen, Dick Tyldlesley. *Front row* George Stevens, Frank Haxell, Frank Foulkes, Bob McLennan, E. J. Turner, Tom Vincent, Jock Byrne.

Jock Byrne, General Secretary (1961–6).

Frank Chapple, Executive Councillor (1958–63), Assistant General Secretary (1963–6) and General Secretary (1966–84).

Les Cannon and Frank Chapple, photographed with civic dignitaries at the Isle of Man Conference in 1965. On the far right is Deputy Prime Minister George Brown MP and standing on the left is the legendary American Electricians' trade unionist, Harry Van Arsdale, whose advice and friendship was much valued by Cannon and Chapple.

Les Cannon, President (1963–70), lecturing at Esher Place in 1968.

TUC Delegation in 1965. This picture includes active members and officials as the leadership changes took effect in the 1960s. Second from the left is Paul Bevis, then Colin Lowry and Fred Gore. Sixth from the left is Doug Hepburn, then Eric Hammond and Bill Blairford. Eleventh from the left is Jack Ashfield, then Les Cannon, Jock Reynolds and Frank Chapple. On the extreme right is Peter Snadden, then Bill Blair and Harry Cooper. Fifth from the right is Albert Owen, Harry Gittins and Alf McLuckie.

1968 – the Plumbers arrive. The Amalgamated EETPU Executive Council: *Standing, left to right* Bill Blairford, Ernie Hadley, Charlie Lovell, Dan Fraser, Harry Gittins, Tom Breakell, Bill Blair, Fred McGuffie, Don Sheasby, Jack Ashfield, Eric Clayton, Eric Hammond, Jim O'Neil. *Sitting, left to right* Jim McKernan, Les Cannon, Frank Chapple.

Hayes Court, on the outskirts of South London, the Union's head office since 1947.

(*Right*) Esher Place in Surrey, the first trade union training centre in Britain, bought by the ETU in 1952.

(*Left*) Cudham Hall in Kent, the Union's second training centre, bought in 1974. It specializes in technical and vocational courses in electronics.

Buxted Park, the Union's country estate in Sussex, which provides hotel and leisure facilities, including trout fishing and a fitness centre. In the 325-acre grounds is the only trade-union owned herd of deer in Britain.

Demonstrations and marches sometimes have to be part of the Union's propaganda effort. (*Right*) Women-workers striking for union recognition in 1955 at the Lowestoft factory that is nowadays the home of 'strike-free' Japanese TV company Sanyo. (*Below*) A London march during the contracting strikes of February 1954.

There is no such thing as a typical electrical worker; these two photographs illustrate the range of skills provided by EETPU members. (*Below*) An overhead linesman repairs storm damage caused by the hurricane of October 1987. (*Below left*) Wendy Packer, who became an electronics technician after gaining technical qualifications with the Union's help.

Eric Hammond, Executive Councillor 1963–84, General Secretary 1984–

The Executive Council in the Centenary Year 1989–90. *Left to right* Bill Gannon (Plumbing National Secretary), Lew Britz (S. London and the South-East), Frank Chapman (Midlands), Harry Hughes (W. London and N.W. Home Counties), Bill Hayes (Yorks.), Eric Hammond (General Secretary), Barry Davis (North-East), Brendan Fenelon (E. London and East Anglia), Ken Jackson (Merseyside and Lancs.), Paul Gallager (President and Manchester and N. Wales), Hector Barlow (Scotland and Ireland Plumbing Section), Jim Egan (N. Plumbing Section), Alf McLuckie (Scotland), Wyn Bevan (Wales and South-West).

25

THE BOTTOM LINE: NEGOTIATIONS
IN THE MODERN UNION

TRADE UNION MEMBERS PRIMARILY judge their union's performance in terms of the standard of living the union's negotiations produce. It is impossible to look at all the agreements that the union holds, but several significant features of the union's negotiating performance are worth examining.

First, the two 'touchstone' agreements in electricity supply and contracting demonstrate that where the union is the dominant negotiating union or the sole negotiator, the comparative standards of its members have improved dramatically since 1970. Second, the union has confronted a different challenge in the manufacturing industries. There, the developing skill of the maintenance electrician has been increasingly recognized in a multi-union environment. The use of productivity bargaining techniques in support of companies who seek to grow has enabled the union's membership in manufacturing to break out of the stranglehold of the common craft rate.

Electricity Supply 1970–89

The key turning point in the history of negotiations in electricity supply was the national dispute that took place in December 1970.

In the autumn of that year, the electricity supply negotiators approached the talks with unprecedented determination. Average male earnings had risen by 14.9 per cent from September 1969 to September 1970. In manufacturing, it was 15.2 per cent. Prices had risen by 7 per cent from September 1969 to September 1970. An independent inquiry had awarded dustmen and other local authority workers an increase of £2 10s 0d a week. On 27 October, new Tory Chancellor Tony Barber had introduced a mini-budget that increased health service charges, the price of school meals and introduced cuts in public spending. The bleak outlook of confrontation and inflation was intensified by the publication of the Government's industrial relations reform proposals which were to try to make agreements legally enforceable, abolish the closed shop, set up new courts and impose 'cooling off periods'.

In the minds of the EETPU negotiators, now led by Frank Chapple as Les Cannon lay terminally ill in bed, was a growing feeling that the members in supply were being taken for fools. In October 1970, average earnings per week for all adult males (with a much higher proportion of unskilled and semi-skilled workers than supply employed) were £28 0s 11d. In supply, weekly earnings were £25 6s 6d. Of course, supply workers worked less hours – four per week to be exact. Nevertheless, they worked these hours often on shifts and staggered patterns and remained a huge £3 11s 9d per week behind average earnings in manufacturing.

The claim was presented at the NJIC on 10 September. It demanded 'substantial' increases in salary levels, an 'urgent' re-aligning of differentials, increases in shift allowances, to make the rate of pay the rate on which overtime would be calculated, extra holidays and a reduction in the working week. The next meeting was held on 29 October. In between, Les Cannon had written in the *Sunday Times* and it was re-published in the October edition of the union's quarterly magazine, *Contact*. His last contribution to the industry was a desperate plea that productivity bargaining should not be disgraced as an idea by a parsimonious approach by the employers. 'It must be obvious that no group of workers will go on giving REAL increases in productivity for MONETARY increases in earnings which lose most of their value in the ensuing twelve months. If these negotiations do not at the beginning redress this grievance, I fail to see how they can succeed. ... In view of the real and exemplary contribution of electricity supply workers over the past six years, it must not be permitted that they suffer any relative deterioration in their salary levels.' The same thing was being said by the usual people associated with the unofficial movement: a handful of power stations banned overtime and called meetings in mid-October. On 29 October, the boards' members revealed the pressure on them from Whitehall with a roundabout declaration that 'inflationary' wage settlements didn't help anyone. The new Conservative Government, although this was not openly admitted at the formal negotiations, had a new type of incomes policy – so new it was reminiscent of Selwyn Lloyd's 1961 pay pause. The Government had abolished the Prices and Incomes Board and the setting of 'norms'. Instead, it wanted to lean on nationalized industries and the public sector paymasters to drive down the level of settlements. By setting a good example in the public sector it was to be hoped that private industry would take the hint about high wage deals. Apart from the fact that local authority workers got £2 10s 0d a week increase, this approach gave no credit to Cannon's point about productivity bargaining. On 9 November, the NJIC unions quantified their claim. They wanted the industry to spend £35 million on raising wages. If it was equally divided, each supply worker would get an increase of £5 16s 0d each (25.8 per cent). The claim was justified by looking at two aspects of productivity. First, the industry set aside each year in depreciation allowances £35 million more than they actually spent per annum on the replacement of plant and machinery. Secondly, the voluntary severance scheme of 1968 had been working very well from the employer's point of view. The workforce in generating stations had fallen by 11 per cent since 1965–6 and 25 per cent in the area boards. Consequently, the 1969 settlement of 10 per cent in the industry should have raised the wage bill by £14 million. Actually, it only went up by £1.9 million. The unions argued that if men continued to leave the industry at the average rate of the previous two years, the wage bill would only rise by £19.4 million. This would be a 13.5 per cent increase on the total wage bill; but wages were such a small proportion of the industry's total costs, the rise in electricity prices would only have to be 1.5 per cent.

The unions held a meeting two days later on 11 November with representatives from every works committee, district joint council and each of the unions concerned, with Frank Chapple in the chair. The rising tide of enthusiasm for action was clear from that meeting: the negotiatiors were told of the men's determination to press the claim to the limit.

The employers response was nowhere near this level of expectation. On 19 November, the boards offered £1 15s 0d with a promise to look at conditions in the near future. The unions there and then gave notice of a ban on overtime and a work-to-rule to start on 7 December 1970. On 2 December, last-ditch negotiations produced an offer of one more paid public holiday, a rise in the rates on which overtime was paid and an increase on the rate of just £2, around 9.7 per cent. The employers then invoked the last clause in the agreement – that arbitration should be used to settle the question. The work-to-rule and overtime ban went ahead on 7 December; arbitration procedures were not trusted by the unions. The cause was just, they thought. The members were ready – and not just the persistent unofficial elements. From the moment the action started, men no longer accepted temporary up-grading or down-grading. Skilled men refused to drive vehicles. No stand-by or call-out duties were done outside normal hours. The action was immediately effective. Available capacity on the first day fell by a quarter, largely due to men in power stations insisting to the letter on manning levels and refusing their normal co-operation in moving round the locations and up-grading/down-grading flexibility. On the distribution side, the refusal to drive vehicles and the insistence on clocking-on at the depot instead of travelling direct to a job added to the collapse in the service. Industry and domestic consumers, hospitals and agriculture – the whole country suffered power cuts and voltage reductions. It was later made clear that area board engineers sometimes did not fall over themselves to shut down cement works and keep hospitals on supply.

The public reponse to the strike was amazing. There were many letters of support sent to Hayes Court – particularly from local branches and committees of trade unions and constituency Labour parties. However, Stourbridge trades council wrote a furious letter of condemnation. Secretary of State for Industry John Davies, speaking on the television programme *24 Hours*, urged members of the public to let the power workers know what they thought of them, 'by quite clearly demonstrating their absolute disapproval of what is happening at the moment'. David Frost's television programme on 12 December enticed five lay trade union representatives from the power industry onto the programme. They were to 'debate' the issue with people whom the producer described to EETPU member Tom Diss as 'a load of middle-class housewives who had been shopping in Sainsbury's'. One of the union's supporters subsequently complained to the Independent Broadcasting Authority, particularly about the constant barrage of shouting at the power workers, culminating in Tom Diss being hit by an irate poultry farmer. It was left to *The Guardian*'s labour correspondent, John Torode, to bravely attempt a justification of the power workers' case. Even Lord Aylestone, the Chairman of the IBA, acknowledged that the five supply men were ineffective due to their 'unfamiliarity with the atmosphere of a live television show'. That was the point. The supply men were overwhelmed by the anger of the studio audience. This David Frost programme was simply the most spectacular, televised abuse of a sort that was repeated up and down the country. A sympathetic newspaper shop owner wrote to Frank Chapple from Sunderland warning of his customers plans to attack known power workers. Newspapers printed hundreds of letters complaining about the 'blackmail' of the old, the sick, the hospitalized. Typical was one nurse from Sussex who wrote to Frank Chapple. 'I heard you speak on the radio yesterday and you did not seem a callous man – a man who enjoyed being faced by a man whose wife had died during an operation or a mother whose premature baby died as a result of a sudden power cut.' A thirteen-year-old girl wrote from Newcastle saying that her homework was suffering from being written in the dark and, slightly more impressively, that her best friend had fallen in the dark while searching for candles and broken her arm. One woman wrote that her social worker daughter had visited an eighty-five-year-old man sitting in the dark in his overcoat during a blackout whose wife had died just that afternoon. In the midst of dozens of lunatic letters that referred to Chapple as a 'dirty bastard gangster' and, laughably, as 'Communist scum' who should go back to Russia, there were hundreds from the old and chronically sick which were genuinely affecting in the stories they told. This fear of the dark and cold raised unbridled forces in the public against the union and its members, egged on by the newspapers. Cartoonists like Jak in the *Evening Standard* and Cummings in the *Sunday Express* drew unpleasant cartoons like one of Cummings' which showed a power worker laying a wreath on the grave of the 'Sick and the Old' who 'died to give the electricity men a rise'.

The effects on the members in electricity supply of the work to rule were to last for years. They have great power. They have a cause for good treatment, given the crucial service they provide and their productivity-based contribution to keeping electricity prices down. And yet the effects of taking industrial action on their neighbours and, indeed, themselves, gives them pause. This set of contradictory emotions was best expressed by the wife of one of the union's shop-stewards in the industry living in Leamington Spa. On the seventh day of the work to rule, 14 December, the action was called off. The steward's wife wrote privately to Frank Chapple in complete frustration. 'For fourteen years, I have had to struggle to bring up a family on a miserably inadequate wage, while my neighbours, whose husbands have been in better paid employment, have been able to shop in comfort, without the humiliation of deciding what you can do without this weekend. The reason given for your sudden withdrawal was that you did not wish to be unkind to the nice public. Well, the nice public did not mind being unkind to us. We were barred from shops, insulted by perfect strangers or heard our husbands described as criminals. All this on top of the general inconvenience which we had to put up with like everybody else.'

Frank Chapple was always sensitive to the potential devastation involved for society in a power strike. In 1979 he gave a long, thoughtful and personal speech to the Royal Institution in which he mused long on the impact on society of the public sector strikes that could be so harmful, concluding 'it is trade unionists and their families who invariably bear the hardest burden in these recurring crises'.

The work-to-rule and overtime ban were called off on 14 December 1970, two days after the Government declared a state of emergency, in the face of rising abuse and physical violence aimed at the supply workers.

The dispute was called off to allow the union's claim to be examined by a court of inquiry. There was little enthusiasm for this procedure on the union's side. First and foremost, the Government insisted that the terms of reference for the court of inquiry included specific reference to the 'interests of the public and of the national economy'. This only added to the union's suspicions of the three-man tribunal appointed on 29 December. Frank Chapple publicly expressed these fears in talking directly to Lord Wilberforce, the chairman. He said: 'We are impelled to refer to the suspicion which has stuck deep into the minds of our members that the court is prejudiced before it opens. ... There is yourself, whose associations are fairly well known. You could not be described as one whose sympathies lay in any way with the interests of the unions. There is Sir Raymond Brookes (chairman and chief executive of GKN) who was chosen presumably to represent the employers, and it has been well and clearly stated that his company has contributed to the Conservative Party funds, and indeed, he was in the first honours list of this present government.' John Mortimer was nominally the union's nominee, but neither his trade union career at the left-led Draughtsmen's Union or his new job as personnel director of London Transport would please Frank Chapple much.

This combative and aggressive start to the proceedings did not obscure in any way the revolutionary nature of the union's submission to the court. The case was assembled by Eric Hammond, using the expertise of seconded shop-steward Fred Franks, who came from Northfleet power station in Kent, who also gave persuasive evidence in person on the hard work needed to implement the massive changes in the 1960s. West London supply's Tom Spellman also gave first-hand evidence. The NJIC union's evidence ran to seventy-five pages plus seventeen appendices. It was, in the opinion of the chairman of the employers' side of the NJIC, R. D. V. Roberts, 'the most comprehensive statement of its kind ever prepared by the NJIC trade union side' that led to the inquiry's hearings being 'urgent and committed, tolerant and rational'.

The case was fundamentally lodged on the fairness due to power workers because of their co-operation with productivity bargaining. The union's negotiators thought that the dispute was justified on those grounds – indeed it had been their *duty* to pursue the issue. 'Our joint efforts which have been successful in improving productivity far beyond that of industry generally, must be used to achieve a corresponding increase in earnings beyond that of the rest of industry. Without such a parallel movement, the whole concept of producivity bargaining would be justifiably denigrated.'

Looking at the increase in productivity since 1948, there were 0.6 workers per million kilowatts generated in 1969, compared to 2.4 in 1948 – an improvement of 300 per cent. On that basis, earnings in supply should average £26; and taking into account the fall in the value of money, £57 10s 0d. Since 1965, the amount of electricity generated per hour of staff labour had increased by 77 per cent: the amount supplied by area board staff per hour, by 93 per cent. The number of staff employed on the area boards had fallen by 38 per cent. However, wages had only risen by 34 per cent, while prices had risen 27 per cent. Echoing Les Cannon's last word on the subject, the union's evidence concluded that this 6.9 per cent real increase was pretty small reward for the effort expended. 'The industry and the country have been given real increases in productivity, real men have left the industry and those remaining have given real co-operation. We have had in return, if not a dud cheque, one very much devalued.'

The board's reply to all this was to seek to undermine the case by urging the court to ignore the union's figures which concentrated on the productivity produced by massive capital investment and concentrate instead on the more modest figures on labour productivity produced by the 'yardstick' technique now common throughout the industry (4.5 per cent in 1969–70).

The court was to be treated to one more element of pure theatre when the Government sent top Treasury civil servant Sir Douglas Allen down to the inquiry to draw attention to the need to fight inflation by keeping down public-sector wages. Frank Chapple pushed him straight back on the ropes by asking Sir Douglas how he justified his *own* recent wage increase from £9,800 to £15,000 – what 'broad criteria' was it based on? Sir Douglas replied it was determined by various comparative criteria by an outside body. Senior civil servants 'do not make claims ... we have given up the right to claim, the right to strike, and our pay is settled by an independent body rather like a court of inquiry'. Contrasting this with the power workers position, Chapple instantly enquired, 'Can we get *this* claim before *that* court?'

Wilberforce's recommendations, published on 10 February 1971, were later adopted after negotiations with the supply authorities on 22 March 1971 (an adoption that Eric Hammond disapproved of, losing his seat on the NJIC negotiating team as a result). It gave the unions what Chapple described as 'a victory for the workers on almost every count'.

The court was keenly aware of the rise in prices and other average earnings. They were particularly keen that productivity emphasis in the industry should be encouraged. Consequently, they urged that the weekly rates should be raised by £2 per week. Craftsmen and foremen were to get an extra £35 per year. Three-shift workers got a £20 rise in the shift premium. Everyone got three days' extra holiday. In order to encourage the faster introduction of comprehensive incentive schemes across the industry, everyone should receive 'lead-in' payments of £1 a week, rising to £2 in January 1972 to encourage acceptance of the schemes. The payments would stop when the incentive schemes were finally in place. The final agreement also included a greater emphasis on the voluntary severance scheme whose terms were improved. The settlement was to be worth 15.9 per cent. It raised the weekly earnings of supply workers to £30.82 by October 1971, a leap in the wages league since 1964 from forty-seventh to twenty-fourth on weekly earnings and from sixty-eighth to tenth on hourly earnings. Better was to come.

Supply Negotiations after Wilberforce

The NJIC negotiators were led in the post-Wilberforce period by Frank Chapple and, latterly, by national officer Fred Franks. Frank Chapple's negotiating style was very different from Les Cannon's or Fred Franks's. He rarely read the paperwork in great detail, although his grasp of the industry was encyclopaedic – particularly after he served on the Plowden Inquiry into the industry. He always grasped essentials and sustained the impetus of 1970–1 in raising the supply workers' comparative earnings position within industry. Fred Franks in some ways was vastly different. He was a deeply analytical man, and his negotiating style reflected his total dominance of the complex information thrown up by the industry. Not only did his NJIC colleagues defer to his almost total control of the problems in the industry, he was widely admired by the senior management in the industry. His thoughtful and authoritative style produced further progress for the industry's workforce when compared to other industries.

Throughout the period, the salary structure review committee in the industry largely consolidated the bonuses and 'lead-in' payments into the basic rates, gathered in five 'bands' with several service increments payable. Major controversies remained such as just which types of skilled men would and would not be allowed in the highest band 5. The interminable sense of injustice still rankled when craftsmen were compared with the engineers in the industry. Their determination to hang on to a differential meal allowance was only equalled by their complete refusal to allow craftsmen to enter the engineers' grades through public exams and technical qualification. Nevertheless, no one can deny the comparative success of the supply negotiations since 1970. Then, it will be remembered, the average supply workers earnings were exceeded by the average earnings in manufacturing and the average earnings in all industry alike, despite the high percentage of craftsmen in the supply workface. In 1972, that position changed for the first time: supply men got £34.90 per week compared to £34.50 in manufacturing and £32.80 on the overall index. By 1980, the gap was widening. Average supply earnings were £131.40 per week, manufacturing £115.20 and the overall index, £111.70.

The position had also been rectified in terms of average hourly earnings: in the past, supply workers had only come close to other groups through huge amounts of overtime. By 1980, working a thirty-eight-hour week, average hours worked were 40.1 hours, compared to 43.8 in manufacturing and the average hours in all industry of 44.8. By 1986, the industry enjoyed a clear comparative advantage over 1971; its place in the 'league table' of average earnings has risen to tenth on the weekly index and sixth on the hourly earnings index compared to its post-Wilberforce levels of twenty-fourth and tenth respectively.

In 1989, Fred Franks and his EETPU colleagues, Frank Chapman, Ken Jackson and Brendan Fenelon, achieved the highest basic wage rate increase of that year's wage round – 9.2 per cent. This basic rate increase will lead to further substantial increases in earnings when overtime, shift, stagger and the other payments are taken into account. The basic rate for a band 4 craftsman – the standard, jobbing craftsman in the industry – with five years' service is £11,340 per annum. His top-rated craft colleague in band 5 now earns – as a basic rate – £11,766.

Contracting 1970–89

Contracting has always been the central industry for the EETPU. The launch of the joint industry board in 1968 produced political uproar in the union that has never completely died away; nevertheless, the vast improvements in rates of pay and conditions of service in the last two decades of the union's hundred-year history have been remarkable. They have been increasingly envied by electrical workers outside the industry – particularly in the public sector – as a mixture of incomes policy and public sector cut-backs has undermined public service pay settlements. Inside the NHS, national officer Peter Adams's success in keeping the Health Service electricians linked to the JIB rate throughout the 1970s and into the 1980s was a legendary piece of skilful negotiating.

In the contracting industry itself, the union sustained the value of the rates of pay to electricians and approved electricians. They were, however, dogged by the twin challenges of other trades' site bonuses on large sites upsetting JIB electrical companies and the opposite problem of small numbers working for small employers on provincial sites virtually without local trade union representation. The first challenge has been met by a mixture of large site allowances and local negotiations on a guaranteed number of hours' pay (irrespective of hours actually worked). The second problem has always been addressed by protecting the integrity of the national rates in the JIB agreement itself. (This was done most spectacularly in 1979 when the Labour Government's attorney-general had to go to court to admit that the union's legally enforceable agreement with the ECA took precedence over the Government's attempts to dictate wage rates through threatening the employers with the removal of contracts.)

This balancing act has been all the more remarkable given the nature of the industry. It remains an industry whose typical employers are small, but who belong to an association – the ECA – where the dominant company representatives are relatively large. By 1981, there were 2,671 employers in the JIB employing 31,998 people with 61.6 per cent of those approved electricians and nearly 26 per cent electricians. The remaining workers were technicians (7.3 per cent) and labourers (5.2 per cent). By 1988, the structure was remarkably similar. There were now 31,334 workers, with the proportions of approved electrician and so on virtually the same as in 1981. They worked for marginally fewer employers (2,590), of whom 1,593 employed five workers or less; only forty-nine employed over 100. These large employers, however, employed 9,696 of the 29,000 skilled workers in the industry. The workforce remains predominantly young – 10,848 out of the 31,334 are between twenty-two and thirty-one. Only 9,653 are aged over forty-one. Throughout the 1970s and 1980s the type of work undertaken by electrical contractors deepened and broadened – often with the union's technical training experts egging them on beyond the technical boundaries apparently erected by developments in electronics like optical fibres.

The industry undertakes a wide variety of work, ranging from simple electrical installations in private houses to the electrical work associated with the construction of a power station. All sorts of other specialized installation work – instrumentation, micro-electronics, security devices and detectors, computer peripheral equipment including remote terminals, robotics, data communication equipment, ship work and the maintenance of all types of electrical installations – is also undertaken by contracting firms.

The JIB model is now well established. Its example was enthusiastically taken on board by the plumbing industry, allowing the plumbers to set up their own JIB. This gave the plumbers control over their own negotiations, and they rapidly pulled away from the building industry joint negotiations. (Between 1976 and 1984, for instance, the plumbing rate rose by 127 per cent compared to the craft rate for the Building Industry National Joint Council of 87 per cent.) By 1975, the plumbing JIB had introduced the first industry-wide pension scheme in the construction industry, a feat only equalled by the electricians in 1988. Charlie Lovell, their long-term national secretary, often compared the independent growing role of plumbers within the EETPU with the virtual demise of the Heating and Ventilating Engineers Union. They had first been amalgamated with the sheet metalworkers and then been swallowed by TASS. By the time MSF emerged in the late 1980s and the sackings of officials started, the old heating and ventilating industry concerns were all but obliterated – particularly by comparison with the thriving plumbers.

Two further problems presented themselves in electrical contracting. First, the growth of electricians employing themselves and offering themselves to the industry, in a time of skill shortage, as self-employed craftsmen. Between 1986 and 1988 this problem was reaching crisis proportions. Clearly, self-employed electricians operating on a 714 tax-exemption certificate posed a serious danger to collectively bargained standards in the industry. As early as 1986, all electrical work in the Thames Valley was being carried out by such labour. In London, the figure was 40 per cent and rising fast. In mid-1987, president Paul Gallagher persuaded the union's leadership to confront the problem. There was no strength of feeling for strikes in the industry. The process was too far outside the union's control. The employers were desperate for labour. Paul Gallagher's innovative response was to set up a labour agency in conjunction with the employers to supply '714' labour to the industry under some sort of control. The agency was called ESCA Services, and its initial period of work promises that the union will be able to protect the JIB standards that have taken so long to build up. By October 1988, the agency had 4,000 electricians registered with them, and began opening offices all over the country, handling plumbers as well as electricians. All of the craftsmen registered are graded in line with JIB standards and advised of the advantages of direct employment in terms of the better conditions of employment involved. The rules of ESCA Services require that no electrical contractor can retain these temporary '714s' for longer than three months and these men must not exceed 30 per cent of any one site's workforce. This insistence on a 70 per cent permanent JIB workforce has protected the necessary training environment to continue the supply of apprentices to the industry. Money from the agency fees is also set aside to fund mid-life re-training schemes for electricians; with both these provisos, the union sought to control the influx of self-employed craftsmen while protecting the future of the permanent workers in the industry.

It is this aspect of the union's concern for the industry's apprentices that is so impressive. In 1982, the contracting employers were reluctant to employ apprentices. A registration level of 4,052 in 1978 had fallen to 1,794 in 1981 and was going down fast. In 1982, the employers planned to take on a measly 650. In the face of this crisis, the union had to face up to a stark alternative. After talking to the Government, it was clear that there was around £8 million available to the electrical contracting employers if they continued to take on apprentices as part of a YTS scheme. However, such young people could not be paid the generous percentages of skilled men's rate while undergoing training in the first year. Equally, the employers were anxious that they should not have to retain apprentices for years on end out of respect for craft traditions. The union, too, were keen to do several things. First, if they made the sacrifice on apprentice rates during the first year, high levels of apprentice trainees would continue to be taken on, and kept on, at a time of scandalous youth unemployment amidst a plethora of low-paid, dead-end youth schemes that had the main purpose for the Government of concealing the awful levels of unemployment among young people. This ambition was amply supported by subsequent events. By 1988, there were 12,952 apprentices under training in the industry, compared to 28,858 qualified craftsmen. This is an unheard-of ratio in any other industry, producing skilled and qualified people with a real future. The apprenticeship training is designed with enormous union input; the union even provides one of the country's testing stations for the final achievement measurement test at its own training college at Cudham Hall. This skilled workforce is trained to standards nowadays, not time, and the lessons learnt by the union are being applied in assisting unemployed people in taking up the skill of electrician in the national interest.

Towards the end of the 1980s, there was an enormous demand for skilled labour in contracting. The wage rates in contracting remain the highest in the construction industry. The 1990 rates will pay an approved electrician in London £5.24 per hour and his provincial colleague £4.91. In parts of the South-East, the JIB rates are sustained by guaranteed hours payments, with earnings of over £500 to £600 not at all unusual. The 1989 New Earnings

Survey revealed that average earnings among the contracting industry manual workers were £273.80 for 50 hours' work – the highest average earnings in the construction industry by far.

Progress in Engineering

The union's leadership could feel a justified pride in the comparative position of electricians in electricity supply and contracting. In those two industries, the union's dominant numerical position gave it a better chance of implementing its industrial philosophy based on higher pay for higher productivity. The union had no such advantage in the engineering and other manufacturing industries. Despite the fact that the largest sector of the union's membership worked in manufacturing, they were rarely concentrated in great numbers. The typical group of skilled members would often number under a dozen, although in certain areas of television, telecommunication and electronics manufacture the union has sometimes succeeded in recruiting the production workers alongside their skilled colleagues.

The maintenance electricians would usually operate a plant agreement that steadily grew further away from the minimum time rates in the discredited national agreement. However, their rates were often scrutinized by an aggress-ive generation of production workers, proud of the TGWU slogan 'Second to none'. Electricians' rates were also closely scrutinized by AUEW members whose traditional fitters' and toolroom skills were always in numerical superi-ority to the electricians. It was going to be difficult to establish claims with employers that made the case for *more* for electricians rather than the *same* for electricians as everyone else got. It meant another revolutionary break-out from the past, comparable to the union's efforts in supply and contracting. In engineering, craftsmen of all sorts were paid the common craft rate. This rate encompassed the static skills of the building craftsmen employed in engineering like painters and plasterers as well as the engineering fitters, turners and their doyens of the craft, the toolmakers.

The comparative position of electricians was never going to be helped by the multi-union negotiations carried on industry-wide between the Con-fereration of Shipbuilding and Engineering Unions (CSEU) and the Engin-eering Employers' Federation (EEF). These national negotiations set minimum earnings levels that suited the smallest, most reactionary, least competitive and least modern engineering company. The larger companies, particularly in the car industry, would then top up earnings on the basis of plant bargaining, bonus schemes and higher piecework rates. The national negotiations therefore bore very little relevance to the actual earnings of engineering workers, beyond their effects on overtime, shift and other pay-ments that retained a formal link to the national negotiations.

The EETPU's desire for justice for maintenance workers in engineering goes back to pre-First World War days when Jimmy Rowan recognized that the maintenance electrician is probably the only craftsman who understands the whole system he is maintaining rather than the specific part of the machine's function that he is called upon to repair. The electrician's diagnostic skills of the relationship between electrical power and mechanical movement is rarely reciprocated by a mechanical craftsman's understanding of the electrical control over the machine. His training does not usually include the principles of electrical power, let alone electronics.

Throughout the 1960s, the gradual introduction of electronics into engineering factories produced a rising concern among maintenance electricians that the increased skills expected of them found no echo in their wage packets. They were constantly held back at plant level by a crude unwillingness of engineering craftsmen to recognize the growing skills of the electrician. Following the union's protest at not being placed in a job-evaluated top grade, one Ministry of Labour inquiry into a dispute at Pressed Steel Fisher at Cowley was told by the AEU:

> Further, we would not tolerate a seventh grade to accommodate 'differentials', alleged or real, to certain other unions. Any departure from the six grades by an addition of a further one means, and we would insist upon, an automatic upgrading across the board to all members, irrespective of unions. ... With regard to the electricians, under no circumstances will this union agree that any additions paid to the electricians would solely go to them. On the contrary, any such monies would still need to be paid nationally to all, irrespective of trades, grades, or unions. Never will this union accept that electricians would receive a 'differential' as against the toolworkers as to put the toolworkers at a disadvantage.

This sort of attitude, compounded by the employers' natural reluctance to part with anything, topped off by their fear of repercussions from other unions if they *did* pay electricians more, produced a mountain for the union to climb.

As early as 1964, the union's Coventry Central delegate to the first engineering shop-stewards' conference described the problem perfectly. Brother Haywood said:

> The *position* of the maintenance electrician, the *image* of the maintenance electrician of the past must be destroyed once and for all because this is a thing which is affecting all the negotiations. [Employers] still look at the maintenance electrician as the chappy who goes round mending a fuse wire, then applies a screwdriver, and that is his sole contributions. But now, I think, there are very few members in this hall who don't understand that the first thing that goes wrong with any machine, whether it is an automated thing or whether it is purely hydraulically operated, the first man that they

call is the electrician. He diagnoses the fault and he attends to it whether it's electrical or not.

Les Cannon identified the same problem in 1968. He saw that national negotiations would never grant national recognition of the maintenance electricians' entitlement to break out of the common craft rate. The only way forward was on a company basis; often, on a plant-by-plant basis. Once again the main engine for reform was to improve the productivity of electricians willingly, measure it, and ensure the just reward for the indisputable technical value of the electrician's work.

To this end, the union had developed since 1969 the work study department at head office. This department, and its generic successor, the productivity and technical services department, have given EETPU members advice and guidance on job evaluation and the measurement of work, identified training needs to assist in the development of skills and agreed on criteria for measuring and identifying skill. Fashions change in industrial relations, and the stereotype personnel officer with a stopwatch being monitored and undermined by a sly shop-steward no longer applies.

But the unique trade union philosophy behind a willing acceptance of improving productivity in the EETPU has not changed since the late 1960s. The national officer in charge of work study and productivity bargaining techniques was Paddy McMahon. He was largely responsible for fostering this creative attitude towards building a case for achieving higher earnings for maintenance electricians. He always emphasized that trade union obstruction of developing work practices in new technology areas was unlikely to work. First, employers would always find someone to do the work – unskilled people, supervisory people or members bribed sufficiently well. Second, production workers working new machinery, and achieving higher earnings, would set the pace of maintenance workers' earnings whether they deigned to negotiate on the subject or not. He was convinced that work study, job evaluation and its modern equivalents, designing multi-skilled job content, was a better way of ensuring trade union standards being applied to maintenance workers earnings. The union had to have a positive attitude to making employers in manufacturing efficient in an internationally competitive world. 'If anyone argues that it is easier to get money from a poor employer or an inefficient industry than it is from an efficient one, then they are not dealing with realities. ... In making organizations efficient, we create the basis for bigger and better deals in the future.' He confronted the so-called 'trade union' argument head-on that sought to argue that traditional work practices protected jobs. First, he would always argue that a shut factory employed no one; he also pointed out that many of these traditional practices were simply strategies for creating overtime. An efficient and smaller workforce ought to seek to achieve reasonable earnings without the social crime of overtime. Paddy McMahon's final justification for productivity bargaining was always based on his concept of industrial democracy. If the union was a close, indispensable partner to the company in creating wealth, not only would the membership concerned be better paid, but they would also be closer to minimizing the impact of the employer's 'right to manage' – the institutionalized sense of hierarchy and status that so disfigured traditional British engineering companies.

Paddy McMahon could use a considerable fund of stories to illustrate his support for productivity bargaining, even though his first experience of productivity bargaining was a sad one.

He had been a merchant seaman during the war. The dockers in Middlesbrough were paid extra to handle the loading of explosives onto Paddy McMahon's ship. He represented the seamen in a similar claim, hoping the local seamen's union would take up their case. The canny old seamen's official had clearly got a unique approach to productivity bargaining. He told Paddy McMahon and friends that if his ship carrying the explosives was torpedoed at sea, none of the crew would return to spend any extra bonus they might be entitled to. On the other hand, if they did sail safely home, they wouldn't have earned it!

Productivity bargaining techniques have always featured prominently on courses at Esher and at the union's industrial conferences. Paradoxically, the strength and reasonableness of this approach provided the fierce determination to use every ounce of the union's strength when employers would not recognize the justice in the union's claims.

Chrysler 1973

The most significant turning point in this argument with both employers and other unions occurred at the Chrysler motor car works in Coventry in 1973, and altered the self-esteem of the maintenance electrician throughout the union, for ever.

At this time, 156 members of the union worked for Chrysler at Coventry. The dispute had a long gestation period. In 1965, in common with the union's skilled maintenance membership throughout industry, a claim was pursued through to central Conference level that yielded agreement to achieve parity with the toolroom by 1967. These talks were largely the result of negotiations conducted by Jack Ashfield and the cool, dapper Coventry area secretary, Maurice Crofts. In 1969, the Chrysler factories changed, as many did so painfully in that era, to measured daywork. In reaction to that, the AUEW members, urged on by their local district committee, re-established the link for their toolroom members with the Coventry Toolroom agreement, taking them beyond the internal Chrysler 'A' grade for skilled workers. The EETPU members demanded that the link with the toolroom be maintained; the company spent long weeks trying to persuade the AUEW to come within the factory agreement. The pot boiled even fiercer in 1971 when the EEF gave notice of terminating the Coventry toolroom agreement. In 1972, the EETPU membership first insisted on separate negotiations – talks that would only take place when the company had sorted out the AUEW toolroom claim. The electricians were not going to be cheated of their parity claim again – a parity that they had achieved from 1967–9. Chrysler settled with the production workers; they then offered to toolmakers 'staff status', granting an annual salary of £2,500. The deal was set to be paid from 1 July 1972.

More bad luck awaited the hapless electricians. On 6 November, when their negotiations started, Ted Heath's emergency ninety-day pay freeze was already in operation. The company and union alike beseeched the Department of Employment to allow the parity claim for the £2,500 to go ahead as it had been agreed for many months that the electricians would get whatever the toolmakers got out of the 1972 deal. The department would not hear of it. The electricians reluctantly accepted a 'Stage II' pay deal of £1 + 4 per cent (backdated to October 1972). On 7 February 1973, the company said that if the newly-established Pay Board would allow it, they were willing to grant the 'staff status' agreement. If they were not allowed to do that, they would pay the maximum payment – £250 per year – with effect from 1 July 1973.

These frustrations were but nothing as compared to what happened next. On 30 July, the Pay Board rejected the union's claim for the honouring of the staff status commitment. The union then turned to the company for the £250 at the very least. Suddenly, Chrysler lost their courage. Due to the aggressive insistence of the two big unions at Chrysler – the AUEW and TGWU – the company could not pay the electricians without paying everyone else. On Wednesday, 8 August, 156 members of the union went on strike. The strike lasted fourteen weeks, and produced the greatest imaginable pressure on the members and officials alike. The AUEW and TGWU instructed their members to cross the electricians' picket lines and happily condoned the attempted performance of the electrical work by supervision, senior management and outside contract labour.

The EEPU pickets outside the factory were in a black mood. One contractor arrived at the gate with a snarling, yapping Alsatian in the back of his van. Voices were raised. Tempers frayed. The contractor jumped out of his vehicle and shouted to the dog to seize the pickets. The dog leapt from the van, took one look at the pickets, and didn't stop running until he turned the corner of the street! The big unions used their power within the CSEU and TUC to pressurize the union's officials, while claiming all along that they were neutral in the dispute between the company and the electricians. Chrysler then threatened to close down their whole British operation, making thousands redundant. This type of sabre-rattling only stimulated further efforts by the other unions to urge the electricians to give up their strike. The electricians, however, were roused; on 27 August, 20 EETPU members working for Hill Precision, a Chrysler subsidiary, went on strike in support of the Coventry strikers. The members in the Birmingham-based parts division and twenty-eight in the Luton–Dunstable works came out in early September. At Linwood, in Scotland, 200 EETPU members struck in sympathy with the Coventry members from 5 September to 24 September. The management attempted to do their work and 6,000 members of the other unions came out in support of the electricians.

The CSEU called a meeting of all shop-stewards at the Coventry plants at which the other union convenors said they had no part in holding back the EETPU – it was all Chrysler's fault. The Chrysler management repeated that they had been told by the convenors, in no uncertain terms, that such statements were public relations exercises and if the electricians were paid the £250, there would be strikes from the other unions.

The union accepted that an inquiry might help. Consequently, from 19 to 22 October, Professor Archibald Campbell conducted the inquiry into the dispute while the wary strikers in Coventry stayed on strike: they were wise to do so. The professor exonerated the company and the other unions, producing a furious reponse from the union's executive on 29 October. 'His recommendations amount to an approval of the conspiracy between the company and the representatives of the other trade unions. ... Professor Campbell manages to reduce the deep principle which is at the heart of this dispute to a mere arithmetical calculation about amounts of money ... whereby wage relativities are determined not by the intrinsic value of different jobs, but by a willingness to resort to industrial blackmail.' The leadership denounced the company's refusal to pay the £250 as 'sabotage'. Professor Campbell's report 'about the role of the other trade unions is naive to the point of absurdity. They were willing partners in the conspiracy. ... Throughout this dispute, we have made clear *our* position ... our determination to obtain proper financial reward for the skills of electricians and our resolve to resist attempts by other trade unions to veto agreements with employers that bring such recognition.' Still the strike continued and engineering national officer Roy Sanderson led the union back into negotiations. Pressure was now intensified by the promptings of company, government and self-righteous national representatives of other unions, all apparently concerned about Chrysler's withdrawal threat, all as aware as Roy Sanderson of the local threats made by the Chrysler convenors.

The final agreement was reached on 12 November 1973. It gave the electricians staff status at a salary of £2,650, parity with the toolroom, separate negotiating rights, a basic rate increase to £1.20 per hour, an ex-gratia payment of £51 each and a belated recognition of their great skill in clause 6 (b) of the final agreement. 'The company will not hold the electricians responsible for any electrical work carried out during the course of the dispute. ... The electricians will, immediately following resumption, give their full co-operation to ensure that all electrical equipment is restored to full operational capability.'

This dispute was, and remains, of central importance in the history of the union. It came at the height of the movement to establish the maintenance electrician's place in the sun. It was engineering's echo of the contracting agreement. It was a replica in manufacturing of the supply struggles. It showed the world that the union was determined to use whatever rational techniques were available to measure the genuine contribution to a company's success made by the electricians in a technologically developing world. Having made that measurement, the union was going to get its just deserts in terms of the members' pay packets. It was not going to be deflected by government pay policy, employer resistance or the envy of larger groups of workers who could not produce the same rational argument based on higher skill and higher productivity. The Chrysler dispute demonstrated all this with exceptional clarity.

The union had supported the strikers with some enthusiasm. Voluntary contributions to the strike fund – particularly from other groups of electricians in the West Midlands – amounted to £4,324 – nearly £2,000 of which sustained the expenses of the Coventry pickets as they suffered the organized abuse of the other unions' members. Each striker received £145.60 strike pay during the fourteen-week strike. Academic research by John Gennard in his book *Financing Strikers* showed that the union's triple strike pay amounted to 22 per cent of the strikers' income during the dispute, compared to 12 per cent from wives' income, 24 per cent from savings and 14 per cent from tax rebates. Roy Sanderson was understandably delighted: 'It has been the policy of our union for over a decade to obtain financial recognition for the increased skills and responsibility of our skilled members. Coventry was the battleground on which our members had to defend that policy, both against a multinational corporation and against the unprincipled opposition of other unions. The victory at Chrysler was a victory for the whole union and we owe the 156 electricians at Chrysler a massive debt of gratitude.'

The dispute had internal ramifications at the same time. The sense of unity between the officials, the national leadership and the local shop-stewards and membership was truly inspirational. The union's senior shop-steward at Chrysler was the hilarious figure of Woolfie Goldstein, a burly man with a sense of determination equalled only by his noisy sense of humour. All trade unionists will be aware of conference chairman who strictly time a speaker's contribution. When Woolfie Goldstein was attending his last engineering shop-stewards' conference at Scarborough, already holder of the union's gold badge, he was reminiscing with the delegates from the rostrum, about, among other things, the Chrysler dispute. Chairman, Tom Breakell, activated the orange light on the rostrum to show Woolfie Goldstein he had one minute left. Still Woolfie went on, chatting; the red light appeared, notice of the Chairman's indication he had used up all his speaker's time. Woolfie Goldstein did not stop. Instead, to massive cheers and applause, he reached out and unscrewed the red light, put it in his pocket and kept talking!

Other disputes have occasionally had to be fought and won to prove the same point – that electricians who possess higher skills must not be held back from their higher pay levels by a mixture of other unions' jealousy and employer timidity. Disputes at Brooks Motors and Metal Box in the late 1970s were needed to prove this point yet again.

Nevertheless, overall, the net results in engineering have achieved the ambitions of the 1964 conference in raising electricians' wages both in cash terms and comparative terms. National officer in engineering from 1970–87, Roy Sanderson, presided over the period in which this triumph was achieved in thousands of small negotiations leading to the modern aggregate position. The point is best made by a few simple key statistics.

The department of employment new earnings survey tell a clear story. Since the mid-1960s, the electrician has become the highest paid craftsman in the processing, making, repairing and related industries (metal and electrical) – group XIV in the standard industrial classification. In April 1988, the installation and maintenance electrician was paid an average of £250.60. This was comfortably the highest average weekly earnings, and the hourly earnings [exclusive of overtime] of £5.29 were only exceeded by gas fitters earning £5.54 per hour. The comparisons with the much more numerous conventional engineering craftsmen show how much progress has been made. In 1964, maintenance electricians and maintenance fitters hourly earnings were the same at 39 pence. The toolroom fitter led with hourly earnings of 44 pence. The first year the electrical skills edged in front of the toolroom was 1972. The statistics then listed maintenance electricians on 79.9 pence per hour. Maintenance fitters were getting 76.9 pence per hour. Toolroom fitters and turners were earning 83.7 pence per hour. The new classification, however, of electrical/electronic fitter was getting 87.1 pence per hour. Over the years since, the picture has emerged even more clearly in the electrician's favour in engineering. Choosing a handful of years at random, by 1977, the average earnings of toolmakers per hour were £1.68 compared to £1.74 for the electrician. By 1982, with the manufacturing industries spiralling into decline, the electricians who installed and maintained plant and equipment were now earning 28 pence per hour more than toolmakers on their rates, exclusive of overtime. The 1988 new earnings survey (see Table 7) shows the position to have been consolidated.

Table 7

	Average weekly earnings	Average hourly earnings
		(exclusive of overtime)
Toolmakers	£228.70	£4.85
Maintenance Fitters	£242.90	£4.96
Electricians	£250.60	£5.29

There is still much to be done in engineering. Throughout the post-war period, the union has organized women in production worker grades. Their efforts to achieve equal pay for work of equal value has often been thwarted by the inadequacies of the equal pay legislation. In 1975, the union mounted equal pay 'roadshows' when officials of the union toured the country to speak to meetings of shop-stewards – men and women – who represented women at work. The union has always supported the granting of skilled cards to women factory workers earning skilled rates in occupations like inspection and quality control. Local traditionalists have occasionally objected, but as with the increasing number of women apprentices, the demand of industry for skilled workers is a more powerful force than blind tradition. Since 1945, the union has followed the youthful Les Cannon's dictum to organize the electrical industries and not just the electricians in them.

26

LEADERSHIP, RULES AND POLITICS, 1970–89

THE EVENTS OF 1971–89 reflected the developments that arose out of the reforming years 1962–70. All trade unions tend to become associated in both public and members' minds with their leading personalities. For the EETPU, the union's name, policies and character have been associated in modern times with Frank Chapple and, latterly, Eric Hammond. Nevertheless, for most ordinary members, the union really lives for them at work in the unchronicled activities of the members themselves and their shop-stewards. Occasionally they may see a local full-time official at the far end of a canteen meeting in the midst of some local crisis. More rare is the appearance of a national figure in the union. Both Frank Chapple and Eric Hammond have often chuckled in the author's presence at the low level of recognition of leading trade union figures – including themselves – revealed by modern opinion polls.

Nevertheless, for the activists – the shop-stewards and branch officials, the conference delegates and the local industrial committee representatives – eras in the union's life *are* associated with prominent figures in the leadership. Most of those would agree that the 1970s and 1980s have been associated with the same body of ideas, even though in September 1984, Eric Hammond took over from Frank Chapple as general secretary.

Frank Chapple had been chairman of the TUC from September 1982 and had chaired the Congress meeting at Blackpool in 1983. He remains the only member of the ETU ever to have chaired the TUC, and his year of office strengthened the forces of moderation during an exceptionally gloomy twelve months for the Labour movement. During the 1983 General Election, he backed his old friend John Grant in his constituency in London, even though Grant had left the Labour Party to join the Social Democrats. This personal support found no echo in the union's institutional support for Labour – however much the electorate rejected the Labour message that year. It was in the aftermath of that dreadful electoral defeat that Frank Chapple both chaired the TUC and was the union's main leadership spokesman at its own conference for the last time at Blackpool in November 1983. His speech to the TUC impressed with its calm evaluation of the need to accommodate the Thatcher revolution or risk the complete sidelining of trade unions in society. His introductory speech to his own union's conference was much more of a personal statement to the EETPU. He emphasized themes made familiar since 1962. First, there was a need for trade union leadership to be, above all, representative of its membership. He was convinced that the union's post-1962 democracy, based on secret postal ballots, was responsible for the union's policies emanating from a representative EETPU leadership. He was proud of the union's successes – the growth in the number of delegates and shop-stewards at policy and rule conferences, the computer-based newspaper bulletin services to the membership, the technical training, the pensions expertise and, above all, the reformed financial position. He finished on an uncharacteristically emotional note.

Despite the worst recession in living memory, we are providing services to our members that reflect their real concerns as workers. Recent opinion polls showed our members to have the highest recorded satisfaction rating with their union.

I cannot pretend that the last twenty-two years have been a bundle of fun for me personally. I have been physically attacked, abused and libelled times without number. But I could not have made my contribution to this success story if I hadn't had you standing shoulder to shoulder with me through it all.

This will be my last Policy and Rules Revision Conference. I want to say to my colleagues on this platform, the hundreds of you in this hall and to the thousands of our members outside, that this union is no one-man band and never will be. The credit is ours and not mine.

He continued as general secretary until September 1984, when Eric Hammond took over from him. When he was made Lord Chapple of Hoxton, he delighted in the free parking space in the centre of London and chuckled at the fact that both he and author/playwright, Ted Willis, veterans alike of the Shoreditch Labour League of Youth and the Young Communist League, made it to the House of Lords. Even without the long perspective of time to place Frank Chapple's leadership in some sort of context, it is clear already that his contribution to the union was as important as any other single individual's in the union's history. The short period in the 1960s he shared the limelight with Les Cannon was arguably the ten years that revolutionized the position of electrical workers in society. The instrument of their emancipation was their union. Their union was reconstructed out of the ruin of political jobbery and financial corruption by Frank Chapple. He is famous for his unrelenting bravery in the face of left-wing attempts to return the EETPU to the left-wing fold. He ought to be better known for the practical ways in which he elevated the behaviour of officials and staff of the union back onto a scrupulous and honest plane. He made the union's finances impregnable at a time of raging inflation and mass unemployment. He was careful with investments, canny with property deals and strong in support of spending projects that extended real services to real members. Most of all, his example enthused thousands of others at local and national level to stand their ground and speak their minds.

Eric Hammond took over the reins in 1984 after two years' running in tandem with Frank Chapple as general secretary-elect. There was no perceptible change in policy, with the possible exception of a more genuine and personal commitment to the tribal delights of the Labour Party. He announced that the EETPU's leadership was *not* going to change its style in spectacular fashion through a pounding attacking on the GLC at the 1983 TUC conference. Eric Hammond comes from north Kent; his father worked at Bowaters' Thameside paper mill. Evacuated to Canada during the war, he returned to England at the end of the war to do his electrical apprenticeship at Bowaters. He served his national service in Egypt and spent his early trade union life in contracting in and around north Kent and Thameside, working on power station contracts, the BP oil terminal on the Isle of Grain and other contracting sites. As we have seen, he was first elected to the executive council in 1963 as a young left-winger who could discuss the editorials from the *Daily Worker* on building sites with little sense of embarrassment. He became convinced of the need for the Joint Industry Board in the contracting industry and was first of all disappointed that his colleagues on the left in north Kent could not see the possibilities in the new deal. He was then incensed at their threats to work against him, promising their backing only if Eric Hammond dropped his support for the JIB. He would not do that, and steadily provided more and more of the driving intellectual force behind the union's innovations, especially in administration and in particular after the death of Les Cannon. He remains a man who gives as much passion to his family, his love of rugby and his other outside interests like gardening and photography as he does to the union's concerns.

The Modern Rules: 1971–89; a Political Battleground

Both Frank Chapple and Eric Hammond have shared the key perspective of sustaining the union's modern rule-book, so tortuously changed under Les Cannon's huge influence in 1965.

The modern rule-book largely emerged from the 1971 rules revision conference in the rain and cold of a Blackpool conference in November that year. (This conference was four days tagged on to a six-day policy conference. A two-week conference has never been repeated since. So deep was the impression of exhaustion and misery that year that for a short while afterwards there was serious, if unfulfilled, talk of holding the union's next policy conference in 1973 in Rimini in Italy.)

The 1971 conference had to put together the twenty-rule 'general' rules that had been agreed at the time of the amalgamation with the PTU in 1968, the leftovers from the 1963 PTU rules and from the 1965 ETU rules. The mechanics of the conference were immeasurably lightened by agreeing a 'dummy' rule-book put up by the executive council in the first place, and then amending it with branch amendments.

There was an initial flurry of activity in which the conference quickly reinserted the traditional socialist aims of the union back into its 'objects' – 'to provide legal means and to support legislative action to improve members' financial and social conditions, especially by supporting policies which will ultimately give workers ownership and control of industry.' After the recent death of Les Cannon, Frank Chapple was in the chair for the full fortnight and established his leading position once and for all. This was important against the background of what was happening elsewhere in the union, as shall be seen.

For Frank Chapple, the rules revision was to concentrate on several import-ant issues. First and foremost was the level of contributions in the newly decimalized world of inflation and the protection of the union's funds from any of the possible difficulties associated with the Industrial Relations Act. Second, was the possibility of the return of area committees. Third, was the acrimonious question of discipline and disciplinary appeals. Fourth, was the question of appointment versus election of area and national officials. And fifth, was the ban on communists.

Financing the Modern EETPU

During the 1960s, the union first employed professional accountants to advise the general secretary in a thoroughly cool, practical attitude to trade union finance. For many people in the Labour movement, the efficient management of trade union resources is nothing less than collaboration with international capitalism. They would prefer to spend money on unconstitutional disputes, endless foreign delegations, expensive hotels and entertainment for the union's leadership and delegations. If that puts the union in financial difficulty, so what! The movement is about struggle, not collecting ten-pence pieces. Frank Chapple and Eric Hammond, scrupulously advised by Andy Cunningham's accounts department, have never had any time for that view of trade union finance. There were very real financial difficulties for the union in the early 1970s. Membership growth masked the fact that higher expenditure in an inflationary world was leading to the funds per member falling from £8.09 in

1968 to £7.92 for 1970. These figures looked worse still when adjusted for inflation. Nevertheless, in 1970 the EETPU's 15p skilled contribution compared well with the engineers' 17½p and the post office engineers' 20p. The semi-skilled auxiliary section was paying 10p, compared to the GMWU's 18p and the TGWU's 16½p. The modern contribution is still designed to be demonstrably cheaper than the 'competition'.

Throughout the 1970s and 1980s, attention to the finances was always a crucial concern of the general secretary's office. The growing sophistication of the union's computer installation allowed a much greater quality of financial information to be in the leadership's hands on a regular basis. Contributions were steadily raised from 20p in 1972 to £1 in 1989 for the skilled section of the union. These increases always lagged behind general inflation and also fell as a proportion of an hour's pay in contracting. At the end of 1971, the provincial contracting rate was nearly 60p and the 20p skilled rate was therefore thirty-three per cent of an hour's pay. By 1989, the same approved contracting rate was £4.55 and the £1 a week contribution was twenty-two per cent of an hour's pay.

Contribution increases became part of the membership's expectations of inflationary times. In 1979, the conference decided to allow the executive to raise contributions by 5p per week each year, so long as it was retrospectively confirmed by the following biennial conference. Steadily, the much more efficient method of collecting contributions from the 'check-off' schemes and annual payment in advance, contributed to the stability of the union's finances. It also reassured the Union's Co-operative Bank managers who could check the union's predictions of income and expenditure against the check-off/annual payment figures from previous years. This avoids any pressure of cash-flow problems when 86,000 of the union's members, who *do* still pay cash, fall temporarily into arrears while lazing on foreign beaches in the summer sun! In 1970, only 71,405 members paid by check-off. By 1975, 138,000 paid by check-off and 8,000 paid annually. By the autumn of 1989, over seventy-five per cent of the paying membership were paying contributions in these efficient ways: 212,000 were paying by check-off, 31,000 annually.

A new financial scheme was introduced that helped both the member and the union's administrative machine: 2,000 members paid by direct debit into the union's bank account in the first year. The presentation of the accounts is remarkable: there is first, the conventional annual accounts, and then every member of the union is sent an illustrated 'popular' version of where his money is going.

During the 1970s and 1980s, the union had fundamentally altered the structure of its benefits provision. General secretary A. J. Walker in 1891, was convinced that the provident benefits of the union were central to its very existence; they both prevented the pauperization of the members' families and also had an important collective bargaining function. No employer could starve the members back to work in a strike or generally attack the level of district wages in times of high unemployment. Strike benefits, unemployment benefit, accident benefit and funeral benefit were the social insurance payments for the early trade unionists. However, paying huge amounts of benefits could potentially destroy the union. In the aftermath of the First World War, thousands of members lost their jobs in the early 1920s depression. Their claims for unemployment benefit, particularly coinciding with a high incidence of strikes, bankrupted the union. During the early 1970s, despite the massive success for the movement since 1945 in the emergence of the country's social security system, the same thing looked like happening again. With the Industrial Relations Act controversies seeming to herald a new storm of industrial disputes, they coincided with a rise in unemployment nationally to over one million. Two pounds a week unemployment pay may not sound a lot. However, many branches took to attempting to pay benefit on a daily basis to people who were not wholly unemployed but were on short-time. In 1971, the benefit cost the union £169,000. In 1972, it cost £156,000. Accident benefit cost £50,000 and £44,000 in the same year. The 1973 conference abolished the unemployment benefit, and the accident benefit was retained for another decade by which time sick-pay at work and the Government statutory sick-pay entitlement between them made the benefit redundant. Nevertheless, the branch general purposes fund would be sustained at a level that could afford the £1 a day accident benefit for a maximum of sixty days. By 1988, the union's main financial benefits were those that the Welfare State does not exactly replicate. For 1988, the union spent £701,155 on financial benefits – £404,318 on strike pay, £114,267 on funeral benefit, £113,770 on retirement grants and £68,200 on fatal accidents.

The modern union, however, rather than advance small cash payments direct to members, now spends tens of thousands of pounds providing advisory and recreational services to members that they cannot get elsewhere at such a price. The new membership services department has grown out of Alan Pickering's increasingly sophisticated advice service to pensions negotiators and union pensioners. His new department now offers a complete set of financial services to ordinary members way beyond its original pensions basis. Investment advice, help with buying houses, cars and insurance are key features of the 'Moneywise' scheme. The union's legal services, for many years restricted to the industrial accident cover that Jimmy Rowan would have recognized, now spreads to a national network of solicitors who offer initial free legal advice to any member in any legal situation to do with his work or personal life. The modern union has also turned its attention to the provision of recreational opportunities. The union bought Buxted Park in Sussex for £6 million in 1987. This marvellous mansion is set in over 300 acres of countryside with three fishing lakes and the only trade union-owned deer herd in Britain. Eric Hammond has often described it as a 'Robin Hood' venture where the money earned from its weekday use as a conference centre is used to subsidize weekend and summer holidays for union members. The decision to purchase it was not unanimous – a minority of the executive felt that the provision of such services was straying too far from the 'core' activities of the union. Whatever the truth of that, the union received a serious offer for the estate of over £12 million just two years after its purchase, thus doubling its value in two years. Buxted Park can be seen to offer the opportunity of broadening the benefits associated with trade union membership away from the negative, if vital, protection against disaster that the old 'benefits' represented. Nowadays, the union's 'benefits' are positive benefits aimed at raising the standard of living of individual members and their families – a complete change from past practice. This newest and highest ambition represented by Buxted Park builds on the union's experience gained in its education services. We have seen how Esher Place has become a central part of the activists experience since it opened in 1953. For many shop-stewards, a course at Esher has represented their first contact with the union as a national institution, and has convinced them that trade union activity is to be an important part of their lives in the future; for some, it has been the first step on the road to a full-time career as a union official. In 1974, the union added Cudham Hall in Kent to its educational effort and augmented the buildings' facilities in 1980 to a capacity of forty-nine bedrooms. It was to be at Cudham Hall that the union at last answered the hopes of the pioneers on the question of technical training. Since Jack Ball's day, the union had sought to be associated with the establishment of high technical standards in the industry. The union was anxious to be represented on the City and Guilds and, much later, Business and Technicians Education Council, to help in the definition of technical standards for electrical, plumbing and electronic work. Throughout its history, the union has been involved in the design and supervision of the content of apprenticeships. It was only natural that the union would take an interest in the new electronics industries. For the union's skilled membership, there was an inherent danger in the new technologies. If the average electrician could re-train in mid-career to take on electronics, he would enhance his job security and job control and therefore his wages and standard of living. If he could not, and he was restricted to lesser electrical work, the higher earnings and greater security would pass to specialist 'technicians', usually catered for by other unions or working as self-employed in small specialist companies, brought into factories on a sub-contract basis. In 1979, Dave Rogers ran the first tentative three-day course at Cudham Hall in the general principles of electronics. Initially, many companies refused to even pay the wages of electricians attending the courses. However, since then, under national officer

Dave Rogers's guidance, the union has steadily expanded the range and coverage of its technical education. Employers and government departments alike were convinced of the academic respectability of the courses, some of which were certificated by City and Guilds. The courses were practical – very short technical explanations supported by generously-equipped practical experiments. Members do this practical work in circuit-building and fault diagnosis on everything from the simplest electronic circuit through to a systems approach to the interrelationship between computers in industrial control environments.

By the mid-1980s, the union was providing over 4,000 teaching weeks of electronics training per annum. Cudham Hall remained the centre where courses were taught and developed, but the technical training tutors could put most of the equipment for the basic courses on to the road, and most of the union's larger offices, converted specially for the job, can now host technical training classes on a convenient non-residential basis in the members' localities. The technical training is a new 'benefit' for the membership. Not only do they get training in their vocational skills, but the union gains expertise in the crucial modern area of skills training for the new economic frontiers that industrial society has still to cross. The EETPU's own expertise with its own programme has made its representatives uniquely authoritative on training issues in discussions with semi-governmental bodies like the Training Boards and the Manpower Services Commission (and its successors). All of this is a far cry indeed from 1905 when the executive council minutes recorded: 'London branch asked permission to spend £5 on technical education in the branch. Resolved that permission be given them when the funds of the branch would permit.'

Area Committees

The second main constitutional issue addressed in 1971 was the attempt to reintroduce area committees into the structure of the union. Now that Les Cannon was dead, if Frank Chapple did not handle key issues himself at conference, they often became the responsibility of Eric Hammond. He had finally fallen out politically with his erstwhile left-wing friends in London and north Kent, in 1966, after the Colwyn Bay industrial conferences. In the 1970 elections, where Bill Blairford and Bill Blair nearly lost, Eric Hammond beat the credible left candidate Fred Morphew by 4,770 votes to 2,899. Sometimes it was said in the 1970s that Eric Hammond 'could not carry a conference' – in apparent contrast to Frank Chapple who always could. Eric Hammond was clearly able to destroy that speculation when he became general secretary-elect in 1982. His increasingly powerful platform performances, sometimes televised to great effect at the TUC or Labour Party, were to draw a series of compliments from commentators. Typical of these were remarks of journalist Edward Pearce who wrote on 11 September 1988 that Eric Hammond 'is high-temperature physics, and eloquent with it. He is/was arguably the TUC's best debater, only spoiling with bottomless scorn the points he makes with jagged-edged felicity.' It is also not often recognized that at the polls, within the union, as an executive council candidate, he proved impossible to beat. Throughout the union's recent elections, higher turn-outs of thirty-five to forty per cent have led to highly creditable victories being achieved – president Paul Gallagher won his Manchester executive seat with 7,446 votes in 1987. Scotland's Alf McLuckie won with 7,878 the same year. Harry Hughes polled 8,417 votes in 1986 in North-West London and the Home Counties. As far back as 1975, Bill Blair had decisively beaten Fred Gore, 9,518–3,810, in the same seat. Nevertheless, only one executive council election has ever been won with more than 10,000 votes, and that was Eric Hammond's divisional election in December 1980.

There was nothing wrong, either, with his 1971 presentation of the case on area committees. He was particularly keen to emphasize that the union's focus of influence was moving from the old style of area organization on the basis of branch representation. The modern way was the new style of industrial conferences and committees based on the shop-stewards in each industry in each area of the union. The arguments of the 1965 conference were sustained, along with the addition of area industrial committees of shop-stewards to advise the local full-time official. These committees were elected by the annual area conferences and usually became the delegation to the biennially-held national industrial conferences. In 1977, further responsibilities were gently shifted to the shop-stewards' movement in the union when the area industrial conferences had to provide 200 or so directly elected delegates to join the 600-plus branch delegates for the biennial policy/rules revision conference. There has been no going back on the gradual industrialization of the union's decision-making.

Discipline

The third main area of concern springing from the 1971 conference was the question of disciplinary appeals. We have seen how the late 1960s opposition to the executive focused on unofficial marches, meetings and protests, largely about the JIB agreements and, to a lesser extent, the supply productivity deals. Such protests always involved being in breach of the union's rule about bringing the union into disrepute and therefore often became subject to discipline from the executive council. The final appeals committee in the late 1960s was elected by the biennial conference delegates: it quickly became the focus of frantic politicking, given the entitlement it had to overrule the disciplinary decisons of the executive council. At the 1971 conference, following the 1969 ballot vote abolition of the 'rank and file' appeals committee, Don Sheasby spoke for the executive. He started by justifying the appeals committee being half the executive council while the original disciplinary committee was the other half of the executive. As the debate unfolded, however, it was clear there was unease, even amongst the executive's supporters; Frank Chapple read out loud Les Cannon's contribution on the subject to the 1969 conference. Even so, it all boiled down to the delegates' perception of whether the executive members on the *appeals* committee could be genuinely dispassionate in judging the verdicts of their colleagues on the *disciplinary* committee side of the executive. Pat O'Hanlon from Motherwell supply branch summed up the conference's unease when he said that neither the final appeals committee (of which he had been a member) nor the executive council solution

... represents justice. I believe that this union is not competent to provide an independent final appeals committee and every final appeals committee ought to be independent .... The psychological effect of a member who has been charged by the executive council and goes through the procedure still only dealing with the executive council, to my mind, gives him a lack of confidence ... and there was no question about [the final appeals committee] – a political power struggle did go on within the final appeals committee.

His appeal for a third force outside the union was quickly and gratefully picked up by chairman Frank Chapple. Within hours the executive withdrew its own proposition, met, and happily got Vic Feather, general secretary of the TUC, to agree that the TUC would nominate three experienced trade unionists to be the union's final appeal committee. This successfully took the vexed issue of internal discipline outside the union for final resolution – a job now done by the Advisory, Conciliation and Arbitration Service (ACAS). However, at the 1989 rules revision conference, the executive council did away with many of the rules that gave rise to all the trouble in the first place. Divulging the union's business outside the union and criticizing the executive by pamphleteering are now all perfectly allowable within the union, subject only to internal discipline for wilfully attempting to break up the union, and, just like everyone else, to the law of libel.

The Election/Appointment of Full-Time Officials

The next major reform of the 1960s, under fire in the 1970s but then simply part of the landscape after 1983, was the question of the election of area/national officials against their appointment by the executive council. The ballot vote in 1969 to set up the appointments system in preference to election was narrowly confirmed in 1971, sustained by three to two at the 1977 rules revision conference and overwhelmingly maintained by the 1983 conference.

This issue, along with the ban on communists holding office, has always provided the biggest set-piece, dramatic debates at the union's modern conferences. It was *the* issue on which the pamphleteering concentrated most longingly. It was an issue that was not wholly discussed in terms of whether a delegate supported or loathed the executive – although for the left it was axiomatic to support the return of elections. The debate was stimulating in 1971; it was thrilling theatre at the cavernous Norbreck Castle at Blackpool in November 1977. At that conference, the weather was atrocious. Windows were blown in by gales at the conference centre on the North Shore. Although the sound system was often confused and muddled, no one missed a word when the appointment/election debate was held on the morning of Thursday 25 November 1977. To start with, the executive council moved the rule as it stood. This, of course, enabled them to have the right of reply as the original mover at the end of the debate. The main amendment was to be moved by Fred Gore and seconded by the left-wing periodical *Flashlight* candidate in the Manchester region, Harry Shaw. Throughout the week, the whole conference was busy trying to convince each other in the hotel bars and receptions of the pros and cons on this issue above all others.

The debate started in an almost academic fashion. Eric Hammond talked the conference through an executive council background paper on the issue in careful detail.

He first of all explained that the appointment of officials was related to the much more efficient organization of the area office. In the 1950s and 1960s, the union had run as many as forty-six offices – most of them one-man operations. A local official was supposed to be in touch with all the agreements of his membership in all the average-sized towns of Britain.

Throughout the 1970s, the union had concentrated its offices close to the motorway network, and shut outlying one-man offices. With up to half-a-dozen officials in one office, each one could then specialize in particular industries across a whole region. Driving Vauxhall cars across the motorway network made that service to the members more economic and less random than one official per large town. Typical of this development was the situation in the West Midlands where the Shrewsbury and Coventry offices closed while the centrally-placed Birmingham office, on the Coventry Road, became the focus of mobile, specialized officials. By 1977, the union was running only twenty-seven area offices, of which eleven had three or more officials and only Michael Brennan in Dublin, Jack Varty in Windermere, Laurie Hancock in Scunthorpe, Dick Williams in Chester, Tom O'Neil in Tilbury and Dick Allum in Reading were operating on their own.

For Eric Hammond, these larger areas were vital in the provision of efficient service; but they were likely to lead to huge areas where personal contact with the local membership would be a practical impossibility. Only political factions organize across regional boundaries. The only people to get elected as area officials would tend to be the nominee of the political pre-meeting that owed *nothing* to 'democracy' (because the names on the ballot paper, following the nomination caucuses, would be provided only by unaccountable political factions). From 1977, anyone could apply to be an area official – whether he was from a dominant huge factory in an area or a bright unknown television engineer with half-a-dozen members from a small provincial town. In 1978, the appointments system was considerably refined. Instead of being interviewed by a panel of executive councillors, a sophisticated assessment process was introduced. All the applicants over a period of time – perhaps twenty or so – would go to Esher Place or Cudham Hall or Buxted Park for a few days. They would then take part in a carefully planned course which would include individual, group and plenary sessions covering the complete range of the union's concerns – both internal and external. All of the applicants are observed by an appointments committee (composed of executive councillors, serving area officials and national officers). Following a final formal interview with the appointments committee, chaired by the general secretary, the applicants are recommended to the full executive council on the basis of their immediate suitability for an official's job – when one becomes vacant – or have pointed out to them the gaps in their experience and just how the union can help them to improve their suitability. This process probably tests aptitude and experience slightly more rigorously than the rough-and-tumble of elections. In the late 1970s, cost was still a consideration. With twelve officials in London, each one's election would cost £1,200 for one-way postage – money better spent on appointing *more* officials than otherwise the union could afford.

Appointing officials also allowed the leadership to replace plumbers with plumbers or exploit white-collar recruitment potential by appointing people with the appropriate expertise. Perhaps the key argument, emotionally put forward by the pro-election lobby, was that area officials should be 'account-able' to their electorate with the clear implication that if they were inadequate they would be dismissed by the votes of the members.

First, this argument forgot the anguish suffered in the union's past until 1935, when it had become clear that area officials *had* to be responsible to the executive council. The alternative was between the choice of loyalty to the local office or head office, producing rivalry and anarchy in the manner of the London district committee in the 1920s and 1930s. It is the *executive*, elected by *all* the members, who are to be held to account for the performance of the local officials who are the union's civil servants, implementing the policy of the executive, advised by the union's committees and conferences.

Second, it was clear in practice that few officials ever got removed in an election. This dubious distinction was shared by only three officials in the whole period from 1945–69, and one of those was re-elected the following year. The sitting candidate had a huge advantage in being recognized by the membership, whatever his competence.

Eric Hammond's final point did not duck the issue of the rules revision conference of 571 delegates being *entitled* to change the policy. He reminded them of the 1969 ballot of the members – 47,560–14,725. He then gently, delicately reminded them of the 9,000 votes he had personally received in his recent election, in which this subject was an important part of his rejected opponent's case. He then told the conference straight. Only 8,000 members had attended the 571 branch meetings that had elected the delegates in front of him (just 1.85 per cent of the total membership) and not all those 8,000 had voted for the successful candidates. His final appeal was to recognize the higher democracy of the ballot vote, and retain the appointment system.

Fred Gore introduced his amendment that would have reintroduced the pre-1969 situation of electing all national and area officials every five years. It is always difficult to convey the feeling of a conference hall; a week in a seaside hotel in intense political debate – often with a glass in hand – bears no relationship to real life at all and yet purports to discuss the most intensely real issues of industrial, political and social life. It is a world of its own; as such, it is possible to argue that it is just that unreality of conference life that leads to so many things being said and decisions being taken that open up a gap between trade union activists and the membership in whose name all those decisions are taken.

Delegates to such conferences, whatever their political principles, are usually the last people to notice the bizarre life they are living. Having said that, conference can be pure theatre. Fred Gore that day was masterly. He made his real points by saying something else. The 1969 vote by the membership of 47,560–14,725, was not a ballot – it was a 'referendum', because only the executive's view accompanied the ballot paper. He rejected the idea that area officials would be better chosen by an informed executive council, who knew what was required, by a clever appeal to the deeply-held convictions of the largely middle-aged skilled membership sitting as delegates in front of him. Fred Gore speaks well, slowly but not tediously in a clear, slightly London accent.

The electrician ... is required to have a far wider range of qualifications in order to equip him in the advancing technology. Who, therefore, better than the members to know of [the official's] ability and who knows better if he or she – let us look forward to the day when we have female union officials in this union also – has the ability that is required. I believe that the criteria for a candidate to accept a position in this union are three-fold: (1) he should be a competent craftsman both in the practical and the technical sense; (2) he should have above all a dedication to his fellow workers and to their aspirations for a future and better life; and (3) he should be competent to act and negotiate on their behalf. Les Cannon, our late president, when giving evidence to the Donovan Commission, said that in many unions, and ours included, the electoral system has given us some excellent officials and along with that you get some that are not quite up to that standard. On the other hand he said: 'It is my experience that in unions where they are appointed, again they have some excellent officials, but also they have mistakes. The effectiveness of an official in our organization will most often depend on his relationship with those that he negotiates and acts for. The best negotiators that we can have in this organization are those who emerge from the workshop floor in the course of struggle.'

After cleverly appealing to the middle-of-the-road delegates with the dual incantations of skill and Les Cannon, he attacked the appointed officials as the 'personal supporters' of the executive councillors. He quoted the other skilled unions that still elected their officials and once again, sensitive to his audience, finished his speech by saying: 'I know that in this conference hall today there are many delegates who have the ability and aptitude for these positions and would be prepared to stand for office under such an electoral system.'

There was no mention in any of this of the politics of elections that had nearly overwhelmed the union. No mention of caucuses, conspiracies, pamphlets, ballot-rigging and the pre-selection of candidates by pre-meetings. Harry Shaw, the seconder, was not in Fred Gore's league; he had been left the two points to make that the original ballot in 1969 only involved 62,000 out of the union's 381,000 members and that elections would once again create 'a union where the individual member continues to wish to be a direct participant in the important decisions of the union'.

Support for them came from Tony German from Barry Dock in South Wales, again denying any political involvement, apparently only interested in reintroducing elections as an antidote to 'apathy and cynicism within our ranks'.

Two delegates from the union's white-collar section, the Electrical and Engineering Staff Association (EESA), supported the executive council. The representative from Plessey EESA (Mr Finnigan) felt that service to the membership was best assured by 'officials who are able to devote all of their time to the service of the membership instead of having to spend a great deal of their time electioneering to ensure tenure of office'. His colleague, Mr Donovan, from Newport EESA, complained that only candidates from larger branches stood any chance of election – particularly those who were funded in their travels by their friends. Throughout the late 1960s and the 1970s, there were a handful of delegates from the floor of the conference who supported the executive council on the key political issues: one of these was the Manchester Press delegate, John Weaver. He raised the temperature of the debate by tearing into the proponents of elections by exposing the complete absence of the political dimension from their contributions.

John Weaver was the last delegate selected by chairman Tom Breakell before getting the movers to wind up the debate. From this strong position in the running order, Weaver went straight at it in his instantly recognizable Mancunian accent. Not for the first time in the union's history was Manchester pitched against London. He was in favour of the appointment of officials.

We have been able to place in important jobs men with real commitment to the union and a desire to be of service to the members; people who, under the old system, we would never have even got to know because they did not have a power base of one kind or another to support them. . . .

If we adopt this amendment, in my submission, we open the doors to a bloody-minded struggle for positions and the adoption of political attitudes which are irrelevant to the real needs of our members. . . .

I put it to conference that these people are not motivated by a wish to be of service to the membership or indeed to the movement at large. They are motivated by narrow sectarian political attitudes which are repugnant to the overwhelming majority of our members. . . .

It really will not do for Fred Gore to come to the rostrum of this conference and object to some of the things that Eric Hammond has had to say. Fred knows as well as any of us what the position was in this union fifteen or sixteen years ago when we had the old electoral sytem and the old executive. This organization, to a large extent, was an employment exchange for communists and communist-sponsored candidates, and the maintenance of their positions was of prime importance to the extent that when the tide was turned against them they had to resort to ballot-rigging to maintain a situation unacceptable to the membership.

Fred Gore's reply was cool, reflective and deeply effective. He bemoaned the introduction of the 'cold weather' introduced by John Weaver. He said that what went on before 1960 was not to be held against delegates in the hall, many of whom were much too young to have been at work then. He promised the plumbers that they should elect their own officials. He then asked the delegates, in a rising crescendo of cheers, to think about their own branches and who had sent them. He finished on that note. 'All of you pause and think, think of the debate that has ensued; think of your branch members, the workers that you rub shoulders with in your place of occupation. You know over the years their feelings and attitudes on this question and I know when we take the vote that you will overwhelmingly support the amendment to Rule 15.'

Thunderous applause greeted this; sustained for political effect, no doubt. Much of it was genuine appreciation of the debater's art.

What came next was quite simply the best speech of that conference and, arguably, of any other in living memory. If the vote had been taken after Fred Gore magisterially strode through the delegates to his place in the hall, elections would have triumphed.

Frank Chapple rose to confront the left once more.

He spoke in an emotional torrent straight over the microphone, face to face with the conference, without long pauses to consult notes during the debate. His final reference to a personal appeal was his last card and it proved to be a winning ace.

He started with the politics of the issue and finished with the politics of the issue.

I would like to invite those of you – and I think there are many sincere, honest and reasonable people among you – who support the argument for a return to elections, I invite you to consider the company you are in. Just consider the company you are in. Look around you. You have suffered the intimidation and the pamphleteering this week and I will leave you to reflect on that while I am making the rest of my remarks. Brother Gore, in his reply, indicated he did not like the cold weather. He never did. Brother Gore likes a one-sided debate in which he and his comrades, as he calls them, can pour on the intimidation and we will all bend to it. . . . I tell you, it is not a question of whether we go forward with Brother Gore's 'democracy' but whether we go backwards with Brother Gore's 'democracy'. . . . It is no use Brother Gore complaining about [1961] being past history because we relive it every day and we relive it at every conference. Do not let anyone imagine that we are ever going to be able to escape from it. Until this executive, by a majority, turns into the willing puppets of left-wing minority groups, we will *always* be subjected to it. The only defence we have is to appeal to you the way that I do at this conference. There is no more important issue to this union that this issue of the appointment of officials. . . . Yes, it's true that every delegate here *is* entitled to stand for election. That is not the issue. The issue that Eric Hammond put to you squarely is how many of *you* would be elected, how many of *you* would have the support of these secret meetings that turn out *Militant* and *Flashlight*, with the daily scurrilous pamphlets that pervade this union and have done so since 1961? We have had pamphlet after pamphlet, year in and year out, ever since we changed the rule by ballot and let me remind you it was confirmed by conference decision too [in 1971]. . . . Let me say this to those who say that when we put things to ballots and when they are changed in that manner, they do not get debated, it's the most utter and arrant nonsense I have ever heard. I have only to bat an eyelid and there is a leaflet round the union explaining it to everybody and explaining how foully I do it. One further point and I will sit down. In every election that I have taken part in since 1969, the major point of all of my opponents has been this issue of the election of officials and in every case the members have decisively rejected those opponents of mine. I say this to you and I have never done it before at any conference. I have never put in a personal appeal to the conference before. I do not believe in such things as a practice. I do not have any vested interest in this at all. I have no more elections to face, under the rules anyway. I put this to you. The issue is whether we go forward with a union that is comparatively free of internecine warfare or whether we turn the union back. . . .

I put it to you this will be regarded by our friends, by most of the members as a serious turn for the worse and I urge conference to support the existing rule and reject all the amendments.

The vote was briskly taken. Hardly anyone abstained. The appointment of officials was upheld by a comfortable three to two majority. It was the common consent of every delegate, left or right and every full-time official and conference steward that it was Frank Chapple's victory.

The Ban on Communists

The last major issue confronting the 1971 rules revision conference that was still being discussed in 1989 was the issue of the banning of communists from holding office in the union, first introduced in 1965 after a ballot vote of the members.

In 1971, the executive council did not put the ban on communists into their 'dummy' rule-book that was to be the basis of the amalgamated union's rule-book. Indeed, they were initially of a mind to let the rule slip out of the amalgamated rule-book. The motivation for this apparent change of heart was probably associated with the requirements of the two big unions which the union was seriously discussing amalgamation with at the time – neither the engineers nor the municipal workers had such a rule. The left in the Amalgamated Union of Engineering Workers (AUEW) would warm to the prospect of an amalgamation with the electricians where communists were apparently rehabilitated after the dreadful deeds of a decade before. But just before the conference, the pamphleteers and their friends at the *Morning Star* newspaper started to imply that the executive was on the run and issued detailed advice on how delegates should vote. The executive voted, 8–5, to recommend the ban once more be inserted in the amalgamated rule-book. The five dissidents were Eric Hammond, Don Sheasby, Jack Ashfield, Bernard Clarke and Jim McKernan. The plumbers voted for the ban; others were impressed by the argument that as the policy had been decided by a ballot of all the members, it should only really be changed by another ballot, so the executive had no right to withdraw it. It was not until the 1989 biennial conference that this general principal was to be written into the rule-book – that any ballot decision could only be changed by a further ballot of the whole membership. The 1971, 1977 and 1983 conferences all reaffirmed the ban on communists. In the early 1980s, a green pamphlet called *End the Ban* was widely circulated. At the 1983

Flashlight pre-conference meeting, it was 'the most important issue facing the conference', according to Stan Davidson, bewailing his non-eligibility as a delegate as one who 'has had my sentence renewed every six years.' Each conference is preceded by a *Flashlight* meeting on the Sunday evening and they usually feature prominent left-wingers from inside and outside the union. In 1983, Tony Benn was the guest speaker and apart from saying that he read *Flashlight* and thought it of 'fundamental importance', mentioned at one stage of his speech his recent trip to Cuba. When the end-of-meeting collection was taken, it raised over £100 from the visitors present, and 5 pesetas. Unkind people drew their own conclusions. In 1985, the pre-conference speaker was Dennis Skinner MP. These meetings were usually held at the Blackpool Library. Skinner opened by telling his audience that he had had to explain to his daughter what he was doing at a 'broad left' meeting on a Sunday in a library. He said that he had told her that the reason the left in the EETPU met in a library was 'because they had to keep quiet!'

Flashlight's demand for the end of the ban was ignored by increasing majorities, particularly when it was linked to the other mainstays of the left's constitutional 'reforms' – the election of officials and the right of the conference to 'instruct' and not 'advise' the elected executive council. In 1989, after the union's expulsion from the TUC, the executive council felt that the ban was at last incompatible with the union's attitude to individual freedom. Eric Hammond moved that it was now not appropriate to make such a song and dance about members sending circulars to each other or campaigning in elections. The 'interference' in elections was an outmoded concept. It had never bothered the *Flashlight* brigade, anyway. They had sent circulars and pamphlets during every election. In the same way, Hammond did not think there was any modern need for the rule banning communists. 'Our most dedicated enemies are not touched by it and the years have made the declared target of the clause irrelevant.' London Airport's Fred Gore and Ken Holmes, of Cwmbran, long-time opponents of the executive on this issue, welcomed the change, as they had supported the abolition of the ban in previous years. No one had bargained for the explosive reaction of the moderate delegates. Liz Poulter, a senior shop-steward for the union at Ferranti's, was against the idea with some passion – but nothing like the passion exhibited by Walsall's veteran delegate Don Cook. He had never been a platform yes-man; each conference had been enlivened, and senior union figures occasionally irritated, by his specific and waspish interventions against nuclear power and in pursuit of detail on the union's financial affairs. His speech won the conference: 'Are we never going to learn? When I find the left are leaning over backwards to support our executive, I *know* we have got it wrong.' He alleged it was *really* being done to facilitate an amalgamation with the engineering workers (something else he was opposed to!). The communists had cost Jock Byrne and Les Cannon their lives. He opposed lifting the ban 'not for the next five years, not for twenty-five years, but for ever'. If Don Cook's passion was persuasive, so was Alf Goodson's modest charm. Alf Goodson had been branch secretary of Boston, in Lincolnshire, branch for many years. He was a union gold badge winner. He had been a witness in the High Court for Jock Byrne twenty-eight years before. He urged retaining the ban. The conference voted comfortably to endorse all the other liberalizing measures; but voted equally emphatically to keep the ban.

The third main issue that the left sought to use to regain control of the union was to insist that all conference decisions should be binding on the executive council. Branches were attended by few people and offered a better chance for organized political groups to gain control than postal ballots for executive Council elections. The constitutional position advanced by the leadership over the years is that conference is important, but not supreme. Eight hundred delegates elected from every branch and shop-steward conference look good in the great conference halls of Britain. Nevertheless, the delegates are elected by less than two per cent of the union's total membership, compared to nearly forty per cent turn-outs in secret postal ballots for leadership elections by the late 1980s. In any case it is rare for conference to fall out with the leadership. One great issue where it did occur was at the 1981 conference. The union's negotiators in the contracting industry had been trying to establish an occupational health screening service for the wandering contracting electricians. The National Health Service (NHS) could not provide a national scheme. The employers found the private health care company British United Provident Society (BUPA) would, but only if the scheme taken out for the contracting membership was a comprehensive one. In June 1979, the employers offered the scheme. Contracting electricians were offered the private treatment involved or a cash benefit of £91 per week in lieu when they were eventually treated by the NHS.

The union's national committee for contracting accepted the deal – just one area official on the committee was against. The 1980 contracting shop-stewards conference at Eastbourne did not have a single motion of opposition put up to the scheme. The first 3,500 members screened at mobile centres across the country in the first eighteen months of the scheme revealed evidence of over sixty serious diseases.

For the union it was a genuine quandary. The members in contracting had been offered a genuine improvement in their standard of living. The union leadership did not feel it could oppose it in the interests of Labour's defence of the Health Service and a principled objection to private health schemes. They accepted the idea. This brought a storm of abuse at the TUC from unions who turned out to have similar schemes for groups of their members and the Health Service unions like the Confederation of Health Service

Employees (COHSE) and NUPE – who appeared to have preferential health arrangements for their own full-time officials, never mind members!

The 1981 EETPU policy conference was not dogged by hypocrisy like that. However, the clear majority of delegates felt that in defence of the Health Service, the union should not have signed the contracting scheme. Eric Hammond's long, sensible, and cool explanation of the factors involved reads better than it sounded, as he himself said it would at the time. The executive were defeated. They dealt with the constitutional difficulty with some sensitivity. Despite their own convictions and the demands of many other groups of members for similar deals, the executive would not negotiate new schemes while still maintaining that the contracting deal stuck.

Elections in the Modern Union

The executive council had been shaken by the strong electoral challenge of the left to sitting executive councillors in the elections that spread over from 1970–71. In Scotland, the left's candidate was Charlie Montgomery, whose father before him had been the left's candidate against Willie Turnbull from 1928–38. In the early 1970s, the left in Scotland was vocal, well-organized and energized by the examples of Upper Clyde Shipbuilders (UCS), the Scottish miners' leadership and the anti-Tory atmosphere engendered by the early days of the Heath Government's attack on the unions associated with the Industrial Relations Bill. In trade-union politics, no prize could be greater for the left than a return to electoral triumph in the EETPU. The eventual investigation into the executive election in Scotland that had taken place at the end of 1970 was to reflect this keen determination on both sides of the political divide. The country was deluged with pamphlets, stickers and a travelling band of supporters of Charlie Montgomery visiting building sites and factories with considerable frequency. Pye at Airdrie was a typical case where electricians from Glasgow Corporation had come out to see the shop-stewards' committee in the factory canteen to press Charlie Montgomery's case. They handed out literature and pamphlets to be distributed amongst 1,000 of the union's members in the plant at that time. Charlie Montgomery's riposte to all this was that it was unfair to blame him for leaflets he did not write or distribute personally. Anyway, it was more than suspicious that just at election time, the amount of phone calls to shop stewards, circulars from the office over sitting executive councillor Bill Blairford's name and visits to sites by full-time officials had dramatically increased. All this on top of a failed attempt to have him expelled from the union the previous year for taking part in *Flashlight* meetings (*Flashlight* had become the unofficial newspaper which faithfully reflected the Communist Party's view of union affairs).

The union rules had always been quite clear. The executive council could set aside an election result if the pamphleteering and 'interference' involved with the propaganda being disseminated during the campaign interfered with the eventual result. Charlie Montgomery had 'won' the election by 4,201 votes to 3,598. The executive launched an investigation into the election. Bill Blairford and Charlie Montgomery gave evidence, along with other officials, staff and shop-stewards in Scotland. Blairford revealed details of the year-long campaign against the union's leadership which (given the president's death in December 1970) reached a new low of tastelessness in the delivery of two coffins to the union's area office – one for Les Cannon and one for Bill Blairford. In August 1971, the executive voted, 7–4, to call for a fresh election. Charlie Montgomery challenged this decision in the courts. On 17 November 1971, Mr Justice Megarry effectively supported the executive council's action. He was also convinced about the pamphleteering affecting the result. 'As to the contention that there was no evidence on which members of the executive council could, as reasonable men, reach conclusions that there had been a breach of rule, I can only say that there was ample evidence.' In December 1971, the election was rerun and Bill Blairford this time retained the seat by 4,614 votes to Charlie Montgomery's 3,088.

This feeling of resurgence on the left was underlined by the very strong showing of Fred Gore in the North-West London seat at the same time. Bill Blair held on there, having virtually doubled his own vote since 1966, but only achieved a tiny majority of 2,967–2,830 over Gore. When the third candidate's, Bill Capell's, votes were redistributed, the gap was even narrower, 3,392–3,278. This election, too, produced reams of election material in support of Fred Gore. The campaign was enthusiastically linked to those of the other 'progressive' candidates running for the executive at the end of 1970. A complete slate was published by *Flashlight* across the country (including Charlie Montgomery) which was dutifully reported in the *Morning Star*. Stickers and professionally printed circulars backed Fred Gore's campaign. These circulars would contain, from the leadership's point of view, infuriating allegations that, if true, would do the leadership great harm. The anonymously-written pamphlet that was distributed for Fred Gore asserted as proof of the undemocratic leadership of the union that: 'Rule changes have been engineered to abolish elections of officials, of area committees, of rank-and-file appeals committee, and rank-and-file trustees.' The key word is 'engineered'. It implies clever, malevolent, evil, deliberate hoodwinking. In actual fact, the changes to the rules regarding the appointment of area officials, the appeals committee problem and the trustees replaced by a legal, conventional and unremarkable company for holding the union's property were all decided by a secret postal ballot of the whole membership by huge majorities – nothing to do with leadership manipulation. Area Committees were abolished at a properly constituted rules revision conference in 1965 attended by a delegate from every branch.

Evidence emerged from previously keen supporters of the left of the extent of the campaign: an organizing committee had been set up in Blair's division as far back as February 1970 to organize policy decisions at the industrial conferences and then the branch nominations at the executive council election in the autumn. The committee met at regular monthly intervals in Hendon and organized others at Wealdstone and South Harrow Co-op Halls. It was alleged that Stan Davidson, a member of the Communist Party, was the link between the organizing committee in Blair's division, the other divisional committees who were supporting the 'progressive' candidates and *Flashlight* magazine.

During the first six months of 1971, the sense of political tension rose in the union. The context here is important. Just ten years after the ballot-rigging trial, the left had regrouped round a new band of standard-bearers. The general political atmosphere, in the wake of the power workers' dispute and the Upper Clyde Shipbuilders controversy was very promising for the left. Unemployment was rising fast towards one million. Within the Labour Party, a ferocious row had emerged over membership of the European Economic Community (EEC). Despite the executive's support for the EEC, they balloted the membership on the issue. The members voted, 68,797–35,002 – the biggest ballot in the union's history – to reject entry into the Common Market. The Industrial Relations Bill debate had crystallized into a requirement by the TUC that unions should de-register from the Government's list of 'approved' unions. Frank Chapple, in his speech to the special Congress at Croydon in March 1971, was cautious in his approach. His suggestion of a strike-free year to demonstrate to the country that the unions could control themselves was greeted with derision. That derision found an echo on the executive council. Jack Ashfield told the engineering area conference of shop-stewards on 23 March that Chapple's statement was not executive council policy and that his pledge of a year of no strikes – to 'Kill the Bill' (Industrial Relations Bill) by kindness ... brought the union into disrepute and Brother Chapple should be censured.' Ashfield did not get very far on the executive, losing 10–2 (along with Charlie Lovell) about the speech itself and later in the year drawing a narrow vote of censure on himself for going round area industrial conferences criticizing the union's leadership. Although quoted in the *Flashlight* magazine, Jack Ashfield was not motivated by pro-communist ideas. His motivation was slightly more straightforward, as we shall see. Frank Chapple knew that there were important tax benefits for registered unions (worth £30,000 in 1972). More important, only registered unions were to have access to the courts in recognition ballots and other legal proceedings that would prevent smaller unions winning recognition in large national agreements held by conventional unions. This was particularly worrisome, at least potentially, for the EETPU in electricity supply. Since 1966, the unions in supply were occasionally pestered by the Electricity Supply Union (ESU), a tiny 'union' founded in 1966. They had no structure, no officials and the general secretary was a market gardener. In 1970, the ESU had spent £68! Its total assets were £716 and it apparently neither spent not received any money in 1971. Notwithstanding all this, the registrar had allowed the ESU on to the register. They promptly applied at the National Industrial Relations Court for negotiating rights within the industry on the grounds that they had sufficient members at Ferrybridge 'C' Power Station. The court turned down the application. However, the left in the union portrayed the leadership's fears of the ESU as secondary to the scandal involved in the union ignoring the TUC policy in its determination to defend the EETPU's interests in the 'Tory courts'.

Disputes in the Leadership

In March 1971, a national officer, Mark Young, commenced legal proceedings against the executive council to demand the holding of prompt elections for the post of general president of the union – a post no doubt for which Mark Young intended to run. In October 1970, knowing he was dying, Les Cannon had visited the executive for the last time. All staff members were excluded from the room and Les Cannon gave the executive members a last talk concerning his view of the union's future, including possible developments in its structure. He was convinced that the union should not keep the post of general president. Having two senior national positions in the union could only lead to rivalry and confusion in the members' minds. The union was indeed lucky that there had been no trouble between Cannon and Chapple (apart from the day Les Cannon interfered with the general secretary's responsibility under the rule-book by dealing with his own office removals, which Cannon had once attempted without permission). The role of the general secretary had always been the premier position in the union, and Les Cannon was now recommending that after he went, there should simply be the general secretary, perhaps assisted by three assistant general secretaries. In the early months of 1971, newspaper articles started to appear that gave fulsome praise to Mark Young's record in the Reform Group and his contemporary expertise as a competent, personable national officer of the union. Vincent Hanna, writing in the *Sunday Times* on 17 January 1971, described Mark Young as an 'able, tough bargainer, and regarded as left of centre. He stands on a reformist ticket.' Kenneth Cooper wrote in the *Newcastle Evening Chronicle* of Mark Young as 'the man most likely to succeed the late Les Cannon as general president of the powerful ETU.' This particular article in

Young's home-town newspaper spoke of his family background in the Scots-wood Road and his passion for Newcastle United. Almost reaching the level of a fan-club magazine, it gushed on: 'Mark Young has travelled a well-trodden path, carrying from his working-class background the burden of social injustice, through the ideological furnace of the Communist Party into the mellowing atmosphere of practical trade unionism.' The sense of a gathering campaign building behind Mark Young was further underlined by the publication in the *Radio Times* of a picture of Les Cannon, advertising the programme *Testament of Courage* about his life – with Mark Young alone sitting next to the late president.

In parallel with the desire in certain quarters to speed up the general president election, a fierce controversy broke out surrounding the arrangement for the general secretary election in March 1971. Here, the focus of dispute was the slightly unlikely figure of Jack Ashfield, the Midlands executive councillor. Ashfield maintained that as legal opinion said executive councillors like him could not stand for the general president election as they were already on the executive, the same thing applied to Frank Chapple who was going to apply for re-election as the general secretary. There was confusion between the general rules – in force from 1968–71 – the old ETU rules and the old PTU rules in advance of the 1971 rules revision conference of the amalgamated EETPU. Ronald Waterhouse QC's legal opinion said that any member could stand for election, based on the 1965 rules, for any official's job in the union (and at that time all area officials as well as senior national office holders were all elected) so long as they were not full-time executive councillors at the time – unless they resigned first. The same counsel, on 10 February 1971, was asked if any other full-time officials (i.e. national officers like Mark Young) could run for general president. Here, the legal opinion also turned on the 1965 ETU rules which said a full-time official could not run for the full-time executive council – the intention in 1965 being that the executive was for the first time to become full-time and therefore it ought to have formerly lay-members on it, rather than full-time officials. Consequently, full-time officers like national officers could *not* run for general president, as the general president was an integral part of the executive council – chairing their proceedings and possessing a casting vote. However, the general secretary, although a full-time officer, was described in the rules separately from other executive councillors; on that basis he could be nominated for the job of general secretary (or general president) on the grounds that he was probably *not* an 'executive councillor' in the same way as the president was.

All of this is very confusing. However, it had very clear political implications. Firstly, the February executive council meeting decided to postpone the general president election by seven votes to five (Charlie Lovell, Jack Ashfield, Don Sheasby, Ernie Hadley and Jim McKernan). This produced legal action from Mark Young on two grounds; first, that it was illegal for the union to postpone the election, and second, Mark Young was surely entitled to be a candidate when the election was held. In mid-May 1971, Justice Ungoed-Thomas decided that the executive had power to delay the general president's election until after the rules revision conference had met to produce an amalgamated rule-book. The 1968 Instrument of Amalgamation had said as much; that the executive council could postpone executive council vacancies at their discretion until the rules revision conference made clear the future shape of the executive in an amalgamated union. Cruelly for Mark Young, and his gathering campaign, the question, therefore, of his eligibility to stand did not come into it.

By May 1971, the executive had to review the candidates for the general secretary election. Mark Young had not taken his disappointment lying down. He had got himself nominated for general secretary – just to see the level of support he had in the branches, which was to prove considerable. Just before the election, he withdrew his nomination and it was widely understood that his supporters were recommended to vote for Fred Gore, who had come so close to beating Bill Blair in that executive election the previous year. Jack Ashfield got as far as writing his election address before he was ruled out on the basis of the previous legal advice. He attacked Frank Chapple by implication by saying that the union existed for its members, 'not merely to build up big central funds'. He also claimed that 'the idolatry of individuals is the road to nowhere' and referred to his negotiating expertise and a concern about administrative matters. The eventual election result must have come as a mighty relief to the leadership in the midst of this legal and political maelstrom. Frank Chapple, in *his* election address, spoke of 'doubling the general funds' among many other things. He got 65,231 votes – three times as many as in 1966. Fred Gore got 18,132 and the Socialist Labour League's Jimmy Dormer got 12,007, whether because he called for an 'indefinite General Strike' or in spite of it, it is hard to judge.

After the 1971 rules revision conference was over, the executive called for nominations for general president in January 1972. The election was held in June. Once more, the election was held against a rising sense of crisis as the union's leadership put off a decision to de-register under the Industrial Relations Act, threatening potential confrontation with the TUC. Fred McGuffie had narrowly won his Northern Plumbers executive seat by under 300 votes. The reorganization of London branches, with opposition centring on the appointment of full-time branch officers like Bill Seaman in London West, was providing further grounds for left-wing activity.

The candidates in the election for president included Roy Sanderson, the newly appointed national officer for engineering. He came from Sheffield originally, but had worked at Rotax in Hemel Hempstead where he became the union's convenor. Without having much to do with the Foulkes/Haxell head office manifestation of communist influence in the union, he had been directly elected by the party's congress to its executive for four years, resigning in 1965. He said then that the party was ineffectual, did not complain about Khrushchev's demolition, failed to properly react to the ETU ballot rigging and attributed its difficulties to its failure to throw off the prejudices of the Stalin era which 'owes its origin not to truth and proven facts but to lies and historical distortion'. He had worked for the union for some years as an area official and assistant education officer, before becoming a national officer. He got 3,834 votes, but put down a 'marker' of his intentions to take a prominent role in the future. Jimmy Dormer once again took advantage of the union paying for the free circulation of the Socialist Labour League's manifesto dressed up as his election address. This time he got 5,820 votes. Eric Hammond also ran in this national election, but his candidature was not the central issue on this occasion and he got 7,108 votes. The left-backed candidate as usual was Fred Gore, and he got 10,747 votes.

The real attention in this election was always going to be spotlighted on Mark Young. His campaign attracted much support from union officials as well as branches and shop stewards who remembered his prominent role in the Reform Group. He was no left-winger, but supported the popular policy of electing all officials. He enjoyed significant support in the media and was perceived as a dangerous candidate on the basis that members could vote for 'change' (i.e. against Frank Chapple) without feeling guilty about electing an obvious left-wing *Flashlight* man like Fred Gore. He must have been disappointed with 10,942 votes. The result was declared in August 1972. The union's charismatic education officer, Jock Haston, for one, was so disappointed he resigned in October 1972. His later work for the GMWU and for countless management groups was always appreciated; for Jock Haston, though, Esher Place remained his spiritual home. Just before he died, he attended a cele-bration at Esher of thirty years of trade union training where he held a cheerful conversation with Frank Chapple and told the current national officer for education that he wished he'd never left Esher.

For Mark Young, his challenge to Frank Chapple had failed. Chapple got 44,623 votes – four times Mark Young's vote – and proceeded to use his mandate on this constitutional issue. On 20 August 1973, Mark Young's mandate as an elected official ran out and he applied to the executive for appointed status. He was not reappointed, by ten votes to two (Charlie Lovell and Don Sheasby). After a brief period keeping the wolf from the door at the ASTMS as a research officer, he was appointed general secretary of the British Airline Pilots' Association, a position he has filled with notable public success.

Throughout the mid-1970s, the left were not down-hearted. They had genuine electoral success at last. In February 1973, the union's new area boundaries and executive council division boundaries were tidied up to accommodate three plumbing executive divisions (North of England, South of England, and Scotland and Ireland). With the retirement of Harry Gittins in London from the executive, London and the Home Counties were rearranged to give three executive seats radiating out into the Home Counties. The fourth seat, previously held in London, was reallocated to the North and North-East, in advance of Ernie Hadley retiring in September 1973. There were now two Northern seats – one for the North-East from Middlesbrough northwards and the other for Yorkshire and Lincolnshire. In December 1973, the two new seats held executive elections, along with the Scottish plumbers' seat. This election only became necessary when Ian Clark, the Scottish Plumbing executive member, died dreadfully prematurely on 20 January 1973. He had been a courageous and articulate supporter of the amalgamated union and had brought real spirit to his contributions to the union's leadership. He was a keen admirer of some of the main themes that Les Cannon had been fond of – particularly the pursuit of productivity bargaining to raise the living standards of craftsmen. He was instrumental in the establishment of the Plumbing Joint Industry Board. For the first time in construction and elsewhere, Plumbers were in control of their own negotiations rather than having to join in with the Building Workers Federation or to depend on the CSEU. Ian Clark launched that independence, along with his colleagues, and he was specially missed for years after by Charlie Lovell, the Plumbers' national secretary.

In the North-East, the seat was won by Phil Ramshaw. He got 1,447 votes to local recruitment officer Barry Davis's 1,161. Sunderland's Steve Alcock got 1,033. Three other candidates got over 1,300 votes between them. In Yorkshire, one left-winger, Harold Best, after resigning as Leeds City full-time branch officer, was opposed by three well-known moderates. He received 1,596 votes. Brothers Barker (1,395), Nelson (1,210) and Wright (889) well and truly split the moderate vote.

In both elections, the single transferable vote was used, and the process of eliminating the bottom-of-the-poll candidates started with their second preference being reallocated.

In both elections, however, most second votes were not used at all. Phil Ramshaw got 2,027 against Barry Davis's 1,702 in the final count – well under fifty per cent of the votes cast. Harold Best's final score was 2,031 against Brother Barker's 1,870 – again, well under fifty per cent of the votes cast.

There was no getting away, however, from the resurgence of the left. Hector Barlow, in Scotland, the favoured candidate of the 'Plumber's Action Group' only had his 'victory' disallowed because 2,350 ballots sent to plumbers in Eire did not have the necessary pre-paid envelopes included. The election became a controversy in its own right, constantly postponed as each candidate complained about each other and there occurred the usual arguments about the content of election addresses. In December 1975, Hector Barlow was at last elected by 2,035 votes to John Gaffney's 1,546 and P. Sweeney's 447.

All three in 1973 sought the election of full-time officials. Phil Ramshaw's election address was fairly obvious in intent. He wanted the union, according to *Flashlight*, to 'hear our union once again described as left-wing, to end prevailing apathy in branches and in jobs'. He was 'disgusted' at Frank Chapple holding both main jobs in the union. He thought Mark Young's sacking was 'vindictive'. Hector Barlow bemoaned the ending of the small pension paid to superannuated plumbers, even though the 1973 conference had abolished 'Table Z' payments as an obvious drain on the union's funds. He also wanted the return of district committees. Harold Best wanted greater consultation with members before agreements were signed.

In the meantime, Frank Chapple and the majority of the executive were determined to press on in getting the shape of the leadership machine right. They brought in a consultant – Jim Houston, the neutral chairman of the JIB – who recommended the abolition of the post of general president at a saving of £10,000 a year. The general secretary's administrative duties could be formally devolved, to an extent, to the divisional executive councillors and the residual, important jobs for a president – chairing the union's executive and conferences – could be done by the executive council electing one of their members annually to do the job. The executive accepted this in 1974 by eight votes to four (Harold Best, Phil Ramshaw, Eric Hammond and Don Sheasby) and balloted the members, who also agreed with the idea by the huge majority of 77,943 to 17,221 in December 1974.

The leadership of the union was never let alone. We have seen how the union's rule changes since 1965 provided clear internal priorities for left activity. This was reinforced by their campaigns against the Conservative Government incomes policy in the early 1970s, the Industrial Relations Act and the development of productivity bargaining. One special issue stood out as a continuous internal concern that the left hawked round the rest of the movement in order to increase the pressure on the EETPU's leadership.

'Remember the IRO'

As a deliberate attempt to do something about rising unemployment on Merseyside, the Wilson Government allocated an enormous office block to the town of Bootle for an Inland Revenue Office (IRO) for the North-West region. This site had a chequered history from the late 1960s onwards, and when McAlpine took over as main contractors, they paid all sorts of bonuses to people in order that the contract should not slip too far behind in time.

This resulted in a familiar problem; the sixteen electricians on the site were being paid JIB rates by James Scott & Lee & Beesley's. Their earnings were far behind the wages of labourers, whose earnings were boosted by site bonuses, let alone other craftsmen. From 11 February 1971 to 6 January 1976, there was a virtually continuous series of strikes by the electricians on the site. They were led by John Byrne, a young articulate Communist Council candidate who immediately spotted the potential of the IRO dispute. First, there was the justifiable grievance of pay on the site. For him and his friends, this justified the strike, without any reference to the negotiating machinery. The fact was that the JIB was negotiating the thorny problem of extra payments for large sites. However, the political dimension of the strike became apparent very quickly. Byrne, and his close associate, Tommy Henderson, organized regular marches round the site, sent leaflets and speakers to all sorts of other sites attacking the JIB and the union's leadership's apparent refusal to help the strikers. Stan Simpson, the union's local official, had a rough ride at their hands as he tried to sustain the constitutional position; the union could not support unofficial strikers who were trying to smash the negotiating machinery that had been designed by and signed by the regularly elected leadership of the union on behalf of 60,000 contracting electricians – virtually all of whom were working normally.

The strike dragged on; the IRO propaganda was never-ending. Money was collected everywhere for the brave strikers – most of whom worked quietly 'on the lump' and shared out over £35,000 collected over the years. The issue was raised in Parliament. The local trades council tried to involve the TUC. There were attempts by Byrne to call himself shop-steward – although under the rules, a communist could not hold office. Labour Party conference delegates were leafleted. A six-point 'peace' plan, drawn up by the local newspaper, the *Bootle Times*, was actually put to Frank Chapple to sign on a live edition of the TV programme, *24 hours*. The employers were a difficulty throughout. McAlpine were not JIB members and the union leadership feared they would collapse; in a sense they did. In 1974, they negotiated directly with the strikers and got them paid on a different construction industry agreement, 'borrowing' the electricians from the JIB firms so as to avoid having to pay JIB rates. No sooner, however, had they done that than they felt obliged to sack Byrne for various absences and misdemeanours – real and imagined – round the site associated with his trade union and political activity. The union would not support them until the strikers undertook to obey the rules (which meant among other things stopping the Communist Party member, Byrne, being the shop-steward) and so it went on. The real significance of the dispute, however, remained the evidence it produced of organized, supportive activity for Byrne and friends in the increasingly intense left-right war in the union. After the McAlpine concession, a 'victory' dance was held in Bootle for over 300 supporters, with invitations going out to Fred Gore (who was presented with a commemorative plaque), Frank Foulkes and Charlie Montgomery. The leadership of the union stood firm. It was a confrontation they had to go through with in defence of the JIB. Throughout this period, other groups of anti-JIB activists made a sporadic impact in strikes in places like the St Thomas's Hospital site and the Alcan site at Lynemouth. Nevertheless, the integrity of the JIB was sustained, however much the left and *Flashlight* urged the union's members to 'Remember the IRO'.

Slipping away from the Left: Elections 1975–88

We have seen how the 1977 biennial delegate conference saw decisive victories for the executive council on all the main rules revision ambitions that the left had assembled for Blackpool at that conference. Their electoral ambition, elevated to a new height with the victories of Phil Ramshaw, Harold Best and Hector Barlow, was now to go into seemingly irreversible decline. It had already started to wane. At the end of 1975, Eddie Sabino's prominent support for the IRO strikers did him no good at all in the executive council elections. He improved his 1970 votes by 104 to 3,004. However, his opponent was Tom Breakell, the new president, elected now by his executive colleagues. Breakell had been in the middle of the IRO issue locally. He had taken the abuse for accusing the Shrewsbury pickets of being 'gangsters' when they had been imprisoned for conspiracy arising out of violence on picket lines. None of this hurt him at all with the ordinary members. His vote shot up just over 5,000 to 8,694. Bernard Clarke in Wales beat the left-supported Wyn Bevan, 8,236–3,766. Bill Blair destroyed Fred Gore, 9,518–3,810, and Eric Clayton comfortably beat Ford electrician John Aitken, 7,483–2,788. Before the election, most attention concentrated on Eric Hammond's seat where he was under challenge from popular local full-time official Bill Banning. He got 3,549 votes, but Hammond had doubled his 1970 vote to 8,611. *Flashlight* candidate Jim Atkinson came nowhere with 1,692 votes and the Trotskyist left-winger Ginger Pearse got 649 votes. These victories in 1975 were truly decisive in giving the leadership some feeling of confidence once again that the left were not going to make a decisive comeback. This feeling was confirmed in mid-1976 when the general secretary election was held. Frank Chapple was favourite to win, but all eyes were on how close executive councillor Harold Best would get to him. Best was known for his leftist views, although he never had the raucous manner and the personal association with the intimidation and ferocity occasionally revealed by some of his supporters with a contracting background. Neither Fred Gore nor John Byrne wanted to be the *Flashlight* standard bearer. Harold Best looked better on the ballot paper, given his executive status and experience within the union. He was still beaten out of sight. Frank Chapple added over 19,000 votes to his 1971 total and beat Harold Best,

83,902–24,278. The rather excitable Welsh contracting candidate, a member of the Socialist Workers Party, Billy Williams, got 10,274.

There was one last decisive victory for the left in the 1970s. At the end of the decade an election was held to replace Bernard Clarke, who had tragically and suddenly died in September 1978. Wyn Bevan was a noted opponent of the executive council. He was a steelworker who had been the union's convenor at Port Talbot for ten years. His appeal concentrated on skilled men getting paid for their technology-based skills, but added the election of officials and the reintroduction of area committees. Apart from the Socialist Workers Party's Billy Williams, Bevan was opposed by four opponents – local official Don Jones, a fellow steelworker from Ebbw Vale, Colin Hudson, a senior shop-steward in engineering, Alan Slocombe, and Devonport Dockyard shop-steward and branch secretary John Crabb. The election result was extremely close. On the first ballot, Bevan was top of the poll with 1,903 votes, Williams bottom on 991, with 8,678 votes cast between the six candidates. Bevan eventually defeated John Crabb, 3,166–2,467, but once again most second preferences were not exercised. Nevertheless, the election was rerun because of the enormous amount of pamphleteering, in particular because of the way that Billy Williams urged all his voters to vote for Wyn Bevan as a second preference. A second ballot was held and declared in July the following year. This time, Wyn Bevan got 2,904 first preferences: by the time the second preferences were redistributed he beat EESA's Welsh hospital engineer Wally Haines, 3,698–2,677. Wyn Bevan's membership of the executive council took on an important association with the crucial single-union deals, several of the most important of which were situated in his division. We shall look at that in a moment.

One of the side-effects of the Bevan election and others was a change in the rules affecting executive council elections. If no candidate achieved fifty per cent of the votes cast, even after the second preferences had been allocated, then a second run-off ballot was to be held. This proved to be a necessary reform both in the election of August 1981 when a run-off was needed for Harry Hughes to replace Bill Blair by beating Dick Allum by 224 votes, as well as when Frank Chapman beat Len Sturgess in a second ballot, 6,041–5,466, to replace Jack Ashfield in the Midlands.

If Wyn Bevan's eventual victory was a victory for the 'left' – at least at the time – their other standard bearers, Harold Best and Phil Ramshaw, fell in elections at the end of 1978. Bill Hayes, an EESA member and a senior manager at electrical contractors N. G. Bailey's, beat Harold Best, 4,147–3,712, an astonishing feat he repeated in 1983 by 6,628 votes to 4,298 in a thirty-eight per cent turn-out. In the first election Best complained that over 400 votes at Hayes's old workplace, N. G. Bailey's, had been distributed at work, rather than sent to each member's home. The Electoral Reform Society pronounced the election perfectly fair, given that the members got their voting papers, unopened, via the company's internal post.

Barry Davis this time beat Phil Ramshaw into third place and defeated Caterpillar Tractor's shop-steward John Jorden, 2,722–2,640, with the help of second preference votes. The modern executive council was augmented in 1978 by the election in Scotland of Alf McLuckie by 5,339 votes to Charlie Montgomery's 4,576 (a good total that would have nearly beaten the retired Bill Blairford if achieved five years earlier). In Manchester, replacing Don Sheasby who had died, was Manchester Central's full-time branch officer, Paul Gallagher, who beat the *Flashlight* candidate Harry Shaw, 4,401–3,431. In 1982, Paul Gallagher was re-elected unopposed. In 1987, he destroyed Harry Shaw in a thirty-eight per cent poll by 7,446 to 3,154 votes. He was later elected president after Tom Breakell retired in 1985. Alf McLuckie by then had two clear victories under his belt against the latest Scottish left-winger to try his luck, John O'Brien, the *Flashlight* unilateral nuclear disarmament specialist at conference. When Eric Hammond became general secretary in 1984, Lew Britz, who had been London area secretary, beat Paul Bevis for the vacant executive council seat by 5,956 votes to area official Paul Bevis's 3,744. When Eric Clayton retired in 1986, John Aitkin must have felt he had a chance. A prominent critic of the union, chairman of the pre-conference *Flashlight* rallies, he had first stood against Eric Clayton in East London and East Anglia in 1971. His opponent was Brendan Fenelon, who had come to London as a research officer of the union after his career as a shop-steward at British Leyland subsidiary, SU Carburettors. He had rapidly become an area official in London and eventually a national officer with responsibility for TV servicing and other service industries. Once again, it was not Aitkin's lucky day. Brendan Fenelon beat him, 6,135–2,846 in a $27\frac{1}{2}$ per cent poll. In the plumbing section of the union, the plumbers continued to elect Hector Barlow in Scotland and Ireland. After Fred McGuffie retired in 1985, Sellafield senior shop-steward Jim Egan beat the left's prominent conference speaker Ian Brown, 4,910–3,167. When Charlie Lovell retired in 1987, Bill Gannon beat Ian Brown for the national secretaryship, 7,642–6,580. This concluded a remarkable long march for the gently-spoken Irishman whom Les Cannon identified as a clever and unscrupulous opponent of the executive's in 1969. Bill Gannon beat Dave Fraser in a nation-wide election in 1971 to first win a seat on the executive, clearly to the leadership's chagrin. He was elected unopposed in 1975 and by miles in 1980 and 1985. He negotiates for the union's thousands of plumbers in local councils, the Health Service and throughout the plumbing industries and is widely respected throughout the movement, particularly by the other trade unions in construction. The significant feature of all these recent elections has been the rising turn-out. It is usually more than thirty per cent. Alf McLuckie's election in 1987 was a forty per cent turn-out, as was the contest when Hector Barlow thrashed a *Militant* newspaper supporter in 1985. The most recent endorsement of the leadership's general direction was of course Eric Hammond's re-election in July 1987 when, again in a forty per cent turn-out, he became the first general secretary in the union's history to exceed 100,000 votes when he beat John Aitkin, 108,146–36,684. Jimmy Rowan would not have believed such voting figures possible!

The Union and the Labour Party

The union's modern relationship with the Labour Party has, in some ways, mirrored its uneasy relationship with the TUC. But not in all ways. Members of the EETPU are to be found in high elective office throughout the movement and the union's support for its sponsored MPs and the financial backing given to local election candidates is unrivalled. Throughout the country, the union's officials and shop-stewards are active Labour Party members in their own right: over 1,000 are delegates to local constituency Labour parties. Many are agents and election organizers. Labour Party activity, for all its political frustrations, is an important part of their lives. Eric Hammond's experience as a Labour councillor and active canvasser remains an important example of the union's commitment to Labour by countless individuals as well as by the union as an institution.

Throughout the periods of Labour government in the 1960s and the late 1970s, the union gave its support to the Labour leadership under siege from an unfriendly world and an unfriendly left. That support was not uncritical. In the 1970s, for instance, the union was frustrated by Labour's economic policy, which appeared to do little for an embattled industrial base. The endless deputations to see government ministers to complain about the unopposed and unregulated flood of Japanese imports had little effect. The failure to provide a steady ordering programme for power stations kept the heavy engineering industry on tenterhooks. The Government in the mid-1970s allowed the Post Office to close down whole factories through slashing orders for tele-communications equipment whilst at the same time setting standards for electronic equipment that would be virtually unexportable. Rises and falls in consumer credit and VAT also disturbed the consumer electronics industry, on which 'hi-tech' companies ought to have been able to rely as a source of steady income for other investment. After the dreadful winter of 1978–79 – the winter of discontent – the union viewed with despair the self-destruction of the Labour movement through aggressive trade union behaviour. The defeat of Jim Callaghan's Government in the summer of 1979 brought to an end the era in which British trade union leaders could walk in the front door of no. 10 Downing Street. It was an era in which they probably did not make the best use of the opportunities presented: certainly, the public perceived them as greedy, selfish, aggressive if not downright violent – even unpatriotic. They had become 'the enemy within'.

Without the diversion of talking to the government of the day, the trade unions and the Labour Party fell to fighting themselves on an unprecedented scale. The union entered the constitutional and policy wars within the party after 1979 with several clear aims that lay behind each and every individual crisis. First, the trade unions were not and should not be a government in exile. The Labour Party was clearly disadvantaged in the public mind by its links with trade unions. The party must assert its separateness. The party's leaders had to avoid at all costs the impression that they were in the pockets of trade union barons. Second, the union was appalled as the left assault on the party's constitution from 1979–81 produced one important and dreadful misapprehension within the movement. The victories and manoeuvres of committees and conferences, where decisions were taken by the cynical purchase of affiliation power, were misrepresented as some sort of leftwards shift in the theoretical and political aims of the British working class. What was worse, this crazy misrepresentation was happening at the same time as Mrs Thatcher's Government was steadily persuading more individual citizens that the individualist market-based society offered them more than Labour's apparent reliance on state intervention and what were represented as crypto-communist sympathies. The Tories were able to create an impression that Labour was an obstacle to the good life, equivalent, at its best, to the Gas Board, or, at its worst, to the Gulag archipelago. The union was also determined not to let the intensifying faction war inside the Labour Party enter the union's affairs, and was therefore anxious to throw its weight behind 'moderate' causes within the party.

With those aims in mind, the union modernized its own political organization, starting with a change in the financial arrangements. By September 1974, the union's national political coffers were reduced to £36,000. And yet there was £45,000 in the branch political funds, much of it simply accumulated by branches who rarely affiliated to local parties or contributed to local Labour Party campaigns. The branch funds were amalgamated into the national funds, and all local affiliations paid by Head Office. A new local structure was designed in October 1975; piloted in London, it then became standard throughout the country. Each year, in each Labour Party region, the union holds a conference of all its delegates from branches to local management committees of Labour Parties within that region. In London, there are around 120 such delegates to 92 constituencies. These conferences are timed to take place just before the annual regional conference of the party, and the EETPU conference elects the delegation and discusses the agenda. Each regional conference also elects their representative to the union's delegation to the national Labour Party conference (taking such responsibility from the biennial delegate conference). They also elect annually a regional political advisory committee who administer £1,500 a year in extra political grants to local political causes, on the application of branches or the local Labour Party itself. Money has been spent on issues like helping local parties to computerize, pay for special events on unemployment or the NHS, and to underwrite the costs involved for the increasing number of parties who use one person/one vote in the selection of candidates for office. Finally, the regional annual political conferences of EETPU branch management committee delegates elect a representative to the national political advisory committee who advise the executive council on regional feeling among members, and on the union's political activities. They receive their own quarterly *Political Bulletin* to keep in touch. All this amounts to a responsive and participative political structure at both local and national level.

This structure is also more predictable in its financial commitments as the regional committees are allocated their money at fixed periods of the year. The union nationally retains its responsibility to pay all constituency affiliation fees and the whole union's national affiliation fees to the party; this figure has dropped over the years. Since 1975, the union has not affiliated on the basis of the number of members paying the political levy, which remains at the high percentage of ninety-two per cent. Partly because of policy differences, partly because the Labour Party's chaotic administration pushed up fees much faster than the union's contributions (one week's contribution is the political levy per year); partly because the union would prefer to make grants to members standing for local councillor than pour it down the throat of the Labour Party's insatiable head office; the size of the contribution is the same (£102,500) for an affiliation level of 136,000. The union also pays £1,500 a year to the Labour Party leader's office.

The union has had its ups and downs with its sponsored MPs – but never over how they should vote in either internal Labour Party matters or over policy issues. Tom Cox, MP for Tooting in south London, has been joined in recent years in Parliament by Stuart Randall, representing Hull West. David Stoddart lost his Swindon seat, but remains a prominent party spokesman in the House of Lords. Walter Harrison, the MP for Wakefield, retired in 1987 after years of service in the Whips' office, inside government and out. He was particularly helpful in the days of Labour government in gaining the union access to ministers. In 1982, the union's national officer for research, John Spellar, became the first Labour man to win a by-election from the Conservatives in years when he took Birmingham Northfield. Unfortunately, he was defeated at the 1983 and 1987 general elections, although he is currently the prospective candidate at a Warley seat with good prospects. The union's national political advisory committee and the executive councillors who have led the union's political effort (Eric Hammond and, recently, Ken Jackson) would be the first to recognize the debt the union owes John Spellar in the political field. He has worked tirelessly to make the regional structure work. He has chivvied and encouraged hundreds of the union's activists to add political work to their industrial activity. He has built an unrivalled network of contacts throughout the moderate groups in the unions and party alike. He is well known by his opponents. His robust demands for the party to throw off the imposition of revolutionary ideas peddled by the Militant Tendency led them to describe him as 'John Ex-peller!'. He was also an articulate proponent of the union's 'one-member-one-vote' philosophy. At the 1985 Labour Party conference, he spoke of making a choice between the conspiring party where committees ruled and a campaigning party where a mass membership governed. He was particularly scathing about the implications of left-wing arguments against one member/one vote.

I must say, one of the worst aspects of the debates over the years has been the disparaging way that the ordinary party members, the rank-and-file party members, are referred to in these debates. The élitism is, frankly, appalling. It smacks more of the aristocracy and squirearchy of bygone days than it does of the modern principles of democratic socialism. And it's backed up by a parrot cry of 'massive press interference'. It's as though we have two classes of members in the party. Those who can read the press and all these leaflets that we are handed on the way in, and it doesn't affect them at all, and ordinary party members who will be completely bemused by them. That is utter and arrogant élitism. I suppose we might, in the future, say they should be having special party cards for general committee members, just to show how special they are.

If those élitists arguments were being put anywhere else in the world we would reject them out of hand, and we should reject them here today.

In June 1976, the union sponsored an MP for the first time who was not a member of the union. John Grant, MP for Islington, was a junior minister in the Department of Employment. He had previously been a sympathetic journalist on the *Daily Express* at the time of the ballot-rigging and just after. As such, he knew the union's leadership well. The sponsorship reluctantly had to stop when he left the Labour Party to join the Social Democratic Party in December 1981. He later worked for the union as the editor of its magazine *Contact* after his defeat at the 1983 General Election.

During the 1970s and 1980s, the Labour Party was dominated by the internal war over the attempts of the left to change the party's constitution and policy to its liking. The EETPU, of course with others, was opposed to these developments and in conference or committee opposed them. In December 1976, the union was appalled at the failure to publish the Underhill Report on the activities of Militant; better late than never when action was at last taken to expel its leading figures and then confront the Liverpool councillors associated with the tendency. As early as 1977, the union made its views known on the election of the Labour leader. In February that year, the Union's policy was decided. The EETPU thought on balance that the Labour MPs should choose the party leader. If the 'widening of the franchise' was felt to be an overwhelming imperative, then the union would only support a complete one member/one vote solution. When the issue climaxed during the Tony Benn-inspired campaign at the Wembley Conference in 1981 (which led to the setting up of the Social Democratic Party), the union was still disappointed that the 'electoral college' was preferred to one member/one vote. The union was convinced that the British people were fearful of any Labour leader elected by the manipulation of forty per cent of the electoral college by the buying of extra affiliation levels in trade union bloc votes.

The EETPU would have preferred Denis Healey as Jim Callaghan's successor and was disappointed when its sponsored MPs did not vote unanimously for him. It was later to withdraw sponsorship from its Plumbing section-sponsored MP, Bob McTaggart, who represented Glasgow Central, for being too closely lined up with Benn's deputy leadership campaign in 1981 and the defence of Militant. Here too, fences were mended later in the decade and the sponsorship restored. It was a great disappointment when Bob McTaggart died suddenly in 1989.

In August 1981, at the height of the ferocious Healey–Benn deputy leadership election, Benn wrote to the executive council soliciting their support. Tony Benn was not the man he had been in 1969 when as Minister for Technology he addressed the union's biennial policy conference and 'wished them well'.

Any residual affection he felt for the EETPU was probably dissipated on receipt of the executive's response. Frank Chapple signed the letter accusing Tony Benn of 'duplicity' and of actually being part of that left-wing intellectual crowd who were in reality 'anti-Trade Union'. The letter was clear in its drift. 'The aggravation and conflict generated by those supporting your position are devastating the Labour Party and are unlikely to leave us in the position to attain the political power which we would clearly need to develop "the politics of partnership" of which you speak.'

With the mandatory re-selection of MPs and the electoral college introduced for party leadership elections, the union redoubled its concern to introduce one person/one vote into the party's internal electoral procedures. So disgusted were the leadership over the lack of internal democracy in the party that they decided not to take part in the 1983 leadership election in which Neil Kinnock and Roy Hattersley were first elected. The vote on the executive was only carried on chairman Tom Breakell's casting vote. This was not intended to reflect any lack of confidence in Neil Kinnock personally. The EETPU leadership had admired his courage (or 'balls' as Frank Chapple put it, slightly more colourfully) in standing out against the tide on Welsh devolution, effectively scuppering Tony Benn's deputy leadership campaign, and his informed support for other issues the union held dear like the rejection of worker directors as a panacea for industrial democracy and his keen support for industrial retraining for mid-life adults. Indeed, in 1984, the union resumed its £1,500 donation to the leader's office and grew increasingly impressed with Kinnock's reformation of the Labour Party machine and his confrontation with Militant.

All of these developments made sure that the overwhelming majority of the union's officials and activists stayed solidly in the Labour Party, despite the immense initial success of the SDP. John Grant had left the party and lost his sponsorship, and the retiring Frank Chapple took up his seat in the House of Lords on the cross-benches. None of this deflected the union's leadership from a strenuous campaign in 1985 to guarantee a 'yes' vote in the political fund ballot. The Government had required all unions to ballot on whether they kept their political fund or not. Initial opinion polls showed that only the NUM and the EETPU were likely to vote in favour. The movement as a whole did very well in sustaining the political funds. The EETPU campaigned hard. The union was unequivocal about the link with the Labour Party. The shop-stewards' quarterly review said in December 1984: 'Many of the privileges and freedoms we have enjoyed, and sometimes take for granted, are the product of the relationship between trade unions and the Labour Party.' John Spellar's campaign within the union boldly appealed to non-Labour voters. He argued that parliamentary democracy itself was at stake. For Parliament to function properly, it must have a legitimate opposition and alternative government. Labour could not fulfil that role without trade union financial support. In the union's special *Contact* supplement in support of having a political fund, shop-stewards who voted for the Alliance or the Conservatives warmly endorsed this fundamental political point. All sections of the Labour Party within the union campaigned hard as well. The result of the ballot involved the largest turn-out in the union's history – forty-five per cent. Eighty-four per cent (140,913) voted to retain the fund, and sixteen per cent (26,830) voted not to – an enormous endorsement of the leadership's position. The union used its usual methods of secret postal balloting which made the result all the more conclusive. F. E. Sims had attended the founding conference of the Labour Party at the turn of the century, when the union had only 956 members. The political loyalty of the ordinary members to Labour – whatever the policy differences that so infuriated the union over the years – remained steadfast. As the decade finished, the policies of the Party, following the 1989 policy review, returned to the mainstream which the EETPU had never left. No wonder that Eric Hammond told the hecklers at the Party conference that he could not understand why they didn't share his perception that the new policies had given him his best-ever week at a Labour conference.

27

THE EETPU AND THE MARCH TO INDEPENDENCE

THROUGHOUT THE 1970S AND 1980s the union has debated the role of law in trade union affairs within its own counsels and the counsels of the wider Labour movement. Since the 1960s, in the wake of Donovan, both Conservative and Labour governments have been interested in the proposition that the law could curtail disruptive trade union activity. It was vital to do so, since strikes had apparently destructive effects on the performance of the British economy. Unofficial strikes were the prime targets for government legislation, but related to the issue of stopping damaging strikes was the need to weaken trade union organizing conventions that made both unofficial and official strikes effective.

Within the union, and between the union and the majority view at the TUC, the fundamental issue was the trade unions' right to disobey or ignore the law. Most EETPU officials and shop-stewards would prefer the law to keep out of collective bargaining. There is a near-universal concern about lawyers' tricks, the class loyalty of judges being antipathetic to trade unions and the sheer complexity of American-style contract-based negotiations. But the left always overlaid this natural and traditional trepidation for the legal process with the bald assertion that 'bad' law could be broken with deliberate, virtuous determination. Jim Atkinson at the 1971 policy conference called the Industrial Relations Act 'the most vicious, politically-motivated class legislation since the early 1700s ... we hear that we should not oppose the elected government of this country. This is something that had our ancestors done, we would be working 100 hours a week for ten shillings a week, because we only advanced on the basis of the struggle ... a struggle which has meant deportation and imprisonment.' It is almost obligatory in such discussions to say, as D. C. Wildey, the Castle Donnington delegate, said in 1971: 'I would remind you when members are coming to the rostrum and talking about acting outside the framework of the law, the Tolpuddle martyrs worked outside the framework of the law (applause).' The same sort of remarks prefaced contributions at conferences throughout the 1980s in reaction to the two-yearly instalments of trade union legislation from Mrs Thatcher's Government. Throughout the period, the union's leadership were quite clear that however much they disliked certain parts of the legislation, the fundamental point was that there should not be industrial action to break the law or in seeking a confrontation with the properly elected government of the day. The basis of this view was best articulated by Eric Hammond at the Wembley TUC special conference in 1982, a conference called to organize the unions' opposition to the proposals associated with Secretary of State Norman Tebbit. Arthur Scargill had been arguing for industrial action in breach of bad law and justified this approach by quoting the example of the suffragettes' fight – against the law – for the vote. For the EETPU that was just the point. The suffragettes eventually won and in Britain we now have universal adult franchise. That changes everything. To organize industrial action against legislation proposed by a Government elected by universal adult franchise is to organize *against* democracy and not in its defence. Therefore, the union was always looking at ways to live with foolish anti-trade union law and to redouble its support for the Labour Party who would remove the foolish elements in that law. Of course, it has always been a further conviction of the modern leadership of the union that 'political strikes' alienate voters further from the trade unions and because of the close links with Labour, further distance the Labour Party from the possibilities of power. In dealing with Ted Heath's Industrial Relations Act, the union's leadership was in favour of registering under the Act in order to be able to defend itself in the Industrial Relations Courts, use the facility of applying for recognition of the union and use the industrial tribunals that were set up by that legislation. The TUC's policies, while rejecting industrial action against the law, was eventually to 'instruct' all unions to de-register and, therefore, by ignoring the legislation, make it inoperable. Frank Chapple spoke at the special Congress in March 1971. He did not think the law would help industrial relations. 'I do not know what sort of twisted reasoning can conclude that the right of trade unions and large employers to sue each other will improve the climate of industrial relations.' However, people started shouting at him when first he suggested that trade union eccentricities had cost Labour the 1970 General Election, and brought the house down when he suggested the TUC offer the Government a strike-free year of honoured agreements in return for the withdrawal of the legislation.

The union prevaricated on the question of coming off the register. The executive council itself was split on the subject. Charlie Lovell and Jack Ashfield registered their disapproval of Frank Chapple's Croydon speech. The executive put off a decision until the November 1971 biennial delegate conference, thus keeping an increasingly insistent TUC at bay. They accepted a motion at that conference that called on the union to support the TUC and de-register. In early 1972, a special executive council was held to consider the TUC's 'instruction' to de-register by 30 June 1972. Once again they postponed a decision and invited Vic Feather to explain the TUC's position to the executive at the June executive meeting. Jack Ashfield, Bill Blair and two plumbing executive members – Charlie Lovell and the impressive, thoughtful Scottish plumber, Ian Clark – wanted to ballot the members; the rest of the executive wanted to wait till June.

By this time, the union had tried to use occasional bits of the legislation, stretching the word 'defensive' to its utmost to keep in line with TUC policy. Resisting the ESU's application for negotiating rights was one thing; allowing the recruitment officer, Jack Britz, to use the recognition procedures to get the union to supplant a staff association for British Relay Television Servicing Managers was quite another.

Vic Feather came to the executive and urged prompt de-registration. The executive now agreed to ballot the members on the subject, with a recommendation to stay on the register in defiance of TUC policy. Jim McKernan and Eric Hammond voted against adding the recommendation. The other ten councillors clearly backed staying on the register.

On 24 July, the union was in receipt of a summons from the TUC to appear under Rule 13 (bringing the movement into 'disrepute'). They were due to appear two days later, on 26 July, to accept disciplinary action that would lead to expulsion from the TUC. In the meantime, five TGWU trade unionists had been sent to prison for refusing to obey a National Industrial Relations Court instruction to stop picketing at a container depot outside the dock areas. The 'Pentonville Five' aroused spontaneous and widespread industrial action; the TUC were planning national action in their defence. The executive's position was untenable with trade unionists in prison and they unanimously voted to de-register the union on 24 July 1972. The union's leadership, however, were then appalled by the merciless persecution at the 1972 congress of the smaller trade unions who *had* remained on the register. The National Graphical Association (NGA) were expelled, despite their rules preventing them legally coming off the register. The Seamen and Equity were expelled for registering to get an 'approved' closed shop that alone stopped both their different industries from being flooded by adventurers and amateurs. Frank Chapple was deliberately not called at the Congress that was busy hearing appeals and expelling the smaller unions. He used an old propaganda trick to great effect: 'The speech they would not let me make!' which was highlighted throughout the media; it drew attention to the TUC's blunt refusal to treat the other unions' cases as exceptions and highlighted the ostrich-like insistence of Congress in refusing to negotiate with the Government over the necessary changes to the Industrial Relations Act. That must have made good breakfast-time reading for Frank Chapple's General Council colleagues.

The opposition to the 1980s legislation was a pale echo of the opposition to the 1971 Industrial Relations Act. It centred around the Wembley conference of trade union executives held on 5 April 1982. The 1980 Act had extended the opportunities for people seeking to leave closed shops and had prevented the use of secondary pickets, restricting picketing to trade unionists' own places of work. It had also made it illegal to engage or get rid of sub-contractors on the basis of their compliance with the demands of trade unions in terms of wages or union membership. The 1982 legislation, introduced by Norman Tebbit, further developed these ideas by requiring all existing closed shops to have a massive endorsement in a secret ballot or anyone dismissed from a closed shop would automatically be entitled to hugely enhanced compensation payments that the union may be partly liable for. Fundamentally, Tebbit altered the definition of a legal dispute to effectively ban most types of 'secondary' action – blacking, boycotting, sympathy strikes. The penalties would be imposed by allowing employers to sue unions for damages for any breach of the law; they could also use injunctions to end action that would attract punitive fines for contempt if the action complained of didn't stop immediately.

The union had a growing ambivalence about the operation of the closed shop. Arguably, the union grew at a faster pace in its early years through the judicious use of refusing to work with non-unionists, of appealing for strong groups not to handle the work of the weak until their employers played fair with the newly organized workers. Electricians and plumbers in construction do not expect their unions to be sued when they seek to prevent underqualified, low-cost, cowboy contractors undermining the terms and conditions of workers on larger, organized sites. Over the years, the union has become less theological about the closed shop: the tenor of the times is not in favour of dragooning people into unions, even if the law of the late 1980s allowed it, which it doesn't. The modern EETPU tends to make a virtue instead of the union's membership all being volunteers – a type of membership from whom you can normally rely upon slightly more in an emergency than 'pressed' men. The union's earlier reaction to Jim Prior's legislation at a TUC conference of principal officers held on 22 January 1980 revealed its principled determination to treat each proposal on its merits. The union had no argument with postal ballots funded by the Government. As far as the closed shop went, 'It would be quite wrong for us to insist that workers with long service should be sacked for refusing to join a trade union. Additionally, some unions had been using [the Labour Government's closed shop] legislation to deliberately exclude other affiliated unions from organizing in particular workplaces and industries.' The ban on secondary picketing, however, was different (and entirely divorced from the debate about violence). 'The picketing proposals were far more serious and the TUC should deal with them exclusively and not handicap itself with having to oppose the public funding of secret ballots and the Government proposals on the closed shop.' The executive had in mind disputes like that at Tates Radio in the autumn of 1978.

Tates Radio was a regional television rental company on Teesside where the union had around thirty-five members. Their company was bought by Rediffusion who had a closed shop agreement with the GMWU. The company refused to allow the Tates men to have any sort of representation in the negotiations for the bigger company. The GMWU demanded they join them and leave their own union. The Tates membership refused, and went on strike. Weeks later nothing had happened; Rediffusion men, GMWU members, did their work. Eventually, the union's national leadership had to force the issue at Rediffusion by applying pressure to another company within the same conglomerate. Thames TV was the target. Shop-steward Harry Woolff organized supporting action by refusing to cross Tates Radio picket lines at Thames TV headquarters and later at Wembley Stadium, where Thames were covering an international football match. Blank TV screens brought Rediffusion back to the negotiating table. Secondary picketing had allowed the strong to help the weak.

On most occasions the police have taken a cool view of picketing, as they are mainly interested in preventing breaches of the peace. It is only occasionally that individual police officers reveal an excess of zeal. One such occasion was in the city of Durham during the nurses' dispute. When the night shift finished at Mullards at Durham, the highly successful television tube factory, several EETPU shop-stewards turned up at the local hospital at just after 6 a.m. They stood at the gate with the hospital's nurses, helping them organize their picket for the 'day of action' in defence of the NHS. An earnest young constable, aware that the EETPU shop-stewards were not nurses, sternly asked them: 'Are you secondary pickets?' 'No,' came the reply, 'we got here first!' The young policeman had the good grace to smile and retire despite the fact he had the letter of the law on his side.

Eric Hammond's Wembley speech looked at the TUC's eight-point 'Recommendations'. The union voted for them in order to prevent the Government exploiting the differences in the movement. However, the EETPU were not convinced of the policy in certain key regards. First, the need for a campaign. There was no argument about this, although the suggestion that the Industrial Relations Act had been destroyed in 1974 by the union 'campaign' based on de-registration was wrong. The Industrial Relations Act had been replaced by an incoming Labour Government – proving once and for all the primacy of the ballot box.

The union was sceptical of the proposition that by not holding the required ballots, the closed shops could be preserved and it could not see how keeping trade unionists off industrial tribunals would stop individuals leaving closed shops with huge pay-offs. As we shall see, they were not impressed with the flat refusal to take government funds for the postal costs associated with union ballots. There was no argument about support for unions in trouble with the law and for closer working between unions, along with a £39,500 levy on the EETPU to help pay for the campaign and defence fund. Nevertheless, Eric Hammond implied at Wembley and Frank Chapple said later on the TUC General Council, no one should use the TUC defence fund to launch and support an illegal dispute that dragged the whole movement into a political strike against the legislation.

There was just one issue on which the union felt a higher principle was at stake than respect for the law. On 25 January 1984, the Government withdrew various employment rights from 7,000 employees at the GCHQ electronic listening stations and banned them from remaining members of trade unions. Most of the members at GCHQ belonged to various civil service unions. The EETPU had around twenty-four members involved in site maintenance. The union's view was that action resisting this decision of the Government did not involve simple politics; it was action in defence of 'fundamental human rights', a view later confirmed by the International Labour Office.

The union's leadership was appalled at Mrs Thatcher's insinuation that trade union membership at GCHQ was synonymous with betraying Britain's secrets. Nevertheless, by March that year, over ninety per cent of the staff had been bribed or intimidated into leaving their unions. In frustrated fury, the TUC withdrew its national economic development office delegates; the Government failed to fall. The EETPU, however, took a serious and principled stand. On 1 September 1985, the executive announced that if anyone was sacked for holding on to their membership of a trade union, the union would ballot its membership in electricity supply to take action on the GCHQ's members behalf. Without a doubt this threat stayed the Government's hand. The union supported the campaign in Cheltenham financially, and Eric Hammond led a huge deputation of EETPU members on the commemorative march in Cheltenham in January 1986. Even there, the Trotskyists shouted at him!

Alastair Graham was general secretary of the civil service union, CPSA. He had led the civil service unions in doing everything possible to meet the Government's fears (real or imagined) of strikes in this key defence installation. The civil-service unions even offered the Government an undertaking that there would never be any disruption of GCHQ activities in the future – in effect a 'no-strike' deal. The Government ignored them. Alastair Graham thought Eric Hammond's and the EETPU role in GCHQ 'impeccable'. When the Government backed off sacking the handful of trade unionists, Peter

Jones, the secretary of the Council of Civil Service Unions, wrote to Eric Hammond.

Just a short note to express my personal thanks for your major part in securing the Government's climb down over GCHQ dismissals. Your speech at last year's Congress and the subsequent continued support of the EETPU have been the most significant factor in persuading the Government of the need to avoid confrontation. Whilst the overall battle will still continue, I think the tide is now beginning to turn. When we eventually get our union rights back at GCHQ, we will make you an honorary member.

Tragically, the Government got its way eventually. The EETPU joined with the TUC 'Day of Action' on 7 November 1988 when the last handful of trade unionists were sacked. Members in supply took action short of all-out strikes but the Government had effectively won.

Tied into this problem of respecting the law – particularly just how should the movement react to bad law – was a concern about rising violence in the movement. The union deplored shouting at conferences, the threatening behaviour on conference sea fronts, and all those other echoes of the depth of hatred revealed between 1957–65 inside the old ETU. They were to become particularly concerned with the growing problem of violence on picket lines.

The world is nowadays a more violent and divided society. Deference is everywhere on the retreat; defiance has occasionally slipped into violence in industrial disputes. Throughout the Chapple and Hammond years, they would never tolerate, on behalf of the union, violence in support of any cause, however justified. This often led to a rising tide of resentment against the union, whose leaders were always disappointed that a good case could be ruined in the public's eyes by televised violence between trade unionists and the police. (The union was to speak at the TUC in 1980 in support of the police, appealing for a recognition of their very real problems.) The EETPU was always certain that such publicity did not raise the consciousness of the working-class or expose the fascist nature of state repression leading to a greater determination to strive for the emancipation of the workers. The EETPU was always convinced that in a mature democracy, a Labour government was less likely to be elected and recruiting new members into trade unions made less likely by the linking in the public mind of violence and trade unionism. It did not matter that the union often sympathized with the issue behind the uproar. All that was left in the memory of left-wing activists in other unions was the impression that the union's revulsion against violence was in some way an indication of how the union was in the Tories' and the employers' pockets! The union spoke out when others were silent on the Shrewsbury pickets arrested during a national building strike and imprisoned on 'conspiracy' charges that emerged from the violent picketing. Tom Breakell was shouted down at the 1975 TUC over that issue. The Grunwick union recognition dispute in 1976–77 was deflected by the mass picketing in those North-West London streets, and although the union would have cut off electricity to the factory if it could have been isolated from the rest of the locality, it deplored the violence once again. The outburst of televised strike activity by lorry drivers and health service workers deciding who comes in and out of Great Ormond Street Hospital in the 'Winter of Discontent' was also unpopular. Some unions, who were trying to impose effective secondary picketing through the sheer weight of numbers, often presented an intimidatory spectacle in itself. The picketing of the private steel companies during the 1980 steel strike, the violence associated with the miners and News International picketing, drew strong condemnation.

This issue of violence was closely tied to the unions' attitudes to the fashion for one-day strikes against government policy. The first, organized by the TUC on 14 May 1980 was publicly opposed by the union as 'unwise and untimely'. Frank Chapple always asked the question of supporters of such strikes: 'If the Government does not change course, will we have more "Days of Action" until they do?' All such opposition did was to threaten a general strike at the end of the line, make trade unions unpopular and give the Conservative Government some sort of justification for moving against trade unions legislatively. The union was directly involved in this descent into violence in 1979–80 at the Isle of Grain.

Isle of Grain 1979–80

Inside and outside the union, an industrial dispute at the Isle of Grain once more attempted to elevate greed and sharp practice to the status of principle. Once more picket lines were set up to convince others that anything goes in the name of solidarity. Outrageous behaviour should not only be tolerated by other workers, but actively supported through the act of not crossing picket lines.

In August 1979, the laggers at the Isle of Grain Power Station site were in dispute with their employers, CDN Installations Ltd. The Isle of Grain in north Kent had a long history of lucrative trade union activity. It had been known since the 1950s as 'Treasure Island' by active trade unionists. The laggers (men who insulate boilers and pipework in the power station construction industry) had all been laid off due to a separate scaffolders' dispute. When that strike finished, CDN said they could re-employ the laggers on a phased basis. The laggers wanted to all come back at once. At the same time, CDN were also trying to renegotiate the bonus system downwards. At the end of October, the employers announced the end of the bonus. The laggers were earning twice the wages of craftsmen on site. The highest-paid electrician there was the man providing the comparatively simple task of temporary lighting, paid from a whip-round by the laggers themselves. The strike went on, with workers across the site having collected thousands of pounds for the laggers (although most of them has apparently gone off to work elsewhere, leaving a token picket of only four). On 31 October 1979, the Company offered the laggers through their union, the GMWU, a package deal involving re-instatement, a £550 ex-gratia payment, pay for August Bank Holiday and a minimum earnings level to be paid while talks started on a new bonus scheme. The CEGB were pressing for work to begin once again on a power station contract already an astonishing four years behind. The GMWU recommended to their national laggers branch to accept the deal and to accept a new sub-contractor for the lagging work. In December 1979, the lagging branch said no. CEGB cancelled CDN's contract and brought in Cape Contracts. The lagging branch still refused to work for them, despite the national officials of the GMWU recommending the deal. The CEGB now threatened to close the site completely, with a loss of 2,000 jobs, by June 1980, and started with 600 redundancies. The CEGB finally tried to put the work with GEC and Babcock's; again the lagging branch of the GMWU refused to supply labour.

At that moment, the seven unions on the site agreed to the emergency training of sixty trainee laggers. It may be difficult to reconcile with the amount of forthcoming abuse of the EETPU on this issue, but only one of the trainee laggers was a member of the EETPU. Nevertheless, the mass picket of the site was an ugly and violent affair. Coaches crossed the picket lines. Eric Hammond, then the local executive councillor for north Kent, joined John Baldwin, general secretary of the Constructional Engineering Union (now part of the AEU), on the front seat of the coaches rejecting the arguments of the pickets. Two thousand construction jobs were at risk in the middle of a great recession in the building industry. The laggers did not apparently care about that, only the 'principle' of the picket line. They continued to reject the advice of their own union and the job security of fellow-workers, all enforced with mass picketing.

The TUC were involved under the inter-union machinery and the unions concerned ordered to support the return of GMWU laggers to the site in steady replacement of the trainees. As it happened, the lagging work was completed by the trainees and life went on as much as before. Threats of TUC discipline against the unions concerned became unnecessary, although Eric Hammond and Charlie Lovell had to attend the general council of the TUC. Their 'defence' was a robust attack on the perceived weakness of the GMWU leadership for backing their laggers, despite their rejecting three union recommendations and risking 1,400 jobs on the site. Nevertheless, the EETPU members locally knew that the TUC's support for the laggers had put at risk the 1,400 other jobs on the site. Eric Hammond was gratified to receive support from real trade unionists locally to offset the televised abuse by left-wingers on the question of inviolate picket lines. The Gravesend branch wrote: 'The role played by our union has been one where our members have had full consultation throughout the period of the problem and every move that has been dealt with, [has been done] with their agreement. The settlement last week meant that 1,400 jobs were secured, jobs that are desperately needed in the construction industry.'

Solidarnosc 1980–89

The union's running feud with the GMWU was not helped by events unfolding in faraway Poland. The union had always taken a stringent line on human rights – particularly for free trade unions. The policy was to support any and every manifestation for free trade unions and human rights everywhere in the world – in South Africa, Brazil, Czechoslovakia and Russia. The TUC international committee appeared to the EETPU to have double standards. It was all right to publicly denounce right-wing fascist regimes for their failings, but Eastern European regimes were better handled by the quiet word in the ear on relatively discreet high-powered delegations. Curiously, it was frequently necessary to visit communist countries but not appropriate to visit semi-fascist regimes. The economic committee of the TUC, where the GMWU's David Basnett was the leading light, planned to visit Poland in the autumn of 1980. Apart from the EETPU attempting to make sure that the delegation raised the issues of dumping cheap goods in Europe as a result of cheap labour in Poland, the events in Gdansk in August 1980 radically altered the basis of the planned visit. The birth of Solidarity, led by shipyard electrician Lech Wałeşa, riveted the EETPU active membership. They were thrilled to watch free trade unionism emerge from under the gun barrels of the Polish state police. Frank Chapple was appalled that the TUC economic committee did not plan to meet Solidarity, preferring instead to meet the 'stooge' unions effectively run by the Polish government. He made a fuss at the general council and an even bigger fuss in public when Congress met at Brighton that year. The invitation was withdrawn at the last moment by the Polish government. The EETPU's record of support for Solidarity was to prove unrivalled. There was no TUC-style equivocation at Hayes Court. The union sustained the British office of Solidarity throughout the dark days of suppression for the union from 1981–89, printing the regular Solidarity pamphlets throughout the period, collecting money at the union's two colleges and paying for duplicating equipment to be sent to Poland. The union supported pro-Solidarity demonstrations in the snow with the ancient banner to the fore, and awarded Lech Wałeşa the union's gold badge in 1983. This support was spontaneous, non-denominational and fierce in its belief that the cause was right. This conviction only highlighted further some British unions' equivocation on the subject and added to the store of left-inspired embarrassment and resentment of the voice of the EETPU.

The Miners' Strike, 1984–5

In March 1984, the NCB announced the peremptory closure of Cortonwood pit in Yorkshire. The resulting strike, picked up by the Yorkshire area and then spread via regional sympathy strikes, produced an attempted national miners' strike. In the absence of a national ballot, some pits, notably in Nottinghamshire, were reluctant to strike. They were subjected to ferocious picketing which in its turn provoked a police presence on the streets and on the approach roads to mining villages never before seen in Britain. Aided and abetted by the media that the miners leaders affected to despise, the violence of the picket line accompanied by doom-laden political rhetoric was brought nightly into every living room in Britain. The miners' strike was of immense significance in the post-war history of the movement. No active trade unionist was left untouched by it as it dragged on from March 1984–March 1985. The strike raised the central question of whether a trade-union could or should mount a challenge to the State itself. Every trade union branch, conference and national executive council discussed the strike and took up an attitude to it. Every Labour Party, trades council and joint shop-stewards committee was involved. Activists contributed money, sometimes directly to the NUM, sometimes for children's holidays, food parcels or Christmas parties.

For most of the vocal supporters of the NUM, the miners' strike represented a head-on collision with Mrs Thatcher's Government and the whole economic system she represented. Following on the defeat of the NGA at Warrington, it was a heaven-sent opportunity to deploy in the field the Labour movement's Praetorian Guard, the miners. They had defeated the Tories in 1974. Mrs Thatcher wanted her revenge. She should not be allowed to have it. The miners must not fail.

From that perspective, any cautionary words – any concern about a few bloody noses suffered by scabs in Nottinghamshire – was treachery. It was against this background that the EETPU's leadership considered the strike. The union's most immediate concern was with the several dozen union members involved. These men were largely concentrated in Yorkshire, where they held dual membership in the EETPU and the NUM. They were paid lock-out benefit throughout the strike. This cost the union £39,000, and those members who were in dispute from beginning to end of the strike received £921 each.

There was no doubt that the union at every level was as sympathetic as anyone else to the miners' basic demands of support for their communities through a growing role for coal in the economy. EETPU men who opposed the strike politically were often organizers of the fund-raising support groups in the coalfields. Since the early 1970s, the union had worked in great detail with the NUM leaders to urge upon the TUC and, through them, the government of the day, a balanced energy policy. This had been achieved, and it meant in practice support for high outputs of coal, but, equally, support for the TUC fuel and power committee's united pledge for a gas, oil and nuclear power component in the nation's energy needs. Not only was there unity on the policy side of the equation. During the 1972 and 1974 miners' strikes, the union's members in the electricity supply industry had greatly assisted the miners. In 1974, in particular, their identification of the exact nature of failing coal stocks in direct contradiction to the Heath Government's propaganda was greatly appreciated by the NUM, along with their help in not moving or accepting new coal into power stations.

In the 1984 dispute, the NUM initially ignored the TUC, fearful of its 'taking over' the dispute. Arthur Scargill had long made clear his derision for the TUC energy policy. He defended his anti-nuclear stand in a debate in Worksop with EETPU national officer Peter Adams, but few were convinced by his reasoning and, at the Windscale enquiry, observers were left with the impression that Scargill had little grasp of the subject. The conduct of the dispute rapidly turned the union's sympathy for the NUM into opposition. The NUM's leadership aims quickly became more grandiose. They were clearly not just interested in the protection of village communities from the precipitate closure of pits the country still needed. Quietly and discreetly, general secretary-elect Eric Hammond wrote to Peter Heathfield, the new NUM general secretary, in May 1984: 'Yesterday's general council and the breakdown of NUM/NCB talks moves me to write to you on a personal basis because of my growing concern that your present dispute could result in a considerable setback for the NUM – a setback that could adversely affect the rest of the movement.' He then quoted what he had said at the union's conference in Scarborough.

All of us who have spent our lives in this movement have been raised with a respect for miners, for their loyalty and steadfastness, and their security and reward should be beyond doubt, and differences over the continuation of particular pits could surely be determined by agreed criteria or even an independent commission. The ingredients of an industrial victory for the miners are there, if only their leaders would move to secure them and in the process they would gain the support of the whole movement.

His letter continued:

My union is absolutely opposed to law-breaking and the political use of strikes to bring down elected governments. The overlaying of this dispute with political rhetoric and objectives is an obstacle to our support. To put it bluntly and privately: could the

NUM disown the overt political objectives of some spokesmen, maybe in the form of making it clear that their sole objective is securing the future of their industry through an honourable negotiated settlement? Could they even at this stage unite their union with a national ballot?

I ask these questions, because if you did, I would use all my power and influence to bring assistance to the NUM. I mean by that, I would recommend to our executive that we ballot all our members in coal-fired stations to stop work in your support.

Frankly, without the moves from the NUM that I have indicated, such a recommendation would not have a chance and I certainly would not initiate it.

Peter Heathfield replied in a pleasant enough tone that unfortunately the strike *was* political and the responsibility for the violence lay with the police. And that was that. The miners' main chance of supporting action in the power stations was turned aside. During the union's industrial conferences at Scarborough, Eric Hammond was warmly applauded when he told the power station shop-stewards and their area board colleagues that the EETPU was wary of the NUM's attempts to apparently organize a general strike in the miners' support: 'It is *only* the Nottinghamshire miners with their proper and honourable insistence on a national ballot that have stood in the way.' Eric Hammond saw from the start that the strike was doomed to defeat on the totally plausible grounds that the State could not be overthrown in this way. 'There are other powers exerting their will in our society – some of them who command disciplined men with guns in their hands. If we remove – if we provide the justification for removing – the muzzle of law from these hands, we will not quickly be forgiven.' In his support, yet again, of the primacy of parliamentary democracy, he was fearful that if a Conservative Government was overthrown by industrial action, the police and the army under Mrs Thatcher could not stand aside.

Support for a general strike in support of the miners would bring all unions to defeat in the wake of the miners' defeat; all unions and the Labour Party would suffer from the movement's association in the public's mind with violence and disrespect for the law. He had in mind also the Scottish TUC and the Yorkshire and Humberside regional TUC's calls for one-day strikes in support of the miners (fearful of the same demands escalating into more extensive disputes).

The picketing itself coloured many of the union's activists' attitudes to the miners' methods and, eventually, their actual cause itself. The picketing of the steel industry gave special offence – particularly at Ravenscraig. There, the plant was suffering with another round of fears of total closure. The NUM did not apparently care about 'the Craig's' special problems and many shop-stewards, let alone ordinary members, were deeply resentful of the picket-line insults they had to suffer.

Throughout the summer and autumn of 1984, further attempts were made to picket key industries in support of the miners. Considerable selfless support was advanced by the railwaymen: however, the TGWU could do little about the virtual replacement of rail transport with flotillas of lorries across the country. They had promised much and could deliver little. Electricity supply was to be a target for the pickets in the late summer and early autumn of 1984, either side of the 1984 TUC.

The annual meeting of the TUC often produces a furious row between unions, an embarrassment to the Labour Party leadership or a threat to government. Each year, the media play up the big issue, one general secretary after another appearing live on television from 7.0 a.m. in the morning until 11.0 p.m. at night. The big controversy is always prominently discussed, possibly because the journalists are all there in the hot-house and the studio equipment is all in place – it just has to be used. September 1984's TUC was naturally dominated by the miners' strike. For the TUC itself, the strike presented many problems. The TUC itself was embarrassed by the violence, the failure of the miners to win and the nightly acid comments of Arthur Scargill laying about him with equal abandon against the Government, the NCB and elements in the Labour movement itself who were delaying the inevitable victory. Congress week just had to be got through with as little damage as possible. At the same time, there might be a better chance of resolving the dispute itself if the TUC could 'take over' the conduct of the negotiations. For the miners, this must have had shades of the train-drivers' flexible rostering dispute in which ASLEF thought they had been betrayed by the TUC and the TUC officials were always convinced the union's leadership were discreetly grateful to Len Murray and friends for getting them off the hook. For whatever reason, the miners allowed the TUC to offer its help. The statement put to congress after considerable drafting discussions pledged support for the miners fight to save jobs and communities and urged all affiliated unions to assist the miners by refusing to move coal – or the increasingly important substitute oil supplies. The TUC knew a routine 'support the miners' statement would be resisted in electricity supply and probably steel as well with little real effect on road transport. So they added a key phrase. This support would be provided for the miners only 'after detailed discussion with the General Council [who therefore would gain control of the strike] and agreement with the unions which would be directly concerned'. Senior TUC figures came to the EETPU and attempted to sell this 'support ... but' motion to them. EETPU delegates at that conference remember with distaste the explanations advanced to them as to why they should support this motion. 'It will get us through the week' and 'it doesn't actually *mean* anything; we can insist on the miners changing their tactics when we get back to Congress House' or 'our members in the power stations won't change their minds because of this – so why not support it' and 'there are important elections on in our union – we've got to be seen to be supporting the miners: this empty promise lets us do that.'

No one who was in the conference centre at Brighton that day the strike was discussed will ever forget it. It took place after lunch, with the gallery awash with miners and miners' supporters, who, after months of the strike, had now made a way of life out of fund-raising, touring Labour movement meetings and picketing their opponents' conferences. When Arthur Scargill spoke, the emotional intensity of the occasion successfully fused the atmosphere associated with religious revivalism, intensely fought local football matches and the political excitement that comes from being at an event that next day will be on the front page of every newspaper. Into this ferocity strode general secretary Eric Hammond. The bellowing, fist-shaking, hissing and swearing from some delegates and the majority in the gallery was almost tangible – particularly to the union's three national officers sitting bravely in the gallery. This conference was always going to be significant for Eric Hammond, as at the end of it Frank Chapple was to formally retire. After nearly two years as general secretary secretary-elect, Eric Hammond was about to assume the role of general secretary in his own right.

The speech he made attacked the General Council's statement at the heart of its contradictions. It was 'dishonest and deficient'. The nature of the dishonesty he tried to convey, in the midst of shrieking and interruption, hinged on the impression it gave of imminent powerful action on behalf of the miners. 'Dazzled by this prospect, it is easy to understand the smile on Arthur's face,' said Hammond. Catching the atmosphere of the smoke-filled rooms, he went for the General Council fixers. 'But are the miners deaf? Can't they hear the backstage whispering to unions like mine?' To gain the assent of the power workers, they had been promised that there would be no official picket lines at power stations without the power unions' agreement. Now either the power workers or the miners were being deliberately misled. Given the power workers' concern about power cuts, 'all industrial activity and the means of civilized life will end,' and given their well-publicized concerns about violence and the attack on democracy represented, in their minds, by the political rhetoric used by the miners, it was unlikely that the power unions would agree to such picket lines being organized with their acquiescence. 'Either the power stations stop or they don't. And my union is not going to stop them as a result of this statement or ten thousand like it.'

The statement, was, therefore, objectively going to betray the miners and was designed to do just that! All those on the General Council who voted for it did so in the sure knowledge that the power workers' refusal to implement it would save all of *them* from the consequences of their support for turning the nation's lights out. Eric Hammond crashed on through the abuse to accuse other union leaders of doing this out of 'fear of being branded right-wing; fear of being put under pressure in their own unions'. The statement was also crucially 'deficient' in that it failed to condemn the violence associated with picketing. This silence was all the more disgraceful, in Hammond's view, as it ignored the TUC's own guide to peaceful picketing issued in the ghastly aftermath of the 1978–9 Winter of Discontent.

In a memorable phrase among many others – shouting through a continuous storm of noise – Hammond finished by telling the baying crowd one more home truth. 'The General Council has spoken in this statement. Today Congress will speak, but I tell you, brothers, your members have yet to be heard.'

It is tempting to divert further into the significance of the miners' strike. The temptation must be resisted; however, the 1984 congress cannot be left without recognizing the huge courage displayed in support of Hammond's views by EPEA general secretary John Lyons and the blast-furnacemen's spokesman N. Leadley. Everyone else sat on their hands.

The union's leadership were shaken by the ferocity of the opposition to their view and disappointed with the craven lack of resistance to the rampant confidence in revolutionary trade unionism revealed by Scargillism. With some sense of deeply reassuring pleasure, the executive council decided, alone among the NJIC unions, to test opinion in the electricity supply industry. They balloted EETPU members in October. They put before them not only the executive's views but also the TUC statement. The members voted, 20,042–3,864, to support the union's view in a fifty-seven per cent return. Dozens of letters of support were received at Hayes Court, thanking the union for allowing the members to declare a view. Letters and petitions were received from hundreds of members of other unions, including dozens of signatories from Ferrybridge Power Station wishing to transfer to the EETPU. National officer Fred Franks played straight with his NJIC colleagues, and did not take the men into membership. Nevertheless, the union's stock in the industry rose with its own membership through the simple virtue of balloting them at all – particularly in the absence of the other unions' doing so. That response was pleasure enough for the EETPU leadership.

In all the increased concentration on the picket-line violence, heightened by the death in Wales of taxi-driver David Wilkie, the union's leadership also knew that the prospect of eventual success due to the onset of winter was also illusory. It was yet another cruel trick played on the striking miners. Coal stocks remained high throughout the winter. New TUC general secretary Norman Willis was told this. No doubt the unions leaders knew it too. On 8 January 1985, the CEGB satisfied the highest demand on record for electricity ever – 44,748 megawatts and beat that three times in the next fortnight.

The whole sorry experience was an issue of immense gravity where the views of ordinary members and the activities of trade union bureaucrats and activists were miles apart. Once again, in front of TV cameras this time, the EETPU's leadership would not ignore the majority voice of their own members. They went further and exposed the cynicism and apparent indifference of their equivalents in other unions. It made it more difficult for other unions leaders to love the irritating EETPU's leadership, whose home truths were unwelcome news. It made it difficult for such leaderships, embarrassed and occasionally ashamed, to contradict their own activists, whose Pavlovian reaction to any ideas from the restless, challenging, thinking EETPU is to denounce it as collaborative support for monopoly capitalism. There was only grim satisfaction for Hammond by mid-1985, when the movement's spokesmen all suddenly decided the whole thing had been a disaster. The habit of shrieking at Eric Hammond started to become ingrained, particularly when he insisted at the 1985 Labour Party conference that the NUM leadership, not the State, was fundamentally responsible for the dismissed and fined miners. Indeed, the miners were the victims of the strike in the same ways as their benighted forefathers on the Somme – 'lions, led by donkeys' (a phrase he first used at the union's 1984 industrial conference). The left was also convinced that the strike had been badly organized. The Communist Party analysis was that 'there should have been an early condemnation of the violence'. The Labour Co-Ordinating Committee was equally blunt. 'Failure to hold a ballot was bad politics. Violence weakens support for the strike.' There is rarely any willingness, in any walk of life, to warmly embrace the man who says 'I told you so'. That is human nature and trade unions are human institutions. It remains undeniable that hindsight totally justifies the EETPU analysis of that dismal turning-point in trade union affairs. It is also undeniable that the union won few friends for telling others the truth.

Against the background of fury, disappointment and misery with a rejuvenated Tory Government, many trade union leaders preferred to finger the EETPU for this failure instead of the left 'adventurists' who had really created the issue in the first place. With that in mind, the 1985 congress was to be dominated by one issue in the same curious way the 1984 congress had been dominated by the miners' issue. And not many people were predisposed to examine the content of the EETPU's principled stand on the issue of accepting public funds for trade union ballots.

1985: The 'Ballots' issue

On this occasion, the EETPU had a powerful ally – the AUEW (the engineering, construction and foundry sections, without TASS – the Technical and Supervisory Section). The engineering workers, soon to revert to their traditional title, the Amalgamated Engineering Union (AEU), were in a quandary of their own. They had adopted secret postal ballots for their elections in the early 1970s. They also elected all their officials every three years. The Government had offered state support for the bulk of postal costs associated with postal balloting undertaken since March 1981. The TUC had thrown out this offer in its eight-point rejection of the 1982 Employment Act at the 1982 Wembley conference. The Government had announced a time limit of February 1985 for applications for public funds for ballots dating back to March 1981. Just before Christmas 1984, the AUEW balloted their members on whether the union should accept the public funds. The engineers voted by over twelve to one to take the money. The EETPU executive council had voted in principle to accept the funds as well. The AUEW, whose financial position at the time was giving cause for concern, had a clear financial imperative alongside their principled support for postal ballots. The EETPU, too, stood to gain – just over £190,000: for the AEU it would be £1.2 million. Throughout the first six months of the year, various TUC committees advised the two unions not take the money. Norman Willis visited both executive councils to plead with them to keep to the 1982 Wembley conference decisions and not take the money. In June, the AEU got their £1.2 million. In July, the finance and general purposes committee of the TUC voted thirteen to one to discipline the AEU. Once again, as congress assembled, the EETPU was involved in a high-profile row with the rest of the movement, this time in support of the engineers who shared their view about the supremacy of their membership's wishes in comparison with the authority of the TUC.

The EETPU's attitude to this controversy was plain and blunt. The 1982 Wembley conference decisions certainly included the recommendation (not instruction) not to take the money for ballots. However, it also instructed union members to withdraw from industrial tribunals in closed shop cases. Nothing had happened about those trade union tribunal members who had remained in place. More to the point, the Wembley decisions also banned unions from holding ballots to sustain closed shop agreements in line with the 1982 Act. This decision was being ignored by all the large unions affiliated to the TUC, and yet nothing was being done about that. Could it just be that the General Council majority – virtually none of whom used postal ballots, most of whom never faced periodic election of any sort, some of whom had never been directly elected by any sort of electorate within their unions and one of whom was the losing candidate in an internal election (given his union's General Council nomination as a consolation prize) – could it be that these people were attacking the *form* of popular election used by the AEU and EETPU? Finally, the other unions' attitude was based, back in 1982, on not taking wicked Tory gold because it might be made the subject of restrictions in the future that interfered with the independence of union elections. No one advanced this argument in the parallel issue of accepting Government funds (around £1.75 million per annum) for trade union education. Some unions thought this was a different issue, because the money was administered by the TUC itself from a bloc grant from government. This was a complete non-argument, ignoring as it did the fact that government *does* insist on which sort of trade union courses attract grant and which don't. Without the government support for trade union education (half of which goes to the TUC and half is shared between the individual unions) the TUC programme at both its own centre at Hornsey and throughout the country would collapse.

The EETPU's executive voted unanimously that if the TUC suspended or expelled the AEU for taking the ballot money, the EETPU would leave Congress in their support. The union's Blackpool branch was even more specific in its support. If the two unions were disciplined, they made it clear that the Opera House in Blackpool would have to continue its deliberations without microphones or lights!

As the weeks progressed, more and more smoke-filled rooms produced more and more failed attempts at compromise. There is no doubt that the EETPU's leadership, waiting patiently in the Norbreck Castle for news, fully expected the AEU to be disciplined and for the EETPU to have to honour their pledge to go with them. At the last moment, a compromise was reached. No action for the moment would be taken against the AEU if they balloted their members again, this time making clear the TUC's position based on the 1982 decisions and also including the threat of suspension.

The EETPU decided to ballot its members simultaneously with the AEU. In December, the engineers' second ballot voted eight to one to ignore the TUC's strictures and take the money. The EETPU's vote was nine to one to do the same thing. Within a few weeks, the TUC policy quietly changed. No one was expelled; nowadays everyone takes the money.

The central significance of the ballot money issue was two-fold. Once again, the union was prominent in a fundamental row about the nature of trade union democracy. When the union's 1985 policy conference debated the issue, the overwhelming majority of delegates voted to take the money in clear support for the principle of postal balloting itself. Jim O'Donnell, representing Hotpoint service engineers, with the recent miners' strike in mind, said all unions have to 'demonstrate, through ballot returns, that they are representative of their members – otherwise they run the risk of losing public sympathy and support'. Brian Kendrick, the Birmingham supply delegate, pointed out that the 1984 Act on strike ballots, added to leadership ballots, made it even more important to take the money to pay for the ballots. Jim Boyle from Bury St Edmunds made the political point even more starkly. 'We believe that the campaign against secret postal ballots is an attempt to retain in office leaders who are unrepresentative and who, in a properly conducted election, would be overwhelmingly defeated.' Peter Barnett from Waltham Forest had a novel view on taking government money for ballots. He worked for a nationalized industry and admitted he had been taking government money in his wage packet every week. 'It does not seem to bother me very much as long as I get enough of it!'

The second major lesson of the ballot money issue in 1985 was the way in which the union's leadership and membership first looked seriously at the prospect in life without TUC membership. For the first time, the TUC was trying to impose its authority on affiliated unions over a serious issue that affected the unions' policy (over ballots) and finances.

Eric Hammond identified this as the main concern. 'I told my TUC colleagues openly and candidly that our members elected our executive council. They were elected to be responsible for the finance and government of the EETPU. The General Council of the TUC were not elected by our members to carry out that duty ... for our part, we cannot surrender the authority given to us by our members to the General Council ... The TUC is an alliance of free, independent organizations. It proceeds together by consent and calls for rigid discipline and strict adherence to rules and policy will inevitable destroy it.' The authority of the TUC was not going to be placed above the authority derived from EETPU ballots, executive council decisions and conference resolutions – as the TUC were to find out three short years later.

Wapping

Relationships between print unions have never been cordial. In the 1950s, the ETU and the engineering workers were kept out of the Printing Workers Federation, and forced into disputes to achieve negotiating rights with newspaper owners. In modern times, new technology has revolutionized all manufacturing industry. The impact on the traditional methods of producing newspapers has been particularly acute. The Society of Graphical and Allied Trades (SOGAT) is the result of amalgamations of print unions for the semi-skilled operators and other non-craft workers in the industry. They sent a delegation to America, which reported in 1985, to see how new technology had cut jobs, made whole crafts unusable and allowed journalists to type their stories straight on to the page via computers. SOGAT's new general secretary, Brenda Dean, quickly realized that the American experience showed that a rejection of new technology was an invitation to proprietors to set up de-unionized new technology facilities, thus bypassing the traditional locations of newspaper production. The leadership of the NGA were also aware of the problem. Tony Dubbins had said to his own 1978 conference ... 'the general desire of our membership is to look back to the days when they had control over origination, and when entry to the union was solely through a craft apprenticeship'. He thought that opposition to change would lead to 'a massive tidal wave of changing techniques sweeping over this industry with the creation of an alternative non-union industry or an industry organized by alternative unions'.

Lots of other people knew what was coming. Electricians in the industry were less terrified. Electronics and computers promised an extension of their responsibilities and job security. The union worked with its London Press branch, despite the permanent political gulf between the branch's leadership and the union's national leadership, to introduce access to technical training to help its members into the electronic age.

The other people who knew what was coming were, of course, newspaper proprietors. The American example was first copied with real conviction by Eddie Shah, the entrepreneurial free-sheet publisher from north-west England, who attempted to publish a new newspaper, *Today*, using the new technology. He was not successful, but the breach had been made in the traditional methods of newspaper production.

Rupert Murdoch's News International conglomerate was particularly anxious to use the new techniques to maximize the potentially cash-rich popular newspapers he printed at the old *News Chronicle* building in Bouverie Street and the traditional home of *The Times* in Gray's Inn Road.

He had built a multi-million new printing works at Wapping in London's redeveloping derelict dockland. He wanted to work the building with economic manning levels, apparently for a new London evening paper, the *Post*. The print unions wanted to work it with traditional manning levels, their caution reinforced by a fear that Wapping would be used for printing the *Sun*, the *News of the World*, the *Sunday Times* and *The Times*. They were frightened that Wapping would eventually lead to net redundancies at Bouverie Street and Gray's Inn Road.

So much for the background of an impending technological hurricane in Fleet Street. The employers wanted it to happen, and News International had a purpose-built facility ready in Wapping. The two traditional print unions knew it was coming, realizing that the fall in the number of production jobs and the virtual abolition of types of skill posed threats to both their memberships. The electricians were concerned to remain indispensable by being capable of covering the electronics skills involved.

In 1983, the jockeying for position among the unions broke out into open rivalry. The NGA were anxious to come to some understanding with the EETPU about job demarcations. The NGA were engaged in both London and in the provinces in a series of disputes with journalists about the computer equipment used to set newspapers' pages. For the EETPU, relationships with the NGA in London, although always wary, were generally warm at national level. Not only was there a mutual respect for skill, but the political leadership of the unions, particularly in the London Labour Party at the height of the left's dominance at the GLC, was mutually supportive. In 1981, agreement had even been reached on who did what in the photo-composition area: an agreement unfortunately rejected by the NGA's national council.

The de-stabilizing element in an already unstable blend of trade union interests was the EETPU's London Press branch. This branch had the rights to supply labour to the newspapers, and had often used these rights over the years to fill Fleet Street with electricians who supported the left campaigns against Jimmy Rowan, Ernie Bussey and the modern leadership alike. After the ballot-rigging scandal, the expelled leaders were quickly accommodated in highly lucrative, relatively undemanding jobs in Fleet Street, despite their non-union position as expelled members. In modern times, other left-wingers have sought solace in Fleet Street from political harassment from the majority opinion. The London Press branch minutes showed that from 1977–83, forty-nine people joined the union, mostly apprentices. However, head office records showed 107 extra members directly admitted to the union by the branch secretary himself.

The branch and the individual 'chapels' always administered their own levies, to give them financial independence from the union's control of the general purpose funds. It is fair to emphasize that much of this money over the years has gone to benevolent causes, in very generous amounts, inside and outside the union. Some of the money is widely believed to have supported candidates in elections who are opposed to the modern leadership.

In December 1982, leading members of the London Press branch met senior officials of SOGAT privately at a hotel at Gatwick Airport. They were concerned that between the NGA and the EETPU, the new technology was going to exclude SOGAT. The electricians' branch leadership, FOCs and prominent non-office holders, recognized as long-time communists, were then offered an exciting vision. If the Press branch electricians left the EETPU and joined SOGAT, they could be the skilled section of SOGAT and work together with the production workers in the industry to suppress the craft dictatorship in Fleet Street exercised by yesterday's men in the NGA. The electricians would control their own negotiations and would have their own national officer and executive representation in SOGAT's structure. For the EETPU communists and fellow-travellers in that room, the attractiveness of political liberation from Frank Chapple's union must have been a powerful one.

On 17 December 1982, the London Press branch secretary, Sean Geraghty, reported back to a meeting of FOCs and deputy FOCs: meetings of members in each location were attended and urged by Sean Geraghty to get out of the EETPU and join SOGAT. On 17 March 1983, SOGAT officials were to be invited to address a London Press branch meeting and receive application forms for SOGAT. On 20 May 1983, the London Press branch issued a

manifesto urging members into SOGAT. Its politics were brazen. In addressing their fear that members might retain a residual loyalty to the EETPU,
they wrote:

... it might be useful to look at loyalty and what it really implies. Simply a habit,
which like all habits may be good or bad. Loyalty to the *old* ETU for instance, *really*
means loyalty to a union leadership which emerged during and after the war and lasted
only fifteen years or so until it was smashed in the High Courts by an anti-Communist
power-hungry gang led by Cannon and Chapple. As our more mature members can
confirm, the pre-war ETU of Lord Citrine and his ilk was little better than the
EETPU is now, just a bit less ruthless perhaps. So to those who resort to stealing
Frank Chapple's worn-out demagogic thunder by referring to ballot-riggers – Frank
only uses this to wake up his slumbering conference zombies anyway – it seems
pertinent that they be reminded of the fact that these people were the old ETU, or a
considerable part of it anyway. Let us hope history deals more kindly with these grossly
maligned pioneers in trade union democracy than the sheep-dip tactics of their piffling
detractors permit.

The pamphlet then insinuated that the union was recruiting dog handlers,
prison yard sweepers and chemists (a reference to an EETPU branch political
delegate to a London Labour Party constitutency management committee).
Not only that, the London Press branch now had plumbers in it, by executive
diktat! It ended up by bemoaning the lack of control over the entry of labour
into the industry that the executive had taken away from the branch the
minute the conspiracy came to light. This was a clever appeal, although it
stretched the truth to breaking-point to describe the union's leadership of
1945–61 as 'grossly maligned pioneers in trade union democracy.' It relied on
prejudice against non-skilled workers and included plumbers amongst the
great unwashed (even as the branch's practical help was being deployed behind
the left-wing challenge to Charlie Lovell, the Plumbing Section national
secretary, in his late 1982 re-election campaign).

The union turned to the TUC in mid-March 1983 to require SOGAT to
stop this: despite some attempts on the General Council to make allowances
for SOGAT, general secretary Len Murray was clear that this was an obvious
case of poaching and ordered SOGAT to return the members concerned.
They were very slow in doing so, and had to be threatened with suspension
from Congress until they agreed to return the members concerned on 2
November 1983. SOGAT's own conference in 1984 was extremely revealing
about both the technological base of their desire to recruit electricians and the
political inspiration behind the desire to do the EETPU down. They openly
debated a motion that regretted the SOGAT's executive failure to 'support'
the electricians who joined SOGAT and 'deplored' their failure to pursue a
successful resolution at the 1983 SOGAT conference which had demanded

that non-print unions should give up their memberships in the print to the printing unions. This 1984 conference discussion was dominated by the London Machine branch delegate who said: 'The London Machine branch as a committee was the instrument used by the [SOGAT] executive council and the general secretary to bring the electricians into this union. We acted on the advice and guidance of the general secretary [then Bill Keys].' In further condemnation of eventually handing back these members, another SOGAT delegate said:

How dare we as a trade union say to members of the EETPU, 'Come in, we need you, particularly at this point in our history with modern technology creeping over us like a cancer. We need you because you are a powerful unit.' And then when people like Frank Chapple and Len Murray, and the like of these, start to pressure us, we drop them like a hot brick ... The [SOGAT] membership in London wanted these electricians, and if the membership in London had got them, we could have had them all over the country. The power it would have given us in the new technology fight would have been formidable.

By June 1983, the union had reconstituted a London Press branch committee loyal to the union. Members were won back from SOGAT before November by these brave, loyal and still left-wing members. The branch's right to restore labour to the industry was restored. Sean Geraghty was suspended from holding office for twenty years for attempting to break up the union, reduced by the executive council on appeal to five years and later reduced by a TUC-appointed independent appeals tribunal to a single year. The union's campaign to clean up the London Press branch activities was led by national secretary Tom Rice. Tom Rice had led the EESA section since 1971 and its success in recruiting several key staff associations into the union led to him taking up a non-voting seat on the executive council to directly represent the union's growing white-collar section on the executive council. Since he first came over to London from Ireland, he had immense experience as a branch official in the old Fulham branch and as a shop-steward in the contracting and paper production industries. He had also had extensive experience on the union's political life either side of 1961 and had an unrivalled network of political and industrial contacts across London. He was given responsibility at national level for press matters, and was responsible for a systematic inquiry into the motivation of EETPU members who left to go to SOGAT. Individual members were canvassed for their views, revealing in one electrical overseer's words (a foreman on the *Sun*) that the motivation was in three parts – partly a small element of political appeal; secondly, a fear that there might be something in a carefully fostered rumour that the union were going to dump the membership in the NGA anyway and mainly the cool evaluation that they would support whichever union promised 'to keep the gravy train going in

Fleet Street'. The union got its members back. The EETPU even voted for SOGAT nominees to the Labour Party's National Executive Committee and persuaded other unions to do likewise.

It is worth going into this painful episode in detail to properly understand the union relationships existing in Fleet Steet when News International made its move in 1985.

Wapping stood waiting in 1985, as it had been for nearly two years. News International had told the unions that they had six months to come up with negotiated arrangements for working the plant. This virtual ultimatum would expire at Christmas 1985. In the meantime, a specialist labour recruitment agency set about recruiting the final installation and commissioning staff to get the press and all their auxiliary equipment up and running ready for the end of the year. The print unions complained in early September 1985 that the arrangements being made to make Wapping ready to run a new London evening paper by approximately eighty members of the Electricians' union recruited in Southampton (due to labour shortages over all the South-East regions) included those electricians working on dummy runs of papers as production workers. On 10 October 1985, the union's Southampton office was told to stop helping the recruitment agency in its task of recruiting the commissioning workforce for Wapping. Talks were now underway at Wapping by each of the printing unions separately, and the EETPU's London Press branch handled them without national control. The Printing Industries Committee for the TUC had never met frequently. Indeed, it had not met at all in 1984 and for most of 1985. Each union was suspicious of each other and it proved impossible to agree to a joint approach to News International. SOGAT in particular insisted that it proposed to negotiate on the subject unilaterally, and so each union approached the negotiations on their own. The key issue was the status of Wapping as a 'greenfield' site, and each union was considering its tactics on that basis.

Rupert Murdoch was prepared to look at the possibility of moving the *Sun* and the *News of the World* to Wapping alongside the *London Evening Post*; the unions wanted this because the working conditions in Bouverie Street were medieval by comparison with Wapping. However, whatever he printed there, Murdoch wanted a completely new type of agreement. On 9 December 1985, the Printing Industries Committee met and each union said that they were getting nowhere with Murdoch's proposals and so they now thought a joint approach to News International was necessary. Both the London Press branch and the executive council of the EETPU had not exhausted or broken off talks on behalf of *their* members at all. On 10 December, the union's executive council said that it was negotiating with News International, and Tom Rice was to tell the company and the Printing Industries Committee alike that the EETPU did not entirely rule out Murdoch's proposed agreement. The

Company proposed legally binding agreements and this would be tolerable if they were negotiated and not imposed. Equally, the union had no difficulty with management's 'right to manage' so long as there were counterbalancing rights of consultation and involvement in the company's affairs. The EETPU was not frightened of a 'no-strike' deal. The EETPU was not going to insist on operating a Fleet-Street style pre-entry closed shop. They believed that closed shops were only desirable after a proper ballot, if that's what the members wanted. The company should be committed to encouraging trade union membership with or without a closed shop.

At this point, the web of suspicion and unpleasantness grew firmer. The print unions were convinced the EETPU was about to sign a single-union, no-strike deal at Wapping. They then threatened to organize strikes to achieve recognition at Wapping and on this basis were able to persuade Norman Willis to write to Eric Hammond on 17 December. He told the EETPU not to enter into bilateral negotiations with News International and not to arrange for EETPU members to do any work on printing at Wapping. EETPU protestations that their negotiations were not concluded and anyway the TUC had no right to insist on who could and couldn't talk to an employer at a greenfield site were ignored. Brenda Dean reportedly now shifted SOGAT's priorities. 'Our NEC decided that if we could not get into Wapping by negotiation, then we had better set about protecting jobs in Bouverie Street and Gray's Inn Road.' Despite claiming that nothing should happen without its affecting all the unions, NGA'82, SOGAT and the AEU drafted a claim on News International on behalf of their Gray's Inn Road and Bouverie Street members. SOGAT's Bill Miles wrote to News International on 23 December 1985. He demanded 'Jobs for Life':

The unions are concerned about the security of their members' employment at Bouverie Street and Gray's Inn Road and to this end we seek. . . .

a) amendment of the contracts of employment of the members of the unions to provide a guarantee of continuity of employment at Bouverie Street and Gray's Inn Road – as the case may be – to their normal retirement date. The contract of employment to be further amended at the same time, to provide that future wage increases will not be less than the annual retail price index . . . and

b) on amendment to the contract of employment of the unions members to provide that should there be any transfer to alternative premises [Wapping] of the origination, advertising, printing, publishing or distribution of work carried out at Bouverie Street and/or Gray's Inn Road, you will guarantee that the members of unions concerned will be offered employment at the alternative premises with full continuity of employment at their prevailing wages and conditions, and with a provision for their future annual increases at a minimum of that equivalent to the retail price index increases. Additionally, a further assurance that all existing union memberships and recognition arrangements will apply in any establishment to which work is transferred.

This continuity of employment idea had apparently been discussed before by the company with the unions – however, the letter finished: 'We would like to make it clear that we would wish to avoid taking industrial action, but if you are not prepared to discuss these matters with us and guarantee our members, employment and conditions, you leave us no alternative course of action.'

Rupert Murdoch's six-month deadline had now expired. The print unions were balloting on strikes in support of the 'Jobs for Life' claim. Murdoch's aggressive demands would probably guarantee a strike. One took place. This may always have been his ambition – to provoke a strike. Early in the new year, a letter from News International solicitors, dated 20 December 1985, was made public: the letter from the solicitor said: 'I have advised that if a moment came when it was necessary to dispense with the present workforces at Times Newspapers Limited and News Group, the cheapest way of doing so would be to dismiss employees while participating in a strike or other industrial action,' and the letter then dealt with just how to do it.

Everyone could see it coming. Norman Willis worked mightily throughout early January to avoid the bust-up. By 14 January 1986, the EETPU's negotiations were being organized from head office: the union felt even more isolated given the strike ballots and the intensified abuse about the motives of those working in Wapping. On 15 January it became clear that News International were planning to produce an advertising supplement for the *Sunday Times* on 19 January. This dramatically altered the picture: now Wapping was to do work previously associated with Bouverie Street and Gray's Inn Road. Norman Willis put it to the EETPU that they could stop their members working on the supplement. Legal advice made it clear that the union would be liable for damages and certain to be restrained by injunctions. There was nothing the union could do now, although they accepted TUC advice not to meet News International unilaterally any more.

On Friday 24 January 1986, the sky fell in. Five thousand members of the other print unions went on strike at the four papers. EETPU members were told to work normally at Bouverie Street and Gray's Inn Road. News International sacked the strikers and in a spirit of bravado and determination, printed the *News of the World* and the *Sunday Times* at Wapping that weekend.

The management had turned down an unprecedented agreement offered by the unions. As late as 17 January, under Norman Willis' shrewd chairmanship, the other print unions now offered Rupert Murdoch everything he could possibly want from: recognition of the company's right to manage; a common commitment to 'profitability, efficiency, harmonious relations, productivity and flexibility, and job security'; joint agreements arrived at by the company and a joint union council (to avoid the pitfalls of individual union negotiations); limitation of number of chapels; 'binding arbitration on any difference, to be triggered unilaterally'; inter-union rivalries to be decided by binding adjudication of the TUC.

News International were now being hard. The company would not negotiate beyond their Christmas 1985 deadline. They would not allow the print unions into Wapping. It was to be war to the finish.

The strike lasted from 24 January 1986 to 6 February 1987. Picketing was fierce and occasionally violent. Saturday nights were particularly unpleasant for police and pickets alike. The company were unmoved. They sent all four titles to Wapping; only thirty-two journalists out of around 700 left rather than work at the new plant. Around 400 ex-SOGAT and other print union members worked at the site. The distribution was handled by Murdoch's lorry firm TNT, employing TGWU drivers, rather than the railways. The 180 EETPU members, originally employed to commission the equipment, rapidly learnt how to operate it.

With the strike now in full swing, the furious, desperate print workers turned on the EETPU. The union was charged under seven headings at the TUC. The hearings were arranged for 5 February 1986. They took over fourteen hours to complete, with the small EETPU delegation sitting virtually incommunicado in an ante-room.

Eric Hammond presented the union's defence against the charges brought by the print unions. His prepared statement told the General Council of the TUC:

I repeat the facts:

that some EETPU members were recruited during 1985 for commissioning and installation work at News International's Wapping plant;

that two of our area offices were asked for labour by an agency;

that in the course of their work, the members concerned showed that they could not only commission but also operate much of the equipment at Wapping;

that News International announced that the Wapping plant would produce a new paper with the new technology and subsequently it appeared that those employed on commissioning have become involved on a continuing basis;

that other print unions sought to negotiate a 'jobs for life' agreement for all their existing members in employment with News International but we were excluded from this claim;

that their failure to reach agreement on the claim led to the present strike and the transfer to Wapping;

that the union had no agreement with News International or any of its constitutent companies, concerning Wapping;

that we cannot instruct those presently employed there to stop work without putting the union's funds in jeopardy.

For their purposes, the originators of the 'complaint' have put *their* construction on these facts:

a construction that puts us in collusion with News International and places upon the EETPU the responsibility of the unemployment of Fleet Street workers.

We *totally* and emphatically reject that construction. The immediate responsibility for that unemployment lies with the bad judgement – yes, I must say, for the matters at stake demand plain speaking – with the incompetent leadership of SOGAT and the NGA.

If we are to totally accept *their* version of events, it involves a plot by Murdoch in some way aided by the EETPU to create a situation whereby their existing members would be *provoked* into strike action and Murdoch would then claim justification for transferring to Wapping. Perhaps there was a plot. But I tell you unequivocally that we had no part in it, no knowledge of it. But, I must say this, there was widespread speculation that Murdoch was planning to switch existing titles to Wapping.

Let me give some other facts and the construction *we* put on them as to why we are here today ...

that on 30 January, the *Guardian* ran an editorial which said ... 'This time round then, the electricians may well find themselves isolated, exposed and ultimately expelled. The problem is that people on both sides – among them TUC Chairman Ken Gill, whose white-collar engineering TASS organizes many on the fringes of EETPU territory – are spoiling for a fight. Mr Ron Todd's TGWU has motor manufacturing ambitions. Both men's unions find Mr Hammond's populist 'market unionism' deeply distasteful. They believe that, together, they could poach EETPU members in tens of thousands once the protection of the TUC Bridlington Agreement was removed.'

That is an echo of the gaffe in the *Morning Star* last July when Mr Gill, our [TUC] Chairman, was reported as saying he was confident the AUEW would be expelled over the ballot money issue and with lip-licking anticipation ... 'I would be surprised if they had half of their membership after a year outside the TUC.'

That we received a letter from our South Tyneside MDC senior steward who told us that at a meeting of all senior stewards ... 'I was informed, during this discussion by the senior steward for the TGWU that in the event of the EETPU being expelled on leaving the TUC he had been instructed by his union to begin recruiting electricians and plumbers within this authority into his union. He also informed me that he had been supplied with extra recruitment forms for this purpose' ... and ... 'I hope the information I have given will be of help to you and I am sure South Tyneside is not an isolated case, as the TGWU steward in question is also delegate to that union's regional and national committees.'

That at a recent NALGO [National and Local Government Officers' Association] executive, a member described the EETPU's suspension as a 'golden opportunity'.

The left press, headed with missionary zeal by Mick Costello of the *Morning Star*, called for our heads. He wrote on Monday ...

'There can be no compromise with union members who break union instructions not to work at Wapping or assist News International in any way. To argue that expulsions from, say, the NUJ [National Union of Journalists] or TGWU for strike breaking would weaken those unions is untenable. To retain in membership (with all the benefits that flow from that) those who break ranks is tantamount to arguing that the TUC itself would be strengthened by keeping in membership a union like the EETPU which is co-operating with the employer in the destruction of jobs and other workers' rights.'

And on Saturday, an editorial called for 'defiance of the law', seeing the EETPU as some kind of subversive influence seeking to get the rest of you to operate within the law.

Ken Cameron, writing in a similar vein in *Labour Herald*, said ... 'At the last TUC congress, a "compromise" was reached with the engineers' and the electricians' unions in which they agreed to put forward the TUC's views to their members when they re-balloted on the question of accepting Government money for ballots. But this did not really happen. Having got one "compromise" at Blackpool, the AUEW and, particularly, the EETPU have since been working as hard as they can to move the TUC undemocratically away from the decisions at Wembley' ... and ... 'so there is no doubt that the TUC has got to say "enough is enough". It would clearly be a tragedy if there were to be a split in the TUC, but so be it.'

Now what construction do *we* put on all that. I'll tell you ...

that feeling sore about the Duke of York marching over the ballot money issue, you've decided, regardless of our answer, to rid yourself of the EETPU;

that some unions have calculated they can take our members;

that some of you are under pressure from the several factions of the left who are making their cause the destruction of the EETPU.

All this does not inspire confidence in us that everyone here can or will deal with this complaint fairly.

You are probably outraged that I should doubt your integrity or political backbone, but is it a stranger construction on facts than that which you are asked to accept in the complaint?

The TUC's procedures have been used in a special and discriminatory way. If the problem is the production of News International's titles at Wapping – titles previously printed at Gray's Inn Road and Bouverie Street – how is it that we alone are formally complained of and arraigned.

The labour involved is considerable and diverse:

The originators – over 700 NUJ members.

The production and maintenance staff – best estimates are about 500, of whom it would seem about 180 are electricians but also including NGA'82, SOGAT and AUEW members.

The distribution – up to 700 TGWU drivers and they do have an agreement with their employer. It's one thing to make gestures of solidarity and another to deliver.

Yet we are alone in the dock.

The General Council were not over-impressed. They voted to direct the EETPU not to help News International to recruit staff; not to recruit new starters at Wapping or the Scottish plant, Kinning Park; and to inform the EETPU members at both sites that they were doing work previously done by sacked union members of Bouverie Street and Gray's Inn Road; not to sign any agreement with News International; to join with the other unions in the talks aimed at achieving recognition for the print unions and not to enter into any sole negotiating agreement with News International. The real drama, during the night was the print unions attempting to get the TUC to instruct the EETPU, on pain of suspension from Congress, to order its members to stop working at Wapping. This would have been clearly illegal, and the General Council voted narrowly to recognize the fact. At the EETPU executive council's meeting on 11 February, they accepted the TUC directives in total.

The print unions' frustration increased as they tried again to toughen the discipline on the EETPU. They wanted to proceed with a motion at the September 1986 TUC that urged further discipline against the EETPU, ignoring the constitutional points that the General Council was the discpline body and that Congress itself was the appeal forum; in any case, the union had been disciplined on 5 February and natural justice demanded it could not be tried twice. Throughout the summer, the union's leadership had to put up with what the executive council minutes eventually referred to as 'public threats and private entreaties' from the print unions. Given Murdoch's refusal to discuss the matter in a conventional negotiating atmosphere, there were increasingly desperate and ritualized confrontations with the police outside 'Fortress Wapping'. The only people who had access to the News International management was the EETPU leadership. Acting with Norman Willis, the

EETPU were instrumental in trying to achieve access for the printworkers to future jobs at Wapping and redundancy compensation for the 5,000 sacked printworkers. During April, Murdoch offered to the unions the Gray's Inn Road site to print their own newspaper. The unions developed their concept of a joint negotiating council to deal with all unions, operating a refined version of Norman Willis's 17 January offer which, as we have seen, included complete acceptance of Murdoch's right to manage imperatives, including binding arbitration. Talks took place on 25–26 May at Heathrow Airport with all five unions and the TUC represented. News International presented their 'final' offer – Gray's Inn Road plus a redundancy pay award of four weeks' pay (maximum of £155) for each year of service. This offer was balloted on by the print unions, who rejected it. Still the print unions needed Eric Hammond and Tom Rice to fly to America to try to persuade Murdoch to improve the redundancy settlement and accept the joint union negotiating team at Wapping. Still the printers support groups insulted and abused EETPU representatives and property. They made it obligatory for Eric Hammond to be accompanied to many public functions by bulky members of the union to protect him from a repetition of the kicking he received outside Congress House. His wife was pestered by vile phone calls. The union's college at Cudham in Kent was daubed with petrol, with matches left on top of the can, with the slogan 'next time we set light to it, you bastards', scrawled on the entrance. On and on the dispute dragged, with no change in the company's attitude, until in September 1987, they offered to increase the four week pay-out of £155 to £205 per year of service, a national consultative committee with the print unions (but no direct negotiating rights at Wapping), and the unions to provide lists of names of dismissed printworkers from whom new starters at Wapping would be selected at management discretion. This offer too was balloted on, and rejected. The company withdrew the offer and set about making settlement with previous employees on an individual basis. After a book on the dispute entitled *The End of the Street* by Linda Melvern had been published, making further allegations about EETPU involvement in the pre-strike period without once consulting Tom Rice or Eric Hammond, the print unions once again sought to reopen the whole debate. They managed to get a small victory at the 1986 TUC in which the General Council's report on the subject was 'referred back'. Much scurrying to and fro took place at Congress House, but the General Council voted not to reopen the whole business again.

There was the most ferocious demonstration of all on the anniversary of the strike, 24 January 1987. Under pressure now from News International to stop organizing illegal picketing, SOGAT gave way to the real likelihood of having the union's assets sequestered, and ended the dispute on 5 February. The other unions called their disputes off rapidly afterwards.

The six directives remained in force on the EETPU. The issue was hardly dead; but it was fading somewhat into the background when just before the 1987 Congress, Patrick Wintour, the *Guardian*'s labour correspondent who had trailed round the meetings on this issue with immense application, published some further 'revelations'. These were provided by disillusioned people inside Wapping who alleged the EETPU were in serious breach of the 'six directives'. The Sunday before Congress opened, the executive council set up a committee of inquiry, composed of president and Manchester-based executive councillor Paul Gallagher, North-East Coast executive man Barry Davis, who was also the union's chairman of standing orders committee (the EETPU's equivalent of other unions' general purposes or finance and general purposes committees – the key sub-committee in the union). They were joined by the northern divisional plumbing executive member, Jim Egan.

This committee reported on 19 October 1987. They were able to conclusively prove that the allegations in Patrick Wintour's article were of little consequence. First, the allegation of 'frequent' meetings with News International resolved itself into no more than half a dozen meetings held by Tom Rice with the company – largely to do with the attempts made on behalf of all the print unions to set up a decent redundancy scheme and eventual access to Wapping for the conventional print unions. Second, it was just untrue that the union held a 'check-off' agreement with the company. Third, the 1987 wage claim was not produced by head office staff, but by the in-house Salaried Staff Council, although Tom Rice's occasional meetings with them could be misinterpreted. Fourth, the recognition agreement in which the Salaried Staff Council regularized its own position with the company was specifically forbidden from including the union's name by Tom Rice. The fifth allegation, that the union had circularized Wapping members for a general docklands earning survey covering other union members as well, after getting the Wapping members' addresses from the company, was innocent in intention; nevertheless, the committee thought it probably should not have been done, given the huge suspicion eveyone felt given any contact with the company whatsoever.

One extra item that had nothing to do with Patrick Wintour's allegations. The Committee of Inquiry found to their horror that twenty further members at Wapping had been admitted to the union by Tom Rice's secretarial assistance – even though 330 other applications had been rejected in line with the TUC directives over the previous year-and-a-half. These twenty were immediately excluded and the report forwarded to the TUC. The pressure of all this got to Tom Rice. He had been in an impossible position for over a year and a half. He was attempting to ensure the union's disengagement from Wapping in line with the six directives. Yet he was also expected to be the main source of contact with the company that could ensure other unions' eventual recognition. The strain and exhaustion involved turned him towards taking early retirement on health grounds.

Eric Hammond had to take the pressure now. At the Finance and General Purposes Committee of the TUC, over 300 questions were tabled at their meeting of 14 December arising out of the union's Committee of Inquiry Report. Throughout the first few months of 1988 the Finance and General Purposes Committee and General Council pursued the issue, despite the lack of substance in the complaints, the union's *own* revelation of the twenty members inadvertently admitted to the union and promptly expelled. In May 1988, they went quite outside their own rules in proposing to summon the union's executive council for a 'censure'. The executive were not having that. In any case, other, more serious divisions had opened up with the TUC.

The EETPU Committee of Inquiry's Report of 19 October 1987 gave a pointed, unequivocal internal evaluation of the effects of Wapping on the union itself. Paul Gallagher as chairman, Barry Davis and Jim Egan signed their names to this.

The Wapping issue has been an unmitigated disaster. It has given the EETPU's opponents an almost unlimited armoury of weapons upon which to impale us.

Our general secretary, Brother E. A. Hammond, has been subjected to the worst possible vilification, both in work and at home. The health of Brother T. J. Rice has suffered immense damage. Our members, full-time officials and staff have been derided on an unprecedented scale and the attacks that we have all suffered have been through political vindictiveness.

Notwithstanding this situation, the general secretary was recently re-elected by the members of the EETPU with the largest vote ever recorded in the history of the union. Subsequently three members of the executive council have been re-elected. That level of support and loyalty shown by members of the EETPU is unprecedented. Had we not had the background of Wapping, that support would have been more than generous, but with it, the loyalty of our members has been magnificent and it is in recognition of that, that this Committee of Inquiry owes it to the membership of the EETPU to produce as thorough an investigation as we can.

We also respect the courage of those members of the General Council who have been prepared to take decisions that resulted in our continued membership of the TUC and, in the process, found themselves under considerable pressure. That pressure could have been avoided had they taken the easy way out and voted against us, either in February 1986 or in later votes at the General Council.

We also regard highly the role played by Brother Norman Willis, General Secretary of the TUC, and we freely pay tribute to his consistently high level of integrity and fairness.'

The Wapping issue was always linked to the minds of the union's opponents with everything else they detested about the union. It was probably going to

632   *Light and Liberty*

present such people with a heaven-sent opportunity to pay the union back for everything they had said and done since 1961.

For the union's activists, the Wapping issue proved a serious test of loyalty that the overwhelming majority came through with a keen sense of deter-mination to defend their union. This was partly because most of them so approved of the general drift of the union's political and industrial stance that they were not prepared to abandon the union, despite being aware of what the *New Statesman*'s editor John Lloyd called 'the sharpest of sharp practice' at Wapping. Once again, televised picket-line violence in the name of largely unpopular printworkers did not impress the EETPU activists and general public alike. EETPU activists were also not impressed with the under-reported existence of ritual support for the printers from the Transport Workers whose general secretary said the right things, but was clearly not going to put at risk the large number of members his union had working for Murdoch's subsidiary TNT – despite the fact that their activities led directly to the loss of railmen's jobs in loading papers on to trains. At the 1987 biennial policy conference, the union leadership's position on Wapping was overwhelmingly endorsed, despite the opposition of Sean Geraghty as London Press delegate and the apparently knowledgeable opposition contributions from the union's Southampton area.

Eric Hammond told the delegates of the long history of the dispute – the Press branch 'treachery', the SOGAT recruitment, the long rivalry between all the print unions. He was supported by Tommy Benson, the delegate from the union's Manchester Press branch, who described the gap in negotiating style between the print unions and the maintenance unions over the years. This was now being confronted by the newer generation of aggressive newspaper proprietors, backed up by the new labour laws. *Mirror* newspapers and *Express* newspapers had forced through redundancy, but the EETPU and its members had never been so well organized in terms of the members, local officials and national leadership working together. He pointed out how much work had to be done to keep up to date technologically in the light of NGA'82 ambition. He blamed the Wapping strike on the print unions' precipitate challenge to Murdoch, irrespective of the restrictions always going to be imposed on them by the legislation. The only criticism he made, and it was one widely made at the time, was that the leadership of the EETPU did not reveal the basis of their opposition to the printworkers' allegations weeks before the 5 February 1986 at the TUC hearing. Their silence looked like admission of 'guilt'. 'That left us on the shop floor taking some stick, particularly those of us in the industry.'

Opposition speakers said that the union ought not to recruit in areas it did not belong in – irrespective of the trends that were expanding electrical and electronic technology in the printing industry, and irrespective of other unions' attempts to recruit both national and, in particular, electricians on provincial newspapers. Eddie Duffy from Scotland seized that point. 'I can understand why certain unions recoil at the sight of EETPU people. They have a vested interest in the demise of this union. What I cannot understand is the sight of some of our own members falling over themselves in the rush to join the pack.'

Sean Geraghty's speech was interesting. He appealed for politics to be left to one side, and insisted that he had never been a member of the Communist Party. What was surprising about his contribution was his unequivocal confirmation of Eric Hammond's assessment of the genesis of the strike. 'We did not endanger this union,' said Geraghty, 'we did not engage – we did not want to become engaged in a dispute with Rupert Murdoch, because at that point in time we had no need to be – we were still at the negotiating table ... our positions are quite clearly misunderstood.' He had warned the other unions that Murdoch was looking for a strike, and the EETPU were not in a rush to give him one. Notwithstanding that, he thought the union should support the strikers in the current atmosphere of anti-trade unionism. (How anyone could persuade workers at Wapping to give up their jobs as a gesture in support of printers was not explained. The new workforce were earning in mid-1987 an average of £17,000 when their salaries had been, on average, only £8,000 on engagement.)

They were still anxious to publicly pore over the details of the union's Southampton office involvement in the original recruitment. So were the south coast delegates from Gosport, Hythe and Southampton Central, whose delegate was Ginger Pearse; he described meeting Wapping workers in a pub who had been told not to talk to Ginger about the whole business. Alex Hampson from Wythenshawe sought to criticize the leadership over Wapping in a slightly less frontal manner by concentrating on the executive's propensity to 'dive in' – when they did that, they produced problems for him. 'When you are on the shop floor, people come up and wink and ask what our comical union is up to – the other day I was accused of belonging to the union that puts people out of work and on the breadline.'

However much the activist EETPU shop-steward was teased or insulted by colleagues in joint shop-steward committees and so on, most stood firm by the union to a remarkable degree. For them, Wapping was unfortunate – and as Eric Hammond was to say, they could have done without it. But it did not deflect them from overwhelming support for the union's leadership in the bigger battle that was to come.

28

NEW RECRUITS FROM A NEW INDUSTRIAL WORLD, 1979–89

SEVERAL INFLUENCES HELPED THE Union to recruit in the 1960s and 1970s. Chief amongst those was the atmosphere set by government that public sector trade unionism was to be encouraged – an example that private industry found hard to resist (particularly the large manufacturing corporations). The EETPU, like all unions, was helped by the legalization of the closed shop and its formal application in written agreements (euphemistically re-titled 'Union Membership Agreements') and occasionally by the quasi-legal recognition procedures presided over by ACAS under the Employment Protection Act 1975. In 1979, all that changed: the pro-union legislation was replaced by decidedly anti-union legislation. Most important of all, *all* employers, public or private sector, quickly got the message that modern, snappy, reforming companies had every encouragement to avoid trade union recognition. Traditional supporting action to encourage employers to allow new locations to become unionized was illegal. Unemployment and depression in the early 1980s led to the devastation of areas that had enjoyed the highest densities of trade union membership in Britain.

For the EETPU, the 1980s proved bad, but not terminal. TUC affiliation figures, notoriously exaggerated, fell from 12,172,508 in 1980 to 9,243,297 in 1987 – a decline of twenty-four per cent. EETPU membership reached a peak in 1979 and declined thereafter, overall, by sixteen-and-a-half per cent between 1979 and 1988. The membership decline would have been greater had it not been for the growing number of retired members and the welcome increase in the union's recruitment of managerial and supervisory grades. The decline in those members paying subscriptions was 20.7 per cent. Slight encouragement could be taken from the fact that the decline in membership in the skilled, managerial and apprentice sections was also only 16.5 per cent, and that there was a tiny upturn in membership in 1988 (see table 8).

Table 8

	1979	1988	Total Increase/ Decrease	% Increase/ Decrease
Skilled	253,857	203,497	− 50,360	− 19.8
Technical, Supervisory & Managerial	26,214	34,945	+ 8,731	+ 33.3
Apprentice	27,198	17,930	− 9,268	− 34.1
Auxiliary, Clerical & Administrative	105,574	70,406	− 35,168	− 33.3
Honorary	2,524	2,383	− 141	− 5.6
Life & Retired	28,254	41,208	+ 12,954	+ 45.9
TOTALS	443,621	370,369	− 73,252	− 16.5

Throughout the period, the Union's computer could analyse where the membership was and where it was in decline. The union's recruitment strategies in the 1980s were based on reasonable statistics, but also began to pay attention to the rapid changes in the nature of the British workforce with all the implications this contained for the possibility of trade union recruitment.

Fascinating books are written about this subject. Here one can only test the reader's patience by sketching in the trends without listing all the essential statistics. The British trade union density in manufacturing in 1984 was seventy per cent, according to the Workplace Industrial Relations Survey. It was only forty per cent among the service sector. However, all sorts of manufacturing were in decline during the 1980s. Between 1981–8, employment levels fell in metal manufacturing by twenty-three per cent and in mechanical engineering by twenty-two per cent. In construction, where self-employment trends have accelerated, the decline in the collectivist tradition in which unions thrive, employment fell by ten per cent. In food and drink, twenty per cent less were employed in the same period. Even within manufacturing itself, two other trends have spelt further bad news for trade unionism. Shipbuilding and motor vehicles, steel manufacture and consumer durable employment levels have fallen, to be replaced by 'manufacturing' jobs associated with the computer industries and their satellites. Such companies are typically small, entrepreneurial, often foreign-owned and tending to be in towns like Cambridge, Reading and the South-East. Such towns are nothing like as promising material for the trade union movement as a decent-sized engineering works on the outskirts of Manchester.

The nature of the workforce has also changed dramatically, again in directions which are unpromising on the surface for traditional trade union recruitment strategies. The Engineering Industry Training Board figures show that in the late 1980s, the engineering industry was losing 10,000 craftsmen's jobs a year and only recruiting 4,500 craft trainees across all that great industry's different skills per year.

Full-time male manual workers in manufacturing are fast becoming less common than part-time women workers in service industries. The banking and finance sectors of employment now employ 2,380,000 people – an increase between 1981–8 of thirty-nine per cent! Hotel and catering now employs 1,077,000, an increase of sixteen per cent. Neither of these industries is a watchword for trade union strength.

The very nature of the workforce has altered in traditional class terms, and this has been most clearly demonstrated in voting patterns. All of these trends again do not bode well for the trade union fundamentalist. The total Labour vote in 1987 was only 30.8 per cent of the electorate who voted, largely because more of its natural class base does not vote according to the class stereotype expected of it. That's partly because of the 'embourgeoisement' of the working-class. Opinion polls show that seventy per cent of EETPU members own their own homes. Conservative propagandists are fond of reminding people that more citizens are shareholders than trade unionists. Recent studies summarized in Steve Blunt's unpublished LLM dissertation concerning the Bridlington agreement show Labour only attracting half of the 'working-class' vote at exactly the same time as the size of the 'working-class' part of the electorate declined from forty-seven per cent in 1964 to only thirty-four per cent in 1984.

Arguably, no union's membership, with the possible exception of the AEU, has been subject to all these sociological influences to the same extent as the members of the EETPU. The union's skilled membership in an advancing technological world have become a scarce commodity; yet the decline in manufacturing and shipbuilding, self-employment in construction, the onrush of productivity based job-shedding in electricity supply, food and drink, steel and the assault on employment levels in local authorities and other public services has more than offset the plus advantage the union's skilled based might otherwise have provided for the union. On top of that, the decline in manufacturing has shattered industries like telecommunications manufacture, television manufacture and white goods manufacture in which the union's female and auxiliary sections used to thrive.

Recruiting Strategies

In the last years of the 1980s, the union needed to recruit around 35,000 members per annum just to stand still. The first thing the union did in the face of the maelstrom in the 1980s was tighten up what it had. It tried to make sure apprentices were approached while apprentices and not after they came out of their time. With the advent of government training schemes, membership of the union became free to under-eighteens, both those lucky enough to be doing apprenticeships and youngsters on the schemes. Secondly, the union's officers had to tour all the local government training schemes to recruit people under training who might just be lucky enough to find work after their training. Thirdly, the hospitals, local authorities, government departments and other obvious places where the union was already recognized were tightened up. It is often surprising that without constant vigilance, new starters are not approached with the alacrity they might be. Since the effective demise of the closed shop, the responsibility for trade union recruitment has often passed back to the shop-stewards from the personnel department – which may be no bad thing.

The fourth main strategy has been with the recruitment of what used to be called 'white-collar' workers. Like most manual workers' unions, the EETPU has had a section specially geared up to recruit staff workers. The Electrical Engineering Staff Association was inaugurated in 1971 on the basis of an agreement to represent staff employees in the contracting industry. Tom Rice was appointed to run the section and built it up from nothing. From there it grew to its 1988 size of 35,000 in two main ways. First, it broke new ground by direct recruitment in unorganized industry. It was particularly successful in the staff areas of the television servicing industry. Here, both clerical workers, and later shop and depot managers, joined the union in large numbers to enable EESA to win recognition ballots in most television retail/rental chains. The union has been particularly successful in Granada, where it not only organizes staff in the field, but has a large membership at the company's Bedford headquarters. Perhaps its most dramatic success was in the early 1980s when its huge recruitment of hospital engineers – to add to its planner estimator membership – forced NALGO to concede a Whitley Council seat to EESA. The other main recruitment strategy EESA developed from the start was to offer arrangements through which staff groups who were in their Associations could join up with EESA. In September 1972, the BICC (British Insulated Callender's Cables, the world's largest cable-making company) staff association voted, 2,391–421, to join EESA. In 1977, the 500-strong Association of Managerial, Electrical Executives (AMEE) joined EESA. Persuading this staff union for senior managers throughout electricity supply to merge with EESA was indicative of just how attractive EESA's package was to become for independent, if small, groups. Fundamentally, they were all offered the right to handle their own affairs and organize their own negotiations, committees and conferences, so long as they submitted to the larger union's financial oversight, and paid the union the skilled contribution (they often charge more – in keeping with professional association fees – and can then spend that extra money as they please). Finally, they have agreed representation at the union's conferences, and vote in the union's elections. By June 1977, EESA was affiliated in its own right to the CSEU. The Telephone Staff Association (organizing international and night telephonists) joined EESA in 1978, as did Lawrence Scott's Foremen's Association. In December 1979, the United Kingdom Association of Professional Engineers voted, by over 3–1, to amalgamate with EESA, adding an extra dimension to 'staff' organization of qualified engineering graduates. By the mid-summer of 1980, the largest group of all voted, 4,099–1,360, to join EESA. The Steel Industry Managers Association claimed 10,000 members at the time of amalgamation, and brought to the union expertise and experience of middle-management trade unionism in a huge national industry that was about to embark on the traumas of closure, strike and privatization. These traumas led to a thirty-three per cent fall in membership by 1985. In 1982, EESA entered yet another significant area of British industry when the British Transport Officers Guild voted, 1,717–336, to transfer its engagements to EESA. The Rolls-Royce Managers Association was followed into EESA in September 1983 by the Association of Management and Professional Staffs, who largely organize middle managers in the chemical industry, particularly ICI. These separate organizations would often co-ordinate their activities via their Council for Managerial and Professional Staffs, but the hallmark of EESA membership for each of them was the independence they were allowed in negotiating areas. At the end of 1987, following Tom Rice's early retirement, Roy Sanderson moved from the engineering brief to take up the EESA national secretaryship. By mid-1989, he had presided over further successful transfer of engagements with seven further staff associations, including the Professional Divers Association, the Airport Firefighters and the Ministry of Defence Staff Association. By the end of 1989, EESA and all the other groups were re-organized under a new umbrella organization called the Federation of Professional Associations (FPA). The Fire Officers Union and the Institute of Journalists were quicky attracted to the new structure.

Amalgamation with the AEU

In 1986–9, amalgamation talks were held in earnest. To avoid EETPU fears of being 'swamped', the executive first tried to interest a handful of unions to make up a balance with the AEU. Perhaps the EETPU, UCATT and the IPCS or even ASTMS would equal the sheer numbers of the AEU and prevent its apparently dominating any amalgamated union. This idea came to little: after the ballot money issue, the two unions, the AEU and EETPU, found their political friendship was bringing them closer together. By 1988, amalgamation talks with the engineers were producing results. The two general secretaries published a joint statement on 12 January 1988.

The discussions included the following principles:

From Vesting Day, management and control of the union to be under one executive based on equal representation. There will have to be further examination of the developing executive position post Vesting Day and the agreement of a timescale of change.

It was envisaged that the policy making/rules conference would involve a larger number of people. The conference should comprise one delegate from each branch with additional shop-steward representation from integrated industrial conferences. It is estimated that the resulting conference would be about 2,500 delegates and would take place every two years. Further consideration would be given to the method of resolving differences in policy positions between the executive council and conference, and to involving the whole membership in this process.

Local and national industrial conferences and committees would be operational as soon as possible after Vesting Day in order to harmonize the industrial work of the new union and to facilitate the widest possible shop-steward involvement. Further consideration would be given to the AEU's district committees *vis-à-vis* the proposed strengthened industrial committees.

It was agreed that prior to the next meeting discussions should take place at staff or executive level on the following topics:

1. A full audit of resources.
2. A comparison of contributions and benefits, including other unions'.
3. A comparison of salaries and pension arrangements and financial implications.
4. An examination of the structure of the white collar section in the integrated union and a discussion with the EEF regarding recognition.
5. A comparison of political structure.
6. A comparison of computer and membership systems.
7. An evaluation of comparative office resources.

It was agreed that both organizations should stress to their officials and staff the priority to be given to work on this amalgamation.

The talks produced their own problems. The union's negotiating team of Paul Gallagher, president, Barry Davis, chairman of standing orders, and Eric Hammond, found it reasonably easy to be discreet with the details of the talks. They were constantly frustrated when bits and pieces appeared in the newspapers emanating from AEU headquarters, giving rise to rumours throughout both unions.

Nevertheless, a solid framework was drawn up for recommendation to both unions' conferences in the early summer of 1989.

In essence the ambitions of 1988 were to be achieved. The new union would have an industrial consultative base, rather than a branch and district base. A large biennial policy conference was the ambition of the new union, and in the event of the union's executive disagreeing with the conference, a ballot of members would be held. The thorny problem of appointing officials (which the EETPU did) and electing all of them (as the AEU did) was to be left for a transition period. Each section of the new union would continue its current practice and then ballot on the subject. Contributions and benefits were to be harmonized.

By this time, the EETPU were outside the TUC, and the political angle was played very hard within the AEU's national committeee, their supreme policy-making body. In terms of replacing themselves with a huge policy conference, the industralization of policy-making and more ballot votes, the national committee would be no more in an amalgamated union. They were like turkeys being asked to vote for Christmas. They voted, narrowly, by three votes, to break off the talks. This was not wholly unexpected. What was unexpected was the AEU's executive council's decision to accept the national committee's verdict and not ballot their members. The talks ground to a halt before the EETPU activists could be asked to express their concerns. These have been based for decades on the electrical craftsmen's minority position in AEU-dominated manufacturing plants. Other analysts in the union did not want to import into the union the AEU's almost formal right-left political caucusing – a way of life that the EETPU felt themselves to be emerging from after the 1960s, 1970s and early 1980s. The talks were suspended leaving both leaderships a mite frustrated in the emerging world of mega-unions as others amalgamated with each other freely. Friendship with the AEU at a national level, in particular over political matters, technical matters and inter-union relations, remains strong and genuine. Bill Jordan, president, told engineering shop-stewards of the EETPU that they 'could not build an electric fence round their jobs forever'. We shall see. Having talked for a hundred years to the AEU, off and on, about amalgamation, it would be a brave man that bet against the union talking to them in the future, once again.

Single-Union, Strike-Free Deals: Independence in Action

Such recruitment strategies – tightening up in traditional areas of organization and the careful series of amalgamations with small groups under EESA's wing – has not been enough. All trade union membership figures fell in the 1980s, despite the uncomfortable fact that there were more people at work at the end of the decade than at the start of it.

The EETPU were anxious to arrive at a new formula for recruitment. This formula would pay attention to the key truth of British industrial relations; the growing tide of non-unionism in new technology industries. It would lie somewhere between the polar opposites of a traditional engineering factory's multi-union, multi-problem atmosphere and the arid quietness of the non-union plant. It would break down both management and employee fears of trade unionism. No one gave this problem as much thought as Roy Sanderson, the union's national officer for engineering throughout the 1970s and 1980s until he moved over to lead the union's white-collar section, FPA. Roy Sanderson's first agreement that was to shake the whole movement's attitude to organization to its foundations was signed with Toshiba at Plymouth in April 1981.

Rank Radio International brought together a handful of traditional British consumer electronics companies, and was operating out of the Rank factory at Ernesettle in Plymouth, a location used by the Company since 1947. Rank Radio International was making colour television sets with a wild abandon in the early 1970s; the booming market would take every set the company could make. In the mid-1970s, despite the Labour Government's twenty-five per cent VAT on sets and the steady invasion of Far East imports, the company still employed around 3,000 workers throughout the decade with the EETPU the largest of the usual complement of engineering unions. In 1978, recognizing the better quality and innovative design of Japanese television manufacturers (who were anxious to manufacture in Britain to gain access to EEC markets), Rank Radio were happy to go into partnership with Toshiba at Plymouth. Between 1978 and September 1980, however, the Rank-Toshiba Company failed to satisfy each other's hopes for the future, and the joint company broke apart, with Toshiba left as the sole owner of the site. On 20 March 1981, the Ernesettle plant closed, making 2,600 people redundant (on top of the several hundred sacked already at Redruth in Cornwall).

The company were prepared to talk to the union about the possibility of its restarting an operation at Ernesettle, but it would never be like the Rank radio days again.

Roy Sanderson dealt largely with Geoffrey Deith, the joint company's managing director and the first managing director of the new company set up after the closure, Toshiba Consumer Products. By 4 May 1981, when the new company opened with a tenth of the previous workforce, the new agreement had been worked out and was ready for implementation. Roy Sanderson was later to describe the genesis of the agreement. On a plain piece of paper, the company listed their view of the failings of the previous workforce. The union, for their part, listed the management style and personnel department mistakes that Roy Sanderson thought had contributed to the factory's bad industrial relations record. The Toshiba agreement was the result of this process.

The Toshiba Agreement, 1981

Much has been written about this agreement and its derivatives already. No doubt much more is to come. Its significance for the union, however, is already clear. The central features of the agreement offer the company a package of reforms. Toshiba get things from the union that traditional engineering companies are amazed at. No account of the deals, on the other hand, would be complete without the most insistent emphasis placed on the innovative advantages the union is given by the employer.

One of the most telling recommendations of the Toshiba agreement is the reaction of conservative British engineering companies – a reaction that recognizes the package has a net result of significantly reducing the right of management to dictate factory life in the traditional British way. In that sense, the British engineering management of the late 1980s are as wedded to their 'right to manage' as were their aggressive forebears in 1897 and 1922.

Geoffrey Deith's Toshiba management were made of different stuff. Although this agreement is the key part of the modern EETPU's philosophy in action, the work of the company's managing director after Deith, Des Thomson, and his personnel director, George Harris, cannot be underestimated. They recognized the distance the union was prepared to move and came energetically to meet it. Des Thomson knew precisely what he was moving away from in a curiously similar way to Roy Sanderson. Des Thomson had been a senior manager in British Leyland during its strike-ridden precipitate decline, just as Roy Sanderson had become convinced that the class war in manufacturing was failing the membership in an international industrial environment.

The first element of importance in the Toshiba deal is the single-union component. There is no doubt that no employer would chose to negotiate with more unions than he had to. The sheer time it takes to accommodate the rivalries and competing claims of different groups within a workforce is only compounded by their membership of separate unions. Where one union organizes all grades of a workforce, the rivalries and competing claims are usually sorted out at trade union meetings before the single union reaches the negotiating table with the employer. In a multi-union situation, this is often not the case. From an employer's point of view, then, a single union to negotiate with is a self-evident advantage. From the union's point of view, the advantages in terms of membership, income and influence are equally obvious. All unions take the same view, whatever their public utterances. The author was told by a senior figure in the TGWU that 'the only thing wrong with a single-union deal is when it does not have "TGWU" at the bottom of it!'

The next element within the Toshiba deal that drew considerable attention to itself was the new role for the union in the collective bargaining machinery.

This revolved round the system of worker participation in the company's government. The union had rejected the concept of worker directors in the 1960s, and again in 1976–8 while the Bullock Committee looked at the possibility of legislating for worker directors once more. (The EETPU evidence to Bullock was the only union's evidence to be separately quoted in the Report. Its main point was that the union must represent the workers at all costs. To be on the board meant a trade union representative had to wear 'two hats'. The workers would eventually lose their trust in someone so fatally compromised.) Participation of the workforce in the running of the company at Toshiba was subtly different from this. Toshiba has a company advisory board. (In other companies with these deals, the name is slightly different but the functions very similar.) On this advisory board sit elected representatives from each of the separate departments in the factory, along with senior management and the senior shop-steward of the EETPU 'ex-officio'. The senior shop-steward is the only union officer on the advisory board as of right. All of the workforce (non-unionists included) can stand for office on the advisory board and vote in the departmental elections. In the early days, non-unionists were elected to the board. In modern times, the union's shop-stewards for the departments concerned tend to get elected to the advisory board. The shop-stewards perceive that their capacity to influence events for the membership is enhanced by their election to the advisory board. They take that attitude because the advisory board is obliged to reveal information to the representatives there on every imaginable subject – investment plans, production figures, quality implications, working conditions proposals – everything. The company advisory board, therefore, has a coherent, constantly updated picture of the company in action. The EETPU representatives contribute their members' concerns and experience to the advisory board; that same coherent overall understanding of the company's prospects and problems can then be brought to bear when the time is appropriate for discussing the annual wage round in the midst of all the other demands for the company's resources.

If the advisory board cannot agree on any subject, particularly on wages, of course, the union can then revert to a conventional trade union – management relationship. The area full-time official in Plymouth and the national officer for engineering can then assist the shop-stewards locally in trying to persuade the company to concede more. If they fail, they have come to the end of the line. In a conventional agreement, it would now be time to 'put up or shut up' – accept the company's offer or start the process of organizing a strike.

'Strike Free' Deals

But not at Toshiba. The feature of the agreement that has excited the most comment is the union's willing renouncement of the strike. At the end of the advisory board/conventional negotiating procedures, the Toshiba agreement precludes the issue being resolved by a strike. The union will not officially organize or condone its members' striking for higher wages or anything else at the end of the procedures. However, it thinks it has found something better than strikes, *from a wholly trade union perspective*.

Strikes have never been a test of the virtue of the workers' case. They have always been a test of strength between the union and the employer, who usually has much more of it, backed by money and law. Jimmy Rowan understood this in 1912: 'The fact cannot be ignored that the worker fights on his stomach and the employer on his bank book.' Not much has changed since then. Certainly, many strikes are provoked by employers who force change on a defeated workforce rather than negotiate change with social partners represented by trade unions. In the Toshiba agreement, the reference to power and strength that the strike represents is not on the agenda. The final test of the employer's or trade union's case is pendulum arbitration.

At the end of any dispute – at the end of advisory board/conventional bargaining – if the issue remains unresolved, arbitration often splits the difference between the employer and the union. Not in pendulum arbitration. It asks the arbitrator (usually appointed by the conciliation service ACAS) to choose between the company's last offer and the union's final claim. Someone is going to be 'right'. Someone is going to be 'wrong'. Pendulum arbitration is a most effective deterrent to the arrogant use of power by an employer and the excessively imaginative tendency to claim the earth by a union in negotiations. The fact that a pendulum arbitrator waits patiently at the end of the line – after the company advisory board and conventional negotiations – gives all concerned pause for thought. Add to that the fact that the union negotiators are extremely well-informed about the whole of the company's operations, and a picture emerges of a new style of collective bargaining. The company now is not frightened of the union's capacity to disrupt his operations; he respects the union's capacity to argue a case and present its demands in a logical, rational way, aware that if the case is powerful enough, he will *have* to concede it. The time-honoured managerial response to most trade union claims is to say 'No – and what are you going to do about it?' At those companies with pendulum arbitration, such a managerial style is likely to fail when the arbitrator examines the objective evidence of a trade union claim (movement in prices, increases in productivity, comparable wage rates in the locality or the industry, shortages of skill and many more measurable criteria). There is nothing wonderful about being on strike, from a trade union perspective. Things are said that are never forgotten. Passions are raised, humiliation endured. Members lose money, even when they 'win' a strike. Modern trade unionists are least of all impressed by traditional rhetoric that associates strikes with the vanguard of the assault on capitalism. This last aspect is perhaps the source of the politically inspired opposition to 'no-strike' deals, as they are called in the popular press. If trade unionists win justice within the market economy, the possibility of trade unions being used as the revolution's eventual battering-ram recedes even further into the distance.

Roy Sanderson, the architect of the Toshiba agreement, summed up the importance of pendulum arbitration in speaking to the EESA conference in October 1988, seven years after the signing of the Toshiba agreement.

Arbitration has become a very emotive issue in British industrial relations. It carries a connotation because it means that arbitration is a substitute for strikes, that we are somehow infringing on the freedom and democratic aspects of our society. There is almost an implication that any denial of the right to strike, no matter what it is replaced by, is linked to some form of suppression and totalitarianism.

For some I think, strike action is seen as a weapon of the class struggle, as a means of revolutionary change, and I would imagine no matter how many arguments you deployed you would stand little or no chance of convincing them that there was a legitimate and proper alternative to strike action. But if you look at recent British history, I think a very powerful case can be made for searching for an alternative.

In the eighties, the use of strikes has declined. The British workers have either experienced at first hand or witnessed from the actions of others that strikes do not really pay. They are very costly, they are very damaging as we saw in the miners' strike, especially to the miners and their families, and there is mounting irrefutable evidence of their increasing ineffectiveness.

If you look at the eighties, I think all the evidence points to the need for trade unions to examine very carefully whether or not there exists an alternative mechanism, for settling disagreements, to the strike, and one of course that still retains for the trade unions the essential principles on which they are based. In fact, such an alternative does exist.

The seventies were a decade in which British militancy, the use of industrial action, reached its peak. Yet if you look at the end of the decade and compare it with the beginning, British workers have actually slipped further and further down the international league table when it came to pay, living standards and, most important of all, job security.

The fact was that in those countries where strikes were rarely if ever used, those conditions, that job security, had forged ahead far quicker than in Britain. You only have to look at Japan and West Germany where by comparison in the seventies there were few if any strikes and yet, during that decade, they moved ahead quite substantially compared with the British workers.

The strike weapon, far from being the harbinger of better pay and conditions, let alone the means of worker emancipation as the advocates claim, is actually of declining value in industrial relations and political terms.

Could I also rebut the charge that some of our critics make that we have surrendered the right to strike? The implication of this charge is that we have somehow left workers naked in the face of an all powerful employer. That is not the case. We have never surrendered the right to strike in any of the agreements we have concluded. We have merely exchanged it for a superior method of dispute resolution, that of arbitration. We will never tire of rebutting our critics' allegations because what they avoid analysing is just what a strike is.

A strike is nothing more than a means of settling a disagreement between an employer and a union who cannot settle it by negotiation. That is all it is. It is very damaging, it is very costly, and it is increasingly ineffective. Worse than that, industrial action settles disagreements not on the basis of equity and justice but on a trial of strength. Whoever has the most industrial muscle wins the disagreement. You can have the most powerful and formidable case under the sun, but if you have no industrial muscle you are never going to win that disagreement with the employer. The reverse is true; you can have the worst possible case but because you have plenty of muscle you are bound to win the disagreement.

Arbitration, I think, meets the requirements that trade unions face in the modern world. It is more effective, and when you look at the response of our critics to arbitration they are left in some disarray. I can recall a little while ago, Arthur Scargill halfway through the long-running dispute with the British Coal about their disciplinary system, finished up by demanding that British Coal drop their ideas and replace it by binding independent arbitration, and if they did that then they would be prepared to settle on the disciplinary code that they were putting forward. It is also ironic that the hard left in British trade unions finish up agreeing with those reactionary employers. The problem we find is, talking to employers of the sort of hard 'no' school, it is they who most determinedly resist any ideas of surrendering their economic power. They feel that surrender comes about by agreeing to arbitration and they find that the only allies they really have in the trade union movement are the hard left, our severest critics.

The relevance of pendulum arbitration is that they are part of the agreements that we have introduced in the last several years, the so-called 'strike free' agreements. And they fit the culture of it. In those agreements we are attempting to replace the old adversarial system with a system based on harmony and co-operation.

Pendulum arbitration is just one part, an essential part but just one part of a total package. The theory that attracted us to it was that it does compel both parties from the very start of the bargaining process to advance their most sensible, their most reasoned claims and offers. There is no bonus whatsoever for doing other than that. So we are convinced that pendulum arbitration has one great virtue over compromise [or ordinary] arbitration and that is it encourages, from the outset, responsible collective bargaining.

It encourages genuine collective bargaining because both parties can see that at the end of the process there is always the possibility that if they do not shift their ground slightly in the negotiating arena they could lose all when the issue is decided by the arbitrator.

Like the strike, in a sense, pendulum arbitration has a great merit of hanging over the negotiators like a sword of Damocles compelling both parties to genuinely search out an agreement rather than passing it on to the arbitrator for him to decide.

We have thirty-five strike-free agreements. We have had most of them now for the best part of eight years, and the pendulum arbitration clause has only been flickered three times. That is hardly evidence to suggest that if you introduce this system of dispute resolution then bargaining ends, people end their responsibility to search out acceptable solutions and really just pass on the responsibility. Three times it has been used. Three times we can fairly claim that the verdict came down on the side of the employees in the disagreement; so not only is it rarely used; when it is, it happens to work out in our favour, and that is another reason why we find it a very acceptable system.

Pendulum arbitration is an issue that separated us from the traditionalists and the hard left within the TUC. And I think the reason for it is not some objective, careful consideration of what the merits of pendulum or compromise arbitration are versus industrial action. What is unacceptable to our hard-left critics is the belief that in a market economy it is possible to create industrial relations that are based on trust, harmony and co-operation. That they find totally unacceptable, totally alien to their political belief and creed. They believe there has to be two sides of industry, but they are locked in combat almost like trench warfare and there is no possibility of making progress by evolutionary means through ironing out some of the pretty obvious problems that exist in the industrial relations system.

We think we have to go out now and start campaigning for the introduction of arbitration as a preferable, better means of resolving industrial relations disagreements than those which we traditionally have.

The union not only gets access to an unsurpassed quality of management information and a means of resolving disputes that does not rely exclusively on a trial of strength; it has achieved at Toshiba and elsewhere the goal of a single-status workforce. For generations of manual workers, the minor perks and privileges of office workers and managers – 'the staff' – have long rankled. The Toshiba agreement was not the first one to encourage the abolition of what Eric Hammond called 'industrial apartheid'. The agreement has, however, allowed the union to demonstrate its success over single status at Toshiba with considerable effect elsewhere. Canteen facilities now provide uniform standards at the company's 'restaurant' for all visitors to the plant and workers at every level alike. There are no reserved car parking spaces for the great and the good. The holidays, sick pay, release from work schemes are enjoyed by production workers and production managers alike. The only distinctions now sustained are those of salary levels.

The single status in the factory was underlined by every employee wearing the same short blue coat while working. This uniform gave the agreement's main author, Roy Sanderson, a good reason for being grateful for this sartorial evidence of single status. In March 1982, Roy Sanderson was due to speak in the factory to a joint course of supervisors and shop-stewards. While sipping coffee in a corridor outside the meeting room as the previous session was coming to a close, Roy Sanderson noted that his trouser zip had failed. He was appalled by the prospect of standing up in front of this important group who were looking forward to hearing his explanation of the agreement's genesis. He was saved from complete embarrassment by quickly donning one of the company's blue work-coats whose near-knee length comfortably covered any embarrassment. The talk was given and the applause genuine. Senior Japanese executives present congratulated Roy Sanderson on his genius for the right gesture – wearing the company blue coat was a masterstroke by the union's national officer expressing solidarity with the Toshiba philosophy!

The granting of single status helped the company in getting full value out of their key requirement for labour flexibility – in production, craft and office areas of work alike. In return for regular access to training which improves every worker's capacity to do more around the plant, the company has a workforce that will allow itself to be deployed around the factory in reaction to the changing demands of outside market forces in the consumer electronics world. Everyone is paid, therefore, not on the basis of what they are actually doing each day; rather, they are paid on the basis of what they can do, if required. Pay is related at every level to qualification. The Toshiba agreement says:

In reaching this agreement the trade union recognizes and supports the complete flexibility of jobs and duties within the company, both within departments and between the various departments of the company, subject to individual skills and capabilities. In return the company recognizes and accept the need for training and retraining in the broadening of skills and in new technological developments as they affect the company's efficiency as a manufacturing operation.

Reaction to Toshiba, 1983–9

It is possible to argue that this agreement led to the union's expulsion from the TUC in 1988; certainly, the nature of the agreement, and the EETPU's desire to sign plenty more of them, led to a reaction from the rest of the movement that drove the EETPU down the path to independence.

Some criticism of the strike-free deals from within the movement has been politically inspired, as we have seen, revealing as it does a wholly misplaced emphasis on the effectiveness and virtue of strikes. The criticism also fails to take into account the need in the modern world to accommodate the preferences of the employer if there is to be any sort of trade unionism at all. Some have suggested the EETPU strike-free deals are granted only as a condition of recognition. This is untrue. All of the strike-free deals are first of all balloted on by the membership before being signed: they all include a three-month cancellation clause so that if relationships deteriorate to the level of the traditional adversarial set-up, such relationships can be reinstated and the strike-free obligation done away with. Employers in recognition talks are also not exclusively interested in strike-free clauses: their final decision is based on other criteria like the union's general image, its attitude to flexibility, training, the use of computers and so on. Every union advertises itself to employers in competition with others. Some of the EETPU's fiercest critics are now advertising themselves as the 'quiet option' for employers seeking to avoid any contact with the 'strike-free' but controversial EETPU. The final irony of the whole series of manoeuvres to get rid of the EETPU out of the TUC because of the single-union, strike-free deals is that the EETPU now is the only major union not affected by the TUC's draconian rules!

It is probable that the Toshiba deal in itself did not cause a crisis. It is possible that the Hitachi deal did. In some respects, the Hitachi story paralleled the Toshiba story. The union had mounted a relentless and successful campaign in the late 1970s to prevent Japanese companies setting up on their own and destroying indigenous British television manufacturers. The campaign was waged most fiercely over Hitachi's ambitious plans to come to Britain. The EETPU was not opposed, however, to joint ventures, reasoning that Japanese products, product design and manufacturing methods would provide clapped-out traditional British television manufacturers with at least some sort of future. Hitachi went into a joint venture with GEC at its television factory at Hirwaun in the heart of Welsh coal-mining territory near Aberdare. By 1984, when GEC withdrew from the factory, the business was technically bankrupt. Hitachi were left with the same choice as Toshiba. Shut the plant or start again from scratch. In April 1984, the company wrote to all the seven unions at the plant enclosing a brutal, direct ultimatum. They would keep the factory open only in the following circumstances. Hitachi would only recognize one union, and that union was going to be the EETPU (who had 716 members at the time, compared to 482 between the other six unions officially recognized and 115 non-unionists). The company's proposals also included demands for over 500 redundancies, a seven per cent pay increase (which was a sweetener in a plant which had had no increase at all in the last years of its joint venture life and suffered numerous assaults on the bonus scheme earnings), single status, flexibility, company 'members' board and the no-strike alternative – pendulum arbitration. The redundancies went through and eighty-seven per cent of the remaining workforce voted to accept the new proposals, and they came into effect on 8 August 1984.

The Hitachi agreement, painfully overseen by Roy Sanderson and local executive councillor Wyn Bevan, produced an angry response from the unions who were de-recognized. The debate about the nature of collective bargaining produced by these agreements was about to be replaced by a wholly more sordid approach that sought to prevent the EETPU from signing them. The age-old battle between unions to recruit membership in competition with each other moved to another battleground in reaction to the Hitachi deal.

The TUC rules governing membership of unions and how to resolve arguments concerning which union people should be in, in the event of controversy, are called the Bridlington Agreement. The 'principles' concerned were decided upon at the 1939 Trades Union Congress held at Bridlington, building upon some earlier commitments decided at the Hull Congress of 1924. Fundamentally, Bridlington prevents unions affiliated to the TUC from recruiting members from other unions who already enjoy negotiating rights at a particular location: in short, they are aimed at preventing one union from 'poaching' the members of another TUC affiliate. If one union suspects another of any untoward behaviour, it can report the other union's behaviour to the TUC. A disputes committee of senior trade unionists who are not directly involved is then obliged to sort out the problem and order a union found 'guilty' of breaches of Bridlington to hand the members concerned back to the original union. There is no appeal against a dispute committee 'award'.

Part of the Bridlington Principles urged that 'unions should have regard to the interests of other unions which may be affected [by signing sole negotiating agreements] and should consider their position in the drafting of such agree-ments.' The other unions excluded at Hitachi from August 1984 onwards used this 'principle' to attack the EETPU for signing the Hitachi ultimatum. The TUC disputes committee recognized in a back-handed way that the EETPU had no choice, just like the other unions, although no one at the EETPU ever failed to recognize that, in a group of losers, the EETPU lost less than the others through the company's choice of the union as its sole negotiating partner. The TUC disputes committee gave three instructions to the EETPU. They were to make sure that new starters could join their traditional union if they wanted to; that the officials of other unions should be allowed to represent their members in individual cases like discipline (a point the EETPU was not in a position to prevent or allow – that was in the company's power); and the EETPU should create some sort of machinery that would allow the views of other unions to be taken into account by the EETPU negotiators at the factory. Nevertheless, one union involved at Hitachi was particularly infuriated at the turn of events. APEX, the clerical workers union led by the impeccably moderate Roy Grantham, was the EETPU's unlikely prime tormentor in the

Hitachi affair. APEX officials and EETPU officials were often extremely friendly in the corridor politics at the TUC and Labour Party conferences. At one stage, careful overtures were made to APEX that might have led to a full amalgamation between the two unions. However, at the 1985 Congress, APEX demanded a tightening of the Bridlington rules. Roy Grantham got the TUC to extend the Bridlington requirement about having 'regard to the interests of other unions'. No union would be allowed to enter into any sort of single-union recognition agreement that would exclude other unions from their membership rights – even when an employer imposed a solution as Hitachi had done. It was never explained how disputes committees decisions on this question could be imposed on employers. If the TUC disputes committee had told the EETPU not to sign the agreement in 1984, as they would have had to in the post-1985 TUC era, it must have been more probable that Hitachi would have slid into non-unionism rather than the company's management be told by a TUC disputes committee which union or group of unions it should recognize.

The argument then took a further twist. The TUC were clearly not going to like the unions signing single-union deals at existing plants (strike-free or not was immaterial in *this* context; although the usual political bias was bound up in the opposition to single-*union* deals based on the fear of no-strike deals). The question then arose as to the situation at 'greenfield' sites. The EETPU was the main union involved at the Ferguson (Thorn-EMI) television plant at Gosport near Portsmouth. In 1985, the company wanted to move some of the work from its multi-union plant in Gosport to a new 'greenfield' site at High Wycombe in Buckinghamshire. The EETPU achieved a single-union deal at the new plant and was reported to the TUC. The EETPU argued it was a new factory and therefore it did not have to 'have regard to the interests' of other unions. The TUC disputes committee decided that as it was doing ex-Gosport work, it was not a new site. Now it went much further. There were no other unions involved to give back the High Wycombe membership to: the TUC, amazingly, ordered the EETPU to 'terminate its sole recognition and negotiating agreement forthwith and immediately cease to meet the Thorn EMI Specialist Components Division or its parent company on issues relating to collective matters'. The plant lapsed into non-unionism, as the employer would not accept a Gosport-style multi-union recognition agreement. Non-unionism made a significant return in an area where trade unionism was not part of the local tradition. Trade unionism was the loser. In March 1987, another case came before the TUC. This case affected Yuasa Batteries in Ebbw Vale, again in South Wales. By this time, the union was organizing new factories with a greater attempt at marketing the union direct to employers. Ken Biggs, the Blaenavon branch secretary and ex-tertiary college lecturer, was appointed national organizer in January 1985. The union had formally closed its recruitment 'department' in 1980, preferring all local officials to be their own recruitment officers. However, an important co-ordinating role – particularly in the new technology industries – remained. He would visit new factories with a carefully prepared package. He would show a short video film that explained the union's philosophy. It emphasized the secret postal ballot democracy, the provision of mid-life training skills, the need to welcome technological change. Biggs's briefcase would bulge with copies of the Toshiba agreement (updated as other companies added extra elements to the general principles first implemented at Toshiba in 1981), copies of the union's glossy brochure which contained testimonials from successful companies who dealt with the union and copies of many other union publications stressing its commitment to modern non-ideological trade unionism. If the companies liked what they heard, Biggs and his local colleagues would then be given permission to address the workforce and commence the conventional battle to recruit workers into the union. If these approaches failed, the union would always try the car-park leafleting, the standing outside windswept factory gates, the rather self-conscious meetings in city centre hotels attended by ten potential members (of whom five would be supervisors reporting back to the management). This approach still has to be used frequently. NEC Semi-conductors in Scotland have proved particularly irritating in this regard and remain impervious to any sort of trade union recruitment – via the 'front gate' method or the 'back door' method.

At Yuasa Batteries, there was a new twist to the tale. The TGWU recruited dozens of members at Yuasa: the EETPU had recruited 140 of the 300 total employees at the plant. Eighty-two per cent of the total had accepted the agreement drawn up between the company and the union. The TGWU reported the EETPU to the TUC. The disputes committee ordered the EETPU to exclude its ex-TGWU recruits, leave it for eight weeks while both unions tried to recruit and then jointly approach the company. If the joint approach was rejected, then the company could sign an agreement with whoever was by then the most representative union. A bemused Yuasa management eventually signed a single-union deal with the EETPU.

Yet another disputes committee in 1986 awarded the EETPU single-union status at Shotton Paper Mills, to the fury of SOGAT. Here the disputes committee agreed that the deal had been signed before Roy Grantham's TUC speech changed the rules. It also had to admit it was a greenfield site of an employer from Finland who was not intending to join the industry-wide negotiating machinery in which SOGAT dominated the trade-union side.

The TUC decided at its 1987 congress to set up a special review body on trade union organization that could analyse the reasons for the deepening crisis affecting trade union recruitment battles. By now, the problem was being discussed alongside the parallel problem of Wapping. Eric Hammond identified the political basis of the union's unpopularity; he drew together the increasingly hostile attitude to single union-deals with their occasional strike-free companions. He urged the special review body to take into account the agreement's real achievements, in contrast to the political whim of the agreement's opponents.

All that we have done is to articulate the commonsense experience of ordinary people and we have been prepared in the process to take on the political theorists and the revolutionaries. There are plenty in our movement who hide behind the labels of 'left' and 'Marxist' who do nothing to gain wide support, who pose impossible claims, and, when they lead, lead to defeat. They pose no threat to the entrenched privilege of our class system. In fact, they reinforce it. The establishment welcomes a choice between them, the status quo, and the phoney revolutionaries. Ours is a truly radical challenge to the established order. . . . We are the future and we are not going to go away.

The union expected the worst concerning the special review body. Its draft reports, circulating in the early summer of 1988, were clearly aimed at the 'tighter discipline, rigid rules and dire penalties . . . the gallows of expulsion' that Eric Hammond feared. In any case, two further Disputes Committees ruled against the Union in April 1988. The first company was another new South Wales electronics company, Orion Electrical. To start with, all the unions with an interest first of all agreed not to recruit until each had had an opportunity to make presentations to the company. However, in early 1987, the TGWU claimed thirty-eight employees in their union, although they were not paying subs. The EETPU, starting from scratch, recruited seventy-two members in a week. On 23 April 1987, a workplace secret ballot was held. A 96.4 per cent turn-out voted for the EETPU to represent them by 136 votes to two against, and the agreement was endorsed by 129 votes to ten. The TGWU were extremely angry, having already suffered the rebuff at Yuasa and having got in first at Orion, although they never got an agreement out of the company. The TUC disputes committee ordered the EETPU to 'forthwith withdraw' from the agreement and only approach the company in tandem with the TGWU – a solution which the company would not tolerate for a moment. The other decision to go against the union at the same time involved the distribution company Christian Salvesen. They were a well-known distribution company who had set up depots to supply dry goods to Marks & Spencer. This company was called Salstream and was opening depots throughout the country, two of which were at Warrington and Brentford. The company made it known that it would recognize unions, but only from among the ones already recognized in Christian Salvesen (TGWU, GMWU, USDAW, AEU and EETPU). It also emphasized it did not want five unions per depot, and so organized 'beauty contests' to decide which union would organize which depot. The EETPU won single-union no-strike agreements at the new Warrington and Brentford sites. The three general unions (not the AEU) complained to the TUC. They did not mind losing one of these contests to each other, but fought like cats to prevent those two depots going wholly to the EETPU. On the usual grounds of not paying regard to other interests, and the claim that Salstream depots were integral to Christian Salvesen and therefore not 'greenfield' sites, the disputes committee told the union to withdraw from the agreement. It then went much, much further when it ordered the EETPU to 'forthwith exclude all those individuals whom they have recruited within the Salstream depots'. For the first time, the Bridlington procedures were used to tell a union to exclude previously non-union members from the union in defence of other unions' 'rights' to possibly organize a specific plant where the workers themselves had already freely voted to accept the EETPU as their union. What really sent the EETPU leadership up the wall was the revelation within days that the GMWU had signed an exactly similar single-union binding arbitration deal at the next available Salstream depot in Neasden. The *Financial Times* reported this event on 12 May 1988, adding that the GMB were probably in breach of the 'greenfield' consideration like the EETPU. 'The GMB would have difficulty persuading a disputes committee that its depot was a different case. It is unlikely that the GMB will be reported to the disputes committee which is what particularly angers the electricians.' Paul Bevis, the union's national officer responsible for putting the union's case, along with Ken Biggs, to the disputes committee, highlighted other aspects of the inadequate disputes committee awards. He wrote to the *Daily Telegraph* on 1 July 1988.

The three other unions also bid for sole recognition at the two depots in question to cover all workers, including the electricians. They did not consult with the EETPU and, in the case of a further depot, they all declined to consult, even though the EETPU had asked all unions concerned for consultation.

While the hearing was taking place the General Municipal Boilermakers Union, one of the complainants, was bidding for this other depot and subsequently gained recognition, using an agreement exactly the same as the EETPU's. That recognition, once again, was for all the employees, including electricians. The agreement was signed two days after the TUC award against the EETPU.

On 10 May 1988, the EETPU executive council met at Hayes Court with the three strands coming together. First of all, the General Council had issued its demand that the executive council turn up to receive a censure at a future general council meeting. The union itself had revealed that a handful of new members had been admitted to the union at Wapping and then just as promptly expelled in line with the TUC's directives. For this, the union was to be censured without being charged by the General Council. Second, the union's executive had to decide what to do in reaction to the disputes committee awards on Orion and Christian Salvesen. Third, the union had to anticipate the likely opposition of the special review body to the so-called 'no-strike' deals.

The executive council were decisive and unanimous, whatever the political or skill differences between them. Electricians and plumbers, 'left' and 'right', all knew what was *the* issue behind all three TUC attacks. 'The executive council were agreed that it must be the union's members and elected representatives, not the TUC, who determine the nature of the union's agreements.' Consequently, the executive unanimously decided not to turn up to receive a censure, not to accept the Orion and Christian Salvesen awards and finally, turning as ever to the members, to ballot the membership on a rule change. This would make it explicit that the union's affiliation to such bodies as the TUC would only be continued while it was consistent with the union's ability to enter into agreements with companies that were determined by the union, not by anyone else. The members were urged to vote 'yes' for the rule change.

The TUC would not wait for this ballot. Despite the whole of the movement and media commenting on the subject, the TUC general secretary attacked the secret postal ballot as one-sided, because it was accompanied by the executive's endorsement of a 'yes' vote. While the ballot papers were out, the union's industrial conferences met at Scarborough. The general secretary of the TUC, Norman Willis, had his invitation to speak cancelled when the TUC would not postpone the 'suspension' hearings for the EETPU from its mid-conference date of 22 June and in advance of the membership's ballot vote result. Willis compared the union's ballot with the way the 'Albanian electorate are encouraged to reject the official party candidate'. Hammond's speeches to the industrial conferences were received with mature, steady and prolonged applause. All eyes waited for the membership's verdict, particularly as the General Council went ahead with their hearing on 22 June. Eric Hammond travelled down to London with president Paul Gallagher. When they arrived at Euston station, they were fortified for their forthcoming ordeal by a railway porter telling them to give the TUC what-for. The union was given two weeks to comply with the directives to obey the disputes committee awards or be suspended from Congress from 8 July 1988. On 15 July 1988, the union's ballot was closed. In a forty-three per cent turn-out, the members voted by 128,400 to 25,680 to accept the executive council's recommendation, clear in the knowledge that it implied possible expulsion from the TUC at the September Congress. Once again, the members supported the executive council and ignored the *Flashlight* line. Their main leaflet urged a 'no' vote. They wanted a delegate conference before any irrevocable decision was taken; they insisted that it was 'democratic' for the TUC to instruct the EETPU.

They thought Ken Gill was right to suggest that outside the TUC the union would 'bleed to death'.

The executive council pressed on: they decided to 'appeal' to the September 1988 Congress. This involved the payment of around £150,000 in affiliation fees, but the money was felt to be well spent in that it gave Eric Hammond a priceless televised opportunity to explain to the TUC and the public beyond just what had led up to the union leaving the TUC.

The single-union deals had to be defended for a variety of reasons. First the union was conscious of something approaching a conspiracy against it ever since the *Financial Times* on 23 February 1987 reported:

Leaders of the GMBU are considering asking the TUC to draw up a code setting minimum standards for union recognition deals with employers. They believe this would halt a weakening of trade unionism through such developments as single union and strike-free deals. Mr John Edmunds, GMBU general secretary, has informally discussed the idea with leaders of the TGWU and the NUPE. The move indicates how much unions have been affected by developments such as strike-free deals, signed mostly by the EETPU and the AEU engineering union, even though the agreements are few in number. The initiative's aim would be for the TUC to set down a code establishing a model procedure for resolving disputes but which would preserve employees' rights to take industrial action. It would be enforceable under the TUC's Bridlington Procedures, and a proven breach of the code would require any agreement to be renegotiated or terminated, or the union disciplined under TUC rules.

The intention had been clear for a long time: tighten the rules and force the union out of the TUC. There was at base here a rivalry over recruitment. The general workers' unions in Britain have long arrogated to themselves the right to recruit members anywhere. From their perspective, the EETPU ought to remain strictly occupational (although when the union rather flippantly offered the return of all lorry drivers to the TGWU in Christian Salvesen in return for all electricians in the TGWU elsewhere in the company, there was a stony silence!). For the GMB under John Edmunds, the EETPU has proved a particular irritant. When Granada took over Rediffusion, the GMB members were delighted to join the EETPU and enjoy the higher standards of the electricians' union within Granada. When Matsushita opened an electronic printers' factory in Newport, the Company and its employees chose the EETPU rather than have the GMB recognized as it had been at the same company's Cardiff television factory. Indeed, the union's prickly relationship with the GMB was central to the opposition to the union at the TUC. The EETPU exposed the GMB's changes of position bordering on immense hypocrisy. The GMB attacked single-union deals while they sought to add to the dozens they had had for years. They denounced strike-free deals while not only operating them historically but continuing to sign them in the late 1980s.

They denounced financial packages for trade union members as irrelevant to their needs and insulting to poorer people; they were eventually to introduce a comprehensive package of similar benefits topped off with a most potentially financially damaging credit card.

In reaction to this deepening hostility, Eric Hammond offered the TUC a new system whereby disputes over membership could be resolved. Instead of the panoply of Bridlington, threatening 'the gallows of expulsion', he suggested that members should decide in ballots which union they wanted to be in. Unions could negotiate 'free movement' agreements that would respect the members' votes.

The special review body discussion documents at the TUC found this suggestion appalling in its implications.

If it became the practice to seek workers' views, it would be difficult to resist the claim of such views to be paramount. While the arguments against this are not always comfortable to advocate, the fact is that after a division in the union – say during a strike or after a change of official or after an unpopular settlement – there is sometimes disgruntlement with the main union responsible. It would introduce a major element of instability into the disputes machinery.

An earlier reference discussing the same matter of letting members decide, said:

The SRB could not accept the principle in all circumstances that if workers voted for something, they must be granted it. This could lead to damaging results for the trade union movement.

The convenience of Union bureaucracy was to be preferred to the views of union members. The EETPU took delight in rejecting such talk.

EETPU Members' View of the Agreements

The most influential voice within these deals is that of the members most directly concerned. It is the voice least heard by the TUC decision-makers; it is the most decisive voice heard by the EETPU executive council.

Toshiba remains the first example of this reaction. Philip Basset, in his book *Strike Free*, published in 1987, described the union's senior shop-steward's view.

In 1981, Toshiba became the first company to feature the strike-free package in practice. The testbed of the idea, it has since become almost a social laboratory, peered at by teams of delicately probing industrial relations experts. 'On the shop floor,' says Joan Griffiths, 'we feel we are in a goldfish bowl, we get so many visitors'. Popular, expansive, every inch a Devonian, she marshals the tours round the factory, the company's personnel people studiously dropping back. She is the agreement's best advertisement: 'People are still not believing that our system can work. We're sick to death of telling people that it *does* work.' But she is hardly promulgating a glowing, copywriter's whitewash: 'Let's not fool ourselves,' she says. 'I'm not going to be that naive to say that it's all wonderful. Of course there are times when I think that management are totally wrong. We are bound to have problems. But it's not the fact that we get problems – it's how we try to deal with them.' Her refusal to accept Toshiba's system uncritically only goes to reinforce the genuineness of her enthusiasm for it.

Joan Griffiths was to say in 1985 that: 'It is not the Garden of Eden, but it is not a battlefield littered with lost jobs either.'

Throughout the companies affected, the union has struggled to equip its shop-stewards with the necessary support to enable them to face up to their extra responsibility under the agreements. Some companies, though not Toshiba, have occasionally given the impression that the union's commitment to flexibility is a green light for management to introduce whatever change they want, when they want it, with a minimum consultation with the workforce. The union's traditional responses are still sharp when faced with such occasional displays of arrogance. Nevertheless, the traditional help of less than starry-eyed area officials of the union keeps the show on the road.

The single-union deals have been attacked, to little effect, at the union's own policy conferences. Joan Griffiths again told the 1985 conference some home truths. 'Working people are more concerned with the right to work than with the right to strike. If you do not believe that, you are just not listening to them, maybe not even talking to them, much less representing them.' She was most proud of the expansion of jobs involved at Toshiba to close on 1,000. The Baglan Bay Chemicals branch delegate, Gareth Thomas, hit the nail right on the head at the same conference. 'Our union has hundreds of agreements with employers. They are all different. Some have provisions for voluntary arbitration, others for compulsory arbitration. Some involve other unions; others are single-union agreements. What is important is not the type of agreement but whether the members themselves are happy with their arrangements and whether it offers them the best protection.'

The opposition, largely from Scottish branches like the Rosyth Dockyard and Falkirk, suffered from having to admit none of them had actually read any of the agreements, and Wyn Bevan for the executive was able to make much of this and the political basis of the criticism. The union's policy conferences, members in the factories concerned and shop-stewards conferences understood the realities of these agreements and support their development with enthusiasm.

The 1988 TUC

The union's 'appeal' against expulsion at the 1988 TUC was not an 'appeal' in the proper sense of the word. The union did not think it had done anything 'wrong'. Armed with a huge ballot majority, a unanimous executive council, constant private opinion-polling evidence, the applause of EETPU conferences, the support of weekly shop-stewards' courses, no general secretary of the union had ever been better fortified with the most impeccable of representative credentials.

Eric Hammond's speech to the 1988 TUC did not dwell on the minutiae of the TUC committee procedures, the failings of the rules, the jealousies of rivals. He spoke beyond an uncharacteristically silent Congress to British workers everywhere. He spent weeks on the speech; it was to be the most considered exposition of EETPU policy made in recent times. It brought together the political understanding gained since 1961 and carefully laid out the EETPU's total faith in the membership of trade unions and its hearty lack of confidence in much trade-union leadership. It was spoken with a view to the future. It was in clear contrast to Norman Willis's speeches which dwelt on how the EETPU had broken the rules – that the rules were sacrosanct and had to be obeyed. There was no appeal against disputes committee decisions. It was the same for everybody.

Eric Hammond started and stayed on a wholly higher plane. The 1961 ballot-rigging – the last time the union was expelled from the TUC – was a 'pivotal' starting point. In reaction to that corruption, based on fiddling ballots, the union had introduced elections based on secret postal ballots. This finally broke the dominance of minorities based on the branches.

The new leadership could only base itself upon the ordinary members. With secret postal balloting, managed and counted by the independent Electoral Reform Society, our members made decisions on who was to lead them, what rules were to apply and what policies we were to pursue. As the voice of the member grew, so we diverged from many of you, our TUC colleagues.

How could it be otherwise? You listened to and were part of the unrepresentative politicos. We were at one with our members. That difference has meant that the opposition of our members – all our members – to unilateral nuclear disarmament finds no echo among Congress decisions. There is public scepticism, to say the least, about the moral and practical effects of nationalization which is ignored by our composites. Our members' attitudes to strike ballots, law in society and violence in disputes are disregarded. There is a pathological, racist anti-Americanism here which finds little echo amongst our members. Above all, our members reveal an enthusiasm for the market system and its values which infuriates the sherry-party revolutionaries with their model resolutions and conference hall rhetoric.

These questions are fundamental to the reputation of trade-unionism as represented by this Congress. But this Congress constantly rejects the known views of members. For this Congress, the members are now the problem. If you seek to please the activists, it is necessary to outwit the membership. That is why trade union structure is, as Citrine said, 'a function of our purpose'. If you continue to allow committee decisions to have precedence over the views of members, the structure becomes part of the conspiracy against the members. You constantly say that you are democratic, in that the decisions of conferences are represented as the views of the members. The reality is the opposite. The work of our activists is important but they are not the union. None of us will survive if we continue to ignore the views of the average, the normal and regular member. . . .

You obviously see the TUC and its rules as paramount. We do not. Above you, above your rules and above us are our members and any majority decision they may make. It is right and democratic in the present difficult circumstances that we should test their continuing assent to TUC affiliation. . . .

The particular [dispute committee] awards that we are now concerned with would result, if we accepted them, in no agreement and no members for any union. We are convinced that that is a state of affairs that our critics would prefer. Better no union than it be the EETPU.

Colleagues, what is the future facing our movement? History teaches us that after every war there is a settlement, even if the war goes on for thirty or more years. It may be that the trade union leaders have wound themselves up to a position where a separation is inevitable. We neither seek nor desire that, but I am realistic enough to recognise the symptoms of Salem, of the witch-hunt. I also recognize the danger for the TUC as it is today. The problem is not so much that our members support or oppose the TUC as that they see it as wholly irrelevant to their needs. I say very coolly and carefully to the members and officers of other unions, particularly the craft unions, that if you vote for our expulsion today and for extending the TUC grip on your affairs, you are fashioning weapons to deal with us which will be turned against you tomorrow. You will not be able to curtail the ambitions of the general unions, especially not if the machinery of the TUC is at their beck and call. . . .

The birth of our independent union today does create a new situation. It springs from our members' insistence on the right of the individual to choose. I have to say to you that our policy is that of the open door. We will protect our members from intimidation and arm-twisting from you or from any other quarter. If any EETPU member wishes to join any other union, there is nothing we will do to stop him. The door is open. It is also open for anyone to come in. When you expel us today, you provide all trade unionists and all potential trade unionists with a choice, with freedom. The choice today is yours. The choice tomorrow is the members'. Will they choose the future or the past? Will they choose independent, secret and individual votes or the cornflake ballot box rattled under their nose, reality or hypocritical humbug, partnership and co-operation or hard-left class war conflict? We are convinced that they will choose freedom as our members have chosen independence.

'Ah', our friends say to us, 'all these things which you oppose are changing'. It is not our fair-weather friends whose unions were pleased enough to accept our support when they were in the firing line but now rush forward in their eagerness to denounce us, but our genuine friends who have some strong arguments. They will say, 'Why leave now when we are winning and things are moving our way? We beat the dinosaurs on the issue of ballot money; we moved them on Poland; everyone in practice is moving our way on financial packages, single-union deals, binding arbitration and single status. The Labour Party has moved to one member, one vote. We have moved the hard-left majority on the General Council and the NEC. The General Council document on 1992 marks a major turn-round on Europe. Further – they say this quite legitimately – with the new laws on union elections the days of the ballot-riggers are numbered and the notoriously dirty elections will be cleaned up. All unions will then shortly be marching to the tune of their members and all union members want sensible and moderate trade unionism.

It is a powerful and attractive argument, but I have to say to those friends that we do not just have a responsibility for the policy of the movement as a whole, although I do not think it can be said that we have shirked in this respect. We have worked, organized and incurred unpopularity in our mission to change the overall situation. We have a primary obligation, and that is to our own members and our own union. That obligation I have been trying to discharge this morning. However, we have considered carefully the representations of our friends right up to this eleventh hour. Is there any proposal we could make consistent with the seemingly irreconcilable positions of our union and that of the General Council?

We believe that there is. We put it forward as an honourable alternative to the recommendation of expulsion. Our movement faces an ever widening split. Our hand reaches out before the gap becomes too great. The EETPU is prepared to accept the dispute committee awards in respect of Orion and Christian Salvesen subject to an affirmative vote of the members concerned. Will you do the same? Will you let the members decide?

This last-minute appeal was brushed aside by Norman Willis. He also rejected the idea of a conspiracy by rival unions as 'absolute rubbish'. He continued to emphasize the Rules – rules that the EETPU had occasionally been a beneficiary of. Indeed, the whole issue was not a 'matter of left and right; it has been a matter of right and wrong'. The EETPU were wrong to break the rules. The TUC could not allow votes on which union people should be in. 'The fact is we cannot take those decisions and then say you should hold a vote on them [dispute committee awards]. We know that means anarchy. That would be the response of every union towards every decision we ever took.' The EETPU's Delegation had already left the hall.

The union was not immediately affected by the expulsion from the TUC. It is too early to judge if there are to be any long-term effects. Most other unions appear to want to negotiate in the normal fashion, particularly at local level, alongside their EETPU colleagues. The union retains its affiliation to the Labour Party where its long-held policy of membership democracy appeared at the 1989 conference to take precedence at last, alongside other EETPU policies such as the rejection of unilateral nuclear disarmament and wholesale renationalization without compensation. A small number of *Flashlight* supporters attempted to set up a breakaway union: in the first year they had recruited precious few members and achieved no negotiating rights of any substance. They even suffered the indignity at the 1989 Labour Party conference of being berated by Charlie Montgomery at their fringe meeting. Charlie Montgomery, Fred Gore and many others stood firm within the EETPU whilst never sacrificing their left-wing contributions to the union's debates. Manufacturing, Science and Finance appeared to prefer directly recruiting such members as did leave the EETPU, rather than hold them on behalf of the breakaway union. The union saved nearly £400,000 in affiliation fees and other expenses associated with TUC membership.

The feeling of independence abroad in the union as it approaches its second century of existence will surely sustain it, whatever happens in the immediate future. Two recent labour editors of the *Financial Times* are perhaps best placed to have observed and analysed the essence of the EETPU – what it means, what it stands for. The final verdict on the spirit of the union can be left with them.

Firstly, John Lloyd, writing in the *New Statesman* on 27 May 1988.

The electricians' union should stay in the TUC. Not because to leave would create the focus for a split union movement. Not because it should learn to obey rules, though it is clear it has flouted some; but because the electricians, together with the engineers, *are now making the case for production and they have a long way to go before their case is complete.*

The right has played this role, in a somewhat muted, almost embarrassed, form, for the past three decades. The left gave up on the old consensus over production, a renunciation which contributed to its decline. The left seemed to forget, at least in its public utterances, that its salient projects of increased democracy, higher pay and better conditions and shorter hours implied, indeed demanded, a very large growth in productivity both absolutely and relative to those countries, like the other west European states and crucially Japan, which were all getting more productive faster. It was not that left-wing union officials did not sign productivity deals; but they did so for as large a price as possible and as quietly as possible. It was not, in the main, the currency of the conference rostrum. Nor was it that the employers were not largely to blame for shirking what was their prime responsibility; they were, but sooner or later they were bound to realize that fact and either give up or do something about it. Much of what we call Thatcherism is their doing something about it – spurred and aided, of course by the Government.

Lacking a production ethic of its own, whether a left or right-wing version, the Labour movement has floundered. But now it has at least two major unions – the electricians and the engineers – which are prepared to make the deeply unpopular argument that industrial production, though leaner, really is fitter, should get fitter still, and that the dislocation that will cause will be as nothing to the further dislocation to be caused if we don't carry on getting more efficient. They remain wedded to the left in this sense: that while this more efficient production will take place within a private sector, it should be framed within a context of a society prepared to legislate for social justice, prepared to provide collectively and prepared to put a reasonable partnership in industry on to the agenda once more.

This echoes Jimmy Rowan's and Les Cannon's insistence that the union should be associated with skill, with progress, with the future.

Philip Basset, in *Strike Free* underlines this awareness of the union's key commitment to productivity, but places it in a historical and political context that explains the EETPU's resilient determination.

The EETPU is wholly coherent, in its philosophy, its practices, its organization, its politics: no other British union can match the depth or the consistency of its approach. Partly, that is a matter of history: the aftermath of the communist ballot-rigging scandal in the union in the 1950s saw the new leadership slice through the union to its very bone, cutting out the supporters of the ousted old guard and methodically replacing them with those believing in the new order. The result is a near-total hegemony, unnerving many of its opponents – and they are many and various – by its sheer homogeneity: left-wingers charge it with ideological cloning, so that listening to one EETPU official resembles nothing more closely than listening to another EETPU official. They are right; and it is that constancy which both gives the union strength, sustaining it against all opposition, and leads to its isolation, to its position as the UK Labour movement's principal maverick. Its aggressive certainty is rooted in the two crucial elements of its make-up. First, there are its absolute, governing beliefs: it believes in its members, and it believes that its own stance utterly reflects theirs. Second, there is the union's realization of industrial change, its perception that technological shifts are at once marginalizing many other unions and bringing to prominence the EETPU.

Its pragmatism, its voluble rejection of the posture of revolutionary industrial militancy, ensures that it both exemplifies and encapsulates the strands of thinking which came to be known as the TUC's new realism. The EETPU's approach is so interwoven – its philosophy on trade unionism, for instance, both completely informs its attitude towards other trade unions and stems from them; its political stance both springs from the nature of its membership and consistently reinforces it....

In the end, the union is an institutional reflection of the typical member. Norman Willis intended to say to the EETPU Scarborough 1988 conference, if he had given his speech: 'You have never been the most easy member of the trade union family to live with. Traditionally, electricians are individualists and that is as much a feature of your union as it is of the factory "sparks".' His distinguished predecessor was Walter Citrine – Lord Citrine, as he had become by 1947 – who publicly expressed his view of the exclusivity of electricians at the ETU conference at Margate in 1947. He ought to know, having been an electrician on pre-First World War Merseyside.

I have said many times that it seemed to me to follow that a union whose members had essentially to equip themselves with a considerable depth of theoretical knowledge in order intelligently to understand their work, must apply that same sort of analytical sense to the problems of the working class. It seemed to me to be inevitable that the membership of this trade union would – without any sense of distinction or arrogance or anything of that kind – tend to be on a somewhat higher intellectual level than that of the rank and file of trade unions who were not concerned with these problems.

The members might be individualists, different, special. Their motivation in trade union affairs remains a universal one.

For Eric Hammond, his inspiration was first publicly expressed by him in 1963. 'I know what it is for me – a decent home, a secure, reasonable wage, a decent education for my children and a world at peace to allow me to enjoy these modest gains.' Most EETPU members would say 'Amen' to that.

Appendix I

THE UNION'S LEADERSHIP
1889–1989

(i) THE EXECUTIVE COUNCIL
1890–1990

1890–1907 (*The London Executive The union's executive council was elected in the branches across the country, but only members living in London could be executive councillors to avoid the costs of executive members travelling.*)

1901–04	F. Austin	1905–07	H. Blatch
1898–9; 1901	C. Bowles	1899–1902; 1907	J. Brebner
1901; 1903–04	J. Brixey	1890	C. Brush
1904	G. Buchanan	1900	F. Bugden
1907	J. G. Butler	1894–1907	A. Calipé
1891–8	T. Cannon	1907	A. Carrier
1894–5	W. Charman	1902	O. Choppin
1896–9	H. Constable	1891–2	H. Cork
1905–07	J. Dibdin	1901–05	F. Donaghue
1903–04	H. Durtnall	1902–03	J. Earl
1890	T. Everard	1899–1900	J. Farenden
1890–2	T. Forster	1899–1901	T. Foster
1899–1901	J. Gardiner	1891–2: 1899–1901	W. Gooday
1895	H. Grant	1896–8	J. Hart
1894–5	J. Hilliard	1891	F. Hilling
1892	A. Hines	1898–9	T. Honey
1906–07	R. Howes	1906	H. Jessop
1896–7	R. Lang	1903–06	J. Marshal
1894–5	G. Montague	1891–8	J. Moon
1906	C. Moore	1904–06	S. Morris
1904–07	J. Murdon	1891–4	A. Norman
1903; 1905	H. Oakleigh*	1894–5	S. Pannington
1896–9	J. Pearce	1903–05	J. Pearce

1900–01	G. Pegg	1898–1902	A. Rossin
1894	F. E. Sims	1890–1	R. Steadman
1890	T. Sullivan	1890–2	W. T. Tebb
1890	A. Terry	1900	E. Tice
1892	C. Thirlwell	1900–05	F. Trevis
1891	J. Trower	1894–7	T. Welsh
1898	C. Williamson		

* Elected also in later period.

1908–14   *There were six executive seats, nominated by branches in the division, but elected annually by the whole union, thus providing a national executive council.*

1911	J. Carrick	Merseyside & North Lancashire
1913–14	G. Dawson	Midland, Wales & South Yorkshire
1908–10; 1913–14	A. Garner*	Merseyside & North Lancashire
1908–10	J. Kinniburgh	Scotland
1908–14	W. McKay*	Manchester
1908–09	B. McMillan	North East
1912–14	W. Noble*	North East
1908–09	H. Oakleigh	London & The South
1910–11	G. Olley	North East
1910–14	T. Philpott	London & The South
1908–12	F. Soughton	Midlands, Wales & South Yorkshire
1914	A. Stewart*	Scotland
1911–13	T. Stewart	Scotland
1912	A. Wright	Merseyside & North Lancashire

* Elected also in later period.

1915–35   *There were nine executive council divisions, with the members voting in each division simply for their own executive councillor. With slight alterations to boundaries, there were annual elections until 1925 and thereafter for two-year periods of office.*

1922–44	T. Anderson	Glasgow & West Scotland
1916; 1919–25; 1928–31	J. Bellamy	Yorkshire & Lincolnshire
1919–21; 1923–24	H. Bolton	North London & Suburbs
1916	J. Bryan	Glasgow & West Scotland
1922	E. Bussey	North London & Suburbs
1915–20	J. Collins	Midlands, Wales & South West
1919–20	J. J. Collins	Ireland
1924–5	T. Corbett	Merseyside, North Lancashire & North Wales
1925	J. Costello	Glasgow & West Scotland

1916–17	W. Day	South London & Southern England
1919–20	J. Dennison	Glasgow & West Scotland
1921–5	W. Finn	Ireland
1926–7; 1930–31	S. Fitzpatrick	Ireland
1921	G. Foster-Curtis	Midlands, Wales & South West
1915–17	A. Garner	Merseyside, North Lancashire & North Wales
1928–9; 1932–3	E. Hainge	Midlands, Wales & South West
1918	J. Hampton	Merseyside, North Lancashire & North Wales
1918; 1923; 1925	G. Humphreys	South London & South East England
1919–23; 1926–31	J. Illingworth	Merseyside, North Lancashire & North Wales
1925–35	E. Irwin*	Manchester
1917–18	W. Jackson	North East
1934–5	F. Johns*	Midlands, Wales & South West
1918–19	E. Jones	Manchester
1915–19	E. Kidd	Ireland
1926–7	G. Ladd	North London & Suburbs
1915	J. Law	East of Scotland
1916; 1920	D. Low	East of Scotland
1928–33	J. Lyons	North London & Suburbs
1917	E. Lyson	Manchester
1920	P. McArdle	North East
1915–16; 1913–34	W. McKay	Manchester
1932–5	G. McKernan*	Merseyside, North Lancashire & North Wales
1934–5	G. Millar*	North London & Suburbs
1922–7; 1930–1	W. Minor	Midlands, Wales & South West
1921–2; 1924–29; 1934–5	F. Morrison	East of Scotland/North East
1922; 1926–33	H. H. Morton	South London & South East
1917–21	J. Muir	North London & South London
1915–16; 1923	W. Noble	East of Scotland/North East
1924; 1934–5	J. H. Smith*	South London & South East
1917–18	W. J. Smith	Glasgow & West Scotland
1932–3	R. Smyth*	Ireland
1915–19	C. H. Stavenhagen	North London & Suburbs
1915; 1919–21	A. H. Stewart	Glasgow & West Scotland
1928–9	J. Swidenbank	Ireland
1926–35	W. Turnbull*	Glasgow & West Scotland
1917–18	J. Waterson	East of Scotland/North East
1916–17	W. Webb	North London & Suburbs
1925–6	W. Westfallen	North London & Suburbs
1915	F. Whitehead	South London & South East
1926–7	A. Williams	Yorkshire & Lincolnshire
1930–3	W. Wise	Yorkshire & Lincolnshire

* Elected also in later period.

1936–47   *There were now eleven executive council divisions: the two extra seats were formed by giving an extra seat to London and the Home Counties and by splitting the East and West Midlands and South Wales, the South and South West England. The electoral period remained two years.*

1937	C. R. Bond	West & North West London, Oxford, Luton
1942–7	E. Breed*	West & North West London, Oxford, Luton
1938	W. H. Bryant	West & North West London, Oxford, Luton
1946–7	L. Cannon*	North Lancashire & Merseyside
1944–7	T. Carter*	West of Scotland & Glasgow
1938–45	G. Cole	North Lancashire & Merseyside
1936–7	W. Creyk	North East England/East of Scotland
1944–7	J. Deans	North East England/East of Scotland
1936–47	L. Gregory*	South East/South West London, Kent, Sussex, Surrey
1940–3	F. Haskell	East & North East London/East Anglia
1941–3	G. Haslam	Manchester & Lancashire
1938–40	A. Hatton	Manchester & Lancashire
1938–9; 1944–7	F. Haxell*	East & North East London/East Anglia
1944–7	E. J. Haynes*	East/West Midlands
1936–7	E. Irwin	Manchester & Lancashire
1938–41	C. Innes	North East Coast/East Scotland
1936–7	F. Johns	Wales & South West and South
1936–43	E. R. Lee	East/West Midlands
1942–3	W. Lilbury	North East Coast/East Scotland
1938–42	A. A. Martin	West & North West London, Oxford, Luton
1936–7	G. McKernan	North Lancashire & Merseyside
1936–7	G. Millar	East London/East Anglia
1944–7	E. Morrow	Northern Ireland
1943–7	J. Potter*	Yorkshire
1945–7	L. Price*	Wales & South West & South
1942–3	J. Simpson	Yorkshire
1942–3	J. Sinclair	Northern Ireland
1936–7	J. H. Smith	South East/South West London, Kent, Sussex, Surrey
1938–9	R. A. Smyth	Northern Ireland
1944–7	G. Stevens*	Manchester & Lancashire
1936–41	H. Thorpe	Yorkshire
1936–7; 1939–41	R. Todd	Northern Ireland
1936–43	W. Turnbull	West of Scotland & Glasgow
1938–44	H. F. Turner	Wales & South West & South

* Elected also in a later period.

1948–63 *Still eleven executive council divisions: Scotland now was one division for the whole country, and the North East Coast went in with Yorkshire. There were now four seats for London and the Home Counties. These were the last executive elections in the branches (two years). The introduction of secret postal ballots was first used for executive vacancies in 1963.*

1963–	J. Ashfield*	(First executive council man elected by secret postal ballot in March 1963) East & West Midlands
1948–57	A. C. Batchelor	West/North West London, Bucks, Herts, Middlesex
1962–3	W. Blair*	West/North West London, Bucks, Herts, Middlesex
1961–3	W. Blairford*	Scotland
1962–3	T. Breakell*	North Lancashire & Merseyside
1948–54	L. Cannon	North Lancashire & Merseyside
1948–9	T. Carter	Scotland
1958–63	F. Chapple	East & North East London/East Anglia
1960–1	I. Davies	Wales and South West
1955–61	J. Feathers	North Lancashire & Merseyside
1954–61	J. Frazer	South West/West Central London, Surrey, Herts Berks
1962–3	H. Gittins*	South West/West Central London, Surrey, Herts, Berks
1955–61	S. Goldberg	East & West Midlands
1948–54	L. Gregory	South West/West Central London, Surrey, Herts, Berks
1960–3	E. Hadley*	Yorkshire
1948	F. Haxell	East & North East London/East Anglia
1957–61	J. Hendy	West & North West London, Bucks, Herts, Middx
1948–59	J. A. Humphrey	South East/East Central London, Kent & Sussex
1948–9	F. McGrath	East & West Midlands
1960–3	J. McKernan*	Northern Ireland
1949–55	F. Murphy	Scotland
1962–3	J. O'Neil*	Wales & South West
1948–59	J. Potter	Yorkshire
1948–9	L. Price	Wales & South West
1960–1	R. Sell	South East/East Central London, Kent & Sussex
1962	F. Sharman	East & West Midlands
1950–5	P. Snadden	East & West Midlands
1948–56	G. Stevens	Manchester & Lancashire
1962–3	L. Tuck	South East/East Central London, Kent & Sussex
1949–57	T. Vetterlein	East & North East London & East Anglia
1956–60	C. Walker	Scotland
1958–63	H. West*	Manchester & Lancashire

*Elected also in a later period.

1963–89 *From March 1963, all executive council elections were held with secret postal ballots. From 1963–5; every two years. From 1966 onwards, the executive council has been* *full-time and elected for five years. From 1971, the three plumbing divisional members have been elected similarly. In 1973, London and Home Counties lost one seat which was given to the split divisions of Yorkshire and the North East Coast.*

1964–82	J. Ashfield	East & West Midlands
1976–	H. Barlow (P)	Scotland and Ireland
1974–8	H. Best	Yorkshire
1980–	W. Bevan	Wales & South West
1964–81	W. Blair	West & North West London, Bucks, Herts, Middlesex
1964–78	W. Blairford	Scotland
1964–85	T. Breakell	North Lancashire & Merseyside
1984–	L. Britz	South East/South West London, Kent, Sussex, Surrey & Hampshire
1982–	F. Chapman	East & West Midlands
1971–3	I. Clark (P)	Scotland & Ireland
1971–8	B. Clarke	Wales & South West
1964–86	E. Clayton	East & North East London/East Anglia
1979–	A. B. Davis	North East Coast
1986–	J. Egan (P)	Northern England
1987–	P. B. Fenelon	East & North East London/East Anglia
1978–	P. Gallagher	Manchester & Lancashire
1971–8	W. Gannon (P)	Southern England
1964–72	H. Gittins	South West/West Central London, Surrey, Herts, Berks
1964–73	E. Hadley	Yorkshire and North East
1964–84	E. Hammond	South East/South West London, Kent, Sussex, Surrey & Hampshire
1979–	W. Hayes	Yorkshire
1981–	H. Hughes	West London, Berks, Bucks & Oxon
1985–	K. Jackson	North Lancashire & Merseyside
1964–85	F. McGuffie (P)	Northern England
1968–75	J. McKernan	Northern Ireland
1978–	A. McLuckie	Scotland
1964–70	J. O'Neil	Wales & South West
1974–8	P. Ramshaw	North East Coast
1964–74	D. Sheasby	Manchester & Lancashire
1964–5	H. West	Manchester & Lancashire

Plumbing National Secretary

1968–87	C. Lovell
1988–	W. Gannon

Appendix 2

THE UNION'S LEADERSHIP

(ii) GENERAL SECRETARY
1890–1990

1890–1900 Appointed by the Executive Council.

1890	R. J. Steadman
1891–4	A. J. Walker
1894–5	R. J. Steadman
1895–1900	F. E. Sims

1900–40 Elected in the branches every three years.

1900–07	A. Ewer
1907–40	J. Rowan

1940–66 Elected in the branches every five years.

1941–8	E. Bussey
1948–54	W. Stevens
1955–61	F. Haxell
1961–6	J. Byrne

1966– Elected by secret postal ballot every five years.

1966–84	F. Chapple
1984–	E. Hammond

Appendix 3

THE UNION'S LEADERSHIP

(iii) GENERAL PRESIDENT
1890–1990

1890–1911 Appointed by executive council annually.

1890	A. J. Walker
1891–3	T. Cannon
1894–5	G. Montague
1896–7	J. Hart
1898–9	J. Pearce
1899–1901	W. Gooday
1901–03	F. Donaghue
1904–05	J. Pearce
1906–07	J. Dibdin
1907–08	S. Morris
1908–11	J. Ball

1911–15 Appointed by executive council, confirmed by branch votes.

1911–15	J. Ball

1916–40 Elected annually by branch votes, biennially after 1925.

1916–31	J. Ball
1932–41	E. Bussey

1941–74 Elected every five years; after 1962 by secret postal ballot.

1941–5	H. P. Bolton
1945–62	F. Foulkes

1963–70   L. Cannon
1972–4   F. Chapple

1975–   Appointed by executive council annually.

1975–85   T. Breakell
1986–   P. Gallagher

Appendix 4

MEMBERSHIP FIGURES
(AT DECEMBER)

1889		1918	31,345
1890	570	1919	48,784
1891	1,123	1920	57,292
1892	1,183	1921	45,561
1893	817	1922	31,345
1894	402	1923	26,165
1895	326	1924	27,589
1896	392	1925	29,241
1897	635	1926	29,058
1898	702	1927	25,712
1899	904	1928	26,187
1900	959	1929	28,612
1901	917	1930	31,453
1902	1,107	1931	31,322
1903	1,105	1932	30,921
1904	1,071	1933	31,100
1905	1,144	1934	34,221
1906	1,261	1935	40,271
1907	1,539	1936	48,407
1908	1,709	1937	58,168
1909	1,689	1938	63,877
1910	1,871	1939	70,065
1911	3,076	1940	80,058
1912	5,214	1941	97,298
1913	7,272	1942	113,361
1914	8,195	1943	124,942
1915	10,861	1944	132,484
1916	12,929	1945	133,033
1917	20,621	1946	161,943

1947	170,141	1968	364,929
1948	181,775	1969	381,102
1949	187,520	1970	420,588
1950	192,339	1971	419,646
1951	197,958	1972	417,087
1952	203,344	1973	425,412
1953	211,512	1974	420,577
1954	215,596	1975	426,812
1955	223,602	1976	428,636
1956	228,158	1977	432,627
1957	239,334	1978	438,269
1958	230,136	1979	443,621
1959	233,579	1980	438,669
1960	242,900	1981	428,595
1961	252,673	1982	416,482
1962	257,464	1983	401,092
1963	271,912	1984	394,283
1964	281,773	1985	384,577
1965	292,741	1986	373,715
1966	293,173	1987	369,244
1967	297,450	1988	370,369

Appendix 5

A NOTE ON SOURCES

1 The Internal Sources

The main source materials for this book have been the union's own published records. These are sketchy before 1910, comprehensive afterwards.

A Rule books 1889–1989 (a complete set)

B Annual reports 1891–1989 (no report was published in 1893)

C Conference reports – A complete set of conference reports exists for every conference from 1893 onwards: Rules Revision Conference 1893–1989 (periodic); Policy Conferences 1936–1989 (annual and biennial); Industrial Conferences 1964–1989 (biennial)

D Union journals *Eltradion* 1905–09
      Electrical Trades Journal 1909–14: 1915–21: 1922–50
      Electron 1950–68
      Contact 1969–89

E Executive Council minutes 1898–1907; 1911–1989

F Sub-Executive Council minutes 1911–1968

G Evidence and judgement of Byrne & Chapple v ETU in the High Court, 1961. (This evidence is mountainous, and includes many of Les Cannon's private papers)

H District, area, branch minutes (various) 1917–1989

I Membership enrolment ledgers 1889–1914

J Circulars, tracts, bulletins, pamphlets and anti-leadership publications

K The appropriate ETU/EETPU speeches and controversies reflected in the pages of TUC and Labour Party Conferences reports, FEST and CSEU reports

2 Books that are wholly concerned with the ETU/EETPU

Joe Wild, *A Souvenir of 50 years of the ETU*, Internal publication, 1939

Gordon Schaefer, *Light and Liberty – 60 years of the ETU*, Internal publication, 1949

John Vickers, *The story of the ETU*, Internal publication, 1952

C. H. Rolph, *All those in Favour*, André Deutsch, 1962

Olga Cannon & J. R. L. Anderson, *The Road from Wigan Pier*, Victor Gollancz, 1973

Frank Chapple, *Sparks Fly*, Michael Joseph, 1985

3 Useful Books that set the framework in which the ETU/EETPU has operated

Hugh Clegg, Alan Fox & A. F. Thompson, *History of British Trade Unions*: volume 1, 1889–1911, Oxford University Press, 1964
Hugh Clegg, *History of British Trade Unions*: volume 11, 1911–1933, Oxford University Press, 1985
Sidney & Beatrice Webb, *History of British Trade Unionism*, Longmans Green & Co, 1920
G. D. H. Cole, *A Short History of the British Working Class Movement*, George Allen & Unwin, 1948
Keith Mason, *Front Seat*, Huthwaite, 1981
Henry Pelling, *A History of British Trade Unionism*, Pelican, 1984
A. J. P. Taylor, *English History 1914–45*, Pelican, 1966
W. E. J. McCarthy (ed), *Trade Unions*, Pelican, 1985
Ken Coates & Tony Topham, *Trade Unions in Britain*, Spokesman, 1982
Eric Wigham, *The Power to Manage*, Macmillan, 1973   •
Barrie Sherman, *The State of the Unions*, John Wiley, 1986
Philip Basset, *Strike Free*, Macmillan, 1987
Martin Adeney & John Lloyd, *The Miners Strike – Loss without Limit*, Routledge & Kegan Paul, 1986
Leslie Hannah, *Electricity Before Nationalisation*, Macmillan, 1979
Leslie Hannah, *Engineers, Managers & Politicians*, Macmillan, 1982
Sir Ronald Edwards & R. D. V. Roberts, *Status Productivity & Pay*, Macmillan, 1971
Walter Citrine, *Men and Work*, Hutchinson, 1964
Walter Citrine, *Two Careers*, Hutchinson, 1967

4 Books which have been useful in specific circumstances

Eric Batstone, Ian Boraston, Steve Frenkl, *Shop Stewards in Action*, Blackwell, 1977
John French, *Plumbers in Unity*, Internal publication, 1965
H. Clegg, A. Killick, R. Adams, *Trade Union Officers*, Blackwell, 1961
Philip Williams, *Hugh Gaitskell*, Jonathan Cape, 1979
Harold Wilson, *The Labour Government*, Pelican, 1974
John Gennard, *Financing Strikes*, Macmillan, 1977
Daniel F. Calhoun, *The United Front. The TUC and the Russians 1923–8*, Cambridge University Press, 1976
E. H. Carr, *The Twilight of the Comintern*, Macmillan, 1982

Index of Names

General Index

Mullards 384, 602
Municipalization 80–1, 120
Murdoch, R. 618, 622–33
Murray, L. 611, 621

National and Local Government Offices
  Association (NALGO) 627, 637
National Arbitration Tribunal 269, 293
National Association of Theatrical Employees
  (NATE) 130, 211–12, 274, 325
National Association of Theatrical and Kine
  Employees (NATKE) see NATE
National Coal Board 608, 609
National Economic Development Council 537,
  603
National Federated Electrical Association 117,
  139, 141, 220, 222, 225–6, 229–30, 237–
  8, 240–1, 268, 296–309, 316, 379–83, 500,
  502, 504–5, 529, 535 (see also Joint
  Industry Board, JIB, ECA)
National Graphical Association 600, 608, 617–
  18, 618–19, 621, 623, 626, 632
National Health Service 547, 577, 602
Nationalization 290, 310–24, 659, 662 (see
  municipalization, public ownership)
National Joint Industrial Councils 116–24, 131–
  2 (see also Negotiating Structures)
National Sailors and Firemen's Union 101
National Union of General and Municipal
  Workers – see General and Municipal
  Workers Union
National Union of Journalists 627, 628
National Union of Mineworkers 325, 596, 608–
  14 (see also MFGB, Miners' Strike)
National Union of Public Employees 315, 578,
  656
National Union of Railwaymen 123, 131
National Union of Seamen 504, 600
National Telephone Co. 17
National Unemployed Workers Committee 164
National Wiring Company 39
Negotiating Structures (general) 116, 205–6
  in Contracting 79, 118–20, 201, 230, 295–8,
    500–2, 547
  in Electricity Supply 120–4, 184, 200, 295,
    310–24, 520
  in Engineering 79, 295, 520–3, 528, 539, 550–
    58
  in Shipbuilding 79, 295
New Communist Party 486
Newcastle Evening Chronicle 581–2
News Chronicle 406, 618
News International 618, 622–30, 633
News of the World 618, 622, 624
Newspaper electricians 153, 178, 387, 632 (see
  Branches, London Press)
New Statesman 413, 418–21, 424, 533, 632
Norbreck Castle 569, 616

North Metropolitan Supply Co. 216
Nottinghamshire Miners 609, 610
Nuclear power 609
Nuffield College 517

O'Brien, T. 211–12
Office of Works 84–5, 86
Olympia 300–1, 303–4, 306, 307
Orion Electrical 653, 655, 661

Pacificism 101, 105, 133, 251
Padley, W. 418
Pannell, C. 465
Panorama 409, 448
Panton, J. 44–6
Parker, Thomas 34–6
Pay Board 554
Peace Congress, Vienna 340
Peace Committee 340–5
Pentonville Five 600
Penwill, L. 205, 227–8, 232, 237–8, 269, 296, 297,
  302, 304, 305, 310, 379, 381, 461–2, 500
  (see also NFEA)
Philips, M. 293, 358, 364
Phillimore, Mr 304–5
Phoenix Electrical 308
Picketing 21, 601–2, 604–5, 606, 608–11, 612–13,
  629
Piecework (PBR schemes) 8, 61–2, 114–16, 263–
  6, 299–300, 356, 357, 381–2, 501
Pirelli 149, 205
Plessey 522
Plumbers Action Group 585–6
Plumbing Trades Democratic Defence
  Committee 519
Plumbing Trades Union (PTU) 40, 51, 192, 296,
  518–19, 585
Polish Solidarity 607, 661
Polish War Veterans 333–4
'Political' strikes 132–3, 138, 305 (see also Miners'
  strike)
Pollitt, H. 164, 167, 215, 283, 285, 375, 398, 419,
  456
Poplar Council 222, 226
Post Office electricians 130–1, 183
Power in the Land 362–3
Power Worker 315, 497, 536
Poznan, 1956 400–1
Pressed Steel Fisher 551
Prices and Incomes Board (PIB) 503–5, 521–2,
  524, 527
Printing and Kindred Trades Federation 387
Productivity Bargaining 290, 292, 294, 297, 503,
  522, 526–7, 529, 537, 540, 544–6, 552–3
Public Ownership 103 (see nationalization,
  municipalization)
Pugh, A. 172